THE ENCYCLOPEDIA OF
ANCIENT
EGYPT

THE ENCYCLOPEDIA OF
ANCIENT EGYPT

GENERAL EDITOR
HELEN STRUDWICK

amber
BOOKS

First published in 2006 by Amber Books Ltd
Bradley's Close
74–77 White Lion Street
London N1 9PF
United Kingdom
www.amberbooks.co.uk

Reprinted in 2007

ISBN-13: 978-1-904687-85-6
ISBN-10: 1-904687-85-7

Distributed in the UK by
Bookmart Ltd
Blaby Road
Wigston
Leicester LE18 4SE

Project Editor: James Bennett
Design: Portland Media
Photographs: De Agostini Picture Library

Front cover image © Jean Guichard/Photos12.com

This material was originally published in partwork form as *The Glory of Ancient Egypt*

Printed in Singapore

CHRONOLOGY   9

HISTORY   10
Egypt, Gift of the Nile   12
Egypt before the Pharaohs   16
The 'Zero' Dynasty   20
King Narmer, The First Pharaoh?   22
The Thinite Period   24
The Old Kingdom   28
Khufu, Builder of The Great Pyramid   32
The Time of Pepy I   34
The First Intermediate Period   36
Herakleopolis Magna   40
Nubia and Egypt   42
The Middle Kingdom   44
Fortresses in the South   46
Pharaoh Mentuhotep II   50
Senusret I – Man of Character   52
Senusret III   54
Second Intermediate Period   58
The Hyksos   60
The New Kingdom   64
Of Workmen and Tomb Robbers   66
Thutmose I   68
Hatshepsut, the Pharaoh Queen   70
Thutmose III   72
Akhenaten's Religious Reforms   74
Nefertiti – Power and Beauty   78
Tutankhamun   80
Pharaoh Horemheb   82
Rameses the Great   84
The Battle of Qadesh   86
Sea Peoples   88
The Priest Kings   90
Libyans on the Throne   92
The Persians in Egypt   94
Alexander as Pharaoh   96
Cleopatra – the Last Queen   98

CONTENTS

RELIGION 100

The Gods of Egypt 102

The Sun Cult 108

Amun, King of the Gods 112

Osiris – God of the Afterlife 116

Isis, Universal Mother 120

Seth and Nephthys 124

Horus, God of the Sky 128

Hathor, Goddess of Love 130

Sekhmet, Goddess of Destruction 134

Bastet – the Cat Goddess 136

Min, God of Fertility 138

The Lesser Deities 140

Foreign Gods on the Nile 144

The Creation Myth of Hermopolis 148

The Sacred Apis Bull 152

The Animal Necropolises 154

Horus, the King's Protector 158

The Sed Festival 162

The Opet Festival 166

Priests, Servants of the Gods 170

Life After Death 174

The Ka, the Ba and the Akh 178

Embalming the Body 180

Canopic Jars 184

Food for the Afterlife 186

The Funeral Cortège 190

The Opening of the Mouth Ceremony 194

The Weighing of the Heart 198

ART 202

Art in Ancient Egypt 204

Painters and Paintings 206

Relief-carving Techniques 208

Stelae, Books of Stone 214

Royal Statuary 220

Coffins and Sarcophagi 224

The Magic of Jewels 230

Ceramics 232

Funerary Masks 238

Furniture for the Afterlife	242
Rahotep and Nofret	246
Building the Pyramids	248
The Sphinx	254
The Statue of Ka-aper	260
Seneb and his Family	262
The Temples of Deir el-Bahri	264
Thebes, 'City of 100 Gates'	270
The Valley of the Kings	276
The Settlement of Deir el-Medina	278
The Tomb of Nakht	284
The Colossi of Memnon	288
The Temple of Luxor	292
The Art of Akhenaten	298
The Mask of Tutankhamun	302
The Tombs of Horemheb	304
The Monuments of Rameses II	310
The Temples of Abu Simbel	316
Nefertari's Tomb	320
The Temple of Khons in Karnak	324
Alexandria, a Royal Dream	328
The Fayum Portraits	334
EVERYDAY LIFE	340
Childhood in Ancient Egypt	342
Educating the Children	346
Marriage	350
Ancient Egyptian Houses	354
Town and City Life	358
Egyptian Society	362
Divine and Worldly Law	366
The Role of Women	370
Clothes and Fashion	374
Cosmetics and Perfumes	378
Hygiene and Body Care	382
Goldsmiths and Jewellers	386
Civil Servants	388
Workers and Patrons	390
Fruits of the Soil	392
Keeping and Breeding Animals	396

CONTENTS

CONTENTS

The Slaughter of Animals 400

Vines and Wine 404

The Brewing of Beer 408

The Hunt 412

Music in Egyptian Life 416

Life in the Oases 418

The War Chariot 422

SCIENCE AND TECHNOLOGY 426

The Nilometer 428

Egyptian Astronomy 432

Mathematics and Measurement 436

Ancient Egyptian Numbers 440

Applied Physics 442

The Egyptian Calendar 446

Measuring Time 450

Medicine 452

Textile Production 456

Boats in Ancient Egypt 460

Weapons 464

WRITING 468

The Rosetta Stone 470

Reading Hieroglyphs 472

Hieroglyphs from Life 474

The Egyptian Alphabet 478

Hieratic Writing 482

Coptic, the Script of the Christians 486

Writing Materials 490

Making Papyrus 494

Temple Inscriptions 498

Coffin Texts 502

Administrative Papyri 506

INDEX 508

Palaeolithic Period	c.700,000–7000 BC
Saharan Neolithic Period	c.8800–4700 BC
Predynastic Period	c.5300–3000 BC
Early Dynastic Period	c.3000–2686 BC
Old Kingdom	686–2160 BC
First Intermediate Period	2160–2055 BC
Middle Kingdom	2055–1650 BC
Second Intermediate Period	1650–1550 BC
New Kingdom	1550–1069 BC
Ramessid Period	1295–1069 BC
Third Intermediate Period	1069–664 BC
Late Period	664–332 BC
Ptolemaic Period	332–30 BC
Roman Period	30 BC–AD 395

CHRONOLOGY

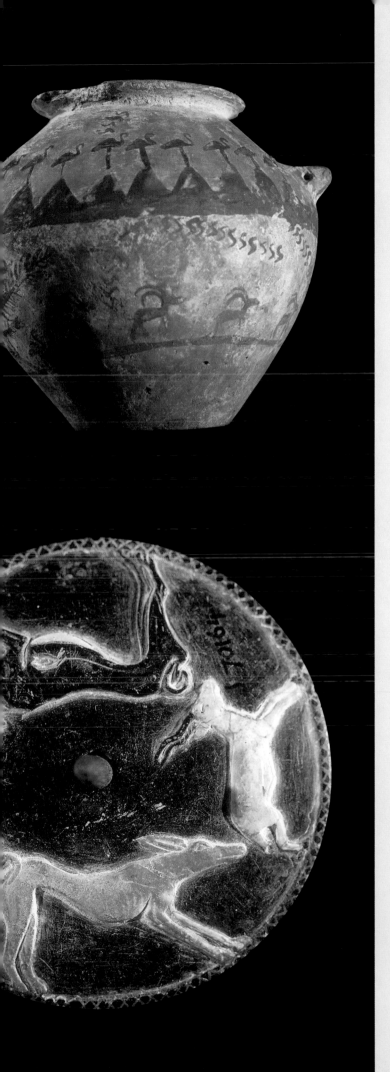

History

Egypt lies in the north-eastern corner of Africa, on the edge of one of the most inhospitable parts of the world, the Sahara desert, where rainfall is negligible. Yet, thanks in large part to the presence of the river Nile, which brought both water and fertile soil, this was the location for the flowering of one of the most important civilizations of the ancient world.

Modern historians divide Egyptian history into dynasties following the system first recorded by an Egyptian priest called Manetho, who wrote in Greek in the 3rd century BC. 'Dynasties' implies that that particular group of rulers belonged to a single family. Although these divisions do not always accord with actual changes in the ruling family, the dynastic system is still retained today.

Kingdoms and periods

The dynasties are usually grouped together into different Kingdoms (Old, Middle and New), which are usually regarded as eras of particular stability. The earliest epochs of Egyptian history are usually referred to as the Predynastic period (prehistoric), and the Early Dynastic period which covers the first two dynasties.

The periods between Kingdoms are known as Intermediate Periods, times when centralized government control under a single king broke down. The last of these (the Third Intermediate Period) came after the New Kingdom and was followed by the so-called Late Period.

Ancient civilization
Ceramics from various periods (clockwise from left): part of a statue of Queen Hatshepsut (1473–1458 BC), Gerzean pottery from the predynastic period (3500–3100 BC) and an alabaster and soapstone disc depicting hunting scenes from the Thinite or Early Dynastic period (3100–2686 BC).

Egypt, Gift of the Nile

Without the Nile, which irrigates the south and north, and forms a vast delta before flowing into the Mediterranean, Egypt would be a huge desert. Fascinated by its unique geography, the Greek historian Herodotus (483–420 BC) called Egypt 'the gift of the Nile'.

Around 5000 BC, climatic changes turned the Sahara grassland into desert and nomadic hunter-gatherers were pushed towards the Nile valley. Here, in the rich, fertile soil they developed arable farming and began to domesticate animals. Stable communities grew up and the economic conditions led to the creation of a state. The Nile became the mortar that would hold together the building blocks of Egyptian civilization for 3,000 years.

The Egyptians were totally dependent on the majestic Nile, in particular its annual flood which replenished the soil of the fields with rich silt. It also supplied fish, waterfowl, papyrus for writing, reeds and grass for baskets and matting, mud for pottery and bricks, and was the main communication route through the country. So important was the Nile

▼ Palm tree bounty
The Egyptian landscape is dotted with majestic date palms, which produce succulent dates, and dom palms, which bear a hard nut containing a gingery-flavoured fruit. This scene, against a backdrop of the pyramids at Giza, with palm trees gently swaying in the breeze and camel, rider and mule reflected in the tranquil water of an irrigation canal, perfectly evokes the Egyptian countryside.

▲ Medieval map
During the Middle Ages, Arab travellers marvelled at Egypt's ancient sites. They described the country, costumes and grand monuments in many works, among them maps which sited towns and villages, as well as natural features.

This ninth-century map shows the Nile and, to the left, the Fayoum oasis linked to the Nile by the Bahr Yussef canal. To the north, as it enters the Delta, the Nile is divided into six branches.

that the Egyptians deified the annual flood, or 'inundation', in the form of Hapy. A symbol of fertility, he was an androgynous figure with female breasts, clothed simply in a girdle, whose green or blue flesh symbolized the regeneration of plants and the waters of the river.

Other deities linked with the Nile are the goddesses Heket, the frog, and Taweret, the hippopotamus, both of whom were associated with childbirth.

The inundation

The entire rhythm of Ancient Egyptian life was governed by the annual inundation of the Nile. Until the opening of the Aswan Dam in 1964, which now regulates the flood, it began around 15 June above the first cataract (set of rapids) near Aswan. The waters continued to rise during the summer before reaching their highest point in September, then subsiding in the autumn.

The period of flooding released a huge labour force from work in the fields, allowing it to be diverted to work on the building of temples and monuments.

▲ **Papyrus**
The lotus and the papyrus were the two plants that symbolized Ancient Egypt. Papyrus, used to make all kinds of objects, such as baskets, boats, furniture and mats, flourished in the marshes of the Delta and was the symbol of Lower Egypt.

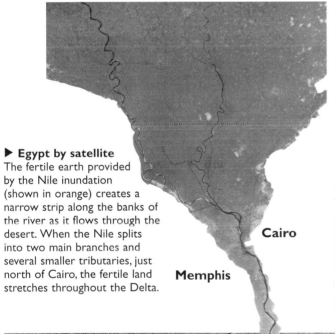

▶ **Egypt by satellite**
The fertile earth provided by the Nile inundation (shown in orange) creates a narrow strip along the banks of the river as it flows through the desert. When the Nile splits into two main branches and several smaller tributaries, just north of Cairo, the fertile land stretches throughout the Delta.

Cairo

Memphis

▶ **Preparing for the inundation**
The nilometer, a series of steps cut into the banks of the Nile, was used to predict the height of the inundation, If high levels were expected, the Egyptians protected their stores and possessions on high ground. If the flood was minimal, they made plans to use stocks of food and animal fodder reserved from previous years.

▼ **Communication route**
The Nile, which traverses the entire country from south to north, was the main route of communication. Light boats made of papyrus, cargo vessels filled with raw materials and wooden ships carrying passengers and goods crisscrossed the river. At Aswan and in Nubia, negotiating the cataracts (rapids) required great skill on the part of the ship's crew.

◀ Dromedaries

The Arabian dromedary camels found in Egypt today were not used in pharaonic times, when the mule was the principal beast of burden. Perfectly adapted to the extreme climates of the desert, the dromedaries were probably introduced in Ptolemaic times and were later used on the caravan routes from the Nile valley to oases and to Nubia.

▼ The Nubians

During the Old Kingdom (2686–2181 BC), the Egyptians extended their domination over Nubia to territory south of Aswan and the first cataract where they began mining gold.

To protect this part of their kingdom, and to subdue any revolts by the Nubians, the pharaohs of the Middle Kingdom (2066–1650 BC) began building huge fortresses.

In November, farmers returned to work and cultivated the earth newly fertilized by silt deposits so that their crops would be ready by the following spring.

To record the height of the river and to predict the likely soil fertility and crop yield, the Ancient Egyptians invented the nilometer, a measuring device which usually took the form of a series of marked steps against which the increasing levels of the inundation could be measured. If the prediction was high, people moved to higher ground; if it was low, it was necessary to use food that had been stored. Drought led to epidemic disease and civil disorder, and it has been suggested that a series of poor floods led to the end of the Old Kingdom in 2181 BC.

▼ Above the waters
To protect themselves from the Nile's annual flood, the Ancient Egyptians traditionally built their towns and villages on high ground, out of the water's reach. Despite these precautions, however, they were not always safe from exceptionally high rises in water level, which could have devastating results.

▲ Lost riches
Since the construction of the Aswan Dam in the 1960s, the waters of the Nile no longer fertilize the land with rich layers of silt each year. The river still teems with fish, however, an important element in the local diet since Predynastic times, using fishing methods that have changed little for 5,000 years.

▼ Irrigation
The Egyptians used different methods to draw water from a river or canal. The most ancient, dating from pharaonic times, was the shaduf (below top), a pole with a bucket at one end and a counterbalance at the other. The water wheel (middle), introduced in the Ptolemaic period, was a vertical wheel equipped with

vessels and driven by oxen. The Archimedes screw (bottom), contemporaneous with the water wheel, drew water by means of a turning screw enclosed in a cylindrical drum.

▼ Feluccas
Today, as in the time of the pharaohs, sailing vessels are used on the Nile, although the rectangular sail on ancient boats has been replaced by the triangular sall of the feluccas. Impressive fleets of this traditional means of transport now offer cruises between Luxor and Aswan to visitors.

Egypt before the Pharaohs

Although we know relatively little about Egyptian life in Predynastic times, archaeological evidence suggests that a sophisticated culture existed before the Pharaonic Age.

Foot soldiers *wearing loincloths are engaging in hand-to-hand combat.*

A naval battle *between three Egyptian papyrus skiffs and two vertical-prowed boats is shown on the middle part of the handle. Bodies can be seen floating between the ships.*

Warriors *with different headdresses confront each other. Although distinctively dressed, they have not been identified.*

As the desert encroached upon the once-rich savannah, the nomadic hunter-gatherers of northern Africa settled closer to the Nile and desert oases, turning to farming and the domestication of animals as a way of life. By 4000 BC, at the beginning of the Amratian period (also known as Naqada I), they cultivated wheat and barley, raised goats, sheep, cattle and pigs, and domesticated the donkey and the cow. They also made the first pottery, bricks, cosmetic palettes and war maces.

The distinctive black-topped, red clay pottery, used for storage and transport, began to be supplemented by pottery incised with scenes of hunting and everyday life. Grave goods included clay and ivory figures

◀ **Knife blade**
Mounted in wooden, bone or ivory handles, prehistoric knives were used for skinning animals and butchering meat.

▶ **Arrowheads**
Barbed arrowheads were mounted on wooden shafts and used to hunt the plentiful wild game of what was once savannah lands, but is now desert.

▶ **Rock art**
As elsewhere, Egyptian prehistoric nomadic hunters developed rock art. These engravings, discovered at Wadi Hammamat in the eastern desert, depicted the hunters' prey, perhaps as a form of sympathetic magic to ensure success in the hunt.

▶ **The Gebel el-Arak dagger**
Made around 3200 BC, this weapon, now in the Louvre Museum in Paris, is among the first masterpieces of Egyptian art. The light-coloured flint blade, with its distinctive, ripple-flaked texture, is embedded in a hippopotamus-tusk ivory handle. Decorated on both sides, it shows a land and naval battle on one side and a bearded man controlling two tame lions on the other – a design of Mesopotamian origin.

▼ **Late flint working**
By the Late Predynastic period, stone blades were finely carved with sharp serrated edges.

and stone vessels. Towards the end of the Amratian period, sprawling but low-density settlements grew up at Naqada, north of Luxor, and Hierakonpolis, south of Luxor.

Second phase

The final phase of the Predynastic period, which lasted from about 3500 BC to 3100 BC, is called the Gerzean period (also known as Naqada II), after the site at Gerza which is situated about 80km (50 miles) south of Cairo. The desert was now at its driest and Naqada and Hierakonpolis had become closely packed towns, but people settled in the Fayum Oasis and the northeast Delta.

Grave goods now included animal-shaped cosmetic palettes, hard stone vessels and maceheads. Pottery, made of pale clay and painted with red ochre decorations, began

Gerzean ceramics

Characterized by a pale clay paste and red ochre decoration, Gerzean pottery (3500–3100 BC) is found beyond the region of Upper Egypt.

INSIGHT

Predynastic fabric

This fragment of fine linen painted in red and black was discovered in a Predynastic tomb at Gebelein in Upper Egypt, about 30km (18 miles) south of Thebes. The damaged fabric was found folded beside the body of the tomb's occupant. It is decorated with two small boats – with slightly curved prow and stern – equipped with two cabins. The boats are propelled by rowers and directed by a pilot. Other fragments of this material show women dancing and a hippopotamus hunt.

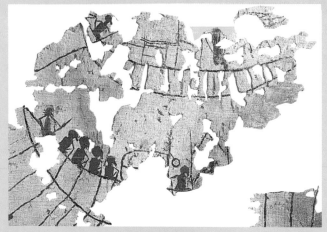

Ibises are depicted standing on small hills.

The goats shown on the frieze around the bottom of the storage jar are similar in style to those found in rock engravings.

▶ **Amratian ceramics**
Black-edged, red ceramics are typical of the Amratian phase (c. 4000–3500 BC). Designs include bowls and, here, large vases 50cm (20in) high.

▶ **Sickle**
The first Egyptian farmers made tools suited to their new agricultural activities. To cut wheat and barley, they used a carved, serrated flint blade embedded in a wooden handle. Highly effective, these tools remained in use until the Pharaonic era.

◀ **Amratian ceramics**
This double vase from the Amratian period (4000–3500 BC) has a glazed, red ochre surface. It is decorated in white with goats and human figures, combined with geometric designs.

to include Palestinian and Mesopotamian motifs. The finest flint tools appear at this time, with their characteristic rippled blades and ivory and bone handles carved with relief scenes of hunting and war. Cosmetic palettes became more ceremonial than practical, and showed scenes of battles and wild animals, both real and imaginary.

Both Naqada and Hierakonpolis now had city walls, and the tombs in the cemeteries began to show a difference in size, suggesting the evolution of a structured society and the development of different classes. The largest tombs were brick-lined, and one at Hierakonpolis had wall paintings – the first recorded tomb paintings in Egypt. The scenes of battle and motifs of power imply the growth of warring kingdoms in the established towns. These undocumented struggles, and the mergers of power, prepared the unification of Egypt from Upper Egypt to the Delta around 3100 BC.

◄ **The god Horus**
This gold falcon's head from the Twelfth Dynasty (1993–1776 BC), came from the temple of Horus at Hierakonpolis. Horus was the patron god of the city.

During the Predynastic period, the city of Hierakonpolis, 80km (50 miles) south of Luxor, was the major population centre of Upper Egypt.

▲ **The paintings of Hierakonpolis**
In the Gerzean period (3500–3100 BC), a prince of Hierakonpolis ordered the walls of his tomb to be decorated with paintings. The hunting and warfare scenes, surrounding six small boats, describe the violent world in which the tomb's owner lived.

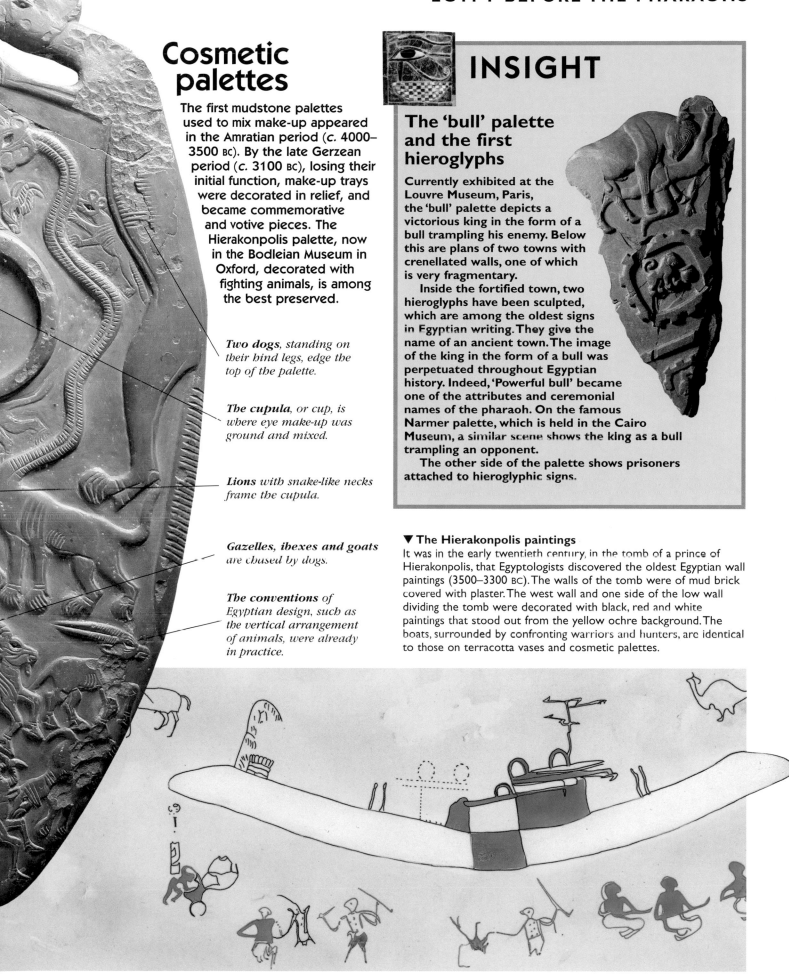

Cosmetic palettes

The first mudstone palettes used to mix make-up appeared in the Amratian period (*c.* 4000–3500 BC). By the late Gerzean period (*c.* 3100 BC), losing their initial function, make-up trays were decorated in relief, and became commemorative and votive pieces. The Hierakonpolis palette, now in the Bodleian Museum in Oxford, decorated with fighting animals, is among the best preserved.

Two dogs, standing on their hind legs, edge the top of the palette.

The cupula, or cup, is where eye make-up was ground and mixed.

Lions with snake-like necks frame the cupula.

Gazelles, ibexes and goats are chased by dogs.

The conventions of Egyptian design, such as the vertical arrangement of animals, were already in practice.

INSIGHT

The 'bull' palette and the first hieroglyphs

Currently exhibited at the Louvre Museum, Paris, the 'bull' palette depicts a victorious king in the form of a bull trampling his enemy. Below this are plans of two towns with crenellated walls, one of which is very fragmentary.

Inside the fortified town, two hieroglyphs have been sculpted, which are among the oldest signs in Egyptian writing. They give the name of an ancient town. The image of the king in the form of a bull was perpetuated throughout Egyptian history. Indeed, 'Powerful bull' became one of the attributes and ceremonial names of the pharaoh. On the famous Narmer palette, which is held in the Cairo Museum, a similar scene shows the king as a bull trampling an opponent.

The other side of the palette shows prisoners attached to hieroglyphic signs.

▼ The Hierakonpolis paintings

It was in the early twentieth century, in the tomb of a prince of Hierakonpolis, that Egyptologists discovered the oldest Egyptian wall paintings (3500–3300 BC). The walls of the tomb were of mud brick covered with plaster. The west wall and one side of the low wall dividing the tomb were decorated with black, red and white paintings that stood out from the yellow ochre background. The boats, surrounded by confronting warriors and hunters, are identical to those on terracotta vases and cosmetic palettes.

The 'Zero' Dynasty

In the final phase of the Predynastic period (5500-3100 BC), a power struggle for control of all Egypt took place between various factions, leading to the emergence of the first nation state.

The surprisingly named 'Zero' Dynasty (*c.* 3150-3100 BC) emphasizes the many gaps in our knowledge of Ancient Egyptian history prior to the pharaonic era. Work carried out by German archaeologists resulted in the creation of this dynasty, which contradicts the records provided by ancient sources. For example, they have discovered that kings reigned before the unification of Egypt. These early rulers were known as 'Horus kings' as their names were written in a serekh - a hieroglyphic symbol comprising the palace façade decoration inscribed with the name of the sovereign - surmounted by a falcon, the bird identified with the god Horus. In later dynasties, the serekh was supplemented by cartouches giving the throne and birth names of the king.

Among the funerary equipment discovered in the tombs of the kings Scorpion I, Herihor and Ka at Abydos, a number of objects bore inscriptions. This proved that the Ancient Egyptians had a writing system by *c.* 3150 BC. Recent discoveries at the site also suggest that Scorpion was probably a title rather than a name.

▲ The red crown
A king, seated on his throne and wearing the red crown of Lower Egypt and the heb-sed coat, is depicted on the relief of this macehead.

Regional powers

Centres of power existed towards the end of the Predynastic period at Naqada, Hierakonpolis and Thinis with its necropolis at Abydos. These came into conflict

The two flags are crowned by the images of two birds - the Horus falcon and the ibis of Thoth.

The royal flags have bands, which hold the arms of the prisoners tied behind their backs.

Vultures and other birds of prey swoop down onto the bodies of the dead soldiers, pecking at their eyes.

◀ Palette with a battle scene
The events leading up to the unification of Upper and Lower Egypt were a popular motif in works of art, which depicted a violent subjugation. Here captives are taken and the bodies of slain enemies are attacked by birds of prey.

The hieroglyph for 'country', with the papyrus thicket on top, means 'land of Lower Egypt'.

The king, in the form of a lion, has brought down an enemy and tears him to pieces in wild fury.

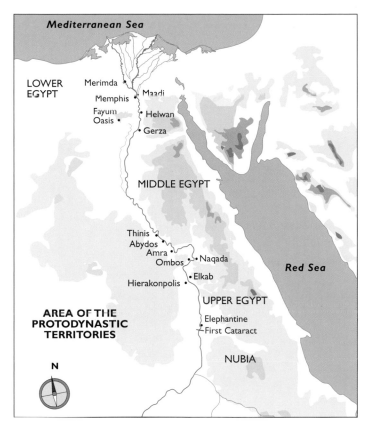

▲ **The phases of the unification**
This map shows the most important centres of power before the unification of Upper and Lower Egypt. The kings of Hierakonpolis conquered Naqada and Thinis, then extended their territory to the Delta in the north and to the First Cataract in the south.

with each other, leading to the development of Upper Egypt, with Hierakonpolis (Nekhen in Egyptian) as the capital. The kings of this region gradually extended their power to Naqada in the north, eventually settling in Thinis.

In sight of unification

The kings reigning from Thinis made offerings at the Horus temple at Hierakonpolis to maintain the relationship with their region of origin. In the so-called Main Deposit of the temple, the ceremonial macehead of a king known as Scorpion, and the celebrated palette of King Narmer, the founder of the First Dynasty, were discovered. From Thinis, the rulers of Upper Egypt extended their territory to the Delta in the north and to the First Cataract in the south.

The kings of the 'Zero' Dynasty were buried at the necropolis at Abydos – which was later the centre of the cult of Osiris – in the so-called U cemetery, the oldest part of the site. Most of their names, however, have not been deciphered. Adjacent is the cemetery now known as Umm el-Qa'ab, which houses the tombs of the pharaohs of the Early Dynastic period (3100–2686 BC). There are strong cultural links between the styles of burial and grave goods in the two cemeteries, and it is possible that the foundation of the Dynastic period should be put further back in time.

▲ **King Hathor**
There is no falcon on this serekh carved onto a clay vessel. The serekh contains the name of King Hathor, a ruler of the 'Zero' Dynasty. As 'Hat' means 'first' and 'Hor' means 'Horus', the name therefore reads 'Horus is foremost'.

serekh	transcription
	Nihor or Nuhor (?)
	Hathor (?)
	Irjhor (?)
	Ka
	Narmer

◄ **Kings of the 'Zero' Dynasty**
The Horus falcon on the serekh is missing in the first two names of the chart, which are read as Nihor or Nuhor, and Hathor. The following sign of Irjhor depicts the falcon, but not the serekh. Both elements appear for the first time in the names of King Ka and King Narmer.

▶ **Knife from Gebel el-Araq**
Objects such as the ceremonial macehead above and this knife (on display in the Louvre in Paris) were signs of royal supremacy and power. Hunting scenes with dogs, lions and ibexes are depicted on one side of the hippopotamus-ivory knife handle. A man in Mesopotamian costume taming two lions is portrayed on the upper part of the handle. On the other side are four rows of battle scenes, with shaven-headed men overwhelming their long-haired enemies. The motif indicates that there was contact between the Egyptian and Mesopotamian cultures at the end of the fourth millennium BC.

King Narmer, the first Pharaoh?

The unification of Lower and Upper Egypt in about 3100 BC laid the foundations of the Egypt of the Pharaohs. Was Narmer the founder and ruler of the combined kingdoms – the first pharaoh?

According to ancient Egyptian tradition, the unification of the two regions of Upper and Lower Egypt was achieved by a legendary ruler called Menes. He is also credited with founding the city between the two lands. Historically, however, the fabled Menes has been linked to two known early rulers – Narmer and Aha.

As there are no detailed records from the time, Egyptologists continue to debate whether Narmer was the forerunner or founder of the 1st Dynasty, and some argue that he and Aha were the same person, while others claim that Aha was Narmer's son and successor. A jar seal impression found at Abudos in 1985, however, lists the eight rulers of the first dynasty, with Narmer first on the list, followed by Aha.

The most important archaeological evidence for the unification of Egypt under Narmer is a splendid ceremonial palette found in Hierakonpolis in 1897. The discovery of the mudstone palette, along with a limestone macehead, from under the floor of the temple of the old Kingdom (2686–2181 BC), can be clearly identified with a king called Narmer from hieroglyphs of his name. Unfortunately, the excavations were badly recorded, but the palette shows the name of Narmer on both sides, with the king wearing the crown of Upper Egypt on one and the crown of Lower Egypt on the other.

On the palette, Narmer is depicted smiting his enemies. This kind of depiction of victorious pharaohs was to be used for about 3,000 years and was repeated, with the individual ruler of the period in a triumphant pose, on every Egyptian temple until Roman times.

The founding of Memphis

It seems likely that Aha founded the new capital Memphis, as his name is the first ruler's recorded at Saqqara, the necropolis for the city. It is, however, difficult to say where exactly the centre of power of the state lay. During the 1st and 2nd Dynasties, huge tombs were built in Saqqara, as well as in Abydos, the most important burial site in Upper Egypt. It could be that by maintaining both traditions, conflicts were avoided and the unification was strengthened.

Although we know nothing about the character of Narmer, his lasting achievment was to forge a state with a national consciousness from regions that were widely different culturally. It is unlikely that this could have been achieved without a strong central ruler who had the vision to put in place an effective administration with all power invested in himself.

The king, wearing a short ceremonial gown and a red crown is seated on the throne of the two countries.

◀ **Royal macehead**
In the late 19th century, excavations at Hierakonpolis (present-day Kom el-Ahmar), the capital of Upper Egypt in Predynastic times, yielded offerings and cult implements of the time.

Among the finds was a ceremonial macehead (left). On the macehead, there is a scene from the sed festival where Narmer is shown seated under a canopy bearing the royal insignia. Behind him are shackled prisoners, while in front there is a figure lying on a litter.

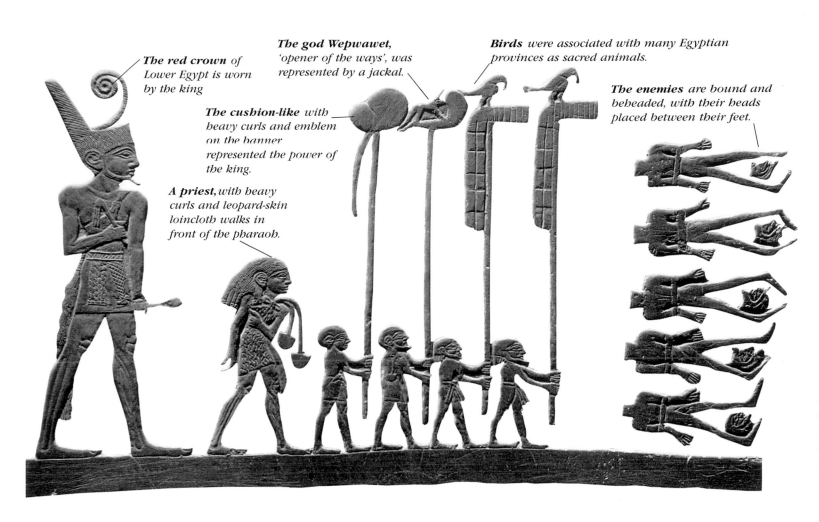

The red crown of Lower Egypt is worn by the king

The god Wepwawet, 'opener of the ways', was represented by a jackal.

Birds were associated with many Egyptian provinces as sacred animals.

The cushion-like with heavy curls and emblem on the banner represented the power of the king.

A priest, with heavy curls and leopard-skin loincloth walks in front of the pharaoh.

The enemies are bound and beheaded, with their heads placed between their feet.

The white crown is the symbol of Upper Egypt.

The ritual clothing Consisted of a short loincloth with a bull's tail at the back.

A mace is raised by the king in readiness to strike the enemy.

The enemy is probably a Libyan, as they were usually depicted as bearded.

▶ **Victor and vanquished**
One side of the Narmer palette shows the king wearing the crown of Upper Egypt. He is about to strike an enemy kneeling before him whom he clutches by the hair. This representation of the submission of enemies became an enduring image in Egyptian art and symbolized the invincibility of Egypt.

▶ **Victory over the north**
To commemorate victory over Lower Egypt, a palette was made which shows various scenes of the conquest. A falcon holds on to the enemy, which is resting on the hieroglyph for 'country'. The six papyrus reeds are a symbol for the delta region. The Horus falcon is a god of upper Egypt, as well as representing the warrior king.

◀ **The 'catfish'**
On both sides of the Narmer palette, the name of king appears in hieroglyphs of a fish (nar) and a chisel (mer), which translates as 'catfish'.

The Thinite Period

The Thinite era, or Early Dynastic period, began with the unification of the country by Narmer, Egypt's first pharaoh. It lasted for 400 years and included the two earliest Ancient Egyptian dynasties.

The Thinite period takes its name from the town of Thinis, near Abydos in Upper Egypt, where the rulers of the first two dynasties originated. Almost nothing is known of the events that marked the reigns of these early kings. Historians are not sure that all of them were recorded, and, even with those whose existence has been established, the order of their succession is not always certain.

It appears that the region was one of the small states that were vying for control of Upper and Lower Egypt at the end of the Predynastic period. Thinis became the seat of power for the first rulers of a united Egypt, but the capital was soon moved to Memphis, which was strategically located between the Delta and Nile Valley. It was here that the state became organized around the king, and the principles that would govern pharaonic Egypt were established.

▲ Stele of Fed
The inscription on this stele, discovered at Abydos and now in the Louvre Museum in Paris, shows some of the earliest hieroglyphs. The phonetic signs give the name of the deceased, a courtier called Fed.

◄ Ivory statuette of a Thinite king
Discovered in the temple of Osiris at Abydos, this statuette shows an unidentified pharaoh wearing the white crown of Upper Egypt.

Draped in his coat for the sed festival (jubilee), the king's arms are crossed over his chest. He was probably holding the royal insignia of the crook and flail. Despite the poor state of preservation of the figure, now in the British Museum in London, it is still possible to admire its fine execution.

The head of Seth has a long nose and squared-off ears. It has been likened to an anteater, but probably portrays a completely mythical beast.

► The god Seth
Seth is one of the earliest gods of Egypt. Originally from Ombos, he was the protector of Upper Egypt. In the Thinite era, the king was the earthly incarnation of Seth and Horus, his counterpart for Lower Egypt.

Integrated into the Osirian cycle, Seth became the murderer of Osiris and a god with an ambiguous personality. Venerated as a powerful warrior, he was also held in contempt for his role as a killer.

This statue is much later in date and is part of a group depicting the pharaoh Rameses III (1184–1153 BC) crowned by Horus and Seth.

Seth was the god of chaos and confusion, but was still venerated during the Thinite period.

The ankh cross signified life and was often shown being presented to the pharaoh by the gods to confer eternal life.

Seth's body is depicted as either that of a man or that of a dog.

One of the major innovations of the Thinite period was monumental architecture, although the mud-brick palaces of the early dynasties have fallen victim to time and only ruins survive. An idea of what they looked like can be gained from images on such objects as the funerary stele of Djet. It is likely that these early palaces were surrounded by a fortified enclosure wall with alternate set-backs and overhangs.

Hieroglyphic writing was also developed during the Thinite period, originally just on objects inscribed with the king's name, but there is evidence to suggest that religious and medical literature first came into existence at this time.

▼ Decorated disc
The tomb of the chancellor Hemaka, who lived around 3050 BC, contained a wooden chest inlaid with ivory. Inside the chest were perforated discs threaded on a wooden rod. They may have been spinning tops.

▶ Thinite cup
This cup from the First Dynasty was discovered in a tomb in Lower Egypt. It is now in the collection of the Egyptian Museum in Munich.

The front of the disc is flat and decorated, while the back is smooth and convex.

The hooves and horns of the gazelles are sculpted from the soapstone.

The black dog has seized its prey by the neck and holds it firmly.

The disc rotates around a wooden rod, which passes through the central hole.

The ochre-coloured dog is pursuing another gazelle.

▼ Animals in art
This vase in the shape of a gazelle, from the east of the Delta, shows that artists already displayed considerable creativity.

▲ Dogs hunting gazelle
This disc, also found in Saqqara inside the tomb of Hemaka, the chancellor of Lower Egypt, depicts a hunting scene with a pair of gazelles being chased by two dogs. The bodies of the ochre-coloured dog and the gazelles are in alabaster, fixed to the black soapstone with an adhesive material.

Chronology of the Thinite Period (3100–2686 BC)

3100 BC The First Dynasty Begins

▲ A king with two names
The names of Aha, of the First Dynasty, are shown in this detail from an ivory label found in the tomb of Queen Neithotep, who was probably Aha's wife. Under the Horus falcon is Aha. The other name is 'Men', giving rise to the idea that Aha and the semi-mythical founder of Memphis, Menes, were one and the same person.

▲ The royal palace
The pharaoh Djer built his royal palace at Memphis, the capital founded by his father. The 'palace façade' (shown in plan and elevation in the sketch) formed part of a motif known as a 'serekh' in which the Horus name of the pharaoh was enclosed. The serekh was the forerunner of the cartouche.

◄ Funerary stele of the pharaoh Djet
This magnificent stone stele is 143cm (56in) high and 65cm 25½in) wide. Made 5,000 years ago, it is now in the Louvre Museum in Paris. The upper portion shows the falcon god Horus; the royal serekh contains the hieroglyph of a snake (Djet was 'the cobra of Horus'). The lower portion shows the typical 'palace façade' design.

▲ The first conflict with the east
An ivory label found at Abydos (now in the British Museum) portrays the pharaoh Den in the act of striking an Asiatic dignitary with a mace. The inscription reads 'first time of striking the easterners' and suggests conflict with Palestine.

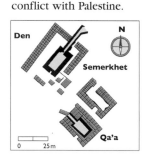

◄ Human sacrifice
This plan of the royal cemetery at Abydos shows the tombs of three pharaohs of the First Dynasty: Den, Semerkhet and Qa'a. The tombs were large and surrounded by satellite tombs. Den's, for example, measured 56m x 25m (184ft x 82ft) and had around it the tombs of 174 sacrificed servants. This practice was soon abandoned, however, and shabti figures eventually replaced the servants for the performance of tasks beyond the grave.

3100	3000 BC	2980 BC	2950 BC	2925 BC	2900 BC

2890 BC

First Dynasty 3100–2890 BC

◄ Aha was the immediate successor to Narmer, the first pharaoh of a united Egypt, and probably his son. His name means 'the fighter'. Two tombs have been discovered – one at Abydos, the other at Saqqara – one of which was perhaps a cenotaph.

► Djer, son of Aha, succeeded his father as pharaoh of Egypt. His name means 'Horus, he who gives succour'. His tomb at Abydos was the first to have different chambers filled with grave goods.

► Djet, also known as the serpent, was interred at Abydos in a wood-lined burial chamber. Close to his tomb was a limestone funerary stele, now in the Louvre, Paris, which bears the hieroglyph of a serpent, of which the phonetic value is 'djet'.

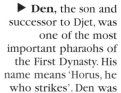

► Den, the son and successor to Djet, was one of the most important pharaohs of the First Dynasty. His name means 'Horus, he who strikes'. Den was the first monarch to boast the title 'king of Upper and Lower Egypt' and first added the title 'he of the sedge and bee' to the royal names. His tomb at Abydos is the earliest example of stone being used in a funerary monument.

► Anedjib, whose name means 'saved is his heart', was the first ruler to add the title of 'Two Ladies' to his name, emphasizing that he was the ruler of both Upper and Lower Egypt. His tomb at Abydos contained a mud-brick, stepped structure which is thought to be the precursor of the stepped pyramid.

► Semerkhet usurped the throne of Anedjib and was in his turn overthrown by Qa'a. His name means 'attentive friend'.

► Qa'a came to the throne after overthrowing Semerkhet. He was the last pharaoh of the First Dynasty. His name means 'his arm is raised'.

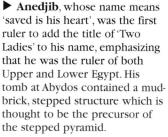

Egypt in the Thinite Period

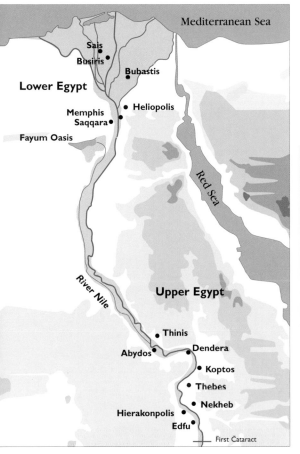

Mediterranean Sea

Lower Egypt

Sais
Busiris
Bubastis
Memphis
Saqqara
Heliopolis
Fayum Oasis

Red Sea

River Nile

Upper Egypt

Thinis
Abydos
Dendera
Koptos
Thebes
Nekheb
Hierakonpolis
Edfu

First Cataract

◄ **A stele with two ladies**
This elegant double stele (48cm x 10cm/19in x 4in) dates from the end of the Thinite period and is one of the most ancient representations of a funerary banquet. It comes from the necropolis of Saqqara and is now in the Louvre Museum in Paris.

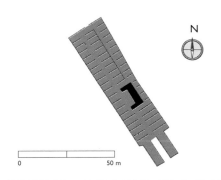

N

0   50 m

▲ **Change of name**
The penultimate Thinite pharaoh began his reign with the name Sekhemib ('of the potent heart'). His serekh was surmounted by a Horus falcon. Later in his reign, Seth was promoted to greater prominence and his serekh was adorned with a Seth animal. He also changed his name to Peribsen ('hope of all hearts').

▲ **A tomb for the last Thinite pharaoh**
Khasekhemwy died around 2686 BC, and with him the Second Dynasty and the Thinite period came to an end. He was buried in a trapezoid mastaba tomb 70m (230ft) long and 17m (56ft) wide at its broadest point. It had a stone-lined burial chamber, 43 storerooms for funerary offerings, and represents the last royal burial in the cemetery at Abydos.

| 2890 BC | 2865 BC | | 2700 BC | | 2686 BC |

Second Dynasty 2890–2686 BC

◄ **Hetepsekhemwy**, founder of the Second Dynasty, established peace between Upper and Lower Egypt. His name means 'pleasing in powers'. He built his tomb at Saqqara, near Memphis, which was now the sole capital of Egypt.

▶ **Raneb** was the second pharaoh of the Second Dynasty. His name means 'Ra is the lord', the oldest evidence for the birth of a cult to this deity, set up by the priests of Heliopolis in Lower Egypt.

◄ **Nynetjer** was the third pharaoh of the Second Dynasty. When the tension within Upper Egypt heightened, he dismantled the fortresses of several cities in the Delta. His name means 'divine'.

Weneg and Sened are known only by their names. It is probable that their power was limited to the Memphis area and that another unknown pharaoh controlled Upper Egypt.

▶ **Peribsen** re-established the capital at Thinis and was buried at Abydos, next to the tombs of the kings of the First Dynasty. It is possible that there was conflict between Upper and Lower Egypt, but seal impressions found at Elephantine confirm that his kingdom stretched as far south as the First Cataract. His name is often followed by the description 'conqueror of foreign lands'.

▶ **Khasekhemwy** was a warrior king who fought a bloody war against the north of the country, in which more than 47,000 of the enemy died. This led to the re-unification of the two kingdoms. His serekh unites Horus and Seth, perhaps indicating a return to religious and political harmony.

The Old Kingdom

In ancient Egyptian history, the Old Kingdom (2686–2181 BC) was a golden age of prosperity, which witnessed the construction of the first great funerary monuments that are now regarded as one of the highlights of Egyptian civilization.

Khasekhemwy (c.2686 BC), the last ruler of the 2nd Dynasty, united Egypt after a period of turmoil and laid the foundations for the development of the Old Kingdom, beginning with his sons, Sanakht (2686–2667 BC) and Djoser (2667–2648 BC).

The beginning of the pyramid period

Of the five pharaohs of the 3rd Dynasty, only Djoser (2667–2648 BC) is well known. He established the necropolis at Memphis as the site for royal burials and built the step pyramid at Saqqara – the first large-scale stone construction in history. Building the pyramid was made possible by the enormous upswing in the Egyptian economy, by increased agricultural production and by well-defined and well-organized state administration.

The 4th Dynasty, starting with Sneferu (2613–2599 BC), saw the power of the pharaohs reach its climax. This was reflected in the size and grandeur of the tomb monuments. Sneferu built three pyramids at Meidum and Dashur, and his son and successor, Khufu (2589–2566 BC, constructed the Great Pyramid at Giza. Djedefra (2566–2558 BC), one of Khufu's sons, seized power after killing his brother, before himself being assassinated by Khafra (2558–2532 BC). Djedefra built his pyramid at Abu Roash, but Khafra kept up the tradition at Giza with the construction of the second pyramid and the Great Sphinx. Little is known about his successor, Menkaura (2532–2503 BC), except that he built the third pyramid at Giza, while the last king of the 4th Dynasty, Shepseskaf (2503–2498 BC), chose to be buried in a mastaba tomb between Saqqra and Dashur.

During the 5th Dynasty, smaller pyramids were built and sun temples were constructed for the increasingly influential cult of the sun god, ras. In the pyramid of the final ruler of the dynasty, Unas (2375–2345 BC), are the first examples of the Pyramid Texts.

The pyramids and tombs of the 6th Dynasty, founded by Teti (2345–2323 BC), are all located at Saqqra. The best-known ruler of this dynasty was Pepy I (2321–2287 BC), who built several temples and married two daughters of a high-ranking official in Abydos. He was suceeded by sons of these marriages, first Merenra (2287–2278 BC), who ruled for just a few years, and then by Pepy II (2278–2184 BC), who governed for more than 90 years and presided over the decline and end of the Old Kingdom.

◄ **Statuette of a woman**
This small ivory figure of a woman from Abu Roash shows the progress in the art of carving at the beginning of the Old Kingdom.

▼ **The statues of Sepa and Neset**
These limestone statues date from the 3rd Dynasty (2686 – 2613 BC) and are on display in the Louvre, Paris. They are among the most ancient examples of private statuary. Although the faces are finely sculpted, their static posture is typical of the style of sculpture in the early part of the Old Kingdom.

Sepa, an official from the 3rd Dynasty, wears a helmet-like, curly wig, characteristic of the Old Kingdom.

▲ The palace-façade decoration
Many memorials of the Old Kingdom, in particular sarcophagi and tombs, display a motif of recessed panelling. This represents the stylized façade of a royal residence, and is a hieroglyph usually associated with Horus, of whom the king was an earthly incarnation.

► Statue of Imhotep
Vizier and building supervisor of Djoser (2667–2648 BC), Imhotep constructed the step pyramid at Saqqra. Posterity worshipped him as the inventor of monumental stone architecture, as well as a writer and a skilled physician.

His reputation lasted for centuries, and by the late period (747 –332 BC) he was revered as a god – a rare honour for someone not of royal birth. From this time, there are numerous small bronze figures which show him as a seated scribe, unrolling a papyrus across his knees.

Neset, the wife of Sepa, wears a heavy black wig which descends beyond her shoulders.

The lower lids of Neset and Sepa were emphasized with broad, dark lines. In life, Egyptians used kohl or green malachite powder to underline the eyes.

Neset's long linen robe has a v-shaped neck.

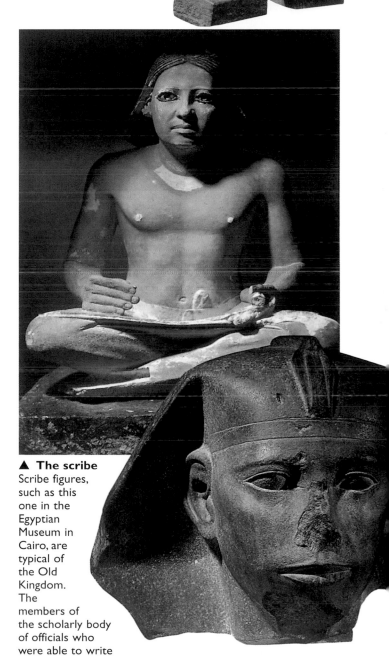

▲ The scribe
Scribe figures, such as this one in the Egyptian Museum in Cairo, are typical of the Old Kingdom. The members of the scholarly body of officials who were able to write were responsible for the fortunes of the state, and often had themselves depicted in this formalized way.

▲ Sphinx of Djedefra
This head of the pharaoh Djedefra (2566–2558 BC) is from a sphinx made from red quartzite. It was found in a boat pit at the king's pyramid site in Abu Roash.

Chronology of the Old Kingdom (2686–2181 BC)

2686 BC The Old Kingdom begins

◀ Tomb complex of Djoser
The second pharaoh of the Old Kingdom, Djoser built the first step pyramid at Saqqara, the largest necropolis in the capital, Memphis. It has been suggested that the monumental tomb complex surrounding the pyramid was a stone image of the capital in which the king's palace was located. The first monument to be built entirely from cut cubic stone, it was designed by the architect Imhotep.

◀ Tomb furnishings of Hetepheres
Hetepheres was the wife of Sneferu, the founder of the Fourth Dynasty, and the mother of Khufu. Her son had her reburied near his own pyramid in Giza after her first tomb had been partially robbed. The well-preserved tomb ornaments found in Giza, such as these bracelets, are a testimony to the splendour of such burials in the Old Kingdom.

▲ Pyramid of Nyuserra
For this pyramid, built north of Saqqara in Abusir, regular stone blocks were used only as an outer casing. The inside of the monument was filled up with poor-quality field stones and scree. After the cut stone blocks were plundered, the pyramid soon began to fall apart. This cheap way of building, however, had been common since the rule of the pharaoh Sahura (2487–2475 BC).

◀ The pyramids of Giza
On the plateau of Giza, at the edge of modern Cairo, the kings of the Fourth Dynasty – Khufu, Khafra and Menkaura – constructed their pyramids. Architecturally, these are the most impressive pyramids in Egypt. Completely made from cut stone blocks, they remain almost fully intact today.

2686 BC	2667 BC	2613 BC		2494 BC
Third Dynasty 2686–2613 BC		Fourth Dynasty 2613–2494 BC		

▼ Sanakht (2686–2667 BC) was the son of the last Thinite king, Khasekhemwy (c. 2686 BC). His unfinished tomb monument is probably in Saqqara, to the west of the step pyramid of Djoser. His Horus name means 'victorious protection'.

▶ Djoser (2667–2848 BC) was probably a brother of Sanakht and the most important king of the Third Dynasty. Imhotep, his building supervisor, constructed the famous step pyramid for him within a magnificent tomb site. His Horus name, Netjerikhet, means 'with a godly body'.

2613 BC End of the Third Dynasty and beginning of the Fourth

▶ Sneferu (2613–2589 BC) founded the Fourth Dynasty. From then, the birth name of the ruler was framed by a cartouche. In search of the perfect tomb image, Sneferu had no fewer than three pyramids built at Meidum and Dahshur. His name means 'the one made perfectly'.

▶ Khufu (2589–2566 BC) was the successor of Sneferu and builder of the largest pyramid at Giza. His name means 'Khnum protects me'. During his 23-year reign, his power remained unchallenged. In Greek texts, he is called a 'loathsome tyrant', but Khufu was one of the mightiest Egyptian pharaohs.

▶ Khafra (2558–2532 BC) was the brother and successor of Khufu's oldest son, Djedefra (2566–2558 BC). He built the second, slightly smaller pyramid in Giza. His Horus name, Rakhaef, means 'Ra appears'.

◀ Menkaura (2532–2503 BC) was the son and successor of Khafra. His name means 'for ever remain the ka powers of Ra'. Menkaura had the third pyramid built on the plateau of Giza.

▶ Shepseskaf (2503–2498 BC) was the last king of the Fourth Dynasty. Unexpectedly, he abandoned the pyramid tomb as a burial form, left the plateau of Giza and built a mastaba tomb in south Saqqara. His name means 'his ka is sublime'.

2494 BC End of the Fourth Dynasty and beginning of the Fifth

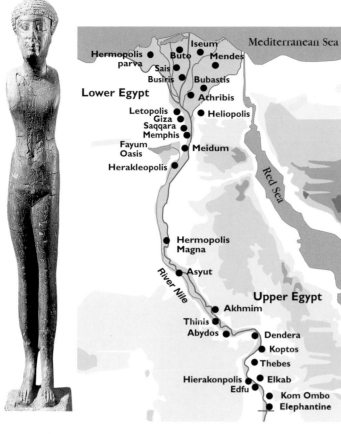

2345 BC End of the Fifth Dynasty and beginning of the Sixth

◄ Egypt in the Old Kingdom

One of the most important aims of the pharaohs of the Old Kingdom was the cultivation of the entire country and the development of town planning. For this reason, large parts of the population were relocated along the Nile.

▼ Pyramid of Teti

This tomb monument, built for the founder of the Sixth Dynasty, is located in north Saqqara. In its building technique and dimensions, it is similar to the pyramids of the Fifth Dynasty, but, in Fourth-Dynasty tradition, the complex contained satellite pyramids for the burial of two queens. The passage in the main pyramid is inscribed with *Pyramid Texts*.

◄ Mastaba of Qar

Statues of Qar and his family hewn into the rock line the walls of his underground burial chambers at Giza. Among his other functions, Qar was the priest for the mortuary cult of Pepy I, and was in charge of the pyramid sites of Khufu and Menkaura.

▲ Wooden statue of a woman

The private art of the Old Kingdom is characterized by a greater naturalism than the royal sculpture of the same time. Numerous styles of statue were created in an abundance of materials, particularly in different kinds of stone. Wood, too, was often used, as shown by this small female figure from the 5th Dynasty.

2445 BC	2345 BC	2321 BC	2181 BC
Fifth Dynasty 2494–2345 BC		Sixth Dynasty 2345–2181 BC	

▼ Userkaf (2494–2487 BC)

was the founder of the Fifth Dynasty. He separated the mortuary cult from the cult of the sun god, Ra. During his reign, the number of titles of the king was extended to five by adding a 'throne name'. Userkaf's name means 'effective is his ka'.

▼ Sahura (2487–2475 BC)

was the brother and successor of Userkaf. His name means 'Ra comes to me'. The core of his pyramid at Abusir consisted of fragmented stone rather than stone blocks. The first expedition to Punt took place during his reign.

▼ Nyuserra (2445–2421 BC)

also had his pyramid built in Abusir. During his reign, the first sun sanctuary was built in Abu Gurab at the western edge of the desert, and is the best preserved sun temple of the Fifth Dynasty. His name means 'the power belongs to Ra'.

▼ Unas (2375–2345 BC)

was the last ruler of the Fifth Dynasty. He built a small pyramid in Saqqara and, for the first time, had its internal walls inscribed with *Pyramid Texts*.

▼ Teti (2345–2323 BC)

was the founder of the Sixth Dynasty, although he was not of royal descent. Several influential viziers are known from his reign, among them Mereruka and Kagemni. Teti built his pyramid complex in north Saqqara.

▼ Pepy I (2321–2287 BC)

was the son of Teti. He developed an active foreign policy, undertook several military expeditions to Asia and colonized the Libyan oases. His pyramid complex in south Saqqara was called Merire-mennefer, probably giving Memphis its name.

▼ Pepy II (2278–2184 BC)

was the successor and younger brother of Merenra (2287-2278 BC). His reign, lasting for about 60 years, was one of the longest in Ancient Egyptian history. Under his rule, the final decline of the Egyptian state of the Old Kingdom took place. His small pyramid in south Saqqara is the last of the period.

2181 BC End of the Sixth Dynasty and the Old Kingdom

Khufu, Builder of the Great Pyramid

Although Khufu, also known by his Greek name Cheops, was the builder of the first and largest of the three pyramids at Giza, little is known about his life and his only surviving image is a small ivory statuette excavated from a temple in Abydos.

Khufu (2589-2566 BC), the second pharaoh of the Fourth Dynasty, was the son of King Sneferu (2613-2589 BC) and Hetepheres (*c.* 2600 BC), a daughter of the last king of the Third Dynasty. Written documents show Khufu in a contradictory light. The

Greek historians considered him a tyrant, but in Egypt he was generally looked upon as a wise and good king.

There is little information about Khufu's personality and his ways of government from contemporary sources, but it is evident that he fortified the kingdom founded

▲ Khufu's seal
The cartouche on the pharaoh's seal contains the hieroglyphs (above right) that spell his name. Khufu is the abbreviation of *Khnum-khuefui* – 'Khnum protects me'. Khnum was the ram god associated with the Nile floods and was one of the gods who created the universe.

▶ Stone blocks
The Great Pyramid at Giza consists of more than two million limestone blocks, each weighing at least 2.5 tonnes. In a building period of about 23 years, the length of Khufu's reign, one block would have to have been moved every five minutes to complete the work.

by his predecessors and increased the power of the state that they had carefully established.

A strictly organized administration ensured that the king's orders were followed, and that the resources of the state were well used. The key positions of government, as well as the highest priesthoods, were held by members of the king's household. Two of Khufu's sons, Djedefra (2566–2558 BC) and Khafra (2558–2532 BC), followed Khufu to the throne.

Prosperity and posterity

Neighbouring countries contributed considerably to Egypt's prosperity at this time. The badly needed wood for building purposes was imported from Lebanon. Sinai provided copper and valuable turquoise, and Nubia gold, while raids on Nubia and Libya yielded rich pickings in cattle and prisoners.

The Great Pyramid, with which Khufu immortalized his reign, was designed to surpass every tomb that had been built previously, and the king's family, household and government officials were buried in the surrounding necropolis. His mother, chief queens and other family are entombed in three smaller pyramids and mastaba tombs.

INSIGHT

Khufu's boat to the afterlife

In 1954, a boat, which supposedly took Khufu to the afterlife, was discovered on the southern side of the Great Pyramid. Separated into 1,224 individual pieces, it was found stowed in a cavity hewn out of rock and covered with stone slabs. After its removal, the boat was reconstructed over a period of years (below), and a museum was built on the spot where it was found. The boat is constructed of cedarwood, juniper and pine, and measures 43m (141ft) long and 5.9m (19ft 4in) wide.

Khufu – the second pharaoh of the Fourth Dynasty

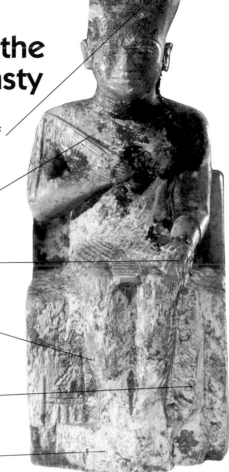

The pharaoh's headdress is the red crown of Lower Egypt.

Khufu holds a flail, the symbol of his royal power, in his right hand.

Regal statues often show the ruler's left hand resting on his knee, as here.

Khufu's throne name appears in hieroglyphs on the right side of the throne.

The hieroglyphs in this cartouche are partially damaged.

The ivory statuette is only 7.5cm (3in) high.

▲ Khufu's image

The only remaining image of the builder of the Great Pyramid was found in the temple of Khentimentiu, in Abydos, and can now be seen in the Egyptian Museum, Cairo. The ivory statuette, only 7.5cm (3in) high, shows the enthroned king wearing the red crown of Lower Egypt. In his right hand he holds a flail, while his left hand is draped over his knee. On the throne, next to his legs, is his name.

▼ The final resting place

The tomb chamber of the pyramid of Khufu was built of red granite. The sarcophagus, made of the same material, was placed on the western wall during the building works. After the entombment of the ruler, the chamber was sealed with three stone slabs which served as trapdoors.

The Time of Pepy I

The Sixth Dynasty (2345–2181 BC) was a time of long, stable reigns, economic growth and colonial expansion, but this age of prosperity was the last great flourish of the Old Kingdom.

Pepy I (2321-2287 BC) was the son of Teti, founder of the Sixth Dynasty, and Iput, daughter of Unas, the last ruler of the Fifth Dynasty. Teti died in 2323 BC, and Egypt was ruled by an obscure figure called Userkara, who was either a regent or, more probably, a usurper, for more than a year before Pepy I took the throne.

Pepy I was an active ruler, sending military and trading expeditions into Nubia and the Middle East, and promoting the building of many monuments, including temples at Abydos, Bubastis, Dendera and Elephantine. None of these has survived, however. The country's economy began to grow and Egypt prospered as the result of blossoming trade with Byblos (modern Lebanon) in the north and Punt in the south. Turquoise and copper were found in the Sinai, gold was brought from Nubia, and calcite and greywacke came from the quarries of Hatnub and Wadi Hammamat.

▲ All the way to Memphis
The pyramid of Pepy I was called Men-nefer, 'established and beautiful', and the name was applied first to the pyramid town and thence to the nearby capital city of Ineb-hedj ('White Walls'). The Greeks hellenized this name to Memphis.

▶ The pharaoh in copper
This life-sized representation of Pepy I, buried under the floor of a side chapel at the temple of Hierakonpolis, is the earliest copper statue ever found in Egypt. Pepy presided over the opening up of copper mines in Sinai.

▼ Provincial powers
The provincial governors, the nomarchs, grew in power from the end of the Fifth Dynasty as their offices became hereditary. They began to assert their power by, for example, insisting on being buried in their province rather than in the capital.

S3 - Rʿ, Ppj

'Pepy,
son of Ra'

Mn-nfr - Ppj

'Perfect and eternal is (the pyramid of) Pepy.'

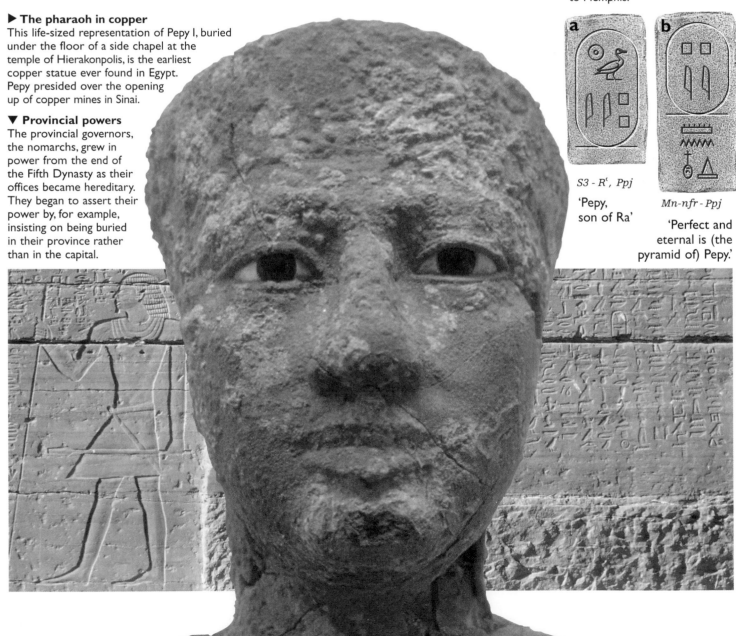

Despite his successes, there are hints that Pepy I had his share of internal political problems. The funerary biography of a courtier called Weni – whose long service began under Teti and ended under Pepy I's son, Merenra – tells of a harem conspiracy and an attempt on Pepy's life. Such treachery, possibly instigated by his first wife, is a clear sign of his loss of authority.

Rise of the nomarchs

Later in his reign Pepy I married two sisters, both called Ankhenesmerira. They were the daughters of Khui, the governor of the nome centred on Abydos. The office of nomarch had become a hereditary one, and some nomarchs began to wield great power and influence, few more so than Khui. The older of the two sisters was the mother of Pepy's successor Merenra, who died young. He was followed to the throne by the infant son of the younger sister, Pepy II. Khui's son, Djau, was vizier to both. Pepy II's long reign saw the gradual collapse of the Old Kingdom, as power gradually shifted to the nomarchs.

▲ Foreign labour
Agricultural production intensified during the Old Kingdom and there were sometimes labour shortages. The pharaohs would send raiding parties into Nubia – then referred to by Egyptians as Yam – to take prisoners and bring them back to Egypt. Most of them were forced to settle and farm in the Delta. Nubians also joined the pharaonic army as mercenaries.

▼ Desert outpost
At the end of the Fifth Dynasty, the Egyptians established a colony at Dakhla Oasis in the Egyptian Western Desert. This was at the crossing of two important trails, one leading from the Nile Valley to the east and the other south to Nubia. The colony was administered and policed by governors appointed by the pharaoh, and flourished during the reign of Pepy I.

▼ A little-known king
The reign of Merenra ('Beloved of Ra') was short; the unfinished state of his pyramid near that of his father in Saqqara suggests he died a premature death. He continued his father's foreign policies in Syria-Palestine and tightened Egypt's grip on Nubia, but left very few monuments. The alabaster vase below bears his name in a royal cartouche and one of his titles.

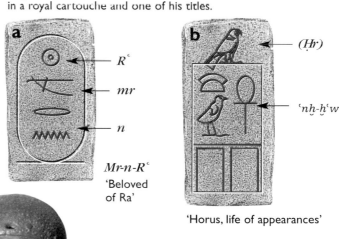

a
R^c
mr
n

Mr-n-R^c
'Beloved of Ra'

b
(Hr)
'nh-$h^c w$

'Horus, life of appearances'

▶ Son and heir
The copper statue of Pepy I found at Hierakonpolis had this smaller statue cached inside it. Before they were buried, the two statues stood alongside one another on the same base. Although there is no inscription on this second statue, Egyptologists usually ascribe it to Pepy's son and successor, Merenra (2287–2278 BC), partly because the face, although it bears a familial resemblance, differs significantly from that of the adult king, and partly because Merenra's name appears on a surviving fragment of the base.

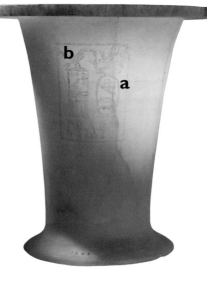

b
a

The First Intermediate Period

As the traditional structure of the Ancient Egyptian state dissolved at the end of the Old Kingdom (2686-2181 BC), Egypt entered a period of political and economic uncertainty with no central figure to lead the country.

At the close of the 6th Dynasty (2345-2181 BC), Egypt suffered social and political decline. Insurrections weakened and divided the central government in Memphis. For more than a century, the country was torn apart by continuing social unrest, political anarchy and invasions by Bedouin peoples. Very little is known about this period, except that it saw the growth of provincial power. The nomarchs, whose position had been hereditary since the 5th Dynasty (2494-2345 BC), reigned supreme in their constituencies.

The trouble began with Pepy II (2278-2184 BC). His old age and long reign caused him to lose control of the country. Many temples were freed from taxation and the chief administrators of the provinces no longer had to pay tributes. The country became bankrupt.

The pharaohs, residing at Memphis, now ruled all of Egypt in name only. Their actual influence was limited to a rather small area, as the Delta, too, was independent. All this led to a rapid turnover of rulers - in the mere 50

▶ **Decline of the Monarchy**
The old Kingdom reached the height of its glory under the great pyramid-building pharaohs of the 4th Dynasty – Khufu, Khafra and Menkaura (right). By the 6th Dynasty, the Egyptian state was in terminal decline as the power of the pharaoh weakened.

▼ **The nomarchs**
Since the late 5th Dynasty, the provincial governors – the nomarchs – had gained more power and began to demonstrate their independence by being buried in their home provinces rather than close to the pharaohs in the royal necropolises.

▼ **The Officials** Up to the middle of the 5th Dynasty, all high ranking officials were appointed by the king and were under his direct control. The rewards were high. Ptahshepses (c. 2445–2421 BC), was given this magnificent mastaba tomb at Abusir.

years of the 7th and 8th Dynasties there were more than 25 kings. The provincial governors of Herakleopolis took over power in the north and founded the 9th and 10th Dynasties in 2160 BC, claiming sovereignty over all of Egypt.

But a second power base developed in Thebes, and the local nobles founded the 11th Dynasty in 2125 BC. Both princely houses assumed the title of king of all Egypt – and with this, a fight for supremacy began that would last for decades.

Renewed Unification of the Country

While the Herakleopolitans tried to expel the immigrants from the Near East, the Thebans started to expand their territory from the Delta, under Intef I (2125–2112 BC) and Intef II (2112–2063 BC). The border of the northern part of their country was Thinis; any further expansion was opposed by the provincial governors of Asyut, who at that time still supported Herakleopolis. Eventually, Mentuhotep II (2055–2004 BC) began to conquer Lower Egypt, reunify the country and found the Middle Kingdom.

▶ Stele of the hunter Intef
Intef was responsible for the stockpiling of supplies for the Theban kings Intef II and Intef III (2063–2055 BC). His career ended under Mentuhotep II, who unified the country.

▼ Herakleopolis
Located close to modern-day Beni Suef, Herakleopolis was the capital of the 20th nome of Upper Egypt, and during the 9th and 10th Dynasties was the seat of one line of pharaohs who claimed the throne of Egypt.

The three women depicted *are wives of Intef.*

The inferior artistic quality of artefacts and monuments during the First Intermediate Period is reflected in the figures' proportions.

The hieroglyphs on the stele list the names and titles of the figures.

◀ Nubian mercenaries
Provincial governors established their own armies comprising numerous Nubian mercenaries, a large colony of whom seem to have existed at Gebelein, about 30km (18 miles) south of Thebes. In the nearby cemetery, several stelae have been found, depicting the Nubians with curly hair, short loincloths with a sash and their weapons. Often they are accompanied by their favourite animals – large slender dogs. This stele belongs to a soldier called Tjehenu.

Chronology of the First Intermediate Period

2181 BC Beginning of the 7th and 8th Dynasties and the First Intermediate Period

▲ Tomb of Ankhtify
A provincial governor of the nomes of Hierakonpolis and Edfu, Ankhtify (c. 2160 BC), was an opponent of the Thebans.

◄ Stele of Heka and his wife Hemet
The only relief decorations in the tombs of low-ranking officials in provincial cemeteries of the First Intermediate Period were small limestone stelae, the work of local craftsmen.

▲ Stele of Khety
Only a few stelae and false doors come from Herakleopolis, the capital of egypt during the 9th and 10th Dynasties. They bear the names and titles of some officials from that time, and are from the badly damaged necropolis of the First Intermediate period.

Year	2170	2165	2160	2155	2150	2145	2140	2135	2130	2125	2120	2115	2110
Dynasty	VII & VIII Dynasty		IX & X Dynasty										

Neferkare
A number of short reigning kings of the 7th and 8th Dynasties took the throne name of Pepy II. In this way, they tried to continue the tradition of the late Old Kingdom and to legitimise their reign. The name of Neferkare is mentioned in the tomb of Ankhtify at el-Mo'alla. It means 'Perfect is the ka of Ra'.

Mentuhotep I
The founder of the dynasty of Thebes, with the birth name 'Montu is content', did not bear the kings title but only that of a provincial governor. The two kings succeeding him to the throne were probably his sons.

Intef I Sehertawy
The first Theban governor, Intef I officially adopted the royal title, thus threatening the rulers of Herakleopolis. According to contemporary texts, at the end of his 12-year reign, after his victory over the provincial governor Ankhtify, he ruled the territory of the southernmost six nomes, from Elephantine to Dendra.

Intef II Wahankh
The reign of Intef II, whose Horus name means 'With eternal life', lasted 50 years, during which time the first serious conflicts with Herakleopolis took place. He extended the sphere of influence of the Thebans almost up to Asyut by conquering the 8th Upper Egyptian province with the towns of Thinis and Abydos. According to the inscription on the tomb stele of Intef II, the northern border of the province in his 50th year of rule was in the 10th Upper Egyptian province at Qau el-Kebir. Among his opponents were the provincial governors of Asyut, who were allies of the rulers of Herakleopolis. The tomb of Intef II is in the northern part of the Theban necropolis. It is called a saff tomb because of its striking facade with a row of pillars (saff means 'pillar' in Arabic).

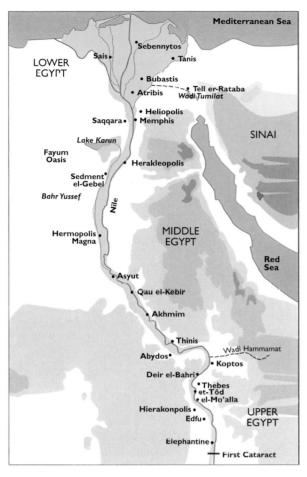

◀ The *Coffin Texts*

The downfall of central power led to a change in political, social and religious affairs. The formerly exclusively royal *Coffin Texts* were written on everyone's coffins, a kind of 'democratization' of the afterlife.

◀ Egypt during the First Intermediate Period

Apart from the two kingdoms of Herakleopolis and Thebes, there were further small city states which, at least temporarily, kept their independence. The most trusted allies of the Herakleopolitans were the provincial governors of Asyut.

▶ Stele of Tjetji

Tjetji, the treasury administrator of King Intef II, writes on his stele of his many years of service, when the country was under Intef's control, in the south to Elephantine and in the north to Thinis.

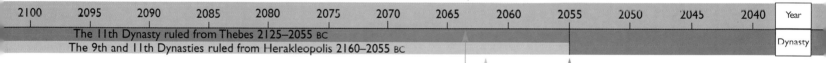

Year													
2100	2095	2090	2085	2080	2075	2070	2065	2060	2055	2050	2045	2040	

The 11th Dynasty ruled from Thebes 2125–2055 BC

The 9th and 11th Dynasties ruled from Herakleopolis 2160–2055 BC

Dynasty

Intef III Nakhtnebtepnefer

The Horus name of this king means 'Strong master of correct actions'. He ruled for only eight years and there is no accurate documentation of his conflicts with the ruler of Herakleopolis, Khety V, and his subjects.

Four documented kings ruled from Herakleopolis during the 9th and 10th Dynasties, the chronology of which is uncertain.

Khety V Wahkara

The most important king of the Herakleopolites and author of The *Teachings for Merykara*, a set of instructions to his son on how to be a king.

During his reign there were several years of peace with the Thebans, and he led campains against the Asian Bedouins ruling in the Delta and drove them out. From that time, trade relations with Byblos are again documented. Khety V erected the so-called Wall of the Ruler in the eastern Delta to secure the border.

Khety IV Meryibra

Little is documented from the reign of this ruler of Herakleopolis, whose throne name meant 'With a loving heart like Ra'. Even his position in the succession of kings of the 9th and 10th Dynasties is not quite certain.

Merykara

The throne name of the only king from Herakleopolis, whose tomb pyramid is at least documented by inscription, means 'Loved in Ka power like Ra'. During his reign, the kingdom of Herakleopolis met serious trouble for the first time because of Theban attacks.

Mentuhotep II

After leading the decisive battles against the kingdom of Herakleopolis, Mentuhotep II unified Egypt once again, founding the Middle Kingdom.

Herakleopolis Magna

Situated in Upper Egypt, Herakleopolis Magna was the capital of the country for a short period during the political upheaval of the First Intermediate period (2181–2055 BC).

Towards the end of the Old Kingdom (2686–2181 BC), the central authority of the pharaoh waned. Local rulers gained power, and the once-united country was separated into numerous small territories. After about 20 years, Khety I, the first ruler of the Ninth and Tenth dynasties (2160–2025 BC), claimed sovereignty over all of Egypt and moved the seat of government from Memphis to Herakleopolis Magna.

Divided rule

While the kings of the Ninth and Tenth dynasties ruled Egypt for a short period, resistance began in Upper Egypt. Under Mentuhotep I and his son Intef I (2125–2112 BC), the Thebans seceded from the Herakleopolitans and announced their independence. This led to the founding of the Eleventh Dynasty and the partition of the country. The three successors to Mentuhotep I all had the name of Intef and regarded themselves as the rightful kings of Upper and Lower Egypt. It was Mentuhotep II, however, who reunited the two parts of the country in 2055 BC and founded the Middle Kingdom.

▲ The capital and the district
Herakleopolis Magna was the capital of the 20th Upper Egyptian nome, the old name of which was naret-khentet, meaning 'the naret (tree) in front'. The tree was probably a species of oleander.

▼ Bahr Yussef
The ancient name of Herakleopolis Magna was Henen-nesw, 'the (house) of the king's child'. This is reflected in the city's modern name of Ihnasya el-Medina. It was situated near the fertile Fayum region on the right bank of the Bahr Yussef channel, and was an important religious centre throughout Egyptian history.

◄ The god Heryshef
The Ancient Egyptian name of the ram-headed creator god of Herakleopolis Magna was Heryshef ('he who is above his lake'). The Greeks identified him with their god Herakles, and named the city Herakleopolis.

The Bahr Yussef is a channel linked to the freshwater Lake Moeris (Birket Qarun).

Herakleopolis Magna was located south of the Fayum Oasis.

INSIGHT

The history of the city

Herakleopolis Magna had its heyday during the Ninth and Tenth dynasties (2160-2025 BC), but this ancient city continued to play a part in Egypt's history. The temple of the local deity Heryshef was enlarged during the Eighteenth Dynasty, and Rameses II (1279–1213 BC) consented to further extensions and renovations.

The city's necropolis is at nearby Sedment el-Gebel and was used from the First Intermediate period to Greco-Roman times. A stele found at Memphis documents that the pharaoh Sheshonq I (945–924 BC), the founder of the Twenty-Second Dynasty, was from Herakleopolis, and a large number of monuments discovered among the ruins of the city are from the Third Intermediate period (1069–747 BC).

Later, Greeks, Romans and early Christian Egyptians (Copts) settled in Herakleopolis, and archaeological excavations have brought to light Christian sculptures, architectural elements and the occasional remains of a building or two. During these excavations at Herakleopolis Magna, the foundations of an early Christian church (above right) were found.

▶ **Shabti**
This Herakleopolitan shabti is holding hoes in its hands to work the fields in the afterlife.

▶ **Mentuhotep II**
During the reign of the last kings of the Herakleopolitan dynasty, Mentuhotep II (2055–2004 BC) launched his decisive attack from Thebes on Herakleopolis and the partially independent viceroys of Middle Egypt. After fierce battles, in the course of which the Herakleopolitan necropolis was destroyed, Mentuhotep II emerged victorious. Around 2055 BC, the reunification of the country was complete, marking the beginning of the Middle Kingdom (2055–1650 BC).

The surviving archaeological remains at Herakleopolis Magna include a temple dedicated to the local god Heryshef and a nearby necroplis of the First Intermediate period, which also houses rock-cut tombs of the Ptolemaic and Roman periods (332 BC–AD 395). The temple complex contained a sacred lake and was enlarged by Rameses II (1279–1213 BC), when a hypostyle hall with granite columns and palm-leaf capitals was added.

A new beginning

The city of Herakleopolis Magna flourished again during the Third Intermediate period (1069-747 BC), and archaeological excavations have revealed a large temple, parts of the settlement and a cemetery dating from this time.

Nubia and Egypt

Lying to the south beyond Aswan, Nubia was rich in gold, copper and semi-precious stones. In addition, it controlled the trade routes to tropical Africa and its coveted supply of ivory, ebony and animal skins.

Compared to Egypt, Nubia had only a small fertile strip of land along the Nile, but it was rich in mineral resources and trade in luxury goods. Archaeological evidence proves that there was contact between Egypt and Nubia as early as the Predynastic period, but in 3000 BC, when Egypt evolved into a hierarchical society with a central government, successive pharaohs set their sights on controlling the southern land.

Initial raids were little more than slave-gathering enterprises, but by the Old Kingdom (2686–2181 BC) permanent Egyptian settlements were established to mine gold, smelt copper and quarry diorite stone, some of which was used for statues in the mortuary temples of Khufu (2589–2566 BC) and Khafra (2558–2532 BC).

▶ **Grave goods**
During Roman rule over Egypt, Nubia was governed by local kings. After their death, they were buried with many tomb offerings in underground burial chambers which were covered by a mound of earth. Many treasures have been found in these graves, such as this silver headdress decorated with gemstones. The Egyptian influence is evident in the uraeus serpent, the sun disc and the stylized feathers of the atef crown.

▼ **The population of Nubia**
Nubians can be easily identified on Egyptian murals and reliefs. Their characteristics are, among others, a broad nose, wide lips, dark skin colour and a distinctive hairstyle, as well as the occasional headdress. Today's population of southern Egypt and northern Sudan – the territory of former Nubia – still displays the same facial features.

The troubles of the First Intermediate period (2181-2055 BC) broke the commercial contact between the two countries, and it was not until the stability of the Middle Kingdom (2055-1650 BC) that Egypt reasserted its power. After military campaigns by Senusret I (1965-1920 BC) and Senusret III (1874-1855 BC), Lower Nubia was annexed and a chain of fortresses was built as far as the Second Cataract. During the New Kingdom (1550-1069 BC), the pharaohs moved the southern border to the Fourth Cataract and divided Nubia into two administrative regions.

Nubians as pharaoh

At the end of the New Kingdom, Egypt's power waned, and an independent kingdom developed in Nubia. Around 750 BC, the Nubians took the pharaohs' throne and reigned until the invasion of the Assyrians in 664 BC.

The conquest of Nubia

During the New Kingdom (1550-1069 BC), Nubia was the target of several military campaigns, which eventually led to the occupation of the country as far as the Fourth Cataract. This relief from the tomb of Horemheb (1323-1295 BC) in the necropolis of Saqqara shows the treatment of Nubian prisoners.

▼ Nubian servants
Egyptians and Nubians were not always at war. Even during the Middle Kingdom (2055-1650 BC), Nubians lived as members of the police troops in Egypt and made up some of the king's bodyguard.

In art, however, they were mainly depicted as servants. This small alabaster statue, dating from the New Kingdom, depicts a Nubian carrying a vessel. It was most probably used to store precious oil or perfume.

The inscription in the tomb of Horemheb describes the Nubian campaign.

An Egyptian guard beats the prisoners with a stick.

The Egyptian soldier is distinguished from the Nubians by his clothes and facial features.

Round, gold earrings were a common feature in depictions of Nubians.

Distinctive headdresses were worn by Nubian soldiers.

A scribe is busy recording the number of prisoners.

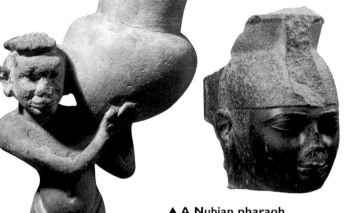

▲ A Nubian pharaoh
Taharqo (690–664 BC) was the third pharaoh of the Nubian Twenty-Fifth Dynasty and inherited the thrones of Egypt and Nubia from his nephew Shabitqo (702–690 BC). During his 26-year reign, he built monuments in the temple complexes of Karnak, Kawa, Medinet Habu and Sanam. Driven out of Egypt in 671 BC by Assyrian invaders, he died in his native Nubia.

▲ Pharaoh power
The Egyptian pharaohs of the New Kingdom had many temples constructed in Nubia. This one at Wadi es-Sebua in the north of Nubia was built by Rameses II (1279–1213 BC), and drawn by Hector Horeau in the nineteenth century.

The Middle Kingdom

During the Middle Kingdom, Pharaonic culture reached a peak. For hundreds of years, the Egyptian era reached great heights in pictorial art and literature, turning this period into the country's golden age.

The First Intermediate period (2181–2055 BC) ended with a 100-year war between Herakleopolis Magna in Lower Egypt and Thebes in Upper Egypt. In 2055 BC, the Theban ruler Mentuhotep II (2055–2004 BC) emerged as the victor of these battles and established rule over the newly unified kingdom, proclaiming himself king.

Mentuhotep II set up his court in Thebes and brought many skilled officials and artists to work there. It was not long before the culture and the economy began to flourish. Today, the Middle Kingdom is seen as one of the high points of Egyptian history.

The conquest of the south

During the civil war, a rich society had developed in Nubia, which was then assimilated by the Egyptian kings of the Eleventh and Twelfth dynasties. They sent many expeditions to the south and established a trade in luxury goods from the Land of Punt. They also gained control of the stone quarries of Wadi Hammamat.

▶ The rise of Amun
Thebes grew from a small provincial town into one of the most important cities of Egypt and, with it, Theban gods also grew in stature and gained a supra-regional importance. Up to the end of the Pharaonic period, Amun remained the highest of the Egyptian gods.

▼ The necropolis of Deir el-Bahri
Mentuhotep II, the first pharaoh of the Middle Kingdom, was laid to rest on the west bank at Thebes, where he had built an unusual terraced funerary complex, which was later copied by Queen Hatshepsut (1473–1458 BC).

The kings of the Twelfth Dynasty (1985–1795 BC) pursued the goal of re-establishing the centralized state of the Old Kingdom (2686–2181 BC), although the regional leaders retained some of their privileges, as can be seen from the rock tombs found at Beni Hasan, Meir, el-Bersha and Aswan. At about this time, the principal royal residence was moved to Itjtawy on the edge of the Fayum region.

Trade and occupation

Trade relations with Byblos and the Aegean Islands were re-established, and the eastern Delta was protected from attacks by Asians and Bedouin by border fortifications. In Nubia, too, fortressses were built, and Egyptian culture was spread by the creation of small temples, most often dedicated to Horus and Khnum.

When there was no successor to the throne at the end of the Twelfth Dynasty, a new period of political upheaval began, ushering in the Second Intermediate period.

▲ **Abodes for eternity**
Like their predecessors in the Old Kingdom, the kings of the Middle Kingdom were buried in pyramids. As these were no longer built with the same care and attention as earlier ones, however, they are in a poor state of preservation today.

▼ **Montu, the god of war**
The pharaohs of the Middle Kingdom were from Thebes, where Montu, the falcon-headed local god of Armant, had been worshipped since the Old Kingdom. In honour of Montu, four rulers of the Eleventh Dynasty gave themselves the name of Mentuhotep, 'Montu is content'. At the beginning of the Twelfth Dynasty (1985–1795 BC), Montu's position as most important deity was taken by Amun, but Senusret III (1874–1855 BC) still built a large temple for Montu at Medamud.

The falcon-headed god
Montu is called 'lord of Thebes' in this inscription.

Senusret III, *whose name and title are written above his head, is standing under the winged sun disc, making an offering to Montu.*

Montu, *the local god of Armant, is usually depicted with a headdress consisting of a sun disc, two tall falcon feathers and two cobra goddesses.*

Fortresses in the South

After the difficulties of the First Intermediate period, the pharaohs of the Middle Kingdom (2055–1650 BC) regained control of Lower Nubia and extended the border to the Second Cataract, where they built a series of defensive fortresses.

From the earliest dynasties, a system of fortifications in strategic and sensitive locations was built to protect Egypt's frontiers. There were fortresses, stockades and even border walls to regulate the paths through the desert. In the Delta, it was necessary to guard against intruders from the Middle East, such as the Libyans, who were constantly trying to move into Egypt.

Securing trade

There were many heavily armed forts in the cataract regions of Lower Nubia. During the Middle Kingdom, Senusret III (1874–1855 BC) built 14 citadels in the area. They stretched along the banks of the Nile between the First Cataract and Third Cataract at intervals of no more than 60km (37 miles). These fortified bastions depended on the fortress at Buhen, a settlement on the Second Cataract that acted as a buffer between Nubia and Sudan, and controlled the only caravan route. Buhen became the administrative centre for the region and the seat of Egyptian power in the South.

▶ **The fortress gate**
This entrance to the Medinet Habu temple of Rameses III (1184–1153 BC) in western Thebes is one of two that were modelled on a common fort design. The reliefs record Rameses III's military campaigns in Syria-Palestine.

▲ **Slate palette**
This detail from a slate palette shows the symbolic destruction of a city. The pharaoh, in the form of a falcon, is tearing down the city walls with his claws.

The garrisons were populated by soldiers conscripted into the regular army and by Nubian mercenaries, but the commanders were Egyptian princes or other members of the royal family. Inside the garrison, the barracks were usually next door to the quarters for the soldiers' families and Egyptian settlers, while the administrative buildings adjoined the various cult temples.

A soldier's life

The soldiers went on manoeuvres, trained daily and also took part in patrols. They were responsible for monitoring the movement of caravans, protecting nearby wells and oases, and challenging suspect vessels sailing on the Nile. Thus, the fortresses served as bases for the pharoah's military campaigns and were responsible for ensuring the safe passage of luxury goods, such as gold, ebony, ivory, leopard skins and ostrich feathers.

▼ Continuity at Qasr Ibrim

About 240km (150 miles) south of Aswan is the fortified settlement of Qasr Ibrim, which now stands on a headland in Lake Nasser. It was first occupied around 1000 BC, and subsequently through successive periods until the beginning of the nineteenth century when it garrisoned Bosnian troops of the Ottoman Empire. When David Roberts painted this watercolour in 1838 it lay abandoned.

Air-dried mud bricks were used to build the fortresses of the Middle Kingdom.

The walls of the fortress were crenellated to provide protection for the soldiers.

Egyptian soldiers and Nubian mercenaries were stationed inside the fortresses.

The ramparts were reinforced at regular intervals by semicircular bastions.

▲ The fortress of Buhen

From the time of the Old Kingdom (2686–2181 BC), Buhen was an important settlement as it was the strategic base for mining expeditions to Nubia. By the Middle Kingdom (2055–1650 BC), the site had developed into a mighty fortress, with walls 11m (36ft) high and 5m (16ft) thick, which contained the governor's residence, barracks, administrative and residential buildings and a temple. In the Eighteenth Dynasty (1550–1295 BC), a second temple was built; both were saved from flooding, while the fort was left to sink below the surface of Lake Nasser.

A gatehouse, with a narrow doorway, made the entrance to the fortress easy to defend.

Chronology of the Middle Kingdom

▲ Royal funerary equipment
Only a few remains of Mentuhotep II's funerary equipment were found in his tomb at Deir el-Bahri – all royal tombs of this period had been plundered in ancient times.

▶ Egypt in the Middle Kingdom
After the end of the civil war between the northern and southern parts of the country, the pharaohs of the Eleventh Dynasty moved the seat of the government of Egypt to their home city of Thebes. At the beginning of the Twelfth Dynasty, they returned to the north, making Itjtawy near the fertile Fayum Oasis their residence.

▼ Art
Art and literature reached a peak in the Middle Kingdom, as documented by murals in tombs and paintings on sarcophagi, as well as in literary works.

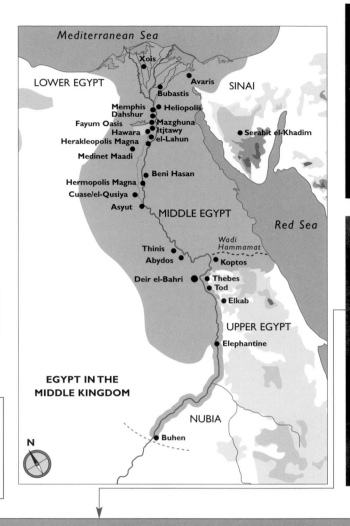

EGYPT IN THE MIDDLE KINGDOM

2055 BC		2004 BC	1992 BC	1985 BC		1965 BC
	Eleventh Dynasty					

Mentuhotep II
Mentuhotep II was the first ruler of the Eleventh Dynasty. His victory over Herakleopolis Magna around 2055 BC resulted in the reunification of Egypt, and he is regarded as the founder of the Middle Kingdom. Immediately following the reunification, he launched military campaigns against Nubia and Palestine. His building projects comprised the temple of Montu at Tod, chapels for Hathor at Dendera and for Osiris at Abydos, and a sanctuary for Satet on the Nile island of Elephantine. At the mortuary temple of the king at Deir el-Bahri there are also tombs with elaborately decorated chapels and sarcophagi of six of his secondary wives. His name means 'Montu is content'.

Mentuhotep IV The last pharaoh of the Eleventh Dynasty, Nebtawyra is documented only by rock inscriptions at Wadi Hammamat in the eastern desert. An expedition under the vizier Amenemhat was sent to Wadi Hammamat to gather material for the king's sarcophagus. Nebtawyra's tomb itself has not been discovered. His name means 'Ra is the lord of the two countries'.

Mentuhotep III During his reign, Sankhkara ('he who lets live the ka of Ra') gave orders for a trade expedition of 3,000 men under the official Henenu along Wadi Hammamat to the Red Sea, and from there to Punt. Both his and his father's tombs are at Deir el-Bahri.

Amenemhat I The birth name of the founder of the Twelfth Dynasty was 'Amun is at the head'. Amenemhat I, probably the same person as the vizier of the same name of Mentuhotep IV, moved the royal residence from Thebes to Itjtawy and reorganized Egypt's administration. Some of his building projects were concentrated on the Delta. Possibly assassinated, he was buried in his pyramid near el-Lisht.

Senusret I Appointed co-regent by Amenemhat I, Senusret I heard the surprising news of his father's death while on a campaign against Libya, as told in *The Tale of Sinuhe*. During his long reign, he took care of the development of the Fayum region. He constructed and extended many temples and monuments, among them the 'white chapel' at Karnak, and secured the conquered territories in Nubia by building several fortresses. His pyramid is at el-Lisht.

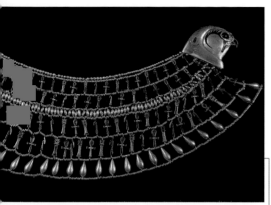

◀ The treasure of a princess
Despite numerous precautions, almost all royal burial sites were plundered. One of the few tombs whose funerary equipment was preserved is the mastaba of Princess Khnemetneferhedjet (1908–1878 BC), wife of Senusret II, at Dahshur.

◀ Senusret III
Senusret III regularized internal affairs and pushed back the southern borders of Egypt to the Second Cataract.

◀ Relief from the 'white chapel' at Karnak
One of the most significant works of art of the Middle Kingdom is the so-called 'white chapel' at the temple complex of Karnak from the reign of Senusret I. The chapel was pulled down in antiquity and rebuilt in the twentieth century.

▲ Amenemhat III
Apart from increasing economic relations with Byblos and Crete, this pharaoh heavily exploited the mineral resources of Sinai.

◀ The viceroys' cemeteries
The magnificent rock-cut tombs at Beni Hasan show that the viceroys initially were allowed to keep their wealth, although the kings of the Twelfth Dynasty curbed their power.

1922 BC	1880 BC		1874 BC		1855 BC		1808 BC			1799 BC	1795 BC

Twelfth Dynasty

Amenemhat II
Little is known of the 44 years of Amenemhat II's reign, apart from a military campaign to Syria – with 1,500 prisoners being brought back to Egypt – and various trade missions. His limestone-encased pyramid is at Dahshur.

Senusret III The most important, and probably best known, ruler of the Twelfth Dynasty abolished the inheritability of a viceroy's office. Four campaigns to Nubia enabled him finally to establish Egypt's southern border near Semna at the Second Cataract. His badly damaged pyramid is at Dahshur.

Amenemhat IV
This ruler, who had the throne name 'Ra is justified', encouraged trade with Byblos, where several artefacts bearing his name were found. Amenemhat IV was probably buried in the pyramid at Mazghuna, near Dahshur.

Sobekneferu
The last ruler of the Middle Kingdom was a woman – Queen Sobekneferu, 'the beauty of Sobek', a daughter of Amenemhat III and the wife of Amenemhat IV. After the latter's death, she ascended the throne and assumed the complete titulary of a male pharaoh, as only Hatshepsut and Tausret did after her.

With the death of Sobekneferu, the Thirteenth and Fourteenth Dynasties comprised minor ephemeral rulers. The Second Intermediate period began 445 years later in 1650 BC.

Senusret II
This pharaoh, 'the manifestation of Ra appears in glory', expanded commerce with Syria, as is documented by the depiction of a trade caravan in a viceroy's tomb at Beni Hasan. The large town site near his pyramid at el-Lahun served on occasion as his residence.

Amenemhat III Amenemhat III was already known to Classical authors because of his famous mortuary temple, the 'Labyrinth', at Hawara. The main achievement in his 50-year reign was the final economic and political development of the Fayum, where he also built several temples with exceptionally worked statues. Inscriptions tell of various expeditions to the quarries of Sinai and Wadi Hammamat and to Nubia. Before he had his pyramid and mortuary temple erected at Hawara, he built a smaller pyramid at Dahshur.

Pharaoh Mentuhotep II

Mentuhotep II unified the two parts of Egypt after the First Intermediate period, a time of political unrest and anarchy. His reign started the Middle Kingdom (2055–1650 BC).

When Mentuhotep II (2055–2004 BC) of the Theban Eleventh Dynasty (2125–2055 BC) acceded to the throne, he ruled over a territory stretching from the First Cataract to Asyut. One final battle assured the fall of the Herakleopolitan Tenth Dynasty (2160–2025 BC), and Mentuhotep II was proclaimed pharaoh of a united Egypt. It took a few more years, however, before peace was fully restored to the country.

The king crushed his opponents and rewarded his allies. He moved his capital from Memphis to Thebes and created political posts for a number of Theban provincial inspectors who were to keep watch over the rest of the valley, and in particular the nomes of Herakleopolis and Heliopolis. He also created the new position of governor of the North and restored the titles of chancellor and vizier.

▼ **The reunification of the country**
After the fall of Herakleopolis Magna, Mentuhotep II finally attained his goal: the unification of Egypt. This relief shows two Nile gods tying the papyrus plant (Lower Egypt) and the lotus (Upper Egypt) around the symbol for 'unite' – the sema-tawi, which Mentuhotep II took as his Horus name towards the end of his reign.

The black skin colour symbolizes the rebirth of the king in the afterlife.

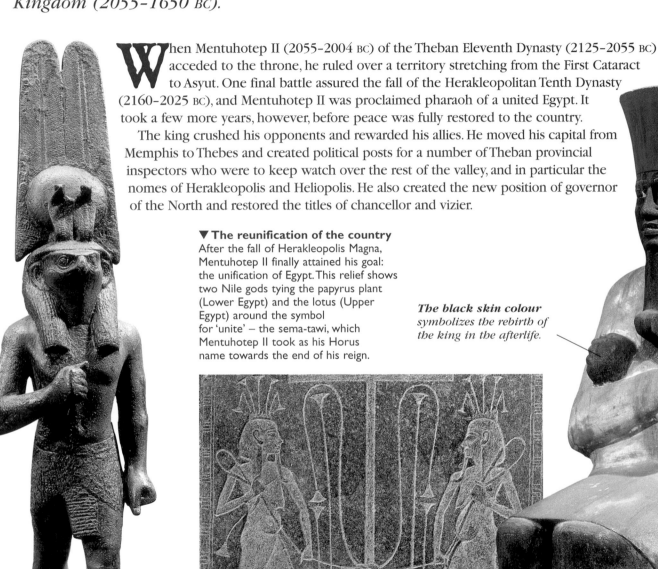

▲ **Montu, the god of war**
There was a close relationship between the king and the old Theban god of war, Montu, as the birth name of Mentuhotep II – 'Montu is content' – attests.

▶ **Statue of Mentuhotep II**
This painted sandstone statue was ritually buried in a chamber under the terrace in the mortuary complex of Mentuhotep II at Deir el-Bahri. The king is wearing the heb-sed (royal jubilee) coat and the red crown of Lower Egypt.

These changes took 30 years to implement fully and, nine years later, Mentuhotep II took the new Horus name of 'He who brought peace to the Two Lands'. The pharaoh actively pursued a policy of restoration of monuments and carried out large building projects, including the construction of the unusual terraced mortuary complex built in the style of the Old Kingdom in the natural embayment in the cliffs at Deir el-Bahri. He was particularly active in Upper Egypt, as shown by his monuments in Dendera, Abydos, Elkab and Elephantine. Temples dedicated to the war god Montu, who at that time was the principal god of Thebes, were constructed at Medamud, Armant and Tod.

Foreign policy

Mentuhotep II revived foreign policy to secure Egypt's borders. He led military campaigns against the Libyans and the Sinai Bedouin and re-exerted influence over Nubia. A mass grave of 60 Ancient Egyptian soldiers who were perhaps slain in battles against the Nubians, or killed in the first assault on the city of Herakleopolis, was found in Deir el-Bahri. When Mentuhotep II died, he bequeathed to his son, Mentuhotep III (2004–1992 BC), a prosperous and stable country. Thebes was transformed into a major political centre, and its little-known local god, Amun, was elevated to the status of a national divinity.

▼ Nubian politics
An important aim of Mentuhotep II was control of Nubia, and thus of the gold mines and the lucrative trade routes with sub-Saharan Africa. Although Mentuhotep II exercised control to as far as the Second Cataract, Nubia held onto the independence it had achieved during the troubles of the First Intermediate period.

◄ The Libyans
After military expeditions against the Bedouin in Sinai and Asiatics in the Delta, Mentuhotep II turned his attentions towards the Libyans in the west. They are identified by the two feathers worn in their hair and their distinctive style of dress.

▼ Dakhla Oasis
After Mentuhotep II rose to power, political refugees fled to the remote oases – in particular to Dakhla in the Western Desert. This gave rise to several military expeditions to that area and led to acts of retribution. Later, the territories were annexed – 'put under the protection of Egypt' – as the oasis with its fertile soil was of immense importance to the country's economy and strategically served to protect Egypt from Libyan incursions.

► The office of vizier
Mentuhotep II concentrated power in Thebes and delegated Nubian politics to his vizier Khety. His chancellor Meru was responsible for the control of the Eastern Desert and the oases.

Senusret I – Man of Character

First governing as his father's co-regent, Senusret I ruled Egypt for 45 years. He established political stability, extended Egypt's territories through trade and conquest, built splendid monuments and encouraged art and literature.

Senusret I, wearing the white crown of Upper Egypt, carries a long crook, or sceptre, symbolizing government.

When the young prince Senusret (1965–1920 BC) returned from a military campaign in Libya, he learned that his father Amenemhat I (1985–1955 BC) had been the victim of a palace plot and assassinated. Having ruled as co-regent with his father since the age of ten, Senusret took control of the throne.

These events inspired the *Tale of Sinuhe*, one of the most popular stories in Egyptian literature. This work recounts the life of a palace employee who, through various trials and tribulations, remains loyal to his king. It was essentially a propaganda piece, intended to reinforce the legitimacy of the new Twelfth Dynasty (1985–1795 BC) founded by Senusret's father.

Senusret continued the conquests which had been made by Amenemhat I. In Nubia he extended his control

◄ King of Upper and Lower Egypt
Close to Senusret's funerary complex at el-Lisht are the tombs of a number of dignitaries. In one, dedicated to Imhotep, the deified architect and priest at Heliopolis, two painted wooden statues of Senusret I were found. One shows him with the red crown of Lower Egypt; the other, now in the Egyptian Museum in Cairo, sees him wearing the white crown of Upper Egypt.

▲ Birth name cartouche
Only the king's birth name and throne name were ever enclosed in a cartouche. Senusret, the pharaoh's birth name, as depicted in this cartouche, means 'man of the goddess Wosret'.

▼ Pyramid ruins
The pyramids of the Middle Kingdom (2055–1650 BC), built with less care than those of the Old Kingdom (2686–2181 BC), were unable to resist the ravages of time. As the limestone exterior disintegrated, the interior structure of mud-baked brick was exposed and soon eroded. At the same time, rising ground water flooded the mortuary chamber, sinking the foundations.

The seated pharaoh

Senusret's funerary complex at el-Lisht consisted of a limestone pyramid 61m (200ft) high, surrounded by nine small pyramids for the king's female relatives, a satellite pyramid and a mortuary temple dedicated to the royal cult. To the northeast of the mortuary temple, 10 life-sized almost identical but incomplete statues of the seated pharaoh were found buried in a ditch.

as far as the Third Cataract, in present-day Sudan, while in the west he reinforced Egyptian garrisons up to the Libyan coast. He entered into fruitful trading relationships with Syria-Palestine, and exploited the gold mines and stone quarries within his territory.

Itjtawy remained the capital of the country under Senusret I. This was located in the Fayum Oasis, a short distance from the modern site of el-Lisht, where the pharaoh built his pyramid complex. He also erected a number of new buildings and embellished old ones, using the stone provided by the quarries for the many statues and monuments that decorate the temples.

Builder and patron

Little evidence remains of Senusret the builder, although he was involved in the enlargement of the temple of Amun-Ra at Karnak. He also restored the temple of the sun god Ra at Heliopolis, of which a 20m (66ft) high obelisk is all that remains. Senusret also encouraged the writers who produced the great classics, such as the *Tale of Sinuhe*, the *Instruction of Amenemhat I* and the *Loyalist's Instruction*. He made his son – the future Amenemhat II – co-regent four years before his death.

The nemes headcloth, adorned with the protective uraeus (serpent), was a common royal headdress.

The ceremonial 'false' beard is typically found on representations of the living pharaoh.

The regal pose of one hand resting on the thigh was frequently adopted in statuary.

The right hand holds a folded linen cloth which represents the hieroglyphs for health.

The feet rest on a pedestal cut into the same block of stone as the statue. The sides of the block are decorated with symbols of the union of Upper and Lower Egypt.

▼ The White Chapel

When the third pylon of the temple of Amun at Karnak had to be completely dismantled for restoration in 1922, the French architect Maurice Pillet discovered the White Chapel's decorated stones among the foundations of the temple.

Built during the reign of Senusret I, the chapel's fine, white limestone blocks had been exceptionally well preserved, and reconstruction was therefore made possible. Originally, the chapel had served as a kind of shelter on the processional route, and provided a temporary altar for the barge of the god Amun.

Senusret III

A great general, a clever administrator and an active builder, Senusret III (1874–1855 BC) was one of the most successful kings of the Middle Kingdom. During his 19-year reign, Egypt enjoyed unrivalled prosperity, her borders were secured and the government was reformed.

In four military campaigns undertaken during his reign, Senusret III conquered Lower Nubia as far as the Second Cataract of the Nile. This region, partially controlled by the Egyptians since the Old Kingdom (2686–2181 BC), became an integral part of Egypt. To protect his conquest from Sudanese incursions, the pharaoh built a powerful defence system, consisting of eight fortresses, erected on both banks of the Nile. These included both Buhen and Semna near the Second Cataract.

On a stele at Semna, Senusret proclaimed that he had fixed the country's southern border at the Second Cataract, and that henceforth only Nubians with peaceful intentions were allowed to cross it.

▼ **The pyramid of Dahshur**
Senusret III's pyramid of raw brick, originally covered with limestone, is part of the southern end of the Memphite necropolis. A granite sarcophagus was discovered in 1894, but there was no evidence that the pharaoh was buried here. Other chambers in the pyramid, however, yielded funeral treasures belonging to the royal women.

▶ **Senusret, 'Man of the goddess Useret'**
The birth name (above right) of the king, Senusret means 'Man of Useret' or 'Man of the Powerful Goddess'. It places the sovereign under the protection of this Theban goddess, usually pictured with a bow and arrows. Useret, however, remained a second-ranking divinity in the Ancient Egyptian pantheon of gods and goddesses.

Senusret's double crown confirms his mastery of all Egypt.

The lined face, with its drooping eyes, suggests that this is a realistic portrait.

▲ **Head of Senusret**
Found in front of the sixth pylon at Karnak by the Franco-Egyptian Centre in 1970, this head of Senusret III is made from rose granite. The beard shows that the king was depicted as Osiris or in his costume for his Sed festival (royal jubilee).

INSIGHT

Mereret's pectoral

In 1895 Jacques de Morgan discovered two treasures in an underground gallery in the north of the pyramid of Senusret III, reserved for the sarcophagi of the women of the royal family. They belonged to Sit-Hathor and Mereret, the king's sister and wife, respectively. Among Mereret's jewels is a pectoral (breastplate) made of gold, cornelian and lapis lazuli. It shows Senusret III as a griffon trampling a Nubian enemy underfoot and striking a Libyan. In the centre, a vulture, the incarnation of the goddess Nekhbet, hovers above the king's cartouche. The design sits inside a shrine framed by two columns with lotus-flower capitals.

The griffon has the head of a plumed falcon.

Nekhbet, the goddess of Upper Egypt, unfolds her protective wings.

The griffon is a mythical animal which has the body of a lion and the head of a falcon.

The pharaoh's throne name, Khakaura, is enclosed within the cartouche.

The garrisons stationed in the fortresses were there to repel warring tribes. To facilitate traffic between Nubia and Egypt, and to allow boats to avoid the rapids of the First Cataract, Senusret III enlarged the Sehel Canal built around the First Cataract at the end of the Old Kingdom.

In the north of Egypt, the king's military activity was less spectacular, and was limited to controlling borders and an expedition to Palestine, which he personally led. Senusret III took the Palestinian city of Sekmem, but did not follow up this conquest.

Trade with the East

Egypt did not yet have imperialistic designs on the Near East, and Senusret III enjoyed flourishing relations with his neighbours in the eastern Mediterranean. Egypt traded with Syria-Palestine, from which it was separated by Mesopotamia and Anatolia. It also traded with Crete, as shown by pottery found there.

Dealing with the nomarchs

At home, Senusret was faced with the serious problem of how to reduce the power of the nomarchs, the governors of the nomes, or provinces, whose duties had been hereditary since the end of the Old Kingdom, and whose wealth and power rivalled that of the pharaoh. The king took a radical step by undertaking a broad reform of regional administration.

The local governors, some of whom had their own troops, were a permanent threat to royalty. To eradicate this danger, Senusret III abolished the nomes that gave these governors their power, and established a new form of regional government.

▼ **Senusret III as a young man**
The diorite statue comes from the temple of Montu at Medamud and shows the young Senusret III wearing the nemes headdress.

▼ **Senusret III in old age**
This statue shows an ageing Senusret III. His face is deeply lined and the eyes droop. The two statues of the young king and the old king, now in the Louvre Museum in Paris, were carved at the same time, and not during different periods of his reign. What is the reason behind these portraits? For some, they serve as a reminder of the sun's cycle – old in the evening, young in the morning and mature at midday. Others think they express a new conception of royalty, in which a long reign was considered the ideal.

▼ **Senusret III in middle age**
In his statues, Senusret III broke with the tradition of idealized portraits that had existed until then and introduced an element of realism. The pink granite head found at Karnak clearly shows the features of a ruler in his maturity.

HISTORY

The pharaoh divided the country into three regions: Lower Egypt, Upper Egypt and the Elephantine (now Aswan) and northern Nubia. Each was under the control of a vizier, a kind of prime minister, who in turn had a number of ministers and officials working under him. The immediate consequences of this radical reform were a significant reduction in the power of the nobility and the rise of the middle classes working in government.

Like most pharaohs, Senusret III was also a great builder. He dedicated a temple at Medamud to the warrior god Montu, and looked after the temples of Amun at Karnak and Osiris at Abydos. For himself, he built a pyramid at Dahshur to the south of Saqqara. He also created a cenotaph (a symbolic empty royal tomb) at Abydos, the holy city of Osiris, god of the dead.

▲ Egypt's enemies
In the south, the Egyptians defended their border, set at the Second Cataract, against incursions by Nubians from the kingdom of Kerma, the centre of which was near the Third Cataract. To the north, Senusret kept an eye on the Bedouins and prevented them from infiltrating the Delta.

Secondary doors, which were used by the priests, led into the temples.

The capitals in the centre are carved as open papyrus leaves; those at the sides are carved as closed buds.

The columns were made up of cylindrical blocks rather than a single monolith.

◀ **The fort at Buhen**
Although a settlement had existed at Buhen, near the Second Cataract of the Nile, since the Old Kingdom, Senusret III transformed it into a large and impressive military garrison controlling the area to the north of the Second Cataract. This view shows part of the mud-brick ramparts of the fortress.

The inscriptions decorating the architraves were not reproduced by the painter of this picture.

INSIGHT

Magic figurines

To destroy their enemies by magic, the Egyptians often made crude statuettes of prisoners with their hands tied behind their backs. Texts were inscribed on these figurines listing the princes and countries to be destroyed if they rebelled. The example (right, showing front and back view) dates from around 2000 BC.

Different regions of Nubia and Syria-Palestine were mentioned in this way. The figurines, buried in the ground, were a kind of magical protection system against the enemy, just as the fortresses were physical ones. The inscriptions were also placed on vases, which were broken while a ritual spell was pronounced.

A large number of vases, fragments and figures were unearthed in the Nubian fortress of Mirgissa, constructed by Senusret III. Some of these items, thrown into a well, were found beside a human skull and a flint blade. It would seem that the magic ritual carried out in this instance involved a human sacrifice.

◀ **The temple of Medamud**
The temple at Medamud that Senusret III dedicated to Montu was restored during the New Kingdom and modified during the Ptolemaic period. It was unable to withstand the ravages of time, however, as shown in this nineteenth-century painting by David Roberts, the Scottish artist and traveller, who faithfully reproduced many Ancient Egyptian monuments in his watercolours.

▼ **Montu, the warrior god**
It was thanks to the princes of Thebes, who reunified Egypt and restored the power of the pharaohs at the beginning of the Middle Kingdom, that Montu took his place among the country's chief gods. The four temples dedicated to him in and around Thebes – Medamud (below), Tod, Armant and Karnak – form a system of defence providing magic protection for the temple of Karnak, dedicated to Amun.

The Second Intermediate Period

With the decline of the Middle Kingdom, groups of Asiatics established settlements in the Delta region and began a time of foreign rule in Egypt, known as the Second Intermediate period.

After Queen Sobekneferu's (1799–1795 BC) death, the Middle Kingdom (2055–1650 BC) entered into a long period of decline. About 70 rulers of the Thirteenth Dynasty (1795–after 1650 BC) reigned for only a few years each, but retained the royal residence at Itjtawy. Relaxation of the borders saw an influx of Asiatic settlers into the Delta and, by the late Thirteenth Dynasty, the Eastern Delta broke away from the weakened central government and was ruled by minor kings of the Fourteenth Dynasty (1750–1650 BC).

In about 1650 BC, the local rulers of the Delta were usurped by kings who the Ancient Egyptians called 'rulers of foreign lands', later named the Hyksos by the Greeks. They established Avaris in the Delta as their seat of government. At about the same time, the Thirteenth-Dynasty Egyptian rulers abandoned Itjtawy and retreated south to found their new capital at Thebes. The Second Intermediate period had begun, but the exact reign dates of the individual rulers are not verified by the archaeological records.

▼ Technical innovations
Using a horse-drawn, two-wheel chariot – unknown in Egypt until then – and the improved bow and arrow developed in the Near East, the troops of the Hyksos were superior to the Ancient Egyptian soldiers in battle.

▼ Kamose
Kamose (1555–1550 BC), the last pharaoh of the Seventeenth Dynasty, continued the conflict against the Hyksos that started with his father, Taa II (c. 1560 BC). In 1857, his pyramid-style tomb was discovered at Dra Abu el-Naga in western Thebes. When his coffin was opened the mummy immediately disintegrated.

Baal is standing under a winged sun disc, in the same way as depictions of Ancient Egyptian gods.

The atef crown, with the uraeus serpent, and a loincloth with a bull's tail are typical attire of the Ancient Egyptian pharaohs and gods.

◀ Baal and Seth
The Hyksos worshipped the Ancient Egyptian god of chaos, Seth, whom they equated with the Syrian-Palestinian weather-god Baal. Other Egyptian deities worshipped were the war goddesses Astarte and Anat, both of whom originated in Syria-Palestine, and were at various times the consorts of Baal and Seth. They were regarded as the divine protectoresses of the king in battle.

The Hyksos extended their control from Avaris, eventually capturing Memphis. Initially, relations between them and the line of native Egyptian kings were peaceful, and the Hyksos adopted the traditional Egyptian form of government – the royal titulary and the few royal sculptures that have been found are in the style of the Middle Kingdom. Literature continued in its conventional form, with new works being composed and older ones, such as the Rhind Mathematical Papyrus, being copied.

The Hyksos were, however, militarily superior to the Egyptians, introducing horse-drawn chariots, an improved bow, the curved khepesh sword and helmets and armour.

Real conflict broke out around 1570 BC when the Hyksos ruler Apepi accused the Theban ruler Taa II of killing hippopotamuses - creatures sacred to Seth, and hence Baal - in the lake at Karnak. Taa II appears to have been killed in battle - his skull bearing a wound inflicted by an Asiatic style of axe. His successor, Kamose, drove the Hyksos back to Avaris and his son, Ahmose (1550–1525 BC), expelled them from Egypt and founded the New Kingdom.

▲ Egypt and the Mediterranean world
Fragments of frescoes from a palace built at the time of the Hyksos were found at Avaris (today's Tell el-Dab'a). The Minoan-style murals show scenes similar to the decorations at Knossos on Crete, such as griffins and bulls. Ancient Egyptian objects with the names of Hyksos kings have been discovered in Crete, Baghdad and Boghazköy, indicating trade relations with the Aegean and the Near East.

▼ Bracelet of Ahhotep I
The mother of Ahmose, Ahhotep I (c. 1590–1530 BC) acted as regent until the pharaoh was 16 years old. Numerous artefacts with the name of her son were discovered in her tomb, among them pieces of jewellery. This gold bracelet, which is decorated with lapis lazuli, shows the king kneeling in front of the god Geb, who raises his right hand in recognition of his divine rulership.

The double crown of Upper and Lower Egypt is worn by Ahmose.

The Theban ruler Ahmose wears the white crown of Upper Egypt.

Cartouches contain the names of Tetisheri and Ahmose.

Queen Tetisheri, Ahmose's grandmother, wears the vulture hood and the tall feather crown.

The titles engraved above the name of Tetisheri are 'king's wife and king's mother'.

▲ The liberation of Egypt
Ahmose, the founder of the Eighteenth Dynasty, who expelled the Hyksos from Egypt, had this stele created for his grandmother Tetisheri. It was erected in a chapel dedicated to her at Abydos. According to the inscription, Ahmose wanted specially to honour his grandmother, who had played an important political role during the reign of her husband, Taa II.

Chronology of the late Middle Kingdom/Second Intermediate Period
(1795–1550 BC)

▲ The ka of the pharaoh
This wooden statue of Hor I from the Thirteenth Dynasty embodies that part of the human soul which the Egyptians called the 'ka'. It was found by Jacques de Morgan in 1896, in the king's tomb at Dahshur, which was located in the pyramid district of Amenemhat III. This is the only known ka statue of an Egyptian king.

▶ Sobekhotep IV
'Sobek is merciful' was the name of several Thirteenth-Dynasty pharaohs. The crocodile god Sobek was the most important local deity of Fayum Oasis, where the capital Itjtawy was located.

▶ Royal wealth
The Theban kings began to regain power towards the end of the Seventeenth Dynasty. Their renewed affluence is demonstrated by their funerary equipment, such as this diadem of Intef I with the royal uraeus.

▼ Relations with foreign countries
Several Ancient Egyptian objects, with cartouches of kings from the Hyksos period, have been found at Hattusas (modern-day Boghazköy), the capital of the Hittites, confirming trade and political contacts.

| 1795 | 1780 | 1760 | 1750 | 1735 | 1725 | 1695 |

Fourteenth Dynasty (in the Delta)

Thirteenth Dynasty

Wegaf Khuitawyra was the first king of the Thirteenth Dynasty, with the throne name 'Ra protects the Two Lands'. A military commander, his reign probably lasted for about a year. Four of his monuments are preserved.

Sekhemrakhuitawy was the third king of the Thirteenth Dynasty, who, according to the Turin Royal Canon, reigned for six years. Several stone blocks from a monument erected during his reign are preserved, and his name is also attested to by seals from the Nubian fortress of Uronarti at the Second Cataract.

Hor I (Awibra) was presumably the 14th king of the Thirteenth Dynasty, who gave orders for the restoration works on the pyramid of Amenemhat III at Dahshur. Hor's tomb, with its well-preserved funerary equipment, was located inside the district of Amenemhat III's pyramid.

Khendjer was the 17th king of the Thirteenth Dynasty, who reigned for about six years. As one of the few rulers who reigned for any length of time, he had a pyramid and a mortuary temple built at Saqqara. The black granite pyramidion, with the name of the king, was reassembled from numerous fragments.

Neferhotep I (Khasekhemra) The 22nd king of the Thirteenth Dynasty ruled for about 11 years. He had the statue of Osiris re-erected at Abydos and donated statues to several Ancient Egyptian temples.

Sobekhotep IV (Khaneferra) was the most important king of the Thirteenth Dynasty, who reigned for about eight years. He led a campaign to Nubia, had contacts with the Near East and had his own statues erected in several temples.

Ihy I (Merineferra) was the 27th, and last, ruler of the Thirteenth Dynasty, whose name is still attested in all of Egypt. The pyramidion of his pyramid, probably built at Saqqara, was found in the Delta.

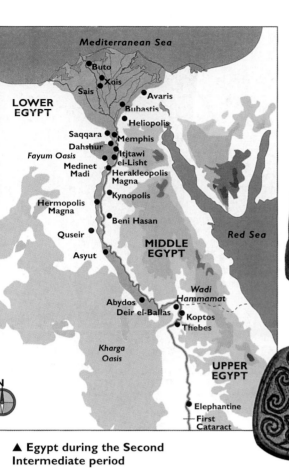

▲ Egypt during the Second Intermediate period
The most important cities of the Middle Kingdom retained their status throughout the Second Intermediate period. The Delta, however, grew in importance due to the Hyksos royal residence at Avaris.

◄ Stele from the Second Intermediate period
The tombstone of the scribe Sobekhotep is engraved on all four faces. It bears two cartouches from the Seventeenth Dynasty of Sobekemsaf II Sekhemrasewadjtawy.

► Statue of Tetisheri
New research has proven that this figure – in the collection of the British Museum in London – is a fake. The bottom part of the real statue, from which the inscription was copied, is in the Egyptian Museum in Cairo.

◄ Scarabs
The numerous scarabs found in all Mediterranean countries demonstrate that Egypt had relations with foreign countries during the Middle Kingdom and the Second Intermediate period. Many of the seals bear the names of kings of the Thirteenth to Seventeenth Dynasties.

1660	1630	1610	1600	1590	1560	1555	1550

Sixteenth Dynasty (Minor Hyksos rulers)

Fifteenth Dynasty (Hyksos)

Seventeenth Dynasty (in Thebes)

Meriuserra Jaqob-her was probably one of the Hyksos kings of the Fifteenth Dynasty. His name is found on scarabs from all over Egypt, and even in foreign territories such as Kerma and Palestine, implying that there were trade relations with these regions.

Khyan (Seuserenra) was one of the most significant kings of the Fifteenth Dynasty. Several monuments with his name have been found in Egypt and abroad, for example, the statue of a resting lion in Baghdad and a granite block at Gebelein in Upper Egypt.

Anat-her Heka-khasw was one of the kings of the Sixteenth Dynasty, a vassal of the Hyksos, who possibly ruled in southern Palestine and not in Egypt. His name is attested on only a single scarab.

Intef VII (Sekhemra-Herwhermaat)  was the 12th king of the Seventeenth Dynasty, ruling at Thebes, probably with a very short reign. His throne name was 'A powerful one, a Ra, who is satisfied with Maat'. His rishi coffin, which was typical for the time, is found at the Louvre in Paris.

Taa II was the 14th king of the Seventeenth Dynasty. According to a papyrus, he fought with the Hyksos king Apepi, to whom he had to pay tribute. Judging by the wounds on his mummy, he fell in battle. His coffin was found at the cachette at Deir el-Bahari.

Kamose was the last king of the Seventeenth Dynasty. He continued the battle against the Hyksos started by his father. His war report is written on two steles, which he had erected at Karnak.

Apepi I was the most important king of the 15th Dynasty, whose 33rd year of reign is attested by the Rhind Mathematical Papyrus. During his rule, the quarrels between the Hyksos kings residing in the Delta and the native Egyptian rulers living in Thebes began.

The Second Intermediate period ended in 1550 BC when the rulers of the Eighteenth Dynasty – founders of the New Kingdom – regained power over the entire country.

The Hyksos

The Hyksos, settlers from Syria and Palestine, rose to power in Egypt during the political vacuum of the Second Intermediate period (1650-1550 BC).

Towards the end of the Twelfth Dynasty (1985–1795 BC), many immigrants from the regions of Syria and Palestine settled in the eastern Delta around the town of Avaris (modern-day Tell el-Dab'a). Although despised by the native Egyptians as Hyksos (rulers of foreign lands), over the next 100 years these immigrants integrated into Egyptian society. During the same period, centralized Egyptian power was breaking down, with some 70 minor rulers claiming sovereignty over different parts of Egypt.

It is unclear if the Hyksos took over the Delta by force, or simply became the majority, but by 1650 BC they ruled over Lower Egypt from their capital, Avaris. From there, they extended their power to Memphis and into Middle Egypt. Meanwhile, in the south, Egyptian kings of the Seventeenth Dynasty ruled over Upper Egypt from Thebes.

The Theban kings, although violently opposed to foreign rule, were militarily weak, and an alliance struck between the Hyksos and Nubia left them threatened from the north and the south. It took an extraordinary diplomatic incident to fuel the flames of war.

▲ **Hyksos scarabs**
The names of Hyksos rulers on their scarabs are one of the most important sources of information about their history. The left scarab bears the inscription of Nikare, a minor Hyksos king of the Sixteenth Dynasty (1650–1550 BC), the one on the right an inscription of Khyan (c. 1600), a king from the Fifteenth Dynasty, which was contemporaneous with the Sixteenth Dynasty.

The mane on the pharaoh's sphinx replaces the nemes headdress, which traditionally framed the face on a sphinx.

The pharaoh's name changed, as a succession of pharaohs had the name of their predecessor removed, and their own engraved instead.

▼ **Near Eastern nomads**
The word 'Hyksos' is the Greek form of the Egyptian *heka khaswt*, meaning 'rulers of foreign lands'.

▲ **Lion sphinx**
This sphinx of Amenemhat III (1855–1808 BC), found in Tanis, shows him almost completely as a lion, and thus a powerful symbol of strength.

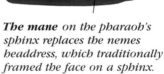
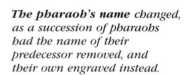

▲ Statue of Ahmose I
Founder and the first pharaoh of the New Kingdom, Ahmose I (1550–1525 BC) was the son of the Theban ruler Taa II (c. 1560 BC) and brother of Kamose (1555–1550 BC), both of whom waged war against the Hyksos. Ahmose I completed the conquest of the Hyksos, by capturing their capital of Avaris and finally driving them out of Egypt.

❛Your heart is weakening, cowardly Asiatic! Look, I shall drink the wine from your vines, which the Asiatics I have captured will press for me.❜

❛Let us divide the towns of Egypt and both our countries will be jubilant.❜

▶ Kamose's lance
This spearhead, with the name of the Theban king Kamose (1555–1550 BC), is from the tomb of his mother, Ahhotep I (1590–1530 BC), in western Thebes. It is on display at the Ashmolean Museum, Oxford.

▶▶ Kamose's stele
The stele of Kamose was found in the temple of Karnak in 1954. It tells of Kamose's victory over the Hyksos king Apepi I, and how the latter wrote a letter to the ruler of Kush in Nubia in which he suggested an attack on Kamose. The messenger was intercepted by Kamose's troops. Being informed of the plans of his opponent, Kamose was able to launch a pre-emptive attack.

▲ Kamose's axe blade
This weapon, also found in Kamose's mother's tomb, bears the name of Kamose. It is now in the British Museum, London.

The Hyksos king Apepi I (c. 1555 BC) wrote to the Theban ruler Taa II (c. 1560 BC) asking him to abolish the hippopotamus hunt practised by the Thebans, as the animal was the earthly incarnation of the Hyksos' major deity, Seth. The Thebans refused and war broke out. Details of the battles are unknown, but the mummy of Taa II shows that his skull was sliced by an Asiatic battle-axe. His son Kamose (1555–1550 BC) took up the fight and, with the help of Nubian archers, drove Apepi I back to Avaris, but did not take the city. Ahmose (1550–1525 BC), Kamose's brother, finally expelled the Hyksos and founded the Eighteenth Dynasty (1550–1295 BC) and the New Kingdom.

The New Kingdom

The period known as the New Kingdom numbered among its rulers such celebrated pharaohs as Rameses II, and was the last glorious period in the history of Ancient Egypt.

The New Kingdom began when the Theban rulers of the Eighteenth Dynasty (1550-1295 BC) expelled the Hyksos kings - foreign invaders from Palestine - who had controlled the country since about 1650 BC. Under a succession of pharaohs, including Thutmose I (1504-1492 BC) and his grandson Thutmose III (1479-1425 BC), Egypt extended its boundaries to Syria in the north and to the Fourth Cataract of the Nile in Upper Nubia (modern Sudan) to the south.

These conquests brought considerable wealth to Egypt in the form of tribute, as well as an influx of exotic ideas and influences. As a consequence, not only the pharaohs of the New Kingdom, but also the nobility and governing classes enjoyed a life of unprecedented luxury and refinement.

A golden age

The reign of Amenhotep III (1390-1352 BC) marked the golden age of the Eighteenth Dynasty. When he became pharaoh, Amenhotep III inherited a peaceful kingdom and a sophisticated, cosmopolitan court. Taking advantage of Egypt's prosperity, he set about

▲ A fortunate accident
The golden mask of Tutankhamun (1336–1327 BC) is one of the finest of the New Kingdom treasures to have survived intact. In about 1140 BC, when workmen were digging the tomb of Rameses VI (1143–1136 BC), they threw the debris onto the tomb of Tutankhamun, concealing both it and its entrance. As a result, it escaped the attention of the tomb raiders who began scavaging in the Valley of the Kings some 20 years later.

▼ The Valley of the Kings
From the time of Thutmose I, Egypt's pharaohs were buried in a desert valley at the foot of the hills west of Thebes. Here the visually impressive but often structurally unsound pyramid tombs of old were replaced by tombs cut into the rock. A team of surveillance officers guarded the site and its treasures.

increasing the splendour of his kingdom by building sumptuous monuments. The most notorious pharaoh, however, was his son Akhenaten (1352–1336 BC), who attempted to sweep away the old religious order and replace it with a single deity, the Aten. Traditional beliefs were restored under the reign of the boy king Tutankhamun (1336–1327 BC), the most famous of the New Kingdom rulers, but about whom little is known; Tutankhamun's fame rests on the fabulous treasures discovered in his tomb.

The Nineteenth Dynasty was dominated by another illustrious pharaoh, Rameses II (the Great), who was celebrated for three things above all: the defeat of the Hittites at Qadesh, the length of his reign and the number of monuments which were built under his administration.

◀ A radical pharaoh
This statuette depicts the Eighteenth-Dynasty pharaoh Akhenaten making an offering. The most radical of the New Kingdom rulers, Akhenaten 'reformed' Egypt's religion by elevating one deity – the Aten – to the unique position as the country's only god. He built a new capital at Amarna and instigated a new artistic style, which is reflected in this statue. The full lips, snake eyes and rounded body are typical of portraits of this ruler, although these features are not as exaggerated as in some images of him.

▼ Invasions by foreigners
During the Nineteenth Dynasty, Egypt had to defend itself against incursions by the Sea Peoples, migrants from the Aegean islands and the southern coast of modern Turkey (below). They were triumphantly defeated by Rameses III (1184–1153 BC), but under subsequent pharaohs, foreign raids on the country, notably by Libya, became common, marking the gradual decline of Egypt as a power.

▲ A vassal king
The New Kingdom pharaohs launched many military attacks on territories in the Near East, and annexed several cities and states. This statue depicts Idrimi, king of one of Syria's city-states, who reigned at the time of Thutmose I.

▼ Karnak, centre of power
Amun-Ra was the pre-eminent god of the New Kingdom, and Karnak was the site of a magnificent temple dedicated to him during this period. A large proportion of the spoils of war, including slaves, animals and precious objects, went towards swelling the treasury of the temple. Consequently, the unrivalled wealth invested with the priests of Amun gave them great power and political influence.

Of Workmen and Tomb Robbers

After the death of Rameses III in 1153 BC, a succession of weak leaders presided over a long slide into economic collapse and social decay. Bribery was rife, and corrupt officials turned a blind eye as tombs in the Theban necropolis were emptied of treasure.

Several papyri, including the Papyrus Abbott and Papyrus Amherst-Leopold II, report a legal inquiry into the plundering of tombs in the Theban necropolises in the sixteenth year of Rameses IX (1126–1108 BC). These 'grave robber papyri' paint a detailed picture of a society in decay, where even such high-ranking officials as Paweraa, the mayor of Thebes West, had profited from the widespread plundering of tombs in his jurisdiction. Two scribes from Deir el-Medina told Paser, Paweraa's rival and counterpart in Thebes East, what was going on. He denounced the thieves and officials to the pharaoh. He also sent his vizier, Khaemwaset, to supervise an inquiry.

It found that for at least three years, several gangs of robbers had been methodically looting the royal and private cemeteries on the west bank at Thebes. One thief they questioned confessed he had once been caught in the act, but had bought his freedom from the scribe who had arrested him with his share of the loot. The officials inspected

▼ **Rameses IX**
From Rameses IV to Rameses XI, Egypt had a succession of weak pharaohs with neither the will nor the power to keep the country and its institutions in good working order. Rameses IX was one of only two to rule for 10 years or more. His action against grave robbers proved largely ineffectual.

▼ **The tomb of Rameses VI**
When Egypt lost its empire and its resources at the end of the New Kingdom, corruption spread as the plundering of tombs and temples for treasure increased. The robbers did not spare the great tombs in the Valley of the Kings, such as that of Rameses VI (1143–1136 BC). A papyrus in the Liverpool Museum in England lists 50kg (110lb) of bronze and copper items stolen by five robbers from this tomb alone.

▼ **An unsafe haven**
The tradition of building pharaohs' tombs near their mortuary temples faded at the beginning of the New Kingdom. A remote spot in the high rocky deserts west of Thebes became the royal cemetery, the Valley of the Kings. So much wealth in one place would prove an irresistible lure to grave robbers.

10 tombs of the Eleventh and Seventeenth dynasties at the royal necropolis of Dra Abu el-Naga and found only one, that of Sobekemsaf II, a pharaoh of the Seventeenth Dynasty (1650–1550 BC), and his wife, had obviously been plundered. The Valley of the Kings at that time was still well guarded, but the tombs of the officials told a different story: many of them had already been robbed.

Systematic plunder

Grave robbing continued. Many tombs in the Valley of the Queens were cleared around this time. There is new evidence emerging that the practice was not only winked at by officials, but was actually organized by them as well. The treasures of earlier pharaohs were being recycled to fill the depleted state coffers.

When the rule of Rameses XI (1099–1069 BC) and the New Kingdom collapsed into civil war and anarchy, the pillage of royal and private Theban tombs began in earnest, orchestrated by the high priests of Amun, who cleared the tombs of treasure in the guise of restoration. Many royal mummies were stripped of their gold, given new shrouds and hidden away. A century or more later they were taken to Deir el-Bahri and put in the family tomb of Pinedjem – one of the high priests who was a grave robber himself.

◀ A Libyan taken prisoner
Adding to problems caused by the disorganization of the administration and strikes by the workers charged with building his tomb, Rameses IX also had to contend, between years 8 and 15 of his reign, with aggressive incursions from Libya. Statues such as this were part of the propaganda battle aimed at reassuring Egyptians that the pharaoh was still in control. The tomb robbers probably took advantage of these troubles as a cover for their own activities.

INSIGHT

Tomb 320 – hiding place of the royal mummies

In 1871, two brothers called Rassul discovered the blocked entrance to a shaft at the foot of the steep rock faces at Deir el-Bahri, on the west bank of the Nile opposite Thebes. They opened the shaft (right) and began digging. At 13m (43ft) deep, they found a 70m (230ft) long corridor leading into the hillside. It was piled with dozens of coffins containing the mummies of kings and other dignitaries stacked one on top of the other, along with a large amount of funerary equipment. The mummies had been brought there by high priests to keep them safe after their tombs were stripped clean at the end of the Twentieth Dynasty.

The Rassul brothers started quietly selling objects from the tomb, and continued for years before the Egyptian Antiquities Service, under its then director Gaston Maspero, realized what was happening. In 1881, Maspero ordered his assistant Emil Brugsch to clean out the tomb as quickly as possible; rumours had begun to spread among the incensed inhabitants of the nearby village of Qurna, where many houses are built above the tombs of pharaonic officials (below), that the Antiquities Service had found immense treasures of gold and precious stones, and Maspero feared an attack.

In just two hours, the coffins and mummies of such kings as Thutmose III (1479–1425 BC) and Rameses II (1279–1213 BC) were pulled up through the narrow shaft and taken to the Cairo Museum. Over the years, tomb 320, also called 'cache' or 'cachette', filled up with rubble and loose rock. The Egyptologist Erhard Graefe uncovered it again in 1998, examining it scientifically for the first time.

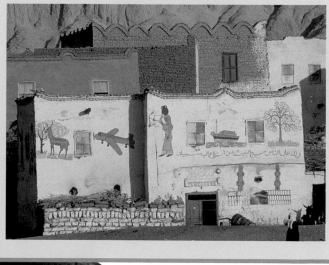

Thutmose I

The third pharaoh of the New Kingdom (1550–1069 BC), Thutmose I extended Egypt's influence to the Euphrates River in the Near East and into Nubia in the south.

The enthronement of Thutmose I (1504–1492 BC) took place under unusual circumstances. The pharaoh Amenhotep I had no male heir, and was succeeded not by a person of royal blood, but by the military commander Thutmose. His origins are obscure, but it seems that, to legitimize his reign, Thutmose I married Princess Ahmose, who was probably the daughter of his predecessor.

Thutmose's achievements

Although his reign was relatively short, Thutmose's achievements in foreign policy were notable. He inherited a well-organized army, and with it pacified Nubia, marking Egypt's southern border at the level of the Third Cataract. His great ambition was to conquer Asia and to make Egypt the most important power of the time. He reached the banks of the Euphrates, successfully confronting the powerful Mitanni people, Egypt's sworn enemies, and was the first of the New-Kingdom pharaohs to gain control of this area in the Near East.

▲ **Birth and throne names**
Two of the five names of a pharaoh were written in cartouches. Thutmose's birth name is represented by the sacred ibis, while his throne name below means 'great is the manifestation of the ka of Ra'.

◄ **A warrior king**
Thutmose continued the expansionist policies of his predecessors. Military campaigns led him to Nubia and the Near East, where he was the first pharaoh to reach the Euphrates and to establish Egypt's rule in Syria.

▼ **Amenhotep I – Thutmose's predecessor**
Amenhotep I (1525–1504 BC), the second king of the Eighteenth Dynasty, had no male heir. Consequently, the succession passed to Thutmose, an army commander.

▼ **Protégé of Thoth**
Thutmose's birth name, meaning 'Thoth is born', placed the king under the protection of the god of writing and knowledge. Thoth was often depicted in the form of a baboon, as here.

At home, Thutmose enlarged and elaborated the temple complex of Karnak, building a colonnaded great hall with two imposing pylons (ceremonial gateways); two obelisks stood in front of the gateways.

Tomb in the Valley of the Kings

The pharaoh also instructed his architect Ineni to construct a tomb for him at Thebes, the first royal burial in the New Kingdom necropolis of the Valley of the Kings. Thutmose's mummy was later moved to another tomb, and may be one of those in a cache discovered at Deir el-Bahri. On his death, the throne passed to Thutmose II, the pharaoh's son by one of his minor wives.

▶ Scarab seal
Seals in the form of a scarab, usually decorated with designs and inscriptions, were sometimes used to authenticate official documents. This example has Thutmose I's cartouche, enclosing his throne name, flanked by the heads of two falcons, with a winged scarab above.

◀ Hatshepsut
This queen was Thutmose I's daughter by his principal wife, Ahmose. She married her half-brother, Thutmose II, and on his death became regent for his son and successor, Thutmose III. Soon after, however, she assumed the role of pharaoh and ruled Egypt as such for about 20 years.

▶ Obelisks at Karnak
During his reign, Thutmose I ordered his architect Ineni to restore and extend the Amun temple in Karnak. As a consequence, a huge columned court was built behind two pylons. Two obelisks stood in front of the pylons, of which only one remains. The obelisk belonging to his daughter Hatshepsut (right) stands just to the north of the one belonging to Thutmose.

◀ Conquered people
Thutmose I expanded Egyptian control over the Nubians in the south, seen here in their traditional dress, and over the people of Syria-Palestine in the north. The main reason for these incursions was to gain access to trade routes for such raw materials as copper, silver, oils, timber and and slaves.

Hatshepsut, the Pharaoh Queen

*During three millennia of amazing rulers, Ancient Egypt saw only three female pharaohs.
The most famous was Queen Hatshepsut, who ruled by proxy from 1473–1458 BC.*

Hatshepsut had a daughter but no sons by her husband and half-brother Thutmose II (1492–1479 BC), so when Thutmose died, the title of pharaoh was inherited by the son of one of his minor wives, Isis. But the child, Thutmose III, was a mere baby, and thus Hatshepsut became regent for her nephew and brother-in-law.

Choosing a woman for this role was not exceptional. Other queens had acted as regent during the minority of their sons – and as the daughter, sister and wife of kings, Hatshepsut was by far the best-placed person to fulfil the role. At the beginning of her regency, however, there was little indication that the first lady in the land intended to become pharaoh herself.

She was always depicted as a woman and constantly gave precedence to her kinsman. But then, in year seven of Thutmose III's reign (1473 BC), Hatshepsut took on the crown of Egypt and began to be portrayed as a man. She had by now carefully consolidated her power, notably by winning the support of dignitaries such as Senmut, the grand steward of Amun and, possibly, the queen's lover.

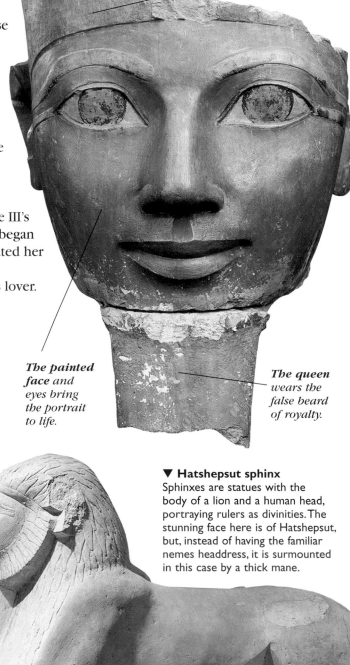

The red crown is the symbol of Lower Egypt.

The painted face and eyes bring the portrait to life.

The queen wears the false beard of royalty.

▶ Serene queen
Reconstructed from fragments, this head was part of a giant statue from the third terrace of the temple of Hatshepsut at Deir el-Bahri. The large eyes and smile help give the statue a less haughty appearance than the famous bust of Nefertiti.

◀ Crowning glories
In year seven of the reign of Thutmose III, while he was still a minor, Hatshepsut had herself crowned pharaoh. Thereafter, she was depicted not in the apparel of a great royal wife, but with the masculine attributes of a pharaoh: the double crown of Upper and Lower Egypt, the plaited false beard, the animal tail symbolic of power attached to her belt, and the royal loincloth.

▼ Hatshepsut sphinx
Sphinxes are statues with the body of a lion and a human head, portraying rulers as divinities. The stunning face here is of Hatshepsut, but, instead of having the familiar nemes headdress, it is surmounted in this case by a thick mane.

To make her seizure of power legitimate, Hatshepsut updated the rituals of birth and coronation, asserting that the king was the son of the gods and their representative on earth. She also set up inscriptions claiming divine birth. Despite this, Thutmose III remained the theoretical ruler, so for 15 years Egypt had a co-regency.

Success and succession

The period was a prosperous one during which the queen sponsored numerous building projects – including a large-scale construction programme in the temple of Karnak, dedicated to Amun, and her own superb funerary temple complex at Deir el-Bahri.

On Hatshepsut's death, Thutmose III, well prepared for his role as king, took over the reins of power, and during his sole tenure the queen's names and images were hammered flat on most of the monuments built in her honour. According to recent studies, these were not destroyed immediately after her death, but some 20 years later, beginning in year 42 of Thutmose's reign. This contradicts the notion, widely held, that a vengeful king immediately satisfied the hatred he bore towards the queen, as the destruction appears to have taken place much later.

Male attire

The relief (below), carved on one of the two great obelisks erected by Hatshepsut at Karnak, depicts the queen dressed as a male pharaoh with the god Amun-Ra.

▲ Thutmose III – Hatshepsut's nephew
Although it is often asserted that the queen hid Thutmose III away in the palace, in fact she had her co-ruler portrayed on all her monuments – in the background – in order to associate him with her important acts of government. Trained from an early age in the exercise of power, Thutmose (above right with the falcon-headed god Horus, from a shrine near Hatshepsut's mortuary temple) was made head of the army during the last years of his aunt's reign.

The god Amun-Ra *can be recognized by his distinctive two-feathered cap.*

The queen *wears the white crown of Upper Egypt.*

The male representation *of Hatshepsut is conveyed by the clothes, the body of a man and the false beard.*

The pharaoh's right hand *grips the mace, a symbol of royal power used to kill enemies of the king.*

INSIGHT

The Land of Punt

Later described in detail on the walls of the second terrace of the temple at Deir el-Bahri, the peaceful expedition to Punt was the grand project of Queen Hatshepsut's reign. The Egyptians had known of this wealthy land far to the south for several centuries, originally as a place of fable and legend inhabited by dark-skinned races. However, trade relations had not existed for more than 300 years when Hatshepsut initiated her ambitious expedition.

Launched from a port on the Red Sea, the expedition covered some 1,000km (600 miles) before reaching the coast of Punt. The Egyptians, welcomed by the king and his hugely obese queen with her donkey, discovered villages with reed-built huts constructed on stilts and entered by ladder, with palms and myrrh trees dominating the vegetation. The queen's agents exchanged necklaces, beads, statues and weapons for gold, ebony and incense trees – often by 'silent trade' (items being negotiated with neither party talking).

On its return to Thebes, the expedition received a triumphal welcome and Punt ('divine land') became firmly etched in the public imagination as trade continued to grow by both river and sea, before declining in the heyday of Lower Egypt. The drawing above, by the talented nineteenth-century French adventurer Emile Prisse d'Avennes from a relief at Deir el-Bahri, shows a Punt trader. For historians, the location of this semi-mythical land has been a matter of some debate, although the consensus is now for present-day southern Eritrea.

Thutmose III

After a faltering start, when he was overshadowed by his aunt and regent, Hatshepsut, the long, extremely successful reign of Thutmose III (1479-1425 BC) was marked by his great successes at the army's head.

The reign of Thutmose III was one of the most splendid periods in the history of Egypt. He extended the borders of the country as no other ruler had, and has been dubbed 'the Egyptian Napoleon' by the Egyptologist James Breasted. It was 20 years into his reign, however, before he established himself as sole ruler.

Regent and queen

He was the son of Thutmose II (1492-1479 BC) and a minor wife, Aset. When his father died, Thutmose III was still a child, and Thutmose II's principal wife, Hatshepsut, became regent. Around 1473 BC, she took on the title of pharaoh, ruling in her own right until her death in 1458 BC. Thutmose III claimed his birthright and began organizing the first of many campaigns in the Middle East, aimed at winning back control of the Levant from Mitanni, a warrior state based in Mesopotamia and Syria. At the same time, he set about eradicating Hatshepsut's name and picture from her monuments in favour of his own.

▲ Name cartouche
Thutmose III shares his birth name, 'Thoth is born', with three other kings of the Eighteenth Dynasty (1550–1295 BC). In those days it was usual for the birth name of the king to be formed with the name of a god. Also included in Thutmose's cartouche are the hieroglyphs that make up the pharaoh's title, 'ruler of Heliopolis'.

Statues of Thutmose III show the ruler with the idealized serene, assured features of a conqueror.

The uraeus, the nemes headcloth and the squared-off false beard all bear witness to Thutmose's royal status in this black granite, seated figure.

The cartouche on Thutmose's belt buckle bears his throne name, Menkheperra.

◄ The great builder
This seated figure, displayed today at the Egyptian Museum in Cairo, is from the temple at Karnak, where Thutmose III was responsible for raising obelisks, building the festival hall, and laying out the sacred lake. As pharaoh, he created many new monuments in Egypt and Nubia.

▲ Defaced and denamed
Soon after Hatshepsut died, the pharaoh began the systematic removal of her image and name from her monuments. This was not done from personal hatred, nor a desire for vengeance, so much as a wish to restore the natural order, outraged that a woman could act as pharaoh.

The powerful prince of Qadesh, a city-state in Syria, allied himself with the viceroys and governors of other vassal states of the Mitannians. Thutmose III – who had almost certainly assumed control of the army before the death of Hatshepsut – met the military threat posed by this alliance by taking on the allied forces in 1457 BC at the Battle of Meggido. A surprise attack routed the coalition army. The survivors fled into the walled city of Meggido, but capitulated after a seven-month siege.

The victorious pharaoh stripped the prince of Qadesh of his possessions. Many of the rebellious viceroys declared loyalty to Thutmose III after the battle; they kept their positions but had to pay tribute to Egypt. In all, Thutmose needed 15 more campaigns to bring the area under total control. Egyptian troops advanced far into Mitanni, to the Euphrates, in 1446 BC. Although no decisive battle took place, a 20-year period of peace in the region ensued.

Thutmose III was not known solely for his empire-building activities. Towards the end of his reign he built many temples, including those at Tod, Medamud and Armant, as well as the famous festival hall at Karnak. Little is left of his mortuary temple at Deir el-Bahari – next to that of Hatshepsut – but his tomb, with its famous decoration resembling a written papyrus, is one of the most impressive sites in the Valley of the Kings.

► **Final campaigns**
At the end of his reign, Thutmose III led his troops to Nubia to suppress a revolt, and took many prisoners.

▲ **Southern limits**
Under Thutmose III, Egypt's area of influence extended into Nubia to the Fourth Cataract. Many mud-brick sanctuaries there were rebuilt as stone temples.

► **Family resemblance**
The slightly feminine, boyish features of Thutmose III were so like those of his aunt Hatshepsut that it is sometimes difficult to tell their statues apart.

◄ **The red chapel**
Hatshepsut had begun a new barge sanctuary at Karnak dedicated to Amun. This sanctuary, built of quartzite, is known today as the red chapel. Like all the monuments she built in Egypt, it bore inscriptions and reliefs that associate the young Thutmose III with the rituals she carried out to honour the gods. Building was incomplete at the time of Hatshepsut's death, and it was finished by Thutmose III. This relief shows the king kneeling in front of Amun-Ra, who honours him by placing the blue crown on his head.

Akhenaten's Religious Reforms

For centuries, Amun was the pre-eminent god in the land, and his priests enjoyed unique power and privileges. However, Akhenaten (1352-1336 BC) revolutionized religious life when he adopted the cult of Aten.

The Aten, the manifestation of the sun god as the solar disk, first appeared at Heliopolis where the earliest known sun temple was located. Worship of the Aten grew in popularity during the New Kingdom (1550–1069 BC), and the god was first depicted in the form of a disk with rays as outstretched arms during the reign of Amenhotep II (1427–1400 BC). But it was Amenhotep III (1390–1352 BC), influenced by his wife Tiy (c. 1410–1340 BC), who popularized the Aten as a major deity.

His son, Amenhotep IV (Akhenaten), driven by both his religious conviction and his desire to break the power of the priesthood of Amun, took this one step further and promoted the Aten as the sole god of Egypt. Without the king's support, the cult of the god Amun was reduced in importance and eventually banned throughout the country.

▲ Changing Names
Amenhotep IV ('Amun is content') changed his name to Akhenaten in about the fith year of his reign and included the name of the Aten in the cartouche.

▶ Aten, the one and only god
Akhenaten only allowed the worship of the Aten, who was depicted as a sun disc, with the sun's rays ending in hands that held the ankh, the sign of life, and the sceptre, symbol of power.

The sun's rays touch the king and his offerings with their hands, and present him with the ankh and the was sceptre.

The pharaoh Akhenaten, wearing the blue khepresh crown, holds up an offering of papyrus flowers to his god, the Aten.

▲ Tiy, the king's mother
The first wife of Amenhotep III (1390–1352 BC), Queen Tiy (c.1410–1340 BC) had considerable influence over her husband and her son, Akhenaten. She visited the latter at his capital, Akhetaten, in the twelfth year of his reign, and possibly had her own palace there. This wooden head, in the Egyptian Museum in Berlin, shows her strong, expressive face.

In about the fifth year of his reign, Amenhotep IV changed his name to Akhenaten and founded a new capital which he called Akhetaten – 'the horizon of the sun disc' – at present-day Tel el-Amarna. Here he built two temples dedicated to the Aten, with open courtyards filled with offerings tables and altars. Akhenaten and his queen, Nefertiti, presided over the open air worship where food, drink and flowers were placed on the offerings tables and music accompanied a ceremony of prayers and hymns glorifying the sun.

To confirm the divine association between himself and the Aten, the pharaoh had the name of the god inscribed in a cartouche similar to his own and proclaimed the sun disc a celestial pharaoh, with himself as the Aten's earthly representation. As the highest priest of the Aten, Akhenaten became the sole mediator between god and humans.

The Return of Amun

This religious revolution, however, barely outlasted Akhenaten's reign itself, and after his death Egypt reverted to the worship of Amun. The city of Akhetaten was abandoned and the systematic destruction and defacement of all references to the pharaoh and his god began.

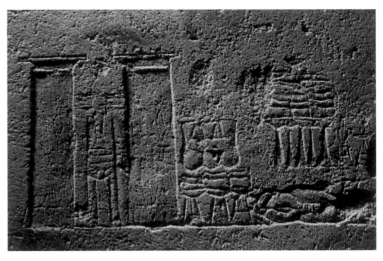

▲ Open-topped
Since the Aten was worshipped in the form of the sun disc, the temples were constructed with roofs open to the sky, so that his rays could reach the sacrificial altars without obstrction. The temples had no dark sanctuaries, but consisted of a number of open courtyards. The relief shows a temple entrance and two altars.

▼ Asiatic enemies
Akhenaten showed little interest in foreign policy and the concerns of Egypt's allies. On the painted floors of the palace at Akhetaten, however, he continued to show defeated and captured Asiatic enemies, such as this bound Asian prisoner on whom the king would have trodden during his daily walks.

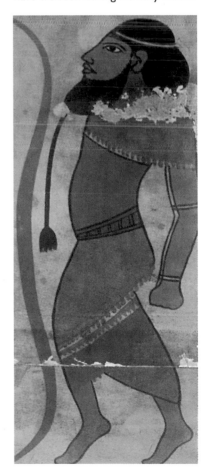

Akhenaten's foreign policy

Under Amenhotep III (1390–1352 BC), Egypt was at peace with its neighbours and the country prospered. However, Akhenaten, his son and successor, seems to have had little interest in foreign policy and the affairs of state. His conviction that, through the sun god, the Aten, all men were good, generous and peaceful was not shared by Egypt's vassal states and allies who found themselves increasingly threatened by neighbouring kingdoms.

A remarkable cache of documents, discovered in 1887 in the ruins of Akhetaten and known as the Amarna Letters, contains diplomatic correspondence between Egypt, Babylonia, Assyria and the vassal states of Syria-Palestine which details the concerns of Egypt's allies. They are written in cuneiform script on clay tablets (left) in the diplomatic language of the time – Babylonian.

They contain pleas from the prince of Byblos who was constantly being attacked by the Bedouin of the Syrian desert, a request from the king of Mitanni, Tushratta (c. 1360 BC), for troops to defend his cities against the Hittites, and complaints from the kings of Assyria, Ashuruballit I (c. 1365–1330 BC), and Babylon, Burnaburiash II (c. 1360–1333 BC), about the amount and the quality of the traditional gifts of gold. The Hittite king Suppiluliumas I (c. 1380–1346 BC) systematically annexed the small kingdoms under Egypt's protection and within ten years the borders of the Egyptian empire had been reduced to the Nile Valley itself.

▼ The Royal Line
Akhenaten had six daughters from his marriage to Nefertiti, but no male heir to the throne. After his death, various blood relatives gained power for short periods of time untill the former general Horemheb took over to end the dynastic succession.

Akhenaten's successors
Prior to his death, Akhenaten made Smenkhkara (1338–1336 BC) his co-regent. The relief below is possibly a portrait of Smenkhkara and his wife Meritaten. Little is known about his origin, and even the exact duration of is two-year reign is not fully documented. Smenkhkara was

Flowers and fruit are offered by Meritaten to her husband.

probably a son of Akhenaten and one of his lesser wives, which would make him a brother of Tutankhamun (1336–1327 BC), who succeeded him. The elderly courtier Ay (1327–1323 BC), possibly Akhenaten's uncle, took over the throne after Tutankhamun's death and married one of Akhenaten's daughters. The last ruler of the 18th Dynasty, Horemheb (1323–1295 BC) had no family connections.

The elongated head is an essential feature of Amarna art.

Meritaten, the young wife of Smenkhkara, was a daughter of Akhenaten and Nefertiti and the former wife of her father

The transparent robe hints at the erotic background of the scene.

◀ **King Horemheb**
General Paatenemheb was the army commander under the pharaohs Akhenaten and Tutankhamun. He succeeded to the throne as Horemheb (1323–1295 BC) and began to dismantle the temples dedicated to the Aten.

▲ **The boy-king Tutankhamun**
Married to Ankhesenamun, a daughter of Akhenaten and Nefertiti, this son of Akhenaten and his other wife Kiya (c. 1350 BC) ascended the throne at the early age of eight.

▼ **An Amarna princess**
One of the daughters of Akhenaten and Nefertiti, recognizable from the shape of her head and a broad strand of hair, praises the blessing rays of the Aten.

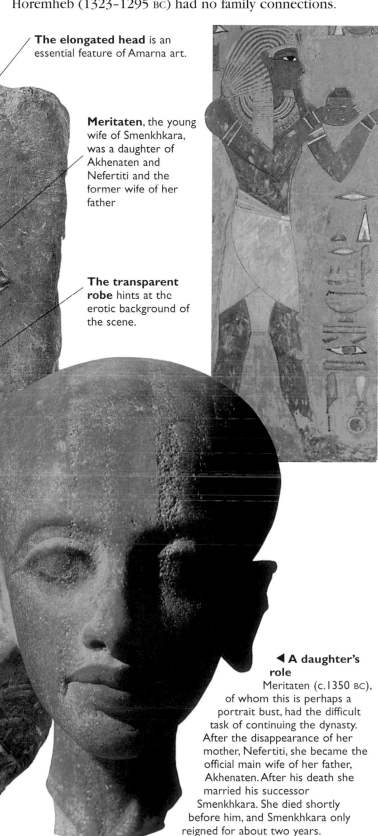

◀ **A daughter's role**
Meritaten (c. 1350 BC), of whom this is perhaps a portrait bust, had the difficult task of continuing the dynasty. After the disappearance of her mother, Nefertiti, she became the official main wife of her father, Akhenaten. After his death she married his successor Smenkhkara. She died shortly before him, and Smenkhkara only reigned for about two years.

Nefertiti– Power and Beauty

Nefertiti's extraordinary beauty is just as mysterious as her personality, but numerous inscriptions and representations show her to have played an important part in political and religious life.

Nefertiti, the principal wife of the pharaoh Akhenaten, is best remembered today for her legendary beauty, but she was also remarkable for the power she wielded. After her marriage, she became so involved in affairs of state, and wielded such a great deal of political influence, that she was often portrayed wearing a pharaoh's crown.

Very little is known for certain about Nefertiti's early life. Some historians have suggested she was the daughter of Ay, a relative of the pharaoh and one of his important officials. There is also frustratingly little detail about her

▶ Regal beauty
Contemporary writers described Nefertiti as 'a noblewoman of many charms', who was 'virtuous in every way'. There is no doubt that her physical beauty caused a great stir at court, and artists paid tribute to her in many forms.

▶ The necropolis of Akhetaten
In 1348 BC, his fifth year as pharaoh, Amenhotep IV marked his religious reforms by renaming himself Akhenaten (after Aten, the sun god) and ordered the building of a new capital, Akhetaten – the horizon of Aten – on the site of an important astronomical alignment. Today, it is known as Tell el-Amarna. The photograph shows the necropolis, or burial place, of the city, where 25 stone tombs have been discovered. Among them are a royal tomb with fragments of the sarcophagus of Akhenaten. Nefertiti's burial place has never been discovered.

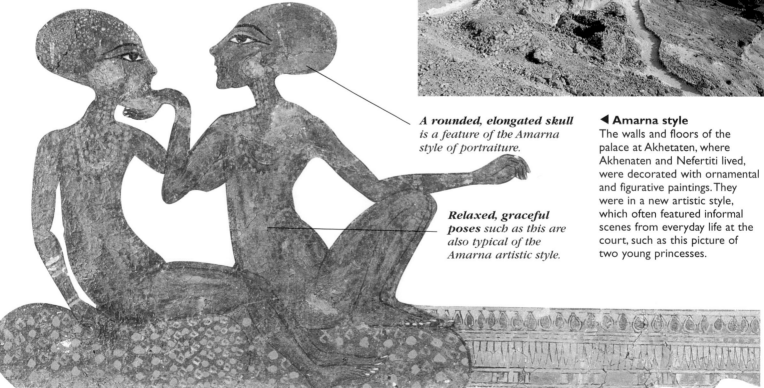

A rounded, elongated skull is a feature of the Amarna style of portraiture.

Relaxed, graceful poses such as this are also typical of the Amarna artistic style.

◀ Amarna style
The walls and floors of the palace at Akhetaten, where Akhenaten and Nefertiti lived, were decorated with ornamental and figurative paintings. They were in a new artistic style, which often featured informal scenes from everyday life at the court, such as this picture of two young princesses.

political activities, but there is no doubt of her power. She is often shown distributing gifts to officials from what is probably the palace balcony, or standing in a war chariot wielding a mace to destroy her enemies.

Such signs of power customarily belonged by right only to the pharaoh, but many traditions were overturned in Akhenaten's reign. Nefertiti is even shown standing alongside her husband as an equal at religious ceremonies.

▼ Nefertiti à la mode
Nefertiti is always represented in reliefs and statues wearing the fashions of the time. This sculpture from the period of Akhenaten shows a woman – possibly Nefertiti or one of her daughters – wearing a robe typical of the time. It is made of gossamer-thin, highly pleated linen – although the sculptor may have employed artistic licence in the number of pleats – cut to show off, rather than conceal, the body of the wearer.

A shawl, tied in a fan-shaped knot below the breast, was worn over this simple robe. The final touch to the royal outfit would have been a decorated headdress.

Her power, along with her extraordinary beauty, led to Nefertiti being venerated in her lifetime as a mother goddess and protectress in Akhenaten's capital, Akhetaten.

Ultimate power?
Around 1340 BC, she seems to have disappeared. She may have died, or been supplanted by another of Akhenaten's wives, but another possibility is that she simply changed her name to Smenkhkara and ruled as co-regent in the last years of Akhenaten's reign, and briefly as pharaoh after he died in 1336. The old order was, though, restored under Tutankhamun (1336–1327 BC). Akhetaten was soon abandoned, and the old gods were restored. Nefertiti's reputation suffered along with that of her husband.

Aten, the sun god

Aten was always shown as a sun disc, with rays stretching downwards. He was worshipped in the Amarna period to the exclusion of all the other gods of Ancient Egypt.

The blessings of Aten rain down on the royal family. The lower end of some of the rays hold the ankh, symbol of life and vitality.

The pharaoh Akhenaten is represented, in stylized form, as a gaunt, androgynous figure.

A cushioned footstool is provided for the comfort of the pharaoh, who is shown wearing sandals.

Nefertiti's daughters are depicted as small-scale adults. The royal couple had six girls, but no sons.

The frame of the frieze is made up of columns carved as stems of papyrus, the heraldic plant of Lower Egypt.

Tutankhamun

Before the opening of his tomb in 1922 propelled him to world fame, Tutankhamun was, ironically, one of the most obscure of all pharaohs.

The reign of Tutankhamun (1336-1327 BC) marked the end of the Amarna period, when Akhenaten established a new, heretical religion devoted to worship of the Aten, and a new capital city, Akhetaten. Tutankhamun was born there, probably to one of Akhenaten's lesser wives, Kiya.

A period of transition

Akhenaten died in 1336 BC, and after the ephemeral rule of the even more obscure Smenkhkara, the nine-year-old child became king. He was then called Tutankhaten, but in the second year of his reign, he and his wife, Ankhesenpaaten – third daughter of Akhenaten – reflected the resurgent power of the priesthood of Amun by changing their names to Tutankhamun and Ankhesenamun. Despite this, his successors had his name removed from the official king lists as he was tainted by the Amarna heresy. As Tutankhamun was still a child, the country was governed on his behalf by his courtiers.

▲ **Too young to rule**
Because of his youth, Tutankhamun had no real power. While the child king was a living god and the titular head of the state and religion, the day-to-day affairs of Egypt were handled by his vizier Ay, the chief general Horemheb (both later pharaohs in their own right) and Maya, his treasurer.

Tutankhamun's face is adapted to that of the god Amun.

Amun's hands are positioned to symbolize the divine protection of the king.

The small statue of the pharaoh is protected by Amun.

▲ **Changing names**
The first mention of the king is in an inscription in the Aten temple at Hermopolis, when he was called Tutankhaten, 'Living image of the Aten' (upper cartouche). Later, he became Tutankhamun, 'Living image of Amun, ruler of the Southern Heliopolis' (lower cartouche).

◄ **The pharaoh's father?**
Akhenaten (left) is generally believed to be Tutankhamun's father, but some inscriptions suggest that it was Amenhotep III who was his father, and that the boy king was Akhenaten's much younger brother.

◄ **Return to tradition**
As early as his second year on the throne, Tutankhamun officially rescinded the innovations of the Amarna period. The worship of the Aten was rejected in favour of Amun, who was once again seen as the highest god of the land. Many statues such as this were dedicated to Amun-Ra in the name of the child king.

The true power brokers in Egypt were the pharaoh's chief vizier and 'god's father' Ay, who had also served Akhenaten; the general Horemheb; and the treasurer Maya. Huy, the viceroy of Nubia; Nakhtmin, another soldier; and two courtiers called Usemonth and Pentju made up the rest of the inner circle.

The regents abandoned the new capital at Amarna and returned the seat of power to Memphis. They reopened and restored the temples of the traditional gods of Egypt that had been closed by Akhenaten. Thebes was once again established as the religious centre of Egypt, and Amun-Ra was restored to his former eminence as chief of the gods.

War – and regicide?

We know few details of the reign of Tutankhamun. Some tomb scenes show the pharaoh as a military leader, although it is enormously unlikely that he ever fought in battle. During his reign, though, Horemheb went on the offensive in Syria against the Hittites – who had profited from Akhenaten's apparent lack of interest in foreign affairs by taking over territories in the region – and won several victories.

Mystery surrounds Tutankhamun's death, at aged 18, as it does his life. He may have been murdered; the mummy's skull shows signs of a possible head wound. His hasty burial – albeit with a fabulous treasure – in a small tomb that was not originally intended for him adds to the puzzle.

▲ **Monuments of Tutankhamun**
The boy king left his mark in the temple at Luxor, where he was responsible for the decoration of the walls of the court around the great colonnade which had been built by Amenhotep III. The reliefs show the Opet Festival. He also had made a beautiful alabaster sphinx for Karnak.

▲ **The successor**
Ay, the king's secretary, was the true power behind the throne. After Tutankhamun's death, he married the pharaoh's widow and became king himself. Ay had been a courtier of Akhenaten, and this stele from his tomb shows him (top right) and two servants with the elongated heads typical of the Amarna style.

▼ **The general**
As the commander of the army, Horemheb was, next to Ay, the most influential figure in Tutankhamun's court. This tomb relief shows him being garlanded with gold necklaces for his military victories. His rule as pharaoh (1323–1295 BC) saw the restoration of order to Egypt.

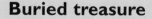

INSIGHT

Buried treasure

Tutankhamun's name had been expunged from the official king lists, and did not appear on any of the known relics of the Amarna period. In the early twentieth century, though, goods bearing his name kept turning up in antique shops.

In 1917, the archaeologist Howard Carter began looking for the tomb of the obscure pharaoh in the Valley of the Kings, as a pit containing the remains of his funerary banquet had been found there in 1907. Carter vowed to strip the Valley of the Kings down to the bedrock if necessary, and his efforts were rewarded on 4 November 1922, when his diggers found a staircase leading down to a tomb consisting of a rubble-filled corridor and four small chambers stuffed with funerary equipment.

The treasures included gilt statues of the king (left), furniture and jewellery fashioned in precious materials such as gold, silver, ivory and gemstones, as well as more everyday items. Carter concluded that thieves had visited the tomb fairly soon after it was dug, but had not done much damage. When the tomb of Rameses VI (1143–1136 BC) was cut into the rockface nearby, the workers had piled up the spoil in the entrance of the neighbouring tomb, then built their cabins on top of it, effectively preserving the site from further depredations.

Pharaoh Horemheb

At the end of the Amarna period, when there was no royal prince to succeed to the throne, General Horemheb (1323-1295 BC), already the de facto ruler of Egypt under King Ay, took over the reins of power.

Little is known about the background of Horemheb, the last pharaoh of the Eighteenth Dynasty (1550-1295 BC), except that he came from Herakleopolis. His parents remain anonymous, although his wife, Mutnedjmet, was possibly Nefertiti's sister. If Horemheb is identical to the military official Paatenemheb - a view held by some Egyptologists - then he would have started his military career under Akhenaten (1352-1336 BC), appearing as Horemheb during the reign of Tutankhamun (1336-1327 BC), when he was appointed King's Deputy.

Soldier and politician

Horemheb led military expeditions to consolidate those borders of Egypt that were threatened by the Hittites, and accompanied Tutankhamun on a campaign into Palestine. By means of military campaigns and shrewd foreign policy he successfully combated the influence of the Hittites on Egypt. After Tutankhamun and Ay (1327-1323 BC), who died without a male heir, Horemheb himself ascended the throne.

▼ Cartouches
Horemheb turned to several gods because of his various names: in the left cartouche, his name is 'Sacred are the manifestations of Ra, chosen of Ra'; in the right cartouche, 'Horemheb, beloved of Amun'.

▶ Under the protection of Amun
Horemheb continued Tutankhamun's restoration of the old order that had been established before the Amarna period. He reintroduced the ancient cults, particularly that of Amun, thus proving himself a true pharaoh who had to establish Maat (the world order).

▼ Horemheb the soldier
Horemheb was the 'great commander of the troops of the lord of the two countries', possibly already at the time of Akhenaten, but definitely during the reign of Tutankhamun. This relief from Horemheb's tomb at Saqqara shows a chariot and soldiers. During his reign he surrounded himself with military officials who had helped him with his rise from general to pharaoh, and whom he now entrusted with important priestly offices, giving him control of the powerful Amun priesthood.

The priesthood of Amun was certainly happy with Horemheb taking over power, as soon after his accession to the throne he had his pharaohship confirmed by Amun during the Opet Festival at Karnak.

The coronation inscription on the back of a double statue, showing Horemheb with his wife, tells that he is under the protection of Horus and appointed by Amun. It reports further that he had the damaged statues of the old gods remade and had temples that had fallen into disrepair rebuilt. For the Amun cult, 'he provided them with servants to the god and lector priests from the military elite'. In a decree on a stele at Karnak, he again officially confirms the restoration of the old order.

A second tomb

Directly after his accession to the throne, Horemheb had a tomb built in the Valley of the Kings, abandoning his earlier one near Memphis. For the first time, scenes from the *Book of Gates* were used in the burial chamber as a decoration of a royal tomb. Horemheb appointed the career general Parameses, who ascended the throne in 1295 BC as Rameses I (1295–1294 BC), as his successor.

▼ The Aten reliefs of Karnak
It is not yet proven whether Horemheb had really exorcized the Amarna period; the great iconoclasm began only after his death. To be able to build for himself, however, he did have the Per-Aten temple at Karnak pulled down and constructed a pylon of the Amun temple with its stone blocks. The reliefs from the Amarna period on those blocks therefore remained fairly well preserved.

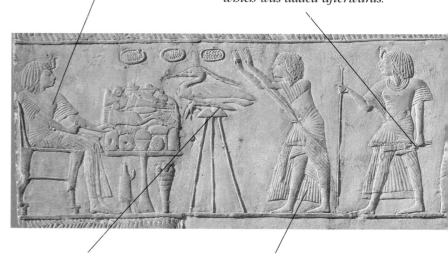

Wearing the typical pleated linen robe of a high-ranking official, Horemheb had himself depicted sitting in front of the offerings table.

Horemheb holds the pole and the sekhem sceptre of a high official, but can be identified as a pharaoh by the uraeus, which was added afterwards.

The benu-bird, regarded as the protector of the dead and as the soul of Ra, is sitting on a stand.

The man worshipping behind the benu-bird is the only figure not to wear a uraeus.

▲ The speos of Horemheb
Once he had become pharaoh, Horemheb took over many of the buildings of his predecessors and had them extended or rebuilt. For example, he enlarged the Amun temple at Karnak and increased the size of the workmen's settlement of Deir el-Medina. Outside Thebes he had a speos (rock temple) erected at Gebel el-Silsila that was dedicated to the Theban triad – Amun, Mut and Khons – as well as to Sobek, Taweret and himself.

▼ The military campaigns
As a general, Horemheb led several military campaigns during the reign of Tutankhamun; the prisoners captured are depicted in his tomb at Saqqara. The relief shows Near Eastern and Hittite men and women in handcuffs being led to the king by Egyptian guards. The handcuffs are attached with ropes to the neck of the captives, so that they are barely able to move their arms and hands.

Rameses the Great

Pharaoh Rameses II was one of the greatest of the Egyptian kings and ruled Ancient Egypt at a time of political and economic strength for an incredible 66 years.

Rameses II, the third pharaoh of the Nineteenth dynasty, ruled from 1279 to 1213 BC. As his statues and mummy show, he was a handsome and physically imposing man, about six feet in height when the average Egyptian was little more than five feet tall.

He was a legendary figure in more ways than one. At a time when most people lived for only a few decades, Rameses was well over 80 years old when he died. He also produced an amazing number of children – more than 100 sons and daughters appear in the official records, and these deal only with the 'official' marriages.

The cobra on the blue khepresh (blue crown) is the uraeus, the burning eye of the sun god Ra, worn by kings and gods as a symbol of their power over life and death.

The crook, or sceptre, in the pharaoh's right hand, represents the royal power to govern granted to kings by the god Osiris.

▲ Rameses the builder
After acceding to the throne, each pharaoh built a series of buildings. Rameses II, however, was unmatched as the greatest builder of them all. His mortuary temple, the Ramesseum in Thebes, resembled a large city. Here, a colossal granite head of Rameses II lies in front of four huge stone pillars which depict the god Osiris.

▶ Rameses II and power
This black granite statue shows the young pharaoh. Wearing a helmet-shaped royal headdress known as the blue crown, and holding the crook of government, he represents royal power. His pedestal is inscribed with nine bows, symbolizing Egypt's nine vanquished enemies.

Nefertari, Rameses' principal wife, is shown here. One of his sons is on the other side.

▲ Throne name
In this oval plate (known as a 'cartouche'), Rameses' throne name, User-Maat-Ra ('The justice of Ra is powerful'), is given in hieroglyphs. Many later kings used his personal name of Rameses.

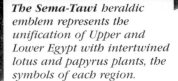

The Sema-Tawi heraldic emblem represents the unification of Upper and Lower Egypt with intertwined lotus and papyrus plants, the symbols of each region.

**◀ Rameses
the warrior**
This picture by the Italian
Egyptologist Ippolito Rosellini
(1800–1843), taken from a relief
in the great temple of Abu
Simbel, shows the pharaoh in his
war chariot, accompanied by
a tame leopard.

He had eight wives (at least two of whom were his
daughters!), but his favourite wife, Nefertari, is the best
remembered. For Nefertari he built an imposing temple
in Abu Simbel and also constructed an elaborately
decorated tomb – one of the most beautiful in Egypt –
in the Valley of the Queens.

Warrior, statesman and builder

From his youth, Rameses excelled on the battlefield, and
at the beginning of his long reign undertook several
military campaigns. The most famous was the battle
against the Hittites at Qadesh in Syria, which led to the
signing of history's first known peace treaty between
the two great powers of the time.

During Rameses' reign, the Egyptian economy flourished;
there was extensive trade with merchants from the Middle
East and the Aegean islands. Outsiders immigrated and
settled, bringing foreign words into the Ancient
Egyptian language and worshipping foreign
gods, such as Baal, a Syrian deity.

In addition, Egypt's status as a world power was
consolidated, with borders extending to Syria in the
east and Nubia in the south. With stability both at home
and abroad, Rameses set out, in the last third of his
reign, to express the wealth and power of Egypt with
magnificent building works.

The entire country was lavishly bestowed with
temples, of which the most famous are the spectacular
constructions at Abu Simbel. His own rock-cut temple
here is dominated by four massive statues of himself
carved in such a way that they stand out in every
condition of light. The pharaoh also founded a new
capital city in the east Nile Delta called Pi-Ramesse, or
City of Rameses, which, according to contemporary
descriptions, was beautiful beyond compare.

▶ Nefertari's cartouche
In the royal name-plate, Nefertari's
name appears as 'beautiful', or even
'most beautiful of all'. This is followed
by her title as the 'beloved of Mut',
who was the goddess-wife of Amun.

Nfr.t-irj

Mwt

n

mrj.t

Nfr.t-irj. mrj.t n Mw.t
'Nefertari, beloved of Mut'

▶ Queen Nefertari
Nefertari was the principal and
most beloved of Rameses II's
wives, and he dedicated various
monuments to her, including a
small but exquisite temple at
Abu Simbel.

In this wall painting from her
large and beautifully decorated
tomb in the Valley of the
Queens, she is shown playing
senet, a popular Egyptian board
game similar to chess. She wears
a long white linen gown, and her
headdress represents Nekhbet,
vulture goddess of Upper Egypt
who, like the cobra goddess, was
a protector of royalty.

**▼ Temples of Rameses II
and Nefertari**
Rameses built two enormous rock
temples in Abu Simbel in Lower Nubia.
On each side of the entrance to
Rameses' 'great temple', seen here on
the left of the photograph, sit four
massive figures of the king. The smaller
temple to the right is dedicated to
Nefertari and the goddess Hathor.
In the 1960s, the temples were
moved to higher ground to
protect them from the
Aswan High Dam.

The Battle of Qadesh

In 1274 BC, the Egyptians and the Hittites fought a major battle for the city of Qadesh, with victory claimed by both. Rameses II celebrated his exploits in numerous temple reliefs and documents.

The city of Qadesh, located in modern-day Syria, was much fought over because of its strategic position on the trade route from the Euphrates to the Mediterranean. Sety I (1294–1279 BC), the father of Rameses II (1279–1213 BC), had conquered the city earlier; however, as soon as he withdrew his military forces, it fell again to Egypt's powerful rivals, the Hittites. These people from Anatolia (modern Turkey) controlled northern Syria and much of the Middle East.

In the fourth year of his reign, Rameses II set out to the northeast of Egypt and captured the provinces of Canaan, Upi and Amurra. He then decided to push on to Qadesh the following spring. His 20,000 men were divided into four divisions, named after the gods Amun, Pre, Ptah and Seth, and an additional élite force, the Na'arn, which

◄ **A Middle Eastern fortress**
The Egyptians depicted the fortifications of their Middle Eastern opponents as tower-like buildings which had to be attacked by bow and arrow.

▲ **The courage of Rameses**
In the Egyptian account of the battle, Rameses II displayed the 'courage of a lion' as he stood alone against the Hittite hordes.

▼ **Hittite soldiers**
Although the Egyptians described the battle as a great victory, neither side gained the upper hand, thanks to the strategic ingenuity of the Hittite commanders and the bravery of their soldiers. The relief below (c. 90 BC) shows Hittites armed with spears, helmets and shields.

was sent northwards along the Phoenician coast. Rameses II and his four divisions eventually reached the Orontes river, just short of the city, where they captured two Bedouins, who claimed falsely that the Hittite army was some way off. Rameses II fell into this trap and led his Amun division across the Orontes to attack the city.

The Hittite king Muwatallis, with an army of 37,000 foot soldiers and 3,500 battle chariots, crossed the river and defeated the Pre division, which was hastily moving its forces towards the front. Muwatallis' troops then stormed the Amun division, routing most of its men. Rameses II was suddenly isolated, with only his bodyguards between himself and the Hittites. The series of stories known as the *Poem of Pentaur* tells how Rameses II

INSIGHT

The empire of the Hittites

The Hittites were an Indo-European people who probably originated in southern Russia and moved to Anatolia around 3000 BC. The majority of the population were free farmers and traders who lived in a confederation of city-states which joined to form the Hittite empire in the sixteenth century BC. They soon extended their rule over all of Anatolia and expanded southward to what is now Damascus in the south, and to the River Tigris in the east.

During the reign of Akhenaten (1352–1336 BC), Egyptian foreign policy was weak and the Hittites gained control as far south as Syria and Palestine, where they harassed the Egyptians. Under Sety I and Rameses II, the Egyptian empire strengthened and Hittite expansion was halted. Hittite ascendancy came to an end with the incursions of bands of settlers who migrated from the Mediterranean and the attacks of the Assyrians. The leading Hittite city was Hattusa (below), 200km (124 miles) from modern-day Ankara, which was made the capital of the empire under King Laburna II.

Egyptian soldiers were armed with shield, lance and battle-axe.

Sherden mercenaries were the bodyguards of the pharaoh, and can be recognized by their round shields and horned helmets.

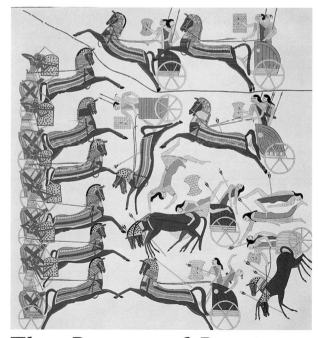

The Poem of Pentaur

A colour reproduction of a relief from the temple at Abu Simbel. This poem of praise to Rameses II forms the basis of many representations of the various stages of the battle of Qadesh. Such works can be found in the temples of Abydos, Luxor, Karnak and in the Ramesseum in west Thebes, as well as in the temple at Abu Simbel. Most show Rameses II in the act of smiting his enemies with the disciplined Egyptians on the left, and the chaotic Hittite forces to the right.

rose above his adversity and single-handedly beat off the Hittites; in fact, he was saved by the timely intervention of the Na'arn, who arrived from the coast and attacked the Hittites from behind. This allowed the Egyptians to regroup and the Seth and Ptah divisions to march north to join up with what remained of the army.

With no decisive outcome to the battle, a ceasefire was arranged, and the Egyptians withdrew their forces and returned home, with both sides claiming victory. The Hittites soon reoccupied the provinces of Amurra and Upi, leaving only Canaan under Egyptian control, but Rameses II's flair for self-publicity made sure his 'victorious' deeds were remembered well beyond his death.

After 15 years, a peace treaty was signed between the two sides, the first such agreement recorded in history, as both joined forces to fight the new threat of the Assyrians. Rameses II consolidated the alliance by marrying a Hittite princess, an event celebrated on the Hittite marriage stele in the temple at Abu Simbel.

Sea Peoples

In the 12th century BC, a loose alliance of peoples from the islands of the Aegean Sea and the southern coast of modern Turkey attempted to settle in Egypt, only to face the might of Rameses III's well-organized army.

A confederation of migrants, known as the Sea Peoples, the name given to them by the Egyptians, formed an alliance in order to invade and settle in Greece and the Near East. By the time of their second attack on Egypt, during the reign of Rameses III (1184–1153 BC), it is possible that they had already brought down the Hittite empire. They had destroyed and plundered some of the coastal cities of Syria-Palestine and now prepared to inflict the same fate on Egypt.

Rameses III reacted swiftly, mobilizing the country's troops and distributing the weapons of the royal arsenal to his soldiers. An intelligent and experienced military strategist, he led his forces into Palestine to confront the invaders before they could reach the Egyptian border.

▼ Medinet Habu
The exterior walls of the temple of Medinet Habu at Thebes are decorated with scenes of Rameses III's naval and land battles with the Sea Peoples.

▶▼ Rameses III
Rameses III was one of the last great pharaohs. Like Rameses II, he built magnificent temples and was a great military strategist, as shown in his resounding victory over the Sea Peoples.

▲ Massacre of the prisoners
Rameses III symbolically seizes his prisoners by the hair and prepares to strike them as they plead for mercy.

Rameses III was well informed of the Sea Peoples' tactics of combining land advances with naval attacks and was prepared for them. The Sea Peoples, slowed down by heavy carts carrying their families and belongings, were quickly and decisively defeated by the Egyptian army on land. Their accompanying fleet, positioned off the coast near Gaza, was also no match for Rameses III's forces. Egyptian archers fired salvos of arrows at the enemy ships and boarded them, engaging in a fierce battle that is depicted on the walls of the pharaoh's temple at Medinet Habu. The Egyptians were soon as triumphant on sea as they had been on land and those enemies that survived the battle were taken prisoner, many later settling in Thebes and eventually becoming a powerful group.

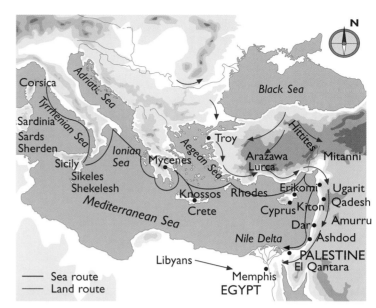

The Peleset wear helmets with feathers or horsehair.

The Sherden from Sardinia wear flat, horned helmets.

The Egyptian soldiers wield clubs and protect themselves with wooden shields.

The prow of the Egyptian boat is in the form of a lion's head, with the head of an Asiatic person in its jaws.

This enemy is recognizable by his headdress and loincloth, which are different from those of the Egyptians.

▲ **Detail of the naval battle against the Sea Peoples**
This relief, from the temple at Medinet Habu, is the earliest known depiction of a sea battle. After the Egyptians had encircled the enemy fleet, they boarded the boats, armed with clubs, spears and bows, and protected by shields. They mercilessly inflicted injuries on their foes, as shown here in striking detail.

INSIGHT

The Libyan campaigns

As well as repelling the advances of the Sea Peoples, Rameses III had to drive out Libyan hordes who were threatening Egypt's western borders. It took two military campaigns – the first carried out in the fifth year of his reign and the second in the eleventh year – to achieve this objective and guarantee the country's safety.

The second of these campaigns proved to be a difficult contest as the king was confronted by Libyan forces led by a military commander named Mesher. However, the final encounter near Memphis resulted in success for Rameses III, and Mesher was taken prisoner.

The relief below from the temple at Medinet Habu depicts Mesher leading a long procession of prisoners before the pharaoh.

The Priest Kings

After Rameses XI's death ended the New Kingdom, the kings of the Twenty-First Dynasty (1069–945 BC) ruled the north from Tanis, while the high priests of Amun in Thebes held sway over southern Egypt.

Rameses XI (1099–1069 BC), the last pharaoh of the New Kingdom, ruled in name only from his 19th year. A Libyan general called Herihor was the most important man in Upper Egypt. As well as being high priest of Karnak, the richest temple in Egypt, he was vizier of southern Egypt, viceroy of Kush, and commander of the Egyptian army. Smendes, vizier of Lower Egypt, effectively ruled the Delta region.

The trappings of power

Herihor (c. 1080–1070 BC) did not hesitate to take on the emblems and attributes of a king. His name appeared on walls surrounded by a royal cartouche and he was depicted in reliefs referring to the cult of Amun on the walls of Karnak, taking on the role of intermediary between the gods and men usually reserved for the pharaoh; one relief shows him wearing the double crown.

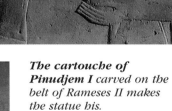

▶ **Amun at Karnak**
The Theban god Amun, seen here on the right facing Senusret I (1965–1920 BC), became the god of the royal dynasty and the nation during the Middle Kingdom (2055–1650 BC). His temple at Karnak, enlarged and embellished by each new pharaoh, was the wealthiest in Ancient Egypt. Its high priests wielded great political and military power, and acted as sovereigns over Upper Egypt from the time of the high priest Pinudjem I (c. 1070–1030 BC).

▼ **Mummy hideaways**
Many royal tombs in the Valley of the Kings were robbed as pharaonic power declined in the New Kingdom. Pinudjem I ordered several mummies, and what funerary treasures remained in the plundered tombs, to be removed to safe hiding places – 12 pharaohs ended up in a shaft tomb at Deir el-Bahri, while eight more were uncovered in the tomb of Amenhotep II (1427–1400 BC), shown below.

*The cartouche of **Pinudjem I** carved on the belt of Rameses II makes the statue his.*

The small female figure standing in front of the king's legs is a wife of Rameses II.

▶ **Pinudjem I**
After the death of Herihor, Smendes (1069–1043 BC) shared the rule of Ancient Egypt with the high priest Pinudjem I, who in 1053 BC adopted the royal titles and protocol, as had Herihor. He also laid claim to royal statues by usurping this colossal statue of Rameses II to the north of the second pylon at Karnak.

Herihor died before Rameses XI, in 1070 BC. It was believed that Piankhi (*c.* 1060 BC), who headed the army of Upper Egypt, then became high priest of Amun, a post that was inherited by his son, who ruled as Pinudjem I. Recent studies suggest, however, another version of events, in which Piankhi preceded Herihor, while Pinudjem I was Herihor's son. Pinudjem I legitimized his position by marrying Henuttawy, whose father, Smendes, founded the Twenty-First Dynasty.

Dynastic marriages

In the sixteenth year of the reign of Smendes, Pinudjem I took on the royal attributes and proclaimed himself pharaoh. One of Pinudjem I's sons would rule in Tanis as Psusennes I (1039–991 BC), while two others, Masharata and Menkheppere, followed him as high priest of Amun at Thebes. This role then descended through Menkheppere, who had married the daughter of his brother, Psusennes I. Although strong familial ties bound the high priests of Amun and the Tanite kings, northern and southern Egypt continued to be governed as separate states.

▲ **The high priest Herihor**
Herihor's reign was a relatively short one, but he did oversee the completion of the hypostyle hall and colonnaded courtyard of the temple of Khons at Karnak. His tomb remains undiscovered; only this *Book of the Dead* papyrus, in which he is depicted as a king wearing the uraeus, and a bracelet bearing his name have been recovered.

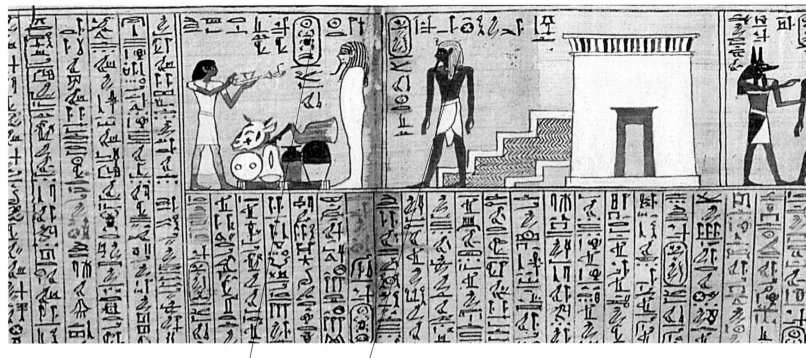

▲ **The *Book of the Dead* of Pinudjem I**
When the bodies of the New Kingdom kings were moved to their new resting places at Deir el-Bahri during the Twenty-First Dynasty, they were accompanied by more than 100 mummies of Theban priests, including that of Pinudjem I. Near his mummy was discovered his well-preserved papyrus of the *Book of the Dead*, which is today on display at the Egyptian Museum in Cairo.

Kheperkaura, the throne name of Pinudjem I, is written in the cartouche before the dead pharaoh's standing mummy.

Pinudjem I, shown standing in front of his tomb, sports the pharaoh's nemes headcloth and loincloth.

▶ **The Delta kings**
The pharaohs of the Twenty-First Dynasty ruled in the Delta while the priestly dynasty was in the ascendancy in Thebes. One of the most significant of the kings ruling from Tanis was Psusennes I (1039–991 BC), the son of the Theban high priest Pinudjem I and his wife Henuttawy, who was herself the daughter of the first Tanite king, Smendes.

Libyans on the Throne

The era of Libyan leadership began with Sheshonq I (945–924 BC) and ushered in a brief revival of the pre-eminence Egypt had enjoyed under Rameses III (1184–1153 BC).

▲ The founder of the Dynasty
Sheshonq I (945–924 BC), a 'great leader of the Meshwesh', was a member of the Libyan tribe from Bubastis. He extended his power base to Tanis and Memphis. In 950 BC he occupied Thebes, and came to the throne in 945 BC.

During the Twentieth Dynasty (1186–1069 BC), the Libyans already represented a powerful colony of mercenaries established in the Delta. On the death of the 21st-Dynasty king Psusennes II (959–945 BC), the Libyan general Sheshonq I seized power and founded the Twenty-Second Dynasty. To legitimize his power, he married Psusennes II's daughter and appointed his son, Iuput, as Governor of Upper Egypt, High Priest of Amun and commander in chief of the Egyptian army.

Wishing to restore Egypt to its former glory, Sheshonq I revived trade links with Byblos and launched military campaigns into Palestine, possibly sacking the temple in Jerusalem and carrying off massive treasure as tribute. This allowed Egypt to re-establish its former frontiers in Asia and also swelled the royal coffers. Reliefs on the exterior wall of Sheshonq I's festival court at Karnak document his victories in Syria-Palestine.

A bobbed hairstyle was used to depict Libyans in reliefs, murals and statues.

Egyptian-style clothes were worn by the Libyans in military and everyday life.

Libyan mercenaries are depicted heavily armed and wearing long tunics.

Two ostrich feathers as a headdress are typical of Libyan clothing of the time.

▲ Libyan soldiers
This relief depicts soldiers from the Libyan Meshwesh tribe, serving as mercenaries in the Ancient Egyptian army.

▶ The sarcophagus of Sheshonq II
In 924 BC, Sheshonq II was appointed to be the High Priest of Amun in Thebes by his father, Osorkon I (924–889 BC). As heir to the throne he held the title (among others) of 'Lord of the north and south'. In the last year of Osorkon I's reign, Sheshonq II was co-regent with his father. Sheshonq II was buried in the royal necropolis in Tanis, encased in this magnificent falcon-headed silver coffin.

After a reign of 20 years, Sheshonq I designated his son Osorkon I as his heir. As pharaoh, Osorkon I (924–889 BC) continued his father's policies and enlarged and decorated temples at Memphis, Bubastis and Karnak. He appointed his son Sheshonq II (c. 890 BC) as his heir, who ruled as co-regent with his father for only one year. Takelot I (889-874 BC), another of Osorkon I's sons by one of his concubines, succeeded them. The next pharaoh, Osorkon II (874-850 BC), was a great builder who restored the temple at Elephantine, embellished Bubastis and began building work at Thebes. The death of Osorkon II led to problems of succession. One of his younger sons, Takelot II (850-825 BC), acceded to the throne at Tanis, while his stepbrother Nimlot became increasingly powerful as High Priest of Amun at Thebes.

The beginning of the end

Under Sheshonq III, the sixth king of the Twenty-Second Dynasty, the Egyptian state started to dissolve. The Libyan commanders of cities such as Leontopolis, Herakleopolis Magna, Sais and Thebes – who were all related or connected by marriage – strived for independence. Pedubastis (818-793 BC) founded the Twenty-Third Dynasty at Leontopolis that was contemporaneous with the last pharaohs of the Twenty-Second Dynasty, while Bakenrenef founded the short-lived Twenty-Fourth Dynasty (727-715 BC). This confusion allowed the Kushite pharaoh, Piy (747-716 BC), to temporarily unify Egypt and found the Twenty-Fifth Dynasty.

▲ Sheshonq III
During his troubled reign, Sheshonq III witnessed the end of a century of Egyptian unity. In the eighth year of his kingship, Pedubastis I from Leontopolis declared himself pharaoh with the backing of the priests of Amun and thus founded the Twenty-Third Dynasty, which ruled at the same time as the last four kings of the Twenty-Second Dynasty. Sheshonq III's power was restricted to parts of the east and central Delta.

A colossal statue, wearing the crown of Upper Egypt, stands in front of the massive entrance.

The royal necropolis of Tanis was built within the enclosure walls of the temple of Amun.

The remains of the gate of Sheshonq III were rebuilt by French archaeologists.

All of the temple blocks originated in other parts of the Delta, most coming from Qantir.

◄ The ruins at Tanis
The rulers of the Twenty-Second Dynasty adopted Tanis, the capital of the preceding Twenty-First Dynasty, as their royal residence, which was close to their city of origin, Bubastis. In 1939, the French Egyptologist Pierre Montet discovered the subterranean tombs of six kings of the Twenty-First and Twenty-Second dynasties, complete with magnificent funerary equipment.

▼ The land divided
Towards the end of the Twenty-Second Dynasty, Egypt had fallen into several areas of influence: in Thebes, the High Priests of Amun held power and contested the throne. The pharaohs of the Twenty-Second Dynasty resided in Bubastis and Tanis, while the Twenty-Fourth Dynasty, which was also recognized by the viceroys of Herakleopolis Magna – where this relief was found – ruled in the western Delta city of Sais.

The Persians in Egypt

The Achaemenid empire of the Persians, a tribe with its heartland in modern Iran, grew inexorably in the sixth century BC, swallowing up Egypt in 525 BC. It remained a Persian province until 404 BC.

In 664 BC, having been successively dominated by Libyans, conquered by Nubians from the kingdom of Kush, and briefly invaded by Assyrians, the Egyptians regained their independence under a dynasty originating in the Delta city of Sais. The Saite pharaohs (664-525 BC) restored the kingdom and encouraged a renaissance of Egyptian art. They fostered close relations with the Greeks – some of whom enrolled as mercenaries in their armies – and the Phoenicians, who put their seafaring skills at their service.

The last Saite pharaoh, Psamtek III, came to the throne in 526 BC. He occupied it for just six months before the Persian emperor Cambyses II (525–522 BC) – who had been guided across the Sinai by Bedouins – crushed his army near Pelusium and took over the country. The defeated pharaoh was taken to the Persian capital, Susa, and later put to death. When Cambyses II ascended the throne in Sais, he adopted the titles of the kings of Egypt. Manetho, the Egyptian historian of the third century BC, considered him the first king of the Twenty-Seventh Dynasty.

▶ The cartouche of Darius
The Persian rulers of Egypt never took up residence there, but they were thoroughly naturalized in Egyptian reliefs, which showed them taking on the robes, attributes and titles of a pharaoh. Cartouches at the temple of Hibis give Darius I the Horus name 'with effective will' and the throne name 'descendant of Ra', as well as his birth name.

▼ A synthesis of styles
The Achaemenid pharaohs ruled Egypt from Susa or Persepolis, deep in the Persian heartland, but Egyptian culture sometimes came to them. The traditional Persian decorations in the palace of Darius I in Persepolis were enriched with Egyptian, Greek and Mesopotamian motifs to create a distinctive new style.

▼ Darius I
The Persians understood that they could maintain order in, and extract tribute from, their 20 or so satrapies by maintaining their institutions rather than replacing them. Darius I was particularly astute at this. He had derelict temples restored and erected a new sanctuary for Amun, Osiris and other gods at Hibis in the Kharga Oasis.

The motif of a gryphon bears a passing resemblance to a winged sphinx, but is Mesopotamian in origin.

A Persian-style headdress is worn by Darius in reliefs at Persepolis. In Egypt, he was shown in traditional pharaonic style.

The winged solar disc was imported from Egypt. It was considered a symbol of the god Ahuramazda in Persia.

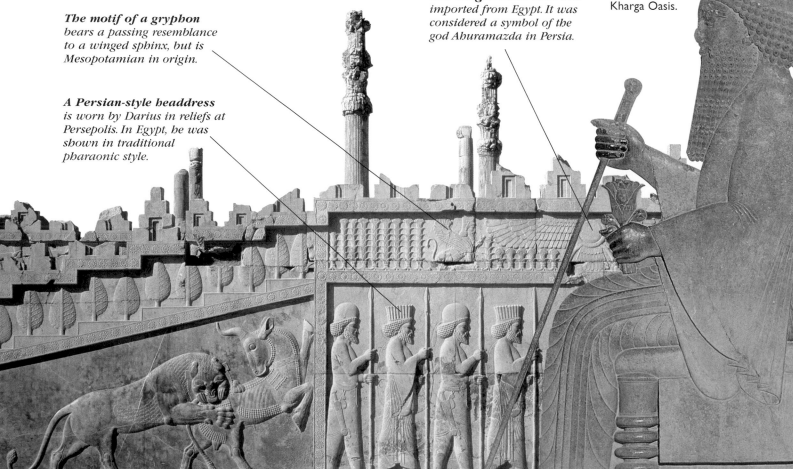

▲ A frieze of archers
The ruins of the palace of Darius I at Susa were excavated by French archaeologists between 1884 and 1886. Among their finds was this relief – now exhibited in the Louvre Museum in Paris – executed in coloured glazed bricks. It shows a row of Persian warriors carrying weapons, but dressed for ceremony rather than battle. They represent members of the so-called 'Immortals', the 10,000-strong Persian élite force. The army also employed mercenaries, many of them Greek.

The politically astute Cambyses II enlisted the support of the Egyptian aristocracy. He favoured Egyptian beliefs and promoted temple building to mitigate the growing influence of the Greeks, the Persians' great enemies.

Cambyses II made Egypt a satrapy, or province, of the Persian Empire. In 522 BC, he named as its first satrap Ariandes, who governed from Memphis. Under Darius I, (522–486 BC), Cambyses's successor, the self-serving style of government adopted by Ariandes brought Egypt close to revolt. The satrap overstepped the mark by minting and issuing his own coinage. Darius had him executed and introduced new policies to develop the province. He reformed the legal system and bureaucracy and oversaw the completion of a canal linking the Nile to the Red Sea.

War and peace

Darius's reforming zeal was, however, curbed by war with the Greeks, and the Persians' defeat at Marathon in 490 BC. Egypt rose again in revolt, but Darius's successor, Xerxes (486–465 BC), re-established order and made his brother, Artaxerxes, satrap. Artaxerxes proved extremely durable. He followed his brother as emperor (465–424 BC), and returned to Egypt to put down a revolt around 460 BC.

Egypt remained under Persian rule for 25 years or so, but by 404 BC, a spirit of rebellion was once again abroad. An uprising led by Amyrtaios of Sais ousted the satrap of the newly installed Artaxerxes II, and the Achaemenids, engaged in dynastic infighting for control of the empire, made no immediate attempt to win power back.

▼ The temple at Hibis
The temple complex at Hibis, at Kharga Oasis in the Libyan Desert, is the largest and best-preserved of the sanctuaries of the Late period (747–332 BC). Dedicated to Amun and Osiris, its sanctuary contains depictions of hundreds of Egyptian deities. Begun by the Saite pharaoh Psamtek II (595–589 BC), it was completed and embellished by Darius I, who appears in the reliefs making offerings to the gods of Egypt. The temple marked the westernmost extent of the Achaemenid empire.

Darius I is depicted in the temple at Hibis as a pharaoh wearing a short loincloth and the crown of Upper Egypt.

The two deities receiving the offering are the ibis-headed Thoth of Hermopolis Magna and his wife, Nehmetaway.

▼ The 'sacrilege' of Cambyses II
Herodotus and other classical writers characterized Cambyses II as utterly contemptuous of Egyptian beliefs, razing temples and going as far as to kill the sacred Apis bull, who was buried in the Serapeum at Saqqara (below). However, these writers drew from sources tainted with Greek propaganda against their long-term enemies. Archaeology has shown, to the contrary, that two Apis bulls were buried with all the honours due their divinity during the reign of Cambyses II, while restoration work was undertaken in the temple of Neith at Sais.

Alexander as Pharaoh

Late in 332 BC, Alexander the Great, having driven the Persians from the Nile Valley, was welcomed as a liberator by the Egyptians, who recognized him as a pharaoh.

Born in 356 BC, Alexander was the son of Philip II, King of Macedonia. After reforming the army to make it the most formidable of the time, Philip undertook a series of conquests to enlarge his kingdom. In 338 BC he conquered the Athenians to complete his control of Greece. He soon familiarized his son with power, and initiated him in the art of warfare by involving him in his campaigns. Philip entrusted his son's intellectual education to the philosopher Aristotle, who left his mark on his pupil more through his lessons on the ideal city and science than through his lessons on politics and ethics. At the age of 20, following the assassination of his father, Alexander inherited both his throne and his ambitions.

Having become head of the Hellenic Confederation, he prepared to conquer the Persian Empire. He went first to Asia Minor (now Turkey), where he captured the Greek cities, and in 333 BC he defeated Darius III at the battle of Issus. After subjugating Syria, Alexander entered Egypt – an event closer to a triumphant procession than an invasion – and displaced Darius as pharaoh.

The following year, in the place where the Nile Delta meets the Mediterranean coast, Alexander founded the first and by far the most prestigious of the many cities that bore his name. Thanks partly to its location, Alexandria became a prosperous commercial centre and a great seat of culture.

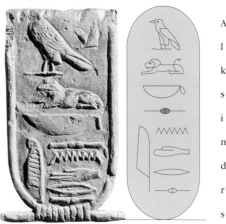

A l k s i n d r s

▲ **Alexander's cartouche**
The hieroglyphs in this cartouche translate phonetically as the name Alexander.

▼ **Alexander the builder**
Alexander restored the temples neglected by the Persians and dedicated new monuments to the Egyptian gods. In the temple of Luxor, near Karnak (below), he built a chapel for the sacred barge.

▶ **Alexander the conqueror**
Egypt was only one of a large number of territories taken by Alexander from the Persians, and by the time of his death his unprecedented empire stretched from the Mediterranean to the river Indus. During his few months in Egypt, Alexander reformed the taxation system on Greek models and organized the military occupation of the country, but, early in 331 BC, he left for Asia in pursuit of the Persians, never to return alive.

▶▶ **Alexander in Egypt**
After his trip to Siwa, Alexander was crowned in the temple of Ptah at Memphis. It appears that the Egyptian people, from priests to peasants, did not find it disturbing that Alexander was a foreigner – nor that he was absent for virtually his entire reign.

Amun wears a feather headdress, with a cap and ribbon.

Wearing the blue crown, Alexander worships the god Amun.

▲ Worship to Amun
The barge chapel of the temple of Luxor is decorated with reliefs that were originally painted. The scenes depict different episodes, as the pharaoh Alexander worshipped his 'father' Amun-Ra. Here he is portrayed in the gesture of adoration.

Amun-Min, with an erect penis, is one of the many forms of the 'king of the gods'.

Alexander prepares himself to worship the image of his 'god father' Amun.

▲ King of the gods
Amun, the head of the Egyptian pantheon and equivalent to Zeus, the supreme god of the Greeks, 'recognized' Alexander as his son in his sanctuary at the Siwa Oasis. Alexander thanked his 'father' by offering him monuments, such as the chapel for the inner temple at Luxor.

INSIGHT

Where is Alexander's tomb?

On his return to Babylon in 323 BC, Alexander died as the result of a fever. Tradition has it that his body was buried in Macedonia, next to his father Philip II, but in fact Ptolemy I removed it on the way to Greece and carried it to Egypt – first to Memphis, then to Alexandria, where it was buried. The conqueror's tomb was much visited in ancient times, and in particular by Octavian, the future emperor Augustus. Its exact location was lost during the first centuries of the modern era.

The sarcophagus known as Alexander's, found at Sidon (right), owes its name to the reliefs depicting the victor.

In order to legitimize the taking of power, and to be recognized as the descendant of the long line of pharaohs, Alexander made sacrifices to the gods at Memphis and went to consult the famous oracle of Amun-Ra at the Siwa Oasis in the Libyan Desert. In the depths of the sanctuary, the god 'identified' Alexander as his son (thus restoring the 'true' pharaonic line) and promised that he would rule over the entire world. The Greeks interpreted this message – one that the gods addressed to all pharaohs – as a prophecy.

As it transpired, Alexander had little time to make a real impact on the political or economic structure of Egypt. After he died from fever, attempts to hold the vast empire together were made during the reigns of his half-brother Philip Arrhidaeus (323–317 BC) and his son Alexander IV (317–310 BC); however, it soon devolved into a number of separate kingdoms ruled by his rival generals and their descendants. In Egypt, control passed to Ptolemy I (son of Lagos), the founder of the Ptolemaic Dynasty (305–30 BC).

Cleopatra, the Last Queen

Celebrated in art, literature and music, Cleopatra is the most famous Egyptian of all. Her suicide in 30 BC brought to an end the last chapter in the 3,000-year story of Ancient Egypt.

▲ The face of a queen
Like many queens before her, Cleopatra wore the vulture-shaped helmet of the goddess Nekhbet, symbol of Upper Egypt.

By the time Cleopatra VII Philopator (51–30 BC) reached the throne of Egypt in 51 BC, Rome was the dominant power in the Mediterranean. Clever and with superb political abilities, Cleopatra, however, was determined to keep Egypt independent. She succeeded her father, Ptolemy XII Neos Dionysos (80–51 BC), at the age of 18, after ruling as co-regent with him. According to his will, however, she had to marry and share the throne with the eldest of her brothers, Ptolemy XIII (51–47 BC), even though he was only 10 years old.

The meeting of Cleopatra and Julius Caesar

Soon after she came to the throne, a power struggle developed between Cleopatra and Ptolemy XIII, who ousted Cleopatra for a short time in 48 BC. All was not well in Rome either. The ruling triumvirate of Pompey, Julius Caesar and Crassus was beginning to crumble. About this time, Caesar defeated Pompey at the battle of Pharsalus. Pompey fled to Egypt, where he was assassinated by supporters of Ptolemy XIII, who had hoped to gain the support of Caesar (who had pursued Pompey to Egypt). Cleopatra, not to be outdone so easily, charmed her way into Caesar's affections.

Caesar stayed for several months in Alexandria, defeated Ptolemy XIII in a civil war and restored Cleopatra to the throne in 47 BC. Their relationship produced a child – the boy Ptolemy XV Caesarion. Caesar and Cleopatra dreamed of a new empire formed from the unification of Rome and Egypt. When Caesar left to put down his enemies in Asia Minor, he convinced Cleopatra to marry and share the crown with the younger of her two brothers, Ptolemy XIV Philopator – at that time still a child.

This Ptolemaic statue lay on the seabed for more than 2,000 years before being rediscovered in 1995.

Powerful jets of water were used to uncover the ancient treasure. The effects of waves and sand, however, have taken a toll on its condition.

◄ Underwater past
Because of the ever-changing water levels of the Egyptian coast, many archaeological sites are now underwater. An expedition in 1995, off the coast of Alexandria, led to the identification and partial salvage of many sculptures and fragments of stone from Cleopatra's palace. She was the last of the Ptolemaic Dynasty, who established their rule at Alexandria.

As queen of Egypt, Cleopatra had her own throne name cartouche.

K
L
O P
T
R
A

NETJERET

IT-ES

MERET

The hieroglyphs translate as: 'Cleopatra, the goddess beloved of her father'.

▶ **Cleopatra's son**
Ptolemy XV Caesarion was the result of the relationship between Cleopatra and Julius Caesar, and was co-regent with his mother from 44–30 BC. After the Egyptians were defeated by the Roman legions, this rightful heir to the throne was executed by Octavian, who saw him as a threat to his power.

On this sculptured stone, or stele (right), Caesarion can be seen on the far left in a ceremony for Amun, the god of the state of Egypt.

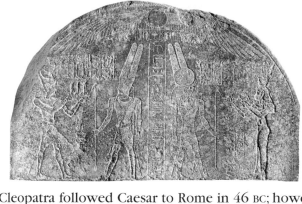

Cleopatra followed Caesar to Rome in 46 BC; however, when Caesar was assassinated in 44 BC, Cleopatra returned to Egypt, and ordered the killing of her brother Ptolemy XIV. She then installed herself and Caesar's son as co-regent on the throne.

Cleopatra and Mark Antony

In Rome, power was shared between Mark Antony, who ruled the eastern part of the Roman Empire, and Octavian (later Augustus), who ruled the west. When Antony ordered Cleopatra to meet him at Tarsus, she arrived laden with gifts as she sailed up the river to greet him.

Mark Antony was immediately captivated and went to Alexandria with her. In 40 BC, Antony returned to Rome to conclude an uneasy peace with Octavian, cemented by a marriage to his sister Octavia. After three years, he realized that his differences with Octavian could not be settled and travelled east again, hoping to use Cleopatra's money to finance a war of conquest against the Persians. His war was a failure, but he married Cleopatra, who bore him twins. Antony now began to give parts of the eastern empire to Cleopatra and her children.

Faced with this open treachery against Rome, and personal insult, Octavian mounted an invasion of Egypt and defeated Antony in a sea battle at Actium off the coast of northern Greece in 31 BC – not least because Cleopatra's fleet inexplicably withdrew and sailed for Egypt. Mark Antony committed suicide a year later.

Cleopatra had no intention of abasing herself before Octavian, nor of being taken by him in triumph to Rome. She killed herself with the venomous bite of a cobra – symbol of the goddess Wadjyt, protectress of the pharaohs – and thus escaped the humiliation of defeat. Her death marked the end of the Empire of the Pharaohs.

▲ **The ancestors of Cleopatra**
Cleopatra was the last in the line of the Ptolemies, who originated in Greece and ruled over Egypt from 332–30 BC. The founder of the dynasty was Ptolemy I Soter (305–285 BC), who became the leader of Egypt after the power struggles that followed the death of Alexander the Great (332–323 BC).

The Ptolemies held on to their Greek culture and language; only Cleopatra identified with her subjects and used their language. In spite of their Greek background, the Ptolemies respected Egyptian religious cults. This relief from the temple of Dendera shows Ptolemy VIII Euergetes II (170–116 BC) and Cleopatra II making offerings of drink and bouquets of flowers to the gods.

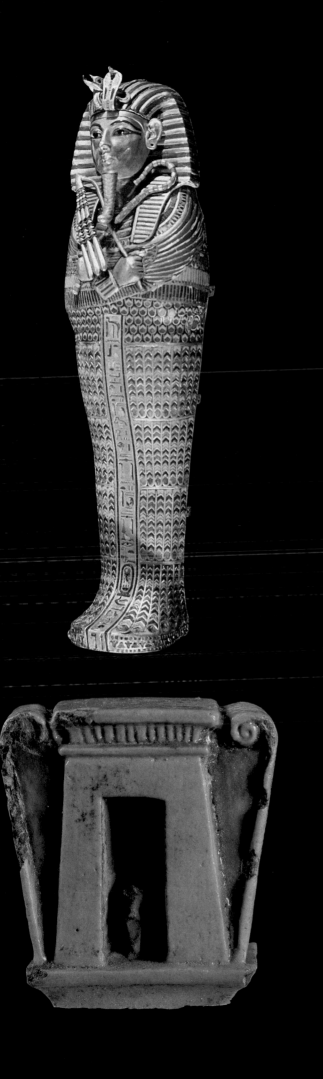

Religion

The religion of the ancient Egyptians often appears very alien to modern eyes, with animal-headed gods and complex temple structures. Their belief in an afterlife, which necessitated the practice of mummification, can also seem strange. Some ancient Egyptian gods represented aspects of the natural environment, such as the sun, the moon, or crocodiles, but they were also seen as complex beings, and it is rarely possible to say they of them that they were the 'god of' something as is common in the later, Classical world.

Temples and festivals

Egyptian temples were the places where the gods lived, and the priests who worked there were their servants ensuring that they were properly cared for. Temple estates provided produce for the god's table, as well as food for the priesthood.

At special festivals the images of the gods might be carried out of their temples in procession, or travel by river to visit other deities. This would be the almost the only chance for ordinary people to interact with the god of the local temple.

Within their homes, Egyptians revered gods related to fertility and child bearing. They believed in an apparently sophisticated form of afterlife, in which various spiritual aspects of a person, including the ka, the ba and the akh, continued to exist and required maintenance. This meant spending considerable time and expense on providing for the afterlife and in preserving the bodies of the dead so that the spirits could return there to be reunited.

Sacred symbols
Min, god of fertility (far left), was one of the most important ancient Egyptian gods. The mummified bodies of the dead were interred in decorated sarcophagi such as this example found in the tomb of Tutankhamun (above left). This small model (left) depicts the protecting walls of the temple, the home of the god.

The Gods of Egypt

The Ancient Egyptians worshipped a number of gods and goddesses, each of whom had different roles or functions, as well as a variety of creation myths.

F or the Ancient Egyptians, the divine nature of the universe was manifested in a multitude of ways. Their gods, for example, could appear in the guise of animals, illustrating a fundamental belief that all forms of life were an expression of the divine. Similarly, the sky and its heavenly bodies, as well as a number of environmental and climatic features of Egypt, were embodied by deities such as Nut, who personified the sky, and Hapy, who was the god of the annual Nile inundation.

The manifestations of the gods

The gods of Ancient Egypt often had several aspects and could appear in different ways. Thoth, for example, was associated with the movement and power of the moon, although he was better known as a god of writing and knowledge, and could be depicted with the head of either an ibis or a baboon.

The process of syncretism, by which two or more deities were combined to form a single cult, was also central to religion in Ancient Egypt. Two of the most important deities, Amun and Ra, for example, were fused to create Amun-Ra. In the Ptolemaic Period (332–30 BC), Ptolemy I (305-285 BC) created Serapis, a combination of the Greek gods Zeus and Helios with Osiris and Apis, perhaps in a move towards political and cultural unity.

▲ **Depiction of hybrid deities**
The solar cult was one of the central features of Ancient Egyptian religion. The sun god, Ra, had numerous forms, including Ra-Horakhty, shown above, a combination of Ra and Horus.

INSIGHT

Osiris, god of the afterlife

Along with the sun god, **Ra**, Osiris, the primary god of the dead, was one of the most important deities in the pantheon. In Ancient Egyptian mythology, Osiris was killed by his evil brother Seth, and his dismembered body was mummified and resurrected by his wife Isis.

During the Old Kingdom (2686–2181 BC), the deceased pharaoh was identified with Osiris and was believed to experience rebirth in the same way that the murdered god did. During the First Intermediate period (2181–2055 BC), however, it seems that it became possible for commoners to be ressurected in the manner of Osiris, as a sort of 'democratization of the afterlife' took place. Mummification was designed to make the deceased resemble Osiris as much as possible, in the hope that this would ensure eternal life in the underworld.

Osiris presided over the weighing of the heart ceremony in the afterlife. In this ritual, the deceased made the 'negative confession', swearing that they had not committed any of a list of offences, then their heart was weighed against the feather of Maat, symbol of truth and harmony. Osiris judged the results of the ritual and was responsible for deciding whether the deceased was worthy of resurrection.

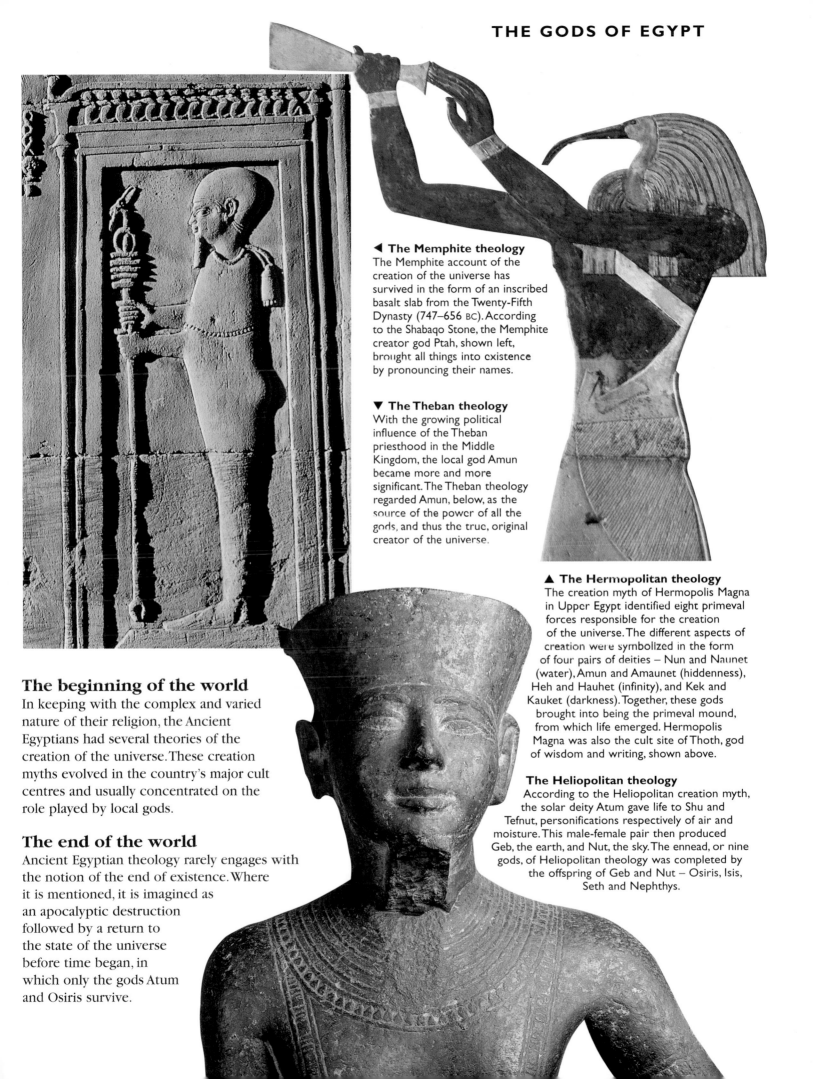

◄ **The Memphite theology**
The Memphite account of the creation of the universe has survived in the form of an inscribed basalt slab from the Twenty-Fifth Dynasty (747–656 BC). According to the Shabaqo Stone, the Memphite creator god Ptah, shown left, brought all things into existence by pronouncing their names.

▼ **The Theban theology**
With the growing political influence of the Theban priesthood in the Middle Kingdom, the local god Amun became more and more significant. The Theban theology regarded Amun, below, as the source of the power of all the gods, and thus the true, original creator of the universe.

▲ **The Hermopolitan theology**
The creation myth of Hermopolis Magna in Upper Egypt identified eight primeval forces responsible for the creation of the universe. The different aspects of creation were symbolized in the form of four pairs of deities – Nun and Naunet (water), Amun and Amaunet (hiddenness), Heh and Hauhet (infinity), and Kek and Kauket (darkness). Together, these gods brought into being the primeval mound, from which life emerged. Hermopolis Magna was also the cult site of Thoth, god of wisdom and writing, shown above.

The Heliopolitan theology
According to the Heliopolitan creation myth, the solar deity Atum gave life to Shu and Tefnut, personifications respectively of air and moisture. This male-female pair then produced Geb, the earth, and Nut, the sky. The ennead, or nine gods, of Heliopolitan theology was completed by the offspring of Geb and Nut – Osiris, Isis, Seth and Nephthys.

The beginning of the world

In keeping with the complex and varied nature of their religion, the Ancient Egyptians had several theories of the creation of the universe. These creation myths evolved in the country's major cult centres and usually concentrated on the role played by local gods.

The end of the world

Ancient Egyptian theology rarely engages with the notion of the end of existence. Where it is mentioned, it is imagined as an apocalyptic destruction followed by a return to the state of the universe before time began, in which only the gods Atum and Osiris survive.

Major Egyptian Gods

◀ Amun

Originally a local Theban deity, Amun achieved the position of head of the Egyptian pantheon with the rise of the Theban priesthood in the Middle Kingdom (2055–1650 BC). He was usually represented as a man with a double-plumed crown, or with the head of a ram. His importance among the gods was due in large part to the way in which he was combined with other powerful deities. With the sun god, Ra, he became Amun-Ra, and with the fertility god Min, he became Amun-Min. As well as being worshipped at Thebes as part of a triad with his consort Mut and their child Khons, he was also regarded as one of the eight gods, or Ogdoad, in the creation myth of Hermopolis Magna. As a personification of air or hidden power, he represented one of the elements that allowed the universe to come into existence. The temple at Karnak, the best surviving religious complex of the New Kingdom (1550–1069 BC), is dedicated to Amun.

▶ Bastet

The local deity of Bubastis in the eastern Nile Delta, Bastet was the daughter of Ra and the protective aspect of the aggressive lioness goddess Sekhmet. Her earliest form was as a woman with the head of a lioness, but by the first millennium BC she appeared in the more gentle guise of a cat or a cat-headed woman, sometimes accompanied by a group of kittens. The ancient town of Bubastis is the site of a red granite temple dedicated to Bastet, as well as a series of mud-brick cat cemeteries.

▼ Bes

Despite his grotesque and ferocious appearance, this dwarf god was one of the most popular domestic deities in Ancient Egypt. He was believed to ward off snakes, and was regarded as a protector of the family, associated with childbirth and sexuality. His image is found on birth houses of the Late period (747–332 BC), as well as on numerous everyday items.

▲ Anubis

Represented as a dog, or as a man with a dog's head, Anubis was a god of the dead, closely associated with the process of mummification and embalming. The priests who perfomed these rituals on the deceased are thought to have taken on the role of Anubis by wearing jackal masks. Anubis features in depictions of the weighing of the heart ceremony in the *Book of the Dead*, assisting in the judgement of the dead. He was also considered to be a guardian of cemeteries, known in this guise as 'lord of the sacred land' and 'foremost of the divine booth'. The cult of Anubis was eventually assimilated with that of Osiris, another major god of the dead.

▶ Apis

The Apis bull, an individual animal chosen according to particular distinctive markings, was the physical manifestation of the Memphite creator god Ptah. When they died, the Apis bulls were buried in the catacombs of the Serapeum at Memphis, discovered by Auguste Mariette in 1851. In the Ptolemaic period (332–30 BC), the Apis was combined with several Greek gods to create the cult of Serapis.

◄ Khnum
The ram god Khnum had his principal cult centre at Elephantine, where he was part of a local triad of deities, probably from the Early Dynastic period (3100–2686 BC). He was associated with the annual Nile inundation and the fertile soil of the Nile Valley, which related to his role as a potter god. In this form, Khnum was responsible for fashioning the unborn child from clay and placing it as a male seed in the mother's body. The best-preserved temple of Khnum is at Esna, built during Greco-Roman times (332 BC–AD 395), where reliefs depict him as the creator of the universe, including gods, humans, animals and plants.

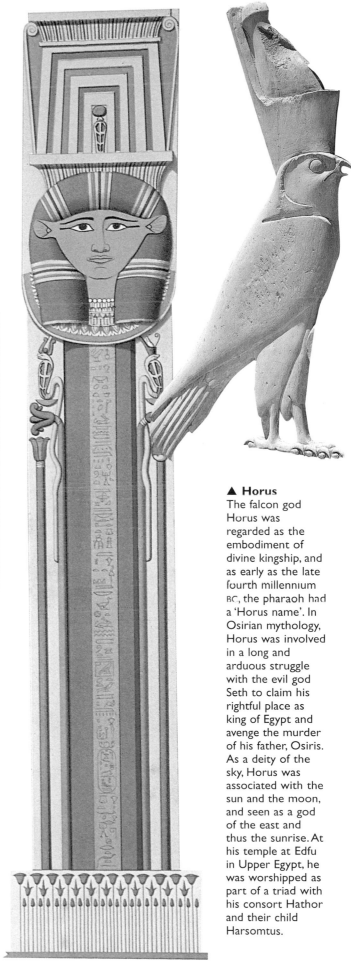

▲ Hapy
Hapy was the god of the Nile inundation, the annual flooding of the great river, and was worshipped as an embodiment of the floods and the ensuing fertility. He was usually depicted as an androgynous figure with a beard, pendulous breasts and a pot belly, wearing a headdress of papyrus plants. From the Nineteenth Dynasty (1295–1186 BC), reliefs are found, such as the one above, depicting two Hapy-like fecundity figures. One is wearing the papyrus of Lower Egypt and the other the lotus of Upper Egypt, in the act of tying together the wind-pipe sema hieroglyph in a representation of the unity of the two parts of Ancient Egypt. Hapy was also closely associated with the creator god Khnum, who was worshipped at Elephantine as the god of the Nile springs.

▶ Hathor
The bovine goddess Hathor was one of the most important deities in Ancient Egypt, and had a variety of associations. She was regarded as the goddess of a number of the pleasurable aspects of life, such as dance, music, sexuality and alcohol. She was also, along with Isis, considered to be the divine mother of the reigning pharaoh, as illustrated in a relief in a rock-cut chapel at Deir el-Bahri showing Hathor in the form of a cow suckling the pharaoh Amenhotep II (1427–1400 BC). In addition to these roles, she was 'lady of turquoise' and 'lady of Byblos', and, as 'lady of the West', was responsible for receiving the setting sun each evening and keeping it safe until dawn. In this funerary aspect, she could also offer protection for the deceased in the afterlife.

▲ Horus
The falcon god Horus was regarded as the embodiment of divine kingship, and as early as the late fourth millennium BC, the pharaoh had a 'Horus name'. In Osirian mythology, Horus was involved in a long and arduous struggle with the evil god Seth to claim his rightful place as king of Egypt and avenge the murder of his father, Osiris. As a deity of the sky, Horus was associated with the sun and the moon, and seen as a god of the east and thus the sunrise. At his temple at Edfu in Upper Egypt, he was worshipped as part of a triad with his consort Hathor and their child Harsomtus.

▼ Isis

The cult of Isis spread far beyond Ancient Egypt, being adopted by the Hellenistic and Roman worlds in post-Pharaonic times. The goddess was the wife of Osiris and mother of Horus, becoming identified, like Hathor, as the divine mother of the reigning pharaoh. As the devoted wife of Osiris, she mummified and reanimated his dismembered body after he had been murdered by Seth, and magically conceived their son Horus in the process. She was also known as 'Isis great in magic', and, as such, had healing powers and the ability to protect the young. In Ancient Egyptian myth, she cured the sun god, Ra, from a snake bite, in return for knowledge of his secret name. She passed this on to Horus, giving him great powers. Her most famous cult site was the island of Philae near Aswan, where a magnificent temple complex was constructed in her honour.

◄ Maat

Maat was the personification of truth, justice and harmony, responsible for regulating the stars, the seasons and the actions of both humans and gods. The maintenance of this divine order was essential for the survival of the Ancient Egyptian state and society, and Maat was thus revered as a central figure in the pantheon. To live by Maat was to act according to a strict code of ethics, as opposed to the chaos that reigned outside Egypt's borders. From the Eighteenth Dynasty (1550–1295 BC), Maat was described as the daughter of Ra, indicating that pharaohs were believed to rule through her authority. She was portrayed as a woman with an ostrich feather on her head, or sometimes represented by the feather alone. In the weighing of the heart ceremony, the deceased's heart was weighed in the balance against Maat, symbolized by this feather.

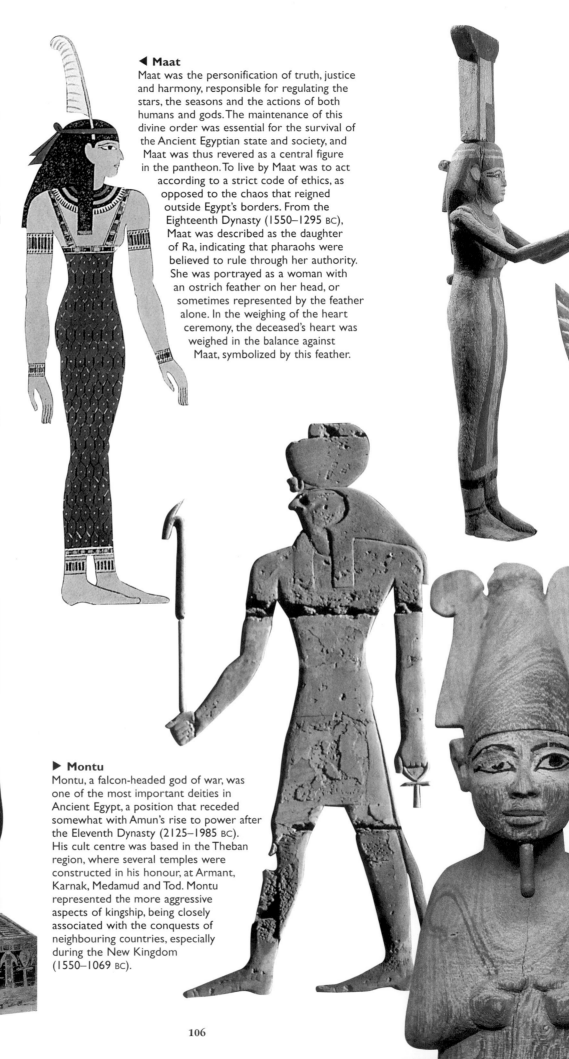

▶ Montu

Montu, a falcon-headed god of war, was one of the most important deities in Ancient Egypt, a position that receded somewhat with Amun's rise to power after the Eleventh Dynasty (2125–1985 BC). His cult centre was based in the Theban region, where several temples were constructed in his honour, at Armant, Karnak, Medamud and Tod. Montu represented the more aggressive aspects of kingship, being closely associated with the conquests of neighbouring countries, especially during the New Kingdom (1550–1069 BC).

◄ Nephthys

The sister of Isis, Nephthys was the wife of the evil god Seth and, in a later myth, the mother of Anubis through a union with Osiris. She was a protectress of the dead, often pictured at the head of the deceased's coffin, with Isis at the feet. Nephthys also protected the baboon-headed Hapy, not to be confused with the god of the Nile inundation of the same name, who in turn was the guardian of the lungs of the deceased.

▼ Nut

In the Heliopolitan creation myth, the sky goddess Nut was one of the nine gods of the ennead who were responsible for the creation of the earth. Numerous reliefs and paintings depict Geb, the consort of Nut and representation of the earth, lying on the ground with the goddess bending above him, touching the ground with only the tips of her fingers and toes as the couple try to be reunited. As the personification of the sky, Nut swallowed the setting sun, Ra, every evening and gave birth to him from her womb in the morning.

► Ptah

Ptah was originally associated with craftsmen, and this connection probably contributed to his elevation to creator god. According to the Memphite myth of creation, Ptah brought the world into existence by uttering the names of things. Ptah was usually depicted enveloped in a close-fitting robe, with his hands emerging holding a staff that combined the djed pillar, ankh sign and was sceptre – symbols of stability, life and welfare. By the Late period, Ptah was combined with Osiris and the hawk god Sokar to become Ptah-Sokar-Osiris.

◄ Osiris

One of the most important of all the Ancient Egyptian gods, Osiris was associated with death, resurrection and fertility. The deceased king was identified with Osiris from at least as early as the Fifth Dynasty (2494–2345 BC), but, by the end of the Middle Kingdom (2055–1650 BC), it was possible for commoners to be resurrected in the manner of Osiris. Osiris was the the father of Horus and husband of Isis, who mummified and reanimated his dismembered body after he was murdered by his evil brother Seth. A number of sites in Egypt were associated with the scattered parts of his body – Busiris, for example, claimed his backbone, while Abydos was said to be the burial place of his head.

◄ Ra

The Ancient Egyptian sun god, Ra, had his main cult centre at Heliopolis in the outskirts of modern Cairo. Worship of Ra reached its peak in the Fourth Dynasty (2613–2491 BC), when the 'son of Ra' title was added to the royal titulary. Such was the importance of Ra in the pantheon that his cult was incorporated into the worship of several other gods, forming deities such as Amun-Ra and Ra-Horakhty. Ra was depicted as a hawk-headed figure wearing a headdress featuring the solar disc.

► Seth

In addition to being the murderer and evil brother of Osiris and enemy of Horus, Seth had a number of aspects. He was associated with the hostile deserts of Egypt, as well as having a protective role in guarding Ra in his dangerous 12-hour journey through the night. Seth was depicted in a variety of ways, sometimes as a boar or hippopotamus, but most commonly with the body of a man and the head of a mythical animal with a long nose and squared-off ears.

► Sobek

The crocodile god Sobek, principally worshipped in the Fayum region and at Kom Ombo, was associated with the strength and power of the pharaoh, as well as being a means of warding off the crocodiles of the River Nile. As Sobek-Ra, he was worshipped as an aspect of the sun god.

◄ Thoth

Depicted with the head of a baboon or an ibis, Thoth was the god of writing and wisdom, as well as a lunar deity. In the New Kingdom (1550–1069 BC), Thoth appeared in illustrations in the *Book of the Dead* recording the results of the weighing-of-the-heart ceremony. His cult centre was at Hermopolis Magna, where two colossal statues of the god still stand.

The Sun Cult

In many respects, the sun was the most important of the Egyptian gods, and was worshipped in a variety of different forms.

With good reason, the Ancient Egyptians regarded the sun as a powerful life force. Along with the annual flooding of the Nile, it produced their crops and ensured their livelihood. The sun god Ra had been worshipped from the Early Dynastic period (3100–2686 BC), but it was not until the Old Kingdom (2686–2181 BC), when Ra became the dominant figure in the Egyptian pantheon, that the sun cult really took off, in Heliopolis (literally 'city of the sun'). There, around 2600 BC, a temple dedicated to Ra in his role as Ra-Horakhty was built. From the time of Djedefra (2566–2558 BC), the direct successor of Khufu, the builder of the Great Pyramid at Giza, the name Ra also appeared as the title of the ruler – calling themselves 'sons of Ra', the pharaohs underlined their divine relationship with this powerful sun god. More significantly, Heliopolis became the cult centre for Atum, the creator of the universe who was also a solar deity and who gradually became fused with Ra as Ra-Atum.

Manifestations of the sun

The sun was fundamental to ancient Egyptian life and was worshipped in many forms, of which the three most often depicted were the sun disk, a scarab beetle (Khepri) and a ram (Atum). Many other gods also acquired a solar aspect. For example, in the New Kingdom (1550–1069 BC), Amun was combined with Ra to become Amun-Ra, the king of the gods, and the warrior god Montu was worshipped as a solar god. Ra also reached into the afterlife, where he and Osiris were fused into one being. During the reign of Akhenaten (1352–1336 BC), the Aten – the sun disc – was elevated to the status of sole god, and an attempt was made to eliminate the traditional plethora of gods and goddesses.

▲ The winged disc
The image of the solar disc with the wings of a hawk was originally the symbol of the god Horus and associated with his cult in the Delta town of Behdet. The sacred cobras were added on either side of the disc during the Old Kingdom (2686–2181 BC). The winged disc had protective significance and was found on temple ceilings and ceremonial entrances.

▼ An offering to the sun
This depiction of a scene from the tomb of Rameses X (1108–1099 BC) shows a mirror image of the pharaoh on either side of the solar disc, with an offering of the wedjat eye (the eye of Horus), a solar and lunar symbol, in his hand. Within the disc are the sacred scarab, representing the rising sun, and the ram-headed god Atum, a symbol of the setting sun.

▼ Ram-headed scarab
This piece of jewellery, dating from the Late period (747–332 BC), is from the collection of Natasha Rambova, the wife of the American star of silent movies Rudolph Valentino. It depicts a scarab with a ram's head and is symbolic of the solar cycle, with the ram's head representing the sun's setting and the scarab beetle its rising. For the Ancient Egyptians, the solar cycle was not merely a natural phenomenon, but a daily affirmation of the triumph of life over death. The shen sign that the beetle pushes with its hind legs symbolizes the eternal cycle of the sun.

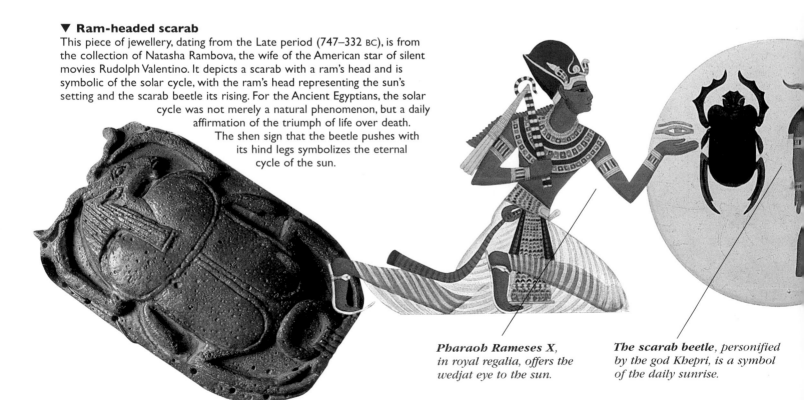

Pharaoh Rameses X, in royal regalia, offers the wedjat eye to the sun.

The scarab beetle, personified by the god Khepri, is a symbol of the daily sunrise.

INSIGHT

The scarab, symbol of the solar cycle and rebirth

In Egyptian art, the scarab was often depicted holding the ball of the sun between its front legs (right). The choice of the dung beetle as a symbol of life and the solar cycle was based on its behaviour of continuously rolling its eggs in dung balls along the ground. Young beetles were seen to emerge from the dung as if reborn from the scarab's own decomposition. To the Egyptians, this was a symbol of resurrection and of the incarnation of the solar cycle of night and day. The scarab was seen as a manifestation of Khepri, a creator god who was particularly associated with the rising sun (left).

▲ **Khnum-Ra, the ba-soul of the sun god**
Like many other gods, the ram-headed god Khnum became associated with the sun god Ra. Khnum was regarded as the 'ba-soul' of Ra, and for this reason Atum was depicted with a ram's head as he passed through the underworld on his solar boat.

The sun disc represents the sun god Ra, who gives life to the world through the sun's rays.

The ram-headed god Atum symbolizes the setting sun.

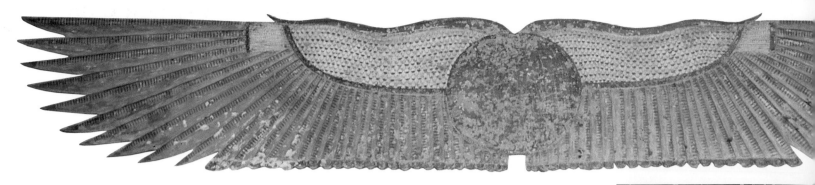

The daily course of the sun was associated with several deities. Sunrise was related to the winged scarab Khepri, Ra-Horakhty represented the sun at its highest point at midday, and Atum-Ra personified the setting sun. All three gods were often depicted in the form of a human figure with the head of an animal.

The daily solar cycle

For the Ancient Egyptians, the day began at sunrise when Nut, the sky, gave birth to the sun in the east. Throughout the day, the sun journeyed across the sky in his day barge before descending in the west at sunset. Here he entered his night barge and sailed into the region beneath the earth called the Duat for his 12-hour nightly voyage. This journey through the netherworld was fraught with dangers, but in the middle of the night the sun met and fused with Osiris, the god of the dead but also of rebirth. Having been given a new life by Osiris, the sun was then able to proceed through the remainder of the night towards resurrection at dawn.

◄ Ra-Horakhty, an aspect of the sun god
In one of his manifestations, the falcon-headed sky god Horus was amalgamated with the sun god Ra to become Ra-Horakhty. 'Horakhty' refers to Horus's identification with the horizon, the place where the sun rose and set, and therefore the home of the sun god. As one of the most powerful gods in the Egyptian pantheon, Ra took on the aspects, or characteristics, of a number of gods. Here, as Ra-Horakhty, he is represented as a hawk-headed human figure with a sun-disc headdress.

▶ Life-giving sun
The scene on this New Kingdom papyrus depicts the rays of the sun giving life to the deceased in the underworld, freeing him from being trapped for ever in the netherworld. It is based on paintings of the sun's nightly journey found on tomb walls in the Valley of the Kings.

The wedjat eyes (eyes of Horus) protect the solar barge on its journey through the underworld.

The sun hovers above the solar barge, its rays lighting up the darkness of the underworld.

The rays of the sun bring life-giving warmth to the dead.

The sign at the prow of the boat is made up of a sceptre and a package of knives. It symbolizes the power of the sun god to enforce his authority throughout the universe.

The solar barge transports the sun god Ra on his nightly journey through the underworld.

The rudder of the barge represents the powers ruling the universe.

The deceased is given life by the rays of the sun.

◄ **Symbol of Horus**

The winged sun disc was a symbol of the sky god Horus from at least the First Dynasty (3100–2890 BC), and represented the heavens through which the sun moved. As Horus was identified with the king, the winged sun disc also came to have royal associations, as well as, by the New Kingdom (1550–1069 BC), being a symbol of protection. The motif is found not only on tomb entrances and ceilings, but also on numerous stelae and funerary jewellery.

INSIGHT

Khepri, the scarab god

The scarab was the personification of the god Khepri, a creator god whose name literally means 'he who came into being'. Khepri, and by association the scarab, was the incarnation of the strength of the rising sun as it prepared to spread its beneficial rays upon the earth. Khepri also symbolized the transformations undergone by living beings from their birth until their death and rebirth in the afterlife.

The Egyptians made many amulets and funerary jewellery in the form of scarabs. They were considered to have the strongest and most efficient powers of protection, as the dung beetle was said to be capable of eternal regeneration. This pendant from the Nineteenth Dynasty (1295–1186 BC) shows the scarab being worshipped by the goddesses Isis and Neith.

▲ **The Aten – an exclusive sun god**

The simplest manifestation of the sun – the disc itself – was elevated to the role of supreme god by the pharaoh Akhenaten (1352–1336 BC). The Aten is usually represented as an orb with its rays ending in hands, some of which hold the ankh sign of life. Only the royal family, pictured above, and not individuals, could worship the Aten directly and benefit from its life-giving powers.

Amun, King of the Gods

By the time of the New Kingdom (1550–1069 BC), Amun was considered the greatest of all Egyptian gods, with his cult centred at Karnak in the largest and richest temple in the land.

Amun was initially the local deity of Thebes, worshipped from as early as the Eleventh Dynasty (2055–1985 BC); however, the rise of the Theban pharaohs, beginning with Mentuhotep II (2055–2004 BC), saw Amun elevated to the most important of all the Ancient Egyptian gods. In the temple of Senusret I (1965–1920 BC) at Karnak, Amun is described as 'the king of the gods', and he was combined with several other gods, most significantly with the powerful sun god Ra as Amun-Ra.

The manifestations of Amun

In one of the Egyptian creation myths, Amun and his female counterpart Amanunet represented air, or 'hidden power', one of the four fundamental elements of life. Although Amun was known as 'the hidden one', he was depicted in a variety of forms. He appeared most frequently as a man wearing a double-plumed crown, an image closely related to that of Min, the god of fertility. As Amun-Kamutef, a self-begotten bull, and Amun-Kematef, a god able to resurrect himself by taking the form of a snake shedding its skin, he embodied the powers of creation. Amun was often shown with a ram's head, or as a goose, both animals also being associated with the creative force.

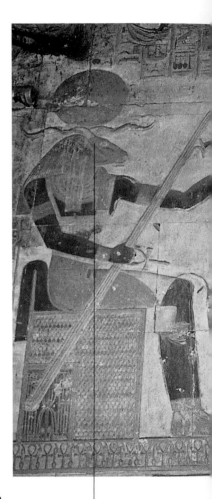

The god Ra-Horakhty, *shown here with a ram's head topped by a solar disc, sits behind Sety I.*

◀ **Ram emblem of Amun**
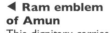
This dignitary carries a macehead with a ram's head crowned by a solar disc – the sacred emblem of Amun used in rituals and festivals in honour of the god.

◀ **Royal couple**
In this statue, Amun is shown with Mut, the goddess and consort with whom he was worshipped at Thebes. Along with their son, the moon god Khons, they formed the Theban triad of deities – the chief gods of this centre.

▼ Images of Amun

This scene from the temple of Sety I (1294–1279 BC) at Abydos shows the pharaoh kneeling before Amun. The painted relief has been remarkably well preserved, with bright colours clearly showing the figures' skin and clothing.

Amun's blue skin imitates the colour of lapis lazuli, which was the most prized stone in Ancient Egypt.

The typical headdress of Amun was a double-plumed crown from which hung a red ribbon.

Amun, holding the ankh sign of life, hands a sword and club, symbols of power, to the kneeling Sety.

The symbol of a unified Upper and Lower Egypt appears on Amun's throne.

PROFILE

Pharaoh, 'son of Amun-Ra'

Amun-Ra, as the supreme god and creator of the universe, was considered to be the father of the pharaoh, and all kings from the time of the New Kingdom were referred to as the 'son of Amun-Ra'. As such, the pharaoh was responsible for maintaining the order of the universe on earth by opposing the forces of chaos. Under his benevolent protection, the movement of the stars, the Nile floods and even human relations remained untroubled.

It was essential to stress the divine nature of the reigning monarch in order to prove the legitimacy of his rule. Reliefs in the mortuary temple of Queen Hatshepsut (1473–1458 BC) depict her divine birth, the result of a union between Amun and her mother, Queen Ahmose. As Hatshepsut was a woman, and because her claim to the throne was under threat from her nephew Thutmose III (1479–1425 BC), these reliefs may have been a direct attempt to prove her right to rule. Amun appears as Amun-Min in Senusret I's White Chapel at Karnak (below left), and on the walls of Medinet Habu (below right) Amun-Ra offers symbols of kingship to (not seen) Rameses III (1184–1153 BC).

▶ Temples of Amun

A number of temples were built in honour of Amun, but the most impressive is at Karnak, where ram-headed sphinxes line the processional way that once linked Karnak with Luxor. The temple of Amun is a huge complex of pylons, courts, columned halls, obelisks and colossi, constructed by successive pharaohs of the New Kingdom, and served by a vast number of priests of various ranks.

Many Ancient Egyptian festivals celebrated the power of Amun. The Beautiful Festival of the Valley and the Festival of Opet both took place at Thebes from the time of the Eighteenth Dynasty (1550–1295 BC). The Beautiful Festival of the Valley involved an annual procession taking the cult statues of the Theban triad (Amun, Mut and Khons) from Karnak to Deir el-Bahri across the Nile. The Festival of Opet also took place annually and lasted for a period of two to four weeks. The divine image of Amun was carried from the temple of Karnak to the temple of Luxor in a procession that symbolized the sexual union of Amun and the mother of the reigning king – and thus confirmed the divine origin of the pharaoh.

The priests of Amun

More than any other god in the Egyptian pantheon, Amun demonstrates the close link between religion and politics in Ancient Egypt. During the New Kingdom, the temple of Amun at Karnak was the largest in Egypt, and its priests became so powerful, economically as well as spiritually, that they threatened the supremacy of the pharaoh himself. Their political strength may have provoked the 'heretical' reign of Akhenaten, who demoted Amun in favour of the god Aten (the sun disc).

However, the Nubian pharaohs of the Twenty-Fifth Dynasty (747–656 BC) revived the worship of Amun, as they believed that the true home of Amun was the sacred site of Gebel Barkal in Upper Nubia. They associated themselves with the cult of Amun and restored his centres of worship.

▼ **Amun at Siwa Oasis**
As well as Karnak, there were many temples dedicated to Amun throughout Egypt. Two Amun temples existed in Siwa Oasis, for example. Alexander the Great is said to have visited the oracle of Amun at Siwa when he conquered Egypt, where he was officially recognized as the son of Amun and the legitimate pharaoh.

The plumed headdress helps to identify the god as Amun.

The ankh sign, held in Amun's left hand, is a protective offering for the pharaoh.

Horemheb's cartouche *appears behind the heads of Amun and the pharaoh.*

The cult of Amun *was restored by Horemheb after the heretical reign of Akhenaten.*

▲ **The sacred barge**
During the festivals of Amun, a statue of the god was taken across the Nile in a sacred barge, which had an image of the ram-headed god on the stern and the prow. Here, the barge's prow is being carried on poles by falcon-headed gods, while Rameses II (1279–1213 BC) offers incense to the god.

◀ **Protector of the King**
During the Amarna period, the era when Akhenaten (1352–1336 BC) elevated the Aten to chief god, other deities were demoted and in particular the god Amun. The last king of that period, Tutankhamun (1336–1327 BC), reinstated Amun and is shown here with that god. A later king, Horemheb (1323–1295 BC), adopted this statue for himself by replacing Tutankhamun's name on it with his own.

▶ **The Greek Amun**
Under the Ptolemaic Dynasty (332–30 BC), Amun was identified with Zeus, the king of the Greek gods. This coin depicts Alexander the Great with the horns of a ram.

Osiris – God of the Afterlife

One of the most important deities of Ancient Egypt, Osiris was the god of the underworld and of resurrection, and ensured existence in the afterlife.

According to Ancient Egyptian legend, the first royal couple – the sky goddess Nut and the god of the earth Geb – were the parents of Osiris, Isis, Seth and Nephthys. Osiris, the first-born, ruled wisely on earth, but his envious brother Seth plotted his downfall.

The deadly wiles of Seth

Seth gave orders to make a magnificent casket to fit the measurements of Osiris. With 72 co-conspirators, Seth threw a great banquet and promised to give the casket to whomever it best fitted. After Osiris had lain down in the casket, the conspirators closed the lid, sealed it with lead and threw it into the Nile. The river carried it to the sea, where the coffin washed up on the Phoenician coast.

Isis eventually rescued the casket of her brother, who was also her husband, carried it back to Egypt and hid it in the marshes. But Seth found the hiding-place and tore the body into 14 pieces, which he scattered all over the country. With her sister Nephthys, Isis collected all the pieces – except for the penis, which had been eaten by a fish – reassembled them and had the body of Osiris embalmed.

Afterwards, she brought the mummy back to life with her magical powers and miraculously conceived a son, Horus, by her resurrected husband.

▲ The sanctuary of Osiris
According to legend, the pieces of Osiris's body were buried in various parts of Egypt and, consequently, his relics were revered in many places. The most important sanctuary was in Abydos, where it was said his head was buried. Here the figure of Osiris was joined with the local god of the necropolises, Khentamenti.

▶ The djed pillar
This ancient magical object in the shape of a pillar, which represented stability and durability, eventually became the symbol of Osiris. Later, in the *Book of the Dead*, the djed pillar was described as the backbone, or spine, of Osiris.

The wife of the deceased, with her hands raised in prayer to Osiris, stands beside her husband.

Offerings such as food, beverages and flowers are stacked in front of Osiris.

The deceased wears a heart amulet around his neck and a perfumed cone on his head.

Osiris sits on his throne in a chapel whose slender columns consist of lotus and papyrus reeds.

▶ Seth, Osiris's killer

Seth, Osiris's violent brother, was depicted as a fabled monster or as a human with the head of the 'Seth animal', which had a long crooked beak, slit eyes and upright ears that were square at the top. Seth was associated with the desert, foreign lands and the border areas of Egypt, where disorder was thought to reign. The Hyksos, the foreign rulers of the Seventeenth Dynasty (1650–1550 BC), equated him with their local god Baal.

▼ Judge of the dead

Ruling as a king over Egypt when alive, Osiris became the ruler of the underworld after death. Every deceased person had to appear before his seat in 'the hall of truth' and be judged by him before he could pass to the afterlife as 'justified'.

Osiris holds the king's insignia, the crook and flail, as well as the sceptre.

The green skin of Osiris symbolizes the colour of vegetation and fertile crops.

▶ The family of Osiris

Found in the king's necropolis of Tanis, this group of gold statues represents the best-known family of gods in the Egyptian pantheon: Osiris sits on a lapis lazuli pillar (middle), flanked by Isis (right) and Horus (left), who protectively hold out their hands.

Horus then set about avenging his father's death by engaging in various contests with his uncle Seth – the so-called 'Contendings of Horus and Seth'. After 80 years, Seth was defeated and Osiris became god of the afterlife and Horus the ruler of the living, leaving Seth to inhabit the desert as the god of chaos and evil.

The master of the underworld

Initially, Osiris embodied the fertility of crops, and his cult seems to have begun in the Nile Delta. There he was connected to Anedjti, a local king god, from whom he took over the role of the ruler of ancient times, as well as the insignia of the crook and flail.

In the ancient capital Memphis, Osiris was associated with the god of the underworld, Sokar. In Abydos, he was seen as the embodiment of Khentamenti, the god of the dead and the necropolises. With this, Osiris had finally become the master of the afterlife, ensuring the resurrection of humans after death, and his cult spread all over Egypt.

PROFILE

The resurrection of the pharaoh

Some Egyptologists think Osiris may have been a former living ruler – possibly a shepherd who lived in Predynastic times (5500–3100 BC) in the Nile Delta, and whose beneficial rule led to him being revered as a god. The accoutrements of the shepherd, the crook and the flail – once the insignia of the Delta god Anedjti, with whom Osiris was associated – support this theory.

In the Old Kingdom (2686–2181 BC), the pharaoh was considered a son of the sun god Ra who, after his death, ascended to join Ra in the sky. With the spread of the Osiris cult, however, there was a change in beliefs.

The Ancient Egyptians now thought that, while alive, Osiris had ruled as a king; after his death, he became the ruler of the underworld. His violent death had led to a power struggle between his brother Seth and his son Horus. To resolve this, Osiris threatened that the underworld would rise in revolt if there was no just solution. Ra and his court of gods therefore declared Horus the rightful ruler. As a consequence, the person of the pharaoh was equated with Horus during his life and with Osiris, the ruler of the underworld, after his death.

The god's shrine, in which sit Horus and Osiris, resembles the royal barge's canopy, under which the mummy was laid out on the journey to the necropolis.

◀ **The imiut**
The image of a stuffed, headless skin of an animal, tied to a pole mounted in a pot, was a symbol associated both with Osiris as god of the underworld and with Anubis, god of mummification. Models of the imiut emblem were sometimes included among a deceased person's funerary equipment.

The falcon-headed god Horus stands protectively behind his father Osiris.

Osiris wears the atef crown (the white crown with two large feathers), and carries the crook and flail as regal insignia.

Osiris – saviour god

At first it was believed that only the pharaoh could become one with Osiris after death. The people's hopes for a similar resurrection, however, centred increasingly on Osiris. By the end of the Middle Kingdom (2055–1650 BC), everyone hoped to proceed to the afterlife in the image of Osiris.

The stela (below), depicting an offering to Osiris, was probably made before the death of its donor, possibly a wealthy official or nobleman.

▲ The fish of Oxyrhynchos

Together with her sister Nephthys, Isis collected the cut-up parts of Osiris from all over Egypt. She did not, however, find his penis, which had been thrown into the Nile and eaten by fish, among them the Oxyrhynchos. This species of fish was revered in the place of the same name, and according to another legend the Oxyrhynchos was created from the wounds of Osiris.

◄ Ptah

The creator god of Memphis, Ptah was merged first with the hawk god Sokar and later with Osiris. Statues of Ptah-Sokar-Osiris usually take the form of a standing figure in the image of a mummy.

▼ The god of rebirth

As part of the Osiris cult, an image of the dead god was made from soil, covered with seed grains and sprinkled with water, so that the seeds grew from the body. Such sprouting 'corn mummies' were also tomb offerings, and were symbolic of Osiris as god of vegetation, and the rebirth believed to be enacted by him.

◄ Representations of Osiris

The typical representation of Osiris shows him holding the crook and flail that symbolized royal authority. As his most important sanctuary was at Abydos in Upper Egypt, he wears the white crown, the symbol of power in that part of the country.

Depictions of his skin colour could be white (mummy bandages), black (the fertile Nile Valley soil) or green (vegetation). The body was wrapped like a mummy, with only the arms showing, crossed in front of the chest. The deceased were put in their coffin after mummification with their arms in the same position.

Osiris wears the false plaited beard, attached to his chin with a strap. This was a sign of divinity.

The donor of the stela brings an offering to the gods; his prayer appears in hieroglyphs behind his figure.

Isis, Universal Mother

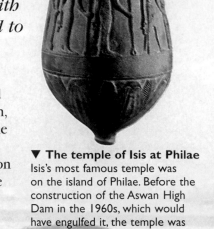

The goddess who exemplified the devoted wife and mother, Isis enjoyed immense popularity throughout Egypt. She was also associated with resurrection, and could use her magical powers to restore life and to help mothers and children.

Accessording to the myth of Osiris, mentioned for the first time in the *Pyramid Texts*, which date back to around 2350 BC, Isis was the daughter of Geb, the god of the earth, and Nut, the goddess of the sky. Her brothers were Osiris and Seth, and her sister was Nephthys. After Seth killed Osiris, who had become her husband, she undertook a long quest to find his body, which she brought back to life with the help of Anubis, the god of mummification. She was therefore associated with the resurrection of the dead and, in funerary scenes, is often depicted hovering over the mummy of the deceased as a kite. Using her wings, she was able to restore the breath of life to the dead person and ensure his existence in the afterlife.

Magical powers enabled her to conceive a son by the dead Osiris and because of this she was considered a protector of children and nursing mothers.

▼ **The temple of Isis at Philae** Isis's most famous temple was on the island of Philae. Before the construction of the Aswan High Dam in the 1960s, which would have engulfed it, the temple was dismantled stone by stone and re-erected on a neighbouring island.

INSIGHT

The myth of Osiris

Jealous of Osiris, who reigned over Egypt, his brother Seth assassinated him in order to gain power. Isis searched for the body, found it in Byblos (now in Lebanon) and brought it back to Egypt. Crazed with anger, Seth cut the body into pieces, which he scattered over the country. Isis took up her quest again, reassembled the body and, with the help of Anubis, mummified her husband. After turning herself into a bird, she brought Osiris back to life, magically conceiving Horus in the process. In the statuette below, from the Twenty-Second to Twenty-Third Dynasty, she is shown standing, with a seated Osiris and the goddess Maat.

◄ **Decorated vase**
This vase, fitted with a handle, held the libations that were used in temples for divine worship and also in funerary rites. The figures of Isis, Horus and Nephthys decorate the vase.

◄ **Emblematic throne**
The emblem that Isis wears on her head is the hieroglyphic sign for throne, and it is believed that her name originally meant 'seat'. Isis is frequently associated with the royal throne and may have been its divine incarnation.

INSIGHT

Isis with infant Horus

Bronze figures of Isis nursing Horus were particularly common during the Late period (747–332 BC). This bronze figurine dates from the slightly later Ptolemaic period (332–30 BC). Made for the faithful, the statuettes were generally thanksgiving offerings dedicated to the goddess Isis as the embodiment of the universal mother. They were placed in sanctuaries to thank the goddess for an easy childbirth, to ask for her protection during pregnancy and childbirth or to look after the young.

Isis is identifiable by the hieroglyphic sign of a throne, or seat, that she wears as a headdress; it is thought that her name originally meant 'seat'. From the beginning of the New Kingdom (1550–1069 BC), she was associated with Hathor, the goddess of love, from whom she borrowed the cow horns holding the solar disc that sometimes replaced the sign of the seat.

Worship throughout Egypt

The Egyptians dedicated sanctuaries to Isis, a universal goddess, throughout the entire country. The best known was on the island of Philae, south of Aswan on the border between Egypt and Nubia, dubbed the 'Pearl of Egypt'. This was her most long-lived sanctuary, and was a place of worship until the sixth century AD, due largely to the importance of her cult to the Nubians. By this time, however, Egypt had become Christianized, and it was the Roman emperor of Byzantium, Justinian (reigned 527–565 AD), who finally sent in the army to close down the temple at Philae.

PROFILE

Isis outside Egypt

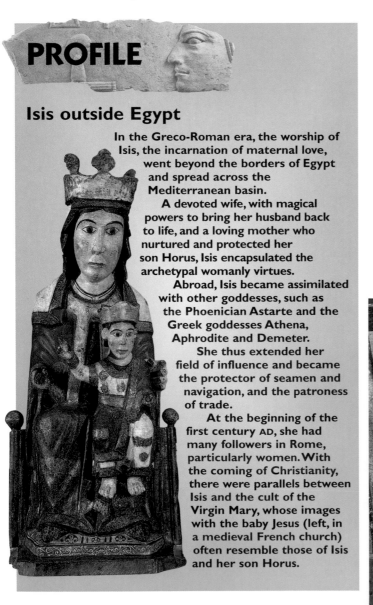

In the Greco-Roman era, the worship of Isis, the incarnation of maternal love, went beyond the borders of Egypt and spread across the Mediterranean basin.

A devoted wife, with magical powers to bring her husband back to life, and a loving mother who nurtured and protected her son Horus, Isis encapsulated the archetypal womanly virtues.

Abroad, Isis became assimilated with other goddesses, such as the Phoenician Astarte and the Greek goddesses Athena, Aphrodite and Demeter.

She thus extended her field of influence and became the protector of seamen and navigation, and the patroness of trade.

At the beginning of the first century AD, she had many followers in Rome, particularly women. With the coming of Christianity, there were parallels between Isis and the cult of the Virgin Mary, whose images with the baby Jesus (left, in a medieval French church) often resemble those of Isis and her son Horus.

Isis, giver of life

In this relief from his tomb in the Valley of the Kings, Rameses III (1184–1153 BC) is welcomed into the afterlife by the goddess Isis, giver of life to Osiris, the ruler of the underworld.

Rameses III wears a royal headdress in the form of a close-fitting cap, decorated with the uraeus cobra on the forehead and ribbons at the back.

As a sign of worship, the pharaoh raises his arm before the goddess.

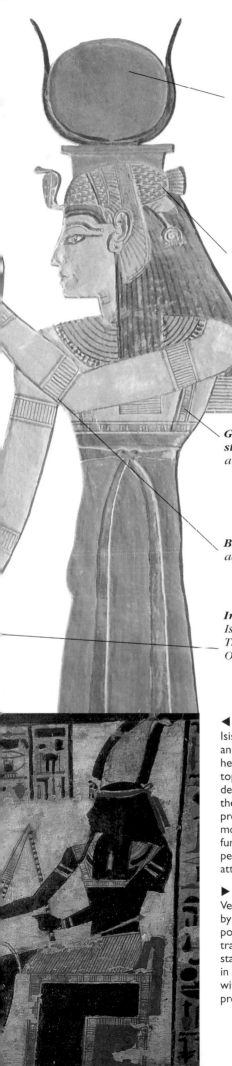

The cow horns surrounding the solar disc are symbols of the goddess Hathor, with whom Isis was closely associated. During the New Kingdom (1550–1069 BC), Isis sometimes exchanged her throne or seat emblem for Hathor's headdress.

A cap in the form of a vulture, the symbol of the goddess Nekhbet, supports Isis's cow-horn headdress.

Gold and semi-precious stones embellish the gown and belt of the goddess.

Bracelets of red beads adorn the goddess's arms.

In a life-giving gesture, Isis holds the king's hand. This denotes his rebirth, like Osiris, in the afterlife.

◄ **Isis and her sister Nephthys**
Isis, wearing the throne headdress, and Nephthys, identifiable by her headdress of a house, or shrine, topped by a basket, are often depicted on coffins. They guarantee the survival of the body and also protect it. They are shown as mourners facing Ptah-Sokar, a funerary deity who, by the Late period, had taken on many of the attributes of Osiris.

▶ **Worship of Isis in Rome**
Veneration of Isis was taken up by the Romans, with her popularity often rivalling that of traditional Roman gods. This statue of the goddess is enclosed in a chapel, framed by columns with papyrus-shaped capitals, and protected at the top by a cobra.

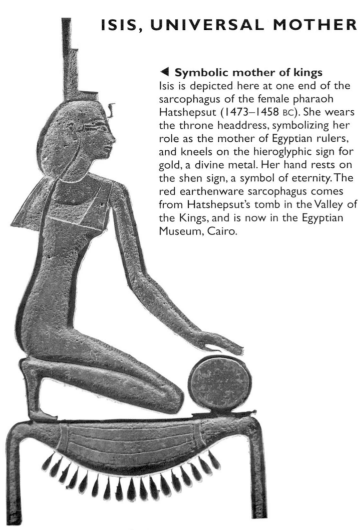

◄ **Symbolic mother of kings**
Isis is depicted here at one end of the sarcophagus of the female pharaoh Hatshepsut (1473–1458 BC). She wears the throne headdress, symbolizing her role as the mother of Egyptian rulers, and kneels on the hieroglyphic sign for gold, a divine metal. Her hand rests on the shen sign, a symbol of eternity. The red earthenware sarcophagus comes from Hatshepsut's tomb in the Valley of the Kings, and is now in the Egyptian Museum, Cairo.

Seth and Nephthys

In Ancient Egyptian mythology, Seth and Nephthys, like their siblings Isis and Osiris, were born to the sky goddess and earth god, and were husband and wife, as well as brother and sister.

Seth is one of the oldest gods in the Ancient Egyptian pantheon, being attested to in the form of a carved ivory artefact from the Predynastic Amratian (Naqada I) period (4000-3500 BC). He was a deity of chaos and confusion, associated with the disorder and barrenness of the desert and foreign lands. Seth was usually depicted with a man's body and the head of a strange animal with a long nose and squared ears.

An ambiguous figure

Despite his role in Osirian mythology as the murderer of Osiris and enemy of Horus, Seth had a variety of aspects and was venerated in certain guises and places. For example, the Hyksos worshipped Seth, possibly because they identified him with the Levantine thunder god Baal. Several New Kingdom rulers, such as Sety I (1294-1279 BC) and Sethnakhte (1186-1184 BC), took the god's name, thus associating themselves with his mythical strength. Seth was also regarded as a 'companion of Ra', accompanying the sun god on his journey through the night and defending him from the serpent Apophis. Most significantly, Seth represented the necessary balance to the order of the universe that was central to the Ancient Egyptian concept of duality.

◄ **The protector of the pharaohs**
Despite his largely negative image, Seth was worshipped at several times and places. For example, the Hyksos venerated Seth at their capital of Avaris in the Second Intermediate period (1650–1550 BC). Some of 7the pharaohs of the Nineteenth and Twentieth dynasties (1295–1069 BC), such as Sety I (1294–1279 BC), shown left, also took Seth's name.

*A **crown** featuring the solar disc and cow's horns appears on Nephthys's head.*

__Seth__ is depicted with the head of a mysterious animal with a long nose and squared ears.

► **Seth and Nephthys**
Despite being husband and wife, Seth and Nephthys are rarely shown together. Nephthys appears more often with her sister, Isis, protecting the deceased. When Seth murdered Osiris, Nephthys helped Isis to reassemble and mummify the dismembered pieces of their dead brother.

◄ **The king's coronation**
The pharaoh's coronation involved a series of elaborate rituals that bestowed divine symbols of power upon the sovereign. In this relief, Horus presents the king with the deshret, the red crown of Lower Egypt, while Seth, pictured left, provides the white hedjet crown of Upper Egypt. Together, these represented the king's power over all of Egypt.

▼ **The fight between Horus and Seth**
The temple of Horus at Edfu, shown here in a nineteenth-century lithograph by David Roberts, features numerous reliefs depicting the contendings of Horus and Seth. In one scene, Seth turns into a hippopotamus and is harpooned by the triumphant Horus.

The 'Edfu Drama', as the battle reliefs of Horus and Seth are collectively known, decorate the walls of the magnificent temple at Edfu.

◄ **The hippopotamus**
The hippopotamus, one of the manifestations of Seth, was a suitably ambiguous animal in Ancient Egypt. It was regarded as a symbol both of disorder and of positive feminine virtues.

From the Third Intermediate period (1069–747 BC), however, Seth's negative aspects were emphasized over his other roles, a trend which coincided with the ascendancy of the cult of Osiris. Seth's defeat at the hands of Horus was widely celebrated, and some statues of Seth were recarved in the image of Amun.

A protective goddess

Although she was Seth's wife as well as his sister, Nephthys had other roles and associations which ensured that she was regarded as a positive figure. She is usually depicted with her sister Isis, the archetypal mother goddess and wife of Osiris. After Osiris's death, Nephthys helped her sister to discover the scattered pieces of the murdered god's dismembered body and resurrect him.

Along with Isis, Nephthys was a guardian of the dead, and the sisters were often depicted at either end of the deceased's coffin. Nephthys was also one of the protective Canopic deities, guarding the baboon-headed Hapy, whose head appeared on Canopic jars that contained the lungs of the deceased. In later mythology, Nephthys was also believed to be the mother of Anubis from a union with Osiris, and in the Late period (747–332 BC), she was worshipped with Anuket, goddess of the First Cataract, at Kom Mer in Upper Egypt.

Nephthys *appears here in her form as a woman with large, outstretched wings.*

Hieroglyphs *spell out Nephthys's name – 'Lady of the Mansion'.*

▼ Protectress of the dead
Through her positive role in the myth of Osiris, Nephthys was regarded as a protector of the dead. In the New Kingdom (1550–1069 BC), she appeared on the external north wall of royal sarcophagi, next to the head of the deceased, often with her arms spread protectively.

▶ Nephthys and Isis
Nephthys was generally depicted alongside her sister, Isis. This stunning pectoral in gold from the tomb of Tutankhamun (1336–1327 BC) shows the goddesses on either side of a djed pillar, a symbol of stability and rebirth, with outstretched, protective wings.

▶ Wailing women
Because of the part played by Isis and Nephthys in mummifying and mourning Osiris, the goddesses are often depicted in funerary scenes. They are shown on this coffin at either end of the deceased, with their hands raised in a gesture of grief. In Ancient Egyptian funerals, two of the female mourners would take on the roles of Isis and Nephthys.

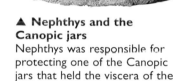

▲ The mummy bindings
Through her association with the cult of Osiris, god of the dead, the tresses of Nephthys's hair were likened to the bandages wrapped round mummies.

The djed pillar is surmounted by the solar disc, a powerful symbol of resurrection.

Isis wears the 'seat' emblem, the hieroglyph for her name, on her head.

▲ Nephthys and the Canopic jars
Nephthys was responsible for protecting one of the Canopic jars that held the viscera of the deceased, along with the other protective goddesses Isis, Serket and Neith. Nephthys was regarded as the guardian of the baboon-headed god Hapy, shown above, who in turn protected the deceased's lungs.

◄ Nephthys and Anubis
Originally, Nephthys was regarded as the wife of Seth, but in later tradition she was believed to be the mother of Anubis, the jackal-headed god of the dead, from a union with Osiris. This, combined with her positive connection with Isis, freed Nephthys from possible negative associations through her relationship with Seth.

Horus, God of the Sky

Not only was the falcon-headed god Horus the god of the sky, but he was also the embodiment of divine kingship and the protector of the pharaoh on earth.

Like most Ancient Egyptian gods, Horus had several aspects, but he is probably best known as the divine manifestation of kingship. He was the god with whom the living pharaoh identified, and his was the first of the five names that all Egyptian pharaohs were given.

According to legend, Horus was the son of Isis and Osiris. His father Osiris had been killed by Seth, his brother, who usurped the throne. When he reached manhood, Horus decided to avenge his father's death and challenged Seth to a series of contests.

Contendings of Horus and Seth

There are several different accounts of their struggles or 'contendings' recorded on stelae and papyrus documents. In one of these contests, Seth is said to have put out one of Horus's eyes (although fortunately, the goddess Hathor was able to restore it), while Horus responded by castrating Seth, thus symbolizing the sterility and treachery of evil. The struggles between the two lasted for 80 years, but ended when the gods decided in favour of Horus.

The defeated Seth was forced to recognize Horus as the rightful heir to the throne, and Horus finally became the ruler of Egypt, like his father and his grandfather. Osiris, who had been miraculously restored to life, became king of the underworld, while Horus became the divine embodiment of the living pharaoh.

▲ **Protector of the pharaoh**
The pharaohs of Ancient Egypt were frequently depicted with their protector god Horus. In this sculpture of c. 1320 BC, he is seated beside Horemheb (1323–1295 BC).

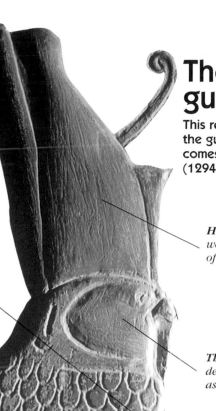

The pharaoh's guardian

This relief depicting Horus as the guardian of the pharaoh comes from the temple of Sety I (1294–1279 BC) at Abydos.

Horus *is usually depicted wearing the double crown of Upper and Lower Egypt.*

The falcon head and body *denotes Horus's manifestation as god of the sky.*

The sun disc, *associated with Horus as god of the sky, is protected by the cobra goddess Wadjet, who holds the ankh symbol of life.*

The rectangular frame, *or serekh, contains the pharaoh's 'Horus name' (one of his five titles). In this example, it can be translated as 'strong bull'.*

▲ **The eye of Horus**
The left eye of Horus was restored by the goddess Hathor and was symbolized by the wedjat eye. As Horus was the god of the sky, his eyes represented the sun and the moon. The wedjat eye was associated with the waxing and waning of the moon, but it was also a symbol of healing and protection, which was carried into the afterlife.

▼ **Horus and Geb**
In one version of the 'contendings' between the gods Horus and Seth, it is the god of the earth, Geb – the father of both Osiris and Seth – who passes judgement on the two and eventually awards the throne to Horus.

This wall painting, depicting Geb (left) and Horus (right), comes from the New Kingdom tomb of Queen Tawosret and the pharaoh Sethnakhte (1186–1184 BC) which is found in the Valley of the Kings.

Hathor, Goddess of Love

The bovine goddess Hathor was one of the most important deities in Ancient Egypt, associated with joy, music and love, as well as being regarded as the divine mother of the pharaoh.

Hathor, variously represented as a cow, a woman with the ears of a cow, or a woman wearing a headdress of a wig, horns and solar disc, was a major figure in the Ancient Egyptian pantheon. She was most commonly regarded as the goddess of the good things in life, such as love, joy, sexuality, music and dance, but also had a wide variety of other associations.

A goddess with many aspects

As well as being the wife of Horus, who was identified with the pharaoh, Hathor was considered to be the divine mother of each king. She was also the daughter of the sun god, Ra, and, as one of the 'eyes' of Ra, she had a destructive role and was depicted in a similar way to the dangerous lioness goddess Sekhmet.

▶ **Sekhmet and Hathor**
In addition to her protective role, Hathor also had a destructive aspect. In this guise, she sometimes appeared in the same leonine form as the aggressive goddess Sekhmet.

▲ **A prehistoric goddess**
The decoration on this cosmetic palette from the Predynastic period (5500–3100 BC) combines celestial and bovine themes in a prehistoric representation of a Hathor-like goddess.

▼ **The divine mother**
In her form as a cow, Hathor was a symbol of motherhood, fertility and protection. As the divine mother of each reigning pharaoh, the goddess was sometimes depicted suckling the king, as in this temple relief, bestowing her favour and support upon him.

◀ Hathor in the tomb of Sety I

The magnificent tomb of Sety I (1294–1279 BC) in the Valley of the Kings, discovered in 1817 by the Italian archaeologist Giovanni Belzoni, features a number of well-preserved reliefs and wall paintings. This is a reproduction of a painting removed from the tomb by Belzoni and now on display in the Louvre Museum in Paris. It depicts the pharaoh being welcomed into the afterlife by Hathor in her funerary aspect. She hands Sety I a large, elaborate necklace, symbolically placing him under her protection.

Hathor offers Sety I a necklace as an emblem of her protection over him.

The goddess takes the king's hand to lead him through the underworld.

▶ Hathor in architecture

This wonderfully vivid illustration from the *Description de l'Egypte*, published between 1809 and 1822 as a record of the Napoleonic expedition to Egypt, shows one of the columns in the temple of Hathor at Dendera. These massive columns, of which there are a total of 24, are surmounted by four-sided capitals carved with the face of the cow goddess. Sadly, many were vandalized, possibly during the Christian period in Egypt (c. AD 395–641).

In her funerary aspect, Hathor was known as 'lady of the west' or 'lady of the western mountain'. She was responsible for receiving the setting sun each evening and keeping it safe until morning. The deceased could also be similarly protected by the goddess in the afterlife.

Hathor was worshipped as the 'lady of Byblos', after the Lebanese coastal town important in pharaonic times for its valuable timber, and as the 'lady of turquoise', as attested to by the temple built in her honour at the turquoise mines at Serabit el-Khadim in Sinai.

Festivals of Hathor

Hathor was celebrated at her cult centre at Dendera during annual New Year processions. The ba statue of the goddess was carried through the various parts of the temple, including the roof chapel, where it was reunited with the solar disc. Her statue was also taken along the Nile by boat from Dendera to Edfu, to the temple of her husband, Horus.

▶ **The temple at Dendera**
Evidence suggests that there was a temple at Dendera in the Old Kingdom (2686–2181 BC), but the surviving buildings date from the Thirtieth Dynasty (380–343 BC) and Roman times (30 BC–AD 395). The façade of the impressive hypostyle hall, with its huge columns, is unique among Egyptian temples.

The winged solar disc shows Horus as a sun god.

Hathor capitals, showing the goddess with the ears of a cow and an elaborate wig, decorate the columns.

The hypostyle hall was erected in the first century AD by the Roman emperor Tiberius (AD 14-37).

◀ **The son of Hathor**
The temple at Dendera is dedicated to the triad of Hathor, her consort Horus and their son, the child god Ihy. Reliefs on the mammisi, or birth house, from the Roman period (30 BC–AD 395) show Hathor suckling Ihy and receiving offerings made by the emperor Trajan (AD 98–117).

The columns, of which there are six on the façade, support the roof of the hall.

◀ **Horus of Edfu**
The falcon god was particularly associated with Edfu in Upper Egypt, where there was a temple dedicated to him, and it was in this form that he was regarded as the consort of Hathor. Hathor's name was written as a falcon contained within the hieroglyph of a building, literally meaning 'house of Horus'.

▼ The Roman mammisi
The temple of Hathor at Dendera has two mammisis, built to celebrate the birth of the child god Ihy. The Roman mammisi, built by the emperor Trajan, is the better preserved of the two, and is decorated with some of the finest reliefs to have survived from Greco-Roman Egypt (332 BC–AD 395).

▶ A Hathor priest
This statuette shows a priest holding a sistrum, a rattling instrument closely associated with the cult of Hathor, decorated with the head of the goddess. During the Old Kingdom and the Middle Kingdom (2055–1650 BC), a number of women of the elite served as priestesses of Hathor.

▲ Hathor at Abu Simbel
Near his great temple at Abu Simbel, Rameses II (1279–1213 BC) had a smaller, rock-cut temple constructed for his wife, Nefertari. The queen appears as Hathor in the colossal statues that flank the temple's entrance. Within, a pillared hall features columns with capitals in the shape of sistrums, the instrument of Hathor, and a sanctuary in which a statue of the goddess protects Rameses II.

Sekhmet: Goddess of Destruction

Among the deities of Ancient Egypt, Sekhmet was feared as a powerful and potentially destructive goddess.

Sekhmet, the lioness goddess and the fire-breathing 'eye of Ra', represented the destructive aspects of the sun; her task it was to destroy the enemies of her father Ra, the creator and sun god. According to legend, Sekhmet was sent by Ra to punish, but not eradicate, the human race who had rebelled against him.

Tricked by the gods

Sekhmet, however, acquired a taste for blood and went on killing until she had to be stopped from destroying all humanity. The gods tricked her into drinking vast quantities of blood-coloured beer so that she fell asleep and the human race was saved. Sekhmet angrily left Egypt, but, without her, the sun was diminished and its reduced power threatened the security of the world – she was persuaded by the god Toth to return.

◀ **Gilded figure of Sekhmet**
This particularly fine depiction of the goddess Sekhmet comes from the Tutankhamun treasures. She wears a solar disc and an elegant, tight-fitting garment with a floral pattern.

Tutankhamun necklace

This sumptuous necklace, which shows Tutankhamun between the god Ptah and the goddess Sekhmet, depicts the coronation of the pharaoh, and was probably made for that occasion.

A crowned falcon sits on the serekh, a stylized drawing of the façade of the royal palace.

Sekhmet, with a solar disc, stretches her arm towards the pharaoh in a gesture denoting affectionate protection.

The ka, or soul, of the king is represented by this figure.

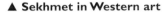

***Tutankhamun**, in a feather robe and short cloak, wears the blue crown and holds the sceptre and flail of kingship.*

***The inscribed gold panels** contain the gods' promises to the king – Ptah offers life, power and health; Sekhmet, eternity.*

***Ptah, the creator god** of Memphis, holds the sceptre, symbol of power, and the ankh symbol of life.*

***Heb, god of eternal life**, kneels below a cobra crowned with a solar disc.*

▲ Sekhmet in Western art

In this detail from a huge painting entitled *Israel in Egypt* by Sir Edward Poynter (1836–1919), Israelite slaves haul a huge statue of a lion to an Ancient Egyptian temple site. It was believed that this represented Sekhmet. In his day, Poynter was a well-known painter of historical tableaux.

▼ 'She who is powerful'

Sekhmet's name means 'she who is powerful', but, if her power was uncontrolled, she could represent a major threat to humanity; thus many rituals were designed to appease her. This depiction of her is from the temple of Sobek and Horus in Kom Obo.

Bastet – The Cat Goddess

In Ancient Egypt, the cat was important as a domestic pet and as the symbol of the protective goddess Bastet. Mummified cats were dedicated to her and her festival was one of the most important in the Egyptian calendar.

Egyptian farmers began to domesticate the native African wild cat (*Felis sylvestris libyca*) before recorded history began. Cats' remains have been found in tombs of the fourth millennium BC. The cat – aptly known as 'miw' in Egyptian, after its cry – was probably first used in grain stores to keep down vermin, but it soon found a privileged place in the home.

Over the centuries, cats graduated from domestic pets to semi-sacred animals dedicated to Bastet, daughter of the sun god Ra, and a protective female goddess. Early images show her with the head of a lioness, but by the first millennium BC she was usually portrayed as a cat, sometimes with a litter of kittens at her feet. The cult of the cat reached its height in the Late period (747-332 BC) with Bastet's main festival celebrated throughout Egypt.

People who sought her help, or who wanted to thank her for a favour, consecrated a cat figurine to Bastet. Alternatively, the priests of Bastet could sacrifice one of the many sacred cats they raised. Its ritually mummified body was then placed in a special underground gallery devoted to cats. The idea was that the animal would immediately seek out Bastet on its arrival in the underworld and pass on a message. Some of these cat cemeteries contained thousands of mummies.

◄ **Lioness-headed Bastet**
Bastet was the goddess of the bas, or ointment jar, and acted like the ointment itself, as a form of protection. She was sometimes depicted with the head of a lioness rather than a cat, as on this gold pendant which dates from the reign of Psusennes I (c. 1039–991 BC).

◄ **Sacred cat figure**
Many bronze cat statuettes, symbols of Bastet, were produced when her cult was at its height. This began during the reign of Egypt's Twenty-Second Dynasty rulers, whose home town was Bubastis in the Delta, which was also the mythical birthplace of the cat goddess.

Papyrus marshes *were home to a variety of birds and geese. To catch them, a snake-shaped throwstick was hurled as the birds flew up from the thickets.*

Three birds *have been caught by the hunter's cat. It has trapped two with its paws and one in its mouth.*

▶ **Mummified cat**
Thousands of cats were bred to be sacrificed and embalmed by pious devotees of Bastet. Priests carried out this flourishing trade and, once paid for, the cat was buried at an important cult site. The idea was that the cat would immediately seek out Bastet in the underworld and intercede on the behalf of the benefactor.

The huntsman's daughter *accompanies her father. She is seated on a boat made of papyrus reeds which have been twined together.*

◀ **Domestic cats**
This detail from an Ancient Egyptian hunting scene shows a cat that has deftly caught three birds for his master, who stands on a reed boat in the papyrus marshes. Household cats were often used for hunting and fowling in the marshes, and are also depicted in domestic scenes, seated beneath their owner's chair.

Min, God of Fertility

As a symbol of fertility, creation and the power of the pharaoh, Min was one of the most important Ancient Egyptian gods, and was celebrated each year in a pre-harvest festival.

Min, who ensured the fertility of both the earth and human beings, was worshipped in an annual festival in the city of Thebes, at which the pharaoh offered the god the first ear of corn from the beginning of the harvest. During the Ptolemaic period (332–30 BC), Min was associated with the Greek god Pan, and the town of Ahkmim, of which he was the principal deity, became known as Panopolis.

Min and other gods

During the Middle Kingdom (2055–1650 BC), Min was sometimes described as the son of Isis. At other times, he was considered to be part of a triad, with Isis as his consort and Horus as their son. In the New Kingdom (1550–1069 BC), he was seen as a manifestation of Amun, and jubilees and coronations incorporated a festival of Min to ensure the potency of the pharaoh.

▲ Min's emblem
From the late Predynastic period (5500–3100 BC), the distinctive symbol of Min was found on pottery vessels, maceheads and palettes.

▼ Colour of fertility
Min's skin and beard are painted black, the colour of the Nile silt from which crops grew. The colour was therefore a symbol of life and fertility.

Min's emblem forms part of the hieroglyphic representation of his name.

The god's headdress, surmounted by two plumes, identifies him with Amun.

The flail seen above Min's right hand is a royal symbol.

A long ribbon trails from his crown.

▼ Depictions of Min

Min is usually shown as a human figure in the form of a mummy, his right arm raised in a smiting gesture, with a flail above it. This stele of Thutmose III (1479–1425 BC) depicts the god in this traditional pose, with the pharaoh standing before him.

◄ Min with other gods

On this drinking vessel, Min is worshipped by a deceased person, with arms raised. Horus, with whom Min was often identified, stands behind him on the left.

► Homage to Min

This relief, from the White Chapel of Senusret I (1965–1920 BC) at Karnak, shows the king, in a triangular loincloth, making an offering to Min.

▼ Fertility and creation

This relief depicts Min in a fertility scene from the boat shrine in the temple of Amun at Karnak. As well as being a symbol of human sexual potency, Min was also an embodiment of the divine power of creation that the gods possessed.

The name of Thutmose III appears in hieroglyphs in the cartouche above his image.

Thutmose III wears the nemes headdress, uraeus and a triangular loincloth.

The erect penis symbolizes Min's role as god of male potency.

Min's body resembles a mummy encased in linen bandages.

The Lesser Deities

In addition to the major deities, such as Ra, Horus and Isis, the Ancient Egyptians worshipped a variety of minor gods. These did not have temples and monuments dedicated to them, but had a domestic role, providing protection and aiding fertility.

The temples of Ancient Egypt were not designed as places where individuals could connect with their gods, but rather as well-oiled machines that maintained the divine order of the universe. In theory, only the pharaoh could enter the inner sanctum of the gods to perform the sacred rites, but in practice this role was delegated to the priests. Official religion was orchestrated by the élite and focused on the issues of the state and the king, as opposed to the personal concerns of the population.

Minor gods for the common people

Although the people of Ancient Egypt were involved in the worship of the major gods, taking an active part in festivals and praying at shrines, they could also appeal to a plethora of lesser deities. These did not usually have temples dedicated to them, but instead appeared in a domestic setting, frequently incorporated into the design of furniture (particularly beds), musical instruments, pottery and other vessels, or in the form of amulets. They often had a protective role, and were commonly associated with fertility and childbirth.

◀ Taweret
Taweret was a household deity, closely associated with the protection of women in childbirth. The goddess took the form of a hippopotamus, usually portrayed with the arms and legs of a lion and the tail of a crocodile, and a full belly that suggested pregnancy. Images of Taweret appeared on amulets, vases and as decoration on beds and headrests from the Old Kingdom (2686–2181 BC).

***The deceased** makes offerings to Renenutet in her role as goddess of fertility and the harvest.*

▶ Renenutet, the snake goddess
Like Taweret, this deity was benevolent, despite her fierce appearance as a cobra or a woman with a cobra's head. She was regarded as the protector of the king and a fertility goddess, responsible for securing and protecting the harvest. Renenutet was celebrated once a year in a festival in the Fayum region, where she was associated with the gods Sobek and Horus.

▲ The companions of Ptah
In the Late period (747–332 BC), the creator god Ptah was sometimes depicted in the form of a naked dwarf, and was regarded in this manifestation as having curative powers against snake and scorpion bites. The Greeks named these strange figures 'pataikoi'.

▲ Showing the regions
The nomes, or administrative regions, of Ancient Egypt were personified by a variety of local gods. These deities were often shown with full bellies and pendulous breasts, symbols of the fertility and abundance of the country. They appear in the lower registers of temples, depicted with local produce, as above.

Hieroglyphs spelling Renenutet's name appear above the goddess.

A crown of feathers sits on the goddess's head.

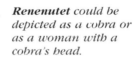

Renenutet could be depicted as a cobra or as a woman with a cobra's head.

A child suckles at Renenutet's breast, emphasizing her role as nurturer and mother figure.

▶ The dwarf god Bes
Despite his grotesque, mask-like facial features and protruding tongue, Bes was an extremely popular god in Ancient Egypt. He was considered to be a fierce warrior, but was also a protector of the family and was associated with sexuality and childbirth – his image is found on all of the mammisi, or birth houses, of the Late period.

The two deities most closely associated with the household and family life, especially women and children, were Bes and Taweret. From the Middle Kingdom, the dwarf god Bes was extremely popular. Despite his startling appearance, he was a beneficient deity, associated with sexuality and childbirth. Similarly, Taweret was represented as a hippopotamus, a dangerous animal, but embodied fertility and protection.

The minor goddesses Heket and Meshkent had similar roles. Heket, who was depicted as a frog, was credited with fashioning the child in the womb and giving it life, while Meshkent was identified with the birth brick on which Ancient Egyptian women delivered their children, and was responsible for determining the child's destiny from the time of its birth.

Protection against dangers

The natural environment of the Ancient Egyptians was fraught with peril in the form of snakes, scorpions, crocodiles and lions. Much of popular religion was concerned with warding off these threats. For example, offerings were made to Renenutet so that snake bites could be avoided or cured, and to the crocodile god Sobek in the hope of protection from the hidden dangers of the River Nile. The scorpion deity Serket was also worshipped to prevent the lethal sting of this insect.

These protective gods were so popular that they persisted throughout the reign of Akhenaten (1352–1336 BC), despite his attempts to promote the Aten as sole god of Egypt. Archaeological findings at his capital at Tell el-Amarna have revealed numerous amulets in the form of these domestic deities, and wall paintings featuring Bes and Taweret.

Heka holds the was sceptre, a symbol of prosperity and well-being.

▶ **Ancient magic**
Magic, personified in the form of the god Heka, was an important part of everyday life in Ancient Egypt. It was regarded as a divine force that could be invoked through rituals or spells to solve problems and crises, such as illness, or to ward off crocodiles or snakes.

The ankh, the hieroglyphic sign for life, appears in Heka's right hand.

The lion-headed goddess Sekhmet stands before the royal couple.

▲ **The goddess Serket**
Serket, along with the goddesses Isis, Nephthys and Neith, protected the Canopic jars containing the organs of the deceased. She was usually portrayed as a woman with a rearing scorpion on her head, or as a woman with a scorpion's tail.

Offerings are made to Heka and Sekhmet by an unnamed royal couple from the Ptolemaic period (332–30 BC).

◀ **Sokar, the falcon god**
This god of the Memphis necropolis was originally a local deity, possibly a patron of craftsmen, although he was also venerated as an earth or fertility god. By the Middle Kingdom (2055–1650 BC), his cult was combined with those of Osiris and Ptah, to form the syncretic Ptah-Sokar-Osiris.

▲ **The goddess of writing**
Seshat was the goddess of writing and measurement, depicted as a woman in a long, panther-skin dress and wearing a star and a bow on her head. Temple reliefs of the Old and Middle Kingdoms show her recording the spoils of war, but from the New Kingdom (1550–1069 BC), she became more associated with the heb-sed festival, or royal jubilee.

◀ **Consort of Montu**
Raettawy, along with another goddess, Tjenenyet, was the consort of Montu, the falcon-headed god of war. At Medamud, just north of Karnak, Montu was worshipped with Raettawy and Harpocrates, the child-like form of Horus, in a Middle Kingdom temple which was dedicated to the triad.

Foreign Gods on the Nile

Egypt's overseas conquests, and the incursions of foreign rulers, brought its people into contact with many different deities; several were worshipped in Egypt, either in their own right or incorporated in an Egyptian god.

The letter of a New Kingdom priestess from Memphis to her counterpart in Thebes asks for a blessing from a long list of deities: 'Ptah who is south of his wall … Baalat, Kadesh, Anat, Baal, Zaphon … and all gods who are in Memphis.' Of these, only Ptah was Egyptian in origin. The text clearly illustrates how gods and goddesses from other countries in the region were apparently worshipped on the same level as the many native members of the pantheon. Although the cults of Baal and Anat had been deeply rooted in the Delta from the time of the Hyksos kings from Palestine (1650–1550 BC), the great majority of these foreign gods had been introduced to Egypt during the New Kingdom (1550–1069 BC), as the pharaohs established strong cultural and trade links with Egypt's neighbours.

A few cults were devoted to gods that originated in Nubia, Libya, or, like Sopdu, the lands east of Egypt, but the great majority of foreign gods in Egypt derived from Syria-Palestine, reflecting the many incursions of pharaohs there during the New Kingdom.

Gods from Phoenicia, Canaan and Syria, including Astarte, Kadesh and Reshef, were widely worshipped throughout Egypt by the end of the New Kingdom. Memphis, a military city with a harbour and the hub of many trade routes, had a particularly large foreign population. Temples and small sanctuaries for Baal, Reshef, Astarte and Kadesh were even built within the confines of the large temple devoted to Ptah.

Min, god of male potency, is the only one of the triad to have originated in Egypt.

◀ **The gods of war**
This small statue adopts a familiar Egyptian pose, stepping forwards with his left leg, and wears a headdress similar to the white crown of Upper Egypt, but is Phoenician in origin. The weapons the figurine once brandished are long gone, but he is identifiable as the warrior god Baal. As early as the Middle Kingdom, but particularly in the Ramesside period, the Egyptian god of chaos, storms and the weather, Seth, became known as 'lord of the foreign lands'. The 'marriage' of warlike Baal and the tempestuous Seth to form the bellicose Seth-Baal was perhaps inevitable.

Three lotus flowers in the right hand of the goddess Kadesh symbolize sexuality and fertility.

▲ **A powerful trio**
The Syrian goddess Kadesh is usually depicted naked (or in a transparent robe) and is shown front-on rather than in profile. She typically stands on the back of a lion, holding flowers in her right hand and snakes in her left. She was so far integrated into Egyptian religious beliefs that she formed part of a triad with another Syrian god, the warlike Reshef, and the ithyphallic Egyptian fertility god, Min.

Hathor's headdress and hair identify Kadesh as a goddess of sex and fertility.

The snake in her left hand signifies the power of Kadesh to ward off evil.

The Amorite war god Reshef is depicted wearing the white crown of Upper Egypt, but with a gazelle's head in place of the uraeus.

▶ A badge of fertility

This sistrum carries an image of Hathor, goddess of love, music and dance in Egypt from the earliest times. Hathor's distinctive curling wig, cow's ears or headdress of wig, horns and sun disc were applied to foreign goddesses introduced to Egypt as a sign of their powers over sex and fertility.

▼ Foreign worshippers, local gods

From the New Kingdom, foreigners who settled in the Nile Valley worshipped their own gods while propitiating native deities. Persians living in Memphis in the Twenty-Seventh Dynasty (525–404 BC) commissioned stelae on which they were shown wearing their own costumes, but carved in Egyptian style, making offerings in front of Egyptian gods.

A mixture of religions

The gods of Near Eastern origin worshipped in pharaonic Egypt generally kept their names. As they were frequently equated with the traditional Egyptian gods and deities, their depictions were often adapted to Egyptian beliefs: thus, their attributes could be the crowns, wigs and sceptres of Egyptian gods. Their cults concentrated on areas where large numbers of foreigners lived and worked. The goddess Kadesh, for example, was much revered in the workmen's settlement of Deir el-Medina.

Foreign gods in Egypt tended to keep their traits, history and human faces – animal-headed gods were rare outside Egypt. Thus Anat, a Syrian goddess, remains a mannish, bellicose figure equipped with a battle-axe and shield. Although they retained their original character, foreign gods were often identified with their Egyptian counterparts. Baal, god of storms, was assimilated in Seth, his equivalent in Egypt, while Kadesh, a Syrian generative goddess, was confounded with Hathor.

The gods of Olympus

After Alexander the Great conquered Egypt in 332 BC, the country's new rulers brought the Greek gods with them. The Ptolemies particularly venerated Dionysos, and held great festivals in Alexandria in his honour, but the local people continued to worship their old gods.

Ptolemy I Soter I (305–285 BC) tried to bring the two cultures together by creating a new god, Serapis, with traits of various Greek and Egyptian gods; his appearance was based on Zeus, the chief Greek god, who had no great cult in Egypt. The veneration of Serapis (the name derives from two Egyptian gods, Osiris and Apis) was centred on the Serapeum in Alexandria, a temple built on classical Greek lines; none of it survives today.

◀ **A new deity**
The Greek pharaoh Ptolemy I Soter I (305-285 BC) introduced a new god with Greek and Egyptian characteristics, to be worshipped in Alexandria. Depicted in Greek style, the bearded Serapis was essentially the Egyptian god Osorapis – himself a fusion of Osiris and Apis – with the attributes of various Greek deities, notably Zeus and Dionysos. Isis was made his consort.

◀◀ **King of the gods**
Zeus, the highest of the Greek gods, was incorporated in the syncretic deity Serapis in Egypt. The cult of Serapis was adopted by the Romans and spread through the empire; a head of Serapis was unearthed at the Walbrook Mithraeum in London.

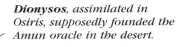

Dionysos, assimilated in Osiris, supposedly founded the Amun oracle in the desert.

◄ **The melding of the gods**
Under the Ptolemies (305–30 BC), the Egyptian pantheon grew ever more crowded as the Greek kings attempted to promote the cultural assimilation of the Egyptian people by merging various gods from the Greek pantheon with native Egyptian deities. Dionysos, god of wine and ecstatic states, was identified, for example, with Osiris. Egyptian gods that did keep their traditional identity – such as Isis – were often depicted in Greek robes and carved in the more detailed, naturalistic style of Ancient Greece.

The cult of Isis, who kept her name under the Ptolemies, continued to be strong throughout the Roman period.

◄ **Hermes Trismegistos**
The Greeks equated Thoth, Egyptian god of wisdom and writing, with Hermes, messenger of the gods (Mercury in the Roman pantheon). The cult city of Thoth, Khmun, was renamed Hermopolis Magna, 'Great city of Hermes', and the Greeks applied the epithet Trismegistos ('thrice great') to Thoth as they did to Hermes. Under the Greeks and Romans, elements of the scientific and arcane wisdom and religious beliefs of the Ancient Egyptians were collected as *Corpus Hermeticum*, so called because Thoth was the scribe of the gods. The *Corpus* was the basis of the spiritual science of alchemy and several European magical systems in what is now known as the hermetic tradition. The secrecy of these writings has led to the use of the word 'hermetic' to mean 'sealed'.

▲ **The birth of Aphrodite**
This piece of decorative fabric from the Coptic Christian period shows the birth of the Greek goddess Aphrodite (the Roman Venus) on a wave. In the Ptolemaic period, she tended to be equated in Egypt with Hathor; Aphrodite was the goddess of love, and Hathor was the 'lady of grace, sweet in love'. Both were capable, too, of a punishing ruthlessness in their dealings with both gods and people who displeased them. The temple of Hathor at Dendera has a Greek inscription that shows the Greeks were fully aware of the correspondences between the two goddesses.

Popular belief

During the Greco-Roman epoch, as in preceding periods, many other gods were more popular with the commoners than those revered by official religion.

The great gods supported by the state presumably seemed too unapproachable to ordinary men and women to be bothered with their everyday needs and worries. Instead, people turned to 'smaller' gods such as Harpocrates, the son of Isis and Osiris. Because of his own fate, having to fend off the manifold dangers of poisonous animals, he seemed perfectly suitable to protect people as well. Numerous terracotta figures of the god are proof of his enormous popularity.

The Creation Myth of Hermopolis

The main cosmologies – theories explaining the creation of the universe – of Ancient Egypt were elaborated by priests in three great religious centres: Heliopolis, city of Ra; Memphis, city of Ptah; and Hermopolis Magna, city of Thoth and the Ogdoad.

The great Egyptian cult-centre of Khmun was renamed Hermopolis Magna in the Greco-Roman period (332 BC–AD 395), but the creation myth associated with it is truly ancient, with some of the gods and ideas mentioned in the *Pyramid Texts* of the Old Kingdom (2686–2181 BC). As with many Ancient Egyptian texts, the cosmology of Hermopolis has not survived as a single account, but has to be deduced from fragments and references in other texts, most of them from the New Kingdom (1550–1069 BC).

It begins, like the other Egyptian myths of the birth of the universe, with a dark world covered by Nun, a featureless ocean of unknown age, depth and extent, symbolizing chaos and the unformed. It is not difficult to see the origins of this image in the way the annual Nile flood covered the land, and, in the same way that the waters silently deposited fertilizing silt on the inundated fields, so the inchoate dark mass of Nun sheltered and nurtured the creative energies that would bring the world into being.

Egg-shaped models are not uncommon in Egyptian tombs. The spiral decoration represents the cracking of the shell as the sun emerges.

The Ogdoad

In the Hermopolis cosmology, this creative force was embodied by four gods and four goddesses, paired up to represent four qualities or principles within the primeval ocean. Known collectively as the Ogdoad, from the Greek word for a set of eight, they were Nun and Naunet, representing water; Kek and Kauket, darkness; Heh and Hauhet, infinity or formlessness; and Amun and Amaunet, air or latent power.

▼ Mythical origins

The annual flood of the Nile, when the rising waters covered its banks and deposited their load of silt before receding to reveal small hummocks of very fertile soil, inspired the Egyptian belief in the existence of a limitless mass of water that preceded creation. This began with the emergence of the first land, known as the primeval mound in other cosmologies and the 'island of flames' in Hermopolis.

▶ The primeval egg

In the creation myth of Hermopolis, the Ogdoad did not create the world themselves, but prepared the way by sending out from the ocean a creator god that had yet to emerge into consciousness. According to one version of the myth, the creative solar god emerged from a primeval egg The Ancient Egyptian sources do not agree on how this egg came into being. One tradition has it that the egg was modelled by the gods and goddesses of the Ogdoad and fertilized by the breath of Amun. In another account, the egg was laid by a bird, which at Hermopolis was identified as the sacred ibis, an incarnation of Thoth. In all versions, though, the egg was placed on the dry land of the primeval mound, where it would hatch out the sun, the true creator of the universe.

◀ **The goddesses of the Ogdoad**
The four female gods of the Ogdoad were represented in the form of snakes, or as figures with serpent heads. As snakes were the first animals to reappear after the waters of the Nile floods had receded, they were naturally chosen as manifestations of the goddesses to partner the frog gods.

▼ **Lords of creation**
The choice of frogs to manifest the male gods of the Ogdoad reflects the Egyptians' keen observation of the natural world. The frog's aquatic habits and origins would have made it at home in the primeval ocean, while its extraordinary life cycle, in which it metamorphoses from tadpole to adult, represented both the transition from chaos to creation and the rebirth of the dead in the afterlife.

▲ **The divine couple**
One of the four pairs of deities in the Ogdoad, Amun and Amaunet, personified the entire male or female force of the Ogdoad. As Amun was raised by the priests of Thebes to be venerated as the main creator god, Amaunet lost her place as his chief wife to the goddess Mut. She is, however, honoured alongside Amun in the temple of Deir el-Hagar in the Dakhla Oasis in the Libyan desert, 300km (186 miles) west of the Nile.

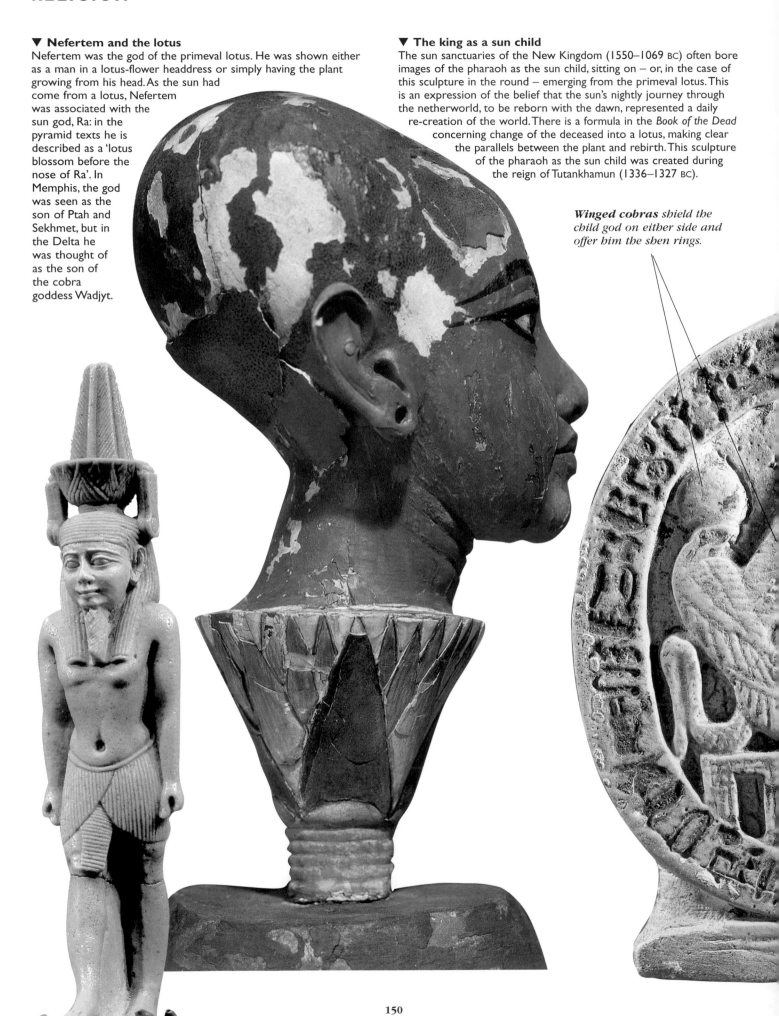

▼ Nefertem and the lotus

Nefertem was the god of the primeval lotus. He was shown either as a man in a lotus-flower headdress or simply having the plant growing from his head. As the sun had come from a lotus, Nefertem was associated with the sun god, Ra: in the pyramid texts he is described as a 'lotus blossom before the nose of Ra'. In Memphis, the god was seen as the son of Ptah and Sekhmet, but in the Delta he was thought of as the son of the cobra goddess Wadjyt.

▼ The king as a sun child

The sun sanctuaries of the New Kingdom (1550–1069 BC) often bore images of the pharaoh as the sun child, sitting on – or, in the case of this sculpture in the round – emerging from the primeval lotus. This is an expression of the belief that the sun's nightly journey through the netherworld, to be reborn with the dawn, represented a daily re-creation of the world. There is a formula in the *Book of the Dead* concerning change of the deceased into a lotus, making clear the parallels between the plant and rebirth. This sculpture of the pharaoh as the sun child was created during the reign of Tutankhamun (1336–1327 BC).

Winged cobras shield the child god on either side and offer him the shen rings.

▼ The amulet of Osorkon

The inscription around this amulet, depicting the creation myth of the primeval lotus, identifies its original owner as Prince Osorkon, whose ancestors became powerful as rulers of a Libyan tribe, the Ma, in the Third Intermediate period (1069–747 BC). A child with a finger placed to his lips sits on an open flower. In his right hand, he holds the heka, or crook, a sign of royal power, while the disc on his head signifies the newborn sun. Two protective cobras offer him a shen ring, symbol of eternity and infinity. The amulet itself is in the shape of a shen ring, making it a powerful charm promoting rebirth into a new life.

The youth curl, a sidelock conventionally used to denote princes in reliefs, helps identify the figure as the sun child.

The band of inscriptions around the amulet's rim lists the names and titles of Osorkon.

There are several versions of how the Ogdoad brought the world into being. One is that their collective will created the first dry land – the 'island of flames' or 'island of fire' – in the primeval ocean. There, the primeval gods created their 'son', an egg, which was fertilized by the breath of air – Amun – producing the god of creation. In Hermopolis, this god was probably equated to Thoth.

Emerging from chaos

Another version is that the Ogdoad propelled a lotus flower from the water; from this emerged the creator in the shape of a beetle (a manifestation of the rising sun), finally taking the shape of a child with his finger placed on his lips – the newly risen sun child.

With their work done, the members of the Ogdoad died and were buried on the west bank at Thebes, on the site of the temple of Medinet Habu. Their demise did not render the eight gods of the Ogdoad inert; from their tomb, they continued to watch over the Nile floods.

▼ Offering the lotus

Many of the abundant aquatic plants in the Nile wetlands have attracted rich religious symbolism, but few more so than the blue lotus, which has flowers that close in the evening and open at sunrise, making it a symbol of creation being renewed every day. The central position of the lotus in the Hermopolis creation myth was expressed in the ritual of 'offering a golden lotus', illustrated in this relief and performed by the city's priests on behalf of the pharaoh: 'Receive the golden lotus that gave birth to creation and chased away the darkness without anyone having witnessed it.'

The Sacred Apis Bull

The Apis bull, symbol of fertility and the physical manifestation of the creator god Ptah, is mentioned in texts from as early as the first Dynasty (3100–2890 BC), and was the most important of all the sacred animals worshipped by the Ancient Egyptians.

The religion of the Ancient Egyptians was closely linked to their natural environment and the creatures they shared it with. As such, many of their gods were worshipped in the form of animals, or as humans with the head of an animal. The sacred Apis bull, an individual animal chosen for its particular markings, is the most significant example of this. Once selected and inaugurated by the priests, the Apis bull enjoyed a life of luxury and veneration.

A Greco-Egyptian god

Apis was originally a god associated with fertility, appearing in texts from the First Dynasty, and later being identified as the physical manifestation of Ptah. The cultural centre of the Apis was therefore located at the ancient city of Memphis, where Ptah was the principal deity and had his main temple.

The Apis had a number of different forms. After his death, he was identified with Osiris, and was described as Osiris-Apis or Osorapis. In the Ptolemaic period (332–30 BC), Ptolemy I (305–285 BC) combined Egyptian and Greek religions, and the Apis was amalgamated with various Greek gods, such as Zeus, Hades and Dionysos, becoming known as Serapis.

Selecting the Apis

The Apis was chosen by the priests of Ancient Egypt with great care, according to distinctive markings and physical characteristics. The Greek historian Herodotus (485–425 BC) wrote that the bull 'was black with a white diamond on its forehead, the image of a vulture on its back, a scarab-shaped mark under its tongue and double hairs on its tail'.

▶ **Memorial stele**
Hundreds of stelae dedicated to the Apis bulls were found in the Serapeum at Saqqara, indicating the reverence with which these sacred creatures were regarded. This example features the Apis, complete with characteristic markings and a solar disc between his horns, being worshipped by a kneeling figure.

An 'image of a vulture' can be found on the back of the Apis bull.

'Double hairs' distinguish the tail of the Apis.

INSIGHT

Sacred bull burials

When one of the Apis bulls died, there was a period of national mourning. The corpse was embalmed at Memphis and taken along the sacred way to Saqqara, for burial in a granite sarcophagus (right) in the underground catacombs of the necropolis of the Apis. Known as the Serapeum, this subterranean cemetery had been in use since at least as early as the New Kingdom (1550–1069 BC) and was discovered by Auguste Mariette in 1851.

The mothers of the Apis bulls were regarded as manifestations of Isis and were buried in a similar manner to their offspring in the Iseum (or 'mothers of Apis' catacomb), located further to the north in Saqqara. The calves of the Apis were also buried ceremonially, but their burial site remains undiscovered.

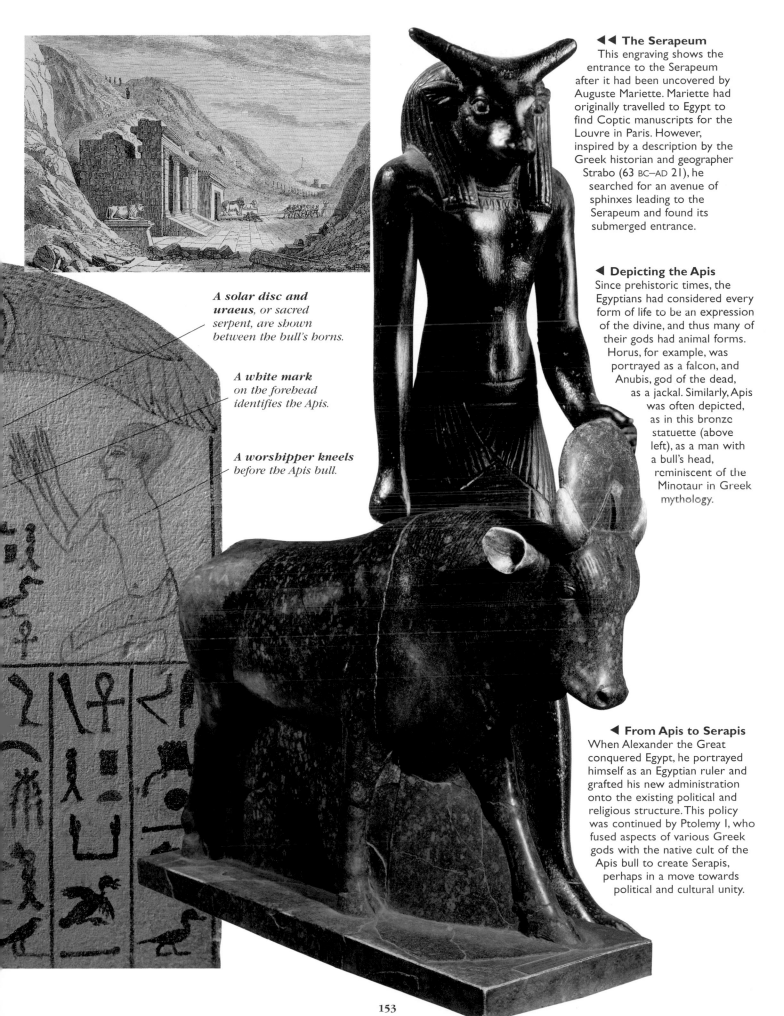

◀◀ The Serapeum
This engraving shows the entrance to the Serapeum after it had been uncovered by Auguste Mariette. Mariette had originally travelled to Egypt to find Coptic manuscripts for the Louvre in Paris. However, inspired by a description by the Greek historian and geographer Strabo (63 BC–AD 21), he searched for an avenue of sphinxes leading to the Serapeum and found its submerged entrance.

◀ Depicting the Apis
Since prehistoric times, the Egyptians had considered every form of life to be an expression of the divine, and thus many of their gods had animal forms. Horus, for example, was portrayed as a falcon, and Anubis, god of the dead, as a jackal. Similarly, Apis was often depicted, as in this bronze statuette (above left), as a man with a bull's head, reminiscent of the Minotaur in Greek mythology.

A solar disc and uraeus, or sacred serpent, are shown between the bull's horns.

A white mark on the forehead identifies the Apis.

A worshipper kneels before the Apis bull.

◀ From Apis to Serapis
When Alexander the Great conquered Egypt, he portrayed himself as an Egyptian ruler and grafted his new administration onto the existing political and religious structure. This policy was continued by Ptolemy I, who fused aspects of various Greek gods with the native cult of the Apis bull to create Serapis, perhaps in a move towards political and cultural unity.

The Animal Necropolises

All along the Nile, from the Mediterranean to the First Cataract, are cemeteries devoted to bodies of several species of animal, including hawks, dogs, baboons, cats, rams, crocodiles and cattle. Some necropolises have yielded hundreds of thousands of mummified beasts.

Many Ancient Egyptian gods were customarily portrayed in the form of an animal. This was not because the beast itself was thought worthy of veneration, but rather because it expressed an essential, otherwise hidden, characteristic of the god. The lion, for example, betrays the aggression of Sekhmet, and the ram speaks of the fertile power of Khnum, while the ibis and the baboon both evoke the wisdom of Thoth.

Living cult objects

In temples, the animal gods were typically worshipped in two different forms: as the cult statue shut away in an inner sanctuary and in the form of an actual animal kept in the grounds of the temple. The incarnation and the effigy shared equal cult status.

When the sacred animal died, the priests would embalm it and bury it with great ceremony in a cemetery reserved for its kind, before – following strict criteria – they chose its replacement. One of the most famous necropolises of sacred animals is the Serapeum at Saqqara, near Memphis. Over the centuries, a network of tunnels and vaults were filled with sarcophagi containing the mummified remains of a long succession of Apis bulls, chosen as the earthly incarnations of the god Ptah.

▼ Sacred to Thoth
Tuna el-Gebel is the necropolis of Hermopolis, the cult centre of Thoth. It has three extensive subterranean animal cemeteries, mostly occupied by baboons and ibises, both sacred to Thoth. They extend below the funerary houses for burials from the Ptolemaic period.

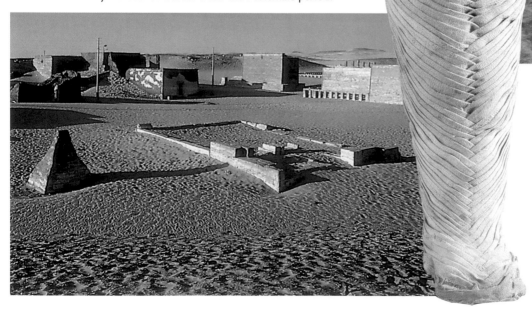

***The site of the Serapeum** is just to the northwest of the step pyramid of Djoser (2667–2648 BC) at Saqqara.*

◄ Ibises by the million
Some experts believe that the ancient custom of killing and mummifying animals led to the disappearance of several native species, including the ibis, from Ancient Egypt. No fewer than four million mummified ibises were interred in one animal necropolis devoted to Thoth at Saqqara.

▼ The Serapeum at Saqqara

In 1851, the archaeologist Auguste Mariette, struck by Strabo's description of an avenue of sphinxes leading to the Serapeum at Saqqara – home of the Apis bulls, incarnations of Ptah worshipped at nearby Memphis – dug for the statues. He followed the avenue to find the unprepossessing entrance to the great underground catacombs where the sacred animals were buried.

The catacombs housed mummies not only of bulls, but also of Khaemwaset, a son of Rameses II (1279–1213 BC) who extended the tunnels and vaults.

Little remains of the cult buildings described by the Greek writer Strabo.

▲ Bull sarcophagi

Auguste Mariette's excavations at the Serapeum at Saqqara, the cult and burial site of the Apis bulls, revealed more than 20 huge granite sarcophagi, weighing up to 80 tonnes, lying in the catacombs. Only one of the sarcophagi still contained a mummified bull; all the others had been plundered, possibly as part of a general persecution of the cult of Serapis by Christian Roman emperors. The oldest known bull burial discovered here was from the reign of Amenhotep III (1390–1352 BC); they continued into the Ptolemaic period (332–30 BC).

◄ The animals of Saqqara

Northwest of the necropolis of Saqqara, about 700m (2300ft) from the pyramid of Djoser, a British archaeologist called W. B. Emery brought to light a number of animal necropolises, including one for the cows that, according to the inscriptions, had calved the Apis bulls. There were also galleries reserved for mummies of ibises and baboons (left), the sacred animals of Thoth, as well as hawks, associated with Horus, and various forms of monkey.

◄ Silent sentinel

A statue of a baboon, crowned with the lunar disc, stands guard over the entranceway to one of the underground galleries in the animal necropolis in Tuna el-Gebel. A system of long interconnecting corridors just below ground houses the mummies of the ibises and baboons ritually sacrificed by the priests at the temple of Thoth in Hermopolis. A chapel in the centre of the catacombs contains a cult statue of Thoth in the guise of a baboon.

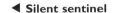

◄ The necropolis of Bubastis
Not far from the cemetery of the citizens of Bubastis in the Delta was an underground necropolis containing the mummies of the cats hastened into the afterlife by priests of Bastet to carry messages to the goddess.

In the Late period (747–332 BC), the sanctification of animals spread to whole species. Any killing – even an accidental one – of an animal venerated in a particular town or region was considered a serious crime.

Killing the messenger

The only exception to this rule was ritual killings carried out by priests, a practice that filled animal cemeteries from the Late period onwards. An Ancient Egyptian who wished, for example, to thank Bastet for answering his prayers, or to beg a favour of her, would approach the priests who served the feline goddess, and purchase one of the cats they raised.

The priests would then kill the cat, usually by breaking its neck, and have the body embalmed according to a strict code of practice. The mummy was placed either in a small sarcophagus or a jar and buried in a cat cemetery. Once it had crossed safely into the afterlife, the cat would seek out Bastet and deliver the petitioner's message.

▲ An image of Bastet
It was the usual practice to wrap the mummies of sacred animals in accordance with the bodily outline of Osiris – with the limbs bound tight to the body, so that only the head made it possible to recognize the animal. This cat, preserved in its natural shape, was an exception, suggesting it had been the pet of a high-ranking person, or was intended as a special offering to Bastet, the cat goddess who protected homes and their occupants.

The deceased cat is shown wearing a broad collar and contemplating a table laden with food offerings.

The cat's epithets, on the side of the lid, include 'the Osiris Ta-Mit (cat), she who is justified by the great god'.

◀ **A well-loved pet**
This limestone sarcophagus discovered at Memphis has inscriptions that show it was made for the favourite cat of Thutmose, the oldest son of Amenhotep III (1390–1352 BC), who died young. The Ancient Egyptians could be very fond of their companion animals, which were often depicted sitting at their feet. They buried them carefully, to ensure they survived in the afterlife to be reunited eventually with their owners. As with human mummies, dead pets were provided with symbolic offerings to sustain them.

The inscription in this column refers to the dead animal simply as 'the cat'; if it had a name, it does not appear here.

The goddess Nephthys kneels above the symbol for gold. Isis appears in the same pose on the opposite side of the sarcophagus.

▶ **Crocodile necropolis**
The temple at Kom Ombo in Upper Egypt, 40km (25 miles) north of Aswan, has some structural remains from the Eighteenth Dynasty (1550–1295 BC), but most of what survives today is from the Ptolemaic and Roman periods (332 BC–AD 395). It was dedicated to two gods, Sobek and Haroeris (an aspect of Horus), represented by a crocodile and a hawk, respectively. A pool in the sanctuary housed a crocodile that was afforded as much veneration as Sobek's cult statue. When it died, the sacred crocodile was mummified and interred in a clay coffin.

▲ **Crocodile mummies**
Archaeologists have uncovered thousands of mummified crocodiles – the sacred animals of the god Sobek – of all ages and sizes in special cemeteries at cult centres such as Medinet el-Fayum. The reptiles' wrappings were often applied with great care to create geometric patterns and motifs. Outside the god's cult sites, crocodiles were generally viewed with fear and loathing, particularly by people, such as fishermen, living and working near the water.

Horus, the King's Protector

The cult of the god Horus, who is usually portrayed as a falcon or a falcon-headed man, was widespread in Ancient Egypt, from Predynastic times (5500–3100 BC) to the Greco-Roman [eriod (332 BC–AD 395).

According to Ancient Egyptian mythology, Horus was the son of Osiris and Isis, and avenged the murder of his father by his uncle Seth following an 80-year battle. Horus was identified with Lower Egypt and Seth with Upper Egypt, and the consequence of Horus's victory was the unification of the two lands. The pharaoh was considered the representative of Horus on earth – a mediator between the earthly and the divine, and responsible for keeping the order of the world – and he became Osiris when he died.

A god in many forms

The Horus cult was widespread in Egypt and expressed in many ways. Haroeris ('Horus the elder') was a battle god, as he was the destroyer of Seth, and the god of the sky, sun and moon. As Horemakhet ('Horus in the

▶ **Horus, protector of the king**
The pharaoh was considered the representative of Horus on earth, and was responsible for the welfare of the country and the upkeep of the order of the world. The king and the falcon god were the same size in many depictions, and thus equal.

Horus wears the crown of Upper and Lower Egypt, the sign of his reign over the entire country.

The ankh sign is handed to the pharaoh by Horus, which was supposed to assure his life and welfare.

▶ **'Horus the elder'**
This manifestation of Horus was especially worshipped at Letopolis in Lower Egypt. As the god Haroeris, or 'Horus the elder', he was the god of light, his eyes representing the sun and moon. The Greeks later identified him with Apollo.

PROFILE

'Horus the child'

Named Harpocrates by the Greeks, 'Horus the child' was a folk god in Greco-Roman times (332 BC–AD 395) and believed to be the personification of the young sun. Together with Isis and Osiris he formed a triad, which was worshipped in many Ancient Egyptian sanctuaries. He was the royal heir, but also a god of fertility. Harpocrates was depicted as a naked child, with his forefinger placed on his lips, wearing the sidelock of youth.

◄ Horus in the royal title
The Horus title is the oldest part of the royal titulary, which totals five titles or names. It was always written with the serekh – a palace façade divided into niches with the royal Horus on top. The name of the pharaoh was written within the rectangle. The Horus title was an expression of the close relationship between the falcon god and the royal court.

The king was considered the representative of Horus in this world and was given the magical power of the god.

▲ Horakhty
Horakhty, 'Horus in the horizon', was already associated with Ra during the Old Kingdom (2686–2181 BC) and subsequently the two gods were combined and worshipped in special sanctuaries. Ra-Horakhty was thought to be the god of the morning sun.

159

horizon') he was god of the east, and hence of the rising sun, and identified with the sun god, Ra. The two deities were eventually combined to become Ra-Horakhty. Harpocrates ('Horus the child') also represented the rising sun and was believed to protect from snake bites and scorpion stings. In his role as Harsiesis ('Horus, son of Isis') he was the god who performed the opening of the mouth ceremony on his dead father, thus claiming his succession to the throne as earthly ruler.

Powerful in battle

Cult sites occur at Letopolis, Hierakonpolis ('the town of the hawk') and Behdet – where Horus was portrayed as a winged sun disc – but Horus is especially associated with Edfu, where he was worshipped as part of a triad that included Hathor and their son Harsomtus.

▶ Horus in the afterlife
The tasks of Horus were not restricted to the world of the living. As the son and heir of Osiris, the god of the underworld, he was closely associated with the mortuary cult; he was to guard the tomb of the deceased and the mortuary offering. This scene from the *Book of the Dead* of Ani, written on papyrus, depicts Horus leading the deceased by the hand and taking her to Osiris.

▼ The sons of Horus
Imsety, Duamutef, Hapy and Qebehsenuef (with human, jackal, ape and falcon heads) were the names of the four sons of Horus. They were thought to be the 'protectors' of the internal organs. From the New Kingdom, Canopic jars had lids in the shape of these protective deities.

▼ The temple of Horus at Edfu
During the Ptolemaic period (332–30 BC), the Egyptians rebuilt the temple of Horus at Edfu, which today is the most complete and best-preserved temple complex in Egypt. The 36m (118ft) high, 137m (450ft) wide pylon is one of the most impressive sights in the country.

Wearing the double crown, Horus accompanies the scribe Ani to see Osiris, the judge of the dead and ruler of the underworld.

Ani is kneeling in front of Osiris. Behind the throne are Isis and Nephthys, with the sons of Horus on the lotus in front of Osiris.

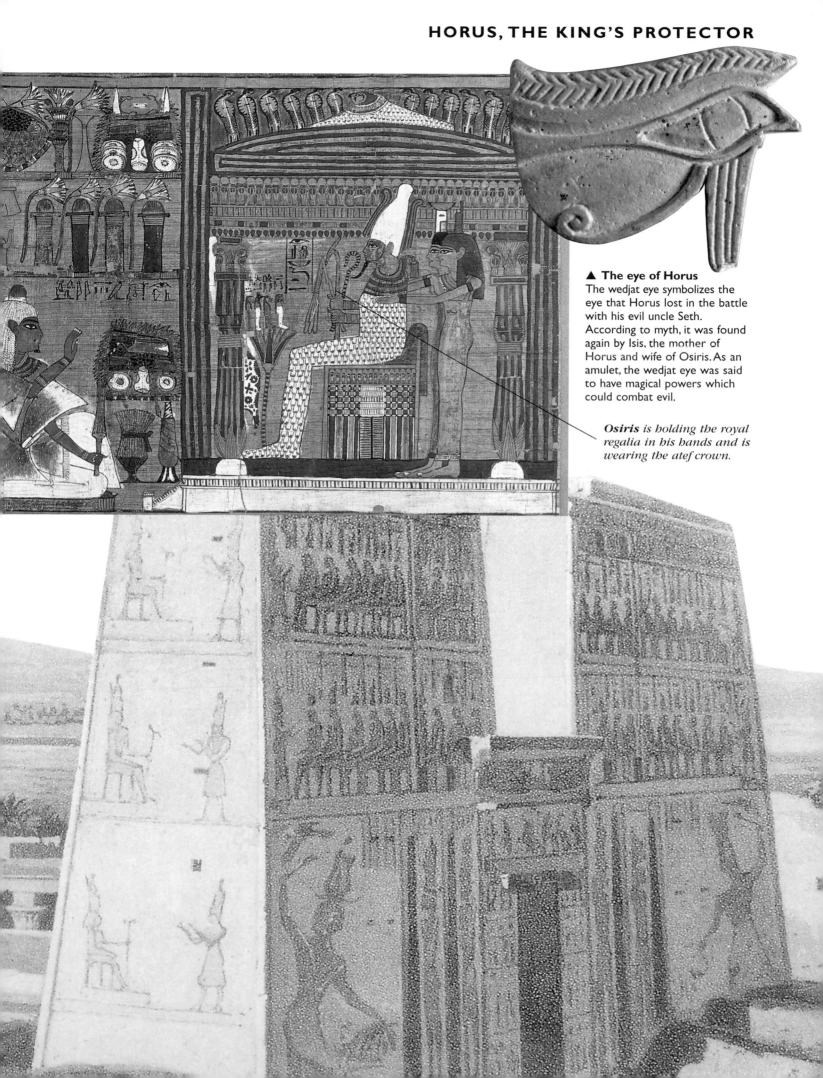

▲ The eye of Horus
The wedjat eye symbolizes the
eye that Horus lost in the battle
with his evil uncle Seth.
According to myth, it was found
again by Isis, the mother of
Horus and wife of Osiris. As an
amulet, the wedjat eye was said
to have magical powers which
could combat evil.

Osiris is holding the royal
regalia in his hands and is
wearing the atef crown.

The Sed Festival

To regenerate his strength and renew his power, the pharaoh celebrated by holding a festival known in Egyptian as the heb sed *(royal jubilee). In principle, this complex ceremony took place in the thirtieth year of his reign and, thereafter, every two or three years.*

Although, in theory, the king could celebrate his jubilee only after a reign of 30 years, in practice, rulers such as Hatshepsut (1473-1458 BC) held it earlier to reaffirm their power. Not all pharaohs had sed festivals; the first recorded one was conducted by Den of the First Dynasty (3100-2686 BC), and the earliest surviving architectural evidence of the ceremony is the sed festival courtyard in the funerary complex of the step pyramid of Djoser (2667-2648 BC) at Saqqara.

The elaborate rituals varied from sed to sed, with some rulers taking a low-key approach, while others, such as Hatshepsut, Amenhotep III (1390-1352 BC) and Rameses II (1279-1213 BC), enjoyed lavish ceremonies that lasted for days.

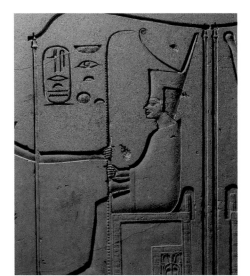

◀ **The costume of the sed festival**
On this relief from the temple of Montu, god of war, at Medamud, Senusret III (1874–1855 BC) is dressed for his sed festival. He wears a long white garment from which only his head and his hands – holding the notched palm branch symbol of longevity – emerge. On his head is the red crown, and to his back a mirror image (not pictured) shows him wearing the white crown. The symbol of the union of the two Egypts is depicted on the side of the throne.

▼ **The courtyard and chapels of the sed festival**
The jubilee was not only for the living king, but also for the deceased. Following his death, the ruler (it was believed) continued to celebrate his sed in the afterlife. In his funerary complex at Saqqara, dominated by the step pyramid, Djoser (2683–2643 BC) built the courtyard and chapels for just such a purpose.

The flail in Queen Hatshepsut's right hand is a symbol of royal authority.

The straight false beard is worn by ruling pharaohs.

The apis bull, the sacred animal of the god Ptah of Memphis, accompanies the ruler during the ritual run.

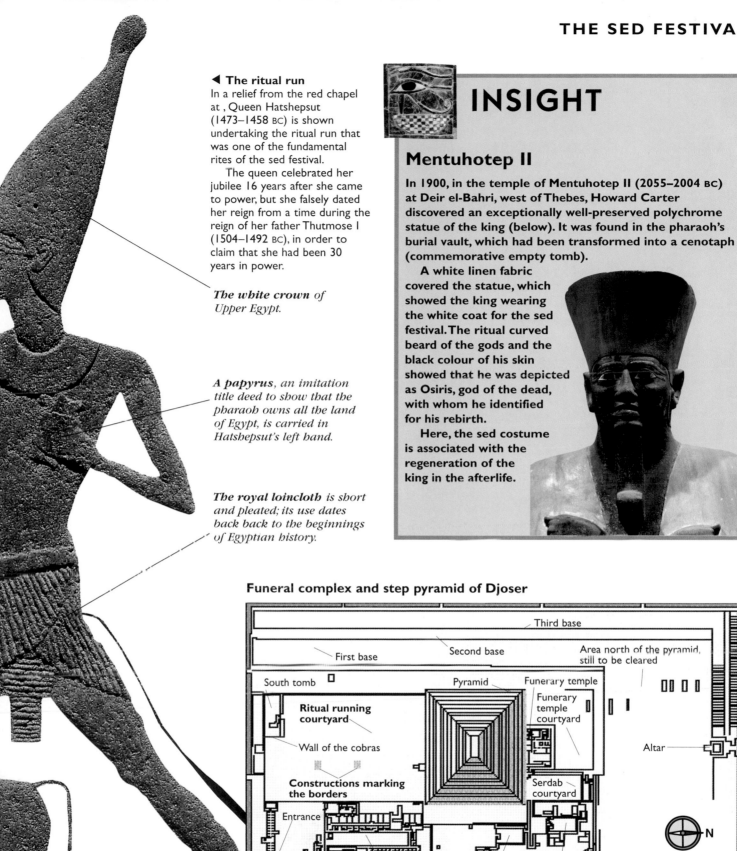

◄ The ritual run
In a relief from the red chapel at , Queen Hatshepsut (1473–1458 BC) is shown undertaking the ritual run that was one of the fundamental rites of the sed festival.

The queen celebrated her jubilee 16 years after she came to power, but she falsely dated her reign from a time during the reign of her father Thutmose I (1504–1492 BC), in order to claim that she had been 30 years in power.

The white crown of Upper Egypt.

A papyrus, an imitation title deed to show that the pharaoh owns all the land of Egypt, is carried in Hatshepsut's left hand.

The royal loincloth is short and pleated; its use dates back back to the beginnings of Egyptian history.

INSIGHT

Mentuhotep II

In 1900, in the temple of Mentuhotep II (2055–2004 BC) at Deir el-Bahri, west of Thebes, Howard Carter discovered an exceptionally well-preserved polychrome statue of the king (below). It was found in the pharaoh's burial vault, which had been transformed into a cenotaph (commemorative empty tomb).

A white linen fabric covered the statue, which showed the king wearing the white coat for the sed festival. The ritual curved beard of the gods and the black colour of his skin showed that he was depicted as Osiris, god of the dead, with whom he identified for his rebirth.

Here, the sed costume is associated with the regeneration of the king in the afterlife.

Funeral complex and step pyramid of Djoser

Third base

First base — Second base — Area north of the pyramid, still to be cleared

South tomb — Pyramid — Funerary temple

Ritual running courtyard — Funerary temple courtyard

Wall of the cobras — Altar

Constructions marking the borders — Serdab courtyard

Entrance

Sed festival courtyard — South house — North house — False doors

N

▲ The sed festival courtyard
During the sed ceremony, the pharaoh proved his physical strength by running a ritual race between two stone structures, symbolically marking the borders of his realm. In the drawing of the funerary complex of Djoser's step pyramid, the immense courtyard for the ritual run can be seen beyond the entrance.

Monumental halls and courtyards were often built to hold the royal jubilee, which began on the morning that the Nile flood began to subside. Surrounded by the royal court and senior dignitaries, the pharaoh would first raise the djed pillar, representing the backbone of Osiris, god of resurrection, and symbolizing stability.

Next, the king re-enacted his coronation, successively mounting two thrones wearing the crowns of Upper and Lower Egypt to reaffirm his authority over all of Egypt. Later in the day, the king undertook a ritual run, often in a specially prepared courtyard, between two sets of boundary markers representing the borders of his domain. Once the ceremonial rites were over, there were days of singing, dancing and feasting on beer, bread and beef, as well as the exchange of gifts and souvenirs.

Varying the rituals

Although there were certain rites central to sed festivals, it appears that the symbolism and events were sometimes adapted to suit the times and the occasion. The introduction of the symbolic travelling by royal barge, to mimic the daily journey of the sun god, appeared during the New Kingdom (1550–1069 BC), and Amenhotep III even had a lake excavated for the journey.

▼ **Hatshepsut's solar journey**
This relief from the Red Chapel at Karnak shows the royal barge being carried to imitate the day and night travels of the sun god across the sky and through the underworld.

◀ **The sed of an unknown king**
This carved ivory standing figurine of an unknown king of the First Dynasty (3100–2890 BC) was discovered in a temple at Abydos. He is clothed in a garment usually worn at a sed festival. The detail of the quilted pattern of the fabric has been exceptionally well executed.

Two journeys were enacted in the royal barge – one for night-time; one for daytime – before the pharaoh was returned to the throne.

▶ Amenhotep III

In the thirtieth year of his reign, Amenhotep III (1390–1352 BC) celebrated the first of his three sed festivals. He built a special hall at Malkata on the west bank of the Nile at Thebes. Preparations for his festival were made years in advance, and Amenhotep III sent scribes to study temple archives and visit the ancient sites to re-create the sed ceremonies of his predecessors.

Hieroglyphs translate as 'Amun-Ra, giver of life and lord of the sky'.

Rising suns symbolize the daily cycle of death and rebirth of the sun and, as such, the regeneration of the pharaoh during the sed.

Participants in the festival were drawn from the royal court and high officials, and sometimes included specially invited foreign dignitaries.

The royal barge carried the pharaoh on the symbolic journey. In some sed festivals, this ceremony took place on a sacred lake.

▼ Singing and dancing

This limestone relief comes from the tomb of Kheruef, steward of Queen Tiys (1410–1340 BC), and principal organizer of Amenhotep III's sed festival. The relief shows two unnamed royal children shaking sistra – special rattles used in the worship of Hathor, goddess of regeneration. She was said to suckle all pharaohs seeking rebirth and renewal of their physical and political power.

The Opet Festival

On important dates, images of the gods were carried through the streets in a procession. One of these events was the Opet Festival, celebrated each year in honour of Amun.

In the temples of Ancient Egypt, only the first courtyard was accessible to the public. Entry to the inner area, or particularly the inner sanctuary where the cult image was kept, was reserved for the priests and the pharaoh. The common people could approach the cult statue itself only during rare and important festivals – but even then it was hidden from view in a shrine.

The journey of the gods

One such occasion was the Opet Festival, celebrated annually in the second month of the season of akhet, the inundation period. Initially, in the Eighteenth Dynasty (1550–1295 BC), it lasted 11 days, but, by the Twentieth Dynasty (1186–1069 BC), it continued for 27 days.

For this festival, the statues of Amun, Mut and Khons were taken from the Karnak temple to the temple at Luxor. In the beginning, the shrines with the cult images were carried overland from Karnak to Luxor on model divine barges; the return journey was made on the Nile. Later, the entire journey took place on the river, in a series of ceremonial boats.

▶ **The god Amun**
The Opet Festival was celebrated at Thebes in honour of Amun. The procession of the divine barges of Amun, his wife Mut and their son Khons from Karnak to Luxor took place with pomp and circumstance. It was the highlight of the festival, during which Amun renewed the pharaoh's right to power, ruling as a god on earth.

▼ **Overland procession**
The divine images were taken on their barges in a festive procession from Karnak to Luxor, as shown in this relief on the walls of the colonnade at Luxor, which was built by Amenhotep III (1390–1352 BC) and decorated by Tutankhamun (1336–1327 BC)

The offerings dedicated to Amun are laid out on offerings tables along the processional route.

Way stations, placed at intervals along the sphinx-lined route, allowed the barge to be rested temporarily.

Several priests carried the divine barge and its shrine.

▼ **Amun's travels**

The priests carried the sacred cult barge of Amun on their shoulders to the river, where it was placed on a large Nile boat to continue its journey. Originally, Amun travelled on the river only on the way back from the Luxor temple to Karnak, but later, the entire journey took place on the water. The Nile boat was towed by the royal barge, or pulled along by ropes from the bank.

INSIGHT

Modern festivals

Some Ancient Egyptian customs and festivals have survived into modern times. At Luxor, once a year, a festival in honour of Sheik Abu'l-Haggâg is celebrated, with the barge procession reflecting the Opet Festival. The high point is the anniversary of the historic arrival of the Sheik at the thirteenth-century mosque of Abu'l-Haggâg (below) at Luxor. There is a boat procession on the Nile, with a felucca mooring at the Luxor temple, just like Amun's barge.

The image of Amun is hidden from view in a protective shrine.

The stern and bow are decorated with a ram's head, the personification of Amun.

The pharaoh walks in front of the barge bearing the divine image.

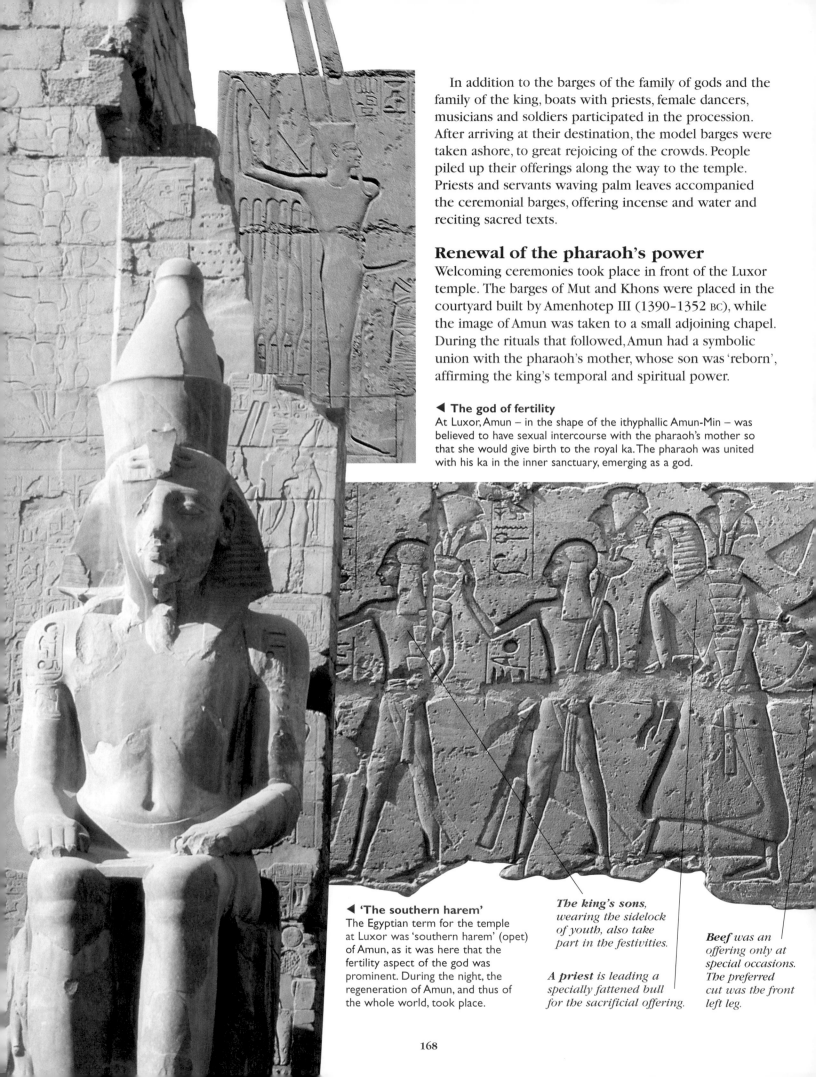

In addition to the barges of the family of gods and the family of the king, boats with priests, female dancers, musicians and soldiers participated in the procession. After arriving at their destination, the model barges were taken ashore, to great rejoicing of the crowds. People piled up their offerings along the way to the temple. Priests and servants waving palm leaves accompanied the ceremonial barges, offering incense and water and reciting sacred texts.

Renewal of the pharaoh's power

Welcoming ceremonies took place in front of the Luxor temple. The barges of Mut and Khons were placed in the courtyard built by Amenhotep III (1390-1352 BC), while the image of Amun was taken to a small adjoining chapel. During the rituals that followed, Amun had a symbolic union with the pharaoh's mother, whose son was 'reborn', affirming the king's temporal and spiritual power.

◄ The god of fertility
At Luxor, Amun – in the shape of the ithyphallic Amun-Min – was believed to have sexual intercourse with the pharaoh's mother so that she would give birth to the royal ka. The pharaoh was united with his ka in the inner sanctuary, emerging as a god.

◄ 'The southern harem'
The Egyptian term for the temple at Luxor was 'southern harem' (opet) of Amun, as it was here that the fertility aspect of the god was prominent. During the night, the regeneration of Amun, and thus of the whole world, took place.

The king's sons, wearing the sidelock of youth, also take part in the festivities.

A priest is leading a specially fattened bull for the sacrificial offering.

Beef was an offering only at special occasions. The preferred cut was the front left leg.

▼ Musicians
Musicians, here playing lutes, formed part of the entourage that escorted the divine barges from the temple at Luxor during the Opet Festival.

▲ Libyans
Recognizable by their feathered headdresses, these Libyans are among the musicians in the procession. They are striking two clappers together, adding rhythm to the proceedings.

Offerings of conical loaves are carried by the priests who walk alongside the sacred bull.

▲ The offerings
During the Opet Festival, numerous cult rituals were performed, with a large number of small altars lining the streets. The king's offering took place at the temple.

Priests, Servants of the Gods

In theory, the pharaoh, as the the high priest of every cult, was the only person permitted to worship the gods. But even the king could not be in more than one sanctuary at the same time, and priests were required for the daily rituals in the temples.

Every city in Egypt honoured its own god, but the importance of the deity – and thus the clergy at its service – depended on the rank of the city. For a long time Amun was a minor god, worshipped in an obscure little town in Upper Egypt; however, when Thebes was promoted to capital, Amun moved up the hierarchy to become king of the gods. Originally, Amun was served by only a few head priests and a modest chapel, but, when he became god of the Egyptian empire, he had the largest clergy in Egypt.

The priestly hierarchy

The clergy in the great temples were organized in a strict hierarchy, although the details vary widely with place and period. At the summit was the chief priest, or 'first prophet', effectively the pharaoh's personal representative, and a few high-ranking priests who assisted him. As the only officials permitted to approach the god's statue enclosed in the sanctuary, these priests wielded considerable power, both religious and secular, controlling the wealth in the temple's treasury and the lands of its estates. They monitored both the 'lector' priests, who wrote the religious treatises and copied the

Water for purifying the food offerings to the temple's god was poured by wab priests from the inscribed hes-vase.

▼ **Dwelling place of the gods**
The temple was entrenched behind a plain brick wall that protected it from attack from the outside world – and from evil influences that could threaten the statue, the receptacle of the deity. The priests had to be pure and clean in order to work in the temple complex.

The terracotta basin collected the water that was poured during ceremonial purifications.

The golden cup was, like the hes-vase, a sacred artefact of temple ritual.

sacred texts in the Houses of Life in the temple complexes, and the more numerous wab priests, who carried out a range of tasks, from purifying the monument to transporting the god's sacred boat.

Most did not hold permanent positions. Divided into four or five teams, or phyles ('tribes' in Greek, but 'saw' or 'watches' in Egyptian), they took turns in the service of their local god one month in every four, and when their term was over they returned to civil life, probably as junior bureaucrats in the case of lectors, or craftsmen in the case of wab priests. These were not unpaid posts; such offices could be lucrative, with priests receiving a fixed proportion of temple revenues. Many of these positions were passed from father to son, while others could be bought.

In addition to these basic ranks there were specialized priestly functions. Two examples were the sem priests, who performed the last rites on the deceased, and the 'hour priests', astronomers who determined lucky and unlucky days, and decided on the most auspicious times for festivals. There was also an array of cult singers and temple musicians, many of whom were drawn from the ranks of noblewomen.

▶ **Priests and priestesses**
When the priests were not in service in the temple, they lived much like other Egyptians; during the months when they devoted themselves to their god, they followed stringent rules on cleanliness and ritual. There were also priestesses, drawn from the elite, who sang and danced in honour of their temple's deity. The clergy of Hathor, goddess of love and joy, were the most likely to admit women, at least during the Old and Middle kingdoms.

The costume of lower-ranking priests – the common Egyptian kilt – is shown in many reliefs to be the same dress as that worn by everyone else.

Osiris and the priest

This illustration, based on the relief in a tomb in the Valley of the Kings, dating from the time of Rameses III (1184–1153 BC), depicts Osiris, receiving offerings from a sem priest dressed in his trademark leopard skin.

Osiris is wearing the solar disc, with a protective uraeus, fitted to the blue crown.

Isis, Lady of the Heaven, reads the hieroglyph above her profile.

▼ **Religious inspector**
Iteti, a dignitary of the Fourth Dynasty (2613–2494 BC), was an inspector of priests in the pyramid of Khafra. During the Old Kingdom (2686–2181 BC), a considerable clergy, attached to the royal funerary complex, worshipped the dead king.

Ruler of the underworld, Osiris was the god worshipped by the dead.

The deceased were also watched over by Isis, the supportive wife of Osiris.

The sem priest purifies the offerings of food and flowers presented to the gods with libations from a hes-vase.

The funerary sem priest is wearing a leopard skin.

Under the leopard skin, the sem priest is dressed in his everyday folded linen clothing.

Offerings to the gods consisted of foodstuffs, flowers and lotus buds, the symbols of rebirth.

◄ **Death in the face of the gods**

The pharaoh was the only person allowed to make offerings to the gods in the temples, and is therefore the only one depicted in the presence of the gods on temple walls. However, in the tombs – dedicated to the worship of the dead, rather than the gods – the deceased had the opportunity to earn favours from the deities by making offerings. In this nineteenth-century drawing by Prisse d'Avennes, Osiris is receiving both an offering and a libation from a sem priest.

◄ **Sacred waters**

The sacred lake of the huge temple complex of Amun at Karnak, near Luxor, was bordered on one side by the priests' houses. Every day after dawn, before entering the monument, the officiating priests climbed down the steps of the rectangular, stone-lined reservoir to purify themselves in the holy water.

When staying within the enclosure of the sanctuary, the priests lived in small houses reserved especially for them. They obeyed very strict rules of physical purity, shaving their heads and bodies, washing four times a day, and wearing only fine linen. Wool and leather were banned, and sandals were made from papyrus. The priests ate light food and obeyed all the dietary taboos.

The priests took part in the ritual of daily worship, the basic ceremony celebrated in the temples. Each dawn the statue of the god of the temple was 'awakened' by a high-ranking priest who entered the sanctuary alone to feed, wash, perfume and dress the deity. Outside the inner temple, priests brought offerings, sang hymns and purified the premises. Thus, the satisfied god would continue to help the pharaoh to maintain world order.

INSIGHT

Carrying the sacred boat

As depicted on the temple walls, most priests fulfilled only subordinate functions, one of which was to bear the model celestial barques that held the god's statue in procession, the shafts resting on their shoulders. This relief from the pillared court of the temple of Amun at Karnak shows priests wearing masks bearing the effigy of the genies of Lower Egypt with the head of a dog. The procession would stop for local people to pray to the god, or to call on the deity to pronounce oracles.

Karnak was the venue for the greatest of Egypt's annual processions, part of the feast of Opet, when a team of priests carried ceremonial boats through throngs of revellers to the River Nile for their journey to Luxor and back.

Life After Death

The Ancient Egyptians saw death not as the end, but as the beginning of a new existence. On their journey to the afterlife, they were accompanied by the material possessions they had used in this life, as well as food and drink to sustain them along the way.

The Ancient Egyptians believed that death was simply an interruption, rather than the end of life, and that the afterlife should consist of the best that was available and pleasurable in earthly existence. This could be brought about by various means. These included piety to the gods and the preservation of the body through mummification, along with the nourishment and protection of the spirit forms which survived death. At its most basic level, enjoyment of the afterlife could be achieved by burying the body with a set of funerary equipment, and at its most elaborate by building the painted and highly decorated tombs of royalty, complete with food, drink, tomb servants and other desirable objects.

The first step was the preservation of the body. As anatomical knowledge grew, embalmers were also able to preserve the internal organs. The body was dried out in natron, a compound of soda bicarbonate found naturally

Anubis and mummification

The jackal-headed god Anubis, watcher of the graveyards and conductor of souls, was the god of mummification. According to myth, he was able to restore life to the body of the murdered Osiris, the god of the dead and the ruler of the underworld, by embalming his corpse and wrapping it in linen.

The head and shoulders of the mummy were covered with a mummy mask, portraying an idealized image of the deceased.

A lion-shaped bier held the mummy. Tables and beds in the form of a lion were part of the mortuary cult as far back as the Old Kingdom.

INSIGHT

Canopic jars: vessels for internal organs

Organs taken from the body were completely dried, then anointed with sweet-smelling ointments, before being wrapped in linen, like the rest of the body, and stored in special vessels called Canopic jars. The name of these jars derived from the town of Canopus, in the Egyptian Delta, where a deity was worshipped in the form of a human-headed jar. The contents of the jar were placed under the protection of four minor gods called the Sons of Horus. The Canopic jars were stored in their own chest, which was drawn on a sled behind the sarcophagus in the funeral procession.

The human-headed Imsety looked after the liver.

The jackal-headed Duamutef guarded the stomach.

The ape-headed Hapy protected the lungs.

The falcon-headed Qebehsenuef looked after the intestines.

PROFILE

Mummy masks

As the dead had to be recognized in the afterlife, the linen-wrapped corpse was fitted with a mummy mask showing the idealized features of the deceased. Usually the masks were made of cartonnage, a material consisting of linen stiffened with plaster, and were often gilded, such as this one of a New Kingdom noblewoman with a vulture headdress (left). According to myth, the flesh of the gods was made of gold, their hair from lapis lazuli and their bones from silver. In the afterlife, the deceased hoped to achieve a godlike form, so in death they sought to imitate this appearance as much as possible.

Embalming priests assumed the identity of Anubis and in certain procedures wore a jackal mask. This was because everybody sought identification with Osiris at death, to ensure resurrection.

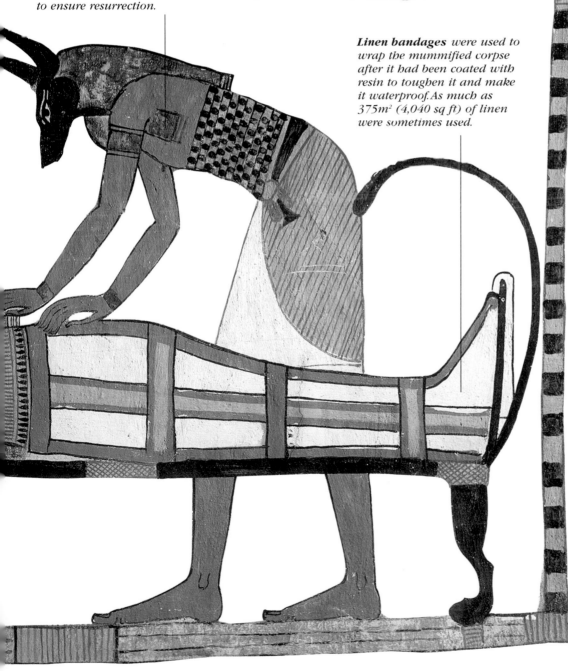

Linen bandages were used to wrap the mummified corpse after it had been coated with resin to toughen it and make it waterproof. As much as 375m² (4,040 sq ft) of linen were sometimes used.

◀ **Decorated tombs**
Much of our knowledge of Ancient Egyptian funerary practices comes from colourful wall paintings such as this one, showing the Anubis priest laying the last hand on the deceased.

It was found in the tomb of Sennedjem, a nobleman who lived during the Nineteenth Dynasty (c. 1200 BC), at Deir el Medina in western Thebes. Domestic scenes of Sennedjem and his wife also decorate the tomb.

▲ **The heart scarab**
Priests placed various protective amulets and charms between the many wrappings of linen. The wedjat eye, or eye of Horus (the symbol denoting the *Insight* box opposite), protected the body from any harm.

Of greater importance, however, was the heart scarab, placed over the heart. It was inscribed with extracts from the *Book of the Dead* (a collection of spells to counteract perils in the hereafter), urging the heart, as the seat of the soul, not to turn against its owner when his or her deeds and life were questioned by the gods during their trial and judgement.

in Egypt, then treated with salves and resins before being wrapped in linen bindings, sometimes as much as hundreds of metres long.

After the prepared mummy was placed in a sarcophagus, and the organs sealed in the Canopic jars, the funeral procession to the tomb began. The heaviest pieces, such as the sarcophagus and the jars, were hauled to the grave on sleds. The relatives and friends, and a long line of bearers, were accompanied by wailing and moaning women – professional mourners. Everything that the deceased needed in the afterlife was taken: chests of clothes and jewellery, furniture, perfumes and food, and sometimes – to show the scholarship of the deceased – writing materials. All of this, along with the sarcophagus and Canopic jars, was sealed in the chamber of the tomb.

The judgement of the dead

Before he entered the underworld, the deceased had first to face the divine tribunal. His earthly deeds were judged by 42 gods overseen by Osiris and many judgement scenes depict the weighing of the heart ceremony. In this ritual, the heart, representing a person's past deeds, was weighed against a feather, symbol of the justice of the gods. This test was only passed when the balance was level or in the heart's favour – and only then could the deceased travel on to eternity and the afterlife.

INSIGHT

Shabti figures

Also known as ushabtis, meaning 'answerers', these statuettes representing servants were placed in the burial chamber to carry out any menial work for the deceased in the hereafter. They have been found in large numbers and were made in a variety of materials, including pottery, wood and stone. Usually, they appear in the form of a mummy and are inscribed with the text from the *Book of the Dead* in which the shabti is commanded to carry out all necessary agricultural work for his master, including irrigating the fields. This typical example (right) is from the New Kingdom tomb of Mutemwija, the wife of Thutmosis IV (1397–1388 BC). Sometimes, tools such as hoes and picks, as well as baskets for grain, appear with the figures. Ideally, a tomb contained one figure for each day of the year, but some royal tombs contained many more.

Funeral procession and burial offerings

Servants carrying grave goods formed a large part of the funeral procession. They transported everything the deceased might need in the afterlife – from furniture, jewellery and knicknacks to food, drink and perfumed oils – all to be buried alongside the body.

Wooden chests *contained valuable belongings needed in the afterlife.*

Furniture, *such as this richly decorated chair with lion-shaped legs and feet, was among items taken to the tomb.*

Perfumed oils *and unguents were contained in vessels such as these, made of stone, faience, pottery or glass.*

▶ The sarcophagus
The mummified body was proctected in an inner coffin, or sarcophagus. Up to the time of the Middle Kingdom, these were coffin-shaped, but during the New Kingdom they evolved into a human shape.

Tutankhamun's mummy was contained in an inner coffin of solid gold, nested within two others of gilded and inlaid wood – and even his inner organs were placed inside miniature coffins similarly decorated (right).

Pleated, white linen garments *were worn by relatives and servants of the deceased. Professional mourners, hired to wail laments for the dead, were often dressed in pale blue.*

Writing tools *for the deceased included a rectangular palette with circular wells for red and black inks, along with several thin reed pens. The holder below contained papyrus leaves. Only a small percentage of the Ancient Egyptian population was literate, and generally only pharaohs, noblemen, professional scribes and government officials acquired the skills of writing.*

The Ka, the Ba and the Akh

For the Egyptians, a person was made up of five parts which included two physical characteristics (his name and shadow) and three invisible elements – the ka (life force), the ba (similar to personality) and the akh (spirit).

The ka came into existence at the precise moment a human was born and continued as the individual's 'double' throughout life and after death. The creator god Khnum, for example, was often depicted modelling both the physical body and the ka on his potter's wheel. After death, the ka continued to live on and, like the deceased when he was alive, required food and drink. Food offerings, or depictions of them on tomb walls, sustained the ka, although he did not physically eat them, but absorbed their life-giving forces. Funerary statues were images of the deceased's ka, and sometimes wore the ka sign of a pair of raised arms as a headdress.

The ba was similar to the personality that makes an individual unique. However, it also represented power and could be extended to the gods and inanimate objects as well. Consequently, the ba was the physical form of certain gods: the Apis bull, for example, was the ba of Osiris. For the body of the deceased to survive in the afterlife, it had to be reunited with its ka every night. As the physical body was unable to do this, it was the duty of the ba to make this journey.

The akh was the form in which the deceased lived in the underworld, and was the union of his ka and ba. Once the akh had been created by this union, it survived as an 'enlightened spirit', enduring and unchanged for eternity.

▶ **The ka of Awibra Hor**
This ka statue came from a wooden shrine in the tomb of Hor, who ruled at Dahshur during the Thirteenth Dynasty (1795–1650 BC). The ka sign of a pair of raised arms is worn as a headdress. The statue, which is 1.70m (5ft 7in) tall, is the only known depiction of a ka as a three-dimensional sculpture.

The inlaid eyes give the statue a lifelike appearance.

The curved beard shows that the ka, like the king after his death, is identified with a god.

A heavy wig covers the head of the ka figure.

The plaster covering the statue cracked and came apart when it was unearthed.

▲ **A bird with a human head**
The word 'ba' has the same hieroglyph as the Jabiru stork. Migratory birds were regarded as incarnations of the ba, which could fly between the tomb and the underworld, so the ba is often depicted as a bird with a human head and, sometimes, human arms.

◀ **The ba**
Humans were not alone in possessing a ba. The gods also had their own, and the apis bull, for example, was the ba of Osiris. The ba was regarded by the Egyptians as a 'physical being', rather than a 'spirit', and as such had its own needs, including food, drink and sex.

The arms, *fastened to the head, show that this is the ka and not an image of the king himself.*

The raised arms *form the hieroglyph that denotes the sound and the word 'ka'.*

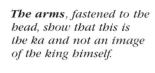

INSIGHT

The statue – substitute for the body

For the Egyptians, the body was an essential element for the survival of the individual in the afterlife. This is why it was mummified and placed in an underground tomb for protection from grave robbers. Despite these precautions, it was not certain that the body could be preserved for ever. The Egyptians, therefore, sculpted statues of the deceased, ready to replace the body if it were to disappear.

The statue could then support the deceased's invisible elements, such as the ka. The ka could be invested in the statue and continue to live on the food offerings made at the tomb, and to sustain the deceased in the afterlife. In the tombs of the Old Kingdom, a windowless room, the serdab (Arabic for 'cellar'), was reserved for the statue of the deceased.

The statue of king Djoser (2667–2648 BC) seen at right came from a serdab near his pyramid at Saqqara.

◀ The akh
The spirit or the 'blessed' deceased, the akh is written with the hieroglyph of the crested ibis. This sign was also used to denote the words 'useful', 'profitable', 'efficient' and 'to shine'. Joined to the ka and the ba, the akh re-created the personality of the individual in the afterlife and ensured his survival throughout eternity.

Embalming the Body

The Egyptians used elaborate mummification techniques on the bodies of the dead which were designed to ensure the soul's unification with the body in the afterlife.

Until the fourth century AD, it was the custom in Ancient Egypt to take a dead body (after a short period of mourning) to the embalming house, where it was given to the priests responsible for mummification – the process that preserved the physical body for use in the afterlife.

The priests began by breaking one of the skull bones and extracting the brain, using a metal hook. They then cut along the body's left flank with a blade of obsidian – a black, glass-like stone – and removed the internal organs to be preserved and buried with the mummy. The stomach cavity was cleansed with palm wine and aromatic essences, and filled with myrrh powder and other substances before the incision was sewn up. The corpse was then covered with natron – a compound of soda bicarbonate – and left to dry for about 70 days.

After this period, the body, now just dried flesh and bone, was cleansed, rubbed with aromatic oils and wrapped in bandages. If the deceased was of high rank,

Anubis – the embalmer

A jackal mask, representing Anubis, the protector of mummification and embalmers, was worn by one of the priests.

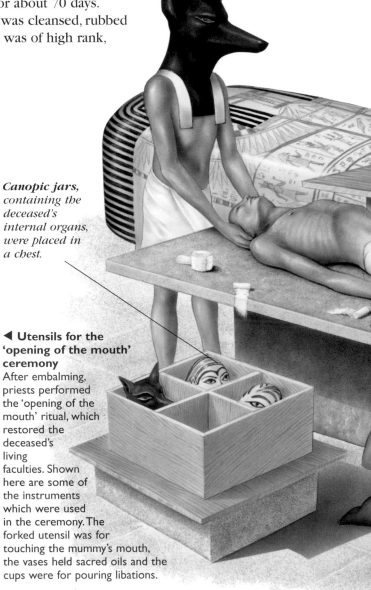

Canopic jars, containing the deceased's internal organs, were placed in a chest.

◀ **Utensils for the 'opening of the mouth' ceremony**
After embalming, priests performed the 'opening of the mouth' ritual, which restored the deceased's living faculties. Shown here are some of the instruments which were used in the ceremony. The forked utensil was for touching the mummy's mouth, the vases held sacred oils and the cups were for pouring libations.

DOCUMENT

The secret life of the mummy

The Ancient Egyptians believed that the souls of the dead needed to return to the body to take in nourishment. In early Egypt, bodies were buried directly into the hot, dry sands, which promoted natural mummification. A switch to using protective wooden coffins ironically hastened decay, and the Egyptians responded by developing a detailed knowledge of the processes of preservation. Some of their mummified bodies have lasted 4,000 or 5,000 years, although little remains of the body except the bones and the skin, which becomes blackened by the various oils used in the preservation process, as this mummy which is part of the collection of the Egyptian Museum in Turin, Italy, shows (left).

The Ancient Egyptians used a powerful chemical to desiccate corpses. White crystalline sodium bicarbonate was mined at the Wadi Natrun in the Libyan desert – from which it derived its name, natron. The body was covered with natron and left to dry for up to 10 weeks.

Protective amulets were placed in the linen bindings.

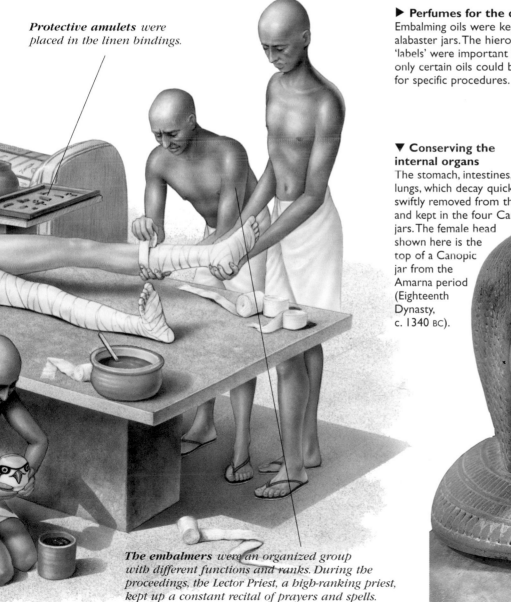

The embalmers were an organized group with different functions and ranks. During the proceedings, the Lector Priest, a high-ranking priest, kept up a constant recital of prayers and spells.

▶ **Perfumes for the dead**
Embalming oils were kept in alabaster jars. The hieroglyphic 'labels' were important because only certain oils could be used for specific procedures.

▼ **Conserving the internal organs**
The stomach, intestines, liver and lungs, which decay quickly, were swiftly removed from the body and kept in the four Canopic jars. The female head shown here is the top of a Canopic jar from the Amarna period (Eighteenth Dynasty, c. 1340 BC).

DOCUMENT

Animal mummies

In Ancient Egypt, certain animals were worshipped as embodiments of the gods. Sacred animals were kept in temples, and after their death were mummified and interred in crypts. This animal cult reached its climax in the first few centuries BC. Mummies of cats (below) were placed in cemeteries in Bubastis, Saqqara, Tanis and Thebes, while there was a vast burial site for ibis and baboons in Tuna el-Gebel.

golden caps were placed on the fingers and toes of the corpse. A gold foil plate, marked with hieroglyphs to ward off bad luck, was put into the incision in the body cavity, and the eyes were replaced with jewels.

The ties that bind

The linen bindings of a carefully preserved mummy could be several hundred metres long. The fingers, hands and feet were wrapped first, then the torso and finally the entire body. The bindings were infused with scented oils, and protective amulets were placed at key locations on the body. The wrappings were sealed with a coat of resin, and painted with hieroglyphs and images of the gods.

A mask was then placed over the head and shoulders. A pharaoh's mask was usually made of gold plate. Others had cartonnage masks – thin layers of linen shaped with stucco, which were gilded and decorated with paint and inlay. Finally, the mummified and bandaged corpse was placed in a coffin, which was then lowered into a stone sarcophagus, a practice which dated from the end of the Middle Kingdom.

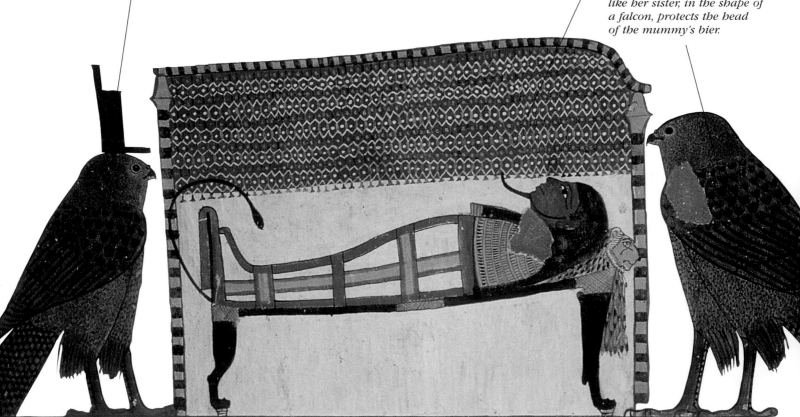

The goddess Isis is represented in the form of a falcon, with the hieroglyphs of her name on her head.

▼ Protected by goddesses
Many pictures show the mummy on a bier under a canopy, protected at both ends by the goddesses Isis and Nephthys, the sisters of Osiris, the god of the dead, with whom the deceased has been united.

A canopy of brightly patterned canvas covers the mummy's bier.

The goddess Nephthys, like her sister, in the shape of a falcon, protects the head of the mummy's bier.

The earliest coffins were simple plank constructions, but they soon became more elaborate. By the time of the Twelfth Dynasty (1985–1785 BC), human-shaped coffins were being made. These were decorated inside and out with a variety of pictures and inscriptions aimed at helping the mummy in the afterlife.

The mummies of pharaohs were protected by up to seven coffins, nestled one inside the other like Russian dolls. The interior coffin was often constructed in gold. The final step was to place the coffins in the tomb in a heavy stone sarcophagus, designed to protect the mummy not only from the elements, but also from robbers.

Mummy and mummy mask

▶ **Cartonnage mummy mask**
This fragment of a mummy mask is made from cartonnage – linen stiffened with plaster – which has been painted and decorated.

Arms clasped across the chest mimic the posture of Osiris, the god of the dead.

Falcons' heads form the clasps of the decorative covering.

▼ **Eye of Horus**
The amulets wrapped in the mummy bandages were supposed to protect the dead with their magic powers and encourage resurrection. One of the most common amulets was the wedjat eye, the falcon's eye of the sky god Horus, which was said to protect everything behind it.

▼ **The wrapped mummy**
The embalmers often wrapped the linen bandages in intricate patterns, particularly over the face and skull.

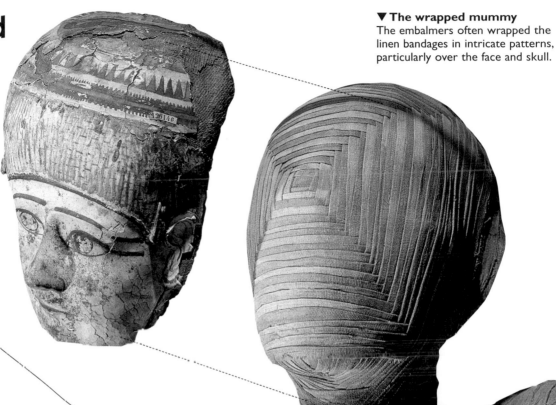

Canopic Jars

Canopic jars held the internal organs of the deceased, and were placed in the burial chamber with the sarcophagus and other funerary objects. They were carefully preserved because, along with the body, they were vital for the deceased's survival in the hereafter.

The Ancient Egyptians believed in the afterlife and rebirth in the hereafter. Great care was therefore taken to preserve not only the body, but also the vital organs of the deceased. These were removed from the body and carefully treated with natron (a natural preservative used by embalmers) and placed in vases that became known as Canopic jars. The name derives from the town of Canopus (now Abukir) in the western Nile Delta near Alexandria, where human-headed jars were worshipped as personifications of the god Osiris. When the early Egyptologists discovered the funerary jars with the deceased's organs, they called them Canopic jars because they resembled those worshipped in the name of Osiris at Canopus.

The sons of Horus

From the New Kingdom (1550–1069 BC), the stoppers of Canopic jars represented the 'sons of Horus' – the protectors of the internal organs – in human and animal form.

The ape-headed Hapy was the protector of the deceased's lungs.

▲ Tutankhamun's Canopic chest
This translucent calcite chest held four gold miniature coffins containing Tutankhamun's organs. Each of the chest's four compartments was topped by an elegant calcite lid in the form of a king's head (possibly Tutankhamun's), wearing the nemes headdress surmounted by the cobra and vulture. Miniature coffins were rare substitutes for Canopic jars, and were generally used only for royalty.

▶ The shape and form of Canopic jars
The style of Canopic jars hardly changed over the centuries. They were flat-bottomed, slightly wider at the neck and were originally sealed by a simple stopper. Later, the stopper took the human or animal form of the god (son of Horus) they represented. The inscription engraved on the belly of the jar recorded the name of the god and goddess concerned and declared the organ under their protection.

▶ Human-headed jars
In the First Intermediate period (2181–2055 BC), simple conical or slightly concave stoppers gave way to ones in the form of human heads. This painted stone jar with the head of a man dates from the Middle Kingdom (2055–1650 BC), and is now in the Egyptian Museum, Cairo.

The falcon-headed god Qebehsenuef protected the intestines.

The human-headed Imsety guarded the liver.

The jackal-headed Duamutef was the protector of the stomach.

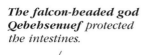

▲ Painted and decorated chests
This wooden chest, decorated with hieroglyphs and a scene from the *Book of the Dead*, once held the four Canopic jars shown beside it. One wood often used for the chests was sycamore, although precious woods, such as cedar, imported from the Lebanon, were favoured by royalty and high officials. The chests were usually placed near the sarcophagus.

Wooden chests were often used to hold the Canopic jars.

Food for the Afterlife

From the end of prehistory to the final disintegration of the pharaonic civilization at the end of the Roman period, the Egyptians customarily surrounded their dead with offerings of food and drink aimed at guaranteeing their survival in the afterlife.

Funerary texts composed by the Ancient Egyptians accord a fundamental importance to the nourishment of the dead. They show that those facing the end of their life on earth were terrified of dying a second, definitive and eternal death of hunger or thirst in the afterlife. This fear is the basis of the funerary cults of Ancient Egypt and the deep-rooted belief in making offerings to the dead. The latter custom goes back to before the pharaonic period, when pitchers of grain were buried next to the deceased to sustain them on their journey to the next world.

The immediate needs of the deceased were met by inhuming a veritable feast - meat, vegetables, fruit, bread and jugs of wine, water and beer - with the mummy. Royal tombs of the Old Kingdom (2686–2181 BC) had several chambers devoted to the storage of food.

The deceased would have left instructions for his oldest son – or perhaps hired a priest – to take responsibility for his funerary cult. An important part of the cult consisted of bringing offerings of food and drink to the funerary chapel every day. These would provide sustenance for the ka, the spirit double or ghost of the deceased, which absorbed the vital force of the offerings.

▲ **The offerings formula**
The Egyptian hieroglyph 'hetep' (circled), which stands for 'offering', is based on a pictogram of a loaf of bread sitting on a reed mat – the precursor of the offerings table in the Old Kingdom.

***Loaves of bread** came in many forms. The shape of this one shows that it was baked in a clay vessel.*

***A groove in the tablet** acted as a drain for the water that was poured over it as a libation.*

◄ **Magical meat**
The left foreleg of an ox was the prime cut of the animal, imbued with magical power, and was an important part of any food offerings ritual. Real and symbolic cuts of meat were ritually offered to gods in their temples, as well as to the dead in their cult chapels.

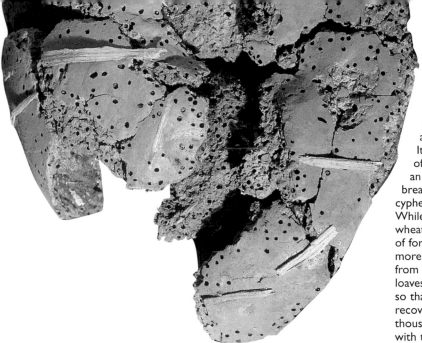

◄ Staple offering

Bread was the staple food of the Egyptians in life, so it is hardly surprising that it should be seen as the food offering *par excellence*. It appears at the very head of the offerings formula: 'May the king make an offering: of thousands of [loaves of] bread.' In this context, 'thousands' is a cypher standing for an infinite number. While almost all loaves were made of wheat, they came in an astonishing variety of forms and methods of preparation: more than 30 distinct shapes are known from reliefs and hieroglyphs. Recognizable loaves of real bread – baked hard and dry so that they did not spoil – have been recovered from tombs some three or four thousand years after they were buried with the deceased.

The left foreleg of an ox – 'khepesh' in Egyptian – was often offered to the honoured dead or to the gods.

The hes-vase, a tall ritual vessel with a short neck and long spout, was used to pour libations of drinking-water over the table.

An offerings formula and the name of the deceased are engraved around the edge of the offerings table.

▲ Offering birds

Geese, ducks, pigeons and quail were all enjoyed by the Ancient Egyptians in life, but the offerings formulae tend to mention birds in general, rather than particular species. From the Old Kingdom, tombs were decorated with scenes of bird hunting in the marshes, with the labourers using nets, while nobles bring the birds down with throwing sticks.

◄ Water offerings

A special vessel, the hes-vase, was used for libations of water poured on the table during the offerings rituals. Other liquids – wine, beer and milk – were offered in containers such as jugs and amphorae, and not poured out. As cult objects with no other use, hes-vases were often elaborately worked; vessels of gold and silver were used in the gods' cult and in offerings for the king. This hes-vase was found in the tomb of the 21st-Dynasty pharaoh Psusennes I (1039–991 BC) at Tanis.

This type of flat bread is very similar to loaves cooked in the region today.

A plucked, prepared goose among the breads on the offerings table is balanced by the ox foreleg opposite.

▲ Offering tablets

The table or tablet on which offerings were left was usually relief-carved with the offerings needed to guarantee the nourishment of the ka after the funerary cult had stopped bringing offerings on a regular basis.

At first, offerings were placed outside the tomb on a reed mat. Later, they were left on an offerings table before the 'false door', the symbolic portal between the sealed tomb chamber and funerary chapel. The Egyptians were not so naive as to believe their funerary cult would last for ever, and took measures to ensure that they would continue to be provisioned long after it was forgotten. They resorted to the magic of the image and the word. Images and lists of foodstuffs could sustain the ka as well as the real thing, as all he was actually consuming was the spirit, or idea, of nourishment.

The deceased at table

One of the most common subjects for tomb paintings and carvings was the deceased seated at an offerings table laden with food (depicted in the typical Egyptian way, as if standing upright on the table) and surrounded by an often long and varied list of provisions. The deceased always holds out his right hand towards the food to indicate his desire to eat it. This motif remained of fundamental importance until the Ptolemaic period (332–30 BC) and can even be seen on steles from the times of the Roman emperors.

▲ A chapel in miniature

This small shrine reproduces a funerary chapel in miniature. In a niche, with a frame resembling the supports of the false door, stand statues of the deceased and members of his family. At the foot of the niche is an offerings table bearing the 'hetep' hieroglyph and representations of jugs and loaves of bread.

▶ Generous offerings

A funerary stele of the Middle Kingdom (2055–1650 BC) shows an official and his wife facing one another across an offerings table piled high with food, including the head and leg of an ox, round loaves, poultry, a bunch of onions and baskets of vegetables.

The blue lotus lent its heady scent to the savours of the offerings laid out for the couple's sustenance.

The head of an ox is included alongside the more usual magically charged foreleg.

▲ At the table

In the Old Kingdom, false doors were topped with slabs decorated with a tableau of the deceased at his offerings table, reaching for bread. Loaves were laid flat on the table, but are artistically depicted standing upright.

▶ Bringing food to the table
Where servants are shown bringing offerings, they usually do so one by one, but two servants are needed to carry this richly laden table in an Old Kingdom relief. Its contents, including bread, courgettes and lettuce, are wildly disproportionate compared with the servants; this illustrates the importance of the nourishment the foodstuffs bring to the ka of the deceased.

The hieroglyph 'hetep', a loaf of bread on a rolled-up reed mat, begins the offerings formula.

Vegetables and fruit such as lettuce, onions and cucumbers were part of the staple diet in Egypt.

A duck or goose is shown ready for roasting on the spit.

▼ A new abundance
Offerings tables in the New Kingdom were shown virtually buried in wide varieties of foodstuffs, although such traditional items as the leg of beef and a bird were always included. This painting is from the tomb of one of the craftsmen who worked on the royal tombs, and lived and were buried at Deir el-Medina.

The Funeral Cortège

Egyptian funerals were ceremonial occasions, which allowed the living to mourn the dead, and helped the deceased on his journey to the afterlife. Funeral processions were frequently depicted on the walls of tombs, particularly during the New Kingdom (1550–1069 BC).

For the life-loving Egyptians, the guarantee of continuing life in the netherworld was immensely important. After a person of high rank died, his corpse was mummified – a process that lasted 70 days; after this, his funeral could take place. The mummy was usually placed on a canopied, open-sided shrine. This was mounted on a boat-shaped bier which sat on a sled drawn by oxen.

Ritual mourning

Servants, priests and relatives all accompanied the funeral cortège. Of particular importance, however, were the professional mourners – wailing women who shouted lamentations, while beating their breasts and striking their heads on the ground (a tradition which persists to this day in North Africa). Various funerary goods and food offerings were also carried in the procession, destined for burial with the body.

▼ **The coffin enshrined**
This scene from the burial chamber of Tutankhamun's tomb shows the king's coffin resting in a canopied shrine decorated with sacred cobras. This is mounted on a boat-shaped bier, which in turn sits on a sled, drawn at the front of the cortège by oxen.

The goddess Nephthys stands on one side of the coffin to protect the deceased pharaoh.

DOCUMENT

Professional mourners

Wailing women – who were paid for their services – were an important presence at every Ancient Egyptian funeral. Usually dressed in pale blue, they let down their hair and tore at it, bared and beat their breasts, wept and wailed loudly, and struck their heads on the ground in a gesture of sorrow. The women's ritualized hysterical behaviour is depicted on this relief (below) from the tomb of Horemheb (1323–1295 BC) at Saqqara. Men displayed their grief in less ostentatious ways: they abstained from cutting their hair or beard for a certain period of time.

▼ A daughter's grief
The daughter of Ipuky, a New Kingdom dignitary, tries to stop his cortège with her hands; a wailing woman offers her hand in sympathy.

▲ Leading the cortège
At the funerals of kings and high officials, eminent dignitaries such as the vizier, here recognizable by his staff of office and distinctive cloak, walked in front of the sled carrying the coffin.

The hieroglyphs identify Tutankhamun with the god Osiris so that, like Osiris, the deceased king will be reborn in the afterlife.

Noblemen and courtiers wear ritual white bandages and white sandals as a sign of mourning.

The mourners use a rope to help pull the sled drawn in the front by oxen.

The two viziers of Upper and Lower Egypt (with bald heads) are among the courtiers who pull the shrine.

Wepwawet, the jackal god whose name means 'opener of the ways' and who protected the deceased on the route into the underworld, is shown on the standard at the prow of the boat-shaped bier.

The funeral cortège often made its way to the edge of the Nile. From there, it was taken by boat to the river's west bank, a voyage that symbolized the deceased's journey from the world of the living – the east bank of the Nile – to the world of the dead – the west bank.

The opening of the mouth ceremony

At the necropolis on the west bank, a tomb was prepared in advance to receive the mummy. Before the body was interred, however, certain rituals were performed. The most important of these was the 'opening of the mouth' ceremony, an elaborate procedure involving incantations and the purification and anointing of the mummified body that restored the dead person's faculties so that he or she could be reborn in the afterlife.

The final separation

Finally, the mummy was placed inside its coffin, which was taken down the vault into a burial chamber. Canopic jars and food supplies for the deceased, along with funerary furniture, were also deposited in the chamber before the tomb was sealed by local masons.

After the burial, family and guests enjoyed a feast of all kinds of food, wine and beer in honour of the dead. This took place outside the tomb, often in a special tent.

The several jars *were probably filled with oil, wine and unguents.*

A servant *carries a chest and the leopard-skin garment worn in religious rituals.*

▶ **Tomb furnishings of Ramose, a New Kingdom vizier**
This scene comes from the tomb of Ramose, governor of Thebes and vizier in the time of Akhenaten (1352–1336 BC). In the afterlife, the deceased hoped to live in the same – or even better – style as he did when he was alive. For this reason, everything he needed in his former life was included in his tomb furnishings.

◀ **Offerings to the spirit of the deceased**
In this scene from the tomb of vizier Ramose, the wailing women are preceded by four women in red and yellow robes with wigs of the same colour. Two present an offering of ritual bowls to the deceased.

INSIGHT

The journey across the Nile

To reach the necropolis on the west bank of the Nile, the funeral cortège had to cross the river by boat. The crossing symbolized the journey from the world of the living to the world of the dead, which was in the 'beautiful west', the location of the underworld.

The boat carrying the deceased was identified with neshmet, the barge of Osiris, the god with whom the deceased was likewise identified. In crossing the Nile, the deceased made a symbolic pilgrimage to Abydos, the site of Osiris's tomb.

This scene from the Eigtheenth-Dynasty tomb of Neferhotep in Thebes (below) depicts a funeral cortège crossing the Nile, accompanied by mourners, officials and relatives. A detail of a similar barge carrying the bier, along with rowers, can be seen at the bottom of the page.

The fan of ostrich plumes was attached to a wooden or metal handle.

An upholstered bed, complete with a black headrest (above the foot) was an indispensable item.

▼ Middle Kingdom mourners

The professional mourners of the Middle Kingdom (2055–1650 BC) can be distinguished from their New Kingdom counterparts by their tunic-style white garments. The displays of grief, however, are the same.

The Opening of the Mouth Ceremony

The opening of the mouth ceremony comprised an elaborate series of acts and incantations that reanimated the faculties of the deceased, and thus ensured their survival in the afterlife.

From the earliest times, the Ancient Egyptians regarded death as only a temporary interruption to life. They believed that eternal life could be ensured through various means, including faithful worship of the gods, the mummification of the body and the provision of funerary equipment. The opening of the mouth ceremony was one of the most important aspects of Ancient Egyptian funerary customs – a ritual that enabled the deceased to see, hear, breathe and receive nourishment in the afterlife.

A complicated rite

The ceremony originated as a ritual used to endow the statues of the dead with the properties of a living being, and thus the ability to support the ka of the deceased. By the Old Kingdom (2686–2181 BC), it had evolved from a statue rite to one which was performed on the mummy itself to restore the use of the mouth, eyes, ears and nose to the dead person. The complex ritual took place in the tomb of the deceased, who stood poised on the threshold to the next world, and involved a variety of acts including purification, censing, anointing and incantation, as well as the touching of parts of the mummy so that the senses would be reanimated.

Jars of water for the purification of the deceased are offered by the priest.

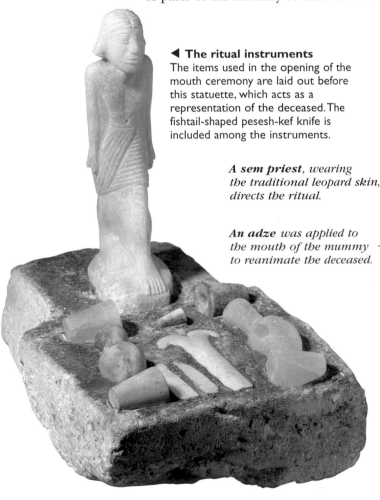

◄ **The ritual instruments**
The items used in the opening of the mouth ceremony are laid out before this statuette, which acts as a representation of the deceased. The fishtail-shaped pesesh-kef knife is included among the instruments.

*A **sem priest**, wearing the traditional leopard skin, directs the ritual.*

*An **adze** was applied to the mouth of the mummy to reanimate the deceased.*

◄ The reviving of the mummy
While the goddesses Isis and Nephthys pour water and unguents on the body, Anubis performs the opening of the mouth ritual with a ceremonial adze.

*The weret hekaw,
a staff in the form of a
ram-headed cobra, was
a symbol of magic.*

**▲ Ceremonies in
front of the tomb**
The opening of the mouth ritual took place in the tomb, after the body had been mummified. In most cases, a sem priest led the ceremony; however, it was sometimes carried out by the son and heir of the deceased as a final act of piety.

*Anubis, the jackal-
headed god of
mummification, takes
part in the opening of
the mouth ceremony.*

*The stele shows the
deceased standing
before Osiris, above an
inscribed prayer.*

**◄ The opening of the
mouth of Hunefer**
This vignette comes from a papyrus found in the tomb of Hunefer, a high-ranking official, and has been dated to the Nineteenth Dynasty (1295–1186 BC). The mummified body of the deceased stands upright, supported by Anubis, while female relatives lament Hunefer's death and priests burn incense and perform the ritual acts with a variety of instruments.

Priests and ritual equipment

The opening of the mouth ceremony was directed by a sem priest, dressed in the distinctive leopard-skin robe, or by the son and heir of the deceased. This helped to identify the dead person with Osiris, god of the underworld, by recalling the filial relationship between Horus and the resurrected god. From the New Kingdom (1550–1069 BC), Anubis, the jackal-headed god of the dead, was often depicted on tomb paintings and papyri playing a central role in the ritual.

A number of implements were used in the opening of the mouth ceremony. Jars and vases contained oils and water for the purification and anointing of the body, while items such as adzes, chisels and knives were held to different parts of the body to reanimate them. In addition, the leg or heart of a slaughtered ox was sometimes extended towards the mummy, perhaps to pass on the animal's strength and vitality.

▶ **Mural in the tomb of Tutankhamun**
Ay (1327–1323 BC) is shown in this wall painting in the leopard-skin robes of a sem priest, performing the opening of the mouth ceremony on Tutankhamun (1336–1327 BC). This representation provided a means of legitimizing Ay's succession to the throne.

The ostrich feather is one of the instruments used by the priest to revive the deceased.

▶ **Wooden instrument**
In the opening of the mouth ritual, the sem priest used a wooden object in the shape of a finger to touch the mouth and eyes of the deceased and thus reanimate and revive him.

Bowls of purifying incense have been placed before Tutankhamun's body.

INSIGHT

Scenes from the opening of the mouth ritual

The superb, well-preserved scenes discovered on the walls of the Theban tomb of Rekhmira, vizier under Thutmose III (1479–1425 BC) during the Eighteenth Dynasty (1550–1295 BC), provide the earliest full illustration of the various acts and rituals that made up the opening of the mouth ceremony.

The sem priest begins the ceremony with purifications, pouring water over the mummy and burning natron and incense, and touches the mouth of the mummy with his little finger. The priest then applies the pesesh-kef knife, one of the most important items in the ritual, to the deceased's mouth. The reanimation of this part of the body was crucial for survival in the afterlife, as it allowed the deceased to receive nourishment.

The slaughter of the sacrificial animal, often an ox, then takes place. Once the animal is dead and has been dismembered, the priest uses certain pieces of the carcass, usually the heart or the thigh, to open the mouth and the eyes of the deceased.

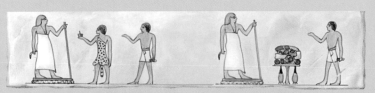

The offerings ritual is carried out after the opening of the mouth ceremony. Food and drink are placed on the offerings table before the mummy, and the offerings formula, or hetep-di-nesw, is recited – a prayer asking for nourishment to be brought to the deceased. Now fully prepared for the afterlife, the body can be buried.

The names of the dead king are listed in the cartouches.

Dressed in a leopard-skin robe, Ay plays the part of a sem priest.

▲ The offering of a heart
During the ceremony, the heart of a slaughtered ox was sometimes used to touch the eyes and the mouth of the mummified body, as in the painting above. The Ancient Egyptians regarded the ox as a symbol of strength, masculinity and fertility.

The leg of an ox slaughtered for the occasion lies between the two kings.

▶ Horus as priest
This mural from the Nineteenth Dynasty (1295–1186 BC), found in the tomb of the official Sennedjem in Deir el-Medina, shows the god Horus performing the opening of the mouth ritual on Sennedjem.

197

The Weighing of the Heart

Every Ancient Egyptian hoped to be reborn in the afterlife in the image of Osiris, the god of the dead, and to be admitted into his kingdom. But before this could happen, the deceased had to appear before a divine tribunal, which examined his conduct on earth.

The idea of the judgement of the dead dates from the Middle Kingdom (2055-1650 BC) but, during that period, the deceased had to undergo trial only if he was guilty of specific faults, crimes or misdeeds. At the beginning of the New Kingdom (1550-1069 BC), the judgement of the dead took on a new form. From then, it applied to all deceased, including the pharaoh himself, and consisted of 'weighing' the heart, which was believed to be the seat of intellect, emotions and conscience - qualities we now attribute to the soul.

The court of justice was presided over by the god Osiris himself. The last judgement of the deceased is the subject of Chapter 125 of the *Book of the Dead*, a funerary text which was composed at the beginning of the New Kingdom, and one of the most important guides to the afterlife. Here, a large vignette illustrates the weighing of the heart in precise detail.

Judgement of the dead

In the weighing of the heart ritual, the deceased's heart, representing his past deeds, was weighed against a feather, symbol of justice. Only after he had successfully passed this test could the dead person begin his life in eternity.

◄ Preserving the body
The embalming of the body and its preservation in a sarcophagus was necessary for existence in the afterlife. It was in this splendid basalt coffin that vizier (chief minister) Gemenefhorbak chose to face eternity.

Hieroglyphs reproduce the text of Chapter 125 of the Book of the Dead.

Osiris, seated on a throne, presides over the tribunal, but waits until told the official result of the test by Thoth.

The Sons of Horus, protectors of the deceased's internal organs, stand before Osiris on a lotus blossom.

Ammut, the Devourer of the Dead, waits to consume the dead whose hearts are heavier than the feather.

THE WEIGHING OF THE HEART

◀ **Preparation for the judgement of the dead**
Before entering the court of justice, the deceased underwent various magical and sacred rituals, and also made offerings of lotus flowers to the gods. The flowers were seen as symbols of birth and resurrection because they open in the morning and close in the evening.

The jackal-headed god Anubis accompanies the deceased to the court of justice, where the weighing of the heart ceremony takes place.

The deceased is led into the judgement hall by the hand.

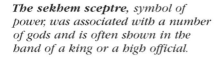

The sekhem sceptre, symbol of power, was associated with a number of gods and is often shown in the hand of a king or a high official.

Thoth, the ibis-headed god and patron of scribes, records the results of the weighing of the heart.

Horus, the falcon-headed god of the sky, checks the accuracy of the scales.

Thoth, this time in the form of a baboon, perches on top of the scales.

Anubis conducts the act of the weighing of the heart against the feather.

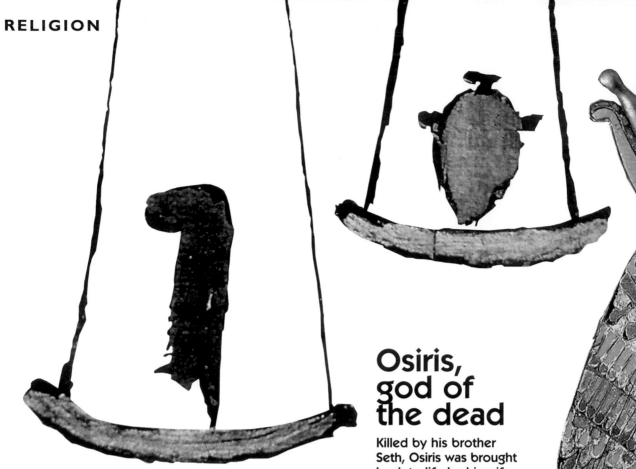

▲ The feather of justice
The symbol of Maat, goddess of justice and order, appears on the scales as an ostrich feather or sometimes as a figurine with a plumed headdress. If the deceased has observed the rules and obeyed the divine law on earth, the heart and feather are evenly balanced and he is granted eternal life.

Osiris, god of the dead

Killed by his brother Seth, Osiris was brought back to life by his wife Isis and by Anubis, who embalmed his body. Osiris, however, did not return to earth where he once reigned, but became instead the god of the dead – who, if his teachings were followed, could also grant eternal life.

The deceased was escorted into the tribunal and stood before Osiris, seated on a throne, and a jury of 42 gods. In the centre of the room was the balance, on which the heart would be weighed. First, however, the deceased had to make a 'negative confession', asserting that he had not committed reprehensible acts, was not guilty of evil deeds or thoughts, and had not acted in defiance of Maat, goddess of truth and justice, or the divine order. He then had to repeat this confession before each member of the tribunal.

The moment of truth

As the heart was about to be weighed, the deceased pleaded with it not to betray him or condemn him, a prayer that was often inscribed on the scarab amulet buried with mummified bodies. The heart was then placed on the scales to be weighed against the ostrich feather that symbolized Maat. If the heart brought the scales into balance, the deceased was allowed access to the afterlife; if, heavy with sin, the heart failed to bring the scales into balance, the deceased faced the open jaws of Ammut, the Devourer of the Dead, a netherworld creature that was part crocodile, part lion and part hippopotamus.

The vulture goddess Nekhbet, wearing the white crown, is the protector of Upper Egypt.

Nekhbet's outspread wings protect Osiris.

The shen sign, in the form of a circle tied at the bottom, symbolizes the eternity that all deceased hoped to achieve.

Tutankhamun, wrapped in a shroud, is depicted in the image of Osiris.

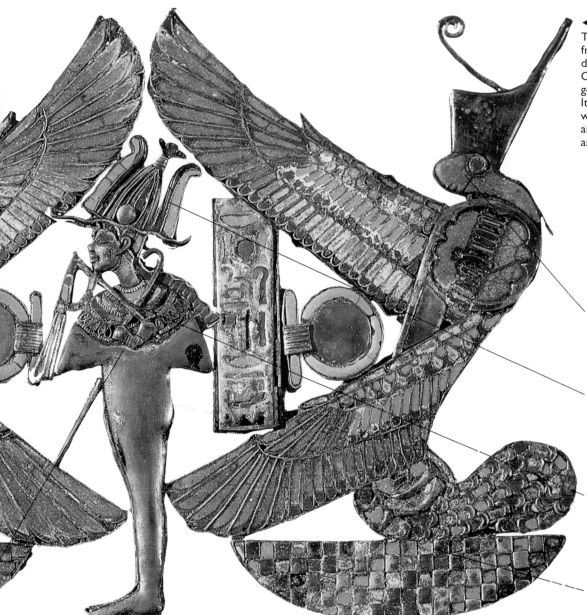

◀ **Osiris as king**
This pectoral (chest decoration) from Tutankhamun's tomb depicts the boy pharaoh as Osiris, protected by the goddesses Wadjet and Nekhbet. It is unlikely that the pectoral was worn during life, and it was almost certainly made for use as a tomb offering.

The cobra goddess Wadjet, deity of Lower Egypt, also protects Osiris with her wings, like the goddess Nekhbet.

The atef crown resembles the white crown, but has a plume on either side supported by the horns of a ram.

The flail and the crook, symbols of royal power, are a reminder that Osiris was once king of Egypt.

Basket-shaped bases support the goddesses Nekhbet and Wadjet.

INSIGHT

Judging the dead – a universal theme

The judgement of the dead, in which evildoers are punished and the good rewarded, is not exclusive to the Ancient Egyptian civilization. Both Ancient Greek and Roman mythologies mention it and describe a 'heaven' and 'hell'. The scales as a symbol of justice also exist in Iran, India, Japan and Tibet, and in the Muslim and Christian religions. Christianity inherited some beliefs from antiquity. In *The Apocalypse*, for example, not only is the Last Judgement outlined in detail, but also the fate, in a paradise or hell, of every individual after death is given the same attention. In the Middle Ages, the weighing of the soul on a set of scales held by a saint, such as St Michael, appears as a motif in many churches and illuminated manuscripts. This thirteenth-century Spanish fresco (right) is one example.

Art

By about 3000 BC, the characteristic appearance of Egyptian art had already developed, and a system of proportions for representing the human form was established.

Unfinished statues and paintings show us the methods used by the Egyptians to produce them. In two-dimensional art, many of the figures were laid out on a grid of squares, although there remained some freedom with the depiction of less important people. Figures were usually placed on a flat horizontal baseline. Differences in size reflect not the actual proportions of what is depicted, but its importance in the scene in question. The same proportional system was applied to three-dimensional work, and there are surviving examples of blocks of stone with grids enabling the sculptor to achieve the correct proportions.

Unknown artists

The names of the artisans responsible for these works are almost never recorded. It is important to remember that although we may regard their products as 'works of art', this may be an interpretation that the Egyptians themselves would not have understood: for example many decorative motifs consist of hieroglyphs representing words ('life', 'dominion') and the vivid scenes on the walls of tombs were almost certainly painted for the purpose of ensuring a continued existence in the afterlife, rather than simply to provide a pleasing appearance.

Timeless treasures
The remarkable works of art featured in this chapter include (clockwise from far left) the mask of Tuyu, the mother of Tiy, the principal bride of Amenhotep III, who was buried in the Valley of the Kings; an iconic alabaster image of Khafra (2558–2532 BC); and the rear of Tutankhamun's gilded throne.

Art in Ancient Egypt

The artistic mastery of the sculpture, architecture, relief carving and painting of the Ancient Egyptians has captivated mankind throughout the ages.

The art of Ancient Egypt is the record of a culture that remained basically the same over some 3,000 years, although styles did change through the different eras. The stonemasons had mastered working in even the hardest stone from very early on, and large stone obelisks and statues made from diorite, quarzite or limestone have decorated temples since the Old Kingdom (2686-2181 BC).

The sophistication of the craftsmen can be seen in the techniques of quarrying. A single, uncracked block had to be cut from rock and often transported hundreds of kilometres to be worked on further. Large teams of craftsmen created the decorations on graves and temples, with draughtsmen, sculptors and painters collaborating to produce works of art. There are very few cases where a work is signed by a single artist.

▶ **Relief work**
The Egyptians decorated temple and tomb walls with two kinds of carving: sunken reliefs, such as in the temple of Sety I (1294–1279 BC) in Abydos, were cut out of the flat wall, while others were raised, with the surrounding stone being cut away.

▶ **Tombs**
The pharaohs spared no expense in the construction of their 'houses of eternity', the most spectacular examples being the great pyramids of Giza. It has never been fully established how the builders and masons managed to make such perfect constructions.

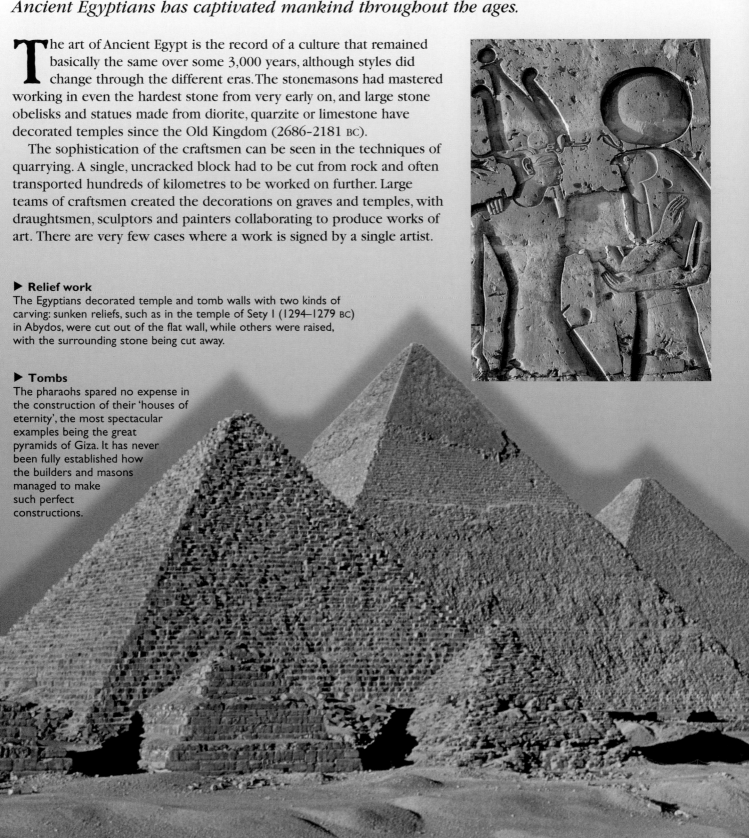

▲ Temples

Countless shrines dedicated to the glory of the gods were built. The most important place of worship, however, was the temple of Amun at Karnak, bordering the Nile, which grew into a large complex of buildings over a period of some 2,000 years.

▲ Painting

In glowing colours that contrasted with the dull tones of the desert landscape, wall paintings depicted scenes of everyday life and religious images. This one, found in the tomb of Horemheb (1323–1295 BC) in the Valley of the Kings, shows gods and the pharaohs in the afterlife.

▶ Sculpture

Stone statues were a form of substitute body for the soul in its life in eternity. The Egyptian artists sought to reflect this idea of timeless existence in their works. In this group, Rameses II (1279–1313 BC) sits between the goddess Mut and the god Amun.

Painters and Paintings

From the Old Kingdom (2686–2181 BC), the art of painting developed in Egypt. Its function was to reflect and perpetuate life and, as such, it was used in tombs and temples for wall decorations and to enhance the sculpture of a relief.

Egyptian art was primarily concerned with ensuring the continuity of life and the universe, and the paintings on the walls of temples and tombs are an idealized reflection of this. The artists did not choose the designs to go on religious monuments. The tomb owners, and the priests or pharaohs of the temples, determined the decorative elements, which generally consisted of faithful but formulaic reproductions of funerary rites, divine cults, myths or historical events.

The slightest failure on the part of the artist in depicting these rituals could threaten the future life of the deceased, or the smooth continuation of the cosmic balance. Scenes from everyday life were also included on wall paintings, however, and here draughtsmen and painters were able to be more uninhibited and lively.

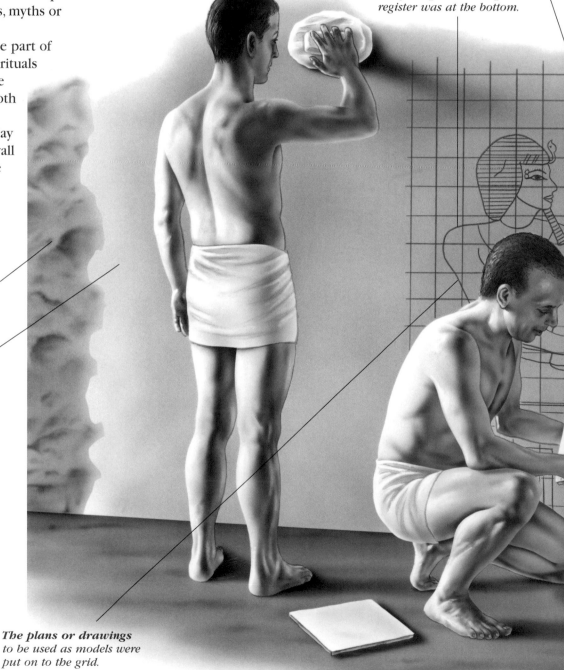

Cords soaked in red paint marked out the grid on the walls.

The first picture strip or register was at the bottom.

A layer of plaster or stucco about 3cm (1¼in) thick provided the surface for the painting. It was wiped and polished to make it as smooth as possible.

Designs and paints were applied directly to the dry wall.

▶ **Step-by-step painting**
Artists worked in teams, with a master craftsman overseeing a number of apprentices. The artists began by covering the wall with a grid, enabling them to copy faithfully from a design drawn up on papyrus. They then traced the outline of the figures in red paint, while their team leader corrected mistakes with black paint. Finally, the painters mixed the powdered pigments with water and an adhesive (acacia gum or egg white). This paint was called 'tempera', and was applied as a flat wash.

The plans or drawings to be used as models were put on to the grid.

Applying the design

To place the design on the wall grid, the draughtsman calculated the number of squares occupied by the figures on the papyrus plan. He then copied them on to the wall, drawing them in the same number of squares so that the proportions were exactly the same.

▼ Artists' equipment
The painters used brushes of different sizes made of plant fibres. They ground the pigments in a stone mortar and mixed them in terra-cotta pots. The sculptors made their incisions by tapping bronze scissors with a wooden mallet.

▼ Paint pigments
The luminous, fresh colours of Egyptian paintings are due to their pigments. Mainly of mineral origin, they were not altered by light. Thus, white has a lime and gypsum base, green came from copper, yellow from ochre, red from iron oxide and blue from azurite.

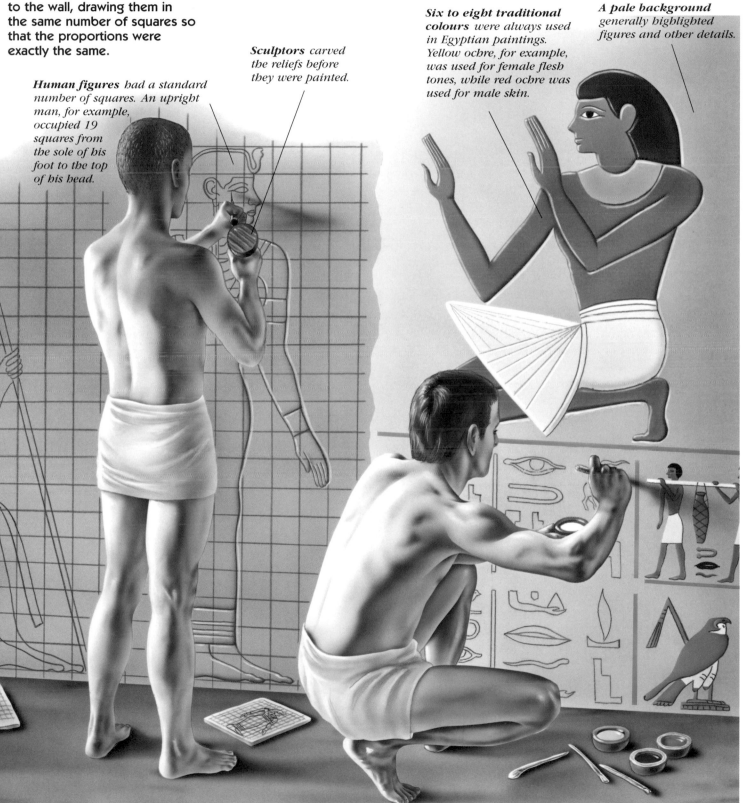

Six to eight traditional colours were always used in Egyptian paintings. Yellow ochre, for example, was used for female flesh tones, while red ochre was used for male skin.

A pale background generally highlighted figures and other details.

Human figures had a standard number of squares. An upright man, for example, occupied 19 squares from the sole of his foot to the top of his head.

Sculptors carved the reliefs before they were painted.

Relief-carving Techniques

Sculpting a relief is much more complicated than painting. For the Egyptians, reliefs were eternal, and were widely used in temples, stelae and in the tombs of high officials, as well as on sarcophagi and other pieces of funerary equipment.

Relief design first appeared in the Predynastic period (5500–3100 BC) on small objects such as cosmetic palettes. It was developed from drawing, from which it took the convention of combining different viewpoints – face-on and from the side – in the same image. From the beginning, relief carvings were usually painted, and only the most important elements of a scene were sculpted in relief. Details, such as wayside plants, woven basket designs or patterned borders on dresses, were added when the stonework was painted to make the picture more vivid.

There are two main types of relief carving. In raised relief, sculptors cut away the material on the outside of a design, leaving it standing proud. In sunken relief, or intaglio, the design is cut into the surface of the stone. The intaglio method was mostly used on outside walls, exploiting light and shade to mould the designs.

▼ Preparing the walls

Before relief scenes could be sketched out, the dressed-stone walls were smoothed and polished, and any cracks and holes filled with limestone mortar. A thin coating of plaster was applied to the walls to make it easier to sketch the designs before carving began.

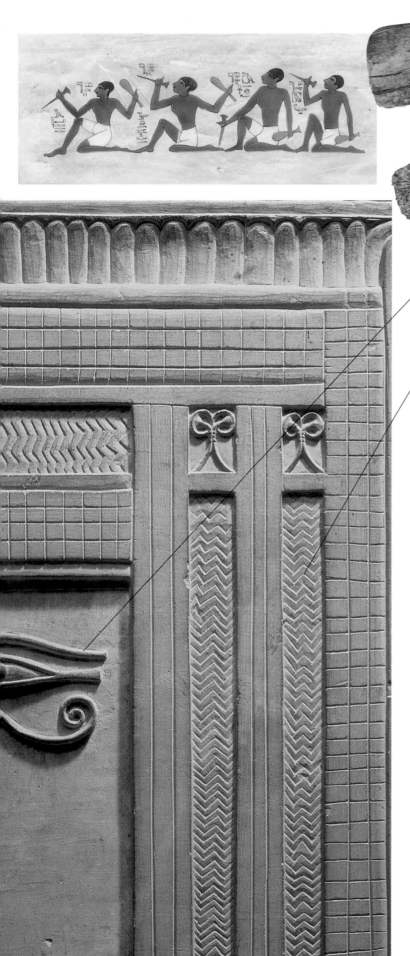

◀ ▼ Tools of the trade
Egyptian sculptors used massive wooden mallets with flat or pointed copper or bronze chisels to carve limestone blocks. Lengths of string soaked in red pigment and stretched between two sticks were used to mark out the design grid on the walls.

The wedjat eye (eye of Horus) is carved in raised relief so that it literally stands out from the design.

Zigzag lines cut into the stone create a simple, repetitive pattern as a decorative motif.

◀ Kawit's sarcophagus
The walls of the tombs of the queens of the Middle Kingdom (2055–1650 BC) were not decorated, but their limestone sarcophagi, such as that of Queen Kawit (c. 2055–2004 BC), bore decorative relief carvings in the palace-façade style.

▼ From sketch to relief
The incomplete tomb of Horemheb (1323–1295 BC) in the Valley of the Kings shows the various stages in the creation of a relief. The wall was covered with a red grid, which helped transfer a papyrus sketch to a larger area. The scene was first sketched in red, then accurately finished in black paint as a final guide for the sculptor. After the relief was carved, the wall was whitewashed and repainted in different colours.

INSIGHT

High and low relief

Throughout the long history of relief carving in Egypt, sculptors worked in what are known technically as bas- (low) relief and haut- (high) relief. Low relief, in which figures and inscriptions are slightly raised against a background that has been chiselled away, was the preferred method. High relief, in which the figures stand out more, and in some cases are almost free-standing statues, is relatively rare, as it involved a great deal more work in cutting away the stone. It did, however, give the carver much more scope for telling detail.

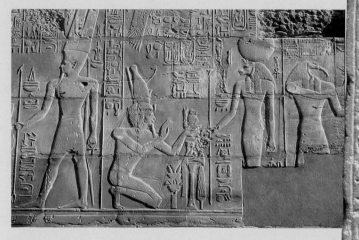

▲ A kneeling king makes an offering to Sekhmet in this low relief from the temple of Amun at Karnak. It dates from the reign of Sety I (1294–1279 BC), a golden age for Egyptian art, and its quality is evident in the fineness of the details.

▼ The Greco-Roman temple of Kom Ombo, dedicated to the crocodile god Sobek and Haroeris, an aspect of Horus, is decorated with reliefs that were mostly made in the first century BC. This carving of a king, with an offering of four sacred vases, shows how high relief can add depth and expression to a face.

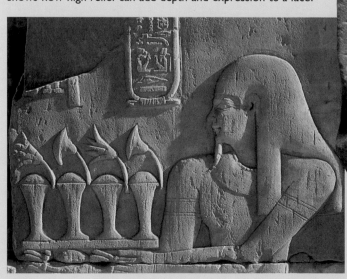

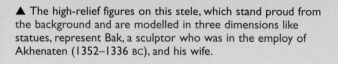

▲ The high-relief figures on this stele, which stand proud from the background and are modelled in three dimensions like statues, represent Bak, a sculptor who was in the employ of Akhenaten (1352–1336 BC), and his wife.

Contrasting styles

Depictions in high relief of four protective goddesses – Isis, Nephthys, Serket and Neith – guard the corners of the sarcophagus of Tutankhamun (1336–1327 BC). The hieroglyphs and wedjat eye are rendered in intaglio, and the contrast throws the high-relief figure of Nephthys into much sharper focus.

The goddess Nephthys uses her outstretched arms and wings to protect one corner of the sarcophagus. She wears a large collar with several strings of beads and painted armlets and bracelets.

The eye of Horus, or wedjat eye, and other inscriptions were rendered in intaglio, using a pointed chisel of hardened bronze. The wedjat eye not only protected the mummy, but also allowed it to view the earthly world left behind.

Sculptors of religious scenes, created in order to maintain the cosmic order in temples and assure eternal life for the dead, were not allowed to give free reign to their imaginations, but had to adhere strictly to designs already set out on papyrus; a grid system was used to transfer these to the walls. The carvers had more freedom in rendering scenes of everyday life, and such reliefs are often filled with flashes of humour and well-observed details.

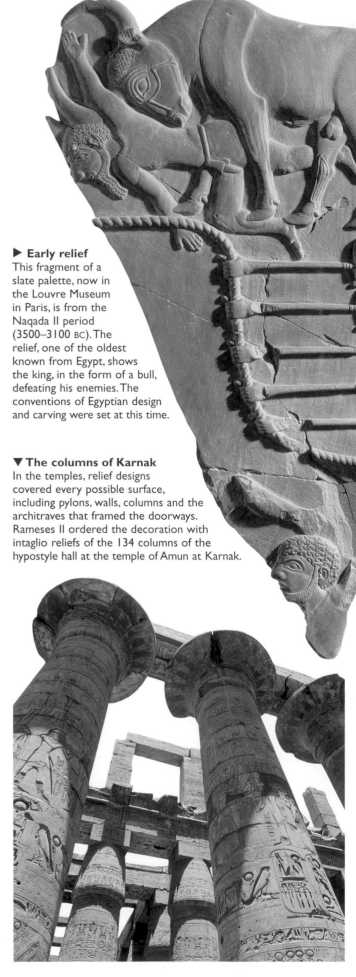

► Early relief
This fragment of a slate palette, now in the Louvre Museum in Paris, is from the Naqada II period (3500–3100 BC). The relief, one of the oldest known from Egypt, shows the king, in the form of a bull, defeating his enemies. The conventions of Egyptian design and carving were set at this time.

▲ Added colour
When low reliefs were finished, the walls were covered with a thin layer of stucco and painted in vivid colours, most of which have faded and disappeared over time.

▼ High-relief massacre
This well-modelled relief on the pylon – ceremonial gateway – of the temple complex of Medinet Habu, across the Nile from Luxor, shows Rameses III smiting his enemies.

▼ The columns of Karnak
In the temples, relief designs covered every possible surface, including pylons, walls, columns and the architraves that framed the doorways. Rameses II ordered the decoration with intaglio reliefs of the 134 columns of the hypostyle hall at the temple of Amun at Karnak.

INSIGHT

Intaglio reliefs

Intaglio, the technique of incising an image into stone or other hard materials, was used to illuminate sculptures on the exterior of Egyptian monuments, and on interior sculptures to highlight figures or scenes. Reliefs of this kind were particularly common during the reign of Rameses II.

▲ On Tutankhamun's Canopic shrine, the figures of Nephthys and the Canopic deity Hapy are cut in intaglio on the gilded wood.

▼ Delineation of the images in this intaglio relief of Rameses II in the temple of Luxor would have been more pronounced when painted.

▲ This deeply incised image of Horus is on one of the pylons of Isis's temple at Philae, and shows the effectiveness of the intaglio technique in modelling with light and shade.

Stelae, Books of Stone

Among the most important antiquities of Ancient Egypt, from the Old Kingdom to Roman times, stelae come in many different types, shapes and decorations.

Stelae were usually made of sandstone or harder kinds of stone such as granite or diorite, but wood was also used in later times. They were between 40cm (16in) and 4m (13ft) in height and could stand free or be built into a wall. Although generally rectangular, with either a square or rounded top, there were countless variations. The hieroglyphs and decorations were carved in sunk relief.

The function of stelae

Stelae fulfilled several functions. There were votive, commemorative and liminal, or boundary, stelae, but the largest group was the tomb stelae. These represented one of the most significant elements of Ancient Egyptian tombs. Their picture area showed the owner of the stele, often with his family, and the inscription listed the name and titles of the deceased after a prayer to one, or several, of the gods of the dead and a request for offerings. Less frequently, an autobiographical text provided additional information about the individual's life.

In the mastaba tombs of the Old Kingdom (2686–2181 BC), stelae functioned as false doors, symbolizing a passage between the present and the afterlife, which allowed the deceased to receive offerings. These were both real and represented by formulae on the false door.

◀ **Cult stele for Rameses II**
This slab belongs to a group of stelae from the Ramesside residence of Piramesse (near modern Qantir in the Delta) that attest to the cult of the deified king. In the upper register, Rameses II (1279–1213 BC) is depicted in front of his own statue offering incense; in the lower one is the donor of the stele, a military official.

Amenemhat is sitting on a stool with lion legs in front of the offerings table and ritual vases.

▶ **Tomb stele of Amenemhat**
This stele from the Middle Kingdom is decorated with depictions of the owner, Amenemhat, and his family. He was overseer of the royal carpenters, and his most important tools – an axe and a saw – can be seen in the bottom row of the picture.

The text under the arch contains the offerings formula that always starts with the words 'hetep dj njswt' – 'a gift which the king gives'.

◀ **Boundary stele**
The Ancient Egyptians used liminal, or boundary, stelae to mark the size and location of fields and the country's borders. Most frontier stelae are from the southern border of Egypt and Nubia. When Akhenaten moved his capital to a new site at Tell el-Amarna, he marked the boundaries of the city with a series of stelae like the one shown here. They depict the pharaoh, his wife Nefertiti and one or several of their daughters praying to the sun god, the Aten. The text tells of the foundation and extension of the city.

▶ **'False door' stele**
This type of stele was particularly common during the Middle Kingdom. It was a false door with an extended picture area, in which the deceased is depicted with or without members of his family — either seated in front of an offerings table or, as shown here, standing.

The deceased is asking for bread and beer, beef and poultry, as well as all other 'good and pure things' for his existence in the afterlife.

▶ **Propaganda stele**
Hewn into the rock next to the entrance of the great temple at Abu Simbel is the double stele of Setau, the son of the Viceroy of Kush at the time of Rameses II (1279–1213 BC). The pharaoh is depicted smiting his enemies in front of Amun-Ra (right) and Horus (left); the lower part shows Setau himself at prayer.

The owner of the stele is not identified by his depiction, but by the name and titles listed.

In the top register of the stele sit Hathor, Horus, Osiris – the father of Horus and lord of the underworld – and his wife Isis.

The high priest Wenennefer, his father Meri and their wives stand underneath the gods.

▲ Stele of Antef
Like most officials of the Middle Kingdom, the chamberlain Antef – who served king Senusret I (1965–1920 BC) – had a chapel with a stele erected, close to the temple of Osiris at Abydos

▼ Stele from Abydos
This Middle Kingdom funerary stele from Abydos depicts three men with their hands raised in prayer. The traditional offerings formulae list the food, drink and clothes that the deceased needs for the afterlife.

Both the throne and the birth names of the ruling king – Usermaatra Setepenra Rameses (II)-meri-Imen – are twice engraved in cartouches in this inscription.

The vertical inscriptions list the names and titles of the men – Wenennefer and Meri – who were both high priests of Osiris.

Votive stelae were exclusively erected in temples by pilgrims to pay homage to the gods or sacred animals. Their picture area showed the donor of the stele praying in front of the deity worshipped at that particular sanctuary. The workmanship of these was often fairly basic, as they were produced in large numbers by local craftsmen, who sold them to devotees.

Deeds and decrees

Commemorative stelae were placed in temples by the pharaoh, or his senior officials, detailing important events of his reign. These include the Kamose Stelae, which recount the defeat of the Hyksos, the Victory Stele describing the campaigns of the Nubian pharaoh Piy as he reconquered the country, and the Restoration Stele of Tutankhamun (1336–1327 BC) detailing the religious reforms enacted after the Amarna period. In Ptolemaic times (332–30 BC), decrees issued by the pharaoh and the priesthood were inscribed on stelae in hieroglyphs, demotic script and Greek, the most famous example of which is the Rosetta Stone.

The simplest boundary stelae marked the edges of fields, while the more sophisticated versions defined the borders of the country, particularly in the south. Uniquely, Akhenaten marked the boundaries of his new capital at Tell el-Amarna with stelae.

◄ **Stele of Wenennefer**
This almost square stele represents a small naos (shrine) with several figures worked in high relief. In the upper niche, the family of gods from Abydos and the goddess Hathor are sitting on a common throne. Below are four praying figures – the high priest of Osiris, Wenennefer, alongside his father, Meri, his mother and his wife.

The goddesses Hathor and Isis are both wearing the sun disc and cow's horns.

Isis, sitting next to Osiris, is identified by her name engraved next to her figure.

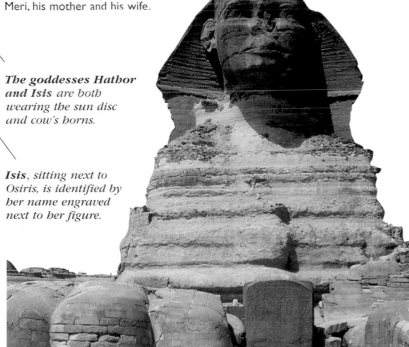

▲ **The 'Dream' stele of Thutmose IV**
Thutmose IV (1400–1390 BC) had a stele erected between the front paws of the Great Sphinx at Giza recording an event from his youth. Hunting close to the pyramids, the young prince became tired and lay down in the shadow of the Great Sphinx, who told him in a dream that he would become king on condition that he removed the sand that almost covered the monument.

◀ Stele of Huni
This stele shows Huni (2637–2613 BC), the last king of the Third Dynasty, being embraced by the falcon-headed Horus. This is among the oldest depictions of the god. Today, the stele is held in the Louvre Museum in Paris, but the location of its discovery remains unknown.

▲ Tomb stele of Itjer
Rectangular stelae such as this were popular in mastaba tombs at Giza from the Old Kingdom (2686–2181 BC). This one shows the deceased Itjer and his wife seated at an offerings table that is piled with loaves. The text lists the thousands of offerings that were made at the funeral.

▼ Stelae at Meidum
On the east side of the pyramid of Sneferu (2613–2589 BC) at Meidum, there is a small chapel with an altar and two high limestone stelae. Unlike the stelae of Sneferu at Dahshur, the Meidum pair has neither decoration nor inscription, as the pyramid complex was never completed.

▶ **Wooden stele**
From the Third Intermediate period (1069–747 BC) to Greco-Roman times (332 BC–AD 395), stelae were made from wood and painted plaster. This example depicts the owner of the stele and his ba praying in front of the sun barge during its journey through the underworld. In the picture area beneath, the deceased is in front of Osiris, Isis, Nephthys and Anubis. To the left are the gods Shu and Tefnut.

▼ **Stele of Hatshepsut**
This arched stele, which was formerly erected in Thebes, shows Hatshepsut (1473–1458 BC) dressed as a male pharaoh offering wine to the god Amun-Ra. Behind her stands her predecessor Thutmose III (1479–1425 BC), wearing the white crown of Upper Egypt.

▶ **Greco-Roman stele**
This tomb stele from the third century AD, today in the Egyptian Museum in Turin, bears an image of Theanous, who died at the age of 49. She is wearing the pleated robe typical of the time and holding a drinking bowl in her right hand.

219

Royal Statuary

In the Egypt of the pharaohs, the most skilled sculptors were at the service of the king. In the royal workshops, they worked as teams, producing the statues that the kings ordered, chiefly for the temples dedicated to the gods and the ruler's funerary monuments.

From the Fourth Dynasty (2613-2494 BC), Egyptian art was created according to a set of rules which were to change little for 3,000 years. This is because art served a distinct purpose - it was not meant simply to depict an image, but also to bring that image to life. The statues in temples and tombs were designed to maintain an ideal world of health and happiness, free from the bad things in life. Death, decay and disease were rarely portrayed.

In the afterlife, a statue was intended to become the person it depicted. To this end, the opening of the mouth ceremony was performed on the finished work so that it could receive offerings of food and drink to sustain it.

It is not surprising, therefore, that the pharaoh, as the most powerful living human and god on earth, should commission hundreds of pictures and statues in his likeness. There were, of course, private statues that were placed in tombs, but nothing on the grand scale as that of the ruler.

◀ **Serene features**
The face of Khafra (2558–2532 BC), sculpted in alabaster, showed the ideal image of the monarch — calm and sure of himself, eternally young and strong, and the guarantor of cosmic order.

▶ **Amun and Tutankhamun**
The god Amun, here depicted with the features of Tutankhamun (1336–1327 BC), sits beside a standing figure of the king. Horemheb (1323–1295 BC), one of Tutankhamun's successors, commandeered the work by having his own names engraved upon it.

◀ **Menkaura and his wife**
The double statue of Menkaura (2532–2503 BC)
and his queen, tenderly holding her husband,
was among the first masterworks of royal
statuary. The shape of the faces and bodies,
the perfect polishing of the granite and the
simplicity of the composition are remarkable.

▼ **Rameses IV offering wine jars**
At the end of New Kingdom
(1550–1069 BC), the weakening of royal
authority affected the production of
royal statues. Fewer in number, they were
also less finished, as shown by this statue
of the pharaoh Rameses IV (1153–1147 BC)
bearing wine jars. Here the legs, in particular,
have been poorly finished.

During the Old Kingdom (2686–2181 BC), statues of kings were placed in the pyramid temples as part of the royal cult, but by the Middle Kingdom (2055–1650 BC), instead of being situated only where offerings were made, they were placed in the temples of the gods. It was during the Middle Kingdom and New Kingdom that the monumental stone sculptures, such as those of Rameses II (1279–1213 BC) at Abu Simbel, became prevalent. Previously, only the Great Sphinx at Giza had been constructed on such a massive scale.

The king was now portrayed in a variety of poses and incarnations. Thus, he might be standing, with his arms alongside his body, or placed on his chest – often with the royal insignia of crook and flail in his hands – or with his hands in front of his loincloth; he could be seated with his hands on his knees, or with one hand on his knee and the other on his abdomen; or kneeling, with his hands outstretched, making offerings.

Sometimes double and triple statues were carved, with the king accompanied by his wife or one or two gods. The face of the god could be a likeness of the king, which is why the features of the gods changed over time.

◄ **Khafra protected by the falcon god Horus**
This masterpiece of Egyptian art, in which Khafra sits on his throne with his head enfolded by the wings of Horus, was found in the mortuary temple below his pyramid at Giza. Buried under the flooring, it was originally one of the 100 or so statues placed in the temple.

▲ **The sculptors' workshop**
The vizier of Thutmose III (1479–1425 BC) and Amenhotep II (1427–1400 BC), Rekhmira was responsible for the royal constructions and workshops of Upper Egypt. For his tomb in Thebes, Rekhmira chose to depict sculptors working on giant statues.

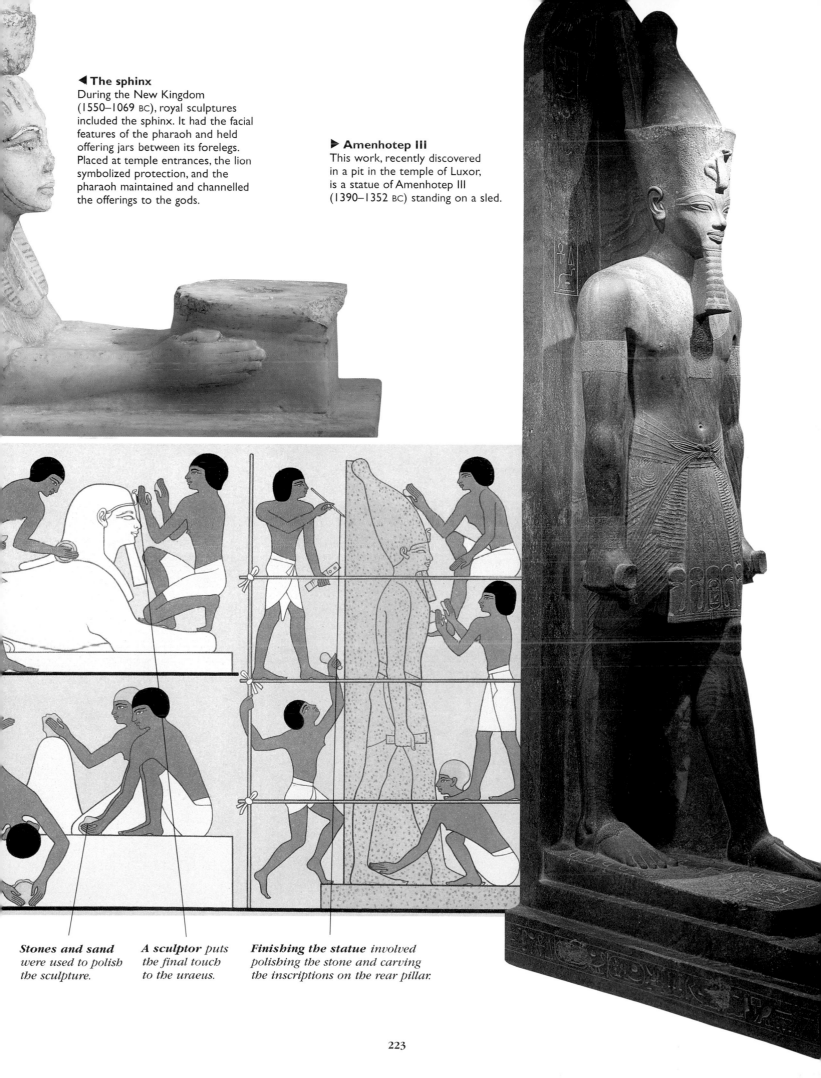

◀ **The sphinx**
During the New Kingdom (1550–1069 BC), royal sculptures included the sphinx. It had the facial features of the pharaoh and held offering jars between its forelegs. Placed at temple entrances, the lion symbolized protection, and the pharaoh maintained and channelled the offerings to the gods.

▶ **Amenhotep III**
This work, recently discovered in a pit in the temple of Luxor, is a statue of Amenhotep III (1390–1352 BC) standing on a sled.

Stones and sand *were used to polish the sculpture.*

A sculptor *puts the final touch to the uraeus.*

Finishing the statue *involved polishing the stone and carving the inscriptions on the rear pillar.*

Coffins and Sarcophagi

Beginning with the Predynastic period (4000–3100 BC), the Egyptians isolated their dead in sand pits by wrapping them in rush matting or animal skins. They subsequently improved these protective coverings and invented coffins and sarcophagi.

The term 'coffin' usually refers to the container in which the Ancient Egyptians placed the mummified body of the deceased, while 'sarcophagus' is generally used to describe the stone container in which one or more coffins were placed. The first coffins, which appeared at the beginning of the Early Dynastic period (3100–2686 BC), were baskets or simple constructions made of wood, clay or terra cotta; they were relatively small and were rectangular or oval in shape.

Emergence of sarcophagi

During the Old Kingdom (2686–2181 BC), the principal material for sarcophagi was stone, although wood was occasionally used. The lids were flat or slightly convex, while the sides were often decorated with a panelling motif known as 'palace façade'. This was modelled on the design of the earliest royal palaces.

▶ Model replica of the afterlife

The basic function of the sarcophagus was to prevent the destruction of the body and to facilitate the rebirth of the deceased. Designed as the final dwelling-place, and furnished with supplies and equipment for future life, the sarcophagus was also a model replica of the afterlife. The texts and illustrations describe the regions of the underworld and the gods that inhabit it, and thus provide a guide for the deceased in his journey to the afterlife.

In the New Kingdom, for example, individuals were thought to be reborn as Osiris; they climbed into the barge of the sun god Ra to navigate through the sky in his company. Like the deceased pharaohs, they identified with the sun, and each morning were reborn on the horizon. On the sarcophagi shown here, passages are engraved from the great royal funerary texts of the New Kingdom – *Litanies of the Sun*, the *Book of Doors* and the *Book of the Secret Dwelling-Place*.

▶ Coffin of Rameses II

To save the remains of their royal ancestors, threatened with total destruction by looters, the kings of the Twenty-First and Twenty-Second dynasties (1070–735 BC) transferred them to different hiding places. They were finally hidden at Deir el-Bahri, and were rediscovered in 1871. Rameses II was found in an unfinished wooden coffin that could well have belonged to his grandfather, Rameses I.

The text on the coffin's exterior describes the wanderings of Rameses the Great's mummy. His remains were carried from the tomb of Sety II to the tomb of Queen Inhapy before being hidden at Deir el-Bahri.

▼ Wedjat eye

The wedjat eyes of the god Horus, the son of Isis and Osiris, were often depicted on coffins. Drawn beside the head of the deceased, they allowed him to communicate with the outside world. Representing the sun and moon, wedjat eyes were considered very powerful protective signs, and were often reproduced as amulets.

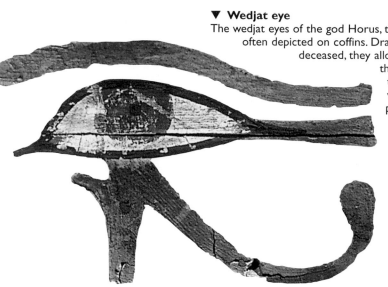

▶ The sarcophagus of Ibu

A provincial governor in the Twelfth Dynasty, Ibu ordered a magnificent limestone sarcophagus with recessed panelling decoration. On the right, the wedjat eyes surmount a false door – the passage taken by the ka, the individual's creative force, as it leaves and returns to the sarcophagus.

Rameses II was buried in a coffin that belonged to Rameses I – after his own tomb had been looted.

The beard, crossed arms and sceptres evoke the god Osiris.

▼ The sarcophagus of Rameses IV

In the New Kingdom, the sarcophagi of the kings became much larger and heavier, a trend typified by the sarcophagus of Rameses IV (1153–1147 BC). This monumental structure is also shown on the plan of the pharaoh's tomb, drawn on a papyrus now housed in the Egyptian Museum in Turin, Italy.

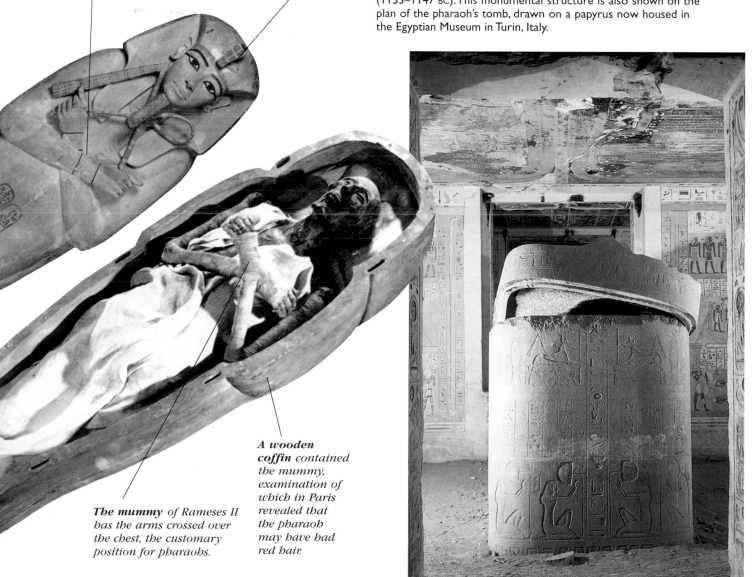

A wooden coffin contained the mummy, examination of which in Paris revealed that the pharaoh may have had red hair.

The mummy of Rameses II has the arms crossed over the chest, the customary position for pharaohs.

Material comforts

The Ancient Egyptians usually made coffins out of wood although, in the New Kingdom, the plaster used for mummy masks was occasionally employed. Most of the coffins were in local woods of mediocre quality, such as sycamore, tamarisk or acacia, but more luxurious examples, intended for royalty and top officials, were made of cedar from Lebanon.

Sculpted, gilded or painted, the coffins were often later placed inside a sarcophagus made of stone, a material synonymous with eternity. Granite, diorite, limestone, quartzite or alabaster were the stones used. The inner coffins of kings were made either of gold (as for Tutankhamun) or silver (the kings of Tanis). The stone sarcophagus shown here, housed in the Egyptian Museum in Turin, Italy, is that of an Ancient Egyptian high official.

Stone sarcophagi now housed the wooden coffin containing the mummy. Coffins were rectangular but were carefully constructed, using large planks of wood joined together.

Painting and decorating

Exterior decoration was enriched with the wedjat eyes of the sky god Horus, depicted on the left side at the end where the head rests. The deceased, lying on his side facing the eyes, could thus 'see' outside the coffin. The eyes also acted as protective amulets. The coffin's inside contained closely written columns of hieroglyphs which reproduced formulae from the *Coffin Texts*, and were intended to help and protect the deceased on his journey to the afterlife. Food offerings were also frequently painted on the inside of coffins – to provide extra sustenance for the deceased in the event of the tomb being disturbed and the funerary paraphernalia, including food, removed.

During the New Kingdom (1550–1069 BC), coffins and sarcophagi underwent a radical development. They now became anthropoid (or mummiform) in shape and were decorated with new images and religious scenes.

An Egyptian funeral parlour

The sculptor Ipuy decorated his own tomb at Deir el-Medina with paintings depicting the manufacture of funerary equipment in a workshop.

A sculptor carves the finishing touches on a coffin.

A woodcutter cuts branches, destined for coffin-making, from a tree.

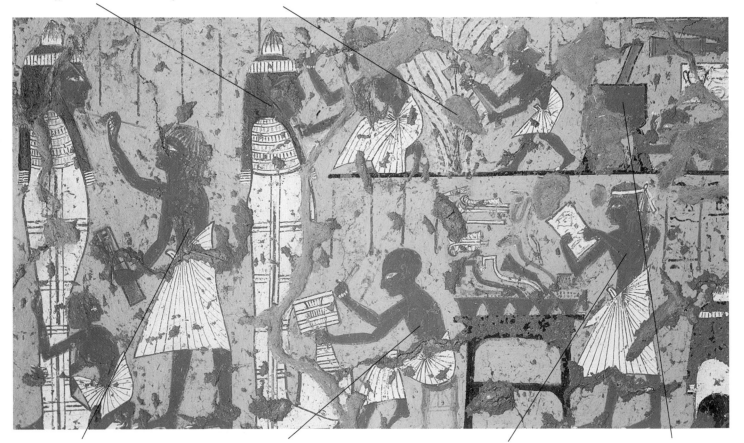

An artist paints a second coffin.

Seated near the table, a sculptor carves a djed pillar for the decoration of the tomb.

An overseer keeps a tally of the materials used in the workshop.

The glue binding the plaster for mummy masks simmers in a cooking pot on the fire.

New developments

Anthropoid coffins and sarcophagi – designed in the shape of the body – first appeared in the Twelfth Dynasty (1985–1795 BC), although they did not really develop until the Second Intermediate period (1650–1550 BC). This new shape gave the sarcophagus the added dimension of a substitute body in the event that the real one was destroyed.

Another development at this time was the rishi coffin, which was characterized by its feathered decoration. The mummified body of the deceased was represented on the lid wearing a heavy wig and enfolded in two large unfurled wings, originally thought to be those of the goddess Isis embracing her husband Osiris, but possibly referring to the ba bird (a manifestation of the physical body).

Although in the same essential style, royal coffins were made of more precious materials – crafted in gilded wood, inlaid with coloured glass and semi-precious stones, or even in silver or gold, such as that of Tutankhamun. These were placed in heavy stone sarcophagi, often in the form of a royal cartouche, and decorated with funerary texts.

In the periods up to Roman times, coffin and sarcophagi styles became even more varied. A few metal sarcophagi were produced, as well as others of highly polished stone, with the entire surface covered in religious scenes. Later, foreign influences from Ptolemaic and Roman art were reflected in Egyptian coffins and sarcophagi.

▲ Sarcophagus of Thutmose III
The quartzite coffin was carved in the form of a cartouche encircling the name of the pharaoh. This type appeared in the time of Queen Hatshepsut (1473–1458 BC), aunt and mother-in-law to Thutmose III (1479–1425 BC). The inside of the sarcophagus lid was hollowed out to leave more room for the coffins to fit inside each other.

▶ Coffin of Intef
The wooden coffin of this prince of the Seventeenth Theban Dynasty is of the rishi type, made throughout the Second Intermediate period (1650–1550 BC). The Arab name refers to the feathers decorating the gilded wooden coffin, and representing the unfurled wings of the goddesses Isis and Nephthys. The gold used for the royal coffins was thought to be impervious to rot – like the flesh of the gods.

▶ Fourth-Dynasty royal sarcophagus
Early stone sarcophagi, such as this example made for a prince of the Fourth Dynasty (2620–2500 BC), were often very simple, undecorated receptacles. The most refined have a 'palace façade' decoration; this geometric design of recessed panelling is said to imitate that of early royal residences.

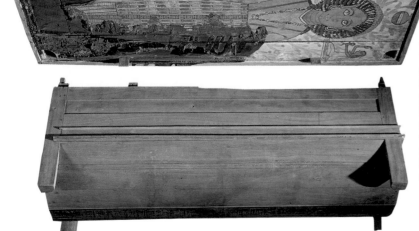

◀ Painted wood coffin
The underside of the lid of this wooden sarcophagus from the Roman period (30 BC–AD 395) depicts the Egyptian sky goddess Nut as an aristocratic imperial woman. Roman artists retained Egyptian motifs, but tended to impose their own artistic styles.

Coffin chapels

Four unique gilded wooden 'chapels' surrounded Tutankhamun's coffins. They had no floor and comprised panels that had been stuccoed and gilded before being assembled actually inside the funerary chamber. The decorations, symbols and texts on the walls told the story of the pharaoh's journey to the afterlife.

On the outer chapel, the protective symbols of Isis and Osiris stood out from a blue background.

Around the second chapel, a wooden frame supported a linen mortuary sheet.

The third chapel was richly decorated with hieroglyphs and illustrations which were taken from funerary texts.

The quartzite sarcophagus containing the pharaoh's coffins was located in the fourth chapel.

Tutankhamun's coffins

The tomb of the Eighteenth-Dynasty pharaoh Tutankhamun (1336–1327 BC) revealed how manificent the funerary paraphernalia of a king could be. Sealed with a granite lid, the rectangular sandstone sarcophagus contained three concentric mummiform coffins.

The cobra and vulture, emblems of the goddesses Nekhbet and Wadjet, and symbols of Lower and Upper Egypt, decorate the king's headdress.

The plaited false beard of Osiris could be worn only by pharaohs and denotes divinity.

Lapis lazuli and semi-precious stones form the outline of the eyes and eyebrows.

Turquoise, cornelian, lapis lazuli, semi-precious stones and coloured glass decorate the coffin's exterior.

Mummy bandages protect the body and conceal the many gold jewels adorning the mummy.

A solid gold mask covered Tutankhamun's head and shoulders.

The shape of the coffin (mummiform) replicates that of the deceased's body. Widest at shoulder level and most narrow towards the feet, it is rounded above the shoulders to form the cavity housing the head.

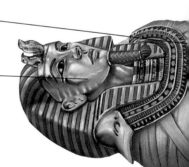

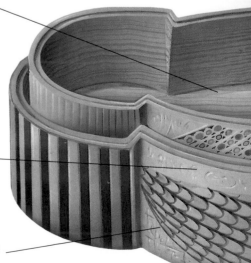

Large planks of wood were assembled with wooden pegs. Up to the Middle Kingdom, joiners used small pieces of wood for economy, but this gradually became less common.

The decoration is sculpted, painted or gilded, and sometimes also enriched with inlaid work.

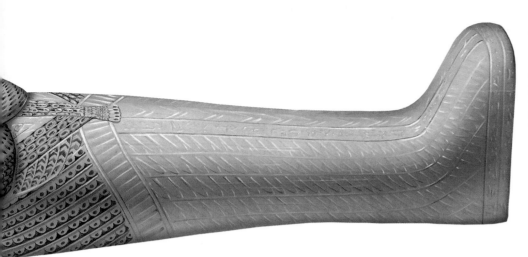

◄ Transformation into Osiris

In order to be reborn in the afterlife and to live for ever, the dead king identifies with Osiris, ruler of the kingdom of the dead. In his coffin, in the shape of a mummy, he takes on the characteristic appearance of the god – the plaited beard, the arms crossed over the chest and the sceptres. The crook and the flail, both royal symbols, recall the time when Osiris ruled the earth.

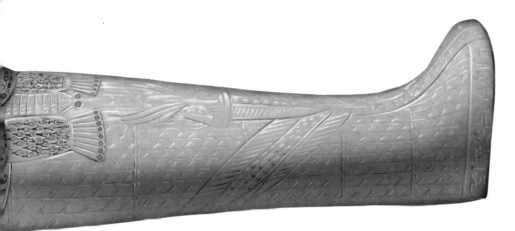

◄ Protecting the mummy

Under the king's arms, the vulture goddess Nekhbet, patroness of Upper Egypt, and the cobra goddess Wadjet, patroness of Lower Egypt, both in the form of birds, keep watch. Below them, the goddesses Isis and Nephtys spread their wings in protection. By moving their wings, they restore the breath of life to the deceased.

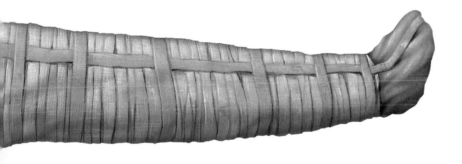

◄ The funerary mask

The Egyptians replicated the features of the deceased on the mummy in a stylized way, so that he could enter the afterlife in the image of Osiris. In the Old Kingdom, the face was simply modelled in linen cloths covering the head, or in plaster applied to the wrappings. The distinctive features of the face, mouth and nose were then painted on to the wrappings. It was in the Middle Kingdom that the masks enveloping the head and shoulders appeared.

◄ Reused coffins and sarcophagi

During the Twenty-First and Twenty-Second dynasties (1069–715 BC), the kings sometimes reused the funerary equipment of their predecessors, if it had not been totally looted or pillaged by grave robbers. They took over stone sarcophagi and wooden coffins by inscribing their names on them, which legitimized their reuse. Moreover, the kings attributed great protective virtues to the funerary equipment of their ancestors.

The Magic of Jewels

The Egyptians wore jewellery from the earliest times. Over the centuries, as the methods of working metals and stones were perfected, so the designs became more complex and sophisticated.

For the pharaoh and his dignitaries, jewellery was an indispensable part of their finery, for the colour of jewels enhanced the delicate white linen garments and heavy curled wigs worn by royal persons and members of the ruling class. Jewellery not only fulfilled a decorative function, however, but also played a magical role both for the living and the dead. Decorative symbols, such as the ankh life sign, the djed pillar of stability, the protecting udjat eye, the scarab of rebirth and images of the gods, dispensed all sorts of benefits to the owner of the object.

Materials and colours were not chosen by chance. They, too, had symbolic significance. Gold, for instance, was a divine metal, regarded as the flesh of Ra and the other gods, while lapis lazuli, which originated in Afghanistan, imitated the appearance of the heavens and was superior to all other metals, apart from gold and silver. The green of turquoise, associated with vegetation, was the emblem of youth and rebirth.

Scarab and goddesses

This detail from Tutankhamun's pectoral, or breastplate (above right), shows a winged scarab framed by the goddesses Nephthys (left) and Isis (right).

Nephthys is recognizable by the symbolic temple and basket worn on her head.

The flesh of Nephthys, a goddess associated with rebirth, is turquoise, the colour of regeneration and eternal life.

A necklace and bracelets on the arms and wrists are among the goddess's adornments.

The cloisonné technique, with inlays of coloured glass carefully cut and fitted, reproduces a net pattern on the dresses of the two goddesses.

▶ Tutankhamun's pectoral
A winged scarab sits in the centre of a shrine of which the roof has been replaced by the solar disc and the wings of the falcon Horus. Elaborately arranged uraeus serpents, with sun discs in their coils, decorate the upper corners (detailed, left).

The winged scarab, or dung beetle, framed by the goddesses Isis and Nephthys, represents the young king, who is reborn every morning like the sun, carried by the wings of Horus, god of the sky. The piece is made of gold, cornelian and coloured glass.

Pectorals first appeared in the Twelfth Dynasty and often hung from a chain or necklace. Shaped like a trapezium or a rectangle, the pectoral was usually in the form of a shrine containing decorative designs.

The Egyptians compared *the birth of the dung beetle, which emerges from a ball, with the sun, symbol of life, rising over the horizon.*

The seat, or throne, is a symbol of the goddess Isis, wife of Osiris and sister of Nephthys.

Gold, a divine metal that never tarnishes, symbolizes eternity.

The goddess Isis, like her sister Nephthys, wears a necklace made up of two rows of red and blue beads.

◀ The scarab and the weighing of the heart ceremony
The scarab, carved from a hard green stone, is engraved on the back with a formula from Chapter 6 of the *Book of the Dead*. This text asks the heart not to betray the deceased during the weighing of the heart, or judgement, held in the court of Osiris.

Ceramics

Although individual pots tend to be fragile, broken pieces of ceramic survive for millennia, providing a vital archaeological resource.

Clay vessels are of special interest to archaeologists, providing them with basic information about the ancient sites that they are excavating. A particular shape of vessel, for example, can identify a building as a grain store or a temple. Evolving design styles and manufacturing methods mean that pieces of broken pot – potsherds – can accurately date the graves or dwellings where they are found. Local and national variations in clay and design mean that they can also give us insights into patterns of national and international trade.

▶ Firing and colour
Pots made of Nile clay are naturally reddish-brown when they are fired in the presence of air, as in a kiln. Robbing the clay of oxygen as it bakes gives the pot a black finish.

▶ Handmade
Ceramics were hand-raised before the potter's wheel was introduced in the Fifth Dynasty (2494–2345 BC). Funerary models continued to be handmade, and the ancient technique of building up large vessels using coils of rolled clay was still used.

▼ Storage vessels
Stone vessels were used for temple or funerary offerings, but earthenware was employed almost exclusively for everyday purposes. These army recruits are receiving their allocation of provisions in the form of jars of beer and basket-shaped vessels piled high with food.

Ceramic shapes were more varied in the New Kingdom, influenced by vessels brought from overseas. This tall jar is typical of the Eighteenth Dynasty (1550–1295 BC).

◀ **The materials**
These pots represent two types of clay used in ceramics by the Ancient Egyptians. The one on the far left is made from the alluvial clay found all along the Nile Valley. This is a dark, blackish-brown clay that dries to a grey-brown. Firing gives it its distinctive reddish-brown hue. Although this clay produced pots with a rather coarse finish, it was by far the most popular material, with almost all everyday items being made of it. The other pot is fashioned from limestone-rich marl (clay with stone in it) that was found in just a few places in Upper Egypt, particularly around Qena. The raw marl is light grey in colour, but changes to yellow-green or pink on firing, depending on the temperature. The silica content in the clay gave the wares a polished finish.

▼ **Faience and glazed soapstone**
Before they began to make complete objects in faience, such as this glazed hippo, the Egyptians carved models in steatite, or soapstone, then covered them with a paste of powdered quartz, limestone and copper oxide. When heated, it formed a thin green or blue decorative coating.

Amphora supports, which were necessary if the round-bottomed pots were to stand upright, sometimes took the form of a ring set into a wooden trestle base.

Ceramic vessels were used mainly for serving, storing and transporting drinks and foodstuffs.

233

Egyptian potters produced mainly vessels – small tableware such as cups and goblets, as well as larger storage jars and amphoras. The hand-turned potter's wheel arrived in the Fifth Dynasty (2494–2345 BC), but came into its own only when the assisted wheel was introduced in the Second Intermediate period (1650–1550 BC). An assistant powering and stabilizing the wheel meant that the potter could use both hands, and faster rotation brought centrifugal force into play in shaping the pots. As a result, pots in the New Kingdom (1550–1069 BC) became slimmer and more elegant, with better formed rims. This time was also the high point of pot decoration. Although the Ancient Egyptians did not use glazes in the modern sense, by the end of the Eighteenth Dynasty they were decorating their pots with geometric or figurative designs applied in paint or slip or incised into the clay.

Making pots

Tomb decorations show how Egyptian potters worked. Cleaned clay was watered and kneaded with the feet to the right consistency. Chopped straw made it more solid and less sticky. Modelled pieces were set aside to dry. When they were 'leather-hard', the potter would decorate them, perhaps smoothing the surface with a pebble, or cutting in a pattern and filling it with a slip of clay in a contrasting colour. Pots were finished by firing – at first in an open fire, but later in kilns at a temperature of 500°–600°C (932°–1112°F).

▼ **Canopic jars**
Potters and makers of stone vessels had certain common items in their repertoires. Canopic jars, made for the storage of the viscera of the dead, were usually stone – such as these in painted limestone – but were sometimes also made in earthenware. The lids, shaped to represent either the head of the deceased or one of the Four Sons of Horus, were always made of the same material as the jars.

▼ **Clay transport**
Tombs from the end of the Predynastic [eriod (c. 3100 BC) contain a great deal of pottery. Along with the customary storage vessels, containing supplies for the afterlife, are pottery figures and models such as this ship, intended to carry the deceased as he accompanies the sun god on his daily journey. In later times, models such as these were more likely to be carved from wood.

◀ **Bold colours**
In the New Kingdom (1550–1069 BC), potters decorated their wares with geometric patterns, or exuberant depictions of plants and flowers, all painted in vivid colours. Vessels recovered from tombs, such as this two-handled jar, or amphora, find their exact match in the scenes of feasting and offerings that were common in tomb paintings of the time.

▼ **Modelled decoration**
The New Kingdom saw a great flowering of decorated pottery. By the end of the period, multicoloured floral or figurative decorations adorned the upper areas of most vessels, while large amphorae often had models such as this antelope's head attached for purely decorative reasons.

▲ **Double containers**
This ingenious and well-proportioned double vase is a product of the inventive potters of the New Kingdom, but makes use of a design from the Predynastic period and subsequently found in every period of Ancient Egyptian history.

◀ **Rounded bases**
Many Egyptian containers had a rounded or pointed base – easier for potters to achieve than a flat one – and were designed to be hung from a beam in a house and transported in nets. Sometimes they were placed in a support made of palm leaves, clay or wood.

INSIGHT

Predynastic pots

In the early nineteenth century, the English archaeologist Flinders Petrie developed a typology for pre- and early historical Egyptian pottery, categorizing finds by date and location. With few exceptions, Petrie's classification is still in use today.

Ceramics from Egypt's Predynastic period (5500–3100 BC) impress most of all through their high quality and richness of design. They are grouped into different styles, according to their culture of origin. The oldest cultures of Upper Egypt were named after finds of ceramics at Tasa and Badari, dating from 5500–4000 BC. Of particular interest are the tulip-shaped containers found at the cemetery at Tasa, with engraved geometric designs. These are similar to finds from Nubia. The mainly thin-walled pots of the Badarian culture

▼ This dark red, tulip-shaped container is decorated with a geometric pattern cut in the clay before firing. It is typical of the Tasa culture, named for the site of an important archaeological find of ceramics. Similar pots were also found further south, in Nubia.

▼ ▼ The red-brown colour, with black lip and inner surface, of this cup is typical of the Badarian culture. They made their pots from very light, sanded clay and fired them at very high temperatures. The black colour was achieved by taking the hot pot directly from the fire and plunging it into ashes.

have a highly polished surface; most vessels are dark red with a black upper band, indicating they were placed upside down in ashes after they were fired. Their smooth, shiny surface was probably obtained by polishing the moulded pot with fine pebbles, or strips of leather, before the clay was completely dry.

The later Naqada culture was also named after an archeological site where a significant find of ceramics was made. This culture can be divided into two phases. Pots of the Naqada I period (4000–3500 BC) have a dark red, polished surface with white decorations, in which, for the first time, people and animals occasionally appear. Naqada II pottery (3500–3100 BC) typically has light pink or yellow pots with figurative or geometric decorations in dark brown. Dark red pots with a black upper band also appear in this period.

◄ The dark red, polished surface, decorated with patterns in a pale slip, is typical of the Naqada I, or Amratian, period (4000–3500 BC).

▼ This full-bodied container, made from a pale-coloured clay decorated in dark red, is from the Naqada II, or Gerzean, period (3500–3100 BC). It has handles and is painted with guinea fowl around a large, flowering plant.

◀ Egyptian faience

Egyptian faience is named for its resemblance to mediaeval Italian, blue-and-white, tin-glazed earthenware. The name is misleading, however, as Egyptian faience is not a true ceramic. It was produced by firing a mixture of pulverized quartz, or quartz sand, with a little lime and natron (a natural carbonate of sodium), water and sometimes gum arabic. The addition of metal salts gave it a colourful, glassy finish, and the Ancient Egyptians called it *tjehenet*, literally bright or dazzling. Its main use was in making jewels, as well as ornaments and small vessels.

▲ Creating colour 'glazes'

Egyptian faience took its colour from the copper oxide added to the basic mix before the piece was modelled. In the heat of the kiln, the copper oxide and alkali salts from the natron migrate to the surface to form the blue-green coating. Other 'glazes' were created in the New Kingdom by substituting different metals for copper. Lead and antimony gave yellow, and cobalt a rich, deep blue.

INSIGHT

Nubian ceramics

In Nubia, north of modern-day Khartoum, pottery of a very high quality was being produced by the late sixth millennium BC. These early pots were decorated with engraved patterns of undulating lines and geometric shapes marked out in dots.

The similarity of Nubian forms to Egyptian ones suggests a good deal of contact with the so-called 'A group' of Nubian culture (3700–2800 BC). Red and brown pots with black upper rims, similar to those of the Egyptian Badarian period, were popular. Egyptian pots of this time possessed rounded bottoms or small, flat standing areas, but the Nubian pots mostly had a pointed base. The Nubian C group culture (2300–1550 BC), produced vessels with flatter bases (above); the design is created by using a contrasting colour to fill in a pattern cut into a polished finish.

The finest Ancient Nubian pottery came from the kingdom of Kerma (c. 2500–1500 BC). Its tulip-shaped vases, their black rims separated from the red lower body by a brilliant grey band, reveal the potters' mastery in their very thin walls and polished finish.

Pots from later periods showed increasing influence from Egypt, Greece and Rome. Vessels of the Meroitic period (300 BC–AD 350), for example, often have painted decoration in a decidedly Mediterranean style, as in the freely expressed floral border on the bowl below.

Funerary Masks

Since the early mummification process was not a reliable one, the Ancient Egyptians covered the face of the deceased with a funerary mask that symbolically preserved the person's features.

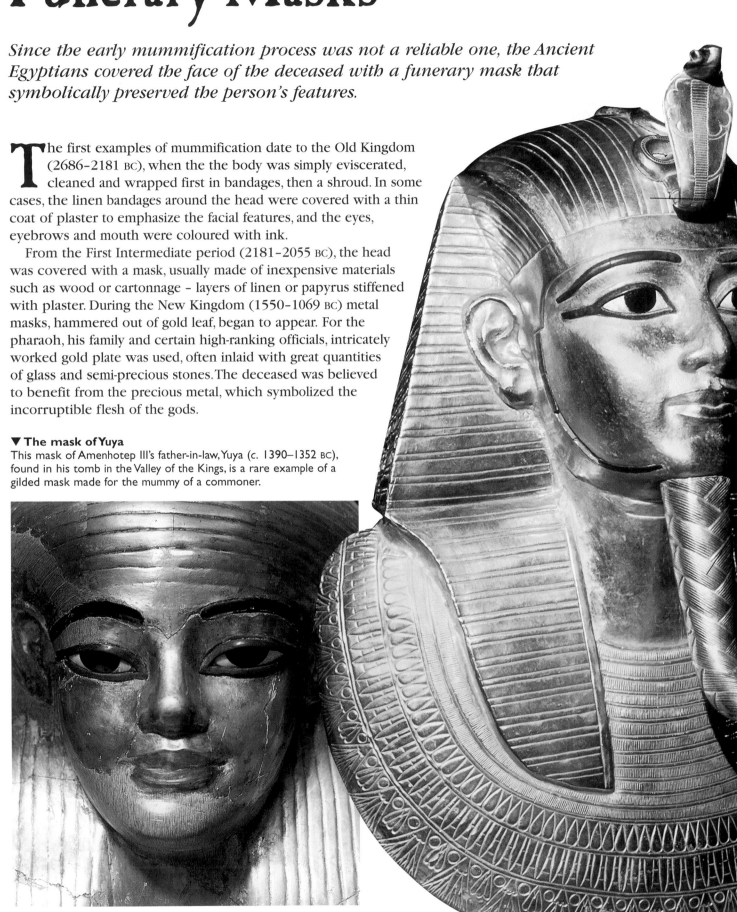

The first examples of mummification date to the Old Kingdom (2686–2181 BC), when the the body was simply eviscerated, cleaned and wrapped first in bandages, then a shroud. In some cases, the linen bandages around the head were covered with a thin coat of plaster to emphasize the facial features, and the eyes, eyebrows and mouth were coloured with ink.

From the First Intermediate period (2181–2055 BC), the head was covered with a mask, usually made of inexpensive materials such as wood or cartonnage – layers of linen or papyrus stiffened with plaster. During the New Kingdom (1550–1069 BC) metal masks, hammered out of gold leaf, began to appear. For the pharaoh, his family and certain high-ranking officials, intricately worked gold plate was used, often inlaid with great quantities of glass and semi-precious stones. The deceased was believed to benefit from the precious metal, which symbolized the incorruptible flesh of the gods.

▼ The mask of Yuya
This mask of Amenhotep III's father-in-law, Yuya (c. 1390–1352 BC), found in his tomb in the Valley of the Kings, is a rare example of a gilded mask made for the mummy of a commoner.

◀ **Psusennes I**

The funerary masks of the pharaohs were usually made from pure gold, such as this one of Psusennes I (1039–991 BC), or at least of wood covered with gold leaf. There are other characteristics: the head was covered with the nemes, the royal headcloth, and the face sported a long, rolled beard. The uraeus, the most important symbol of royalty, was set on the forehead. The masks were supported on a wide, bejewelled shoulder collar.

Psusennes I's mask is made from heavy gold, representing the 'flesh of the gods'.

The eyelids and eyebrows are coloured blue; a reference to the hair of the gods, which is usually represented by lapis lazuli.

The plaited beard, slightly turned up at the end, is symbolic of the divinity of the dead king.

◀ **Mask from the Fayum**

After a break of some 200 years, many masks were made in the Ptolemaic period (332–30 BC). Although they shared the same kinds of features as the earlier masks, their styling was very different. Particularly striking are the luminous colours of the winged sunrays over the brow, the uraeus and the striped design of the headcloth.

▼ **Egyptian and Greco-Roman elements**

This funerary mask is made from gilded stucco on cartonnage. While the sides of the wig show traditional Ancient Egyptian motifs, the pink garland over the forehead is a Roman innovation.

DOCUMENT

The gold mask of Tutankhamun

The funerary mask of Tutankhamun (1336–1327 BC), the child king from the Eighteenth Dynasty, was discovered in 1922 by Howard Carter. It is made from pure gold and inlaid with coloured glass and semi-precious stones. Apart from the nemes and the curved beard, the mask shows the uraeus and the vulture's head, symbolizing both halves of a unified Egypt, above its forehead. The royal robes have a broad shoulder collar inlaid with lapis lazuli, quartz, green feldspar, obsidian and glass. Whether or not the idealized features resemble those of the boy king is not known. The mask is on display at the Egyptian Museum in Cairo.

◀ The Middle Kingdom
The oldest plaster or cartonnage masks with multicoloured decorations come from the First Intermediate period, but they were common in the Middle Kingdom as well. This mask belonged to an Egyptian commander in Nubia. As in later times, the mummy masks from the Middle Kingdom had an extended breastplate, on which a broad pearl-encrusted collar was pictured.

The eyes are inlaid with white quartz and black obsidian; the eyelids and eyebrows are edged with blue glass.

▼ The Second Intermediate period
This mask from the Second Intermediate period (1650–1550 BC) shows the essential elements used in mummy masks until the Roman period – the striped headcloth and the broad shoulder collar with a row of red, blue and green pearls.

The first true mummy masks completely covered the head and upper part of the chest, and, although rare in the First Intermediate period, they were popular in the Middle Kingdom. Only the face, framed by a long wig, and the neck, adorned with a wide pearl necklace, were represented, while the rest was painted yellow or white.

At the end of the Middle Kingdom, bulkier masks appeared. Dainty faces formed a contrast to long, heavy wigs. Beneath the necklace, a column of text indicated the name of the deceased.

Changing styles

In the New Kingdom, masks were smaller and covered just the head and throat and occasionally the chest. Faces were less stylized, but they still possessed a long wig and a necklace of strings of pearls. In the Third Intermediate period (1069–747 BC) and the Late period (747–332 BC) funerary masks became increasingly small, until they covered only the head and neck.

By the Greco-Roman period (332 BC–AD 395), although Egyptian funerary customs remained popular, the overall shape and decoration of the mask had changed. The faces and headdresses had Egyptian gods painted on the sides, and the faces became more lifelike, forming actual portraits of the deceased.

Gold leaf covered the cartonnage to create the illusion of solid gold.

▶ **King Amenemope**
Found in a chamber originally occupied by the mummy of Mutnedjmet, one of Psusennes I's queens, at Tanis, the funerary equipment of the 21st-Dynasty king, Amenemope (993–984 BC), included a golden face mask and copies of his hands.

▼ **Ptolemaic mask**
In the Ptolemaic period (332–30 BC), traditional Egyptian design elements were mixed with Greek styles. The often gilded masks from this time show most of the traditional motifs.

▼ **Roman times**
Even after the Ptolemaic period, traditional elements such as the broad pearl collar remained, while some details, such as the golden earrings, were added.

The shoulder collar of Tuyu consists of several pearls, some of which are worked in the shape of flowers, inlaid with coloured glass.

▲ **The mask of Tuyu**
Tuyu was the mother of Tiy, the principal bride of Amenhotep III (1390–1352 BC). Together with her husband Yuya, she was buried – unusually for commoners – in the Valley of the Kings. The contents of the grave were discovered in 1905 and are now in the Egyptian Museum in Cairo.

Furniture for the Afterlife

Owing to the dry climate, many items from Ancient Egyptian tombs have survived, including wooden furniture and other objects made from transient materials.

The tomb sites of settlement areas were not usually found to contain much furniture because the Ancient Egyptians generally reused their old furniture. Even so, most of our knowledge about the shape, use and construction of furniture, from the simplest to the most luxurious, is based on examples from tombs, or from tomb pictures showing daily life.

Wood – a precious material

Wood, particularly fine timber, was rare in Egypt and had to be imported from neighbouring countries. Especially prized was precious Lebanese cedar, which had to be transported by ship from Byblos. From tropical Africa, including the ancient land of Punt, came ebony, which was used for furniture and veneering.

▲ Symbolic decorations
Furniture found in tombs was often adorned with symbolic decorations, most of which related to permanence, regeneration and power. The ever newly born sun god was closely associated with the lion, seen here forming the graceful legs of this stool.

▶ Everyday furniture
This chair gives an example of the different materials and techniques used to construct furniture. The frame, back and legs are made from wood. The seat is woven from halfa grass or some other plant fibre.

◀ Relief from the tomb of Horemheb
This depiction of Horemheb (1323–1295 BC) comes from his first tomb in Memphis and shows the Eighteenth-Dynasty pharaoh sitting on an elegant chair. The slender legs, shaped like those of a predatory cat, are typical of this kind of upholstered chair favoured by the aristocracy, as are the struts.

▲ Headrests
A wooden headrest such as this one, combined with a pillow to make it more comfortable, was an essential item in the sleeping arrangements of most ordinary Ancient Egyptians.

▲ Bed from Tutankhamun's tomb
This comfortable wooden bed with its vertically panelled headrest, from the tomb of Tutankhamun (1336–1327 BC), has been overshadowed by more spectacular finds from the grave. The bed's surface is made from plant fibres woven in a pattern.

▼ An elegant stand
This wooden stand features a pot, in which a glass of water, beer or wine could be placed. Its surface has been painted with pretty motifs.

Ornate baskets were woven from reed, halfa grass and other plant fibres.

This small, painted wooden box was especially made for use in the tomb.

Smaller objects, as well as food items, were stored in baskets.

▲ Decorations
There were many ways to decorate a chair – different woods were used, or the chair might be inlaid or painted, with delicately woven seats.

By the time of the First Dynasty (3100–2890 BC), many fragments of pieces of furniture were placed in graves – mostly bed and table legs shaped like animals – a style that would persist until the end of the pharaonic times.

Among the usual domestic furnishings would be various boxes, chests and baskets, which were used to store clothes, jewellery and cosmetics. The value of these objects varied according to the material used in their construction and their decoration. Most simpler households had some sort of basic furnishing, although this did not usually include chairs.

Seats for the rich and powerful

For high officials and dignitaries, furniture was a means of demonstrating their status to visitors and servants. Above all, luxuriously decorated chairs were the highest objects of desire. This is illustrated by the Egyptian term *shepes*, meaning 'noble', as it is written with the hieroglyph of a man sitting on a chair.

▼ Upholstered lion bed
This picture is part of the *Monumenti Civili*, a collection of coloured illustrations made by the Italian Ippolito Rosellini in 1829. This magnificent bed was part of the wall decorations in the tomb of Rameses III (1184–1153 BC).

▲ Animal imagery in furniture
Animal-shaped furniture was a symbol of power and regeneration for the Ancient Egyptians. This mural relief depicts three women seated on a long, lion-shaped bed.

▼ Rear of Tutankhamun's throne
The golden throne of the young king was decorated with a variety of symbols, which were made from gold leaf and multicoloured inlays. Most of the contents of the tomb were equally richly decorated.

The fan-shaped lotus thicket, from which two ducks are flying up, symbolized fertility.

The four uraeus with the sun disc on their heads are symbols of royal power.

The cartouches on the back of the throne give the former name of the king, Tutankhaten.

The bodies of the uraeus are decorated with inlays of different colours.

▼ Tutankhamun's throne

Not only is the throne one of the most beautiful and famous pieces of the tomb's contents, but it also shows many interesting historical details: on the armrests and the back are examples of the earlier name of the king, Tutankhaten. This contains a reference to the Aten, who was all-important in the preceding Amarna period (1352–1336 BC).

The armrests consist of winged uraeus wearing the double crown of Upper and Lower Egypt.

The depiction of the Aten is in keeping with the style of the preceding Amarna period.

▲ Tutankhamun's ceremonial seat

The throne-like chair, with its additional back, is similar to a folding chair in shape. Its priming of gold leaf is covered with tiny, coloured inlays of ivory, ebony, faience and different semi-precious stones.

▲ Cosmetic chest of the child king

The decoration on Tutankhamun's chest of drawers consists almost exclusively of hieroglyphs. The two large middle panels express ten times the wish 'all life and well-being' (to the pharaoh).

The four legs of the chair end in lions' paws; two lions' heads decorate the front corners of the seat.

The decoration, most of which has now broken off, shows the 'unification of the two countries'.

Rahotep and Nofret

Masterpieces of art under the Old Kingdom, the remarkably preserved statues of Rahotep and Nofret are among the finest and most lifelike works in the Egyptian Museum in Cairo.

S on of the pharaoh Sneferu (2613–2589 BC) and brother of Khufu (Cheops), Rahotep was a high priest of Ra at Heliopolis. His wife bore the simple title 'known by the king', which suggests that she was a lady-in-waiting. Their mastaba tomb at Meidum was discovered by the Egyptologist Auguste Mariette in 1871. Today, these remarkably well-preserved statues of painted limestone – with the colours still wonderfully bright and fresh – are major showpieces in the Egyptian Museum in Cairo. They are among the finest pieces of art from the early 4th Dynasty (2620–2500 BC).

The intact statues are so realistic that the workman who actually discovered them was terrified. He believed that he was in the presence of two living beings, who fixed their gaze on him in such a way that he felt, for a moment, rooted to the spot in their chamber.

INSIGHT

The Meidum necropolis

To the north of the pyramid of Sneferu at Meidum lie a number of painted tombs from the Fourth Dynasty (2620–2500 BC). One of the most famous is the mastaba tomb of Rahotep and Nofret (below), in which their painted statues were found. A door relief from it is shown (right). Another tomb in the same cemetery contained the celebrated depiction of the Geese of Meidum.

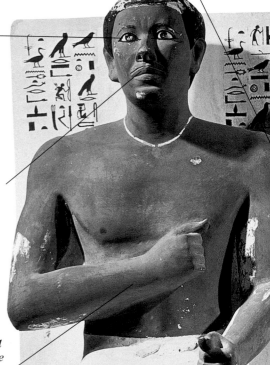

Men's skin was traditionally painted in red ochre.

The eyes, in rock crystal and white quartz, give the statue a lifelike appearance.

Rahotep's full mouth is highlighted by a black-painted moustache.

The right hand folded across the chest indicates Rahotep's noble status. The clenched fist represents male strength and dynamism.

◀ **Nofret, a prince's wife?**
Nofret's sculpture is carved from a single block of limestone. The seat, with its backrest, is therefore an integral part of the piece. The statue of Nofret, 122cm (48in) high, is slightly taller than Rahotep's. She wears a heavy, shoulder-length wig, which is held in place by a headband decorated with floral motifs. Her own hair is flattened on her forehead. Nofret's rounded face is particularly attractive, with delicate features, full lips and large eyes. Around her neck is a throat-piece of alternating colours, ending in a row of pendants. Her white linen garments are close-fitting and reveal the form of her body.

◀ **Rahotep, the pharaoh's son**
With his short hair and fine moustache, Rahotep is a handsome man whose fine-featured face has been carved with great realism. He wears a short, white loincloth and, around his neck, a thin chain and pendant. Like Nofret, he is shown in the rather rigid pose with fixed gaze that was the conventional style of representation. The artist, however, has managed to imbue these statues with remarkable lifelike qualities. This is so that the deceased, who are represented in death by these effigies, can return to their bodies in the afterlife.

Building the Pyramids

At the beginning of the Old Kingdom around 2686 BC, the Egyptians invented a new form of royal tomb – the pyramid – and for more than 1,000 years kings were buried inside these imposing structures.

The first pyramid was built at Saqqara by the pharaoh Djoser (2667–2648 BC) and his architect Imhotep. It was also the first construction to be built in stone, rather than mud-brick. Djoser's pyramid seems initially to have taken the form of a mastaba, a rectangular tomb used for royal burials in the Early Dynastic period (3100–2686 BC). However, it was gradually modified and extended to become a pyramid-shaped structure consisting of six massive steps reaching a height of 60m (200ft). The steps represented the ladder, mentioned in the *Pyramid Texts* (funerary writings to help the deceased king attain eternal life), on which the king could climb to the sky. After unsuccessful attempts by two subsequent pharaohs to replicate the step pyramid, the pharaoh Sneferu (2613–2589 BC) abandoned this type of monument and built the first pyramid with sloping sides.

Planning ahead

Sneferu chose the site with care. It had to face west in accordance with the setting sun, be close to quarries for raw materials and have a rock foundation capable of supporting a massive quantity of stone. In addition, it needed to be out of reach of the Nile's annual flood. Work could commence only after the architect had completed his plan and calculated the amount of materials and men necessary for the construction. The ground also had to be levelled before astronomers fixed precisely the orientation of the pyramid's sides in relation to the cardinal points.

A funerary complex

The pyramid was just one part of a king's funerary complex. There was also a mortuary temple, where various rituals took place, and a causeway leading to the valley temple, where the pharaoh's body was received after its last journey along the Nile.

▼ The funeral procession
The deceased pharaoh's body was transported to the mortuary temple in a sacred boat made of wood. This was a scale model of an actual boat, and it was carried on poles by a slow-moving line of priests.

▶ Valley temple
Situated close to the port, the valley temple marked the entrance to the funerary complex. In one of the best preserved, the granite-built valley temple of Khafra (2558–2532 BC), there are two entrances which were probably protected by two pairs of sphinx separated by an obelisk. Inside, a vestibule led into a large, T-shaped room supported by pillars. Along the walls were statues of the pharaoh.
    According to some Egyptologists, the king's mummification may have taken place in the valley temple, or in a specially erected structure nearby.

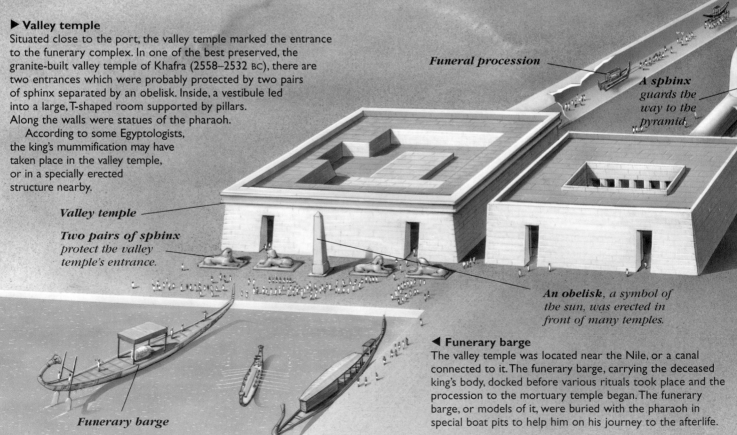

Funeral procession

A sphinx guards the way to the pyramid.

Valley temple

Two pairs of sphinx protect the valley temple's entrance.

An obelisk, a symbol of the sun, was erected in front of many temples.

◀ Funerary barge
The valley temple was located near the Nile, or a canal connected to it. The funerary barge, carrying the deceased king's body, docked before various rituals took place and the procession to the mortuary temple began. The funerary barge, or models of it, were buried with the pharaoh in special boat pits to help him on his journey to the afterlife.

Funerary barge

▶ Burial chamber

The pharaoh's sarcophagus was placed in a burial chamber inside the pyramid, which was sealed, along with the entrance to the monument, with great blocks of granite to deter grave robbers. The king's journey to the afterlife now began as his soul mounted the stairway to the sky to join the sun god Ra.

▶ Sloping causeway

The covered causeway connecting the valley temple to the mortuary temple was situated to the east of the pyramid. It is not certain if the king's funeral procession took this route to the pyramid, as was once believed, as the pathway and staging posts within do not seem large enough to accommodate the royal coffin or a large-scale procession of priest and mourners.

Mortuary temple

Sloping causeway

A surrounding wall encloses the sphinx.

▲ Mortuary temple

Located on the east side of the pyramid, the mortuary temple was where various funerary rites associated with the cult of the dead king took place before burial.

The temple consisted of an entrance hall, followed by a colonnaded court, which gave access to an area containing five niches or shrines for statues of the king. There were also storage chambers and a sanctuary where the priests made offerings to the dead pharaoh.

▶ Obelisks

Generally gigantic, four-sided blocks of stone, obelisks tapered at the top and were surmounted by a pyramidion. They are associated with the cult of the sun god Ra and Ancient Egyptian ideas about the creation of the universe, and represent the 'primeval hill', or place over which the sun first shone. The first obelisks were constructed in the Old Kingdom sun temples, dedicated to Ra, during the Fifth Dynasty (2494–2345 BC).

◀ The pyramidion

The finished pyramid was topped with a distinctive capstone carved from one block of stone. Like the pyramid itself, it is associated with the sun god Ra.

▲ The sphinx

With the body of a lion and head of a king, the Great Sphinx at Giza guarded the way to the pyramid of Khafra (2558–2532 BC).

The construction of the pyramids

Sloping sided pyramids formed part of the royal funerary monuments from the Third Dynasty (2686–2613 BC) to the Second Intermediate period (1650–1550 BC).

After the site had been chosen and aligned, surveyors took over and, with the aid of thick ropes, marked the plan of the pyramid on the ground. The king then officiated at the inaugural ceremony, after which construction work began, as stone-cutters started to extract local medium-quality stone for the core of the pyramid.

Opposite, on the east bank of the Nile, fine-quality limestone from the Tura quarries was mined for the pyramid's exterior. From Aswan, 900 km (560 miles) away in the south of the country, came the hard granite used for sarcophagi, as barriers in interior passages and for the pyramidion, the small pyramid-shaped stone placed at the top of a pyramid or obelisk. This was transported to the site by boat.

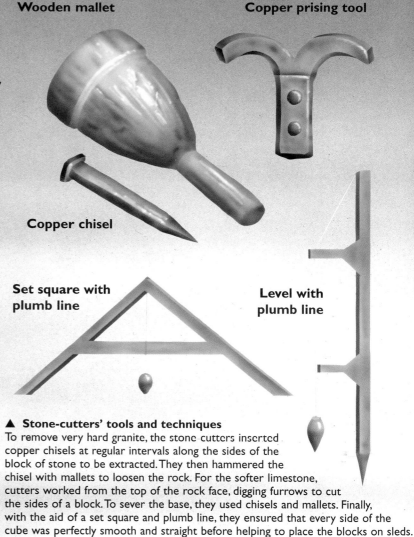

Wooden mallet

Copper prising tool

Copper chisel

Set square with plumb line

Level with plumb line

▲ Stone-cutters' tools and techniques

To remove very hard granite, the stone cutters inserted copper chisels at regular intervals along the sides of the block of stone to be extracted. They then hammered the chisel with mallets to loosen the rock. For the softer limestone, cutters worked from the top of the rock face, digging furrows to cut the sides of a block. To sever the base, they used chisels and mallets. Finally, with the aid of a set square and plumb line, they ensured that every side of the cube was perfectly smooth and straight before helping to place the blocks on sleds.

Thick ropes bound the stone block to the sled to avoid accidents.

Workmen squared off the surface of the blocks.

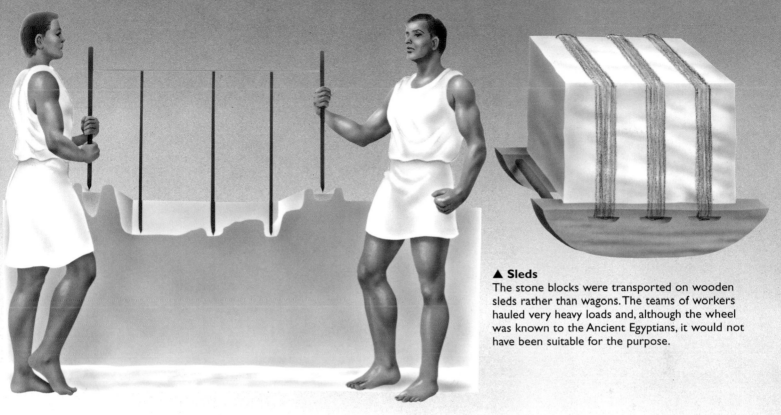

▲ Sleds
The stone blocks were transported on wooden sleds rather than wagons. The teams of workers hauled very heavy loads and, although the wheel was known to the Ancient Egyptians, it would not have been suitable for the purpose.

▲ Levelling the ground
Some Egyptologists believe that the site was levelled by the digging of a grid of narrow channels across the area and filling them with water. The intervening stone 'islands' could then be levelled off. Other specialists suggest that stakes of a known length, connected by a rope, were planted in the ground to measure the level of the land.

Teams of labourers, not pack animals, pulled the enormous blocks of stone.

The workforce did not contain slaves, but was drawn from the entire population below the status of scribe, including farm labourers.

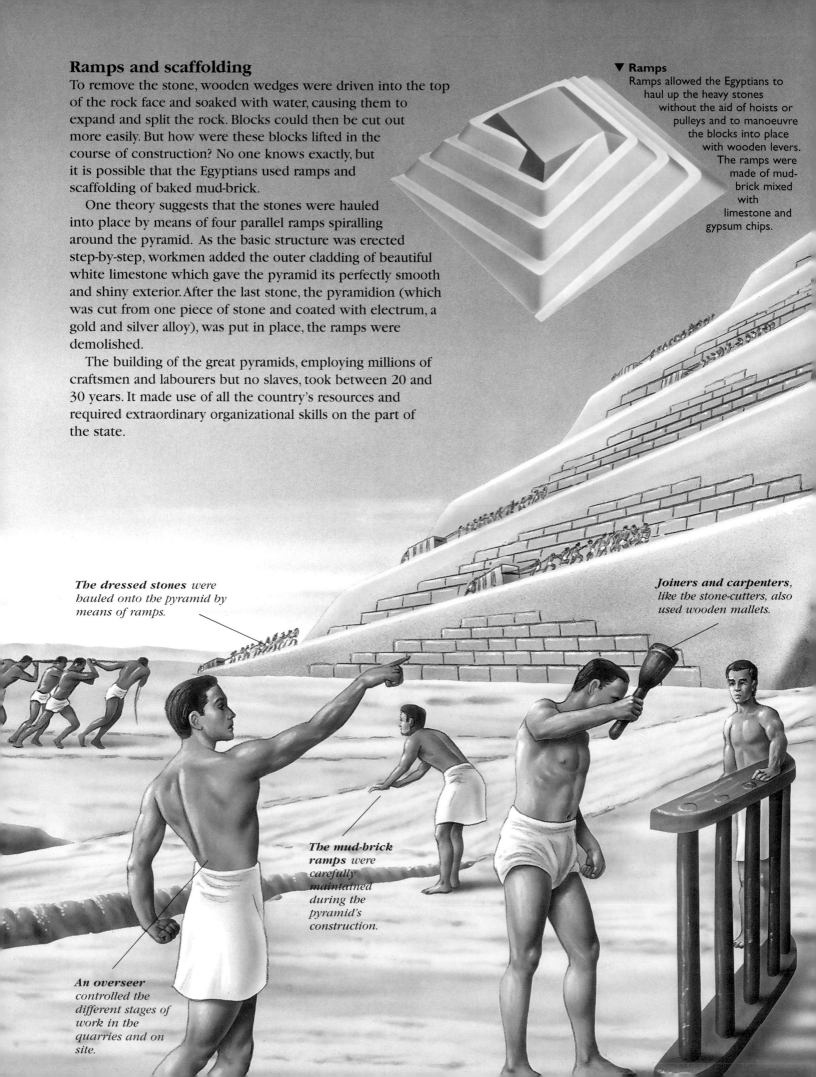

Ramps and scaffolding

To remove the stone, wooden wedges were driven into the top of the rock face and soaked with water, causing them to expand and split the rock. Blocks could then be cut out more easily. But how were these blocks lifted in the course of construction? No one knows exactly, but it is possible that the Egyptians used ramps and scaffolding of baked mud-brick.

One theory suggests that the stones were hauled into place by means of four parallel ramps spiralling around the pyramid. As the basic structure was erected step-by-step, workmen added the outer cladding of beautiful white limestone which gave the pyramid its perfectly smooth and shiny exterior. After the last stone, the pyramidion (which was cut from one piece of stone and coated with electrum, a gold and silver alloy), was put in place, the ramps were demolished.

The building of the great pyramids, employing millions of craftsmen and labourers but no slaves, took between 20 and 30 years. It made use of all the country's resources and required extraordinary organizational skills on the part of the state.

▼ **Ramps**
Ramps allowed the Egyptians to haul up the heavy stones without the aid of hoists or pulleys and to manoeuvre the blocks into place with wooden levers. The ramps were made of mud-brick mixed with limestone and gypsum chips.

The dressed stones were hauled onto the pyramid by means of ramps.

Joiners and carpenters, like the stone-cutters, also used wooden mallets.

The mud-brick ramps were carefully maintained during the pyramid's construction.

An overseer controlled the different stages of work in the quarries and on site.

Mortar was not used to join the stones, which were 'dry-set'.

The architect surveyed the work and constructions of the different craftsmen.

Water was regularly used to lubricate the ramps, making hauling the sleds easier.

Joiners were responsible for the upkeep of the wooden tools and implements, including the sleds which carried the stone.

The Sphinx

With the body of a lion and the head of a human, the sphinx is one of the most characteristic images of Ancient Egypt. But while the Egyptian sphinx was highly revered and benevolent, the Greek sphinx was frightening and cruel.

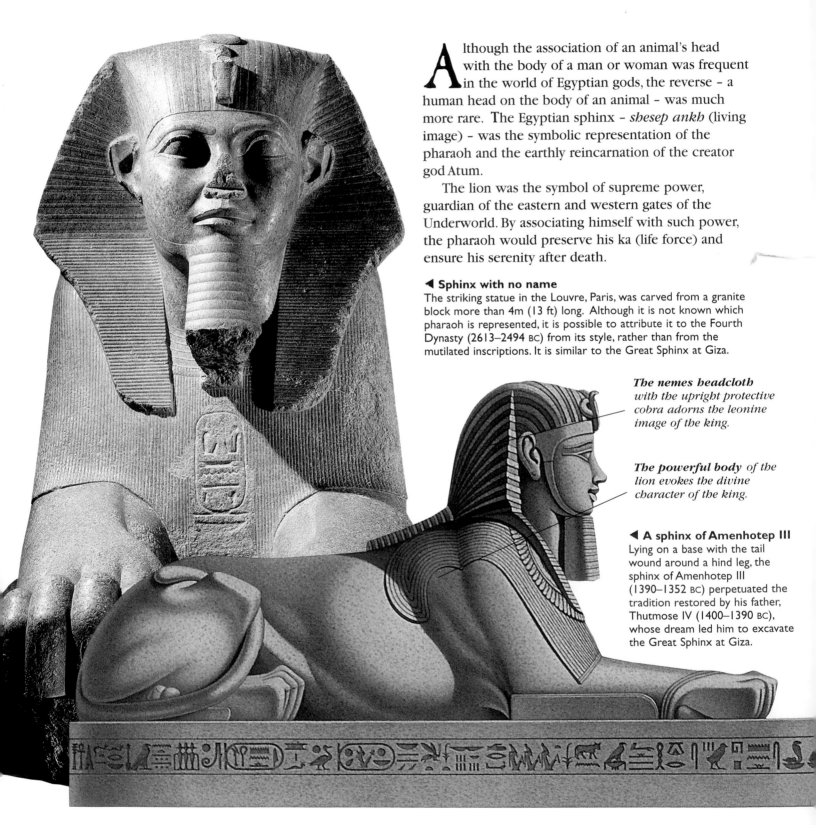

Although the association of an animal's head with the body of a man or woman was frequent in the world of Egyptian gods, the reverse – a human head on the body of an animal – was much more rare. The Egyptian sphinx – *shesep ankh* (living image) – was the symbolic representation of the pharaoh and the earthly reincarnation of the creator god Atum.

The lion was the symbol of supreme power, guardian of the eastern and western gates of the Underworld. By associating himself with such power, the pharaoh would preserve his ka (life force) and ensure his serenity after death.

◀ **Sphinx with no name**
The striking statue in the Louvre, Paris, was carved from a granite block more than 4m (13 ft) long. Although it is not known which pharaoh is represented, it is possible to attribute it to the Fourth Dynasty (2613–2494 BC) from its style, rather than from the mutilated inscriptions. It is similar to the Great Sphinx at Giza.

The nemes headcloth with the upright protective cobra adorns the leonine image of the king.

The powerful body of the lion evokes the divine character of the king.

◀ **A sphinx of Amenhotep III**
Lying on a base with the tail wound around a hind leg, the sphinx of Amenhotep III (1390–1352 BC) perpetuated the tradition restored by his father, Thutmose IV (1400–1390 BC), whose dream led him to excavate the Great Sphinx at Giza.

▲ The sphinx at Luxor
The pylon of the Luxor temple is approached through ceremonial avenues (dromos) flanked by human-headed sphinxes which carry cartouches of Nectanebo I (380–362 BC) of the Thirtieth Dynasty.

▲ Variations on the theme
While the body of the revered lion remained inviolate, not all sphinxes conformed to the Giza model. As well as having the head of a hawk, falcon or other fanciful creature, they could be winged or portrayed standing, lying or sitting.

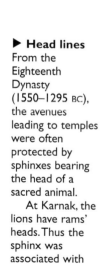

► Head lines
From the Eighteenth Dynasty (1550–1295 BC), the avenues leading to temples were often protected by sphinxes bearing the head of a sacred animal.

At Karnak, the lions have rams' heads. Thus the sphinx was associated with the temple deity, Amun, who was often depicted with a ram's head.

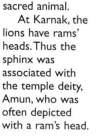

▲ Criosphinx
The name criosphinx is given to a lion with a ram's head. At Karnak, each is fronted by a full-length statue of the pharaoh. The main task of these sphinxes was to hold back the forces of evil.

The Great Sphinx

Together with the Great Pyramid at Giza, which it guards, the enigmatic and solemn sphinx of Khafra (2558–2532 BC) is the most familiar and dramatic statuary symbol of Ancient Egypt.

INSIGHT

The human-headed beast

The sandstone head of King Djedefra (2566–2558 BC), illustrated below, was originally attached to the first known sphinx in Egyptian art. Discovered in the pharaoh's funerary complex at Abu Roash, 8km (5 miles) north of Giza, this is among the most important ancient works in the Louvre Museum in Paris. The priests of Heliopolis were the very first to add a human head to the body of the lion – the incarnation of courage – creating a sphinx to watch over the city. The Greeks gave the name sphinx to the benu bird, the grey heron sacred to Heliopolis, which perched on a sacred stone and ushered in the sunrise. It was this tradition that influenced Khafra to build his monumental statue at Giza. The sphinx, however, was forgotten and abandoned until around 1500 BC, during the New Kingdom, when it was revived as a religious symbol and eventually elevated to the rank of a god. Under the name Horemakhet – to the Greeks, Harmakhis – and translated as Horus in the Horizon, the sphinx became one of the forms of the great sun god, Ra. It had its own sanctuaries where it was worshipped, and its own priests to conduct the holy rites.

The Great Sphinx at Giza watches over the largest necropolis in Ancient Egypt. Measuring 73m (239 ft) long, 14m (46 ft) wide and 20m (66 ft) high, it was carved around 4,500 years ago from a knoll of limestone beside Khafra's causeway.

It has been buried and reclaimed many times since it was created, most famously by Thutmose IV after his prophetic dream. But as early as the Eighteenth Dynasty (1550-1295 BC) the Great Sphinx was in need of repair with limestone cladding. The most recent sand clearance came in 1925, but the monument is under attack from rising water tables, erosion and pollution. Some restoration projects have ended in disaster, causing more damage. However, the Great Sphinx has now been designated a World Heritage Site, protected by UNESCO.

▶ **Buried treasure**

When Ludwig Meyer drew the Great Sphinx during his visit to Egypt in 1804, only the head emerged from the sand. Located below the Plateau of Giza, the statue has never stopped fighting the power of the wind-borne desert sand. At one time painted in bright colours, the head has since lost its nose, uraeus and divine beard.

▼ **View from above**

This aerial photograph gives some impression of the scale of the largest sphinx ever built in Egypt. On the left is the rising road connecting the temple in the valley with the funerary temple attached to the pyramid of Khafra.

ART

▶ **The dream of Thutmose IV**
The New Kingdom pharaoh Thutmose IV (1400–1390 BC) had a stele constructed between the front legs of the Great Sphinx. This tells the legend of how, after falling asleep near the sphinx's head, he dreamed that the Great Sphinx appeared and offered him the kingship if he excavated it from the sand. When he became pharaoh, he kept his promise.

The limestone body of the sphinx has been greatly damaged by wind and water erosion. The face was carved from far stronger rock strata.

Erected by Thutmose IV, the stele recounts how the statue was recovered by the pharaoh after an amazing dream.

The sphinx's front feet, or more accurately its colossal lion's paws, were first restored in the Roman period.

The missing nose has been attributed to barrages by cannonballs and vandalism by religious fanatics.

▶ **Monumental problems**
Cleared from the sand that protected it for so long, the Great Sphinx was again subject to lethal wind erosion. Since 1926, several restorations have been carried out to preserve this statue – the only one of its kind in the world – with the latest completed in 1998.

INSIGHT

The sphinx outside Egypt

In Greek mythology, the sphinx was a hybrid female with the body of a lioness and a human head, sent to wreak revenge on Thebes by Hera, wife of Zeus. At the entrance to the city, the sphinx would pose young men a riddle: 'What walks on four feet in the morning, two at midday and three in the evening?' When Oedipus gave the correct answer (Man – crawling as baby, walking upright as an adult, using a stick as an old man), he drove the sphinx to suicide and thus freed the city from her evil influence.

The Egyptian sphinx was used in Phoenician ivory work, which was greatly influenced by Egyptian art. This ivory sphinx, wearing Egyptian crowns, was discovered in the Assyrian city of Nimrod.

The sphinx continued in Egyptian art until the Greco-Roman period (AD 332–395) (below).

The Statue of Ka-aper

One of the masterpieces of Old Kingdom private sculpture, the life-size standing figure of chief lector priest Ka-aper is remarkable for its astonishing realism, and is among the most frequently viewed objects in the Egyptian Museum in Cairo.

This statue was discovered by Auguste Mariette during excavations in Saqqara in 1860. Local workmen named it 'Sheikh el-Beled', Arabic for 'headman of the village', because of its subject's striking similarity to the chief of their village.

The figure, which bears no inscription, is carved from the wood of the sycomore fig tree, which had a strong symbolic meaning in Egypt: the sycomore was associated with the goddess Hathor and the netherworld.

The sculpture was found in the mastaba tomb of the chief lector priest Ka-aper. Next to it were two further wooden statues – one of Ka-aper's wife, the other of the priest as a young man.

Remarkable realism

The body and head of the figure are made from a single piece of wood, to which the arms, carved separately, were attached. The pose is unusual in Egyptian statuary, in that the legs show a walking movement rather than a rigid stance. This, along with the priest's expressive face and striking eyes, makes the statue remarkably lifelike.

The original cane and sceptre held in his hands were missing, and the cane the priest now holds is a modern reproduction. The legs have also been partly restored. Ka-aper's plump, rounded body is wrapped in a knee-length loincloth, knotted at the waist with a large flap.

The statue is one of the most highly regarded works of the Old Kingdom and perfectly captures the physical and psychological characteristics of the dignified, wealthy man that Ka-aper was.

▶ **Ka-aper, a lector priest of the Old Kingdom**
Measuring 112cm (44 inches) in height, this statue, now in the Egyptian Museum, Cairo, is one of the finest works of art from the Old Kingdom (2686–2181 BC). It is an image of a high-ranking official and chief lector priest – he recited the words of the gods in temple rituals – of the late Fourth or early Fifth Dynasty. It was found in his tomb in north Saqqara near the pyramid complex of the Fifth Dynasty pharaoh Userkaf (2494–2487 BC).

◀ Ka-aper's wife
Two other wooden sculptures were found in the priest's mastaba tomb. This one, also exhibited in the Egyptian Museum in Cairo, is thought to be of Ka-aper's wife. Only the upper part has been preserved, and the fragment, 61cm high, shows her wearing a wig – a sign of nobility – and a sheath dress; originally, an ornate collar was painted onto the statue. Like her husband, she seems to smile softly.

▼ Lively eyes and expressive face
Ka-aper's remarkable, lifelike image is expressed by his striking eyes and lively look. The wooden statue was once covered with a thin, painted covering of gesso, which hid the joins between the torso and the arms as well as irregularities in the wood. The flesh was coloured in the traditional ochre-red and the eyes were outlined in copper, to imitate the lines of eye paint, and inlaid with rock crystal. Physical imperfections were not hidden; indeed, corpulence was a sign of wealth Ka-aper's wide jaw is softened by plump flesh and a double chin.

▼ Ka-aper's profile
From the side, Ka-aper's receding hairline can be seen. The hair itself was painted black on the layer of gesso that once covered the statue. The receding hairline and jowls below the cheeks suggest a man of middle age, and show that the artist sought a realistic, rather than idealized, portrait of his subject.

Seneb and his Family

The group sculpture of the dwarf Seneb, a dignitary of the late Fourth or early Fifth Dynasty, and his family is one of the most unusual and striking pieces of statuary from the Old Kingdom. Discovered in the 1920s by the Austrian archaeologist Hermann Junker, it is now part of the collection in the Egyptian Museum in Cairo.

The remarkable group statue of Seneb and his family, discovered in Seneb's mastaba tomb at Giza, serves as an illustration of both the fine quality of art during the Old Kingdom (2686-2181 BC) and of the high status it was possible for dwarfs to achieve in Ancient Egyptian society. Seneb had several important official positions, being the overseer of the palace dwarfs, chief of the royal wardrobe and priest of the funerary cults of Khufu (2589-2566 BC) - the builder of the Great Pyramid - and his successor Djedefra (2566-2558 BC).

A family group

Seneb has been realistically portrayed, with short limbs and a disproportionately large head. His children, who occupy the space that in other statues would be taken up by Seneb's legs, have their fingers to their mouths and the son wears the sidelock of youth. Senetites embraces her husband affectionately, with one arm around his shoulder and the other hand resting on his left arm. Seneb has his legs crossed in the scribal position, a pose befitting a man of his status.

Seneb sits with his legs crossed in the traditional pose of a scribe.

▶ **The family group**
This painted limestone statue from the tomb of Seneb in the Giza necropolis is regarded as one of the masterpieces of Old Kingdom art. Despite Seneb's diminutive stature, a harmonious composition has been skilfully achieved by the sculptor. The married couple are portrayed in a touchingly affectionate pose, while their children, who occupy the space beneath Seneb's crossed legs, are shown with the traditional attributes of childhood.

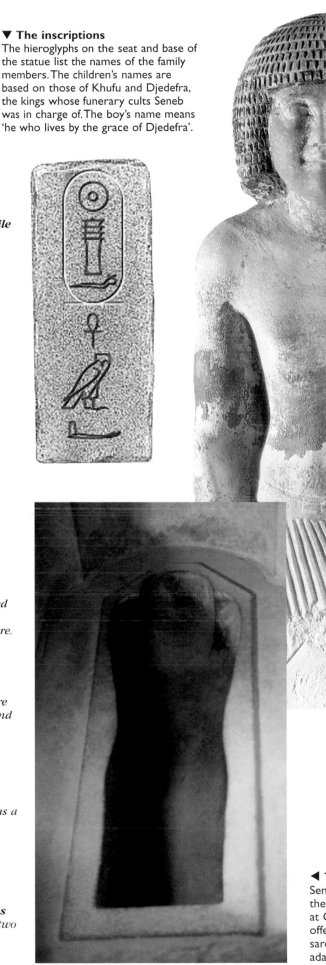

▼ The inscriptions
The hieroglyphs on the seat and base of the statue list the names of the family members. The children's names are based on those of Khufu and Djedefra, the kings whose funerary cults Seneb was in charge of. The boy's name means 'he who lives by the grace of Djedefra'.

A gentle, affectionate smile is shown on the face of Seneb's wife.

A sleek black wig sits on Senetites's head, beneath which her real hair is just visible.

Senetites has one arm around her husband's shoulder, while her other hand rests on his left arm.

Both children are naked, with their forefingers placed to their mouths in a traditionally childish gesture.

The male members of the family are painted an ochre colour, while the mother and daughter are much paler.

The sidelock of youth was a typical sign of childhood.

Hieroglyphic inscriptions give the names of Seneb's two children.

▲ Raherka and Meresankh
This sculpture, which also dates from the Old Kingdom and is executed in painted limestone, shows a married couple in an affectionate pose similar to that of Seneb and his wife. Like Senetites, Meresankh is depicted warmly embracing her husband. The statue now forms part of the collection of Egyptian antiquities in the Louvre Museum in Paris.

◄ The sarcophagus of Seneb
Seneb's tomb was found among the mastabas to the west of the pyramid of Khufu (2589–2566 BC) at Giza. Inside, Junker discovered a variety of offerings, a decorated false-door stele, and Seneb's sarcophagus, pictured right, which had been adapted to fit his unusual measurements.

The Temples of Deir el-Bahri

The natural rock bay in the western Theban hills at Deir el-Bahri was chosen by Mentuhotep II as the site for his mortuary temple and tomb. Now in ruins, the structure is overshadowed by the magnificent, well-preserved temple of Queen Hatshepsut.

The western hills of Thebes were the sacred location of the goddess Hathor, and the rocky amphitheatre at Deir el-Bahri is the site of the mortuary temples of Mentuhotep II (2055–2004 BC), Queen Hatshepsut (1473–1458 BC) and Thutmose III (1479–1425 BC), as well as a number of private tombs.

The architects succeeded in creating monuments that incorporated the sacred hills into their overall designs, so that landscape and building became one structure. Hatshepsut's temple is the best preserved, with its three colonnaded terraces imitating the architecture of Mentuhotep II's new design style, which represented a transition from the funerary monuments and pyramids of the Old Kingdom (2686–2181 BC) to the mortuary temples and separate tombs of the New Kingdom (1550–1069 BC).

Although the other two temples lie in ruins, they have yielded enough archaeological information to allow accurate reconstructions of how they looked in the past.

▶▶ **The first builder**
Mentuhotep II (2055–2004 BC), the unifier of Upper and Lower Egypt and founder of the Middle Kingdom (2055–1650 BC), moved the capital to Thebes and had his mortuary temple built on its western side. The site of the temple at the foot of the hills was considered the sacred area of the goddess Hathor, and the design of the temple integrated its structure into the surrounding landscape.

▶ **The female ruler**
More than 500 years after the death of Mentuhotep II, Hatshepsut (1473–1458 BC) had her mortuary temple erected next to his. It was of a similar design to the earlier temple, but larger and with an extra terrace. Her monuments at Deir el-Bahri often show her in kingly robes and wearing the royal beard to emphasize her position as pharaoh.

▼ Aerial view
The mortuary temple of Hatshepsut dominates the bay of rock at Deir el-Bahri. The modern access road follows the line of the processional route from the queen's valley temple on the edge of the fertile strip of the Nile Valley. Behind the site are the eastern and western branches of the Valley of the Kings.

The ruins of Mentuhotep II's temple lie to the south of the partly reconstructed temple of Hatshepsut.

Hatshepsut's temple is the best preserved of the three temples and is one of the finest monuments in Egypt.

▲▼ The last builder
Little remains of the sanctuary that Thutmose III (below) built between and behind the temples of Mentuhotep II and Hatshepsut (above). In his later years as a ruler, Thutmose III had the name of Hatshepsut removed from the queen's buildings and statues, in an attempt to obliterate the memory of her reign.

The temple of Mentuhotep II

The mortuary temple of Mentuhotep II, with its novel courtyard and terrace design, was the first to be built at Deir el-Bahri. An unusual feature is that it was both a tomb and a temple. The large, tree-lined lower courtyard has a rock-cut shaft leading to unfinished rooms, which were intended as the burial place of the pharaoh. It was not used to bury Mentuhotep II, however, but served as a cenotaph that contained a seated statue of the king.

A ramp led to the upper terrace which was colonnaded on three sides. In the middle was a square building, the roof of which was probably shaped like a mastaba tomb. The complex contained six chapels and tombs for Mentuhotep's wives and family. Behind the upper terrace was a columned courtyard, where a vaulted tunnel led to the king's tomb and an inner sanctuary, hewn into the rock, which was dedicated to the king's cult.

THE TEMPLE SITE OF DEIR EL-BAHRI

▲ **The mortuary temple of Mentuhotep II**
Mentuhotep chose the site of the temple so that it merged into the surrounding hills, with the tomb courtyard leading to an inner sanctuary cut into the solid rock. This contained a statue of the king set in a niche in the rock face.

▶ **Reconstruction of Mentuhotep II's temple**
One of the problems of the reconstruction of the temple of Mentuhotep was establishing the form of the roof on the central building. Originally, it was believed to be a pyramid (as here), but researchers now think that it resembled a mastaba tomb of the Old Kingdom and represented the 'mound of creation'.

The temple of Hatshepsut

The mortuary temple of Hatshepsut was built next to that of Mentuhotep II. Senenmut, the architect and also tutor to Hatshepsut's daughter, took the older temple as an example, but enlarged it by one terrace and added other elements of older temple sites. From the valley temple on the Nile, a sphinx-lined avenue led to the mortuary temple. Behind the outer wall stood the first terrace, decorated with sycomore figs, palm trees and artificial ponds.

From there, a ramp led to a further terrace, with a columned hall. Beside it were the chapels of Hathor and Anubis. On the walls there were painted reliefs depicting Hatshepsut's achievements, including an expedition to Punt, the transport of two obelisks from Aswan to Karnak and the 'godly' birth of Hatshepsut herself.

▼ Reconstruction of Hatshepsut's temple
From the edge of the fertile land in the Nile Valley, an avenue of sphinxes once led to the gate of the temple complex. Although today the site is barren desert, originally it boasted lush gardens planted with sycomore figs and palm trees. Ponds on the lower terrace added to the serenity of the surroundings.

▼ The queen's architect
The construction of the mortuary temple of Hatshepsut was planned and executed by Senenmut, the queen's architect and confidant. He took the temple of Mentuhotep II as a basis for his design, but left out the mastaba and the tomb pit, and constructed a further terrace.

◄ Birth of a goddess
As the widow of the pharaoh Thutmose II, Hatshepsut had to legitimize her claim to the throne. To reinforce her position, she commissioned a depiction of her birth as the daughter of Ahmose and the god Amun.

PROFILE

THUTMOSE III

To the west and above the temple of his step-mother, Hatshepsut, Thutmose III (1479–1425 bc) had a mortuary temple built for himself. It stands on partly walled ground, 20m (66 ft) above the level of the valley, and could only be reached by a ramp. The temple's colonnaded façade fronted a columned hall decorated with reliefs, which led to the inner sanctuary and further halls. This relief in the Anubis chapel of the temple of Hatshepsut shows Thutmose III worshipping Horus.

The shrine dedicated to Hathor has columns crowned with the goddess's image.

The ochre-coloured rocks of the Theban hills tower above the temple site.

The ruined temple of Thutmose III lies between the temples of Mentuhotep II and Hatshepsut.

Mentuhotep II of the Eleventh Dynasty built the first of the three temples.

The shrine of Anubis is set in the northern wing of the temple of Hatshepsut.

The access road to the temple was originally planted with sycomore fig trees.

▲ **The Osiris columns**
Some of the large columns of the temple of Hatshepsut are adorned with impressive sculptures of the queen embodied as Osiris.

INSIGHT

The shrine of Hathor

During the Middle Kingdom (2055–1650 BC), the cow goddess Hathor was worshipped as the 'goddess of the western mountains' who received the sun each evening and protected it until dawn. In Egyptian funerary beliefs, the dead hoped to be in the 'following of Hathor' and so gain her protection in the afterlife.

Both Hatshepsut and Thutmose III dedicated a small chapel to the worship of Hathor in their temples at Deir el-Bahri. At the southern end of the second colonnade in the temple of Hatshepsut, there is a fully preserved chapel. The vestibule is lined with 'Hathor capitals' (right), which show the goddess with cow's ears and a sistrum – the ritual rattle that was shaken during her cult worship – on her head.

Thebes, 'City of 100 Gates'

It was the Greek poet Homer (ninth or eighth century BC) who described Thebes as the 'city of 100 gates', in reference to the grandiose pylons that marked the entrances to the many temples and palaces built on both banks of the Nile.

The temple of Karnak *was once linked to the temple of Luxor by an avenue 3km (almost 2 miles) long, lined with criosphinxes - statues of rams with the bodies of lions.*

On the west bank, *beyond the cultivated land, was the Theban necropolis, with its cemeteries and funerary temples.*

The criosphinxes *between Karnak and Luxor have disappeared, apart from a few outside the southern gate of Karnak. The avenue in front of the temple of Luxor is lined with regular sphinxes.*

The Abu el-Haggag Mosque *was built in the thirteenth century AD over the temple of Luxor, which is partially buried.*

◄ Ancient Waset
To the Ancient Egyptians, the town of Thebes was known as Waset, symbolized by the was sceptre adorned with a streamer and feather. It is written with the hieroglyph uas, symbol of power, the t sign for the feminine and the determiner for the city. It was also called niut, signifying the 'city' in the same way that Rome was designated simply by the word Urbs. It owes its name of Thebes to the Ancient Greeks.

▼ Thebes today
In only a few decades, tourism has transformed the small, sleepy town of Luxor into a rapidly expanding conurbation. Along its banks are dozens of boats which make cruises between the city and Aswan.

Thebes, once the capital of Ancient Egypt, has been built over by the present-day city of Luxor, the name of which derives from the Arabic 'el-Qusur', which describes the forts set up close to the temple at Luxor in Roman times.

A small, obscure town during the Old Kingdom (2686–2181 BC), Thebes was promoted to Egypt's capital after its princes had restored the unity of the country and founded the Eleventh Dynasty (2055–1985 BC). History repeated itself at the start of the New Kingdom (1550–1069 BC), when the Hyksos invaders were expelled and the country was unified under Ahmose.

During the New Kingdom, a succession of pharaohs enlarged and embellished the temple at Karnak, which was dedicated to Amun, Mut and Khons, as well as Montu, the local warrior god and protector of the city. The Luxor temple, situated a short distance to the south of Karnak, was founded by Amenhotep III (1390–1352 BC).

The Valley of the Kings on the west bank became the final resting place of the New Kingdom pharaohs, beginning with Thutmose I (1504–1492), and a long row of mortuary temples and royal palaces was built between the Theban hills and the River Nile.

The temple of Luxor has a majestic colonnade running parallel to the Nile.

East and west banks at Thebes

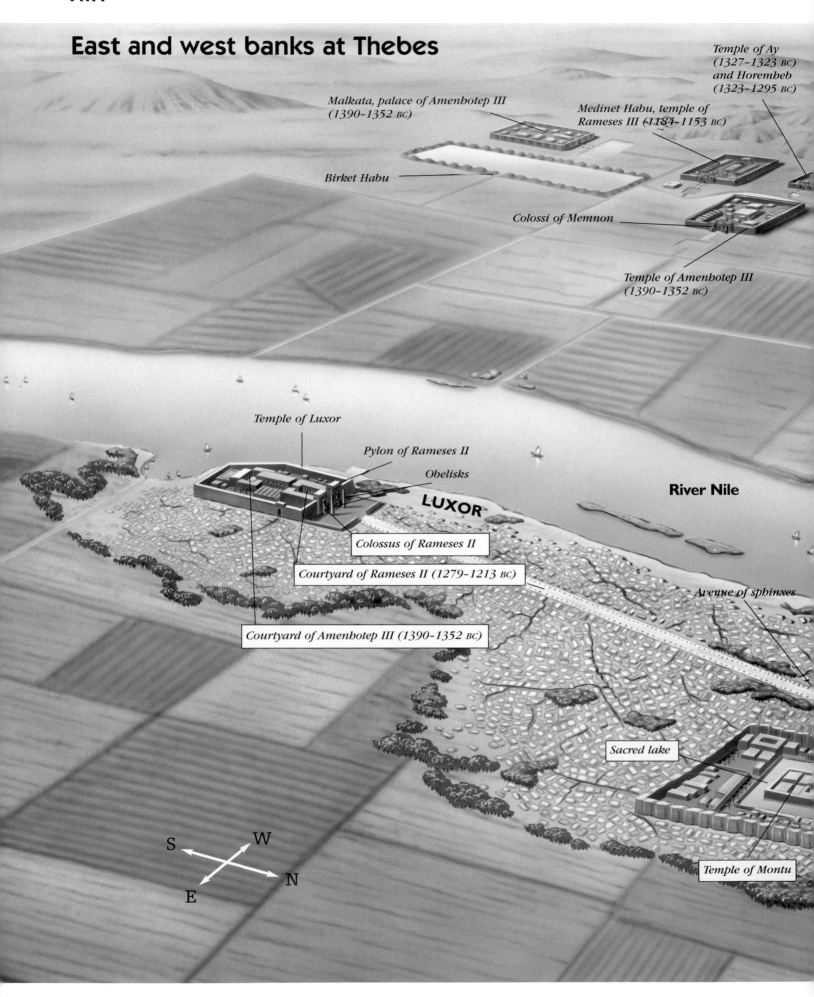

*Temple of Ay
(1327–1323 BC)
and Horemheb
(1323–1295 BC)*

*Malkata, palace of Amenhotep III
(1390–1352 BC)*

*Medinet Habu, temple of
Rameses III (1184–1153 BC)*

Birket Habu

Colossi of Memnon

*Temple of Amenhotep III
(1390–1352 BC)*

Temple of Luxor

Pylon of Rameses II

Obelisks

River Nile

LUXOR

Colossus of Rameses II

Courtyard of Rameses II (1279–1213 BC)

Avenue of sphinxes

Courtyard of Amenhotep III (1390–1352 BC)

Sacred lake

Temple of Montu

S W
E N

272

VALLEY OF THE QUEENS

Temple of Thutmose II (1492–1479 BC)

Theban summit

VALLEY OF THE KINGS

Deir el-Medina: workmen's village

Ramesseum, the funerary temple of Rameses II (1279–1213 BC)

Temple of Mentuhotep II (2055–2004 BC)

Temple of Thutmose III (1479–1425 BC) at Deir el-Bahri

Temple of Thutmose I (1504–1492 BC)

Temple of Merenptah (1213–1203 BC)

Temple of Saptah (1194–1188 BC)

Temple of Thutmose III (1479–1425 BC)

Temple of Hatshepsut (1473–1458 BC) at Deir el-Bahri

Temple of Tausret (1188–1186 BC)

Temple of Thutmose IV (1400–1390 BC)

Necropolis of Asasif

Temple of Amenhotep, son of Hapu (1430–1350 BC)

Avenue of sphinxes

Landing stage

Avenue of criosphinxes

First pylon of Nectanebo I (380–362 BC)

KARNAK

Temple of Amun at Karnak

Temple of Khons

Sacred lake

Temple of Mut

Second pylon

Third pylon

Temple of Amun

Western Thebes

For the Ancient Egyptians, the world of the dead was located to the west, where the sun disappeared in the evening before travelling through the underworld during the night. The Theban necropolis contained several cemeteries and funerary temples. The Valley of the Kings, first used by Thutmose I, houses the tombs of the pharaohs from the Eighteenth to the Twentieth dynasties.

Closer to the Nile, the Valley of the Queens contains the rock-cut graves of princes and royal wives, while the burial sites of nobles and high officials are concealed in the Theban hills facing the Nile river. The craftsmen who built and decorated the royal tombs lived at Deir el-Medina and had their own cemetery inside the village. Some monuments, such as the funerary complex of the pharaoh Mentuhotep II (2055–2004 BC) under the cliffs of Deir el-Bahri, date back to the Middle Kingdom (2055–1650 BC), when Thebes first became the capital of the country. The later funerary temples of Hatshepsut, Sety I, Rameses II and Rameses III are the best preserved on the west bank.

▲ **Medinet Habu**
The funerary temple of Rameses III (1184–1153 BC), stands at the southern end of the west bank, opposite modern Luxor.

▼ **The terraced temple of Hatshepsut**
Hatshepsut (1473–1458 BC) built her funerary temple on three levels under the cliffs of Deir el-Bahri, beside the earlier funerary complex of Mentuhotep II (2055–2004 BC).

▶ **A narrow strip of land**
The cultivable area on the west bank of the Nile at Thebes was flooded in ancient times by the annual inundation. It was bordered by the Theban hills, which contain hundreds of tombs.

▼ **The Colossi of Memnon**
These giant statues of Amenhotep III (1390–1352 BC) are the only remains of his funerary temple that began falling into ruin during the New Kingdom.

▶ **The Ramesseum**
In his funerary temple, with its massive pillars, or pylons, Rameses II (1279–1213 BC) recorded his military exploits at the Battle of Qadesh in Syria-Palestine.

Eastern Thebes

The living inhabited the east bank of the Nile in a collection of houses for ordinary people, residences for dignitaries and royal palaces. This is also the location of temples dedicated to several local gods. They were grouped around the temple of Amun, the head of the Ancient Egyptian pantheon, at Karnak.

Even when the administrative capital was moved to the Delta in the Eighteenth Dynasty (1550–1295 BC), Thebes remained the religious capital. As each king assumed power, he began a substantial construction programme in the temple of Amun, and the pharaohs continued to be buried in the Valley of the Kings.

◀ The criosphinxes
Statues of creatures with the body of a lion and the head of a ram, the sacred animal of Amun, protected the entrance to the temple of Karnak.

▶ The festival of Opet
Each year, Thebes celebrated the festival of Opet, during which the divinity of the pharaoh was renewed for the coming year in the temple of Luxor.

The ceremony began with a procession, on land or by river, carrying the statues of Amun, Mut and Khons from Karnak to Luxor, escorted by the king.

◀ The temple of Luxor
In contrast to Karnak, which was built over a period of 2,000 years, the temple of Luxor shows great unity. It was the work of only two kings – Amenhotep III (1390–1352 BC) and Rameses II (1279–1213 BC). Alexander the Great (332–323 BC) later added a sanctuary for the sacred boat of the god Amun.

▼ The temple of Karnak
The largest of all the temples of Egypt was dedicated to Amun, 'king of the gods'. It housed other temples, including one dedicated to his son Khons.

The Valley of the Kings

A remote desert valley in the hills to the west of Thebes contains the graves of the pharaohs of the New Kingdom, but the treasures of most of these tombs have long since been plundered.

The rulers of the New Kingdom (1550–1069 BC) based their capital in Upper Egypt at Thebes, which was also to become the main burial site for the pharaohs. Tomb robbery was by now a serious problem, and a new strategy for royal burials evolved. The pharaohs would no longer advertise their final resting place with monumental buildings, but hide their tombs away in secret.

The hidden valley

Thutmose I's architect, Ineni, selected a secluded site for the new necropolis in a wadi (dried-out river bed) behind cliffs on the west bank of the Nile – known since the nineteenth century as the Valley of the Kings. The tombs were cut directly into the rock and contained stairways, passages, halls, shafts and burial chambers. There were no overlying monuments, except for the pyramidal form of the mountain peaks that overlooked the valley. Another new development was that the kings' mortuary temples were separated from their tombs and built in a long line on the edge of the desert, linked to the Nile by several canals and at least one artificial harbour.

The Valley of the Kings contains 62 known royal tombs, the earliest belonging to Thutmose I (1504–1492 BC), and the latest to the last pharaoh of the New Kingdom,

▲ **The founder**
Amenhotep I (1525–1504 BC), son of the pharaoh Ahmose (1550–1525 BC) and Queen Ahmose Nefertari (c. 1570–1505 BC), was revered, together with his mother, as the god-protector of the Valley of the Kings necropolis. The nature and whereabouts of his tomb, however, are still not known.

◄ **The 'gates of the kings'**
Biban el-Muluk is the Arabic name by which the Valley of the Kings is known today in Egypt. Many tracks lead across the boulder-strewn hills to the grave entrances.

Rameses XI (1099–1069 BC). The oldest graves are hidden in remote areas at the far end of the valley, accessible only by foot over steep cliff paths.

The earlier graves of the Eighteenth Dynasty were modest, especially when the historical importance of some of the pharaohs is considered. As each new tomb was cut, however, there was a definite development in the layout, decoration and size as the power and wealth of the pharaohs increased.

Incredible wealth

The tomb of Sety I, lavishly decorated over its 100m (330ft) distance from entrance to burial chamber, marks the high point of this development at the start of the Nineteenth Dynasty. The wall paintings in Sety I's tomb are among the most elegant of the New Kingdom.

The fabulous treasures that the two most powerful rulers, Rameses II and Akhenaten, took to the afterlife can only be imagined from the contents of Tutankhamun's tomb.

▶ **The power of pictures**
The best artists of Egypt worked for 500 years to perfect their visions of the afterlife and to immortalize the pharaohs in pictures. This painted relief, from the tomb of Rameses III (1184–1153 BC), shows the king with offerings of incense and drink.

▲ **Rediscovery in the early nineteenth century**
The early travellers who visited the historical sites were followed by treasure seekers and adventurers, but 200 years ago archaeologists began to systematically uncover the hidden tombs. This illustration, published by the English artist David Roberts after his Egyptian travels in 1838–1839, gives an impression of how the Valley of the Kings looked in the first half of the nineteenth century.

The Settlement of Deir el-Medina

The artists and craftsmen who built and decorated the tombs in the necropolises of Thebes, including the Valley of the Kings and the Valley of the Queens, lived in a nearby sheltered valley in the purpose-built village of Deir el-Medina.

At the beginning of the Eighteenth Dynasty, the pharaoh Thutmose I (1504–1492 BC) developed a village on the left bank of the Nile at Thebes, and peopled it with the workers charged with building his tomb. The settlement, now known as Deir el-Medina, continued to accommodate the craftsmen and artists who furnished and decorated the tombs of the royal family and their officials for more than 400 years, until the end of the Twentieth Dynasty (1186–1069 BC).

Excavation history

At its peak, the village, built around a main road and two cross-streets, had 68 houses huddled behind a high enclosure wall. The houses, with stone foundations, were largely built with lime-washed mud bricks. The average house was 72m² (775sq ft) in area, with two main rooms, one or two subsidiary chambers for sleeping, a kitchen open to the sky, a cellar and a terrace.

▶ Pa Demi – a growing community
The Ancient Egyptians called Deir el-Medina Pa Demi – 'the village'. Its growth from the reign of Horemheb (1323–1295 BC) is tied to the changing fashion in royal burials, as they were increasingly dug into the living rock in the form of long corridors decorated with complex painted reliefs rather than just paintings, requiring increasing numbers of able craftsmen.

◀ Ahmose Nefertari and Amenhotep I
Tomb paintings and steles reveal that the workers of Deir el-Medina revered Amenhotep I (1525–1504 BC) and his mother Ahmose Nefertari as protective gods. It is believed that the village was founded by the Eighteenth-Dynasty pharaoh at about the same time that it was decided to use the valleys in the Theban massif as a burial place for all future royalty, creating the need for a permanent pool of workers on the site.

The north gate, a gap in the enclosing wall, was one of just two entry points to Deir el-Medina

A north–south road bisected the village, giving access to the houses.

▶ **Commuter route**
This steep path leads over the rocky slopes from Deir el-Medina to the Valley of the Kings, about half an hour's walk away. When a royal tomb was being built, the diggers and decorators would work for 10 days at a stretch, sleeping in mud-brick huts near the site, before returning to the village for one or two days' break.

The floor plan of the rectangular houses is still picked out in stone walls.

The workers' cemetery is just to the west of the settlement, on the lower slopes of the massif.

◀ **Protective goddess**
A hidden sanctuary, 100m (330ft) from the walls of Deir el-Medina, honours Hathor, Ptah and a cobra goddess worshipped by the inhabitants of the village. Meretseger, whose name means 'she who loves silence', was a personification of the Theban necropolis and a protector of the dead entombed there, helping them in their rebirth into the afterlife. She was thought to live in a cave on the rocky slopes and also personified the pyramidal peak that towers over the Valley of the Kings.

An enclosure wall in mud brick still surrounds the village. It is generally built hard against the side of the houses, but it is sometimes separated by a narrow road or path.

A reconstructed chapel shaped as a pyramid stands proud amid the generally ruinous condition of the necropolis. The craftsmen tomb-builders of Deir el-Medina unsurprisingly had good-quality tombs of their own.

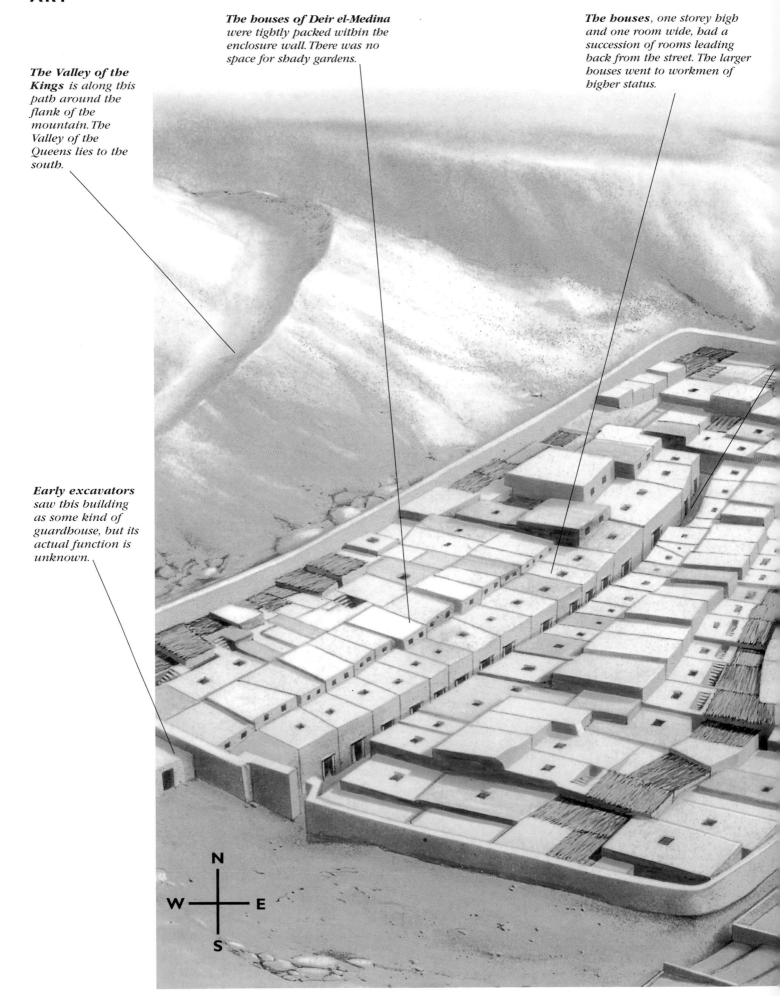

The Valley of the Kings is along this path around the flank of the mountain. The Valley of the Queens lies to the south.

The houses of Deir el-Medina were tightly packed within the enclosure wall. There was no space for shady gardens.

The houses, one storey high and one room wide, had a succession of rooms leading back from the street. The larger houses went to workmen of higher status.

Early excavators saw this building as some kind of guardhouse, but its actual function is unknown.

N
W E
S

A road from the north gate gives access to the far end of the settlement, but the only other exit is to the necropolis in the west.

A sheltered north–south valley between the Theban massif and an outlying hill on the west bank of the Nile was carefully chosen as the site for the workers' village.

Entrance pylons were built in front of the courtyards to several of the workmen's tombs.

Small, steep pyramids in mud brick served as funerary chapels built over the tombs.

◄ **Ancient settlement**
The rectangular grid pattern of a settlement that has been built to order, rather than evolved naturally over time, is apparent in Deir el-Medina. The houses, which were allocated according to the status of the workman, were plastered inside and out, and colourfully painted indoors. The openings in the roofs marked the kitchen, with a fireplace below. A village cemetery was built to the west on the slopes of the hill.

▲ Written on stone
Excavations at an exhausted clay quarry near Deir el-Medina have unearthed chalk and limestone fragments covered with sketches, orders, invoices, instructions and notes made by the workmen. These jottings are a very valuable resource for historians.

Although the workers spent much of their time on site at the various necropolises, their families – women and children, the elderly and the sick – and livestock made sure the village bustled with life. Water was supplied by bearers, whose donkeys hauled the precious liquid up from the Nile, and the state met most of the workers' needs, including a house and a funerary plot, and payment in the form of cereals, vegetables, fish, clothes and tools. This arrangement did not always run smoothly. There are many records of disputes over undelivered goods.

Extra labour was also supplied when necessary to help with the daily work. Temporary workers, along with such auxiliary personnel as water carriers, smiths, potters and gardeners, lived outside the village, higher up the slopes. New recruits to the team of craftsmen were generally chosen from the sons of those in Deir el-Medina, with the agreement of the vizier of Upper Egypt, who was ultimately responsible for the team and its work.

The village was abandoned soon after the Twentieth Dynasty collapsed in 1069 BC. Apprehensive of what the future would bring, the workers fled to the protection of the nearby temple of Medinet Habu.

▼ Statue of Djedi and his son
This double statue, found at Deir el-Medina early in the nineteenth century, shows one of its craftsmen, Djedi, and his son Pendua. The kneeling figures present a stele that bears their names and origins, and honours the sun god, shown travelling in his barge. Statues bearing steles became popular in the New Kingdom. This example was acquired by the Louvre Museum in Paris in 1826 as part of the Salt collection.

▲ A planned community
The lower courses of the walls, built with stones tied together with mud and straw, have defied the passage of time to allow archaeologists to map out the ground plan of the houses. All the houses follow a similar model, and were differentiated only by the fixtures and fittings brought by the workers and their families who lived in them.

▶ Everyday life
Excavations in the tombs of the workers and their houses in Deir el-Medina have unearthed simple furniture — stools, chairs, tables, beds and chests — toilet articles, woven mats, straw baskets and brushes, suggesting they enjoyed a comfortable but not grand lifestyle.

▶ Decorated ointment pot
The tomb of Kha (c. 1430–1370 BC), an Eighteenth-Dynasty architect who oversaw work in the Valley of the Kings, was found unplundered near Deir el-Medina. This small, calcite ointment pot was part of his funerary equipment.

▼ **The Ramesside tombs**
The workmen's tombs built in the Ninteenth and Twentieth dynasties take two basic forms. In the first, the chapel devoted to the cult of the dead is a brick-built, vaulted room topped by a little pyramid. One of these, that of the tomb of the workman Sennedjem (c. 1270 BC), discovered in 1885, has been reconstructed. The second type is cut directly into the rock. The funerary chapel – Sennedjem's is illustrated on the left – gave access to the underground burial chamber containing the mummy via a deep shaft and/or a staircase or two.

The workers' cemetery

The tombs of the workers are mostly in a cemetery to the village's west. Several Eighteenth-Dynasty tombs had not been plundered and provided an abundance of funerary material. Later tombs have magnificently decorated family vaults, worthy of the artists who created the royal tombs. Funerary chapels in the form of little pyramids once stood above the tomb entrances; these have long since collapsed, although one of them has been reconstructed.

▼ **Workers' servants**
Many shabtis were discovered in the excavations of the necropolis at Deir el-Medina. These figures were intended to labour for the deceased in the afterlife, answering Osiris's call to cultivate the fields of Paradise. Their presence testifies to the importance the tomb workers placed on their own survival in the afterlife. Most of the shabtis – such as this one from the tomb of Henuttaneb (Eighteenth Dynasty) – are today on display at the Egyptian Museum in Turin, Italy.

INSIGHT

The temple of the goddess Hathor

Long after the village had fallen into disuse, Ptolemy IV Philopator (221–205 BC) decided to build a temple to Hathor to the north of the site. The work was completed in the reign of Ptolemy IX Soter II (116–107 and 88–80 BC), although the decoration was never finished. The monument is very well preserved. The temple proper is a carefully constructed sandstone building 15m (50ft) long, with two rooms one after the other and three chapels leading off. Around the temple is a court enclosed in a high, mud-brick wall. The temple was eventually taken over by Christian monks, who used the sanctuary as a cloister. The temple came to be known as Deir el-Medina, 'monastery of the town', giving the whole site its current Arabic name.

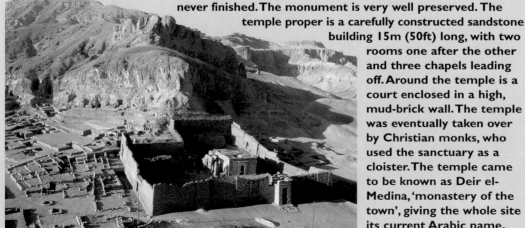

The Tomb of Nakht

Nakht (c. 1400 BC) was by no means the most important official to be buried in the Theban necropolis, but his tomb contains superb paintings of religious ritual and everyday life.

Although unfinished, the enchanting decorations of the tomb of Nakht are among the finest in Thebes. The tomb, uncovered in 1889 near the village of Sheikh 'Abd el-Qurna, is tucked into the low foothills of the Theban mountains, well below the slopes where the great dignitaries of the Eighteenth Dynasty (1550–1295 BC) were buried, and is relatively small. All this suggests that Nakht was a middle-ranking official, and the only titles ascribed to him in the tomb are the relatively lowly ones of scribe and 'hour priest of Amun'.

This means he would have worked in administration and occasionally carried out the duties of an astronomer-priest at the cult temple at Karnak, deciding the precise time at which the daily rituals should begin. This is virtually all that is known of Nakht; no sources other than his tomb mention him, and only a few short texts accompany the paintings. It is the style of these, not the text, that led Egyptologists to date it from around the reign of Thutmose IV (1400–1390 BC).

The layout of Nakht's tomb is typical of Thebes; an open forecourt leads to a transverse hall, here 5m (16½ft) wide and 1.5m (5ft) deep. This in turn leads to a longer room. Only the wide room has painted walls, but these have retained an astonishing freshness.

A throwing stick was used to bring down birds as they broke cover from the marshes.

Dating clues are provided by the subjects' jewellery and styles of wig.

Nakht's wife, a 'singer of Amun', accompanies him on the hunt.

▼ A typical layout

The plan of Nakht's tomb is characteristic of those of officials of the Eighteenth Dynasty. Above ground, a court leads to two rooms in the shape of an upside-down T. The wide transverse hall is decorated with scenes of everyday life; the long room beyond houses a niche for statues of the tomb owner and the opening of the shaft that leads to the subterranean part of the tomb containing the mummy and funerary equipment. This shaft was blocked off after a funeral, to deter robbers.

▲ The officials' necropolis

The hillside village of Sheikh 'Abd el-Qurna, in the foothills of the Theban mountains, now occupies the site of a necropolis containing tombs of several Eighteenth-Dynasty officials, including the scribe Nakht.

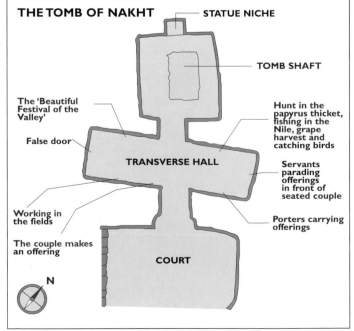

THE TOMB OF NAKHT

STATUE NICHE

TOMB SHAFT

The 'Beautiful Festival of the Valley'

False door

TRANSVERSE HALL

Hunt in the papyrus thicket, fishing in the Nile, grape harvest and catching birds

Servants parading offerings in front of seated couple

Working in the fields

Porters carrying offerings

The couple makes an offering

COURT

N

The papyrus thicket is rendered in a similar way to Old Kingdom tomb reliefs of the same subject at Giza and Saqqara.

Nakht's son, who wears his hair in a youthful sidelock, hands his father another stick.

◀ Hunting and fishing

The eastern half of the north wall is decorated with two symmetrically opposed scenes of Nakht hunting birds and fishing in the Nile wetlands while his family looks on. In the former, shown here, Nakht stands in his boat poised to hurl a stick into the midst of a flock of panicking birds that have been flushed from the papyrus thickets by his approach. His wife braces him with her left hand; in the right she cradles a duckling. The other painting shows Nakht taking his spear from the water, with spray arcing from the two fish impaled on it.

◀ Avatars of abundance

The painted false door in the west wall of the transverse hall is flanked by a pair of goddesses offering whole papyrus plants, heavily laden vines and a platter piled high with food and drink. The trees apparently growing on their heads symbolize fertility and abundance, an identification reinforced by the mass of painted offerings that surround them.

▶ Farm work

The south wall of the transverse hall is painted with scenes from different stages of cereal growing. Here a labourer breaks up the soil with a cross between a hand-plough and a hoe. Other scenes show the seeds being sown in the prepared soil and the grown grain being harvested, winnowed and threshed.

◄ Musical accompaniment
Music was central to the Ancient Egyptian idea of a festival. In the tomb of Nakht, a blind male harpist sits on a rush mat, while three young women dance as they play other instruments; this one plays the lute, recently arrived from the Near East.

▲ A feast for the senses
The guests at the banquet that accompanied the festival celebrations were not only plied with food – although the paintings of tables groaning under their load of food and wine jars suggest they did not go hungry – but also supplied with music to please the ear. The intoxicating scent of blue lotus flowers delighted the nose and induced a sense of spiritual well-being.

A young maidservant adjusts the headdresses of the women attending the feast.

◄ An eye for detail
The paintings in Nakht's tomb are celebrated for the small, beautiful and unusual details that help to bring the pictures to life. In the hunting scene, for example, we see Nakht's wife standing by her husband, cradling a rescued duckling in her hand. The bird's soft down and huddled pose emphasize its vulnerability and thus the tenderness of the gesture.

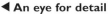

Ointment cones, made from fats impregnated with scent, melted on the head to release their fragrance.

▲ The blind harpist
A nimble-fingered harpist is often to be found in the tomb decorations of the New Kingdom. He was usually depicted as a blind man, but it is not known whether this reflected reality or was simply a conventional way of showing the musician's single-minded devotion to his art.

◄ The festival
The 'Beautiful Festival of the Valley' was a religious holiday when effigies of the Theban triad – Amun, Mut and Khonsu – were carried across the Nile in the divine barge to visit the royal tombs. Even after his death, Nakht expected to take part in the celebrations.

A false door painted on the west-facing wall gives the ka, the vital spirit of the deceased, metaphysical access to and from the tomb. Offerings of food and drink are piled around the door, flanked by goddesses. At the east end of the room porters parade before Nakht and his wife – who are both seated – laden with similar offerings.

There are more offerings at the eastern end of the long south wall, but the other side of the doorway has scenes of agricultural work, showing Nakht supervising his estate from a seat in an arbour. Labourers work the earth and grow and harvest cereals in an undulating landscape, represented by a curved line in yellow ochre.

The great feast

The north wall, to the left of the exit into the long room, shows men and women celebrating the 'Beautiful Festival of the Valley', when an effigy of Amun was taken across the Nile from Karnak to honour the dead. To the right are finely detailed scenes of hunting with sticks and nets, fishing and grape picking. The sheer vivacity of the drawing, the depiction of movement and the delicately skilful way the near-transparent robes of the participants are sketched in all testify to the skills of Theban artists.

The seated women are posed in a way that is typical of Eighteenth-Dynasty art before the rule of Akhenaten.

Non-conventional poses, and a sense of movement in the limbs, suggest the women are dancing as well as playing.

The Colossi of Memnon

Two mighty seated figures keep watch over the west bank of the Nile at Luxor. The colossi of Memnon are the guardians of the burial grounds which extend from the Valley of the Kings, past the mortuary temples of the pharaohs, to the Valley of the Queens.

Amenhotep III (1390–1352 BC), whose rule was marked by an extended period of prosperity and an extensive programme of new building, commissioned two gigantic seated figures to guard over the entrance of his mortuary temple, which today is completely destroyed. The pharaoh entrusted the task of building to his chief royal architect, Amenhotep, son of Hapu (*c.* 1430–1350 BC), who was later deified for his abilities and wisdom.

In his own image

The statues were made from single blocks of pink quartzite, each weighing more than 700 tonnes. The stone was quarried in the Red Mountain close to the old city of Heliopolis, near modern-day Cairo, and was transported several hundred kilometres to its final destination, using wooden sleds and barges for the journey along the River Nile.

Both statues portrayed Amenhotep III sitting on a throne in classic pose, with his hands resting on his knees and the cloth headdress, the nemes, on his head. The throne is engraved with the names and titles of the pharaoh, and images of protecting

The pharaoh carries the coiled cobra on his forehead to ward off his enemies.

The colossus wears the striped headcloth, the nemes, of the pharaoh.

This nineteenth-century illustration of the colossi shows the statues during the annual flooding of the Nile.

The pyramid-shaped mountain el-Qurn dominates the mountains of west Thebes at the Valley of the Kings.

The throne bears the pharaoh's name and title, and the symbols of the unification of Upper and Lower Egypt.

▼ Moving statues

In modern times, as in antiquity, the same methods have sometimes been used to move heavy objects. Giovanni Battista Belzoni (1778–1823), Egyptologist, engineer and exporter of Egyptian art, moved a gigantic figure of Rameses II in 1816. The seven-tonne bust was manually dragged to the banks of the Nile in the same way as it would have been thousands of years before. At first, no boats large enough to carry it could be found, and it took several months before one sturdy enough was available. The granite bust found its way to the British Museum in London in 1817.

PROFILE

Amenhotep III (1390–1352 BC)

The reign of Amenhotep III (below on his battle chariot) saw many changes in religion as he allied himself ever more strongly with the cult of the sun. Whether this was from religious conviction or simply a matter of politics is not known, but it certainly reduced the influence of then powerful priests of the god Amun.

Amenhotep III also elevated his own royal status, decreeing that he was not the son of the gods, but was himself a god, and that his monuments should be accordingly increased in grandeur. His cartouche bears his royal birth name Amenhotep, ruler of Thebes (right).

'IMN

HTP

HQ'

W'ST

Amenhotep, lord of Thebes

▼ **Drawing history**
Artists taking part in expeditions to Egypt in the eighteenth and nineteenth centuries produced accurate images of Ancient Egyptian monuments and artefacts in their sketches and drawings. Their efforts have ensured that, today, ancient monuments which have been damaged, either by vandalism or by construction projects, or which have completely disappeared, can be accurately reconstructed.

Mutemwiya, Amenhotep III's mother, is shown in a small statute to the right of the pharaoh's legs.

Tiy (c. 1410–1340 BC), the principal wife of Amenhotep III, is commemorated in a statue to the left of the pharaoh's legs.

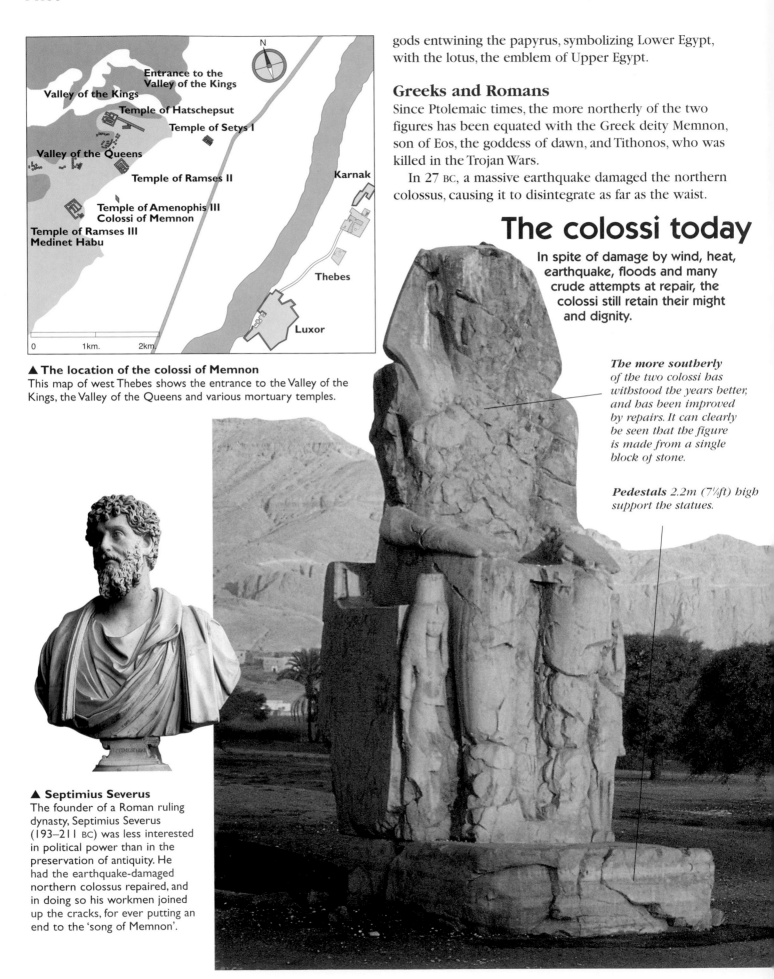

gods entwining the papyrus, symbolizing Lower Egypt, with the lotus, the emblem of Upper Egypt.

Greeks and Romans

Since Ptolemaic times, the more northerly of the two figures has been equated with the Greek deity Memnon, son of Eos, the goddess of dawn, and Tithonos, who was killed in the Trojan Wars.

In 27 BC, a massive earthquake damaged the northern colossus, causing it to disintegrate as far as the waist.

The colossi today

In spite of damage by wind, heat, earthquake, floods and many crude attempts at repair, the colossi still retain their might and dignity.

▲ **The location of the colossi of Memnon**
This map of west Thebes shows the entrance to the Valley of the Kings, the Valley of the Queens and various mortuary temples.

The more southerly of the two colossi has withstood the years better, and has been improved by repairs. It can clearly be seen that the figure is made from a single block of stone.

Pedestals 2.2m (7¼ft) high support the statues.

▲ **Septimius Severus**
The founder of a Roman ruling dynasty, Septimius Severus (193–211 BC) was less interested in political power than in the preservation of antiquity. He had the earthquake-damaged northern colossus repaired, and in doing so his workmen joined up the cracks, for ever putting an end to the 'song of Memnon'.

Soon after, the statue began emitting a musical note each morning. This 'singing' was interpreted as Memnon's greeting to his mother, the dawn, and people flocked from all over the ancient world in order to witness the phenomenon.

In reality, it appears that the morning sun heated the humid night air that was trapped in the cracks in the stone, and as the air expanded and was released, it created the musical note. When the Roman emperor Septimius Serverus had the statue restored in the third century AD, the statue sang no more.

Retaining wall

N

Sanctuary with pillared entrance

Third pylon

Second pylon   **First pylon**

Colossi of Memnon

▲ Reconstruction of mortuary temple's layout
From a few remaining paths and tracks under the orchards and fields, it has been possible to reconstruct the outline of Amenhotep's mortuary temple.

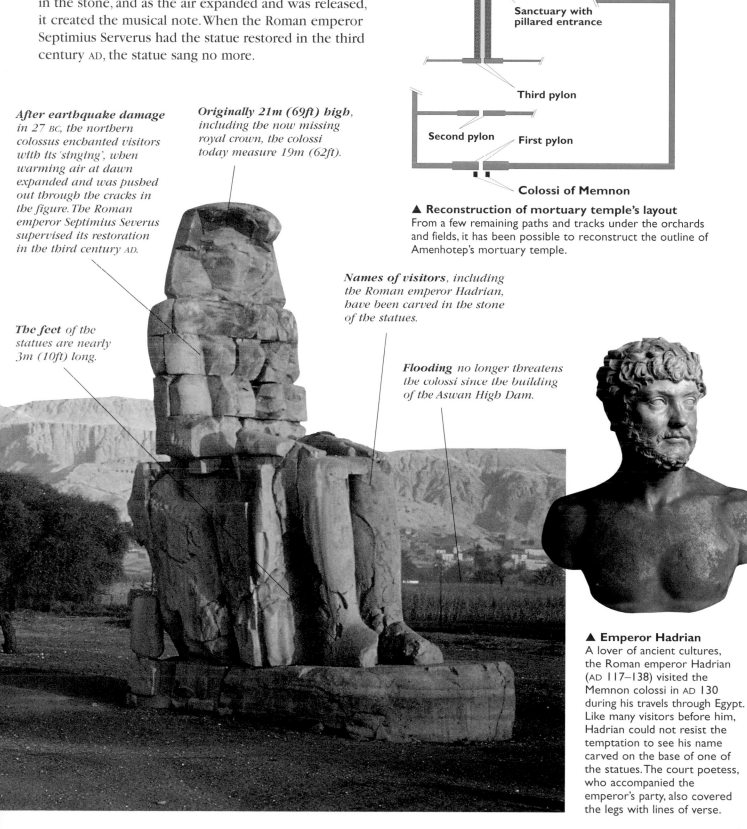

After earthquake damage in 27 BC, the northern colossus enchanted visitors with its 'singing', when warming air at dawn expanded and was pushed out through the cracks in the figure. The Roman emperor Septimius Severus supervised its restoration in the third century AD.

Originally 21m (69ft) high, including the now missing royal crown, the colossi today measure 19m (62ft).

Names of visitors, including the Roman emperor Hadrian, have been carved in the stone of the statues.

The feet of the statues are nearly 3m (10ft) long.

Flooding no longer threatens the colossi since the building of the Aswan High Dam.

▲ Emperor Hadrian
A lover of ancient cultures, the Roman emperor Hadrian (AD 117–138) visited the Memnon colossi in AD 130 during his travels through Egypt. Like many visitors before him, Hadrian could not resist the temptation to see his name carved on the base of one of the statues. The court poetess, who accompanied the emperor's party, also covered the legs with lines of verse.

The Temple of Luxor

Together with the great temple of Amun at Karnak, the temple at Luxor formed a religious complex that was central to the economic and spiritual life of the Theban region.

Set on an artificial embankment to avoid being flooded by the Nile, the Luxor temple was built mainly by two of the greatest pharaohs - Amenhotep III (1390-1352 BC) and Rameses II (1279-1213 BC) - on the site of an older shrine dating to the Twelfth Dynasty (1985-1795 BC). The original temple comprised a collection of small rooms and shrines arranged around the large peristyle court, which is surrounded by a double row of papyrus columns. Work on the temple was abandoned under the reign of Akhenaten (1352-1336 BC), but restarted when Tutankhamun (1336-1327 BC) had the temple decorated with reliefs, which were later made over by Horemheb (1323-1295 BC). The temple at Luxor, however, reached the height of its glory during the reign of Rameses II.

▼ **The avenue of sphinxes**
During the reign of Nectanebo I (380–362 BC), hundreds of human-headed sphinxes were placed along the processional way between Karnak and Luxor.

The pylon is decorated with scenes from the battle of Qadesh (1285 BC), celebrating Rameses II's victory over the Hittites.

One obelisk remains at the temple entrance. The other was given to France in the nineteenth century and is now in Paris.

▼ **The temple entrance**
Rameses II had six colossal statues and two obelisks, each about 25m (82ft) high, erected in front of the pylon. Four niches were cut into the pylon's façade to hold flag poles.

▲ Aerial view of the Theban east bank
Modern Luxor encloses the temple complex, which was once connected to the temple of Karnak by a processional avenue of sphinxes. Further excavations in the city continue to uncover evidence of the avenue.

The colossal seated figures in front of the pylon are images of Rameses II and are inscribed with his name.

Human-headed sphinxes, erected by Nectanebo I along the processional way, guard the temple entrance.

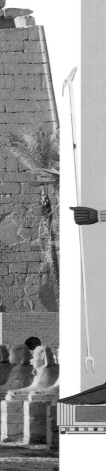

PROFILE

The Theban triad

Amun was worshipped as a local god at Thebes from before the Eleventh Dynasty (2055–1985 BC). With the rise of the Theban pharaohs, from Mentuhotep II (2055–2004 BC) onwards, Amun emerged as the pre-eminent god of Ancient Egypt. At Thebes, he became part of a triad of gods, along with his consort, the goddess Mut, and their son, the moon god Khons. In a nineteenth-century colour plate by Ippolito Rosellini (below), the king, in the centre, is protected by Amun and Mut. In the Middle Kingdom (2055–1650 BC), building started on the large temple of Amun in Karnak, to which almost every succeeding pharaoh added statues or obelisks. Sometime later, the Amun temple in Luxor was built and it was here that the yearly Opet Festival took place.

Accompanied by many musicians, singers and dancers, the cult images of Amun, Mut and Khons were taken in their ceremonial barges along the processional way to Luxor. During the night, the rebirth of Amun took place, and thus the renewal of the world. As the festival took place at the end of the annual flooding, shortly afterwards the plants in the fields began to grow – a visible sign of new life.

Rameses II added a new porticoed court that was much larger than the first built by Amenhotep III. Access was through a massive pylon entrance, in front of which stood two obelisks and six colossal statues. He also decorated the temple with reliefs and inscriptions, mostly celebrating his power and achievements. The two towers of the entrance pylon, for example, are covered with a massive relief depicting the Battle of Qadesh in which Rameses II defeated the Hittites. The last additions were provided by Nectanebo (380–362 BC), who also added the human-headed sphinxes to the processional way. Later, Alexander the Great (332–323 BC) restored the temple to its original state 'in the time of Amenhotep'.

The Opet Festival

The prime purpose of the temple was to host the annual Festival of Opet, in which the cult statues of Amun, Mut and Khons were taken from their sanctuaries at Karnak to Luxor, where the pharaoh repeated his coronation rites before the image of Amun

▶ **The Luxor temple site**
At the top of this aerial view of the temple complex is the pylon and the peristyle court of Rameses II, along with the thirteenth-century mosque. The hypostyle hall leads across the second courtyard to the cult halls. The ascending floor level and the columns' descending height make the rooms seen in the foreground increasingly small and narrow.

▼ **Columns of papyrus buds**
The hypostyle court of Amenhotep III is flanked on three sides by rows of columns. Their capitals, in the shape of closed papyrus buds, support the architrave, the symbol of the sky.

▶▶ **The god Amun**
The temple complex of Luxor was dedicated to Amun, the 'king of the gods'. This statue, from the time of Tutankhamun, shows Amun wearing a plumed crown.

▼ **The processional colonnade**
The columns of the processional colonnade, rising to more than 19m (62ft), were erected by Amenhotep III. Their capitals are in the shape of open papyrus flowers.

INSIGHT

Three millennia of worship

A temple has stood at Luxor from at least the reign of Hatshepsut (1473–1458 BC), but most of what is still standing was constructed by Amenhotep III (1390–1352 BC), extended by Rameses II (1279–1213 BC) and restored by Alexander the Great (332–323 BC). In the first century BC, the entrance to the inner temple was sealed and turned into a shrine for Roman troops (below left) and from the fourth to sixth centuries AD, the entire temple was incorporated into a Roman military camp. After Rome became Christian, several churches were built on the site, one within Rameses' great court, which in turn was built on by the mosque of Abu el-Haggag (below), which remains in use today.

▼ Columns and kings

Rameses II constructed a colonnade of papyrus-bud columns around his great court. Giant statues bearing his name are set between the columns. It was here that people congregated during religious processions and festivals. Statues bearing the name of Rameses II were often not images of the king, however, but ones of earlier pharaohs.

The statues in the peristyle halls of the Luxor temple owe their well-preserved state to the fact that the temple was buried in the sand for centuries.

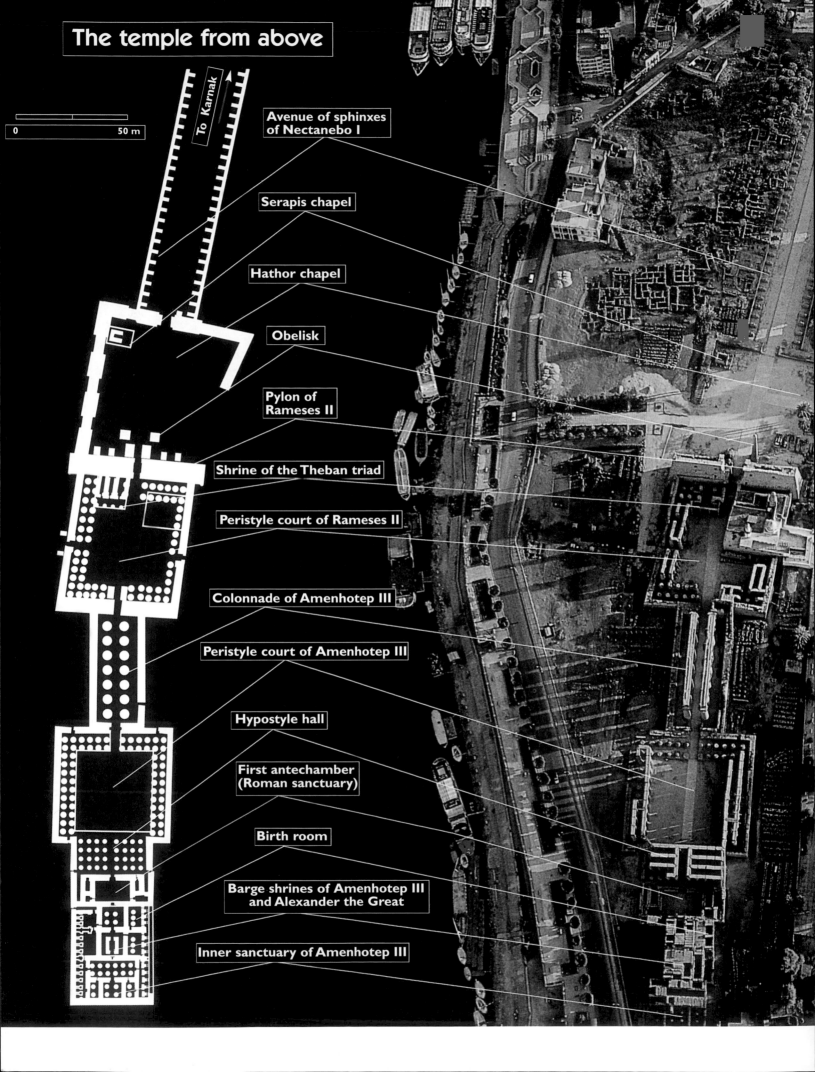

The temple from above

0   50 m

To Karnak

Avenue of sphinxes
of Nectanebo I

Serapis chapel

Hathor chapel

Obelisk

Pylon of
Rameses II

Shrine of the Theban triad

Peristyle court of Rameses II

Colonnade of Amenhotep III

Peristyle court of Amenhotep III

Hypostyle hall

First antechamber
(Roman sanctuary)

Birth room

Barge shrines of Amenhotep III
and Alexander the Great

Inner sanctuary of Amenhotep III

THE TEMPLE OF LUXOR

◄◄ **Ground plan of the temple site**
Comparing the aerial view with the ground plan of the temple site, the early pharaonic buildings can be isolated from the later additions. Although the modern town of Luxor has grown around the temple, part of the broad processional way in front of the entrance remains.

◄ **Rameses II, the great builder**
During his long life, Rameses II built many new temples. Furthermore, he had existing sanctuaries enlarged and a number of statues erected. In doing so, he became the most commonly pictured pharaoh of Egypt. This seated figure of him is located at the entrance to the colonnade of Amenhotep III.

The Art of Akhenaten

Akhenaten's influence on the art of his reign led to a style that showed levels of realism not otherwise found in Ancient Egyptian art. The depictions of the king from this time exemplify this style.

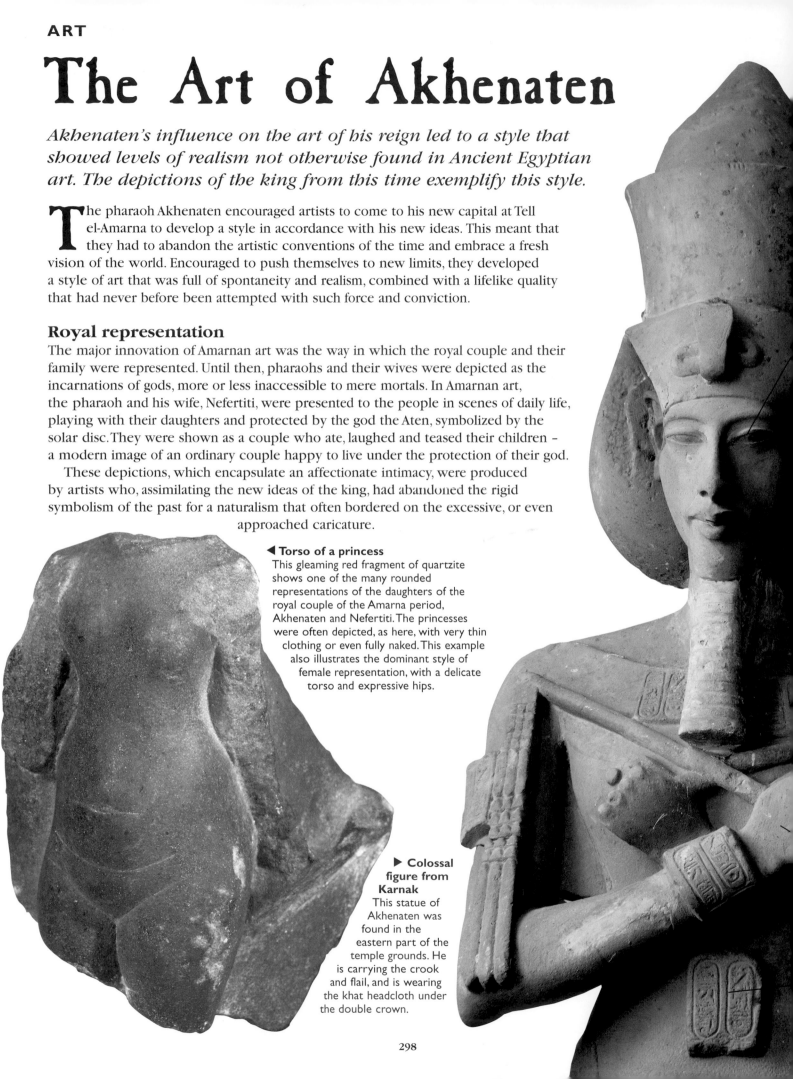

The pharaoh Akhenaten encouraged artists to come to his new capital at Tell el-Amarna to develop a style in accordance with his new ideas. This meant that they had to abandon the artistic conventions of the time and embrace a fresh vision of the world. Encouraged to push themselves to new limits, they developed a style of art that was full of spontaneity and realism, combined with a lifelike quality that had never before been attempted with such force and conviction.

Royal representation

The major innovation of Amarnan art was the way in which the royal couple and their family were represented. Until then, pharaohs and their wives were depicted as the incarnations of gods, more or less inaccessible to mere mortals. In Amarnan art, the pharaoh and his wife, Nefertiti, were presented to the people in scenes of daily life, playing with their daughters and protected by the god the Aten, symbolized by the solar disc. They were shown as a couple who ate, laughed and teased their children – a modern image of an ordinary couple happy to live under the protection of their god.

These depictions, which encapsulate an affectionate intimacy, were produced by artists who, assimilating the new ideas of the king, had abandoned the rigid symbolism of the past for a naturalism that often bordered on the excessive, or even approached caricature.

◀ **Torso of a princess**
This gleaming red fragment of quartzite shows one of the many rounded representations of the daughters of the royal couple of the Amarna period, Akhenaten and Nefertiti. The princesses were often depicted, as here, with very thin clothing or even fully naked. This example also illustrates the dominant style of female representation, with a delicate torso and expressive hips.

▶ **Colossal figure from Karnak**
This statue of Akhenaten was found in the eastern part of the temple grounds. He is carrying the crook and flail, and is wearing the khat headcloth under the double crown.

▶ Harp decoration
This striking head from the Amarna period was used to embellish the foot of a harp. The 20cm (8in) high piece is carved from wood and painted, and can be seen in the Louvre in Paris. The facial features unify all the elements of the Amarna style – the face is very narrow and elongated, with an overly prominent chin, as can be seen in the early depictions of Akhenaten. The slightly protruding lips, the sharp bridge of the nose and the flared nostrils, as well as the almond-shaped eyes and the finely curved eyebrows, are unmistakable signs of a member of the royal family.

The narrow face is dominated by the almond-shaped eyes and protruding lips.

◀ Bust of a princess
Akhenaten and Nefertiti had six daughters, who were portrayed in the same way as their parents, although a typical characteristic of the children's depictions was their elongated skulls.

The impression of femininity is accentuated by the curved lips and the narrow lines of the face.

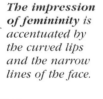

The upper body, with its short chest and narrow shoulders, appears very lean.

Akhenaten's thin arms are crossed over his chest; he holds the crook and flail in his hands.

The slightly protruding belly, with its emphasized navel, is typical of the Amarna style.

▶ Portrait in plaster
Shortly after Akhenaten's death, the royal residence was moved away from Amarna and the site was left to disintegrate. Many interesting finds have been made beneath the rubble of buildings, among which are numerous unfinished works from the workshops of the sculptor Thutmose, including the famous bust of Nefertiti, now in the Egyptian Museum in Berlin. Also in Berlin is this plaster mask that gives a glimpse into the methods of the master craftsmen. For a long time it was thought to be a death mask, until it was revealed to be a mask of a living person, taken by the sculptors in the course of their work.

By banning all representations of any gods other than the Aten, and by having their own images carved on columns around the city to remind the population of their divine status, the royal couple introduced a new way of presenting religious themes. Artists created an icon that gave physical form to the Aten – a solar disc with long rays that ended in hands.

The second major innovation brought by Amarnan art was the representation of depth on a flat surface. The figures that appear on the columns and walls of tombs dating from this period are depicted in a different way.

Lacking in the work of previous artists, perspective came to the fore. In a relief from Tell el-Amarna, Akhenaten is shown holding an olive branch in his hand. This hand is highly expressive and realistic, with no distortion. The artist conveys the impression of depth by giving prominence to the background, where the rays of the Aten can just be made out, and the perspective gives the pharaoh's hand its full symbolic value. For the first time, space was viewed as a whole, rather than a juxtaposition of scenes. Moreover, in contrast to earlier tradition, there is now a clear distinction between left and right hands and feet.

This new artistic vision also introduced the impression of movement. Birds are shown beating their wings in papyrus thickets, brightly coloured fish swim through the waters of ornamental pools, reeds quiver and wheat is blown flat by the wind.

The rays of the god Aten, *in the shape of the sun disc, end in the hands usually holding the ankh sign and blessing the royal family.*

A particular characteristic of the Amarna period is the pleated loincloth sitting low on the hips, emphasizing the curved belly.

◀ A picture of Nefertiti
This relief shows Nefertiti with the projecting, cap-like headgear worn by the royal women in Amarna. This is one of the few characteristics distinguishing her from depictions of the king. The strong assimilation of the facial features of all the members of the royal family has often led to confusion.

▶ Offering scene
This relief shows a man leading a bull to ritual slaughter. The depiction clearly illustrates that the official style was used for everyday scenes, too, but not with the same artistic consequences and strength of expression as with royal motifs. The man does have a projecting skull, narrow shoulders and broad hips, but in a less extreme form.

Akhenaten is depicted wearing the blue crown with the uraeus, and two ribbons streaming down his neck.

Hands extend from the reviving rays of the Aten, reaching out to Akhenaten and Nefertiti.

Nefertiti was considered an almost equal partner of Akhenaten, despite the fact that she is always depicted on a much smaller scale in offering scenes.

The king has a slender figure, a slight torso, rather prominent collarbones and a paunch.

◀ An offering to the Aten
This scene is from a stele of Akhenaten. The king is standing in front of a simple offerings table, accompanied by his wife Nefertiti, wearing a double-plumed crown, cow's horns, a sun disc and carrying a sistrum. The Aten, whose rays shine down on the king and his wife, hovers above the scene in the shape of the sun disc.

▼ The daughters
This fragment of a mural offers an intimate insight into the private chambers of the royal family. On the right, barely visible, are the feet of the queen, covered by a pleated white robe, with the legs of the three princesses standing in front. At the bottom right are another two daughters touching each other tenderly.

▲ Relief of Akhenaten
The numerous reliefs from Amarna depict the king in the same style as that of most of his statues. This example clearly shows the reddish brown skin of Akhenaten and Nefertiti, and the brilliant blue of their crowns that was also used for the hieroglyphs and the cartouches.

The Mask of Tutankhamun

Of the spectacular treasures discovered in the famous tomb of Tutankhamun in the Valley of the Kings, his mummy mask, now displayed among the masterpieces of the Egyptian Museum in Cairo, is one of the most remarkable.

The discovery of the tomb of Tutankhamun (1336–1327 BC) by Howard Carter in 1922 was one of the greatest in the history of Egyptology. Among the young king's rich funerary equipment, Carter unearthed the magnificent mummy mask, made from solid gold with decorations in carnelian, obsidian, lapis lazuli and coloured glass.

The flesh of the gods

When Carter opened Tutankhamun's gold sarcophagus and revealed the mask, he saw a face with the features of a god. The Ancient Egyptians regarded precious metals and stones as divine materials, and their use in the funerary equipment of the king invested him with the attributes of a deity. Gold, for instance, identified the pharaoh with the sun god, Ra.

The nemes headdress is decorated with stripes of lapis lazuli, the blue of which contrasts with the bright yellow of the gold.

▶ **The attributes of the king**
Despite his association with the heretical reign of Akhenaten (1352–1336 BC), Tutankhamun is depicted here in the traditional regalia of the pharaohs. He wears the royal nemes headdress, striped with lapis lazuli and hanging down on either side of his face. The uraeus, or Wadjyt cobra, and the vulture goddess Nekhbet, symbols respectively of Lower and Upper Egypt, and of the king's sovereignty, sit side by side on his forehead, offering him their protection. His false beard, which identifies him with the gods, is worked in a framework of gold with blue glass paste inlaid to create a plaited effect.

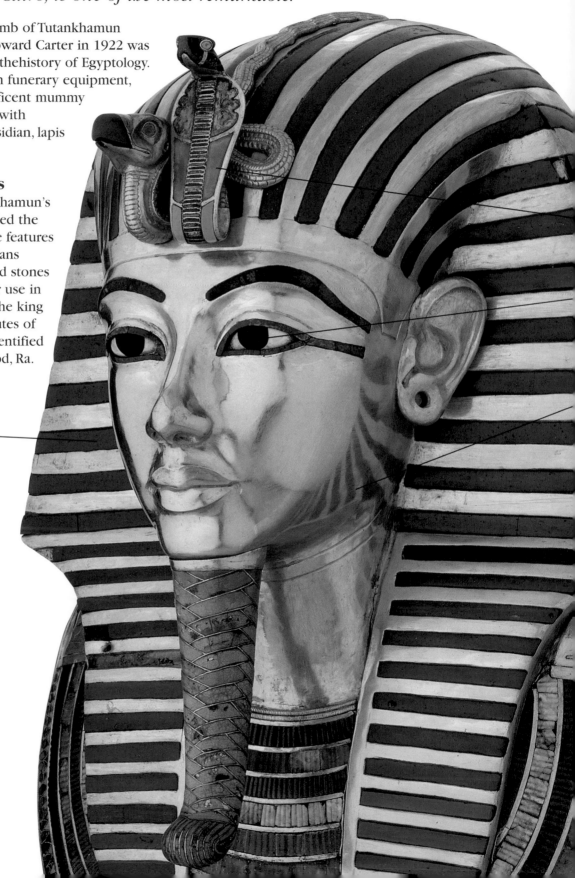

▲ The pharaoh's eyes
Tutankhamun's expressive, almond-shaped eyes are emphasized and extended by eye make-up fashioned in lapis lazuli. The whites of the eyes are made from quartz, while the pupils have been inlaid with obsidian. A touch of red pigment has been added to the corner of the eyes to create a lifelike impression.

The royal uraeus and Nekhbet vulture sit together on the pharaoh's forehead.

A realistic appearance was given to the eyes with the use of semi-precious stones.

The gold of the mummy mask identifies the pharaoh with the sun god, Ra.

The breast collar is comprised of 12 rows inlaid with lapis lazuli, quartz, turquoise and coloured glass.

▶ The depiction of the king
Tutankhamun's parentage is uncertain – his father may have been Amenhotep III (1390–1352 BC) or, according to some Egyptologists, Akhenaten (1352–1336 BC). Although Tutankhamun is shown in the traditional, idealized manner of the pharaohs of Ancient Egypt, the influence of artistic styles popular during the reign of Akhenaten is evident. The facial features – notably the elongated oval of the face, the almond-shaped eyes, the long, slim nose and soft, full lips – are all typical of the Armana period's intimate, expressive portraiture. Tutankhamun's pleasant, youthful face is set in a serene, slightly sad expression.

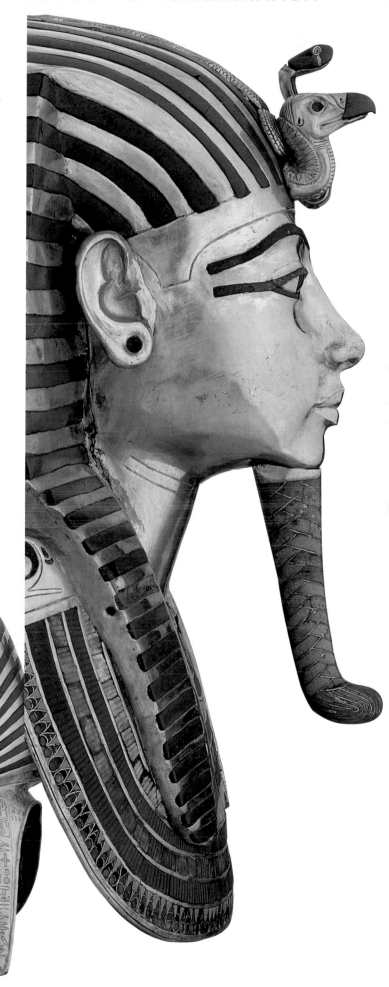

▶ Rear view
The rear view reveals hieroglyphs inscribed on the king's back. These name the limbs of the deceased and identify them with a variety of deities, placing them under their protection. During the New Kingdom (1550–1069 BC), this formula came to be included in the *Book of the Dead*.

The Tombs of Horemheb

While serving as Tutankhamun's general, Horemheb began to build his family tomb at Saqqara. After he became pharaoh, however, he commissioned a new tomb in the Valley of the Kings.

▲ The royal titulary
The cartouche on the left features Horemheb's throne name, Djeserkheperura-Setenpenra, or 'The images of Ra are sacred, chosen of Ra', while his birth name, Horemheb, translates as 'Horus is celebrated, beloved of Amun'.

Commander-in-Chief of the Egyptian army under the pharaohs Akhenaten (1352–1336 BC), Tutankhamun (1336–1327 BC) and Ay (1327–1323 BC), Horemheb (1323–1295 BC) began work on his tomb in the Memphite necropolis at Saqqara during the short reign of Tutankhamun.

The tomb was first located in the nineteenth century by the German archaeologist Karl Richard Lepsius, but was then lost again under the desert sands until its rediscovery by an Anglo-Dutch team in the 1970s. Many of the spectacular reliefs found in the tomb, which were heavily influenced by the Amarna style of art of Akhenaten's reign, are now among the collections of various European museums.

A second tomb

In 1908, a young Egyptologist called Edward Ayrton discovered another tomb of Horemheb, this one in the Valley of the Kings near ancient Thebes. Despite being unfinished, it contained a variety of funerary equipment and featured some splendid coloured reliefs.

Horemheb succeeded Ay as pharaoh at the end of the Eighteenth Dynasty and his reign saw a return to normality after the turbulence of the rule of the heretical pharaoh Akhenaten. Upon his ascension to the throne, Horemheb started constructing a new tomb in the Theban necropolis, where he was ultimately buried.

The first courtyard is surrounded by papyrus bundle columns with closed capitals.

The inner walls of the two courtyards are decorated with fine reliefs of superior artistic quality.

A large part of the building material used by Horemheb is from the site of the step pyramid of Djoser.

A deep shaft in the second courtyard leads to the subterranean burial chambers of Horemheb and his wife.

TOMB OF HOREMHEB AT SAQQARA

side chapel · second colonnaded courtyard · store room · statue room · first colonnaded courtyard · forecourt

side chapel · cult chapel · access to subterranean chambers · store room · entrance pylon

N

0   15 m

▲ The tomb at Saqqara
Horemheb's tomb at Saqqara was originally located by the German archaeologist Karl Richard Lepsius in the nineteenth century. It was comprehensively excavated in 1975 during an expedition undertaken by the Egyptian Exploration Society in collaboration with a Dutch team from the National Museum of Antiquities in Leiden.

◀ Ground plan of the tomb
The tomb of Horemheb is laid out in a plan similar to that of the Ancient Egyptian temples. Its entrance is flanked by pylons, beyond which lie colonnaded courtyards, storerooms, a statue room and several chapels.

▲ The royal tomb

Shortly after he came to the throne, Horemheb began the construction of a new tomb for himself in the Theban necropolis of the Valley of the Kings. In this colourful wall painting, the pharaoh appears several times in the company of deities including Osiris (far left), the god of the dead, and the goddess Hathor, identifiable by her headdress, which consists of the solar disc and a pair of cow's horns.

The entrance pylon led to the first courtyard with its 24 papyrus columns.

The statue room, with several figures of Horemheb and his family, is located between the courtyards.

The floors of the two colonnaded courtyards, the statue room and the cult chapel were all paved with limestone.

▶ Ground plan of the tomb in the Valley of the Kings

The funerary chamber of Horemheb is reached by a succession of corridors, staircases and halls. In the middle of the burial chamber, the king's magnificent red granite sarcophagus still stands.

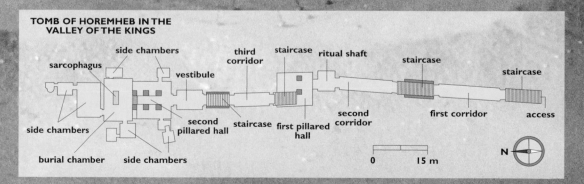

TOMB OF HOREMHEB IN THE VALLEY OF THE KINGS

side chambers
sarcophagus
vestibule
third corridor
staircase
ritual shaft
staircase
staircase

side chambers
second pillared hall
staircase
first pillared hall
second corridor
first corridor
access

burial chamber   side chambers

0   15 m   N

The most notable aspect of Horemheb's tomb at Saqqara is that it was built in stages, growing more sumptuous as the general became more powerful. It was designed to resemble the temples of Ancient Egypt, featuring pylons and spectacular colonnaded courtyards.

A return to tradition

In contrast to the naturalistic, Amarna-inspired reliefs in the Saqqara tomb, Horemheb's burial in the Valley of the Kings was accompanied by images in a more traditional Ancient Egyptian design. The Theban tomb, however, was innovative in its architectural style, consisting of a single straight corridor with side chambers, instead of the 'bent axis' manner of earlier royal tombs. It is also the first example of the *Book of Gates* being used in the decoration of the burial chamber.

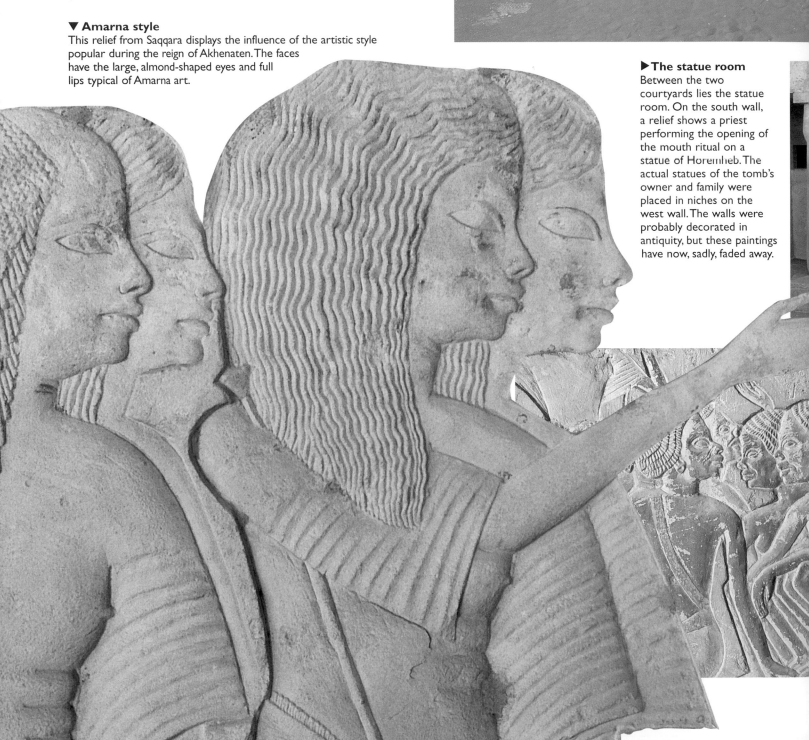

▼ Amarna style
This relief from Saqqara displays the influence of the artistic style popular during the reign of Akhenaten. The faces have the large, almond-shaped eyes and full lips typical of Amarna art.

▶ The statue room
Between the two courtyards lies the statue room. On the south wall, a relief shows a priest performing the opening of the mouth ritual on a statue of Horemheb. The actual statues of the tomb's owner and family were placed in niches on the west wall. The walls were probably decorated in antiquity, but these paintings have now, sadly, faded away.

◄ The first colonnaded courtyard of the tomb at Saqqara
Like all the other walls of the tomb, those of the first courtyard were made from mud brick, originally lined with white limestone tiles. Only a handful of these tiles has been found at the site. The courtyard still contains these elegant, well-preserved pillars.

▼ Horemheb at prayer
This relief from Saqqara shows Horemheb kneeling in prayer before a god, the image of whom has been eroded. In other reliefs, he is depicted making offerings to the gods. The general also erected steles, one dedicated to the gods Osiris, Amun and Ptah, and another to Ra-Horakhty, Maat and Thoth.

General Horemheb wears a layered wig and a thin linen robe with wide sleeves.

The uraeus on Horemheb's forehead was added after he became pharaoh.

With his hands raised and palms facing forwards, Horemheb is depicted kneeling on the ground praying.

As Commander in Chief of the Egyptian army, Horemheb wears a long tunic and sandals.

◄ Nubian prisoners
Some of the reliefs in Horemheb's tomb are remarkably well preserved and retain their original paintwork. This is true of the scene shown left, which vividly depicts a group of Nubian prisoners, identifiable by their loincloths and dark skin.

▲ Foreign envoys
Befitting a man of his military standing, Horemheb's tomb at Saqqara is decorated with images of him receiving tribute from foreign princes. Horemheb collects these gifts, acting of behalf of his pharaoh, Tutankhamun (1336–1327 BC). Many such reliefs are now on display in the museums of Leiden, Berlin and Vienna.

▲ The Valley of the Kings
Horemheb's Theban tomb was discovered in 1908 by the young Egyptologist Edward Ayrton. The vestibule, which leads into the funerary chamber, features colourful scenes of the pharaoh in the company of the gods, including Horus and Isis.

▶ Tomb decoration
The painted, sunk relief decoration covers only certain parts of the Theban tomb. Large-scale depictions of gods can be seen in the ritual shaft and in the vestibule. The burial chamber contains scenes from the *Book of Gates*, a guide to the afterlife that describes the journey of the sun through the underworld. The depiction in the vestibule shows the king before the major deities, and in the company of Osiris, the god of the afterlife, with his crook and flail. The green colour of his skin symbolizes rebirth.

◀ **Horemheb and Anubis, the guardian of the necropolis**
In the vestibule, Horemheb is shown holding the hand of Anubis, the jackal-headed god of the dead. Anubis was responsible for leading the deceased through the underworld, and was also regarded as the guardian of the cemetery of the Valley of the Kings.

▼ *Book of Gates*
Horemheb's tomb is innovative in featuring scenes from the *Book of Gates* on the columns of the funerary chamber rather than from the traditional netherworld text, the *Amduat*. This scene from the second hour of the *Book of Gates*, showing Ra in his barge, appears on the east wall of the burial chamber.

INSIGHT

An unfinished tomb

Despite its spectacular reliefs and architecture, Horemheb's tomb in the Valley of the Kings was never finished. This offers us a unique glimpse at the stages in which the painted reliefs were executed. On this example, the outline grid marked carefully on the limestone is still clearly visible. The artists sketched the images, first in red, then in black, onto the grid. Painting was the final touch, a stage that was never reached in this instance.

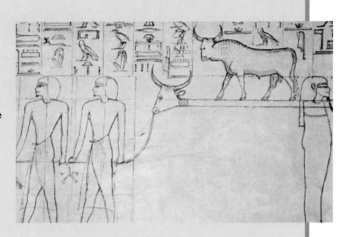

◀ **The sarcophagus**
Horemheb's splendid red granite sarcophagus, identical in shape to those of Tutankhamun and Ay (1327–1323 BC), still stands in the centre of his burial chamber. It was discovered containing a skull and several bones, although these could not be identified as the pharaoh's. The sarcophagus itself is decorated in striking sunken relief and hieroglyphic inscriptions. The lid had been removed in antiquity and shattered across an older break.

The Monuments of Rameses II

During the 66-year reign of Rameses II (1279–1213 BC), Egypt enjoyed a period of peace and prosperity, and witnessed the biggest monument-building programme in its history.

After the Battle of Qadesh in *c.* 1274 BC, and the subsequent peace treaty with the Hittites, Ancient Egypt's northern borders and interests in Syria-Palestine were secure. The gradual annexation of Nubia, with its lucrative trade in luxury goods and natural resources of gold, also began.

Buildings for eternity

The sheer number of new monuments, temples and statues built was breathtaking. In Nubia, Rameses II constructed rock-cut temples at Amara, Beit el-Wali, Derr, Wadi es-Sebua and Gerf Husein, and the magnificent twin temples at Abu Simbel, the larger dedicated to Rameses II himself, the smaller and more elegant one to his favourite wife, Nefertari. The walls of the large temple are decorated with scenes of the Battle of Qadesh, showing the pharaoh vanquishing his enemies – a theme repeated many times in other monuments he built.

◄ **The royal inscriptions**
Statues, such as this standing figure of Rameses II, also served as writing surfaces. On its back is a vertical row of hieroglyphs giving the titles of the king. The bracelets on the wrists are decorated with name cartouches as well. The statue, initially from a temple in Memphis, is today on display in Cairo's busy station square.

The uraeus *protects the king from his enemies.*

The colossal royal statues *in front of the great temple of Abu Simbel depict Rameses II sitting on a throne. They symbolize the power of Egypt over Nubia.*

◀ The great temple at Abu Simbel
Rameses II started building this large rock temple in the sixth year of his reign and finished it in the thirty-fifth year. The front, with monumental statues, imitates the façade of a temple pylon. Like the other six Nubian rock temples, Abu Simbel was not only dedicated to several Ancient Egyptian gods, but also mainly to the deified king himself. The site was rediscovered by the Swiss Egyptologist Johann Ludwig Burckhardt in 1813 and excavated by Giovanni Battista Belzoni in 1817.

Each of the four statues of Rameses II wears the divine beard, the nemes headcloth and the double crown of Upper and Lower Egypt.

The mother of Rameses II, and several of his sons and daughters, are depicted on a smaller scale at the feet of the colossi.

▼ The small temple at Abu Simbel
Rameses II dedicated this temple to his great royal wife, Nefertari, and to the goddess Hathor. The monument's backward-slanting façade is divided into six tall, narrow niches, which house four standing figures of the king with different crowns, as well as two statues of Nefertari in the form of the goddess Hathor.

PROFILE

Augustus and the art of propaganda

A similar policy of self-aggrandizement was employed by the Roman Emperor Augustus (30 BC–AD 14). He had innumerable statues of himself, some of enormous proportions, erected in public places throughout the Roman Empire (below). On the reliefs of some Egyptian temples – for example, on the island of Philae – he had himself depicted performing cult rites in the robes of a pharaoh. A statue of Augustus found at Karnak – now in the Egyptian Museum, Cairo – also shows him as an Egyptian ruler.

Rameses II constructed numerous new buildings in different cities in Egypt, extended existing temples, erecting statues and obelisks in them, and usurping the works of previous rulers. There is hardly a large monument in Egypt that does not attest to his reign – several temples at Memphis, the pylon and court at Luxor, the decoration of the hypostyle hall at Karnak and extensions to the complex, his mortuary temple, the Ramesseum at western Thebes, a new temple at Abydos and the completion of the nearby temple of his father, Sety I (1294–1279 BC).

In his new capital of Piramesse, a harbour town in the eastern Nile Delta, he had several temples built – for example, the main sanctuary for Amun, Ra-Horakhty and the Aten. The importance of Piramesse declined towards the end of the Ramesside period and many of the monuments and statues were removed to Tanis by kings of the Twenty-First Dynasty (1069–945 BC).

▲ The Karnak temple
Rameses II finished the hypostyle hall – with its 134 columns – that had been started by Horemheb (1323–1295 BC). Some of the decorations were ordered by Sety I (1294–1279 BC), but most of the mural reliefs were created under Rameses II.

▶ The colossus of Karnak
Behind the first pylon of the Amun temple of Karnak is an open courtyard with a huge standing figure of Rameses II. It was usurped during the reign of Rameses VI (1143–1136 BC) and later by Pinudjem I, one of the priest-kings of Thebes during the Twenty-First Dynasty (1069–945 BC).

Bintanat, the daughter and wife of Rameses II, wears the tall plumed crown and a tight-fitting sheath dress.

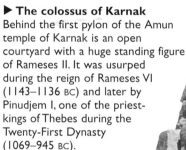

The king wears the nemes headdress and the double crown, and holds the crook and flail, symbols of royal authority.

▼ **Bust of Rameses II**
The head of another colossal statue of Rameses II, wearing the nemes headcloth and the ceremonial beard, lies in front of the entrance pylon of the Luxor temple.

313

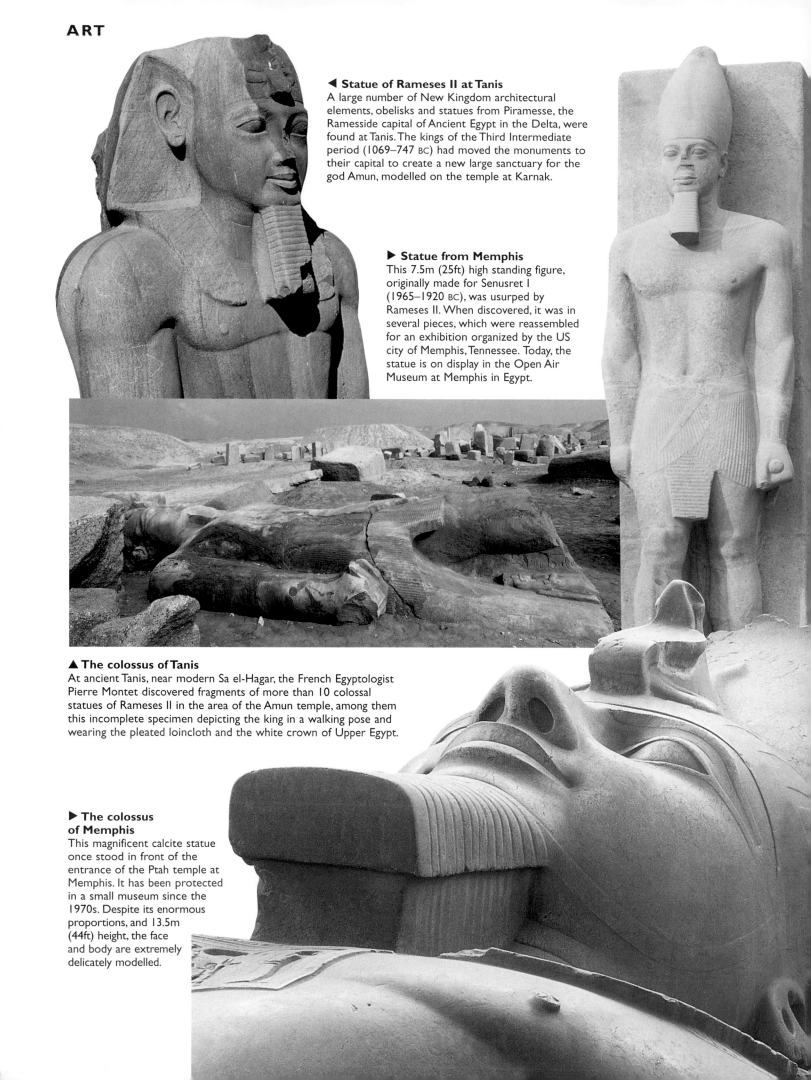

◀ Statue of Rameses II at Tanis
A large number of New Kingdom architectural elements, obelisks and statues from Piramesse, the Ramesside capital of Ancient Egypt in the Delta, were found at Tanis. The kings of the Third Intermediate period (1069–747 BC) had moved the monuments to their capital to create a new large sanctuary for the god Amun, modelled on the temple at Karnak.

▶ Statue from Memphis
This 7.5m (25ft) high standing figure, originally made for Senusret I (1965–1920 BC), was usurped by Rameses II. When discovered, it was in several pieces, which were reassembled for an exhibition organized by the US city of Memphis, Tennessee. Today, the statue is on display in the Open Air Museum at Memphis in Egypt.

▲ The colossus of Tanis
At ancient Tanis, near modern Sa el-Hagar, the French Egyptologist Pierre Montet discovered fragments of more than 10 colossal statues of Rameses II in the area of the Amun temple, among them this incomplete specimen depicting the king in a walking pose and wearing the pleated loincloth and the white crown of Upper Egypt.

▶ The colossus of Memphis
This magnificent calcite statue once stood in front of the entrance of the Ptah temple at Memphis. It has been protected in a small museum since the 1970s. Despite its enormous proportions, and 13.5m (44ft) height, the face and body are extremely delicately modelled.

▶ Torso from the Ramesseum

This part of a black granite colossal statue, found among the ruins of the Ramesseum, is now in the British Museum in London. It belongs to a statue that stood next to the entrance of the hypostyle hall of the Ramesseum. Both face and body are perfectly smoothed, but parts of the loincloth and the nemes headdress were left rough, so that the paints would adhere better.

◀ The seated figures at Luxor

The temple at Luxor was extended under Rameses II. In addition to the huge entrance pylon, the front colonnaded court was built, where several statues were erected between the papyrus columns. Today, only two of the original six seated figures of the king in front of the pylon exist. One of the original two obelisks was removed in 1836 and transported to Paris, where it stands in the Place de la Concorde.

▲ Osiris pillars of the Ramesseum

In the second court of the Ramesseum, the king is represented as Osiris. This reinforced the idea that Rameses II ruled and was reborn as Osiris, and confirmed his divine nature.

▶ Colossus of Abu Simbel

The four 20m (66ft) high colossal statues at the front of the Great Temple at Abu Simbel demonstrate the power of the Ancient Egyptian state over Nubia. The foreign peoples subjugated by Egypt – Nubians, Asians and Libyans – are depicted on the sides of the base. The statues are the largest in Ancient Egyptian art after the Great Sphinx at Giza.

The Temples of Abu Simbel

In a remote part of Lower Nubia, known today as Abu Simbel, two of the great monumental buildings of Ancient Egypt tower over the Nile valley.

Abu Simbel is the location of two of the most extraordinary structures in Ancient Egypt – the huge rock-cut temples of Rameses II (1279–1213 BC) and his queen Nefertari (*c.* 1300–1250 BC). Rameses ordered these stone temples of Abu Simbel to be hewn directly from the solid rock of the hillside. The buildings followed the conventional layout of Egyptian stone tombs and the location was chosen as much for its sandstone as for its position in the hills.

The largest temple is dedicated to the gods Amun-Ra, Ra-Horakhty, Ptah and the deified Rameses II.

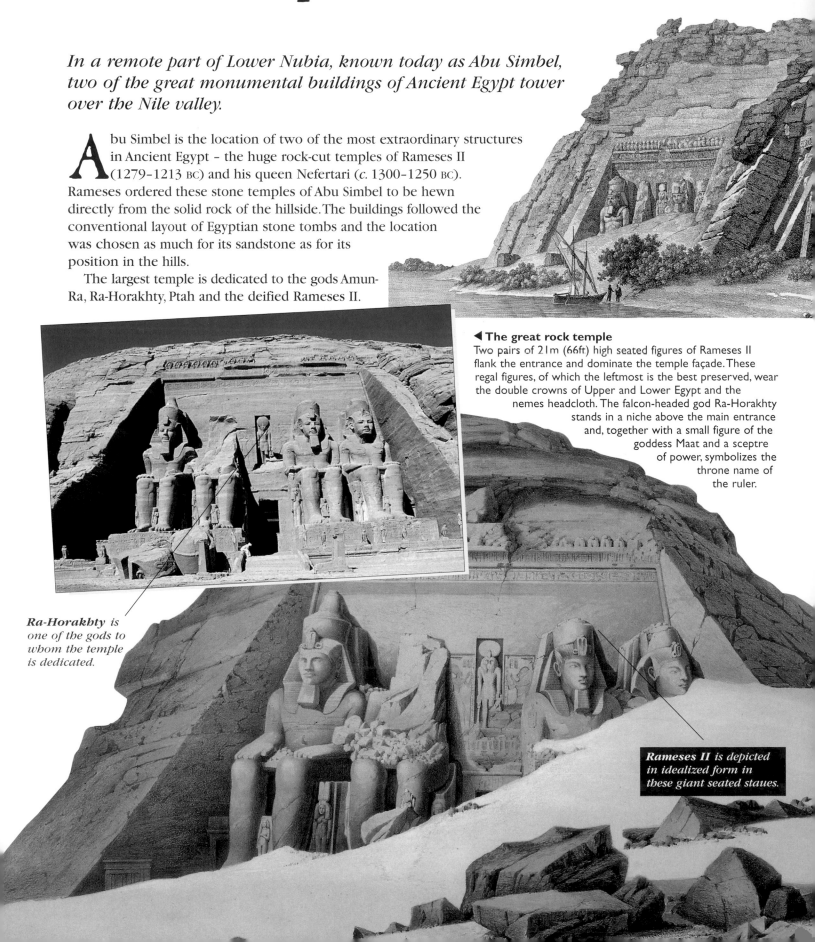

◄ The great rock temple
Two pairs of 21m (66ft) high seated figures of Rameses II flank the entrance and dominate the temple façade. These regal figures, of which the leftmost is the best preserved, wear the double crowns of Upper and Lower Egypt and the nemes headcloth. The falcon-headed god Ra-Horakhty stands in a niche above the main entrance and, together with a small figure of the goddess Maat and a sceptre of power, symbolizes the throne name of the ruler.

Ra-Horakhty is one of the gods to whom the temple is dedicated.

Rameses II is depicted in idealized form in these giant seated staues.

This nineteenth-century engraving shows both temples at Abu Simbel.

The pharaoh's titles and names surround the entrance to the small temple.

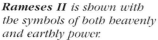

Rameses II is shown with the symbols of both heavenly and earthly power.

Nefertari is shown with the symbols of Hathor.

◄ Abu Simbel's discovery

Abu Simbel was discovered in 1813 when the traveller Jean-Louis Burckhardt (1784–1817) glimpsed the colossal figures at the entrance to the great temple, almost completely hidden beneath drifts of sand. Several years later, in 1817, Giovanni Belzoni (1778–1823) began to excavate the temples from their sandy grave.

▼ The small temple

This east-facing temple dedicated to Nefertari and Hathor is fronted by six 10m (33ft) high statues. Four of these show Rameses II and two show his queen Nefertari, who, unusually for the time, is the same height as the pharaoh. Each of these figures hewn from the rock has its left leg extended. The queen wears the symbols of the goddess Hathor – the double-feathered crown with cow horns and the disc of the sun. The picture below shows the remarkable condition of the temple today, while the engraving, although it exaggerates the scale, gives an impression of the temple in the middle of the nineteenth century after the drifting sands had been removed.

The Master Builder

Rameses II (1279–1213 BC) was the third pharaoh of the Nineteenth Dynasty. Under his reign, Egypt became a world power, with its borders extending to Syria in the east and Nubia in the south. As a mark of his power, Rameses built impressive temples at Abydos and Thebes, in addition to the two temples at Abu Simbel.

The colossi of Rameses, at the entrance to his temple at Abu Simbel (right), have smaller figures under and between his feet, representing the 'nine bows' – the traditional enemies of Egypt – subdued and subjugated by the pharaoh.

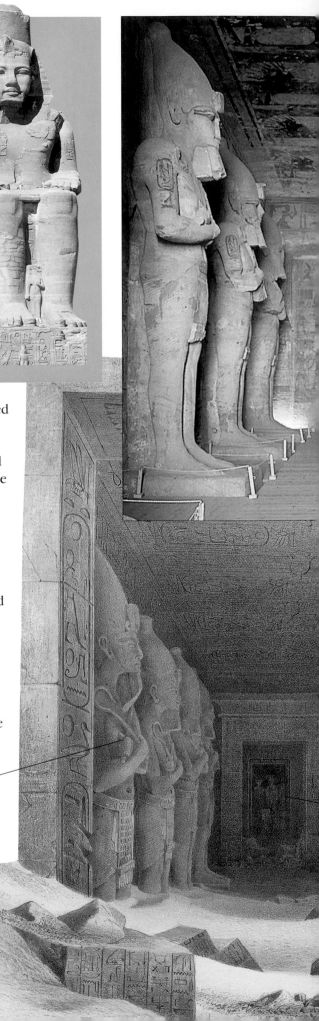

The smaller temple, located a short distance to the north, is dedicated to Rameses' wife, Nefertari, and the goddess Hathor. The two temples, however, have different ground-plans. The great temple consists of two pillared halls and numerous side chambers, followed by a vestibule and a large sanctuary. The smaller temple was restricted to a hall, a vestibule and a small sanctuary.

Inside the temples

The visitor to the great temple enters a huge hall flanked by eight massive statue-pillars which depict Rameses as the god Osiris. Beyond this is a smaller pillared hall leading to a vestibule and the sanctuary, which holds the seated figures of the gods, Rameses, Ptah, Amun-Ra and Ra-Horakhty. Nefertari's temple also contains a hall with six pillared statues of Hathor, a vestibule and the sanctuary, where a statue of Hathor protects Rameses. The interior wall carvings of the temples celebrate Rameses' many military victories, and also show the royal couple in religious rituals.

After the construction of the Aswan High Dam in the 1960s, the temples were increasingly threatened by the rising water levels of Lake Nasser, and had to be cut into blocks and moved 180m (590ft) inland and raised 65m (213ft) to higher ground.

The crown of Upper Egypt is worn by the pharaoh on these statues.

▶ Sand, a natural preservative

The enormous quantities of sand blown into the entrance by north winds closed the temple and ensured the survival of its statues and paintings. The walls of the pillared hall, which show scenes from the life of Rameses II, the massive statues and the ceilings with their paintings of all-protecting vultures were in the same condition and colours as they were before the sands covered them.

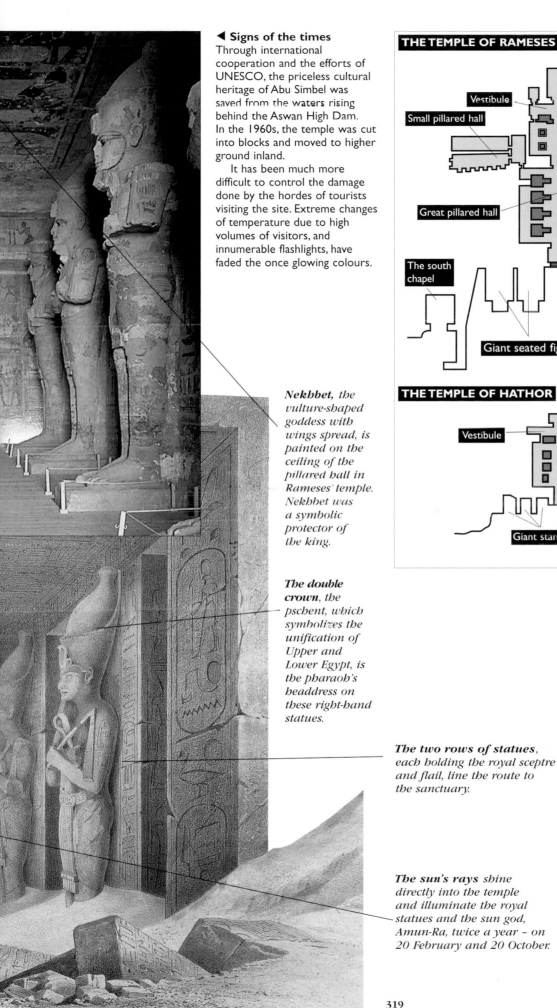

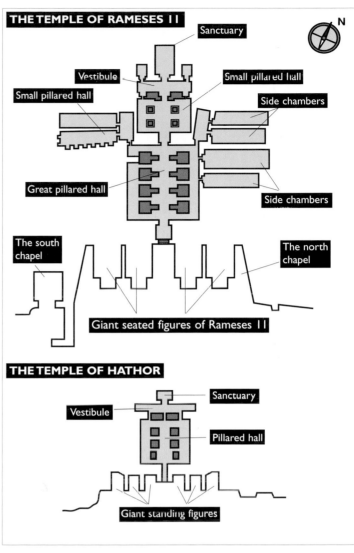

◄ Signs of the times
Through international cooperation and the efforts of UNESCO, the priceless cultural heritage of Abu Simbel was saved from the waters rising behind the Aswan High Dam. In the 1960s, the temple was cut into blocks and moved to higher ground inland.

It has been much more difficult to control the damage done by the hordes of tourists visiting the site. Extreme changes of temperature due to high volumes of visitors, and innumerable flashlights, have faded the once glowing colours.

Nekhbet, the vulture-shaped goddess with wings spread, is painted on the ceiling of the pillared hall in Rameses' temple. Nekhbet was a symbolic protector of the king.

The double crown, the pschent, which symbolizes the unification of Upper and Lower Egypt, is the pharaoh's headdress on these right-hand statues.

The two rows of statues, each holding the royal sceptre and flail, line the route to the sanctuary.

The sun's rays shine directly into the temple and illuminate the royal statues and the sun god, Amun-Ra, twice a year – on 20 February and 20 October.

THE TEMPLE OF RAMESES II

N

Sanctuary

Vestibule

Small pillared hall

Small pillared hall

Side chambers

Great pillared hall

Side chambers

The south chapel

The north chapel

Giant seated figures of Rameses II

THE TEMPLE OF HATHOR

Sanctuary

Vestibule

Pillared hall

Giant standing figures

▲ Layout of the Abu Simbel temples
The two temples at Abu Simbel were carved from solid rock, and are similar in style to burial tombs, rather than temples. There are no pylons at the entrance, which is marked by the colossal figures hewn from the hillside, and the halls and chambers are reminiscent of an underground quarry.

Nefertari's Tomb

For his favourite wife Queen Nefertari (1300–1250 BC), the pharaoh Rameses II (1279–1213 BC) built the most beautiful tomb discovered in the Valley of the Queens.

The Italian Egyptologist Ernesto Schiaparelli (1856–1928) discovered the rock-cut tomb, or hypogeum, of Queen Nefertari in the Valley of the Queens in 1904. Built on the scale of a pharaoh's tomb, it is decorated with paintings of astonishing beauty.

As you enter the tomb from outside, a flight of steps leads into an antechamber decorated with images of the queen with various Egyptian gods. A vestibule and a side chamber lead off this main room. A second flight of stairs gives access to the burial chamber, which is supported by four pillars. On either side of the room are three chambers for tomb offerings, and the decorations retrace the journey of the queen into the afterlife .

Towards immortality

In the higher antechamber, the wall paintings show the queen being allowed access to the afterlife by the gods and being invested with magical powers. Only then can she make her descent into the burial chamber where, after passing through the gates to the underworld, she becomes like the god Osiris and possesses eternal life.

▶ The vestibule
Situated to the west of the antechamber, the vestibule has paintings of the queen being greeted by Neith (far right), before being led by the falcon-headed Horus towards the enthroned figures of Ra-Horakhty, the sun god, and Hathor, associated here with western Thebes. In her funerary aspect, Hathor was the goddess of the Theban necropolis and it was she who received the deceased into the underworld.

◀ Valley of the Queens
This desert valley, eroded by flowing water and wind, is one of the three Theban necropolises of the New Kingdom (1550–1069 BC). Mainly reserved for queens and princes, it contains about 80 tombs, most of them simply shafts. Of the 20 which are decorated, the most important is that of Nefertari.

Orientation of the tomb

Nefertari's tomb is built on a north–south axis, suggesting the course of the River Nile, whereas the journey of the deceased follows the sun from east to west. As she descends into the depths of the tomb, the queen is reborn, like Osiris.

Four pillars enclose the space reserved for the sarcophagus.

One of three small chambers in the burial chamber that held tomb offerings.

BURIAL CHAMBER

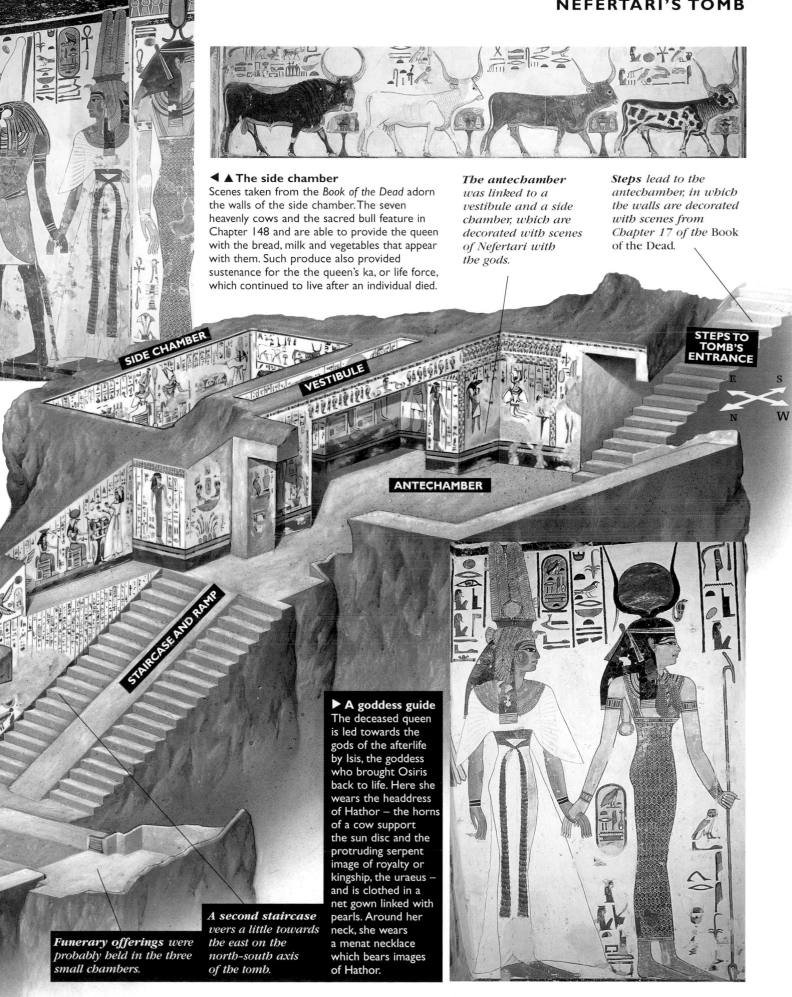

◀ ▲ The side chamber
Scenes taken from the *Book of the Dead* adorn the walls of the side chamber. The seven heavenly cows and the sacred bull feature in Chapter 148 and are able to provide the queen with the bread, milk and vegetables that appear with them. Such produce also provided sustenance for the the queen's ka, or life force, which continued to live after an individual died.

The antechamber was linked to a vestibule and a side chamber, which are decorated with scenes of Nefertari with the gods.

Steps lead to the antechamber, in which the walls are decorated with scenes from Chapter 17 of the Book of the Dead.

SIDE CHAMBER

VESTIBULE

STEPS TO TOMB'S ENTRANCE

E S
N W

ANTECHAMBER

STAIRCASE AND RAMP

▶ A goddess guide
The deceased queen is led towards the gods of the afterlife by Isis, the goddess who brought Osiris back to life. Here she wears the headdress of Hathor – the horns of a cow support the sun disc and the protruding serpent image of royalty or kingship, the uraeus – and is clothed in a net gown linked with pearls. Around her neck, she wears a menat necklace which bears images of Hathor.

Funerary offerings were probably held in the three small chambers.

A second staircase veers a little towards the east on the north-south axis of the tomb.

The tomb of Nefertari was restored between 1986 and 1992 by the Getty Conservation Institute, led by a team of specialist Italian restorers. Since the discovery of the tomb in 1904, the condition of the paintings had gradually deteriorated. The stone, and the layers of plaster which covered and supported it, had been attacked by salt, deposited on the walls by moisture. This included the water originally used to prepare the plaster and the paint, the Valley's infrequent but torrential rain that often flooded the tomb and the water vapour caused by the breath of visitors.

As a result, the paintings were beginning to 'lift' from the walls of the tomb. The restorers have mostly been able to halt the process of destruction, but the only way to protect the tomb further from the ravages of time has been to restrict the public's access to it.

▼ Pillar decorations

One of the four pillars in the burial chamber depicts Osiris and his son Horus. Wearing the leopard skin ritually worn by priests, Horus asks his father to judge Nefertari kindly.

The queen wears a vulture headdress surmounted by a sun disc and tall plumes.

Nefertari's gown is of thin pleated linen.

A wide decorative collar adorns the queen's neck.

Offerings to the gods

The walls by the staircase leading from the antechamber to the burial chamber are entirely decorated. On the upper part are depictions of Nefertari offering food and drink to the goddesses Hathor, Serket, Maat, Isis and Nephthys. Below are pictures of Anubis in the form of a crouching dog and the uraeus protecting the cartouche bearing the queen's name.

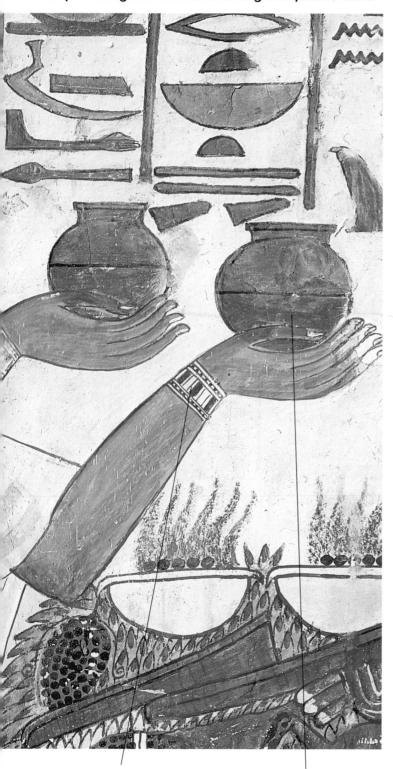

Geometric motifs decorate the bracelets on the queen's wrists.

Jars filled with wine are offered to the gods.

▲ Lost treasure

Several funerary items were found in Nefertari's tomb, one of which was this inlaid amulet of a djed pillar, said to represent the backbone, and thus the resurrection, of Osiris. The queen's tomb, looted since about 1100 BC, almost certainly contained many more riches.

▲ The queen's name

Like the body, the ba (soul), the ka (life force) and the shadow, the name was regarded as an essential element of every individual and had to be included in the deceased's tomb to ensure survival in the afterlife. Nefertari's name, enclosed in her royal cartouche, took the form of a statement: 'beloved of Mut'.

▼ Playing the game

This scene derived from the seventeenth chapter of the *Book of the Dead* shows Nefertari concentrating on a game in which she defeats her opponents in the underworld.

The Temple of Khons in Karnak

Set aside from the large Amun sanctuary in Karnak, the temple of the moon god Khons is a small but nearly complete temple of the New Kingdom (1550-1069 BC).

Together with his parents, Amun and Mut, Khons formed the Theban trinity of gods. His residence was a sanctuary in the south-western part of the temple area of Karnak on the river's eastern embankment in Thebes. A paved processional avenue, framed by sphinxes on both sides, led to an entrance flanked by two impressive towers and forming the pylon. The inner sanctuary was located at the end of a courtyard and a colonnaded hall.

The building of the temple began under Rameses III (1184-1153 BC) in the Twentieth Dynasty, but was completed only in Ptolemaic times (332-30 BC). The relief decorations therefore show pharaohs from various dynasties. Although the temple itself dates back to the Twentieth Dynasty, excavations have revealed traces of a former cult temple.

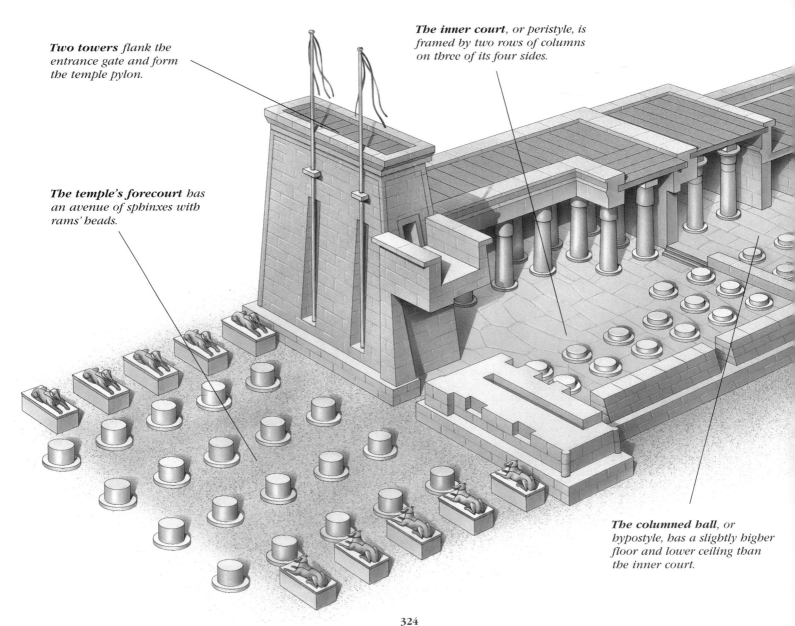

Two towers *flank the entrance gate and form the temple pylon.*

The inner court, *or peristyle, is framed by two rows of columns on three of its four sides.*

The temple's forecourt *has an avenue of sphinxes with rams' heads.*

The columned hall, *or hypostyle, has a slightly higher floor and lower ceiling than the inner court.*

◄ Architectural structure
The Ancient Egyptians used neither arches nor vaults when building temples: structures were supported using vertical and horizontal elements. The various architectural features were decorated with elaborate reliefs and ornate inscriptions.

▲ Access to the temple
The pylon, a massive gateway consisting of two tapering towers linked by a masonry bridge, forms the façade of the temple. In front are the stumps of columns built by the pharaoh Taharqo (690–664 BC).

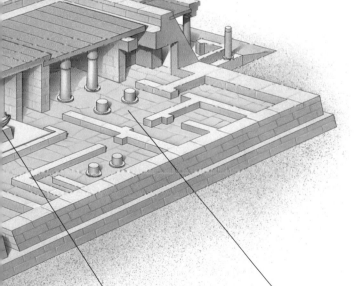

The anteroom contained the barge shrine raised on a pedestal.

The inner sanctuary, or cult chamber, housed an image of the deity; here, the ceiling is even lower than in the anteroom.

◄ Reconstruction of the temple
This 'cutaway' reconstruction of the temple of Khons is how it would have looked durng the New Kingdom (1550–1069 BC). Later additions, not shown, include a gateway built by Ptolemy III (246-221 BC) in front of the pylon. There was also a sun chapel on the roof that could be accessed by stairs leading from the anteroom.

INSIGHT

Elements of the Egyptian temple

An Egyptian temple represents a stone image of the universe. The site was aligned along a longitudinal axis, symbolizing the Nile, and surrounded by massive walls. In general, it comprised the following:

Paved processional way or dromos to the entrance: mostly lined by an alley of sphinxes.

The pylon: a monumental gate with two towers. Both towers rise above a broad rectangular ground plan, with slanting walls. They represent the land through which the Nile flows to Egypt, and the mountains in between which the sun rises. In the niches, there were flagpoles made from cedarwood, with colourful flags flying at the top.

Inner court or peristyle: an open court framed by colonnaded corridors.

Colonnaded hall or hypostyle: a closed, sparingly illuminated hall with a ceiling supported by columns.

The inner sanctuary: a room at the very back and darkest part of the temple that contained an image of the god. It was surrounded by side chapels, storage rooms and the anteroom with the god's barge.

Like most Egyptian temples, Khons has floors which rise in several levels to the inner sanctuary. At the same time the ceilings become lower, and the available light decreases continuously as you move towards the inner sanctum. Here stood the barge shrine of Khons, shrouded in mystic darkness.

Changing rooms

The temple site was redesigned and decorated at different times. The entrance pylon, for example, was decorated by the Libyan general Pinudjem I, who ruled Upper Egypt at the end of the New Kingdom. Reliefs show him with the gods.

The inner court and hypostyle were decorated by Herihor, an earlier general and high priest of Amun, who appears alongside Rameses XI (1099–1069 BC) in the columned hall, but alone in the next court. This probably dates from the time of Rameses XI's death and Herihor's attempt to usurp the throne. The inner part of the temple was decorated when the temple was built, with later additions during Ptolemaic and Roman times.

The last major change took place when the inner sanctuary was turned into a Coptic Christian church. To make it more accessible, the floor was lowered and an altar was built in place of the pedestal with the god's barge.

▶ **Ground plan of the temple site of Karnak**
The sanctuary of Karnak was dedicated to Amun-Ra, the god of the province and the protector of the pharaohs since the Middle Kingdom (2055–1650 BC). Apart from the Amun temple, there were temples for other gods, as well as various buildings, such as living quarters for priests, offices for the temple administration, farm buildings, workshops and warehouses.

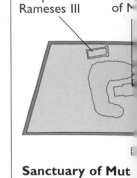

Temple of Rameses III | Tem of N

Sanctuary of Mut

Herihor's cartouches

These cartouches appear in the Khons temple's inner court. They indicate that Herihor, a powerful priest and virtual ruler at the time of Rameses XI, had equal status with the pharaoh.

PROFILE

Rameses III, the temple builder

Rameses III (1184–1153 BC) is considered the builder of the temple of Khons, even though work on the temple site continued until Ptolemaic times. He had several other temples erected at Karnak: one was dedicated to the trinity of gods of Thebes – Amun, Mut and Khons – another exclusively to the goddess Mut. Both temples have a similar ground plan to the Temple of the Dead, built by Rameses III in Medinet Habu (below, detail).

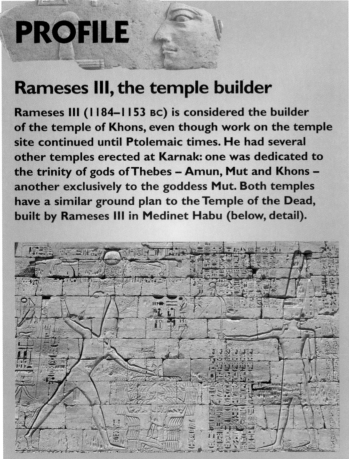

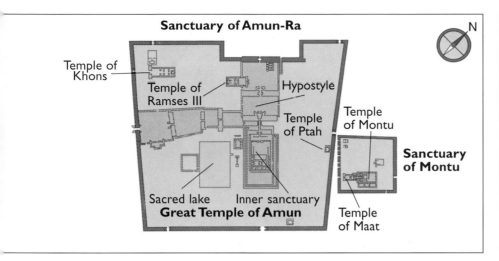

Sanctuary of Amun-Ra

Temple of Khons

Temple of Ramses III

Hypostyle

Temple of Ptah

Temple of Montu

Sanctuary of Montu

Temple of Maat

Sacred lake

Inner sanctuary

Great Temple of Amun

N

The hieroglyphs in the cartouches translate as: 'Herihor Sor-Amun (son of Amun), loved by Amun-Ra'.

▲ The inside wall decoration
The walls of the temple were decorated with colourful reliefs which depicted gods such as the falcon-headed Ra-Harakty.

◄ The inner court
The decoration of the inner court, or peristyle, was completed under Rameses IX (1126–1108 BC), on demand of Herihor, the high priest of Amun who had himself immortalized like the pharaoh.

Alexandria, a Royal Dream

According to legend, the Greek poet Homer visited Alexander the Great in a dream and told the Macedonian conqueror where to found his new city.

Alexander the Great (332–323 BC) conquered Egypt in 332 BC and swiftly established the city of Alexandria on the country's Mediterranean coast, on the site of an earlier settlement called Raqote. Alexander spent less than a year in Egypt and died in Babylon of a fever in 323 BC, aged just 33. His successors, however, became the Ptolemaic Dynasty (305–30 BC) and under them Alexandria grew into the wealthiest and most important metropolis in the ancient world. Its harbours were filled with boats laden with goods and its streets were lined with magnificent buildings.

Centre of science and wisdom

In addition to the architectural and economic wealth of Alexandria, the city also came to be regarded as the cultural centre of the known world. The famous library held around 700,000 volumes and was frequented by some of the greatest minds of antiquity, who gathered there to debate and exchange ideas.

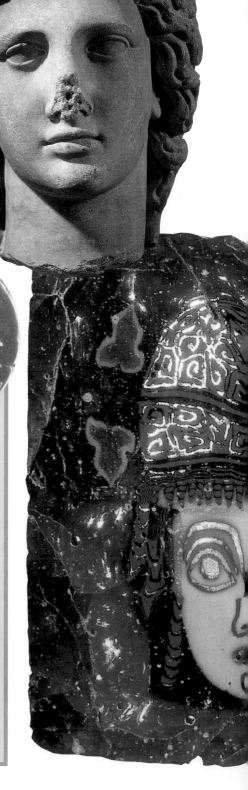

▶▼ Alexander the Great
The city Alexander founded swiftly became the most important trade centre in the ancient world. The coin below, which bears the 'ALEXANDROS' mark and an image of the Greek goddess Athena, was one of many minted in Alexandria and circulated all over Alexander's great empire.

INSIGHT

Underwater archaeology

Since 1996, archaeological expeditions have been undertaken in the waters off the coast of Alexandria in search of remnants of the city's glorious past. Very little of the once magnificent ancient city has survived – the library burned down with all its contents, and the waterfront was engulfed by the sea following a series of earthquakes in the early centuries AD. The lighthouse collapsed in c. 1349.

Led by French Egyptologists Jean-Yves Empereur and Franck Goddio, underwater excavations have yielded results that help us to understand the layout and scale of the city of the Ptolemies.

In addition to numerous artefacts such as jewellery, statues, sphinxes and items of pottery, a series of huge granite blocks, each weighing between 50 and 70 tonnes, has been discovered that might once have been part of the legendary lighthouse of Alexandria.

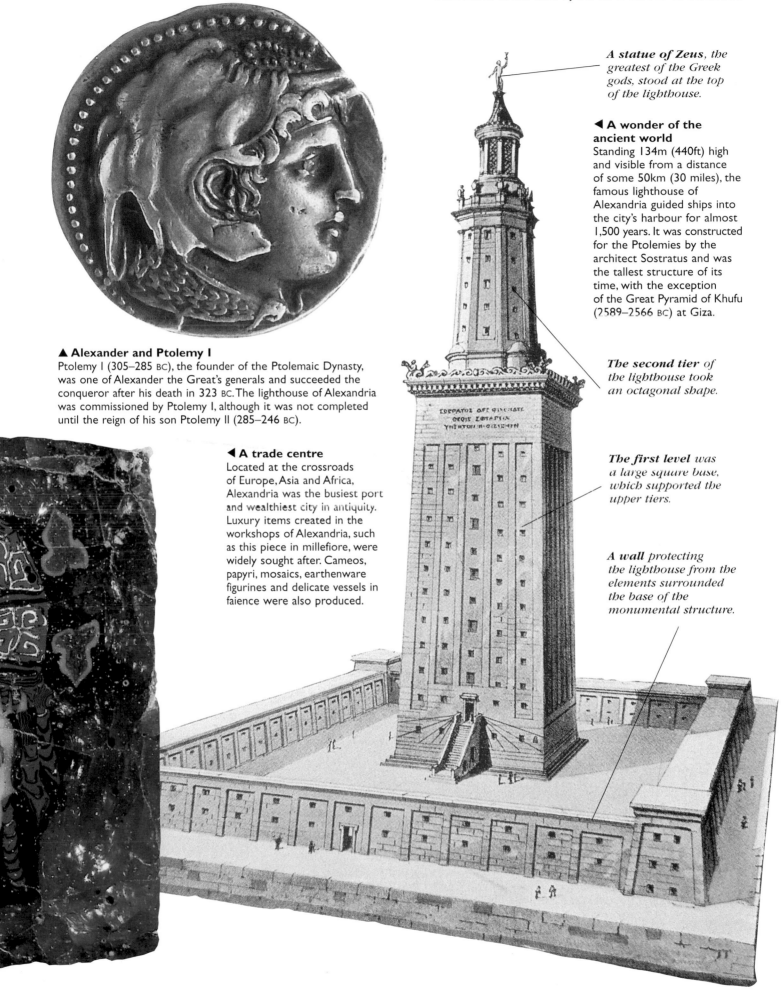

▲ Alexander and Ptolemy I
Ptolemy I (305–285 BC), the founder of the Ptolemaic Dynasty, was one of Alexander the Great's generals and succeeded the conqueror after his death in 323 BC. The lighthouse of Alexandria was commissioned by Ptolemy I, although it was not completed until the reign of his son Ptolemy II (285–246 BC).

◄ A trade centre
Located at the crossroads of Europe, Asia and Africa, Alexandria was the busiest port and wealthiest city in antiquity. Luxury items created in the workshops of Alexandria, such as this piece in millefiore, were widely sought after. Cameos, papyri, mosaics, earthenware figurines and delicate vessels in faience were also produced.

A statue of Zeus, the greatest of the Greek gods, stood at the top of the lighthouse.

◄ A wonder of the ancient world
Standing 134m (440ft) high and visible from a distance of some 50km (30 miles), the famous lighthouse of Alexandria guided ships into the city's harbour for almost 1,500 years. It was constructed for the Ptolemies by the architect Sostratus and was the tallest structure of its time, with the exception of the Great Pyramid of Khufu (2589–2566 BC) at Giza.

The second tier of the lighthouse took an octagonal shape.

The first level was a large square base, which supported the upper tiers.

A wall protecting the lighthouse from the elements surrounded the base of the monumental structure.

ANCIENT ALEXANDRIA

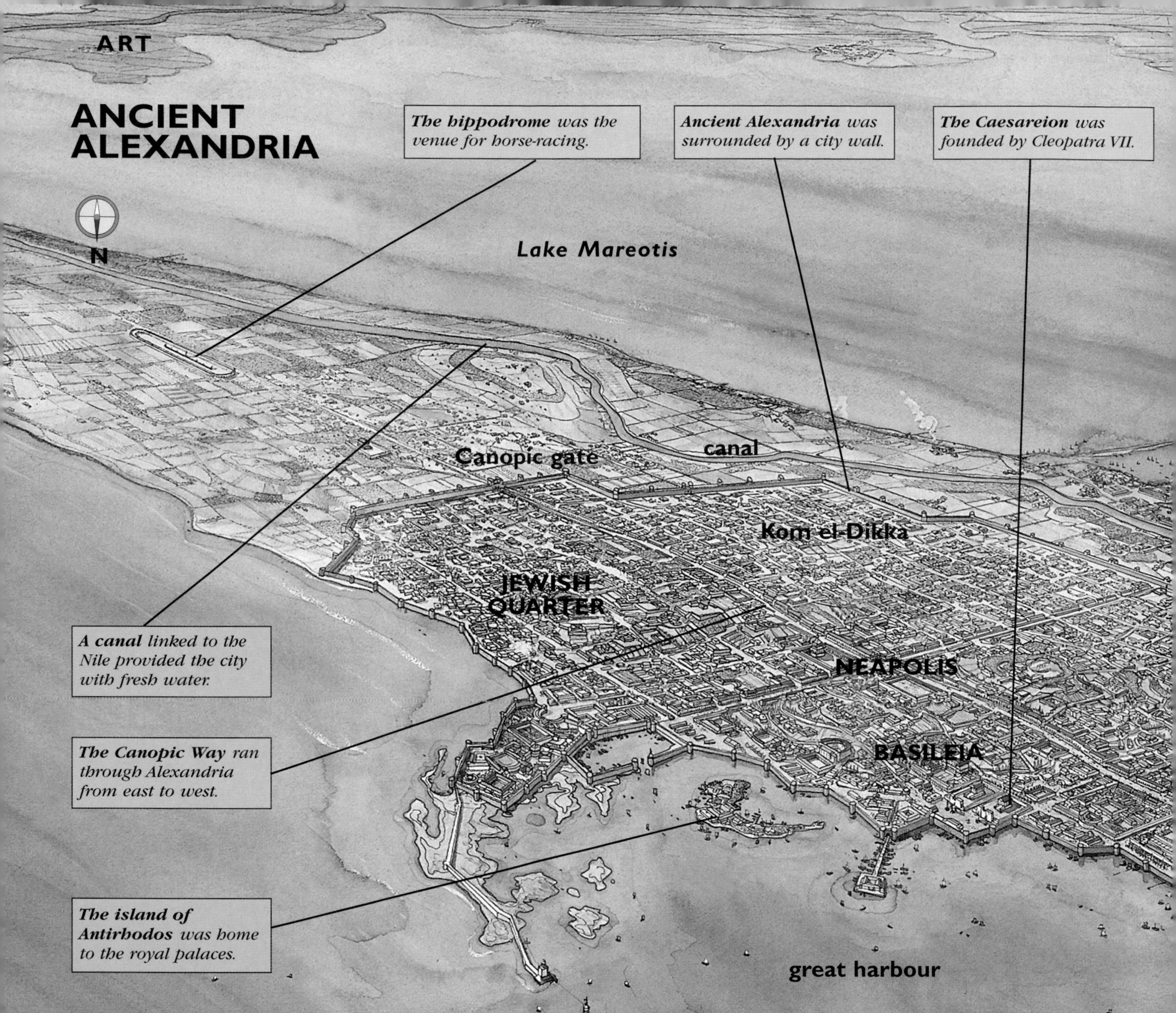

N

The hippodrome was the venue for horse-racing.

Ancient Alexandria was surrounded by a city wall.

The Caesareion was founded by Cleopatra VII.

Lake Mareotis

Canopic gate

canal

Kom el-Dikka

JEWISH QUARTER

NEAPOLIS

BASILEIA

A canal linked to the Nile provided the city with fresh water.

The Canopic Way ran through Alexandria from east to west.

The island of Antirhodos was home to the royal palaces.

great harbour

Pharos Island

◄ **The Pharos of Alexandria**
One of the Seven Wonders of the Ancient World, Alexandria's lighthouse was completed during the reign of Ptolemy II. Over the years, the monumental structure was damaged by a series of earthquakes and by AD 1349 had collapsed into the sea.

MEDITERRANEAN

The fortress of Qait Bey now occupies the former site of the lighthouse.

A temple dedicated to the goddess Isis once stood on Pharos Island.

Alexandria was built on the ancient settlement of Raqote.

The famous library was situated in the Royal Quarter.

◀ Remains of the Serapeum
The Serapeum at Alexandria, built for the worship of Serapis, was one of the city's most important buildings in Greco-Roman times. It was destroyed by Christians when Theodosius (AD 379–395) ordered it to be razed to the ground in AD 391. Only the subterranean sections of the monument have survived.

The Serapeum was dedicated to the Greco-Egyptian god Serapis.

The stadium hosted sporting events.

Raqote

Eunostos' harbour

The Eunostos, or 'safe return', was the main port at Alexandria.

The Heptastadion linked Pharos Island to Alexandria.

The temple of Poseidon stood on the western tip of Pharos Island.

◀ Roman baths
This complex of baths was built on three levels, offering cold, warm and steam baths. In Ptolemaic times, this site was part of a pleasure garden known as the Park of Pan.

▶ **The Canopic Way**
Running at 5km (3 miles) long and 30m (100ft) wide, the Canopic Way was a large avenue that ran through the city of Alexandria from east to west. The road was bordered by engraved columns, shown right in an illustration from the nineteenth century.

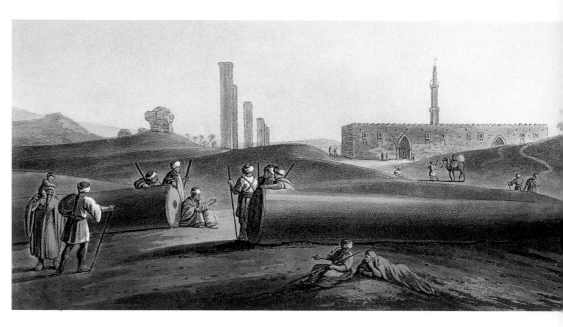

▼ **Canopus**
The city of Canopus was situated about 25km (16 miles) east of Alexandria, at the mouth of the Canopic branch of the Nile. A great temple dedicated to the Greco-Egyptian god Serapis was located here, which many wealthy Greeks visited in order to benefit from the deity's healing powers.

The layout of the city

Legend has it that Alexander the Great's choice of site for his new city was determined by a dream in which the Greek poet Homer, author of the *Iliad* and the *Odyssey*, appeared to him. According to this story, Homer instructed the young Macedonian to build on this strip of land on Egypt's Mediterranean coast.

In terms of its structure, Alexandria was a typically Greek rather than Egyptian city. Designed by the architect and planner Deinokrates of Rhodes, it was built on a gridded street plan, with streets intersecting at right angles from the Canopic Way, the main thoroughfare that ran through the city from east to west.

To the north of the city was the Mediterranean Sea, on which the ships sailed that brought goods in and out of Egypt. To the south were Lake Mareotis and the River Nile, which produced a constant supply of fresh water through a series of connected canals.

▲ **The Odeion**
Alexandria's Odeion was discovered in the 1960s during the demolition of a fort dating from the Napoleonic expedition of 1798–1801. The theatre was originally constructed between the second and fourth centuries AD and was rebuilt several times, even serving as a church at one point.

▼ **Pompey's Pillar**
This pillar, originally part of the Serapeum, was erected to celebrate a victory won by the Romans during the reign of the emperor Diocletian (AD 284–305).

 # INSIGHT

The obelisks of Alexandria

A number of Alexandria's architectural elements were taken from other parts of Egypt to embellish the new city. This is the case with the two obelisks that stood before the Caesarium, which had been erected centuries earlier by Thutmose III (1479–1425 BC) at the temple of Ra at Heliopolis.

These great stone monoliths were among Alexandria's most significant landmarks until the nineteenth century, when Egypt donated them to Britain and the United States. The one transported to England, and known as Cleopatra's Needle, now stands on the banks of the Thames in London. Its twin can today be found in New York's Central Park, where it is sadly in danger of disintegration due to the city's climate and pollution.

◄ **The catacombs of Kom el-Shugafa**
The rock-cut tombs of this subterranean labyrinth date to the first and second centuries AD. The tomb decorations combine Egyptian and Greco-Roman styles.

▼ **Head of a statue**
Found in the waters off Alexandria in 1995, this head possibly depicts Ptolemy II (285–246 BC), who was responsible for building many of the city's great monuments.

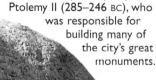

The development of the city

After the death of Alexander the Great, Egypt came under the control of the Ptolemies, who generally employed a policy of maintaining the existing political and religious structure. They took on the Egyptian concept of divine, hereditary kingship, and shocked Romans and other Greeks by adopting the practice of royal incest.

Under the Ptolemies, in particular Ptolemy I (305–285 BC) and his son and successor Ptolemy II (285–246 BC), Alexandria thrived. During the reigns of these two kings, several of the city's most magnificent buildings were constructed, including the famous lighthouse and library. The city's population, made up of Jews and Greeks in addition to native Egyptians, swelled to almost 500,000.

The cultural centre of antiquity

The Ptolemies placed a high value on learning, and supported the community of scholars that thrived in Alexandria. The cultural heart of the city was without doubt its library. The exact location of this building remains unknown, and its vast collection was lost when the library burned down, possibly in the third century AD.

In particular, all branches of the sciences flourished here. The mathematician Euclid (*c.* 330–260 BC), the author of *Elements*, a seminal work on geometry, founded a school in Alexandria in the reign of Ptolemy I, and Archimedes (*c.* 287–212 BC) and Heron (*c.* AD 10–75) invented numerous ingenious machines during their time in the city. Alexandria under the Ptolemies was also the site of significant discoveries in the fields of astronomy and medicine.

The Fayum Portraits

The Fayum Portraits, discovered by Flinders Petrie in the late nineteenth century, are striking depictions of members of the elite in Greco-Roman Egypt and combine Classical styles of art with Ancient Egyptian funerary traditions.

During the Greco-Roman Period (332 BC–AD 395), traditional Egyptian funerary practices and artistic styles came under the influence of Classical models. This is powerfully illustrated by the Fayum Portraits, a collection of mummy masks discovered by the celebrated British Egyptologist Flinders Petrie, at Hawara in the Fayum region in 1888. They were painted in encaustic, a technique that employs a mixture of wax and pigment, creating vivid colours that enhance the strikingly naturalistic depictions of the portraits' subjects.

Images from life

The portraits depict elite members of the Greco-Roman community in Egypt, often in their finest clothes and jewellery, in their prime, or even in their youth. Painted on thin wooden panels, they show their subjects with realistic facial features and an intense, expressive gaze.

▼ The Fayum Oasis
The Fayum Portraits take their name from the Fayum Oasis, where they were discovered by Flinders Petrie in the late nineteenth century. This fertile region in Egypt's Western Desert was an important economic and cultural centre from the Middle Kingdom (2055–1650 BC).

Items of jewellery such as these earrings have been instrumental in the dating of the portraits.

The encaustic technique, which employed a heated mixture of wax and pigment, was used to great effect.

◄ **Depictions of women**
The portraits of women have a delicacy and detail that is absent from those of their male counterparts. A considerable degree of attention is paid to hairstyles and items of jewellery. The necklaces, brooches and earrings that the women are pictured wearing have provided a catalogue of jewellery of the Roman period in Egypt (30 BC–AD 395). In addition, they have helped Egyptologists to date the portraits accurately.

► **Mummy portrait of a man**
This painted and gilded stucco mummy case from the Fayum Oasis dates from the early first century AD and illustrates the combination of Classical and Egyptian styles present in the Fayum Portraits. Traditional Egyptian funerary scenes appear beneath an image of the deceased's face.

Golden motifs have been attached to the bright red cloth wrapped around the mummy.

Typical Ancient Egyptian funerary images decorate the mummy, including a goddess with her arms spread protectively.

The style of the man's beard is one of the elements that has helped historians to date the portrait.

This portrait from the Fayum region has been dated to the second half of the third century AD.

◄ **A distinguished portrait**
As indicated by the bald head and full beard, this portrait depicts a man in middle age. He is dressed in a tunic decorated with pink bands featuring a geometric motif on the shoulders and regards the observer with a direct, dignified gaze.

Painting techniques

Numerous examples of this type of portrait have been discovered in Egypt, in sites as diverse as Saqqara and Aswan, as well as at Hawara in the Fayum region. Earlier pieces were executed in encaustic, but later ones, particularly those dating from the fourth century AD, were painted in tempera – a technique that blended pigment with water and an adhesive material, usually egg white. These watercolour portraits are sadly not as well preserved as their sturdier, wax-based counterparts.

Funerary traditions

The extent and detail of individual characterization seen in the Fayum Portraits led Flinders Petrie to believe that they were painted in the owner's lifetime and were intended to be hung in their home until their death. It appears, however, that after the second century AD most of the portraits were painted after the death of the subject. They were placed over the face of the deceased's mummified body by enclosing the edges of the mask in the outer layers of bandages.

The Fayum Portraits are truly original pieces of art, representing a synthesis of the naturalistic Classical style of portraiture with the Ancient Egyptian concept of death as a gateway to a continuing existence in the afterlife. The portraits have provided Egyptologists with a wealth of information regarding high-status members of Greco-Roman society in Egypt – in particular their clothing, adornment and physical characteristics – as well as being masterpieces of art in their own right. Now mostly detached from their mummies, some of the finest examples are on display in the Egyptian Museum in Cairo and the Petrie Museum in London.

Executed in encaustic, this portrait has been painted directly onto a piece of cloth rather than wood.

The high status of the individual depicted here is indicated by his fine clothes and jewellery.

▼ **The sign of life**
The portrait of Ammonios features the ankh sign, the Ancient Egyptian hieroglyph denoting life. The ankh was eventually adopted by the Coptic church and remains its unique form of the Christian cross, known as the *crux ansata*.

◄ **Roman portraiture**
This Ancient Roman double portrait serves as an illustration of the extent of Roman influence on art in Egypt during the period of Roman rule. The naturalistic depiction of facial features, direct gaze of the subjects and use of light and shade all bear a distinct similarity to the artistic techniques used in the Fayum Portraits. This painting of Terentius Neo and his wife was found among the ruins of their house in Pompeii.

THE FAYUM PORTRAITS

◀ Portrait of Ammonios
This portrait, painted in the encaustic technique on canvas, was discovered in the Roman town of Antinoopolis in Middle Egypt. It depicts an elegantly dressed young man holding a vessel of wine in his right hand and a small bouquet of roses in his left hand. Above his shoulders are the ankh sign and an amulet figurine.

▲ A floral motif
The rose had a symbolic meaning for the Ancient Romans. It was regarded as a symbol of perfection, and Roman emperors sometimes wore wreaths of the flower as crowns.

▼ A golden goblet
The double-handled goblet shown in Ammonios's right hand resembles the communion cups, such as the one shown below, used in the Christian church.

▲ Portrait of a lady
Painted on a background of cedar
wood, this portrait comes from
Antinoopolis in Middle Egypt and
dates from around AD 120. It shows
a young woman, with fair, delicate skin,
swept-back hair and large, dark eyes.
The mantle she wears has been
delicately fashioned in gold leaf.

▲ ▶ Roman fashions
This funerary stele (top right)
shows a woman wearing the
same type of hairstyle as that
of the woman in the portrait
above. The deceased also wears
a piece of typically Roman
jewellery in the form of a large
collar around her neck.

▶ A likeness in tempera
This portrait from the first century AD has been executed in tempera
as opposed to the usual encaustic. The tempera technique, which involves
mixing pigments with a water-soluble binding agent rather than wax, has
the effect of creating strong, translucent colours. When Italian Egyptologist
Ippolito Rosellini (1800–1843) saw the portrait, he was struck by its
resemblance to his own mother.

INSIGHT

An ongoing tradition

The custom of depicting the face of the deceased on their mummies remained an element of Egyptian funerary tradition until the end of the fourth century AD. Some of the Fayum Portraits include decoration delicately worked in gold leaf, a feature of numerous mosaics of the Byzantine period.

A number of other characteristics of the Fayum Portraits are found in paintings of individuals in later epochs. The intense, direct expression delivered by large, dark eyes, the naturalistic features and the use of light and shade are all present in Western portraiture over the centuries. The Fayum Portraits are the earliest such works of art and their poignancy makes them truly enduring masterpieces.

▲ Found in the Fayum region, this portrait is painted in encaustic on wood and dates from the second century AD.

▲ This mosaic from the Byzantine church of San Vitale in Ravenna in Italy depicts the Empress Theodora.

◄ The long face and large eyes in this painting by the seventeenth-century artist El Greco recall the Fayum Portraits.

◄ The elongated proportions seen in early twentieth-century painter Amedeo Modigliani's work create a powerful sense of melancholy similar to that present in some of the Fayum Portraits.

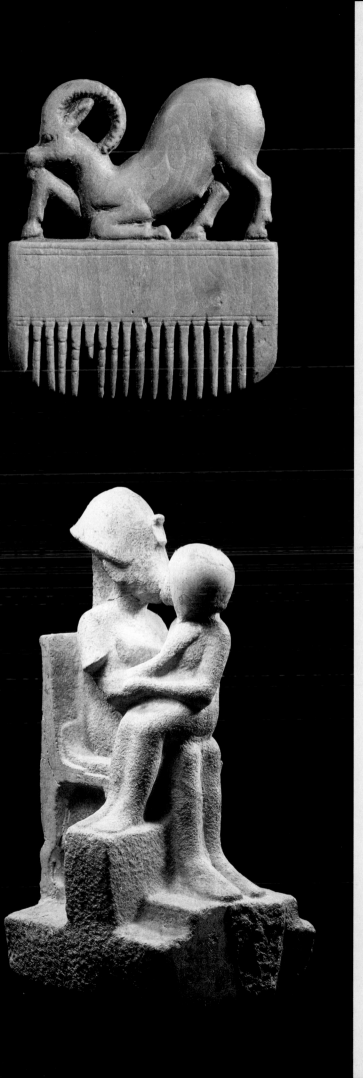

Everyday Life

The inhabitants of Egypt built their settlements within the agricultural land where they grew their crops. Because this land was regularly flooded by the annual inundation of the Nile, remains from these areas have often not survived well, and the continued intensive use of the land means that many sites are simply not accessible.

As a result, much of our evidence about the lives of the ancient Egyptians comes from funerary contexts. For example, tomb decoration illustrates the way crops were grown and harvested, and the remains of objects buried with a person show us actual examples of their furniture, pottery, jewellery and fine linen. Many of these artefacts were made for a specifically funerary purpose and this should always be remembered when we use them to draw conclusions about the lives of the Egyptians.

Archaeological evidence

From the few settlement sites that have been excavated, we know a good deal about, for example, the design and layout of houses, and the types of food consumed. The two best preserved sites were built in the desert: Akhetaten, the short-lived capital city built by Akhenaten, and Deir el-Medina, the village occupied by the workmen responsible for creating the tombs in the Valley of the Kings at Thebes. The latter site has yielded numerous written sources too, from which we can build up a detailed picture of ancient Egyptian life.

Revealing artifacts
Clockwise from far left: statues of the priest Tenti and his wife Imeretef, showing an idealized portrait of a married couple; a decorative comb carved from acacia wood; an unfinished statue of Akhenaten with his daughter on his lap — depictions of private moments such as this were unusual in royal statuary.

Childhood in Ancient Egypt

Children in Ancient Egypt were important, as they looked after their parents in old age and performed the funerary rites that assured them an existence in the afterlife.

Medical papyri and other documents detail the prayers and magic formulas that were used to help women to conceive, have a safe pregnancy and experience a trouble-free childbirth. The deities were also called upon for assistance: the frog goddess Heket was the divine midwife and the hippopotamus goddess Taweret provided protection for all pregnant women. Infant mortality was high, however, with just over half of children surviving to adolescence, leaving a typical Ancient Egyptian family with five living offspring.

Taking a name

All Ancient Egyptian children were given a name at birth, which was kept throughout life. Names could refer to the newborn's first response, such as 'Smiling one', 'Wise one' or 'Bringer of joy'. They might also be placed under the protection of a particular god, such as 'Horus' or 'Daughter of Maat', or simply named after a pharaoh.

Once the young mother had finished a two-week purification ritual, in the 'birth house', away from everyday living areas, her main task was to feed the child. If she was unable to produce breast milk a wet nurse would be employed. Women of high social rank tended to use wet nurses as a matter of course.

▶ Mother and baby
The design of this clay vessel, with the mother breastfeeding her baby and appearing to express milk from her right breast, may point to the possible uses of this container. It could have stored breast milk, which was used to treat certain ailments, or a magical oil to help with milk production. The vessel is on display at the Louvre Museum in Paris.

The rounded handle at the cylindrical spout is typical of medicinal containers.

Breast milk was taken as a remedy for eye, ear and skin diseases.

◀ Children at play
The various games with which children in Ancient Egypt whiled away their time have been handed down in numerous murals and reliefs in tombs. This copy of a mural in tomb no. 17 at Beni Hasan shows two girls with plaits wearing long sheath dresses. Standing opposite each other, they are juggling with three balls each.

▼ Statuette of a small boy
This ivory figure demonstrates the artistic principles employed to portray children. The boy is naked, has the sidelock of youth and puts a finger to his lower lip.

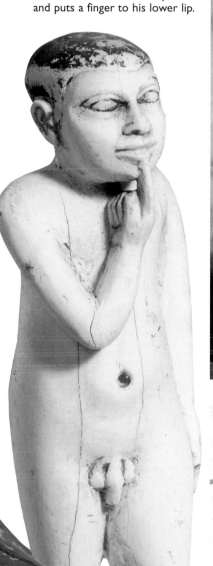

◄ Egyptian children today
Although traditional Ancient Egyptian depictions frequently convey the joys of childhood, today's reality is often the opposite – child labour, overpopulation and poverty. Despite laws requiring universal education, quite a large part of the Egyptian population is unable to afford schooling for their offspring. Consequently, the level of illiteracy is high.

▼ Farm work
This mural from the tomb of Menena from the Eighteenth Dynasty (1550–1295 BC) shows that Ancient Egyptian children were integrated into daily work and, for example, were taken to work the fields. The two men are carrying grain ears in a large net to the threshing floor, while two children fight over the last stalks of wheat. Farm work was mainly a male job, while trades such as weaving and beermaking were almost exclusively female.

Up until the age of four, little children freely played naked with toys, domestic animals or others of their own age. Then, wealthy boys would be sent to school at the 'house of life' at the nearest temple or department of state, where they would learn to be scribes, and study arithmetic, geometry and medicine. As well as academic work, they were taught gymnastics, swimming, ethics, protocol and respect for elders and for social status.

Sons and daughters

Boys from poor families would begin to work with their fathers in their professions, be they farmers, sculptors, painters, carpenters, farmers or fishermen. Girls from both rich and poor families stayed at home, looked after by their mothers or, perhaps, servants. Here they learned how to run a household, the traditional female trades of beermaking and textile production, and the arts of music and dancing.

From at least the Old Kingdom (2686-2181 BC), both boys and girls wore the sidelock of youth, a long tress of hair that trailed down the side of the head. This was shaved off when the child reached puberty, at about 10 or 11 years of age. Boys were often circumcised at this time as a rite of passage into adulthood, while girls were deigned to have become women when they first menstruated. Girls would marry as soon as possible after this, but boys would have to wait until they were 20, by which time they would have learned their trade and be able to support a family.

▶ **Akhenaten with his daughter**
A peculiarity of the Amarna period is the depiction of private activity in royal art. Many reliefs show Akhenaten (1352–1336 BC) in close and intimate contact with his children. This statue gives the impression that Akhenaten is kissing his daughter sitting on his lap, but the details missing from the limestone figure indicate that it was never completed. The stone connecting the faces was most likely to be further carved. If it had been the sculptor's intention to depict a kiss, the statue would probably be an exception.

Akhenaten is holding his daughter sitting on his lap, in a tender, loving way.

The two figures are not completely worked, as can be seen from the surface texture.

◀ **Tomb mural**
This mural from the Old Kingdom (2686–2181 BC) shows the dignitary Meteti sitting in a chair. He receives a cleansing and reviving incense offer from his son, who is holding the vessel with its lid lifted in the direction of his father, so that he can inhale the escaping scent. Compared to the figure of the father, the son is depicted much smaller, as was typical in Ancient Egyptian art. Children and inferior people were always shown smaller to underline their relationship to their parents or to people of higher rank.

◀ **The wet nurse**
This coloured copy of a mural depicts Amenhotep II (1427–1400 BC) sitting on the lap of his wet nurse, Amenemopet. Her son, Kenamun, was described as the king's foster brother and it is likely that the two were brought up together. He rose to become the royal steward, and because of his high rank he could afford a richly decorated tomb, where he had this mural made. Like the royal family, high-ranking families and the upper classes employed wet nurses, who were closely integrated in the family circle.

▼ **The king's sons**
This relief illustrates a procession of the sons of Rameses II (1279–1213 BC) on the occasion of the inauguration of the pylon at the Luxor temple. All the sons are shown in the same pose, each carrying a floral display. To emphasize their youth, the princes are depicted with the sidelock of youth hanging down on one side of their heads. Their titles and ranks are inscribed next to them. As far as it is known, Rameses II had at least 40 daughters and 45 sons.

Educating the Children

Formal education was confined to a privileged minority in Ancient Egypt and, at all levels, training was essentially vocational – farmers' sons learned the age-old ways of agriculture, while sons of craftsmen appear to have served apprenticeships under their fathers from a young age.

Controlled by government departments or temples, Egyptian schools were provided primarily for the sons of civil servants and other dignitaries. In order to supplement their personnel, large institutions needed an ever-growing number of civil servants and welcomed a few boys of lowlier origin. School offered these youngsters the rare possibility of moving up in society, but education was basically for the children of the rich and powerful élite, who were already educated themselves. Although these pupils began school at the age of five or six, most learned only to read and to write in the hieratic or everyday style. Those destined to be priests or artists also practised hieroglyphs, or sacred writing. The boys learned by copying or memorizing texts, and by taking dictation – notably from reports and letters in instruction books, such as the *Book of Kemyt*. They were also taught calculations and basic geography.

Most lessons seem to have comprised committing long passages of text to memory or copying out exercises.

School equipment could include a wooden toy on wheels and (below right) a leather ball stuffed with straw.

▶ **A day in the life of a schoolboy**
Boys went to school very early in the morning and stayed until the early afternoon, taking food to eat during the day. They did their exercises on rough supports – either wooden tablets covered with stucco, or limestone shards called ostraca.

To encourage the pupils and to combat the natural laziness of some, the teacher had no hesitation in using the cane. According to one text, 'a pupil's ear is on his back – he listens when he is beaten.'

After school, the pupil turned to his favourite pursuits. He joined his friends to play outdoors or perhaps to swim in a canal in summer.

A young pupil recites a text to his teacher while seated on the floor.

The teacher used a stick to punish unruly children. Discipline was tough, even for the sons of privileged parents.

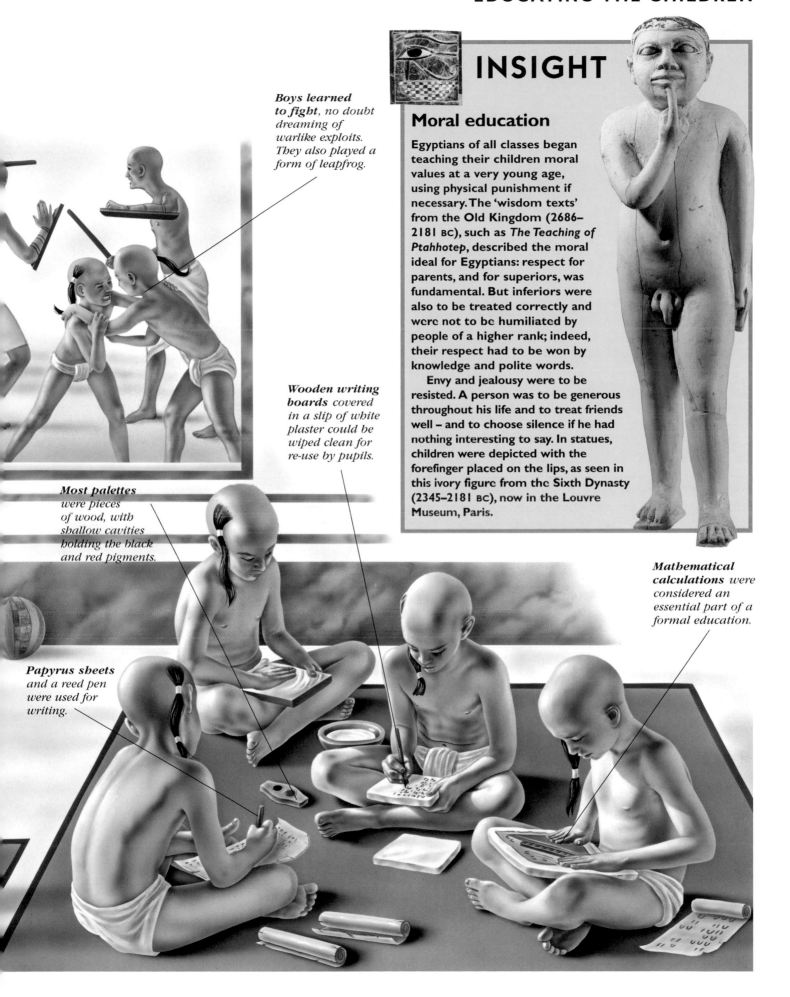

Boys learned to fight, no doubt dreaming of warlike exploits. They also played a form of leapfrog.

Wooden writing boards covered in a slip of white plaster could be wiped clean for re-use by pupils.

Most palettes were pieces of wood, with shallow cavities holding the black and red pigments.

Papyrus sheets and a reed pen were used for writing.

Mathematical calculations were considered an essential part of a formal education.

INSIGHT

Moral education

Egyptians of all classes began teaching their children moral values at a very young age, using physical punishment if necessary. The 'wisdom texts' from the Old Kingdom (2686–2181 BC), such as *The Teaching of Ptahhotep*, described the moral ideal for Egyptians: respect for parents, and for superiors, was fundamental. But inferiors were also to be treated correctly and were not to be humiliated by people of a higher rank; indeed, their respect had to be won by knowledge and polite words.

Envy and jealousy were to be resisted. A person was to be generous throughout his life and to treat friends well – and to choose silence if he had nothing interesting to say. In statues, children were depicted with the forefinger placed on the lips, as seen in this ivory figure from the Sixth Dynasty (2345–2181 BC), now in the Louvre Museum, Paris.

While sons of the élite went to school, the children of peasants followed their elders to the fields, where they began with the least arduous tasks, such as gleaning ears of wheat or watching livestock. The sons of craftsmen, such as potters, cabinet-makers and metal-workers, normally joined their fathers in their workshops to become, effectively, apprentices. After watching the workers in their roles and doing simple tasks, they executed their first works under the supervision of experienced craftsmen.

With the exception of physician, midwife or servant, few professions were open to women. In all social classes, including the wealthy, young girls were raised at home by their mothers, who taught them household chores and how to prepare meals, as well as spinning, weaving and other domestic skills. For fun, the young girls of the working class danced, performed acrobatics, played ball or rocked their rudimentary wooden or terracotta dolls.

Peasant children help their fathers by transferring cereals from small carriers to large baskets.

▼ **Family farming**
Children helped with the cereal harvest by filling and carrying baskets, as shown in this painting from a Theban tomb from the New Kingdom (1550–1069 BC). The father passed on his experience to his sons – notably the eldest, who would take over when the time came, and pass on his knowledge to his own children.

INSIGHT

The education of princes

There is little recorded material about the training of future kings, such as Amenhotep III (1390–1352 BC) (below); however, it is known that the princes attended classes at special palace schools. These also educated the children of the senior dignitaries, such as the sons of the vizier and, often, those of conquered foreign kings.

Once educated, foreign princes were sent back to their own countries, where (schooled appropriately in Egyptian ways) they were meant to behave as compliant subjects.

Physical and military training supplemented the academic education which was given to the princes, preparing them for combat and taking command of the army.

▲ **Help at harvest**
During harvesting, the peasants mobilized all available young people. This painting, which decorated the walls of the tomb of Nakht at Thebes, shows a young girl gleaning the ears thrown on the ground by the male workers, who have cut the wheat with their sickles. Behind her, two workers make a dramatic attempt to close a large overflowing basket.

◀ Noble tasks

The children of the nobility were very privileged. While boys went to school, where they learned to exercise the functions of senior dignitaries, girls stayed at home with their mothers. There they learned how to run a household and manage servants, and how to dress and entertain; this picture shows a daughter literally emulating her mother in the role of hostess. Royal princesses were not merely taught how to read and write, but were also expected to develop a real love of literature. It was literacy, above all, that separated the élite, as writing was the key to both economic organization and civil administration.

Children were expected to help not just at harvest, as shown here, but all year round, including planting.

▶ Women of the court

In addition to their social education, the daughters of the élite classes received strict moral guidance. They also learned to sing, dance and play several musical instruments – and (right) to perform at both secular feasts and religious ceremonies.

Marriage

For the Ancient Egyptians married life was the ideal, and, even though men were permitted to take more than one wife, most marriages seem to have been monogamous.

In Ancient Egypt, the concept of marriage was not bound up in terms of an official ceremony, but rather occurred when a man and woman set up home together. It is not clear what the precise social and legal implications of this were, but documents from the Late and Ptolemaic periods (747–30 BC) have been found that set out the property rights of each partner in a marriage.

Man and wife

Ancient Egyptian men were allowed to have multiple wives, but evidence based on the layout and size of settlements in the workers' village at Deir el-Medina suggests that most marriages were monogamous.

There are, however, some records of divorces. In the Old Kingdom (2686–2181 BC), a man could separate from his wife on grounds of adultery or infertility. By the Middle Kingdom (2055–1650 BC), a law had been established that safeguarded the property rights of a couple's children. This included daughters as well as sons.

▼ Parents and children
Establishing a family unit was the most important aspect of marriage for the Ancient Egyptians. Evidence suggests that most families consisted of a mother, father and about five children, with an average of three or four offspring having died in infancy.

The woman is shown on a slightly smaller scale than her husband, reflecting her lesser status.

The couple hold hands, an intimate gesture rarely seen in statuary of the Old Kingdom.

◀ The priest Tenti and his wife Imeretef
This statue from the Old Kingdom (2686–2181 BC) presents an idealized image of married life. Standing side by side, the couple hold hands for eternity. Although economic interests were a factor in Ancient Egyptian marriages, unions were ideally based on love and affection.

▲ The Egyptian family today
The Islamic faith in modern Egypt permits men to practise polygamy, allowing them to take up to four wives. Largely for economic reasons, however, this rarely happens. Successive marriages are common, though, following abandonment, divorce or the death of a spouse.

▼ Marriage contracts
Documentation of Ancient Egyptian marriage ceremonies is rare, but legal texts, often described as marriage contracts, have survived from the Late period (747–332 BC). These establish the property rights of both partners in the marriage, in an ancient form of pre-nuptial contract. In the event of divorce, a husband could be forced to pay his wife a substantial amount of compensation.

◄ The royal family
The principal wife of Akhenaten (1352–1336 BC), Nefertiti was renowned for her extraordinary beauty, as well as her power and influence during her husband's reign. Numerous reliefs from the Amarna period depict Nefertiti with the pharaoh and their six daughters, in intimate family scenes that were rare in Ancient Egyptian art. In the relief shown left, the family of Akhenaten are shown in the act of worshipping the Aten, or solar disc.

The tall plumes of Tiy's headdress identify her with the gods of Ancient Egypt.

The protective uraeus sits in the centre of Tiy's headdress.

The queen's real hair is just visible beneath her heavy, elaborate wig.

The flail, a traditional symbol of royal power, is held in Tiy's hand.

Unlike the majority of the population, the pharaohs of Ancient Egypt generally had a number of wives. There was usually one principal wife, as Nefertiti was to Akhenaten (1352-1336 BC) or Nefertari to Rameses II (1279-1213 BC), sometimes in addition to a number of diplomatic marriages and a harem of women.

The pharaoh's harem, attached to the royal palace or villa, included his minor wives and concubines, along with their maidservants and sometimes their children. Rameses II reputedly fathered more than 100 children with the women of his harem.

Sisters and brothers

The pharaohs often took their sisters or daughters as wives, a practice that appears to have been confined to royalty. It was once thought that this was because the right to the throne was passed down the female line, but it is more likely that it was done to associate the king with the gods, who frequently had incestuous marriages.

Some of the queens of Ancient Egypt had considerable power and influence within the political sphere. Queen Tiy, for example, the mother of Akhenaten and wife of Amenhotep III, was often shown alongside the king and had an active role in running the country. Similarly, numerous reliefs and sculptures depict Nefertiti, testimony to her significance in the royal circle.

► A queen from the common people
Tiy, whose father occupied the relatively lowly position of chariot officer, was the wife of Amenhotep III (1390–1352 BC). She seems to have wielded a considerable amount of power during the reigns of both her husband and her son, Akhenaten. For example, after the death of Amenhotep III, correspondence from the Hittite leader was addressed directly to Tiy. It is also thought that Tiy encouraged her son to adopt the worship of the Aten as sole god of Ancient Egypt, and advised him of the danger to his authority posed by the priests of Amun.

INSIGHT

The marriages of the gods

The most famous of all divine unions was that between Osiris and his sister Isis. The incestuous marriages practised by the pharaohs of Ancient Egypt appear to have been adopted from this standard, which had the effect of setting the king apart from his subjects and confirming his status as living god.

As the consort of Osiris, Isis was regarded as the embodiment of the ideal wife and mother. Her devotion to her husband led her to retrieve, mummify and reanimate the dismembered pieces of his body after he had been murdered by Seth. Isis was also considered to be the divine mother of each reigning pharaoh.

▶ **Hatshepsut – queen and pharaoh**
The female pharaoh Hatshepsut (1473–1458 BC) had a series of reliefs carved in her mortuary temple at Deir el-Bahri attesting to the divine nature of her birth. This was perhaps part of an concerted effort to legitimize her claim to the throne, which may have been in question due to her gender. The images at Deir el-Bahri represent Hatshepsut as the result of a union between her mother, Ahmose, and Amun, the king of the gods. The relief below shows her as pharaoh, complete with the royal beard, being embraced by Amun.

▶ **The principal wife**
Ahmose Nefertari (c. 1570–1505 BC) was wife and sister to Ahmose I and one of the most influential women of the New Kingdom. She was the first royal woman to be appointed God's wife of Amun, and was involved in founding the workers' village of Deir el-Medina.

During the New Kingdom, it became common for the pharaoh to take the daughters of foreign princes as wives in diplomatic unions. These could consolidate alliances with the Ancient Egyptian empire, or serve as an indication of the subjugation of a foreign state.

Marriage and politics

There are numerous examples of such diplomatic marriages. Rameses II, for instance, took two of the daughters of the Hittite king Hattusilis III as wives to cement a non-aggression pact between the two powers after the Battle of Qadesh in 1274 BC. During the reign of Thutmose III (1479–1425 BC), several princesses from the Mitanni state in western Asia entered the Egyptian king's harem, to offset the threat posed by the Mitanni.

Ancient Egyptian Houses

Our knowledge of Ancient Egyptian houses – and how they were built and used – comes from excavated settlements, models of houses found in tombs and detailed depictions in wall paintings of dwellings and gardens.

The climate of Ancient Egypt was very warm and dry, so houses were built to be as cool as possible. The most common building materials, used since Thinite times, were mud bricks, which were covered with limestone plaster both on the exterior and inside the house. Interior walls were often painted – either with patterns or with scenes from nature. The floors, also of mud, were firmly stamped down or carefully tiled; stone tiles were found in the houses of the rich.

Cool houses and shady gardens

The white plaster on the rather plain walls of the houses was supposed to act as a sun barrier. The few small grille windows set high in the walls let in only a little sunlight, while vents trapped the cool north wind. During the day, inside windows were covered with coloured mats or shades. Additional living space was provided by the gardens surrounding many houses or – within cities – shady bowers on the mostly walk-on roofs.

◀ Building materials
Egyptian houses were built with air-dried mud bricks made from Nile mud, straw and water. For more durability, the kneaded mixture was left for several days, after which it was shaped into bricks using rectangular moulds. The finished bricks were then left to dry and harden in the sun.

Vines and pomegranate trees were among the plants grown in the gardens of the wealthy.

From the outside, a single gate enclosed in a high wall led to the garden of the house.

◀ A view of the past
Many mud-brick structures built by the Ancient Egyptians have remained intact to the present day, and have been little affected by weathering. The use of mud bricks as a building material has endured into modern times and can be observed today in many Egyptian villages. Only in fairly recent times has this traditional method been replaced by fired brick and concrete.

▼ Garden parties
The houses of the upper classes were often surrounded by a garden with shady fruit trees and a pond. The estate was encircled by a high wall, which enclosed a gate facing the house. Parties often took place in the garden, as depicted in this drawing by Ippolito Rosellini, based on a Theban tomb painting.

The sycomore fig was one of the most popular trees because of its wood and dense foliage.

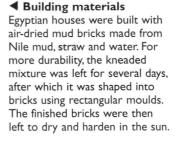

◀ ▲ Interior decoration
In contrast to the plain outer walls of the house, interior quarters were decorated with geometric and floral designs in vivid colours. These examples, reproduced by nineteenth-century copyist Prisse d'Avennes, are of patterns especially popular in the houses of the rich during the Eighteenth and Nineteenth dynasties.

▼ Wooden bolts and frames
Doors were bolted from the inside with mainly wooden but sometimes bronze bolts. Many architectural elements, such as door and window frames, doors, ceiling beams and columns, were made from wood – as was most of the furniture – which was often brightly painted.

Two thin, wooden columns in the shape of a papyrus plant flank the main entrance to the house.

The house's façade features two richly decorated window frames.

The difference between the social classes was also reflected in their dwellings. The poorer classes always lived in small huts with only one or two rooms and an open kitchen yard.

Villas for the upper classes

High-ranking officials could afford large villas. A small anteroom led to a vast, colonnaded entrance hall which was joined to the majestic main room. From here, a staircase led to the roof, where a porch on the north side caught a pleasant cool breeze. At the back of the villa were the private apartments, as well as the bedrooms and the bathrooms with stone basins.

The kitchen and other functional rooms were in adjacent buildings, which also housed the storage cellars.

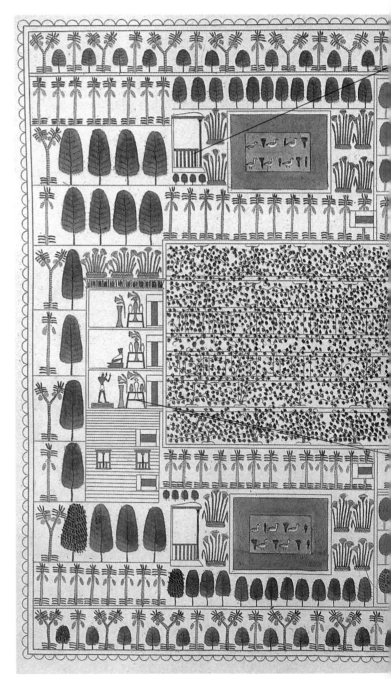

DOCUMENT

The 'soul houses'

For the Egyptians, death meant a continuation of life on earth. Tombs were therefore furnished with everything that was necessary to accompany the deceased to the afterlife, including food, clothing and furniture. Among numerous tomb objects were small models of houses made from wood or clay, such as the example below, which dates from the Middle Kingdom (2055–1650 BC). These are representations of the deceased's abode in the afterlife. Because the models were based on actual houses, they give a good impression of the most common types of dwelling-place in Ancient Egypt, which often consisted of several floors.

▲ **A dignitary's villa**
This ninteenth-century drawing shows a reconstruction of an Ancient Egyptian waterside villa. The building housing the living quarters was located behind a large, well-ordered garden, and the entire property was surrounded by a high wall. Access was via a huge gate, which was flanked by two small side entrances.

▼ A garden in Thebes

This depiction of a magnificent garden, with its sycamore fig, date palm and acacia trees, is found in the tomb of Sennefer, mayor of Thebes under Amenhotep II (1427–1400 BC). The grandeur of the garden reflects the status of its owner. Only wealthy dignitaries, princes and kings could afford such splendour.

The small, colonnaded pavilion near the pond resembles a shrine.

Four ponds, bordered with greenery, provide refreshing coolness, while the papyrus plants beside them add decoration.

A vineyard enclosed by date palm trees occupies the centre of the garden.

A richly decorated gate leads to the garden and the house facing it beyond.

The house, on three levels, as well as the gate and side entrances, are shown front-on – a style typical of Egyptian art.

Ducks swim amid lotus plants in the ponds.

◀ Colonnaded portico

This model from the tomb of Meketra, a high-ranking official during the Eleventh Dynasty (2055–1985 BC), shows a small, colonnaded portico in front of the main entrance to the house. The two rows of four fluted columns are in the form of bound lotus stems and flowers, the bright colours of which have been perfectly preserved. In front of the portico, there is a pond surrounded by sycamore fig trees, the leaves and fruit of which are minutely detailed.

▼ Sumptuous interiors

This illustration is an accurate reconstruction of one of the rooms in a grand Egyptian villa – based on archaeological evidence, wall paintings and tomb models of Ancient Egyptian houses. Brightly painted columns support an upper mezzanine floor inset with windows, while the relatively small windows on the adjoining wall are set high to provide light and minimum heat. The centrepiece of the room is an imposing statue placed amid luxuriant indoor plants.

Town and City Life

The first permanent Ancient Egyptian settlements were founded on the fertile banks of the Nile in around 6000 BC. Some, such as Hierakonopolis, would grow into large towns – by 3500 BC it had 8,000 inhabitants, including many artisans such as potters and weavers.

Archaeological evidence for the form and function of Egyptian towns and cities is unfortunately based on unrepresentative sites such as the abandoned capital city of Akhenaten – Akhetaten – or the planned workers' village at Deir el-Medina. Most of the urban sites on the Nile were subject to annual flooding and are poorly preserved and, over the centuries, many were broken up by farmers who ground the mud bricks into compost for their fields.

House construction

Most houses were constructed out of sun-dried clay bricks set on a foundation of a low stone wall. They consisted of between four to six rooms, a small cellar for storage and a staircase to a flat roof. It is now believed, however, that some houses had an upper storey and that some rooms might have been used to keep animals. The houses were packed tightly together, which created shade on the narrow 'streets', and they had small windows to keep out the heat.

▼ Deir el-Medina, the workers' village
This settlement was inhabited by the workmen who built and decorated the tombs in the Valley of the Kings. Under Rameses II (1279–1213 BC), its population numbered 1,200 workers and their families. They lived in 70 mud-brick houses arranged in 'streets' inside an enclosure wall. Another 40 houses lay close by, probably inhabited by less-skilled workers such as donkey drivers.

▼ Upper-class living
One part of a town would be inhabited mainly by senior officials and priests. Their dwellings would consist of living quarters, storage and work buildings, accommodation for servants and a large garden surrounded by a high wall.

▶ The life of a pharaoh
When not occupied with affairs of state, the king would go hunting in the desert or relax in his sumptuous palace. As well as the royal residence, this had halls, offices, archives and storage facilities, kitchens, bakeries and quarters for servants.

The temples were the only buildings in the town made entirely from stone.

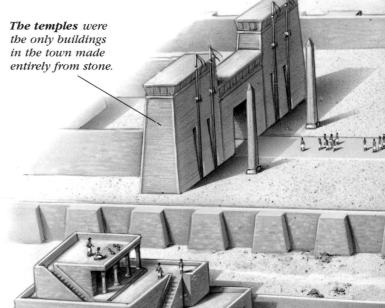

The gardens, full of fruit and vegetables, were an important part of the houses of wealthy Ancient Egyptians.

A broad street crossed the town, allowing easy access to all the main buildings.

▲ The priesthood
Apart from their religious duties, priests were responsible for protecting the temple, guarding its gates and supervising work in the temple workshops.

▶ The vizier
The state's most senior official always lived in the palace.

Artificial lakes in the palace were surrounded by shady trees.

▲ The city quarters
Most towns were divided into quarters. Away from the districts for officials and the wealthy were areas with small houses and narrow streets, where the working class lived.

359

The cities and larger towns were divided into quarters for the upper, the middle and the lower classes. The houses of the wealthy boasted many luxurious rooms, furnished with fine wooden furniture, and perhaps a garden with shady trees and an ornamental pond. Poorer workers made do with mud-brick benches, stone stools and rough wooden tables and wall niches.

Buying and selling

In all cities, there were open-air markets with many lively stalls. Depictions of market life in tombs are rare, but can be seen in the double tomb of the royal manicurists and hairdressers Khnumhotep and Niankhkhnum (c. 2350 BC). The murals show fruits and vegetables, fish and meat, containers of drinks, ceramic pots, baskets, sandals and fabrics being traded and bartered.

Although coins as currency were not introduced until the Ptolemaic period (332–30 BC), every item had a known trading worth. For example, a container of fish might be exchanged for an equally filled container of wine, or a quantity of sycomore figs might be traded for a large pottery bowl.

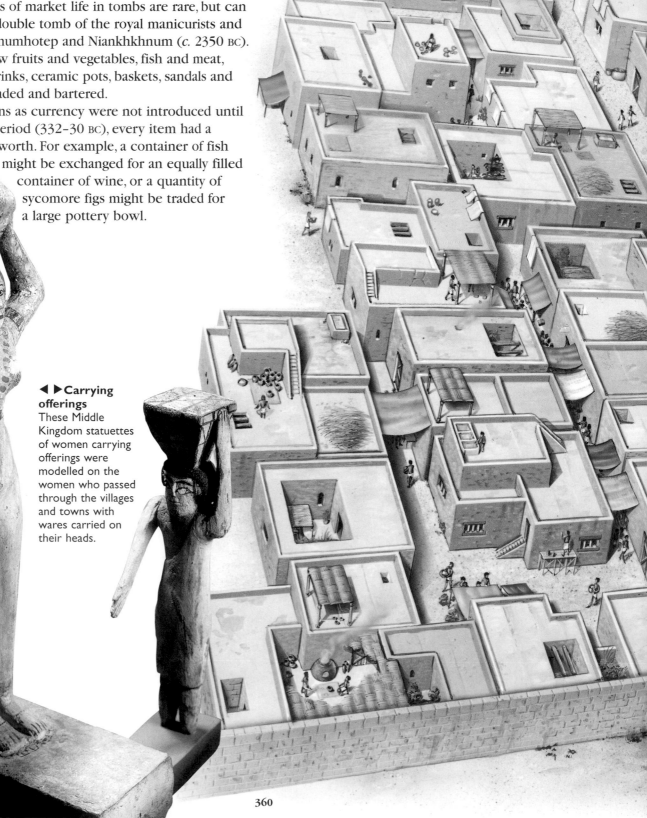

Unfired clay bricks were the main building material utilized for the houses.

The working-class quarters often consisted of tightly packed buildings.

◀ ▶**Carrying offerings**
These Middle Kingdom statuettes of women carrying offerings were modelled on the women who passed through the villages and towns with wares carried on their heads.

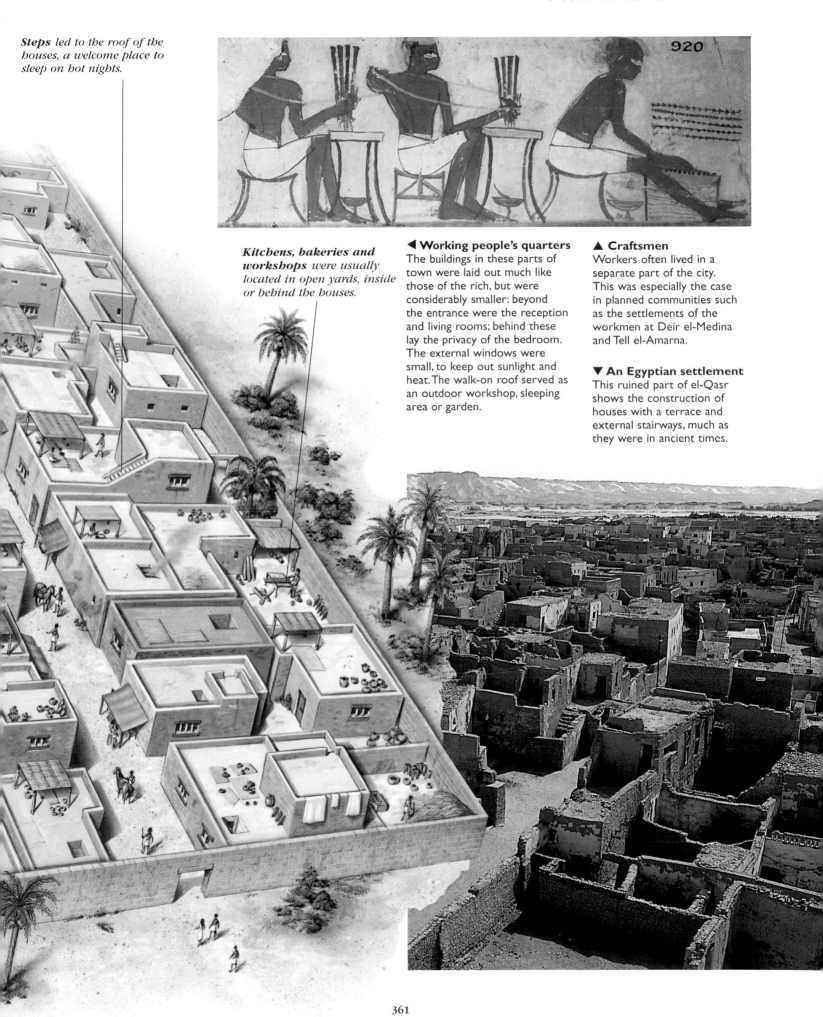

920

Steps *led to the roof of the houses, a welcome place to sleep on hot nights.*

Kitchens, bakeries and workshops *were usually located in open yards, inside or behind the houses.*

◄ Working people's quarters
The buildings in these parts of town were laid out much like those of the rich, but were considerably smaller: beyond the entrance were the reception and living rooms; behind these lay the privacy of the bedroom. The external windows were small, to keep out sunlight and heat. The walk-on roof served as an outdoor workshop, sleeping area or garden.

▲ Craftsmen
Workers often lived in a separate part of the city. This was especially the case in planned communities such as the settlements of the workmen at Deir el-Medina and Tell el-Amarna.

▼ An Egyptian settlement
This ruined part of el-Qasr shows the construction of houses with a terrace and external stairways, much as they were in ancient times.

Egyptian Society

The pyramid, the most characteristic monument of Ancient Egypt, provides a handy model for understanding the strict hierarchical structure of Egyptian society. As the social system was validated by the gods, those at the base of the pyramid tended to accept their lot.

Egyptian society had a distinct hierarchic structure that is often symbolized by a pyramid. The summit of the Egyptian social order was the royal family: the pharaoh, his 'great royal wife', his mother and his children. Titular owner of all the lands, quarries and mines in Egypt, head of government, supreme commander of the army, chief of the priesthood and sole intermediary between the gods and mankind, the pharaoh was all-powerful. He delegated many of his powers to high officials, who were at the head of great bureaucracies. These officials – viziers, generals and high priests of the individual gods – were often related to the pharaoh and made up a relatively small, aristocratic upper class.

The chain of command

The high officials gave their orders to a middle class of functionaries and middle-ranking priests, whose task it was to ensure that their superiors' orders were carried out by such specialists as soldiers, scribes, junior priests, craftsmen and artists, who were paid for their services not in money but in food and other goods.

◀ **The social planner**
Akhenaten (1352–1336 BC) tried to impose a new religion on Egypt and moved the nation's capital to the new city of Akhetaten. The layout perfectly reflected the rigidly stratified nature of Egyptian society.

pharaoh

daughter

wife

high military officials

other

scribes

soldiers

fishermen

servants

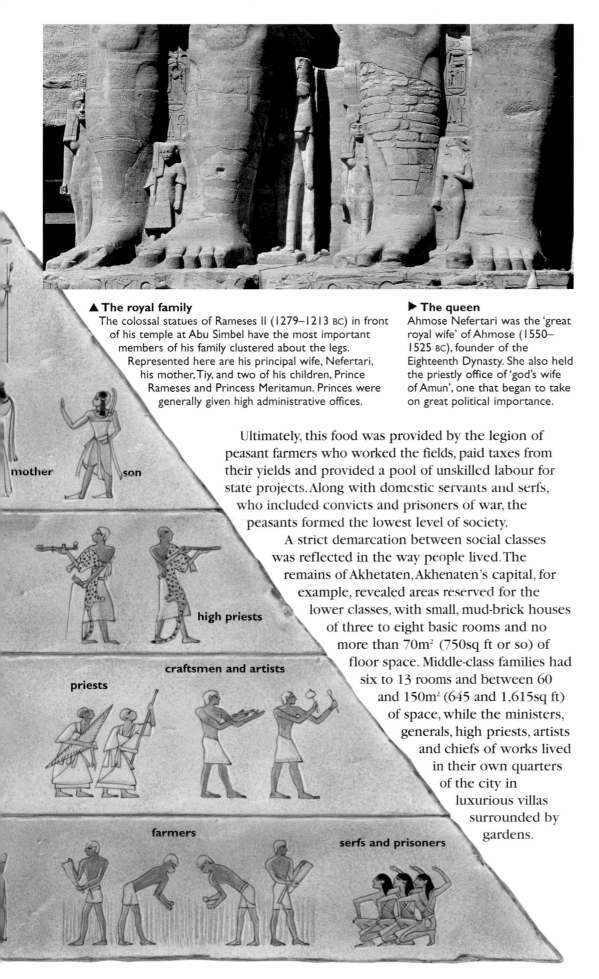

▲ The royal family
The colossal statues of Rameses II (1279–1213 BC) in front of his temple at Abu Simbel have the most important members of his family clustered about the legs. Represented here are his principal wife, Nefertari, his mother, Tiy, and two of his children, Prince Rameses and Princess Meritamun. Princes were generally given high administrative offices.

▶ The queen
Ahmose Nefertari was the 'great royal wife' of Ahmose (1550–1525 BC), founder of the Eighteenth Dynasty. She also held the priestly office of 'god's wife of Amun', one that began to take on great political importance.

mother son

high priests

craftsmen and artists

priests

farmers

serfs and prisoners

Ultimately, this food was provided by the legion of peasant farmers who worked the fields, paid taxes from their yields and provided a pool of unskilled labour for state projects. Along with domestic servants and serfs, who included convicts and prisoners of war, the peasants formed the lowest level of society.

A strict demarcation between social classes was reflected in the way people lived. The remains of Akhetaten, Akhenaten's capital, for example, revealed areas reserved for the lower classes, with small, mud-brick houses of three to eight basic rooms and no more than 70m² (750sq ft or so) of floor space. Middle-class families had six to 13 rooms and between 60 and 150m² (645 and 1,615sq ft) of space, while the ministers, generals, high priests, artists and chiefs of works lived in their own quarters of the city in luxurious villas surrounded by gardens.

To the modern eye, the most remarkable fact about Egyptian society is its stability. Social unrest was rare. Stability was underpinned by the belief that social organization reflected the natural, god-created order personified by the goddess Maat. People accepted their place in society; while workers were expected to defer to social superiors, high officials also had a duty to show respect to their subordinates. Another key to the survival of the system was that it was not totally rigid. People usually stayed in the class into which they were born, but there was scope for movement to and from high office.

The importance of the pharaoh can be seen in the First Intermediate period (2181–2055 BC), when the monarchy collapsed. A new genre of pessimistic literature was born, expressing the deep distress felt by those Egyptians who could no longer cling to their traditional values and verities. The tombs of the wealthy dead were stripped of their funerary equipment as even respect for the dead was abandoned.

As soon as the monarchy was restored, though, the old social order reasserted itself, as the turmoil of the First Intermediate period melted away.

▲ Destined for serfdom
In the New Kingdom (1550–1069 BC), Egyptian conquests in Nubia, the Near East and Libya ensured a steady flow of prisoners of war into Egypt, where they were treated as serfs. Many of them became part of the Egyptian army. Others were pressed into working the fields that supplied the priests, high administrators or successful generals – accepted as one of the perks of the job by the Egyptian elite. Prisoners also became domestic servants in Egyptian families.

▶ The warrior class
Early in Egypt's history there was no standing army. A militia was raised when needed. Only during the Middle Kingdom (2055–1650 BC) did the military come to be regarded as a profession in its own right. The state paid regular soldiers by giving them the right to exploit and profit from pieces of land. Sometimes serfs to work the fields were included. Although the land itself remained the property of the king, soldiers could leave their rights over it – known as usufruct – to their descendants. When army scribes went recruiting, the sons of soldiers were their first call. This figure shows a young officer in the pharaoh's standing army.

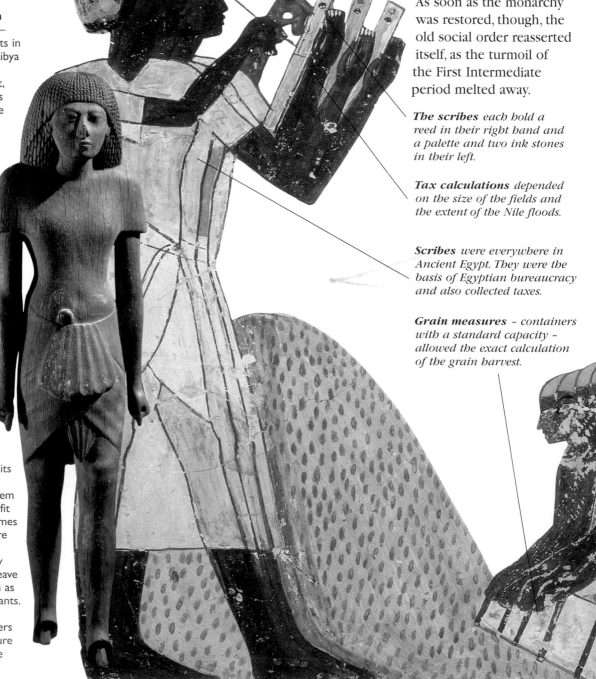

The scribes each hold a reed in their right hand and a palette and two ink stones in their left.

Tax calculations depended on the size of the fields and the extent of the Nile floods.

Scribes were everywhere in Ancient Egypt. They were the basis of Egyptian bureaucracy and also collected taxes.

Grain measures - containers with a standard capacity - allowed the exact calculation of the grain harvest.

▶ The upper classes

The dignitaries and aristocrats who helped the king to rule had fine houses, provided with all contemporary conveniences, and their homes for eternity were no less sumptuous. The rank of an Ancient Egyptian can be gauged by the size of his tomb and the quality of its furnishings and paintings. The illustration here is a copy by the nineteenth-century Egyptologist Ippolito Rosellini of a tomb painting, and shows an official and his wife wearing elegant costumes in pleated linen and a great deal of fine jewellery.

▶ The vizier

This statue shows Neferkari, vizier to Sobekhotep IV (c. 1725 BC). The vizier, a kind of prime minister, was the highest administrative official in , answerable only to the king. He wore an official robe consisting of a long gown with a strap reaching to the shoulders.

▼ Hierarchy In the fields

At harvest time, the peasants were joined in the fields and granaries by an army of scribes, whose job was to supervise the collection of grain and calculate the amount due to the state. They first surveyed the fields when the corn was high, in order to estimate yields – and thus taxes – and were present when the granaries were filled, making tallies all the time.

INSIGHT

The great majority

Peasant farmers made up the great majority of Egypt's population, as the growing of crops and the raising of animals (below) formed the basis of the Egyptian economy. There were around 1.5 million Egyptians in 2500 BC, when the great pyramids were built. Technological developments in irrigation, particularly the invention of the shadoof, increased yields of food and allowed the population to grow, doubling to 3 million under Rameses II (1279–1213 BC) and more than 5 million under Cleopatra VII (51–30 BC). City dwellers, including officials, priests and workmen (right) made up only a small part of the population.

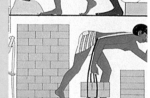

Divine and Worldly Law

From the formation of the Egyptian central state a legal code existed in both the real world and the afterlife.

Ancient Egyptian law was essentially based on the religious concept of Maat – the natural harmonious order which existed when the world was created – personified as a goddess. The Egyptians viewed the universe as being in a permanent state of tension between, for example, good and evil, and light and dark. If Maat broke down then chaos (*isfet*) would follow. The king was considered the guarantor for the justification of the divine laws enacted in Maat – and consequently the legal system.

Legislation in the New Kingdom

Ancient Egyptians always believed in a natural law that embraced social justice and morality. In the course of time, this was supplemented by decrees and laws of the kings, which were kept in writing and archived. The following statement by Horemheb (1323–1295 BC) has been recorded: 'I gave rules to their face (the officials) and added laws to their collection.' Therefore, laws in the New Kingdom were cited as 'Pharaoh's law' or began with the introduction 'Pharaoh says'. In any case, the legal idea of Maat had to be taken into account when it came to passing judgement.

▲ **Maat and the officials**
Even the officials appointed by the pharaoh were legally bound by Maat, who thus represented the ethical basis of the structure of the state. The high-ranking vizier, as well as the low-ranking scribe, was considered to be a keeper of Maat.

◀ **Maat, goddess of justice**
The daughter of the sun god Ra, Maat personified order, truth and justice, among both gods and humans. As the embodiment of the harmony of the universe, she was considered the 'food of gods'. Maat was portrayed with an ostrich feather on her head, which was also her hieroglyphic sign. In the *Book of the Dead*, her symbol was depicted on the scales at the judgement of the dead, and it was weighed against the deeds of the deceased, symbolized as a heart. The weighing of the heart decided the fate of the dead in the afterlife. Maat was also the protective goddess of the judges.

▶ **The pharaoh and Shepsi**
Even the laws and actions of the king were answerable to Maat and had to be in harmony with her, as this was vital for the country's order and economic growth. Related to this was the regular performing of offering rites in the temples by the king. Gods and kings were 'living by Maat', as the Egyptians put it. If the ruler 'lived by Maat', he acknowledged her principles, which can be seen in numerous depictions in the temples, for example in scenes where the pharaoh is portrayed presenting an offering to Shepsi, a manifestation of Thoth. Thoth was regarded as a judge and a mediator.

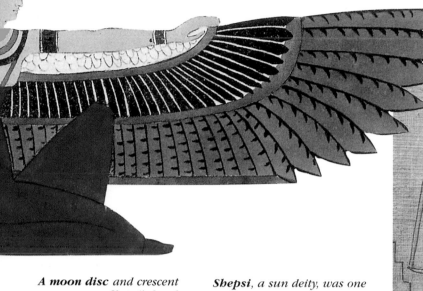

▼ **The weighing of the heart**
At the judgement of the dead, Horus weighs the heart as the seat of the soul and of good and bad deeds, against the feather of Maat. If the deceased spoke the truth in front of Osiris, the scales dipped in his favour to the side of Maat.

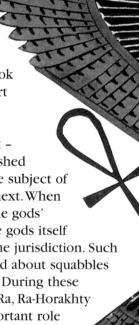

A moon disc and crescent are worn on Shepsi's head.

Shepsi, a sun deity, was one of the manifestations of Thoth.

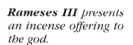

Rameses III presents an incense offering to the god.

A drink offering is poured at the feet of Shepsi by Rameses II.

▼ **Maat as the incarnation of law**
Maat personified both divine and worldly order, as well as the concept of justice. All legal cases, even those concerning the pharaoh, were bound by her. As the highest judge and legislator of the country, the ruler in particular was obliged to honour the enacting of laws and the administration of justice in accordance with Maat. Maat therefore represented supreme ethics and an awareness of right and wrong.

Judgement day

According to Egyptian belief, jurisdiction also took place in the afterlife. Apart from the compulsory judgement of the dead – the weighing of the heart – misdemeanours not punished in this world could be the subject of a judicial hearing in the next. When it came to a conflict of the gods' interests, the world of the gods itself became the place of divine jurisdiction. Such hearings were usually held about squabbles between Horus and Seth. During these hearings, the gods Atum, Ra, Ra-Horakhty and Thoth played an important role as judges and mediators.

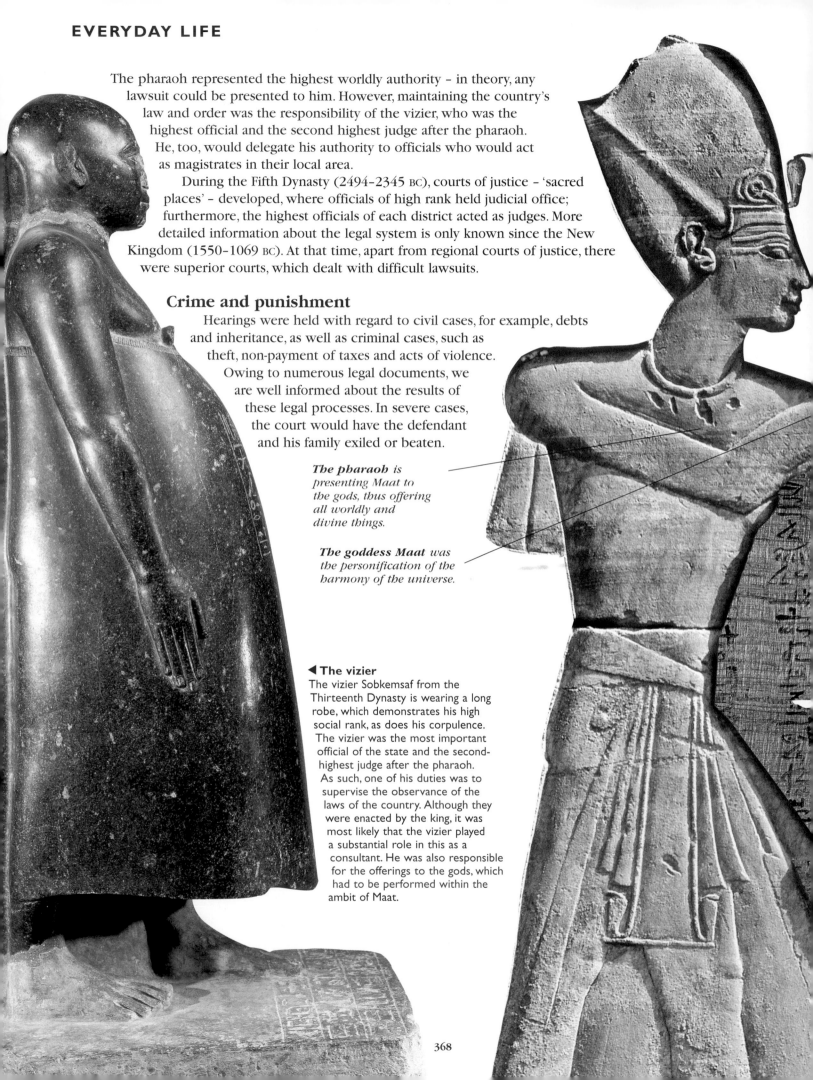

The pharaoh represented the highest worldly authority – in theory, any lawsuit could be presented to him. However, maintaining the country's law and order was the responsibility of the vizier, who was the highest official and the second highest judge after the pharaoh. He, too, would delegate his authority to officials who would act as magistrates in their local area.

During the Fifth Dynasty (2494–2345 BC), courts of justice – 'sacred places' – developed, where officials of high rank held judicial office; furthermore, the highest officials of each district acted as judges. More detailed information about the legal system is only known since the New Kingdom (1550–1069 BC). At that time, apart from regional courts of justice, there were superior courts, which dealt with difficult lawsuits.

Crime and punishment

Hearings were held with regard to civil cases, for example, debts and inheritance, as well as criminal cases, such as theft, non-payment of taxes and acts of violence. Owing to numerous legal documents, we are well informed about the results of these legal processes. In severe cases, the court would have the defendant and his family exiled or beaten.

The pharaoh is presenting Maat to the gods, thus offering all worldly and divine things.

The goddess Maat was the personification of the harmony of the universe.

◀ The vizier

The vizier Sobkemsaf from the Thirteenth Dynasty is wearing a long robe, which demonstrates his high social rank, as does his corpulence. The vizier was the most important official of the state and the second-highest judge after the pharaoh. As such, one of his duties was to supervise the observance of the laws of the country. Although they were enacted by the king, it was most likely that the vizier played a substantial role in this as a consultant. He was also responsible for the offerings to the gods, which had to be performed within the ambit of Maat.

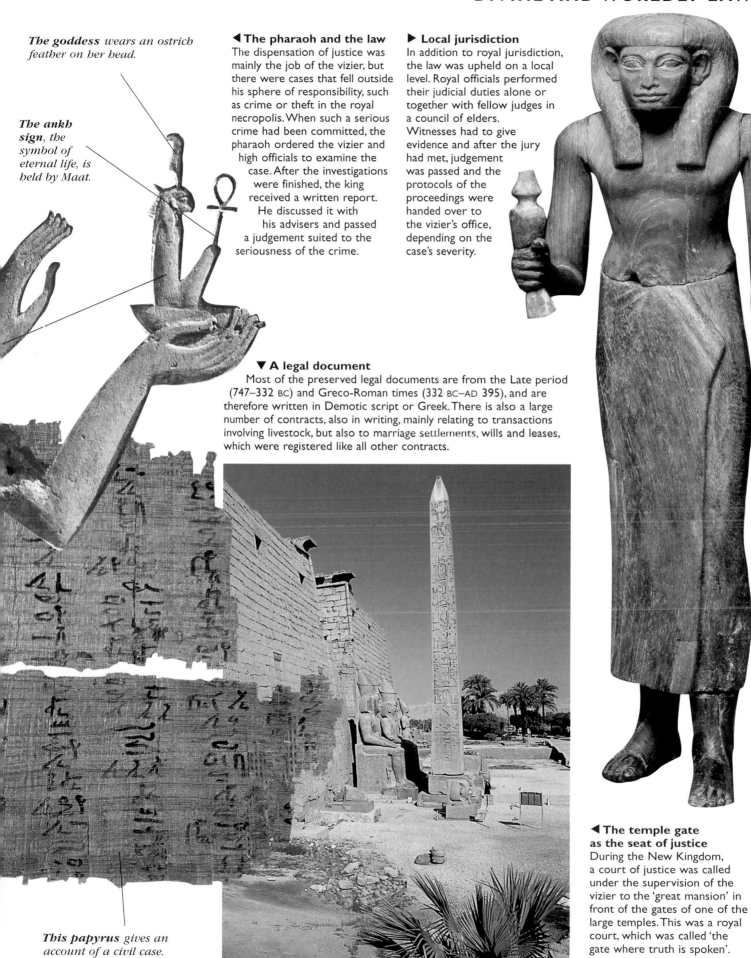

The goddess wears an ostrich feather on her head.

The ankh sign, the symbol of eternal life, is held by Maat.

◀ The pharaoh and the law

The dispensation of justice was mainly the job of the vizier, but there were cases that fell outside his sphere of responsibility, such as crime or theft in the royal necropolis. When such a serious crime had been committed, the pharaoh ordered the vizier and high officials to examine the case. After the investigations were finished, the king received a written report. He discussed it with his advisers and passed a judgement suited to the seriousness of the crime.

▶ Local jurisdiction

In addition to royal jurisdiction, the law was upheld on a local level. Royal officials performed their judicial duties alone or together with fellow judges in a council of elders. Witnesses had to give evidence and after the jury had met, judgement was passed and the protocols of the proceedings were handed over to the vizier's office, depending on the case's severity.

▼ A legal document

Most of the preserved legal documents are from the Late period (747–332 BC) and Greco-Roman times (332 BC–AD 395), and are therefore written in Demotic script or Greek. There is also a large number of contracts, also in writing, mainly relating to transactions involving livestock, but also to marriage settlements, wills and leases, which were registered like all other contracts.

This papyrus gives an account of a civil case.

◀ The temple gate as the seat of justice

During the New Kingdom, a court of justice was called under the supervision of the vizier to the 'great mansion' in front of the gates of one of the large temples. This was a royal court, which was called 'the gate where truth is spoken'.

The Role of Women

Until relatively recently, Egyptologists were little concerned with the role of women in Egyptian society. As females were largely excluded from public life, there was not a lot of information available. In some areas, though, men and women were considered equals.

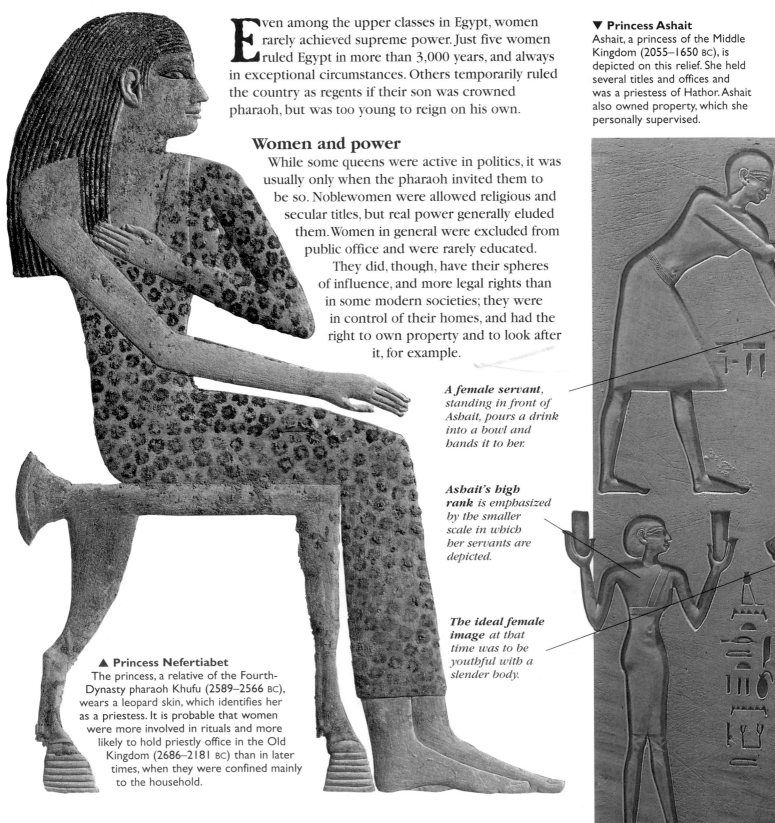

Even among the upper classes in Egypt, women rarely achieved supreme power. Just five women ruled Egypt in more than 3,000 years, and always in exceptional circumstances. Others temporarily ruled the country as regents if their son was crowned pharaoh, but was too young to reign on his own.

Women and power

While some queens were active in politics, it was usually only when the pharaoh invited them to be so. Noblewomen were allowed religious and secular titles, but real power generally eluded them. Women in general were excluded from public office and were rarely educated.

They did, though, have their spheres of influence, and more legal rights than in some modern societies; they were in control of their homes, and had the right to own property and to look after it, for example.

▼ Princess Ashait
Ashait, a princess of the Middle Kingdom (2055–1650 BC), is depicted on this relief. She held several titles and offices and was a priestess of Hathor. Ashait also owned property, which she personally supervised.

A female servant, standing in front of Ashait, pours a drink into a bowl and hands it to her.

Ashait's high rank is emphasized by the smaller scale in which her servants are depicted.

The ideal female image at that time was to be youthful with a slender body.

▲ Princess Nefertiabet
The princess, a relative of the Fourth-Dynasty pharaoh Khufu (2589–2566 BC), wears a leopard skin, which identifies her as a priestess. It is probable that women were more involved in rituals and more likely to hold priestly office in the Old Kingdom (2686–2181 BC) than in later times, when they were confined mainly to the household.

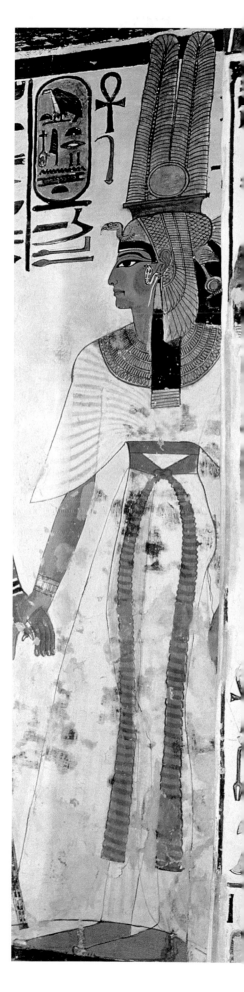

Mut, wife and mother

The basic nuclear family – father, mother and children – was the model for the gods as well as for humans, although the gods tended to have just one child. The goddess Mut was considered the wife of Amun and the mother of Khons. Mut, whose name means 'mother', wears a double crown in this sculpture (right).

▶ **Queen Nefertari**

Nefertari was the first and principal wife of Rameses II (1279–1213 BC) and played an active role in the political and religious life of the time. The pharaoh built a small temple for her at Abu Simbel, as well as a magnificent tomb in the Valley of the Queens, which contains this portait of her. Her husband's divinity was transferred to her, and she was identified with the goddess Hathor. Here she wears the vulture headdress reserved for queens and goddesses, with the plumed double crown and the sun disc.

▲ **Singer of Amun**

While women were generally excluded from work in the temples after the end of the Old Kingdom (2181 BC), several noblewomen from Thebes were recruited as singers for rituals in the temple of Amun at Karnak. This papyrus illustration of one of these priestesses, who were known as 'singers of Amun', is taken from the *Book of the Dead.*

A short, tightly curled wig was the characteristic female style in the Middle Kingdom.

A chair decorated with the head and feet of a lion indicates the princess's wealth and rank.

Ashait is barefoot. In the Middle Kingdom, women did not wear sandals.

The basic division of roles along gender lines was carried into the world of work. Some professions were exclusively taken on by men, and others by women. Women were forbidden from work involving blades, such as reaping, and from working by the banks of the Nile, apparently because of the threat from crocodiles. While women worked mainly as millers, spinners and weavers, men always did the laundry.

In the rural estates of the temples and the nobility, women busied themselves alongside men baking bread and brewing beer. Texts also cite female dancers, singers, gardeners, musicians, weavers and sewers as domestic personnel in great houses. Men had male personal servants, and women female ones.

Farms and factories

Surviving tomb paintings of everyday life in Egypt predominantly show men at work. However, most of these scenes depict outdoor work, such as fishing, hunting or working in the fields. Although women did help gather in the harvest, in general they had nothing to do with agricultural work and animal husbandry. The halls attached to houses where textiles were made – the nearest thing to factories in Ancient Egypt – were generally run and staffed by women.

▶ **Grinding grain**
Woman were very much involved in preparing food. Grain was ground into flour by hand. It was placed on a long stone slab lying on the floor, then pulverized by running a smooth stone back and forth across it.

◀ **Modern fieldwork**
Although the crops have changed, farming methods in Egypt today are often little different from those used thousands of years ago. In areas where agricultural machinery, such as tractors and harvesters, is still a rarity, women's labour is as necessary for the survival of the family as it was then.

A long wig and an ankle-length sheath gown supported by shoulder straps were the characteristic dress of women in the Old Kingdom.

Each woman carries typical produce from the deceased's estate.

◀ **The harvest**
Agriculture in Ancient Egypt was largely a male domain; women looked after the household and raised the children. Women sometimes helped in the fields at crucial times such as harvest, but the prohibition on them using blades meant that men cut the sheaves, while the women gathered them up in baskets.

Women and produce

A tomb in Saqqara, built for Ti, an official of the Fifth Dynasty (2494–2345 BC), contains a relief showing a procession of women with offerings of agricultural produce from Ti's extensive holdings throughout Egypt.

Baskets of offerings, *including fruit, flax and grain, were for use by the deceased in the afterlife.*

Breasts, normally covered by straps, *are conventionally shown exposed in profile.*

Necklaces, and bracelets for the ankle and wrist, were made of faience beads.

◀ **Women in tomb reliefs**
Women actually at work rarely appear in tomb paintings and sculptures. In this relief, they represent the different provinces in which the deceased held estates. The name of the appropriate province appears in hieroglyphs between the figures.

Protector of women

Despite his grotesque looks, the god Bes – usually depicted as a grimacing dwarf with a protruding tongue and a full beard (right) – was a very popular protective deity in Ancient Egypt. His magical powers were thought to protect mothers and children from danger and disease, and small amulets with the deity's image were worn by them. Then, as now, it was considered a blessing in Egypt to have many children.

Sexuality and health were important female issues. There were remedies and magic rituals to promote pregnancy and prevent miscarriages, as well as various means of contraception.

In civil and religious life, Egyptian women had a much higher standing than women in other countries; they were virtually equal to men. Early travellers to Egypt, such as the Greek Herodotus (*c.* 484–*c.* 425 BC), remarked with amazement on the rights of Egyptian women; they could own land, trade without male assistance, and were entitled to inherit and bequeath as they pleased.

Equal legal rights meant that women could appear in court in the same way as men – as plaintiffs, defendants or witnesses. They were fully responsible for their actions and could be called to account for them and punished as severely as men. In public, they could move around unmolested without a companion.

Marriage and divorce

There was no marriage ceremony in Ancient Egypt, but it was customary for couples to set up home together, live monogamously and raise a family. After marriage, women were always addressed as 'mistress of the house'. They kept their own names and continued to supervise their property themselves. They also had as much right to divorce as men. When this took place, women retained any property they had brought into the marriage.

◀ **Brewing beer**
Beer was the Ancient Egyptians' favourite drink, and brewing it was a job for both men and women. This Old Kingdom statue shows a woman pushing moistened barley flour through a sieve as a prelude to fermentation. After several further stages, the barley mixture, thinned with water, was poured into pitchers to ferment and mature into beer.

Clothes and Fashion

Although styles differed for men and women, Ancient Egyptian clothes were generally practical and simple, until the New Kingdom, when men's and women's fashion broke from its rather austere past and became more elegant and refined.

The typical male dress in Ancient Egypt was the loincloth. During the Old Kingdom (2686–2181 BC) and much of the Middle Kingdom (2055–1650 BC), this was a piece of rectangular fabric covering the loins and falling to just above the knee, tied around the waist with a strip of fabric or leather. Only by their jewellery could men from the wealthy classes be distinguished from farmers and artisans.

New Kingdom fashions

It was not until the New Kingdom (1550–1069 BC) that dress became more sophisticated: an apron-like arrangement was often added to the front of the loincloth, and ankle-length skirts and short-sleeved tunics began to be worn over the short loincloth. The full-length robe also made an appearance at this time. This garment had a wide neck and wide sleeves and was gathered at the waist. It is likely that developing relations with other Mediterranean countries played an important role in these new fashion trends.

▶ **Dress of a Twentieth-Dynasty prince**
In this illustration, the son of Rameses III (1184–1153 BC) wears royal garments similar to those of his father. His wide-sleeved tunic of white linen fits over a long, white loincloth, from which hangs a blue and ochre belt.

▼ **The triangular apron**
This garment, worn only by the pharaoh, consists of a loincloth and triangular apron. The end of the coloured sash is decorated with sacred cobras.

▼ **The royal schendyt**
Only the king could attach a lion's tail, symbol of strength, to his short, narrow loincloth, known as a schendyt.

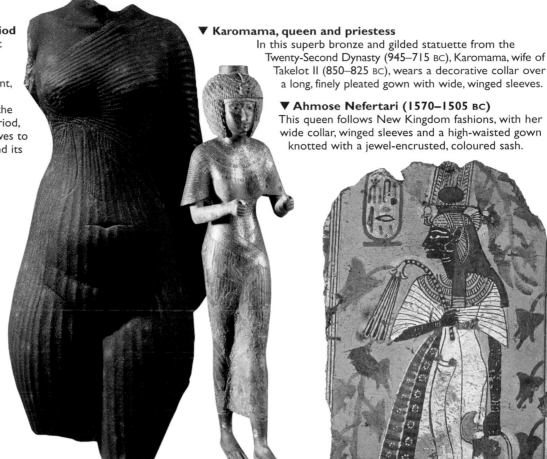

▶ Fashion in the Amarna period
This torso is thought to represent Nefertiti, the wife of the pharaoh Akhenaten (1352–1336 BC). She wears a finely pleated linen garment, knotted under the breasts and leaving the right arm exposed. In the art style typical of the Amarna period, the transparency of the fabric serves to emphasize the body's contours, and its rounded buttocks and thighs.

The richly decorated diadem has a side flap, similar to the sidelock of youth, which indicates that the wearer is a child.

The white tunic covers only the upper arms. The wrists are adorned with costly bracelets of gold and semi-precious stones.

The loincloth is held in place by a wide belt or sash.

▼ Karomama, queen and priestess
In this superb bronze and gilded statuette from the Twenty-Second Dynasty (945–715 BC), Karomama, wife of Takelot II (850–825 BC), wears a decorative collar over a long, finely pleated gown with wide, winged sleeves.

▼ Ahmose Nefertari (1570–1505 BC)
This queen follows New Kingdom fashions, with her wide collar, winged sleeves and a high-waisted gown knotted with a jewel-encrusted, coloured sash.

▼ A ritual garment
Priests and kings often wore a leopard skin when performing religious rituals and on some ceremonial occasions.

▼ Male fashion in the New Kingdom
Fashionable wear in the New Kingdom included the short loincloth topped by a long robe of transparent, pleated linen, with a coloured sash.

INSIGHT

Royal dress

During the Old Kingdom (2686–2181 BC), the simple, short loincloth featured among a king's ceremonial garments. However, by the Middle Kingdom (2055–1650 BC), fashions had changed and more elaborate clothes were worn by the ruling classes. One of the innovations at this time was the starched, triangular apron, which

formed a flap in front of either the short or long loincloth. This was held in place by a coloured, decorative sash. More radical changes took place during the New Kingdom (1550–1069 BC), with the addition of robes and chemises, as well as variable loincloth designs. In the Greco-Roman period (332 BC–AD 395), fashion saw a 'retro' movement and the triangular apron reappeared, decorated, as in this example (above), by the familiar motif of the pharaoh triumphing over his enemies.

Women's fashions

Until the end of the Middle Kingdom, women wore a simple, long sheath dress with one or two broad shoulder straps. A transparent, long-sleeved tunic was sometimes worn over these figure-hugging dresses, as was a sort of decorative mesh tunic.

Women's clothes, along with men's, changed during the New Kingdom. Garments became looser and more sophisticated, and women wore dresses that knotted beneath their breasts and fell away more fully to their feet. Linen became increasingly fine and more highly worked, while draped and pleated effects created some very elaborate fashions. Long sleeves, for example, were often finely pleated and starched to resemble birds' wings. Most of these loose-fitting garments covered the breasts (often bared in earlier times) and the left arm, while the right arm remained exposed.

▶ **Festive garments**
Noblewomen and others of high rank dressed in all their finery on special occasions and for festive banquets, as this wall painting shows.

INSIGHT

Workmen's fashion

Unlike officials, artisans and farmers dressed in plain, inexpensive robes of different fabrics. Before linen came into use, men wore loincloths of reed or palm fibres, leather or fur with broad sashes. Shepherds, ferrymen and fishermen mainly made do with a simple leather sash from which hung a curtain of reeds; many also worked completely naked, at least until the Middle Kingdom – during this time it became rare to see an unclothed worker. Female millers, bakers and harvest workers are often depicted in a long wraparound skirt but with the upper part of the body bared.

The clothes worn by the servants of officials and dignitaries were more refined than those of simple folk. A servant depicted in an Eigteenth-Dynasty tomb (left) wears a finely pleated linen tunic and loincloth with a wide, pleated sash.

376

◀ The linen sheath
This detail from a Middle Kingdom stele shows the typical Egyptian dress of the time – a long, close-fitting linen sheath, supported by straps that reached from below the breasts to just above the ankles. This woman also wears a long wig, and jewellery in the form of a broad collar, bracelets, anklets and toe rings.

▼ A vizier's attire
This bronze statuette depicts a vizier of the Middle Kingdom. His distinctive garment was a long, starched robe that hung from the chest to just above the feet; it was fastened at the back with a cord. In this example, the garment is pleated in broad horizontal bands.

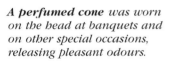

A perfumed cone was worn on the head at banquets and on other special occasions, releasing pleasant odours.

A long, thick wig of tight curls was adorned with an elaborate headdress.

The full-length festive robe of fine linen was knotted above the waist with a cord.

Sumptuous jewellery included bracelets of faience, gold and colourful semi-precious stones, along with large, heavy earrings.

A bouquet of lotus blooms and a single lotus flower across the arm complete the ensemble.

▲ Priestly garments
When carrying out their priestly duties, temple officials often wore the skin of a leopard draped over their shoulder. This dress was initially reserved for the sem priests, who played an important role in regal and private funerary rites and who were responsible for performing the 'opening of the mouth' ritual. In this stele, which dates from the Fourth Dynasty (2613–2494 BC), the priest sits in front of an offerings table.

▶ Pleated tunic
This pleated, linen tunic belonged to Nakht, a chancellor of Egypt during the Middle Kingdom. It was found in his tomb in Asyut, and is now held in the Louvre Museum, Paris.

Cosmetics & Perfumes

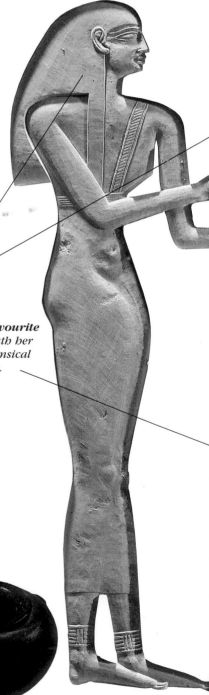

For the Ancient Egyptians, cosmetics and perfumes were not merely for personal adornment – they were associated with the gods and rebirth in the afterlife.

Perfumes were used in Ancient Egypt from the earliest times. Although scented oils and unguents (ointments) were most common, essences extracted by pressing flowers, such as the lily, were also used. Perfumes were originally made for religious rituals, using a wide range of aromatic plants. They were generally produced in the temples, which had their own specialist 'laboratories', making different types of incense and fragrant pastes. Many of the recipes survive and, although some of the ingredients are unknown today, they show that the Egyptians loved sweet, spicy perfumes that filled the air with their heady, long-lasting aroma.

The scent of the gods

Kyphi, the most celebrated Egyptian perfume, was burnt daily in the temple as an incense. Its ingredients included resins, such as frankincense, myrrh, mastic and pine resin; herbs and spices, such as cinnamon, cardamom, saffron, juniper, mint and the patchouli-like spikenard; along with raisins and honey. The burning and offering of incense was a means of communication with the gods, and there are many depictions of pharaohs making such fragrant offerings.

▲ Cosmetic spoons
These small objects held scented unguents for the immediate use of the owner, and were presumably scooped from a larger container.

▶ Unguent pots
The use of cosmetics dates back to early history. Cosmetics and unguents were held in high regard even in Predynastic times, proof of which are these small vessels of hardstone, found in the tombs of the Predynastic Naqada period (4000–3100 BC) and now in the Louvre in Paris.

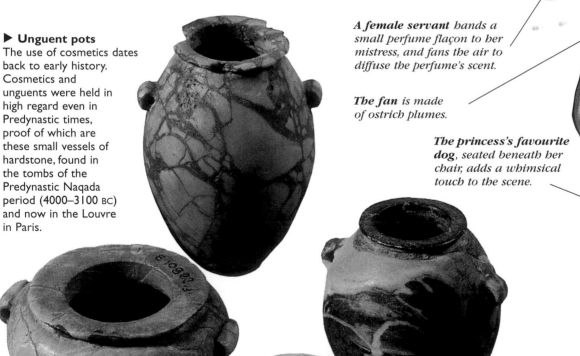

*A **female servant** hands a small perfume flaçon to her mistress, and fans the air to diffuse the perfume's scent.*

*The **fan** is made of ostrich plumes.*

*The **princess's favourite dog**, seated beneath her chair, adds a whimsical touch to the scene.*

▼ The power of perfume

This tomb relief depicts Ashait, a princess of the Middle Kingdom, seated on a bench decorated with the head and the claws of a lion. The Egyptians believed that perfume was a gift of the gods, and it was used in temple ceremonies as well as for personal allure. Its links with sexuality and rebirth made it especially important in the afterlife, and many unguent jars and perfume bottles are found among tomb goods.

▶ Decorative hand mirror

This mirror, which dates from the Old Kingdom (2686–2181 BC), is made of polished bronze and decorated with the figures of Nephthys and Osiris. Its handle was possibly made of wood, metal, faience or ivory, perhaps in the shape of a papyrus stem or human figure.

The sphere-shaped bottle contained perfume or fragrant oils to be used both on the body and for scenting the princess's chamber.

The powerful, hyacinth-like scent of the lotus flower had sexual connotations, and by extension the lotus was a symbol of rebirth in the afterlife – hence its frequent depiction in tomb paintings and reliefs.

▼ Double kohl case

This double cylindrical case, made of wood and ivory, has two compartments with hinged lids for the kohl, and a slot at the back for the kohl stick.

▼ Kohl case

This charming wooden kohl case, with a geometric pattern around the base, is in the form of a palm tree. It was found in a New Kingdom tomb.

During the New Kingdom (1550–1069 BC), perfume began to be used in beauty preparations and for personal adornment, as well as in religious rituals. Fragrant oils and unguents protected the skin in a country where the sun was extremely hot, although few but the rich could afford the exotic scents that now included imported luxuries, such as spicy green galbanum from Persia or rose-scented camel grass from Libya. Then, as now, perfumes were associated with sexuality, and in the divine scheme of things were symbols of rebirth in the afterlife.

Cosmetics – the art of beauty

Cosmetics were already in use in Predynastic times; many cosmetic spoons and make-up palettes date from this period. In Ancient Egypt, the focus was on the eyes, which were outlined with green or black eye paint to emphasize their size and shape. The ground pigments of green malachite, mixed with water to form as paste, were used until the middle of the Old Kingdom (2686–2181 BC), but were then replaced by black kohl, produced from the mineral galena, which came from the mountain regions of Sinai. Significantly, kohl had therapeutic value in protecting the eyes from infections caused by sunlight, dust or flies.

▲ Kohl container
The holes in the top of this vessel contained kohl and the sticks (introduced during the Middle Kingdom) with which to apply it. The monkeys that decorate the container hold the hieroglyph for 'protection', a reminder of kohl's role in preventing eye infections.

▼ Jar in the form of Bes
Many cosmetics containers were in the shape of figures or animals. This faience unguent jar from the Eighteenth Dynasty (1550–1295 BC) represents the dwarf god Bes, who was associated with women, childbirth and sexuality. He is therefore an appropriate image for a container which held a beauty aid to enhance appearance and sexual allure.

▶ Unguent jars
Containers for unguents and perfumed oils came in various shapes and sizes. Some were made of precious materials, such as glass or alabaster, while blue faience was a more commonplace alternative, as here.

◄ Cosmetic palette
Palettes were used to grind pigments such as malachite or galena, from which, respectively, green and kohl eye paints were made. This one is shield-shaped, with two birds' heads at the top. Their use dates from the Predynastic period (5500–3100 BC), during which time they also acquired ceremonial or magical properties; many were found as grave goods in cemeteries dating back to about 4000 BC.

▼ Mummy mask from the Roman period (30 BC–AD 395)
The mummy, or funerary, mask was first used in the First Intermediate period (2181–2055 BC) to help with the identification of the linen-wrapped mummy. This example from the Roman period has the outlined eyes and emphatic brows that were characteristic of the Egyptian style, but the features are more life-like and less stylized than on traditional Ancient Egyptian masks.

Fine brush strokes simulate the hair of these thick eyebrows. Black eye paint was often used on eyebrows to emphastze them.

Kohl was used to colour the eyelids and make the eyes appear larger. It also protected the eyes against infections.

Lip tint was used by the Romans in Egypt, but wall paintings, mummy masks and painted reliefs show little evidence of its use in pharaonic times.

Mummy masks from the Roman period show portrait-like features in the classical style rather than the idealized images that feature on earlier examples.

Hygiene and Body Care

In Egypt, sweltering heat and sanitary problems often coexisted. People went to great lengths to remove dirt from their person and their life. The daily routines included cleansing the skin and mouth, grooming the hair and cleaning the finger and toe nails.

In the ruins of the palace of Rameses III (1184-1153 BC) at Medinet Habu, in the villas of the elite at Amarna, even in the dwellings of the middle classes – chief craftsmen, officials and intermediate priests – archaeologists have discovered bathrooms (or more precisely washrooms) with mud-brick walls protected from the water by slabs of limestone. Egyptians did not take baths. Instead, they poured water from a jug with a spout over their head and body – or, more likely, had a servant do it for them. Sometimes the water – which was never heated – was tipped through a vessel with holes in it, an early precursor of the showerhead. The floor sloped slightly for dirty water to drain away. The sort of homes that had bathrooms would also have had a small room set aside as a lavatory, with a pierced limestone or wood seat raised on some mud bricks, and an earthenware pot half filled with sand beneath.

The houses of the lower classes, by contrast, had no sanitary arrangements at all, and there is no archaeological evidence of public baths in pharaonic times. This does not mean that the general population did not wash – the sheer number of toilet articles that survive from Ancient Egypt testifies to the importance placed on cleanliness and grooming – but that they did so outdoors, either bathing in the Nile or sprinkling water on their face, hands and body from a small bowl and rubbing away any dirt. Water for washing was carried home by women from the river or local wells in big earthenware jars.

▼ Oils and unguents
Ointments based on fats and oils from both plant and animal sources were an important part of body care in Ancient Egypt. There was no soap. Bathers used fats mixed with chalk and limestone dust instead. Other ointments refreshed the skin in Egypt's drying climate, while oil-based fragrances were used to scent the skin. They were kept in precious pots and jars; those depicted here being carried by servants would have been reserved for sacred oils.

Tall, conical pots sealed with flat lids supplemented the smaller, rounded containers. They were used to store fragrant moisturizing oils.

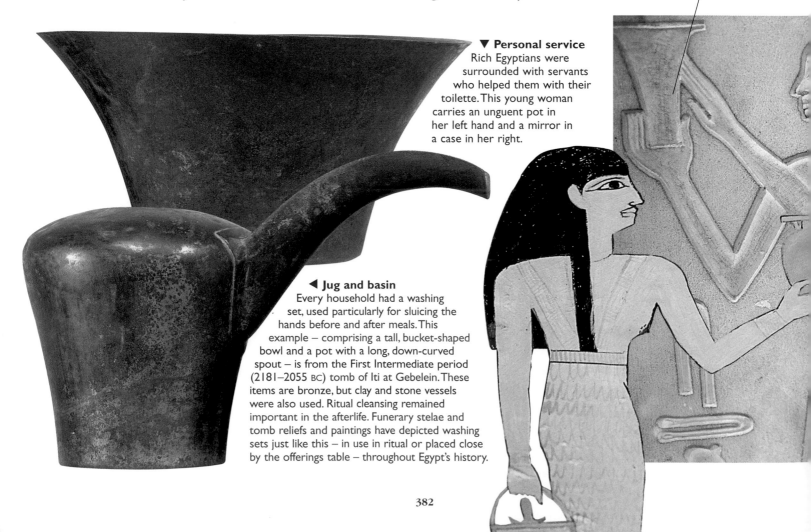

▼ Personal service
Rich Egyptians were surrounded with servants who helped them with their toilette. This young woman carries an unguent pot in her left hand and a mirror in a case in her right.

◄ Jug and basin
Every household had a washing set, used particularly for sluicing the hands before and after meals. This example – comprising a tall, bucket-shaped bowl and a pot with a long, down-curved spout – is from the First Intermediate period (2181–2055 BC) tomb of Iti at Gebelein. These items are bronze, but clay and stone vessels were also used. Ritual cleansing remained important in the afterlife. Funerary stelae and tomb reliefs and paintings have depicted washing sets just like this – in use in ritual or placed close by the offerings table – throughout Egypt's history.

▶ Feet of clay

Divided, rectangular earthenware basins such as this, with
sloping walls and the sole of a foot depicted on the central
divider, are occasionally found in tombs, or carved on
the walls. They may have been used for ritually
cleansing or anointing the feet before entering a
sacred area; water or oil would be poured over
a foot placed on the rest. Feet also received
non-ritual attention in Ancient Egypt. Pedicures —
and manicures — are depicted in the tomb of
a high-ranking Old Kingdom official, Ptahhotep.

◀ Foot relief

The Fourth-Dynasty
mastaba tomb of Prince
Rahotep has a relief that
seems to show (from
above) a basin like that on
the right, but with two foot-
rests rather than one, topped
by a conical vessel (from front-
on). This can be seen as a bucket
of water for washing the feet or
a pot of oil for anointing them.

*Scented sacred oils were
liberally used to perfume the
celebrants of cult rituals and
were offered in libations to
the gods and the dead alike.*

*The young women carrying
the oil jars are the servants of
a daughter of Mentuhotep II
(2004–1992 BC). This relief is
carved on her sarcophagus.*

INSIGHT

Ritual ablutions

Only the pharaoh and his representatives, the priests,
were allowed inside Egyptian temples. Before they entered
the sanctuary to perform their duties, both
ruler and priests had to go through a
cleansing ritual, as nothing from the
profane world was supposed to enter
the sanctuary. According to the Greek
historian Herodotus, writing in the
fifth century BC, 'the priests shaved
their whole body every third
day so that they had no
louse or other pest when
serving the gods ... They
wash twice a day and
twice a night.' The antiquity
of the practice is demonstrated by
the ceremonial palette of Narmer,
founder of the First Dynasty around
3100 BC. It shows a servant carrying
the king's sandals and a water jug
for a ritual cleansing (left) before
the king enters the temple of
Horus to make an offering.

A pleasant fragrance was as important as cleanliness. Scented oils were popular gifts, while lozenges made from myrrh, juniper berries, honey, incense and other ingredients sweetened the breath. Cosmetics were generally applied after bathing. All of these enhanced the appearance, but some of them had a practical use. Eye make-up – green malachite-based pigments used early in the Old Kingdom were later replaced by black kohl, based on galena – made the eyes appear bigger, but also acted as a natural disinfectant, warding off infections, and provided protection from the dazzle and glare of the Egyptian sun.

Household rubbish

The Egyptians dealt with their domestic refuse much as we do today, either burying it in waste ground or piling it up into tips. Some was dumped in waterways. The tips could be quite large – the one associated with the royal palace of Akhenaten was some 200m by 120m (650ft by 400ft) – and can be treasure troves for archaeologists; a refuse ditch dug close by the village of Deir el-Medina yielded literally thousands of ostraca that provide great insights into the everyday lives of the workmen who lived there.

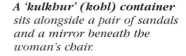

A 'kulkhur' (kohl) container sits alongside a pair of sandals and a mirror beneath the woman's chair.

◄ Looking good
Mirrors were indispensable to the perfect application of make-up. The reflective surface was always a highly polished metal – copper, bronze or silver – disc. Some handles were plain, but most were decorated. They were commonly carved or moulded as a papyrus plant, the fiercely protective god Bes or a naked young woman.

▼ Bowls
These two small bowls – one of Egyptian faience and the other of calcite alabaster – were probably used for hand-washing after a meal, but it is possible they were intended as drinking vessels. Found in the tomb of an official, they are today on display at the Fitzwilliam Museum in Cambridge.

◄ Eye make-up
Egyptians – both men and women – regularly applied 'kulkhur,' or kohl, eye make-up that had a practical as well as cosmetic use, and was kept in small, rounded pots.

► Toiletries for the afterlife
Like anything else that the Ancient Egyptians found useful in life, toiletries and cosmetics were considered to be equally essential for the dead, and they formed an important part of the grave goods of wealthy people. Small containers of wood or basketwork served to store everyday toiletries, while most tombs contained 'kulkhur' vessels of various kinds of stone, glass and faience, along with combs, hairpins, copper and bronze tweezers, razor knives and small whetstones. Cosmetic articles are usually found alongside amulets in the shape of scarabs, which serve to protect health in this life and guarantee rebirth in the next.

▶ Hair care
Combs carved from wood or bone have been discovered in tombs of the Predynastic period (5500–3100 BC). Most preserved combs are decorated with figurative elements. The handle of this acacia wood specimen (today in the Louvre Museum in Paris) pictures a kneeling ibex. The fine quality of the carving raises what is basically an everyday domestic object to the status of a work of art.

The blue lotus, a long-stemmed waterlily that once grew widely along the Nile, was renowned for the perfection of its perfume.

A hunting dog similar to a modern-day greyhound sits by its master's chair.

▲ Pleasant scents
This tomb relief shows a couple enjoying the fragrance of blue lotus flowers, a much-prized scent in Ancient Egypt. The plant owed its popularity both to its heady, even psychotropic perfume and to its status as a symbol of regeneration and rebirth, with the flowers closing each evening to be reborn the following morning with the sun.

◀ Ointment spoon
Flat spoons with elaborately decorated handles have been found in tombs from as early as the late Predynastic period. They were probably intended to offer precious fragrances to the gods, rather than for everyday use.

▲ ▶ Shaving
Razors in various shapes were used to remove and shape head and body hair, as well as facial hair.

▶ Tweezers
Two types of twisted metal tweezers were made: some with pointed ends and others with broad, flattened ends.

Goldsmiths and Jewellers

As early as 5000 BC, necklaces and belts were made along the Nile from beads, plant seeds and various polished stones. From about 4000 BC onwards, the Ancient Egyptians began to use gold, silver and copper to make jewellery.

In Ancient Egypt, both men and women adorned themselves with jewellery, not only as decoration, but also in the form of protective amulets. Virtually every form of jewellery has been recorded, including finger rings, anklets, armlets, girdles and pectorals, necklaces, torques, chokers, diadems, ear studs, earrings and hair ornaments.

Coloured semi-precious stones, such as cornelian, turquoise, feldspar, green and red jasper, amethyst, quartz, agate and lapis lazuli – imported from Afghanistan – were the most commonly used stones. Often, however, they were imitated by coloured glass and faience. Many of the stones were mined in the desert areas of Egypt and in Sinai.

Gold and copper mines were mainly found in the outlying areas of Egypt and Nubia, but during the New Kingdom (1550-1069 BC), much gold was received as

▶ **High-quality gold jewellery**
Objects made from precious metals and precious stones were worn by the nobility in everyday life and used as tomb offerings. The jewellery from the tomb of Tutankhamun (1336–1327 BC) and this gold mask of Psusennes I (1039–991 BC) are of the finest quality.

The eyes and eyebrows, made of lapis lazuli and glass, are set into the thin gold plate of the mask.

The goldsmiths designed the shoulders of the mask as a wide garland of flowers, the so-called wesekh collar.

INSIGHT

Nub – precious metal from the mines of Nubia

In Egypt itself, gold was found in Wadi Hammamat (between Qena and the Red Sea); however, when the pharaohs conquered Nubia, they suddenly controlled a rich source of the precious metal. The Ancient Egyptian word for gold, *nub*, even gave its name to this part of the country south of Aswan.

Expeditions to the gold mines, which lay far away from the Nile, had to be carefully planned. Bedouins, who knew not only the exact location of the mines, but also all the water sources along the way, were hired as guides. Small mounds, called alamats (below), were built as signposts for the routes through the desert.

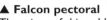

▲ **Falcon pectoral**
The wings of this golden falcon with the head of a ram are inlaid with lapis lazuli, cornelian and turquoise. This pectoral was a tomb offering in the Serapeum of Saqqara.

The golden uraeus serpent was forged separately and attached above the forehead with fine pins.

The cross stripes of the king's headdress, the nemes, were created by engraving the gold plate.

The making of gold jewellery

1. Weighing the gold

2. Smelting the gold in a furnace

3. Hammering and beating the metal into shape

4. Displaying the finished piece

tribute from conquered territories. Egyptian gold was often mixed with a high percentage of silver. This light, or 'white' gold, also called electrum, could be worked at slightly lower temperatures than pure, high-carat gold.

In the Old Kingdom (2686–2181 BC), jewellery-making was a popular theme in tomb decorations. Reliefs show the goldsmithing process, as well as the piercing of pearls and the stringing of necklaces. As craftsmen of the pharaoh, and as makers of protective amulets, jewellers and goldsmiths were held in high esteem.

Civil Servants

Egypt owed its stability and prosperity to a highly stratified bureaucracy that managed the land, its resources and the people with great efficiency. At the top of the hierarchy were senior civil servants who reported to the pharaoh.

Because the pharaoh had to undertake a great number of religious, administrative, judicial and military duties – too many for him to perform in person – he delegated some of his responsibilities to high-ranking administrators. From the beginning of the Old Kingdom (2686–2181 BC), the overall leadership of the regional administration was entrusted to a vizier, a sort of prime minister who ranked as the most important man in the country after the king. So important and difficult was this position that, from the 18th Dynasty (1550–1295 BC), it was split in two, with the king appointing a vizier each for Upper Egypt and Lower Egypt.

Choosing a vizier

Viziers oversaw the administration and government of the land, and also acted as the supreme judges on behalf of the pharaoh. The importance and responsibility of the job, and the risk involved in concentrating so much power in the hands of a single person, meant that the title of vizier was granted only to men who had earned the pharaoh's trust. It could not be gained simply by pursuing a career in administration.

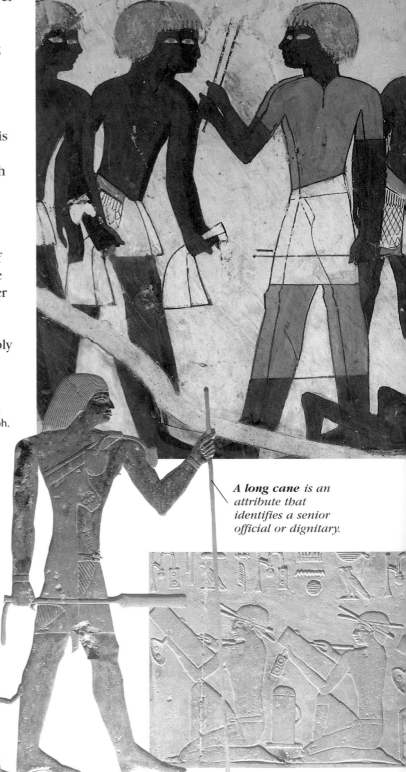

A long cane is an attribute that identifies a senior official or dignitary.

◀ **The sandal-carrier**
From the start of Egyptian history, important people were honoured by serving the pharaoh. Their tasks may appear menial to modern eyes, as in the case of the sandal-carrier shown with the king in the Narmer palette, sculpted around 3100 BC.

▶ **A senior civil servant of the Old Kingdom**
This official holds a long cane – a sign of his office – in one hand and the sekhem sceptre, the symbol of power, in the other. The fact that he wears an animal skin indicates that he is also a priest.

▶▶ **Scribes of the Old Kingdom**
The scribes, the 'foot soldiers' of the civil service, are usually depicted hard at work. A pen case stands in front of the second scribe from the left, while the two on the right have boxes for transporting and storing their writing materials.

Life in the civil service

The tomb of Userhet at Thebes contains representations of the everyday life of an important official. Userhet was a scribe in the service of Amenhotep II (1427–1400 BC), with a particular responsibility for military recruitment. The scenes that decorate the walls of his tomb in Thebes depict him meeting recruits, who bow low as they approach him. In addition to his official duties, the lifelike paintings also evoke the day-to-day personal life of Userhet, such as his penchant for hunting in the desert.

Userhet, wearing the short loincloth of the military, as well as a long loincloth, moves forwards to greet the soldiers.

Recruits wait to be presented to Userhet.

Bowing to Userhet acknowledges his position as a royal scribe.

▲ Vizier Hemiunu
A nephew of Khufu (2589–2566 BC), Hemiunu occupied several important posts, including those of vizier and head of the king's scribes. He was manager of all the pharaoh's building projects, organizing the construction site of the Great Pyramid.

◀ Chief steward Senenmut
The low-born Senenmut became one of the most influential men in the country under Hatshepsut (1473–1458 BC). He was the steward of Amun and director of construction, as well as serving as tutor to the queen's only daughter, Neferura.

Workers and Patrons

Peasants, domestic servants, craftsmen and artists were not free to sell their labour to the highest bidder, but worked on behalf of the state, king, temple or high-ranking officials.

The workers and farmers of Ancient Egypt were as serfs to the keepers of the king's goods and temples. When the pharaoh appointed someone to an office, he lent them the use of the goods and the people living inside the boundaries of that office. Individual enterprises had hierarchical structures within. It was rare for a proprietor to have direct control. A manager or foreman was appointed to ensure the smooth day-to-day operation of the enterprise, along with a scribe to keep records.

Artists and craftsmen operated in teams in workshops; individuals never signed their work. An experienced or particularly talented craftsman was usually made overseer with the idea that he would pass on his skills, but a shop's output was generally very much a joint effort. Younger sculptors, for example, roughed out a piece of stone, while more experienced colleagues did the finer work. Other craftsmen polished the statue, while painters added fine detail and finishing touches. The best workers were employed in royal or temple workshops.

Workshops would generally appoint a scribe to record output and calculate just what would be needed for a job, in order to cut out waste and the misappropriation of such precious materials as wood, stone or gems.

▼ A leader of men
A stele set up in Abydos in 2030 BC vaunts the talents of Irtisen, 'the leader of the king's designers and draughtsmen', a sculptor skilled in working gold, ivory and ebony, as well as stone. Craft secrets were often handed from father to son, as is depicted here.

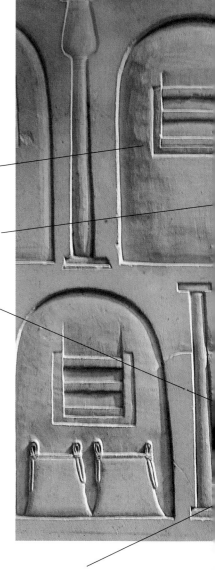

Granaries of the royal estates are depicted in carvings on this sarcophagus.

A scribe controls the filling of the granaries and records the quantity of grain.

Peasants use grain measures to fill the granaries under the sharp eyes of the scribe and the supervisor.

▶ Levels of control
Those who nominally owned and operated land and workshops did not exercise direct control over them. Work was overseen by controllers and inspectors who acted as intermediaries between master and workmen, passing on the former's orders and making sure the latter carried them out. A manager or overseer would be appointed to ensure the smooth day-to-day operation of an enterprise, while a scribe was often delegated to check the work and make a record of it. This relief from the sarcophagus of Princess Kawit (c. 2055–2004 BC) shows grain being measured.

Scenes of workers in action are a common theme in tomb decorations, but are less often seen on sarcophagi.

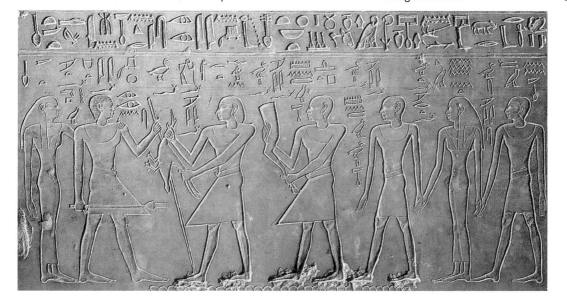

▶ The ship's crew
Virtually any activity represented in tomb paintings or sculptures shows the relative hierarchical status of those involved by means of pictorial scale. On this boat, the oarsmen – at the bottom of the scale, equivalent to simple labourers – are relatively small compared to the helmsman or pilot, those employed to raise or lower the rectangular sail, and the captain on the prow of the boat. Largest of all are the boat's passengers and its owner, who sits in splendid isolation in a small cabin at the bow end.

▲ Domestic servants
Tomb paintings often show processions of servants bringing produce to their masters. Men and women – recruited from among free Egyptians and slaves alike – lived on the premises and cooked, cleaned and acted as personal servants.

▲ The overseer
Like the pharaoh, overseers are shown on a much larger scale than the workers or scribes they control. The long stick is a badge of the overseer's authority.

▲ The king and the clergy
Priests of the great temples, such as those of Amun at Karnak, Ra at Heliopolis or Ptah at Memphis, were organized in strict hierarchies led by a high priest, who was answerable only to the king. This relief shows the pharaoh (right) bringing offerings for Amun. Four shaven-headed priests in long tunics do the actual fetching and carrying.

Fruits of the Soil

Time-honoured farming methods, used thousands of years ago in the fields of Upper Egypt and the Nile Delta by the Ancient Egyptians, are still practised in rural areas of Egypt today.

The Greek historian Herodotus (484–420 BC) exclaimed that 'there was no region in Egypt where the fruits of the soil could be harvested so easily' as in the Nile Delta in Lower Egypt. In reality, however, the conditions in the fields were extremely hard, and the farmers worked simply as labourers, for all the land was owned either by the king or the temples. Farmers also looked after the irrigation system of canals.

The Nile flooded each year from June to August, and, when the floods began to subside, the canals were dammed up and the water held for about six weeks before being released. The first crops were scattered by hand in October and November, and goats, sheep and sometimes pigs were herded into the fields to trample in the seeds.

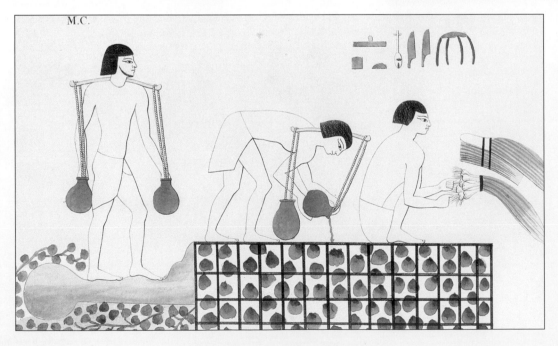

▲ **Irrigation methods**
The shaduf, used to transfer water from river or canal, is basically a long wooden pole with a suspended bucket at one end and a counterbalance at the other. It was first introduced to Egypt in about 1500 BC, but was supplemented 1,000 years later by the Archimedes waterscrew, and later by water wheels driven by oxen. Today, small shadufs are still used to water plants (above).

◀ **Water bearers**
In the earliest form of irrigation, field workers carried vessels of water attached to a yoke. Summer crops and vegetable gardens were often watered using this method.

▲ Ploughing
Today, as in ancient times, oxen can be seen pulling lightweight ploughs through the fertile black soil of Egypt. Arabian camels, however, are newcomers to the job.

Yoked animals, moving at the same pace, made ploughing easier.

Oxen were used mainly as draught animals.

The common wooden plough consisted of a two-part fork and the ploughshare.

◄ Ploughing and sowing
Before seed could be sown, the soil had to be tilled. Yoked oxen were usually used for this job. In ancient times, the soil was also frequently turned over with hoes, as the field labourers could borrow plough animals from the state or temple herds only with official permission.

To prevent evaporation of the groundwater, only the top layer of soil was ploughed. After ploughing, the seeds were sown by hand and various farm animals were used to tread them in.

◄ Harvest
From March to June, during the harvest season, known as shemu, intensive labour was used to reap, thresh, winnow and store the grain. At all stages, a scribe noted the yields to prevent any theft by the workers.

▲ Wooden sickles
Fitted with blades constructed from sharpened flint, sickles were used by workers to reap the barley and wheat.

DOCUMENT

Field work with the family

Men, women and children were all involved in field labour and each was allotted special tasks. Before the harvest began, all the family was involved in keeping animals away from the fields.

Ploughing and reaping were male pursuits, while women sowed the seeds and helped with the harvesting and bundling of the sheaves of grain, as well as with threshing and winnowing. Children were used as gleaners, scouring the fields for the last remaining stalks of grain.

Numerous papyrus pictures and tomb paintings depict men and women working the fields together. These papyrus illustrations (below), now in the Egyptian Museum in Cairo, show ploughing and sowing (top) and harvesting (bottom).

▲ From field to threshing floor

The corn was sheaved and brought to the threshing floor in baskets. There it was spread out and walked on by animals to separate the grains from the husks. The corn was then winnowed with wooden shovels, so that the heavy grain fell to the floor, ready for gathering. This tomb painting shows a donkey and workers carrying loads of corn to the barn.

Clay storage vessels came in different shapes. They were used for storing wine and oil, as well as grain.

▶ Granary

Stockpiling was normal in the barns and corn lofts of the state and temples, as the pharaoh and the priests had to feed the people in times of shortage. Furthermore, all workers, including field labourers, soldiers, craftsmen and priests, were paid in grain. The huge lofts, built of air-dried clay bricks, were ideal for long-term storage, whereas private households stored the grain in stone jars.

Main crops were a type of wheat – called emmer –
barley and flax. The wheat was used for such necessities
as bread and beer, and the flax for the making of linen
cloth and the extraction of linseed oil.

A second crop of plants, such as beans and peas, could
be planted in summer, but the fields had to be irrigated by
hand. Garlic, onions, radish, cabbage, lettuce and cucumber
were grown in small square plots. The harvest yield was
accurately noted by the king's scribe, and a farmer who
failed to reach his grain quota was punished.

▶ Corn loft
The threshed and
winnowed corn was
sometimes stored in hive-like
silos, which were filled through a
hole in the roof, and emptied through a
hatch at the bottom. Models such as the
one shown here were put in tombs to provide
food for the deceased in the afterlife.

*The corn scribe of the loft
kept account books of corn
taken in and out.*

*The threshed corn was
placed in sacks and carried
to the barn by field workers.*

▼ Bread and beer
Grain played a special role in
the nutrition of the Ancient
Egyptians. Not only was bread
made from emmer and barley,
but also lightly baked flat breads,
soaked in water, were used
for brewing beer. The resulting
thin 'beer soup', sometimes
enriched with dates, was rich
in protein and vitamins, and
non-perishable because of its
preserving alcohol content.

Keeping and Breeding Animals

In a society so deeply dependent on agriculture as the Ancient Egyptians', the farming and breeding of domesticated livestock was of enormous economic importance, providing a steady, reliable and predictable source of food.

Domestication of animals in Ancient Egypt began during the Predynastic time (5500–3100 BC), and by about 3000 BC cattle, sheep, goats, pigs, asses and birds such as ducks, geese and pigeons were being farmed. Grazed on the pastures of the Nile Valley and the Delta, cattle were the most important animals, as they provided meat, milk and hides, and could be put into service as draught animals. Most cattle belonged to royalty, the temples or high-ranking officials, although some peasant farmers kept an ox for working the fields.

So important were cattle, as a measure of wealth as well as a source of food, that they were counted each year and their numbers recorded by scribes. In the Old Kingdom (2686–2181 BC), the cattle count was such a significant event that it was used to number the years of a pharaoh's reign.

Beef was considered a luxury and was served only on special occasions. It was also the chosen meat for making offerings to the gods in temples and in funerary rites as food for a deceased's journey through the afterlife.

▲ Cattle breeds
Apart from the indigenous long-horned cattle (above), short-horned varieties were introduced from Palestine, Syria and the Punt (East Africa) during the New Kingdom.

*A **walking staff** was essential equipment and could be placed across the herdsman's shoulder to carry goods.*

*A **vessel** for milk was carried on the herdsman's staff.*

*The **herdsmen** moved with their flocks and herds to remote pastures, and were often naked or scantily clad.*

Sleeping mats were carried, as the herdsmen led a nomadic existence, seeking out new pasture for the animals.

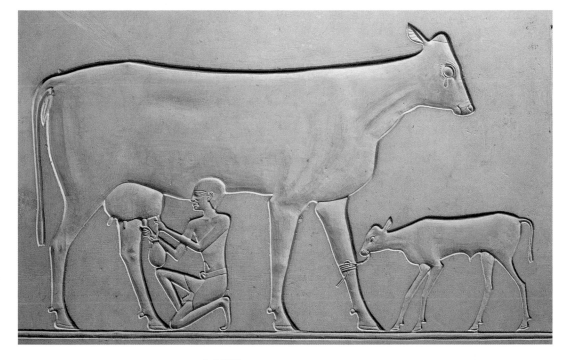

Caring for the herd

The herdsmen chose suitable animals for breeding, helped to deliver the calves and milked the cows. Always on the move in the search for fresh pastures, crossing rivers (below) was a dangerous enterprise, as crocodiles attacked both men and animals.

▲ **Milking**
Cows and oxen were valued as work animals and as a source of milk, meat and hide. On this relief from Deir el-Bahari, the herdsman kneels to milk the cow, while the calf is kept tethered to its mother's leg.

Closely herded together, the cattle are hastily driven through a ford to avoid the dangers lurking in the water.

The calf of the leading cow is carried on the shoulders of the herdsman. Its mother and the rest of the herd follow the two through the river.

INSIGHT

Branding animals

The herds belonging to the temples and the king's court were regularly counted, with scribes checking and recording the numbers. The expected number of newborn animals had been calculated in advance. Each temple and each of the pharaoh's farms had their own branding mark (below), with which the calves were marked during counting. Branding was also important when it came to renting work animals. If an animal died while working, its hide with the brand mark had to be shown to avoid payment for its loss.

Sheep and goats, which could be grazed on the poorer land, were also extensively farmed, providing meat and milk. Wool, however, was never as important as linen for clothmaking. Pigs, although rarely depicted as they were regarded as 'unclean' for religious purposes, seemed to have played an important part in the diet of the lower classes of Egyptian society.

Poultry

During the Middle Kingdom (2055–1650 BC), poultry became an important part of the livestock. Ducks and geese were kept on farmyard ponds and fed on grain, although hens were not introduced until the Ptolemaic period (332–30 BC).

DOCUMENT

Domestication

During the Old Kingdom, there were attempts to domesticate cranes, ibises, hyenas, antelopes and gazelles. The captured animals were force-fed in an attempt to tame them. It appears that the practice failed, however, and there is no record of it in the New Kingdom, when these wild animals appear solely as targets for hunting. The illustrations of antelopes, below, are based on drawings by Ippolito Rosellini of a wall relief from the tomb in Saqqara of court official Mereruka (c. 2350 BC).

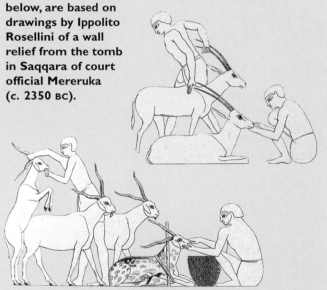

▼ **Favourite roasts**
The most popular meat was beef, but, in contrast to the meat of cows and oxen (below, second from the right) and sheep (below, far right), the meat of ibex (below) and wild antelope (second left) were delicacies reserved for the upper classes.

Goats and sheep

Species differed in the shape of their horns. The dominant sheep until about 1700 BC, for example, had screw-turned horns, whereas animals appearing later had curled horns that followed the line of the ear. This relief from a tomb in Saqqara shows a breed of goat with long, fairly straight horns.

Feeding on the fresh shoots of plants, goats damaged the vegetation.

The birth of new kids increased the size of the herd each year.

▶ **Beasts of burden**
Donkeys, a variety of the Nubian wild ass, were used as pack animals for transporting goods and for agricultural work, such as ploughing and threshing.

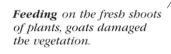

The herdsman *enjoys a rest with the animals, and drinks from his pitcher.*

The dog *of the herdsman, identified by its collar, keeps watch over the herd.*

▲ **Keeping animals in modern Egypt**
Even today, cows, oxen and sheep are the most important domestic animals. Many Egyptian farmers still use cattle as work animals.

The Slaughter of Animals

Animals were killed in Egypt for food and for religious purposes – sometimes for both. The killing of large animals, such as oxen, was often attended by ceremony and ritual, and those in charge of the slaughter usually enjoyed high status.

Only the rich and powerful could afford to eat meat on a regular basis in Ancient Egypt. For others its consumption was limited. The majority of people served or tasted meat only on festivals or other special occasions, such as during offering rituals, when relatives, neighbours and friends were present.

The favourite meat of the Egyptians was beef, obtained from cattle specially fattened at great expense in stables and pastures. Because it was so expensive to raise, beef was generally reserved for the tables of the pharaoh and his wealthier officials, and for the altars of the gods. Servants and the poor might sometimes be given inferior cuts or a beef broth.

Meat on the table

There was, though, a good variety of alternatives to eating beef. As well as the common domesticated animals, such as sheep, goats and pigs, Egyptians also ate game, such as gazelles, hares and antelopes. In addition, hyenas and various types of wild bird were occasionally captured and force-fed for food.

The butcher's knife was always kept sharpened.

A front leg was removed first when cattle were dismembered.

The rear legs were tied together to hobble the cow and immobilize it before it was slaughtered.

▼ **Irukaptah's tomb**
Irukaptah was supervisor of the royal abbatoir in the Fifth Dynasty (2494–2345 BC). This important dignitary was buried at Saqqara in a mastaba tomb decorated with scenes from his working life. This provides an excellent guide to methods of butchery in the Old Kingdom (2686–2181 BC). The wall painting below shows three men in very short loincloths cutting up two cattle, one white and one brindle.

▼ To the slaughterhouse

Cattle were a mark of prestige and prosperity, and often appear in the decoration of the tombs of Egyptian dignitaries. This painting shows animals being selected for slaughter from a herd of oxen with lyre-shaped horns. They are driven to the abbatoir with sticks and dogs. Dairy cows were spared.

▶ Poultry

The Egyptians raised ducks and geese for the pot in huge pens along the Nile, as well as eating pigeons and other wild birds. Although chickens, which came originally from India, were known in Egypt from at least the reign of Thutmose III (1479–1425 BC), they were rarely eaten in large numbers. Trussed and plucked birds were hung on poles to dry, then spit-roasted and perhaps stored in large jars of brine to preserve them.

▼ Ritual killing

The tomb of the princess Idout in Saqqara contains a painted relief, in remarkably well-preserved colours, which shows the ritual slaughter of a cow during a festival. The three men in the scene are a butcher (far left) and his two assistants. The butcher watches while the animal – we know it is dead by the way its tongue lolls from its mouth – is dismembered by his assistants.

INSIGHT

Fattened for the slaughter

Egyptian cattle destined for slaughter were fattened in their stables to improve the quality of the meat. The Egyptians believed that fatty meat made the best eating. They distinguished between 'ioua' cattle, so stout they could move only with difficulty, and thinner, more active 'nag' cattle. Handlers force-fed prime ioua cattle with bread dough (below, in a drawing by Egyptologist Ippolito Rosellini) to increase their weight. Once they reached prime weight, they were taken to the abbatoir.

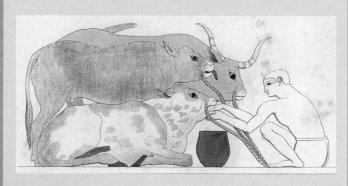

▼ Goose on the menu

In their tombs, Egyptians surrounded themselves with images of feasting, as well as with actual meals and models of foodstuffs. This goose, trussed and plucked ready to be cooked, was found in a tomb of the Old Kingdom (2686–2181 BC).

Slaughterhouses were set within the precincts of temples, in the king's palace and in the houses of the great and wealthy. The slaughtermen and butchers, who were furnished with long-bladed knives, worked in teams of three or more.

In the slaughterhouse

The slaughter of oxen was a sacred ceremony, performed according to set rites. The slaughtermen first tied the rear legs of the beast together, then flipped it on to its back so that it could be killed with a quick, deep incision to the throat. Once it was dead, the animal was carved up, beginning with a front leg, which was considered the choicest cut of meat and also symbolized the vital power of the ox. They then removed a rear leg before skinning and eviscerating the carcass.

As the Egyptians had no way of preserving offal, this was eaten fresh. Freshly killed meat, though, was generally considered to be too tough to eat. As a result, the rest of the animal was cut into pieces, and these were salt-cured or dried to keep them in good condition until they reached the table. Meat was dried by hanging it in well-ventilated rooms. Some wall paintings show cuts of meat hanging from cords stretching between the columns that held up the roof of the slaughterhouse.

▲ Preparing the meal
Most meat was boiled in a cauldron, rather than roasted or fried. Boiling large chunks of meat created a nutritious stock that formed the basis of soups and stews.

The forecourt of a tomb is represented in this model; other soul houses are modelled on domestic buildings, often quite elaborate ones.

Openings in the soul house allowed water offerings and libations to pour away into the tomb.

▼ Removing the hide
Cattle were not slaughtered solely for their meat; their skins were tanned to make leather. This coloured relief from the mastaba of Idout at Saqqara shows a slaughterman skinning a long-horned ox with a large knife. An arc of hide from around the throat and chest has already been removed.

▼ The slaughterer
A slaughterman generally used a long knife with a wide flint blade for killing the animals. Although the men had copper or bronze blades, these were kept sharp for butchery, cutting through the neck and sinews.

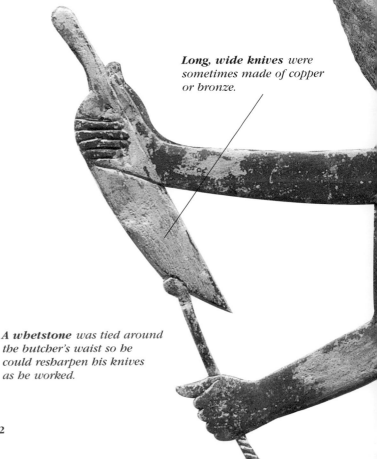

Long, wide knives were sometimes made of copper or bronze.

A whetstone was tied around the butcher's waist so he could resharpen his knives as he worked.

▶ A modern butcher's shop
Butchers in modern-day Egypt often hang their meat from the ceiling on hooks to dry and mature, in much the same way as their remote ancestors depicted on the walls of tombs in Ancient Egypt.

Animals smaller than cattle were generally killed by decapitation. Meat was not the only product of the slaughterhouses. Animal fat was aslo carefully saved for use in cooking and making cosmetics, while hides were taken for treatment to a tannery.

The slaughter of animals in Ancient Egypt also had a symbolic and religious role. The sacrifice of an animal was an integral part of many rituals. The Greek historian Herodotus reported, for example, that it was not allowed in Egypt to eat the head of an animal slaughtered during an offerings ceremony as in the course of the ritual the priests had magically imbued it with all the country's ills.

Slaughtermen were great respecters of the religious calendar. They were, for example, forbidden to kill cattle or any other animal on the twentieth and twenty-second days of the month of Thoth.

▲ All tied up
This graphic relief shows a cow with its throat cut. It clearly shows how the animal was hobbled with a thick rope. This not only made it easier to push the animal to the floor, but also made the slaughterer's work easier, protecting him from any injury from the animal's lashing hooves during its death throes.

A dismembered ox forms part of the clay offerings on this soul house.

The animal's head with its horns is easily recognizable.

◀ A 'soul house'
Clay models found near the burial shaft of some tombs, particularly ones of the Middle Kingdom (2055–1650 BC), were assumed by early Egyptologists to be homes for the spirit of the dead, and were called 'soul houses'. We now know that they acted as offerings tables for those who could not afford a more elaborate tomb. Many of the offerings are in the form of clay, and show a wide variety of foodstuffs, including meat, as here.

Vines and Wine

The luxury beverage of the pharaoh and the wealthy, wine flowed freely at banquets and festivals to the gods. Grapes and wine-making appear in a number of tomb paintings, and the drink was one of many offerings made to the gods and the deceased.

Cultivation of the vine is as old as Egyptian civilization itself. The pharaoh and the temples owned numerous vineyards, while the nobility reserved part of their orchards for vines. Peasant farmers took little interest in wine, which was not a basic necessity and which also required intensive cultivation. Ordinary people were content with beer, which was easy to prepare and inexpensive.

Special care and attention

The soils that produced the best wines were found in the Delta and the large oases of Fayum and the Libyan Desert. Only black grapes are depicted in the tombs of the dignitaries, but various texts also mention white grapes and a number of different varieties. The Ancient Egyptians generally grew their vines upwards on trellises rather than in low-growing rows. Abundant watering was essential to bring the grapes to maturity. Harvesting took place at the end of summer. The carefully picked bunches were poured into presses built near the vines.

▼ Grape harvesting
This scene of grapes being harvested and pressed decorates the Theban tomb of Nakht, scribe and astronomer of Amun, who probably lived during the reign of Thutmose IV (1400–1390 BC). The two harvesters are of different ages – one has black, curly hair, while the other has unkempt, grey hair.

▼ Careful handling
The harvesters placed the bunches of grapes in wicker baskets, taking care not to crush them and thereby to press them too soon. The contents of the baskets were then taken to the presses, large, acacia-wood vats in which the juice would be fermented.

The vine, *attached to a trellis, has produced many bunches of black grapes.*

The bunches *are picked when the grapes are very ripe.*

The grape picker *has placed a few bunches in his basket.*

The harvester *picks the bunches hanging from the trellis.*

◄ **Table grapes**
Grapes were enjoyed not only in the form of wine. The Egyptians were also very fond of table grapes, which, in season, added variety to their diet. Tomb paintings show large-fruited varieties as well as smaller ones, such as the Zante grapes from which currants are made.

▶ **The Tomb of Vines**
The tomb of Sennefer, mayor of Thebes under Amenhotep II (1427–1400 BC), owes its name to its unusual decoration. Its undulating ceiling – instead of a conventional flat one – is entirely covered with grape vines on trellises. The effect, which throws the grapes into relief, is remarkable.

Fermentation of the grapes takes place in large amphorae.

When fermentation is complete, the amphorae are hermetically sealed and labelled.

▼ **Pleasure-loving Hathor**
The goddess Hathor was associated with the pleasurable aspects of life, such as sexuality, music and dance. According to legend, she was prevented from destroying humanity when she was promised huge quantities of wine at her festival, as a substitute for blood. She thus became the goddess of alcohol. Like the other gods, she was offered ceremonial vessels of wine.

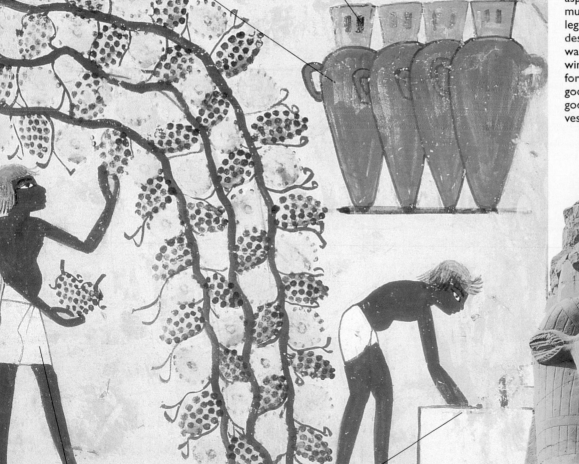

This elderly harvester has a rounded, drooping belly - a sign of age.

A worker cleans out the residue and must that drain from the press into a tub.

Types of wine

The Ancient Egyptians liked very sweet wines that tasted almost like honey. Both red and white wines were made, with white being the more popular. According to ancient records, the wine drunk by royalty and the rich was usually white, sweet and syrupy. There was also a red wine made from a thick-skinned Muscat grape. The less well-off drank palm or date wine.

Among the main types of wine were Mareotic, a mature but light white wine from the Nile Delta with a heavily scented bouquet – apparently a great favourite with Cleopatra (51–30 BC) – and Taniotic, a smooth, sweet white wine with a greenish tinge and a fairly sharp edge.

DOCUMENT

Vigilant scribes

Like all economic activity in Egypt, wine production was closely monitored by the scribes. They noted the quantities of wine produced, the number of jars filled and the reserves deposited in state and temple stores. In these warehouses, they kept an accurate count of what came in and what went out; in the wall painting below, a scribe makes a tally of stores of food and drink. It was also the scribes who labelled the pottery wine jars, either simply by writing the name of the vineyard and the date on them or by affixing baked clay seals to them. These texts provided valuable information on vineyards, vintages and the types of wine produced.

Grape skins and pips from the treading are collected in a pierced canvas bag, which is placed over a vat.

Poles supporting the bag are levered apart to compress it and squeeze out the remaining liquid into the vat.

▶ Treading the grapes

The bunches of grapes were thrown into a large vat, over which was a roof supported by short, papyrus-shaped columns. To prevent themselves from slipping, loinclothed workers held on to ropes secured to a beam as they treaded the grapes.

◀ **Harvesting and storing**
These scenes, copied from an Egyptian tomb painting, show the various stages of wine production. From top to bottom, left to right, they depict the grape harvest; treading the grapes in a long press; extracting the juice using a pierced canvas bag and poles; transferring the wine to jars; and the tallying, by a scribe, of the number of amphorae.

A rope provides support for the grape treaders.

Clay cones are used to seal the amphorae and prevent wine from evaporating through the neck.

▼ **Watertight amphorae**
The amphorae were made of clay, which, even when baked, remains porous and allows liquid to evaporate. They were therefore coated with a type of resin to make them watertight, and were sometimes bound with reed ropes so that they could be carried more easily.

The juice is transferred into larger jars.

A scribe, with his ink palette and reed pens, records the number of jars produced from the harvest.

▼ **Fermenting the wine**
The grape juice, which began to ferment in the small jars, was filtered and transferred to large amphorae, where fermentation continued. Honey or spices were added to the wine before the jars were sealed.

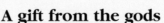

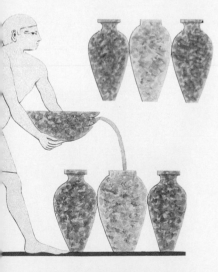

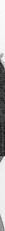

▶ **Flowers and grapes**
This drawing by the French nineteenth-century archaeologist and copyist Emile Prisse d'Avennes reproduces a painting of a young woman bearing lotus flowers and grapes. These offerings of everyday items, depicted in a tomb, represent the continuation of earthly life and its pleasures in the afterlife.

A gift from the gods

For the Egyptians, wine was a gift from the gods and was associated with Osiris, god of death, resurrection and fertility. The goddess of vineyards was the cobra goddess Renenutet, in an extension of her role as goddess of harvest and abundance. Wine also had special significance in the cults of the goddesses Bastet, Sekhmet and particularly Hathor, the goddess most closely linked with alcohol and for whom a 'festival of intoxication' was celebrated. Wine was, in fact, drunk to excess in a number of Ancient Egyptian celebrations and ceremonies.

Inebriation was considered beneficial for communicating with the gods – petitions were more likely to be heard – and it was believed that the gods in turn responded to offerings of alcohol, as it made them more benign.

The Brewing of Beer

Beermaking and breadbaking were daily events in Ancient Egyptian households, with both activities using the same ingredients and being undertaken by women.

▲ Beer containers
Various kinds of ceramic vessels were used in the brewing of beer, and the size varied according to the stage of production. Tall containers were used to ferment the mash, but the finished product was transferred to small pots which were stoppered with lids of straw and clay sealed with plaster. The example above is now in the Louvre, Paris.

Known to the Egyptians as *henket*, beer was both a staple in the daily diet and used as tomb offerings for the deceased's use in the afterlife. Most of our knowledge of Ancient Egyptian brewing is derived from studies of the many tomb paintings, models and statuettes that show the process. The traditional interpretation of these is that 'beer loaves' were made from flour of either barley or wheat. The loaves were lightly baked to brown them on the outside, but leave the inside uncooked.

The cooked loaves were crumbled onto a papyrus sieve and water poured over them. The resulting mixture, the mash, was placed in heated jars to start the fermentation, then stored in large vats. Dates and more yeast were sometimes added – the yeast to speed up fermentation and the dates for extra sugar to produce a stronger alcohol content.

Beer was produced in the household, or by brewers if it was for use by state employees.

▶ Adding flavour
To make beer, water was added to cereals such as barley and emmer (wheat). The resulting mash was poured into conical moulds and heated to cause fermentation. Finally, when the mash had fermented and been strained, liquid flavourings (derived from the boiling or grinding of various fruits, herbs and spices) were mixed in.

◀ Women's work
Both brewing and baking were activities undertaken by women, and numerous statuettes found in tombs show women grinding grain in mills or sifting the resulting flour. This statuette, in the Florence Archaeological Museum, shows a woman working the mash for brewing.

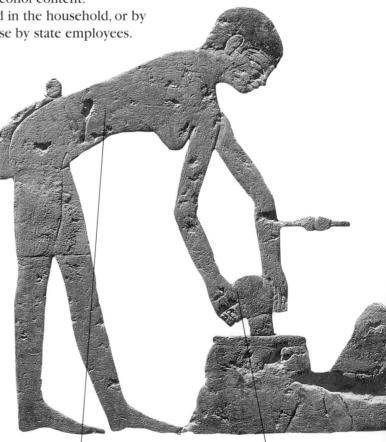

Women undertook the task of brewing beer.

The fresh mash was poured into preheated moulds.

◄ Beer today
Ancient Greek sources claim that beer was invented by the Egyptians, and it continues to be drunk more than wine in Egypt. Adherence to Islam, however, has led to its disappearance from the grocers' shops. This design of the label of a modern Egyptian beer, *Pyramid*, pays homage to its ancient roots.

► Beer signs
The hieroglyphs for beer (*henket*) are derived from objects used as units of liquid measure.

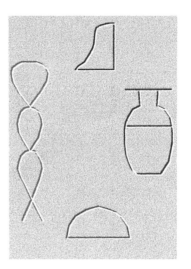

H

nq

t

H̱ nq t
Henket

▼ Beer drinking
Beer was an everyday drink in Ancient Egypt and widespread among all classes. It also had a ritual use: during the feasts of the goddess Tefnut, for example, it was consumed in large quantities in order to induce a state of inebriation.

Beer also occurs in the myths about various deities. On one occasion, Ra sent his daughter Hathor to destroy mankind, but when he relented Hathor refused to stop the slaughter. Ra tempted her away from her addiction to human blood with a lake of blood-coloured beer, which she drank until intoxicated with love and sweetness. This carving from Deir el-Bhari shows beer being drunk in a royal palace.

Spices and flavouring were added to the fermented and strained mash.

Papyrus sieves were employed to strain the fermented mash.

The mash fermented in earthenware cones for several days.

However, new research has suggested that the Ancient Egyptians, particularly of the New Kingdom, did not use bread as the starting point for brewing at all. Residues in ancient jars show that barley and emmer were used, but microscopic analysis implies that the grains were malted – soaked in water and heated so that, as the grain germinated, the starch in the seeds was converted to sugar, which in turn was changed to alcohol by the yeast.

If this is the case, then neither dates nor honey would be needed to provide the sugar content of the brew. They may have been added solely for flavouring, along with other intoxicating herbs, or to produce strong beers for special occasions.

A nutritional brew

Fermentation of everyday beer took a few days, producing a mixture fairly low in alcohol, as the prime purpose of beer was for nutrition rather than intoxication. The outcome was a thick, brothy liquid that had to be filtered through a basket before being drunk. Top-quality beer seems to have been reserved for religious festivals and, along with wine, was consumed in huge quantities – resulting in much drunkenness.

Bread and water were squeezed through sieves to make the brothy mash.

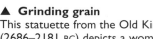

▲ Grinding grain
This statuette from the Old Kingdom (2686–2181 BC) depicts a woman grinding grain between two flat stones. The resulting flour would be sieved several times before being used for baking bread, possibly for brewing beer.

Brewery workers

Although beer was produced daily in most Ancient Egyptian households, there was also large-scale production in breweries for distributing rations to town-dwellers, taverns or 'beer houses', wealthy individuals and state employees. Each brewer had his own mark and the best beer was the most sought after.

Stone jars were used to store the beer.

Workers wait to remove the heated fermenting pots.

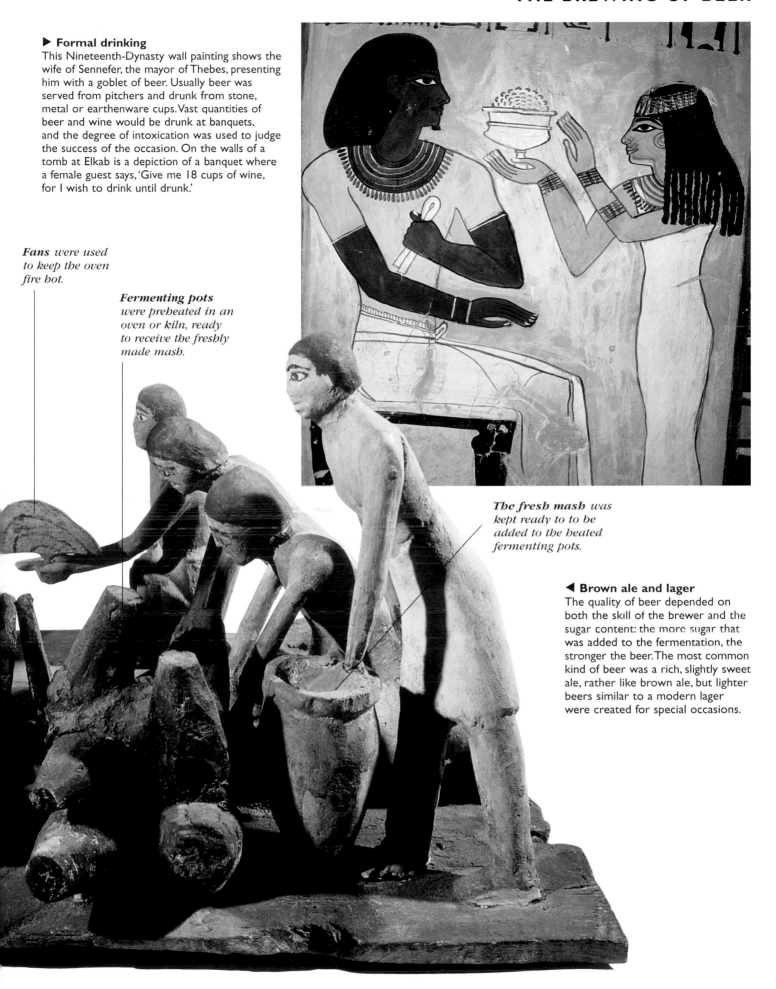

▶ Formal drinking
This Nineteenth-Dynasty wall painting shows the wife of Sennefer, the mayor of Thebes, presenting him with a goblet of beer. Usually beer was served from pitchers and drunk from stone, metal or earthenware cups. Vast quantities of beer and wine would be drunk at banquets, and the degree of intoxication was used to judge the success of the occasion. On the walls of a tomb at Elkab is a depiction of a banquet where a female guest says, 'Give me 18 cups of wine, for I wish to drink until drunk.'

Fans were used to keep the oven fire hot.

Fermenting pots were preheated in an oven or kiln, ready to receive the freshly made mash.

The fresh mash was kept ready to to be added to the heated fermenting pots.

◀ Brown ale and lager
The quality of beer depended on both the skill of the brewer and the sugar content: the more sugar that was added to the fermentation, the stronger the beer. The most common kind of beer was a rich, slightly sweet ale, rather like brown ale, but lighter beers similar to a modern lager were created for special occasions.

The Hunt

In Ancient Egypt, hunting with a bow and arrow developed from a means of obtaining food to a popular pastime of the upper classes.

Vast papyrus thickets up to five metres (16ft) tall stretched along the embankments of the Nile, offering ideal habitats and nesting places for a variety of water birds. Even crocodiles and hippopotamuses used the dense vegetation as a hiding place, while the river itself teemed with fish.

Hunting for food

Both fishing and hunting for birds were of immense importance in providing food for the Ancient Egyptians. Their everyday diet was supplemented with ibex, gazelle, antelope and wild cattle, which were hunted in the drier regions away from the Nile. The number of these animals dwindled from the fourth century onwards, however, as the savannah-like environment turned into an increasingly inhospitable desert.

As a result, arable farming and animal husbandry were developed to provide new sources of food: wild cattle were domesticated and everywhere along the river ducks and geese were raised in poultry farms.

*A **tame goose** at the front of the boat served as a decoy.*

DOCUMENT

Eye-paint palettes

Colour pigments for the eye paint worn by both men and women were ground to powders on often richly decorated palettes of slate. Up to 2700 BC, themes on these were battle and hunting scenes. This fragment of the so-called 'Hunters' palette' from 3300 BC (now in the British Museum) shows hunters stalking hare and antelope.

▲ Hunting in the thickets
Hunting birds with a stick-like weapon was a pastime exclusive to the upper classes. In spring, and in late autumn, the Nile became home to many migratory birds. The hunters moved through the thickets in a papyrus boat.

The hunting scene above is from the tomb of Nebamun in Thebes, probably from around 1400 BC. Today, it can be seen in the British Museum, London.

A crooked stick, adorned with a serpent's head, was used to hunt birds.

The wife and children of the hunter were also depicted, as hunting birds signified the fertility of nature.

▲ Return from the ibex hunt
Servants accompanied their master on his hunting trips. Their task was not only to support the hunter, but also to transport the weapons and spoils. Also in the hunt were dogs which retrieved the prey.

The embankments were covered with dense vegetation, which grew ever denser as more water was brought in by the annual flooding of the Nile.

The family's cat accompanied the hunt, and was fed on fish from the river or water fowl.

▶ Hunting on the Nile
The Ancient Romans were intrigued by Egypt and, at home, commissioned works of art on Egyptian themes. South of Rome, in Palestrina, a magnificent mosaic of the landscape along the Nile was made. This fragment shows hippopotamuses being hunted with spears thrown from a papyrus boat.

413

Hunting soon acquired the trappings of a sporting event. In particular, large and dangerous animals, such as crocodiles and hippopotamuses, wild cattle and occasional lions, were highly sought after by young noblemen intent on proving their skill and bravery. Furthermore, during the pharaoh's ritual hunts, these animals came to symbolize Egypt's enemies, which the pharaoh could defeat and destroy.

The victorious hunter

During the Eighteenth Dynasty, the pharaoh was idealized as an audacious warrior and powerful hero. Texts tell of the hunting successes of pharaohs such as Amenhotep III (1390–1352 BC), who reputedly killed 200 wild cattle and lions in 10 years of hunting. On a chest found among his tomb treasures, Tutankhamun (1336–1327 BC) is depicted as a victorious hunter of gazelles, ibex and lions. In the Nineteenth Dynasty, Sety I (1294–1279 BC) even claimed to have killed a lion single-handed with only a spear.

For the Ancient Egyptians, crossing the Nile in their light papyrus boats was a risky business, as it was teeming with crocodiles and hippopotamuses.

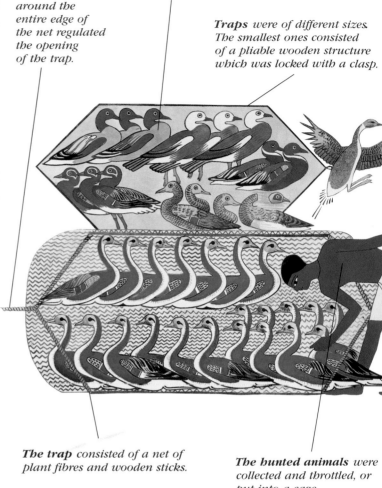

A rope tied around the entire edge of the net regulated the opening of the trap.

Waterfowl, including several species of geese and ducks, were hunted.

Traps were of different sizes. The smallest ones consisted of a pliable wooden structure which was locked with a clasp.

The trap consisted of a net of plant fibres and wooden sticks.

The hunted animals were collected and throttled, or put into a cage.

▼ Hunting hippopotamuses

The hippopotamus hunt was often depicted in the tomb pictures of the Old Kingdom (2686–2186 BC), and showed hunters in boats pursuing the animal with harpoons and spears. This rather dangerous hunt was good for the hunter's image, and also yielded an immense amount of meat. Apart from humans, the hippopotamus had no enemy, although crocodiles always kept a hungry eye on newly born hippos. The relief below is from the tomb of the official Ty (c. 2500 BC) in Saqqara.

▲ Trappers

Hunting birds was not only a pastime of the privileged classes. Birds were also hunted in larger numbers to restock poultry farms, or for food. For this, nets were put into deep waters. When enough animals had settled above the net, the hunters hiding in the papyrus thickets tightly pulled the rope that ran along the edge of the net.

The birds were caught in the mesh and were pulled ashore where they were put in cages for transport. The scene here showing a goose hunt was copied by Ippolito Rosellini (1800–1843) from a rock-cut tomb in Beni Hasan.

▼ The crocodile

Its aggressive nature made the crocodile the symbol of evil. On the other hand, all water animals were considered bearers of fertility. Therefore, the name of the crocodile god Sobek meant 'he who makes fertile'. He became a protective god in the Twelfth Dynasty (1985–1795 BC) and his worship became more widespread. Sobek fought evil and as Sobek-Ra became associated with the sun god.

▲ Hunting by chariot

Hunting in the desert required special techniques. Early on, the hunt was on foot, but, from the early Eighteenth Dynasty (1550–1295 BC) onwards, the hunter stood on a horse-drawn chariot and shot at the prey with bow and arrow. In the picture above, from the tomb of Userhet in Thebes, the hunter is drawing his bow, aiming at a flock of gazelles who are joined in their flight by hares.

INSIGHT

Hunting the wild bull

In Ancient Egypt, cattle were of great importance in almost every aspect of life. The cow was considered a symbol of motherhood, and the wild bull stood for male virility and potency and for physical superiority. As the holy animal of the gods Ptah and Montu, or as an emblem of the pharaoh, the bull embodied the positive attributes of power and strength.

The pharaoh's hunt of the wild bull was a ritual combat. The bull's strength had to be destroyed, while the pharaoh showed his invincible superiority. During such a hunt, drivers cornered the bull, weakened him with arrows and spears and hindered his flight with a lasso. In the end, the bull was killed by the pharaoh with one throw of a spear. This relief from Medinet Habu shows Rameses III hunting a wild steer.

▲ The hippopotamus

Once very common in the Nile, the hippopotamus was absolute ruler of the river. Hunting hippos (left) was a most dangerous activity, as the hunters could not draw too close to the animal, which would attack the boat if it was wounded and not killed immediately. Today, hippopotamuses can only be found south of Egypt, in the wetter regions of Africa.

These huge creatures were revered in the shape of the crocodile god Sobek, who represented male fertility, and the hippopotamus goddess Taweret, who was closely associated with the protection of women and childbirth.

The last crocodile and hippopotamus

Things have changed since ancient times. Today, the papyrus thickets have given way to vast corn fields and many of the smaller animals have lost their natural habitat. Large shoals of fish are no longer found because of dams along the Nile.

When the Aswan High Dam was built in the 1960s, the crocodiles disappeared from the Egyptian part of the Nile, and the hippopotamuses had long since vanished to well south of the Sudan.

Music in Egyptian Life

Across the social scale, music played an important part in the life of the Ancient Egyptians – it was central to religious worship, used to celebrate harvests and festivals, and for pure enjoyment.

ḥ s t
'Heset' designates song/singing in Egyptian hieroglyphs.

Music was everywhere in Ancient Egypt – at civil or funerary banquets, religious processions, military parades and even at work in the field. Most ordinary Egyptian people sang and played some form of instrument. On a grander scale, from the time of the New Kingdom (1550–1069 BC), musicians, who may have been paid professionals, were often part of an organized orchestra, with a conductor to mark time and direct their playing.

We have no record of musical notation or sheet music from the pharaonic era. Instead, music would have been passed down through the generations and played from memory. What we know of Ancient Egyptian music has come from studies of musical artefacts, from depictions of instruments in tombs and temples, and through playing replicas of these ancient objects. The words of New Kingdom love poetry may have been sung or narrated to a musical accompaniment and many of these lyrics have also survived.

▲ Music in hieroglyphs
The terms 'song', 'singer', 'musician', 'conductor' and 'playing music' were formed from the word 'hes'. The sign of the arm in the hieroglyphs above relates to the use of the arm in keeping time to music.

The musician positions his fingers just as players do today.

◄ A musical accompaniment
Musicians often accompanied singers and dancers at festivals and banquets.

◄ Musical notation
The Ancient Egyptians do not appear to have used any form of musical notation. The current system of writing music did not begin to develop until the Middle Ages, when Gregorian monks invented a form of signs to show the melodic line in their chants. In the eleventh century, an Italian Benedictine monk called Guido d'Arezzo established a four-line musical stave, allowing an exact transcription of musical notes. The modern type of stave, made up of five parallel horizontal lines, dates from the sixteenth century.

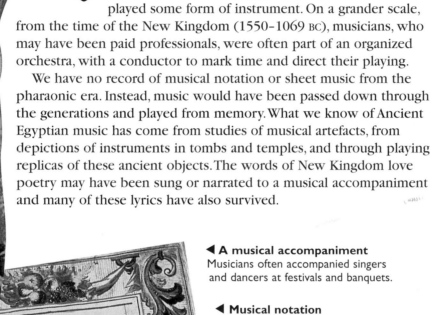

The conductor directs the playing of his companion.

Parts of the Coptic liturgy are still sung in Coptic, a language descended from Ancient Egyptian.

The conductor, like a modern conductor, guides the musicians through hand gestures.

▲ **Keeping time**
This relief from New Kingdom Amarna shows a harpist accompanied by a group of men singing and clapping their hands. The harpist may well have been blind, like many musicians who played this instrument in Ancient Egypt. The harp was played at most official and religious events, and was considered to be a sacred instrument. It was believed that its harmonious tones accompanied the deceased on their journey into the afterlife.

◀ **Orchestra conductors**
Conductors occupied a significant place in Ancient Egyptian culture, as illustrated by their presence in depictions of musical scenes. This example from Saqqara, with its well-preserved colours, shows a conductor, with a hand over one ear to aid hearing and to improve concentration, as he faces the musicians and indicates the passage to be played.

Life in the Oases

The Ancient Egyptians regarded the desert as a place of chaos and wilderness, and the gateway to the kingdom of the dead; however, since the earliest times the lush oases of the Western Desert have been inhabited by thriving communities.

Egypt's vast Western Desert covers an area of some 681,000sq km (262,900 square miles), stretching from the Nile Valley in the east to the border with Libya in the west. For the Ancient Egyptians, the desert was synonymous with chaos and barrenness, as opposed to the ordered prosperity of the Nile Delta and Valley regions.

Islands in the desert

The Western Desert oases of Kharga, Dakhla, Farafra, Bahariya and Siwa, however, represent fascinating islands of fertility in the monotonous, barren landscape, and the people of these isolated oases have maintained their own distinct customs and traditions.

▼ The governors' tombs

The mastaba tombs of Dakhla's provincial governors of the Old Kingdom (2686–2181 BC) were discovered in the 1970s, close to the village of Balat. Like the mastabas of officials in sites such as Saqqara, these were richly decorated with wall paintings and reliefs, such as the one seen below, but have unfortunately been badly damaged over the centuries.

Kharga Oasis, at around 100sq km (40 square miles), is the largest of the oases in the Western Desert.

The remains of ancient buildings can be seen in front of the Roman fortress.

▼ The oases today

In the 1970s, work began on the New Valley project, an ambitious plan to irrigate the Western Desert and relocate landless peasants from the overcrowded Nile Delta and Valley. However, only a small part of the project has been completed, due to financial difficulties and doubts over the subterranean water table. The economic and agricultural health of the oases remains a precarious issue.

▶ Siwa Oasis

Siwa, located near Egypt's border with Libya, is the most isolated and culturally distinct of all the Western Desert oases. One of the biggest issues for the inhabitants of the Siwa Oasis is its excess of salt water, making agriculture difficult. The water table lies only 20cm (8in) below ground level, and land reclamation projects have failed to tackle the problem. Today, the main industries of Siwa are the growing of dates and olives, and tourism.

Massive fortresses were built by the Romans to protect desert trade routes.

◀ Qasr el-Labeka

In pharaonic times, Kharga was one of the most important of the Western Desert oases. It was located at the convergence of several desert trade routes, including the Forty Days Road that brought slaves from the south to Egypt. To the north of the modern town of el-Kharga is Qasr el-Labeka, a Roman fortress built to offer protection to desert caravans on their arduous journey. The remains of the fortress consist of 12m (40ft) high walls enclosing a series of sand-filled chambers, with a ruined, mud-brick temple standing to the north.

▶ Qasr el-Ghueida

The fortified temple of Qasr el-Ghueida, perched on a hilltop to the south of Kharga Oasis, was built by Darius I (522–486 BC) and modified during the Ptolemaic Dynasty (332–30 BC). It features a sandstone shrine dedicated to the Theban triad of Amun, Mut and Khons, as well as a hypostyle hall decorated with scenes of Hapy, god of the Nile inundation, holding symbols of the Egyptian nomes.

During the Old Kingdom (2686–2181 BC), the oases of the Western Desert came under the direct control of the Egyptian state. The oases were of significant strategic importance, operating as stops on the desert trading routes, most notably the Forty Days Road, which linked Egypt with sub-Saharan Africa. The most westerly oases, Farafra and Siwa, also acted as outposts that allowed the Egyptians to guard the border with Libya.

Siwa Oasis had particular importance in pharaonic times as the home of the oracle of Amun. Alexander the Great (332–323 BC), founder of the Ptolemaic Dynasty (332–30 BC), famously visited the oracle in 331 BC to be confirmed as the rightful ruler of all Egypt. Some archaeologists believe that the tomb of the legendary Macedonian conqueror is located in the vicinity of Siwa.

A traditional way of life

The oases of the Western Desert have been affected by modernization to varying degrees. Dakhla and Kharga, for example, have sprawling modern towns, while Bahariya and Farafra essentially remain desert villages, trading in traditional crops such as dates and olives. Siwa, the most westerly of the oases, has probably changed the least, and its glorious isolation and exotic allure has made it an increasingly popular tourist destination.

▼ The camel caravans

The camel was domesticated fairly late in Egypt, in around the ninth century BC. Ideally suited to desert conditions, it soon became an indispensable part of life in this inhospitable region. These resilient animals are capable of covering a distance of 40km (25 miles) per day and carrying loads of up to 250kg (550lb), and of going without water for four or five days. Today, the camel has generally been replaced by faster and more reliable motorized vehicles.

Palm leaves were used by the Ancient Egyptians to make sandals.

Dates were part of most Ancient Egyptians' daily diet.

The wood of the palm tree was used to make furniture.

▲ The donkey
The donkey was used extensively in the Western Desert, especially before the introduction of the camel. These animals have great stamina and are able to carry heavy loads over rocky ground, but their hooves are less well suited to desert sand dunes.

▶ Wine of the oases
From the earliest times, vineyards were cultivated in the oases just as they were in the Nile Valley. Wines produced in the oases of Kharga and Dakhla were very popular, being regarded as among the finest in Ancient Egypt.

◀ Date palms
The existence of underground reservoirs of water allowed the inhabitants of the oases to develop an agricultural system, particularly during the Roman period (30 BC–AD 395). Dates, of which there are approximately 50 varieties in Egypt, were the principal crop produced in the Western Desert, and they continue to play a central role in the economy of the oases.

▲ Desert transport today
The people of the Western Desert oases still maintain some traditional practices, despite steps towards modernization. The sight of men travelling through the desert landscape on their beasts of burden would have been a common one in ancient times.

The War Chariot

Introduced into Egypt around 1650 BC by Hyksos invaders, the chariot revolutionized the art of war, leading to the formation of an élite corps of the Egyptian army – the maryannu.

Lightweight and easy to manoeuvre, the Egyptian chariot consisted of a wooden chassis with wood and leather sides, two spoked wheels mounted on an axle fixed at the rear of the chassis, and a curved shaft ending in a double yoke to harness a pair of horses. The body of the chariot was open at the back to enable the occupants to jump out in an emergency, and they steadied themselves by holding on to a guard rail that ran around the top of the cockpit. As there were no springs or suspension system, high-speed travel over desert sand and stones was extremely bumpy. Very swift, these vehicles could travel 10 times faster than a footsoldier.

Egyptian war chariots held two men – a charioteer, or driver, armed only with a whip and sometimes carrying a shield, and a single fighter armed with a bow. The fighter's weapons consisted of a bow and arrows, and javelins; the use of knives, axes or swords was rare.

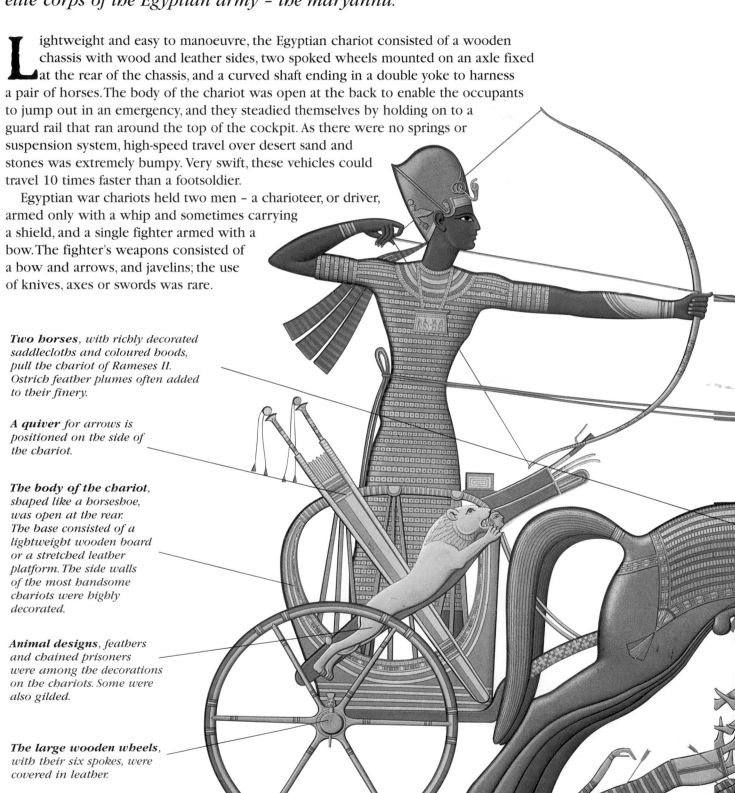

Two horses, *with richly decorated saddlecloths and coloured hoods, pull the chariot of Rameses II. Ostrich feather plumes often added to their finery.*

A quiver *for arrows is positioned on the side of the chariot.*

The body of the chariot, *shaped like a horseshoe, was open at the rear. The base consisted of a lightweight wooden board or a stretched leather platform. The side walls of the most handsome chariots were highly decorated.*

Animal designs, *feathers and chained prisoners were among the decorations on the chariots. Some were also gilded.*

The large wooden wheels, *with their six spokes, were covered in leather.*

INSIGHT

The chariots of Tutankhamun

Inside the tomb of Tutankhamun (1336–1327 BC), Howard Carter discovered the parts of six dismantled chariots. Two of the chariots were highly refined – covered with gold leaf and encrusted with coloured glass and semi-precious stones, such as turquoise – and probably ceremonial; one was less grand and three were most likely for everyday use. After lengthy and painstaking work, restorers managed to rebuild five of the chariots.

Essential equipment for the horses – whips, saddlecloths, leather harnesses and blinkers – were discovered close to the chariots.

Apart from Tutankhamun's vehicles, only five other complete chariots are known, one of which was found in the tomb belonging to Yuya and Tuya (c. 1400 BC), the parents-in-law of Amenhotep III (1390–1352 BC).

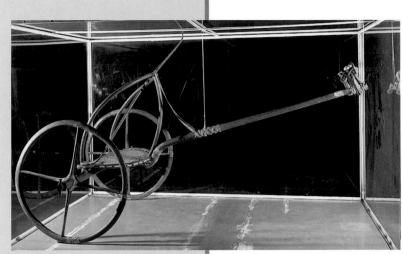

◀ Rameses II in the heat of battle

The battle of Qadesh was fought in Syria against the Hittites. Rameses II (1279–1213 BC) had the conflict depicted on the first pylon of the Ramesseum, his funerary temple in Luxor. The scene reproduced here is the image seen in the photograph, below centre. The reliefs show the Egyptians being attacked by surprise while pitching camp. The king leaps on to his chariot and throws himself into the battle. He rallies his élite troops and manages to reverse the battle when the Hittites have already begun to pillage the camp in the belief that victory is theirs. The Ramesseum reliefs do not describe reality, however, but rather are a propaganda exercise showing the king as a conquering hero aided by the god Amun.

Rameses II's horses are shown trampling Hittite soldiers underfoot. Chariots launched at full speed, and bearing skilled archers, could cause considerable damage to an opposing army.

The war chariot was a tactical weapon that had precise functions on the battlefield: attacking the infantry head-on or flanking it, breaking its ranks, hastening its flight and, finally, pursuing the fugitives. The success of this 'war machine' derived from the fact that it was a mobile platform which moved at high speed, allowing the archers to bombard the enemy with arrows from different, and ever-changing, directions. Chariots could also be combined into a single unit, to create a 'juggernaut' effect that smashed infantry.

Difficult defence

There was very little defence against the chariot beyond the choice of terrain for the battlefield (chariots were effective on the open plain, but not in the hills), the digging of ditches or the construction of obstacles. Sometimes, special troops were employed whose duty was to bring down enemy horses.

▼ **The chariot in war**
At the battle of Qadesh in 1274 BC, Rameses II's army numbered half the size of the Hittite forces. The battle was fierce and spectacular, despite the fact that the military chariot strategy of the Egyptians and their Hittite enemies was crude and far from the efficiency achieved by the Assyrians towards the eighth century BC.

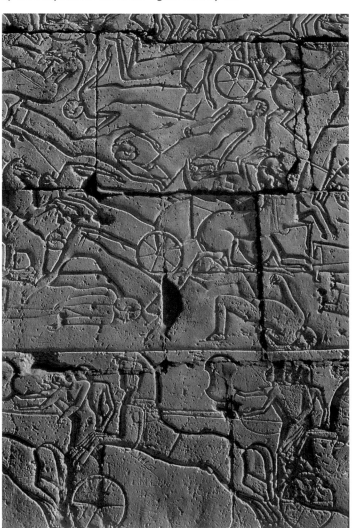

The construction of the chariot

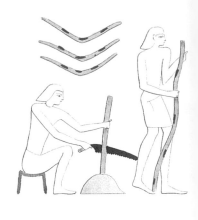

High-quality, light and flexible wood was used to make a chariot. Other materials included leather, bronze, ivory, woven fabrics and, in some cases, precious stones and metals.

The chariot builders were craftsmen who assembled the body of the chariot – the chassis with its side panels, the yoke (a double-arched piece into which the horses were set) and the draft pole, or shaft, that linked the chassis to the yoke.

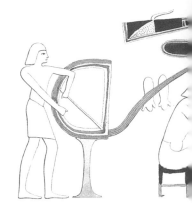

Saddlers made the various pieces of harness: collar, bridle, blinkers, bits and reins. The tack had to be solid and resistant, yet light and manageable at the same time.

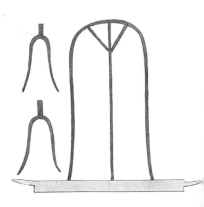

The chassis consisted of the platform and the parapet. Egyptian chariots had no armouring.

Two spoked wheels were the standard pattern for the chariot by the time it reached Egypt between 1650 and 1550 BC. The earliest chariots, however, were built with four wheels.

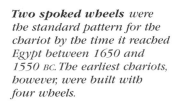

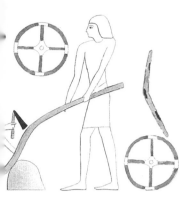

The tools used by the chariot builders were those used by wood-workers (including axes, saws, planes and rasps) or metal-workers (hammers, anvils, and chisels).

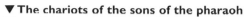

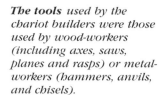

▼ **The chariots of the sons of the pharaoh**
The richly decorated chariots of the sons of Rameses II, with their sidelocks of youth, are similar to that of their father. The young princes were accompanied by a shield-bearer, a feature of the Egyptian chariot not shared by the Hittites and Assyrians.

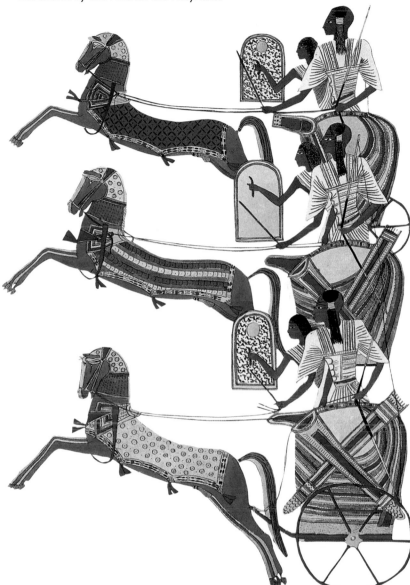

Specialist craftsmen were responsible for the chariot's decoration. Secondary tradesmen such as grooms, saddlers and fletchers (arrow-makers) provided the equipment for the horses and made the weapons.

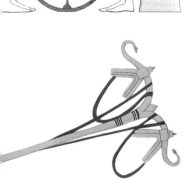

The wheels had four, six or eight spokes, and light composite bent-wood rims often enclosed in leather 'tyres'. The most skilled craftsmen involved in the building of the chariot were the wheelwrights.

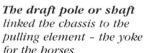

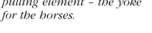

The draft pole or shaft linked the chassis to the pulling element – the yoke for the horses.

◄ **The Egyptian war chariot**
Although it kept certain features of the Assyrian model, such as the spoked wheel, the Egyptian version differed in being drawn by two horses and carrying two men – the charioteer, or driver, and the warrior – instead of the Hittites' three. This drawing by Ippolito Rosellini reproduces a chariot from a tomb in Thebes.

The double yoke fitted over the horses' necks, and forward motion was achieved by the two horses pushing on it.

Pitched battle between chariots was rare and, as a tactic, its effectiveness was dubious. The first documented chariot battle was that at Megiddo in the north of Palestine, fought in 1468 BC between the pharaoh Thutmose III (1479–1425 BC) and an alliance headed by the Prince of Qadesh.

There were two types of war chariot: those for the pharaoh and generals, used in battle for changing positions of command, and the ones which formed a separate, élite fighting corps within the army.

The use of the chariot required both strength and skill, often acquired during campaigning, but also while hunting wild animals in the desert, which served both as a pastime and as military training.

26276

Science and Technology

The Egyptian economy was firmly based on agricultural production, which relied almost entirely on the annual flooding of the river Nile to both irrigate the land and renew the fertile soil. From early times, the Egyptians developed a relatively accurate calendar so that they could predict the rising of the Nile, as well as methods of measuring the actual height of the floodwaters in order to predict the harvest for the year to come.

Practical uses

The Nile was the principal highway through the country and evidence for boat building is found at all periods of Egyptian history. With its current flowing from south to north, it was an easy matter to transport goods northwards, whilst the prevailing north wind could be used to sail southwards. By this means the transport of even large quantities of stone for building projects was relatively easy.

Ancient Egyptian mathematics had a strong geometrical emphasis, probably as a result of the need to be able to calculate areas of land and to specify volumes of stone required for building projects. A number of papyri have survived which demonstrate their mathematicians' ability at problem solving. One even includes a complex technique for calculating the volume of a partially constructed pyramid.

Advanced ideas
Examples of ancient Egyptian science and technology include (clockwise from top) a complex numbering system with symbols representing powers of ten, accurate scales or balances, and wooden sleds for transporting huge stone blocks.

The Nilometer

The flooding of the Nile gave Egyptian life its rhythm. To calculate the flood level with accuracy, the Egyptians developed the nilometer, a simple yet effective measuring tool that remained in use long after the end of the pharaonic period.

Egypt, with its very low rainfall, has always depended on the Nile to irrigate its agricultural land. Until the Aswan High Dam was commissioned in 1964, the country prospered or suffered according to variations in the river's annual flood, which in different years could be insufficient, normal or catastrophically high.

The Ancient Egyptians measured the annual rise of the river's level at the start of summer by using wells that were built alongside it and linked to it by tunnels. The buildings, in which the wells were sunk, had stairways which gave access to the wells and acted as a graduated scale for measuring the water level; each step was one cubit (52.4cm) high. To gauge the eventual height of the water, daily checks were made on the water level and the rate of rise.

▲ Feeding the nilometers
Nilometers either took in water directly from the river, as in this one at Elephantine Island, or were fed from ground-water, as was the case at the temple in Karnak.

▼ Efficient irrigation
The Egyptians took advantage of the early warning system provided by the nilometers by setting up a network of dykes and channels. The former held back the water, while the latter discharged it if necessary. When the flood had reached its optimum level of around 16 cubits (838cm/330in), gates in the dykes were opened to allow the flood waters to inundate the fields.

▼ Nilometers inside temples

Temples such as Karnak were often equipped with nilometers that fulfilled a religious as well as a practical function. They were a symbolic link between the monuments and the primordial ocean, personified as the god Nun. Rites to bring on the flood were performed in the temples.

▶ Access to the nilometer

The dressed limestone staircases that led to the wells were carefully built, as the depth of the steps provided a way of measuring the water level. Officials calculated the strength of the flood by counting the number of steps down to the water level in the well.

▼ Inside the nilometer

Underground galleries and networks of tunnels provided access to the site for measurement and maintenance. The tunnels had to be cleared of silt after each inundation.

Information on the flood level given by the nilometer was entered in the royal records by civil servants. Particularly high or low levels were often marked on the nilometer walls. The records enabled the state to follow the floods over the years and, if necessary, to take preventive measures to limit the famine that would otherwise follow a prolonged drought or a catastrophic flood. The nilometers also gave officials a good idea of how far the water would spread inland, and which fields would be flooded. This enabled them to estimate the harvests and calculate the basis for the forthcoming tax, as well as the grain reserves needed to fill the granaries.

The essential role played by the nilometers in the economy of the country made their upkeep an important duty of the state and the institutions that owned them.

An Islamic nilometer

This nilometer was built by the local caliph in AD 705–715, on a headland on Geziret el-Rhoda, an island in the Nile at Cairo. It was rebuilt in the ninth century and restored in the eleventh century.

▲ A new means of measurement
A marble column in the centre of the well, rather than a set of steps, formed the measuring scale in the Islamic nilometer at Rhoda. The column is held in place by a horizontal beam of around 54cm (21in) wide, and the whole is surmounted by a cupola in the Islamic style.

The drum of the column is marked with gradations in royal cubits so the level of the water can easily be read.

A Corinthian capital surmounts the pillar, which is held upright by a crossbeam.

*A **deep well** communicates with the river via a system of tunnels so that the water level reflects that of the Nile.*

INSIGHT

A basic model

All stone-built nilometers conformed to a basic pattern, with a well that was linked to the Nile or the water table via a system of tunnels, and a stairway that both gave access to the water level in the well and measured its height.

There were several variations on this basic plan. The well was sometimes a rectangular shaft, and sometimes a circular pit (right, at Tanis), while the stairway could be straight or spiral.

Today, the ruined remains of several ancient nilometers – which were typically built as part of a temple complex – can still

be seen. These include one at Medinet Habu, on the opposite bank to Luxor (above), and another which is situated at Tanis in the Delta (below right).

▲ The nilometers at Elephantine

In 27–26 BC, the Greek geographer Strabo took a boat up the Nile and visited the city of Aswan. He left a description of the nilometer that he discovered on the nearby island of Elephantine. 'The nilometer is a well made of dressed stones on the bank of the Nile, marked to show the highest, average and smallest flood levels, because the water in the well rises and falls with the level of the river'. Archaeologists think that this is not the nilometer that can be visited today at Elephantine, but a basin recently discovered south-east of the temple of Khnum, the ram god, whose principal cult centre was on the island.

Egyptian Astronomy

The night sky was a source of wonder to the Ancient Egyptians, who peopled it with their gods. Astronomy was also an important practical skill, marking out the seasons and determining the orientation of monuments and the timing of religious festivals.

From the earliest times, astronomy in Ancient Egypt was the prerogative of the priests, who were taught about the movements of the sun, moon and planets, and the position of the stars, in temple schools.

This knowledge was essentially practical; it was not so much about unravelling the secrets of the cosmos as about marking passing time, the seasons of the year and the hours of the day. Knowledge of the changing seasons and impending flood, vital to Egyptian agriculture, gave the astronomer-priests great power.

Time and place

Each night at sunset, two priests would sit facing each other on a temple roof with a north–south orientation to mark the hours of the night, using no instrument more complicated than a plumb-line to establish the vertical. One man used his companion as a reference point to read the movement of the stars. When they reached a position set out in an astronomical table, both men called out the new hour. As the Egyptians split the night into 12 equal portions, these hours were shorter in summertime.

Before any important building, such as a pyramid or temple, was begun, priests visited the site to make astronomical observations. These allowed them to align the ground plan with the cardinal points of the compass with a great degree of accuracy.

▶ **Anen, priest and astronomer**
Anen was the brother-in-law of Amenhotep III (1390–1352 BC). This statue shows him wearing a priest's leopard-skin garment covered with stars, a testament to Anen's astronomical knowledge. Anen held the position of 'chief star-gazer'.

▲ **A pattern of stars**
A stylized night sky often decorated the ceilings of temples and royal burials – this is from the tomb of Amenhotep II (1427–1400 BC).

◀ The sanctuary at Abu Simbel

At the centre of the temple of Abu Simbel is a sanctuary which was lit by the rays of the rising sun on just two days a year, once in February and again in October, supposedly marking the birthday and coronation day of Rameses II. The sanctuary contains four statues; those of the pharaoh, Ra-Horakhty and Amun-Ra were bathed in light as the sun's rays moved into the sanctuary, while that of Ptah, a creator god with a funerary aspect, was always partly shadowed.

Ptah, god of creation and of craftsmen such as those who built the temple, sits in partial shade.

Rameses II (1279–1213) is flanked by Amun-Ra, with a tall, plumed headdress, and Ra-Horakhty.

▼ Temple alignment

Like most Egyptian temples, that of Amun-Ra at Karnak has an axis aligned to the path of the sun – in this case, to sunset and sunrise at the solstices in June and December. The sanctuary is in the south-east and the entrance in the north-west.

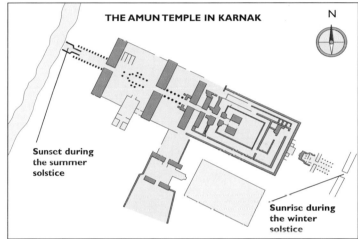

THE AMUN TEMPLE IN KARNAK   N

Sunset during the summer solstice

Sunrise during the winter solstice

Sunlight moves through the antechambers of the temple before reaching the inner sanctuary.

The Osiris columns lining both sides of the axis of the temple depict the pharaoh Rameses II.

A cartouche encloses the name of Rameses II.

◀ The antechamber of Abu Simbel

The precise observations of astronomers were the reason Abu Simbel was chosen as the site of a temple. The builders hollowed out the temple above the Nile, digging out the part of the cliff indicated by the priests. Their calculations mean that the corridor to the inner sanctuary is aligned to catch the rays of the rising sun on only two days of the year, when dawn sends a shaft of light along the 60m (130ft) corridor leading from the entrance to the inner sanctuary.

Heavenly pictures

The best-known astronomical ceiling dates from the first century BC and comes from Hathor's temple at Dendera. By this time, the Egyptians had adopted the ideas of astrology from the Greeks, and the roof shows the signs of the Babylonian zodiac, as well as Egyptian constellations, the planets and two eclipses.

▲ **Pillars of the sky**
Four goddesses function as pillars holding up the night sky in the halls dedicated to Osiris and his rebirth on the roof of the temple of Hathor. The buildings at Dendera were begun in 54 BC by Ptolemy XII, the father of Cleopatra (51–30 BC). The work was continued by his daughter and then, following her death, by the Roman emperors.

*The constellation of **Libra** was symbolized in Ancient Egypt, as it is today, by weighing-scales.*

*The planet **Saturn**, personified by a figure with a bull's head, was known as 'Horus the bull'.*

__Tawaret__, the hippopotamus, represents the constellation of Draco, which winds around the celestial North Pole.

*A **young woman** carrying an ear of wheat embodies the constellation of Virgo.*

*The planet **Mercury**, in the shape of Sebegu, a god associated with Seth, stands above the lion representing Leo and next to the scarab symbolizing the modern zodiac sign of Cancer.*

▶ **Dating the zodiac**
The zodiac of Dendera originally adorned the ceiling of one of the Osiris chambers in the Hathor temple, but was taken to France in 1821 and is now on display in the Louvre Museum in Paris. The star signs used were partly Egyptian and partly Greek. The position of the planets, which are portrayed as gods, allows modern astronomers to put a relatively precise date on the star map, which was made between 12 and 21 August, 50 BC. The lunar eclipse illustrated took place on 25 September, 52 BC, and the solar eclipse in Pisces on 7 March, 51 BC.

*A **jackal**, rather than the modern bear, represents the constellation containing the Pole Star and is at the centre of the map of the night sky.*

*A **cow in a barge** indicates Sirius – Sopdet or Sothis to the Egyptians – the brightest star in the sky. Its rise before dawn in July began the solar year in Egypt and marked the flooding of the Nile.*

__Scorpio__, in the southern hemisphere, is always represented by a scorpion.

*The **leg of an ox** represents the circumpolar constellation we know as Ursa Major, the Great Bear.*

__Gemini__ is depicted not as it is today by male twins, but by a man and a woman holding hands.

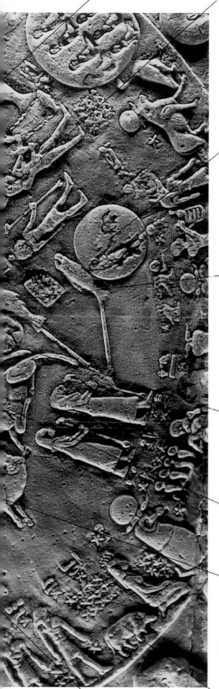

The Greek influence in this map of the heavens is most obvious in the depiction of Sagittarius as a centaur.

Horus the red, representing the planet Mars, stands above the half-goat, half-fish that symbolizes Capricorn.

Aquarius takes the form of Happy, god of the Nile flood, who pours life-giving water from two vessels over a fish at his feet.

The solar eclipse shown here took place on 7 March, 51 BC. A baboon, an incarnation of the moon, is attempting to devour the sun. A woman - probably Isis - tugs at the baboon's tail to pull him away and so save the sun.

Two fish connected with a rope represent the sign of Pisces, in which the eclipse took place.

An eclipse of the moon is represented by the eye of Horus superimposed on a disc. There was a lunar eclipse in this part of the sky on 25 September, 52 BC. This is an important clue for dating the relief.

The ram is the image of Aries, the first sign of the zodiac.

The leaping bull next to Orion represents the constellation of Taurus.

The outer circle of the zodiac contains images and symbols relating to the 36 decans, groups of stars into which the night sky was traditionally divided. Each decan rose just before dawn (heliacal rising) for 10 days in the year.

The constellation Orion, Sah in Egypt, was represented by a man armed with a stick, a symbol of the soul of Osiris.

▲ The tomb of Rameses IX
The ceiling of the sarcophagus room of Rameses IX (1126–1108 BC) is decorated by a night sky in the shape of the goddess Nut. The goddess swallows the evening sun, which passes through her body to be reborn the next day.

▼ Hypostyle hall ceiling
The zodiac is not the only representation of the celestial sphere in the temple of Hathor at Dendera. The ceiling of the hypostyle hall is also decorated with images that trace the movements of the sun and moon across the sky.

Mathematics and Measurement

Neither the Ancient Egyptian system of numbers nor their methods of calculation were as sophisticated and abstract as those developed by the Ancient Greeks, but they were firmly rooted in the practical needs of their life.

The efficient and long-lasting economic system of the Ancient Egyptians was underpinned by a system of mathematics derived from practical experience, rather than the abstract algebra and geometry of the Ancient Greeks. It was mainly concerned with solving problems of construction and administration.

Our knowledge of numeracy in Ancient Egypt comes from four papyrus rolls, two wooden tablets and a leather scroll containing mathematical texts. These show that the Ancient Egyptians had mastered the four basics of calculation – addition, subtraction, multiplication and division. Architects and surveyors were able to calculate the area of triangles and circles, as well as the volume of pyramids and cylinders. While their methods were not absolutely accurate, they were close enough.

Basic numbers

Seven signs were used to denote numbers, representing 1, 10, 100, 1,000, 10,000, 100,000 and 1,000,000 (although the last-named could represent any huge

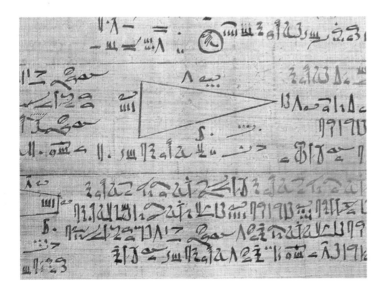

▲ A mathematical discourse
We know about the Egyptian mathematical system from four papyrus rolls used for training scribes. The most important of these is the Rhind papyrus, bought by a Scottish antiquary in a Nile market in 1858 and now in the British Museum. It was made by a scribe called Ahmose around 1550 BC, as a copy of an older work, and contains a series of tables, mathematical problems and formulae for calculating surface areas.

The Ancient Egyptian measuring rod

One palm width, *equivalent to four smaller units, represents one-seventh of the length of the rod.*

The measuring rod *is exactly one royal cubit long. The top is cut with hieroglyphs and lines picked out in white.*

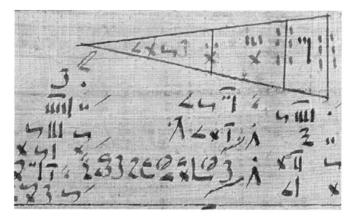

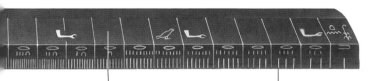

◀ Applied geometry
All the mentions of geometry in the surviving mathematical papyri are to do with solving practical rather than abstract problems. They often involve the calculation of area or volume.

◀ Units of measurement
Measuring rods carved in stone or wood provide information about Egyptian measures. The rods were used by officials and sometimes buried with them.

One thumb's width was the twenty-eighth part of the royal cubit and the smallest unit of length.

Progressive fractions from ½ to ¹⁄₁₆ of a unit - a little over 1mm - mark this end of the rod.

DOCUMENT

Measures of length

The Ancient Egyptians' massive building projects and complex system of taxes and duties demanded exact measuring methods, and standard systems for measuring length, area, volume and time were soon developed.

The basic measure of length – the distance between a man's elbow and the tip of his extended middle finger – was the royal cubit (52.4cm/20⅝in), depicted with the following hieroglyphs:

The royal cubit, subdivided into palm widths and thumb widths, became popular early in the third millennium BC. One palm width, which corresponded to ⅐ of a royal cubit, was shown as:

The hieroglyph for one thumb width, ¼ of a palm width, was:

There were hieroglyphs for multiples of a royal cubit, such as the nebiu, or 1½ royal cubits:

A further multiple of the royal cubit was the het, the measuring unit for 100 royal cubits:

For long distances, the Egyptians used the iteru, which was 20,000 royal cubits or about 10.5km (6½ miles).

◀ Making boundaries
Every year, the flooding of the Nile swept away the stone markers setting out the field boundaries of various villages. As soon as the waters had subsided, officials of the land registry went out to measure the land and re-mark the borders, basing their work on previous surveys.

number, and is often taken to mean 'more than I can count'). All other numbers were represented by repeating the symbols; 137, for example, would be written as 100, three 10s and seven 1s.

Taking measures

A system of weights and measures was also essential to the day-to-day working of the Ancient Egyptian bureaucracy. It allowed scribes, for example, to monitor the collection and delivery of foodstuffs. The records they kept helped to locate food for people when the harvest failed because the Nile's flood was too heavy or too light.

Length was measured in royal cubits, and area in terms of the setjat (later aroura), a square 100 royal cubits on each side. Measures of volume, used to quantify grain and drinks, were based on the hin (about 47cl/16½ fl oz).

Weight was measured in debens (93.3g/3.29oz). Ten debens made a kite. These were mainly measures of gold and silver, but other goods were valued in terms of debens of silver or gold, creating a basic pricing system in a society without money.

Surveying the grain fields

Knotted measuring rope was used by official surveyors to calculate the area of a farmer's grain field, the boundaries of which were marked with stones.

An assistant using a rope is responsible for the actual measuring of the area of the field.

The special measuring rope is 100 royal cubits long, with a knot to mark each royal cubit.

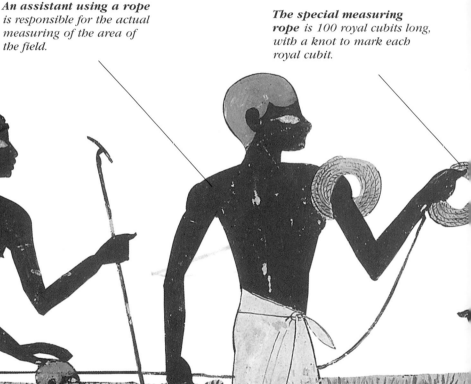

*A **high official** leads the survey of a corn field.*

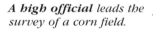

They also had to acquire some mathematical skills. A scribe, depicted here in an ivory statuette from the Middle Kingdom (right), needed to know, for example, how to calculate the quantity of materials required to construct a particular building, or the total amount of corn stored in huge granaries. He also had to be able to keep basic accounts, recording the incoming and outgoing goods in the king's storehouses.

Land registry officials needed basic mathematical skills to carry out surveys, draw up maps and take the census, which was used to calculate tax.

Architects were also excellent mathematicians, and made accurate plans an scale models of proposed building projects, such as the colonnade of the temple of Luxor (right). With their knowledge of geometry, they precisely calculated the angles of the pyramids.

Wheat was the main crop. Estimating how much each field would yield helped the administrators to work out the amount of duty to be raised.

◀ Annual survey by officials

This wall painting depicts the annual surveying of the corn fields before the harvest. Such surveys were the responsibility of scribes from the land registry office, who carried them out with the aid of assistants. The purpose of the survey was to help the administration to estimate the eventual crop yields – and thus the amount of revenue that could be raised in duty – before the event. After the harvest, the actual amount of corn was exactly measured to prevent fraud.

▲ Two measuring rods

These two contrasting rods were found in the tomb of the architect Kha, who worked for Amenhotep II (1450–1425 BC). The gold-plated ceremonial rod was a gift from the pharaoh, while the simple folding wooden stick, found with its leather casing, would have been used on site by the architect. The ends of the golden rod are shown in close-up below.

The beginning of the rod marks out 1 thumb width, 2 thumb widths, 3 thumb widths and 1 palm width.

The end of the golden rod is marked with the hieroglyph for 1 royal cubit.

Ancient Egyptian Numbers

An official system of numbering and calculation was developed early in Egypt's history, a necessary prerequisite to the construction of great monuments and the management of the country's agricultural riches.

Egypt had a decimal counting system. Numbers were carved and written in figures, rather than words, with units represented by a single vertical line and different symbols representing each of the powers of 10 – 10, 100, 1,000, 10,000, 100,000 – up to a million, or 'more than I can count'. Multiples were written out in full; thus nine was nine vertical lines, and 350 would be depicted as three hundreds and five tens. There was no sign for zero.

Number, name and sign

The Egyptians called the first nine numbers wa, senuj, khemet, jfedu, dju, sjsu, sefekhu, khemenu, pesedshu. Ten, medshu, had the sign of a yoke; 100, shenet, a coiled rope; 1,000, kha, a lotus flower; 10,000, dsheba, a finger; 100,000, hefen, a tadpole; and a million, heh, a seated god with upraised arms. Ordinal numbers used in dates and lists were made by adding the suffix -nu or the prefix mech- to the cardinal numbers.

◄ **Dates and numbers**
This scribe holds a record of the arrival in Egypt of the famous Semite caravan from the Near East in the sixth year of the reign of Senusret II (1880–1874 BC). Dates were written using ordinal numbers.

The inscription above the deceased identifies her as the daughter of the king.

◄ **Accounting for the afterlife**
Carvings on funerary steles and the false doors in the tomb chambers of the Old Kingdom (2686–2181 BC) often provide detailed lists of offerings of food and supplies for the deceased in the afterlife. Here, on both sides of the statue, are listed, for example, specific amounts of figs, wine, beer and bread.

A thousand pitchers of beer were among the offerings for the young princess.

▶ **The stele of Nefertiabet**
This stele was found in the tomb of Nefertiabet, believed to have been a daughter of Khufu (2589–2566 BC), at Giza. She is shown as a young woman sitting at an offerings table laden with bread and surrounded by lists of offerings to guarantee her survival in the afterlife. A number is shown for each offering; the lotus flower sign for a thousand appears frequently, and generally expresses the idea of abundance.

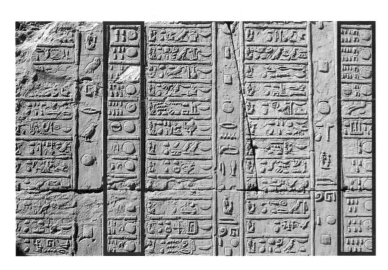

▲ Festival calendar
During the course of the year, many religious festivals were celebrated in Egyptian temples. Their dates were recorded on a calendar of festivals such as this one. It was found at the temple at Kom Ombo and dates from the Greco-Roman period (332 BC–AD 395).

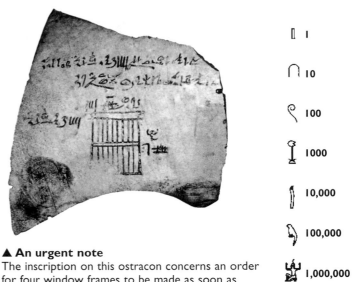

𓏺	1
𓎆	10
𓏲	100
𓆼	1000
𓂭	10,000
𓅆	100,000
𓁨	1,000,000

▲ An urgent note
The inscription on this ostracon concerns an order for four window frames to be made as soon as possible. The rough sketch of the windows has their dimensions written along the sides in hieratic script.

▼ Counting cereal
Scribes throughout Egypt kept a strict tally of the grain harvested and stored in granaries. This enabled the state to calculate taxes, and to manage food reserves to protect the people from famine.

A thousand gazelles (pictured above the number sign), and the same number of oxen and geese are allocated to Nefertiabet for her use in the afterlife.

A separate table deals with fabrics for use in the afterlife, listing them by type of material.

Applied Physics

The Ancient Egyptians never formulated elaborate scientific theories to explain the physical world, but their attempts to find solutions to practical problems led them to develop techniques of lifting and carrying that are fundamental to modern mechanics.

The Egyptians were interested in maths, but their main concerns were practical. Their understanding of geometric shapes and the calculation of area came from their experience of building. This was even more relevant to the principles of physics and mechanics; the applied form of the sciences was part of everyday life, with little or no theoretical underpinning.

Hauling loads and raising water

Five principles were at the heart of all ancient technologies: the wheel, the screw, the wedge, the lever and the inclined plane. As wheels and axles are unsuited to sand and rock, they were rarely used by the Ancient Egyptians, who employed sleds to haul heavy loads. Sled runners (and occasionally rollers) moved much more freely over the Egyptian terrain. Wheels and axles were used on soldiers' chariots, though, while the saqiya, or water-wheel, was used to bring water to the fields. The screw was also important in irrigation. One fitted into a wooden tube could be turned to raise water.

▼ Building the pyramids
Herodotus, the great Greek historian, visited Egypt in the fifth century BC and saw the pyramids at Giza, built some 2,000 years earlier. He speculated that the great blocks must have been lifted into place with a succession of pivoting-beam cranes, like the series of shadufs used to raise water to great heights in Egypt at the time. This theory has since been discounted.

The stones in this illustration have a different shape to those actually used, in an example of artistic licence.

▼ The shaduf
The principle of the lever was embodied in the shaduf, introduced in the Eighteenth Dynasty (1550–1295 BC) to irrigate gardens and orchards. A pivoted beam, with counterweights of baked mud at one end and a bucket at the other, was used to lift water from wells and ditches.

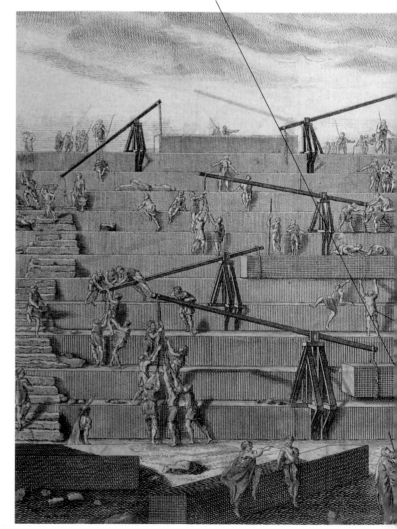

442

▶ Leverage

The principle of using levers to amplify force was widely used and appreciated in Ancient Egypt, from the relatively small scale, such as these nippers, to the massive wooden levers used in the Aswan quarries to extract and move the huge pieces of granite – weighing up to 500 tonnes – intended for obelisks. While levers were used in building projects, they were largely reserved for such relatively simple applications as the positioning of stone blocks; the system of hoisting cranes suggested as the way the pyramids were built were not used by the Ancient Egyptians and would have been impractical. Unfortunately, the usually informative sources of tomb reliefs and murals give us few clues to the technical aids used by ancient builders.

▶ A question of balance

Scales or balances, a specialized adaptation of the principle of the lever, were widely used in the Old Kingdom (2686–2181 BC). Examples have been recovered in excavations, and they are often depicted in tomb paintings, usually in the context of the weighing of the heart ceremony. In everyday life they were used to keep a precise account of precious materials – such as the gold given to smiths so it could be fashioned into jewellery – or to weigh out foodstuffs in commercial transactions.

Pivot and counterweight technology, still used in modern cranes, was not available to the builders of the Old Kingdom pyramids.

Small teams of men, as envisaged by the artist, could not have lifted such heavy stones using the engines shown here.

▼ Levers in action

The long oars used to propel boats up and down the Nile when there was no wind or current to help are an example of the practical use of the principle of leverage. Force applied at one end of the oar by the rower is transmitted and amplified through the lever to the blade at the other end. A large oar in the stern functions as a rudder in the same way, allowing the boat to be steered.

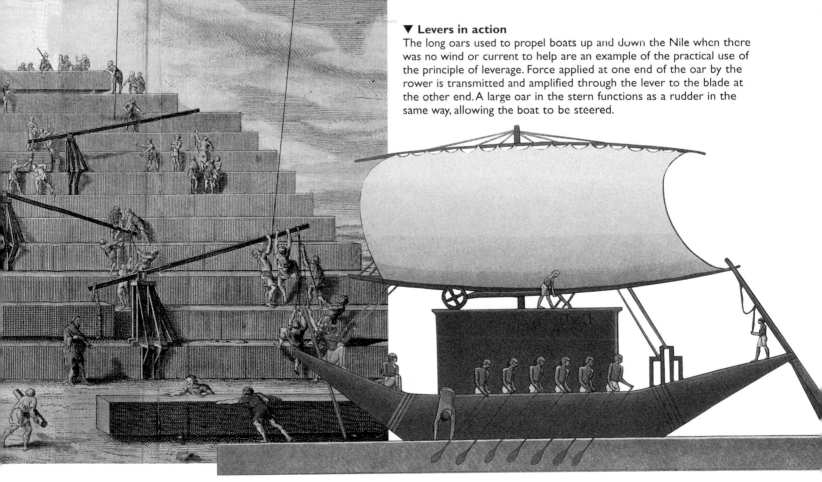

SCIENCE AND TECHNOLOGY

The basic principle of leverage, of amplifying the force applied to an object by using a long beam with an off-centre pivot or fulcrum, was used to raise water in shadufs and to propel and steer boats. It was also important, in tandem with the wedge, for splitting and working stone in quarries, and for manoeuvring the worked blocks into position.

There is no evidence that levers were widely used for raising anything heavier than water. As the pulley-wheel was unknown to them, the Ancient Egyptians used inclined planes when raising stone monuments. At the temple of Karnak at Luxor are the remains of a ramp built from mud bricks. Vestiges of similar ramps have been uncovered around the pyramids. Rather than using levers or hoists, the Egyptians dragged the stones into position up long inclined planes. The only remaining doubt about the use of ramps in building the pyramids is whether they were built at right angles to the sides, or were wrapped around them.

▲ Stone see-saws
This model, found in excavations of a temple built around 1470 BC, is of a sled used for moving stone. Levers would have been employed to tip the block into its carrying cradle and tip it out again once it was in position.

▼ Manpower
According to this painting, it took 172 men to drag a statue of Djehutyhotep, estimated at 58 tonnes, to his tomb at Deir el-Bersha. One man pours water in front of the sled runners to reduce friction and make the task easier.

An overseer stands on the stone block and guides it up a ramp, made of air-dried mud bricks, which could be extended as the building rose.

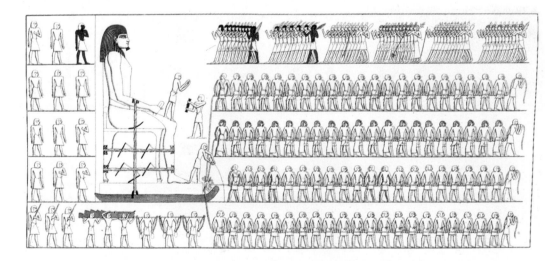

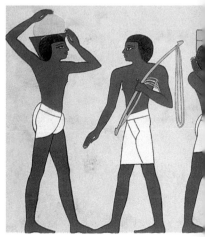

The mud-brick ramp was lengthened and widened as the structure grew. A long ramp and gentle incline minimized the strength needed to lift heavy loads.

▲ The main drag

The best-preserved example of an Ancient Egyptian building ramp rises behind the first pylon at Karnak. It is built entirely from mud bricks. Ramps such as these were used in the construction of pyramids, pylons, obelisks and entire temples, and proved a supremely practical if labour-intensive solution to the problem of raising large stones and other materials to the top of high buildings. They were made of bricks of sun-baked Nile mud that could be produced locally in whatever shape and number were desired, and removed once the project was finished. New layers of bricks were added to the ramps to keep pace with the construction.

◀ Exploiting manpower

Draught animals and wheeled carts were of little use on the sand or bare rock characteristic of Ancient Egypt, so heavy loads were moved by manpower. Blocks of building stone, for example, were dragged from the quarries and into their place in the building by teams of men pulling them along on wooden sleds. This is surprisingly efficient, especially if the team works together. To help the runners glide over the ground, furrows were made, and men were employed specifically to keep these moistened with water as the sled moved through them, helping to minimize friction.

Thick ropes were used to take the weight of the stone blocks. Workers padded their shoulders so that the ropes would not cut into them.

Sled runners provided a fairly friction-free ride on hard or sandy surfaces. The main effort lay in overcoming the initial inertia of the stone.

▼ Building a ramp

This illustration shows workmen constructing a stone ramp, similar to one at the temple of Hatshepsut (1473–1458 BC), which was used not as a building aid, but as the final access leading to a terrace. While a group of workmen transports stones, binder and water, the first workman builds the finishing limestone layer of the ramp.

The Egyptian Calendar

Like all primitive peoples, the early Egyptians measured time by observing lunar months of 29 to 30 days, but around 2900 BC they developed the first calendar not dependent on the movements of the moon.

The first Egyptian calendars combined observations of the moon with the annual cycle of the Nile. The latter was measured with nilometers – reeds with notches cut in them to calibrate the height of the waters. Thus the Egyptian year of 12 months, each 30 days long, was divided into three four-month seasons: *akhet* ('inundation', mid-July to mid-November); *peret* ('emergence', mid-November to mid-March); and *shemu* (perhaps 'low water', the period of harvest from mid-March to mid-July). Each month comprised three 'weeks' of 10 days ('decades'), and each day was divided into 24 hours (12 daytime, 12 night-time).

The Egyptian year was extended to 365 days – the solar year – by the addition of five days following the end of *shemu*. These were regarded as the birthdays of the gods Osiris, Horus and Seth, and the goddesses Isis and Nephthys.

The morning god Khepri *appears as a scarab with a ram's head.*

The sun god Ra *is shown as a solar disc being rolled along like a ball of dung by Khepri, his morning 'self'.*

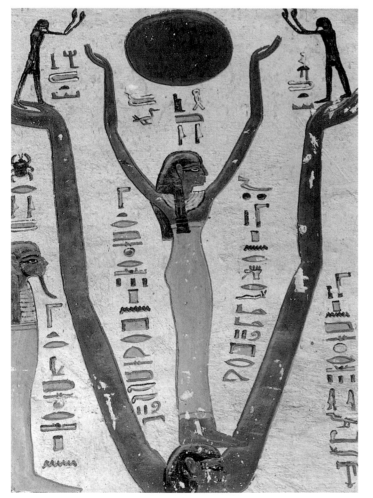

◀ The sky goddess
In the evening, the sky goddess Nut, who is arched above the earth and presides over the movement of the stars and the passing of time, swallows the solar disc, representing the sun god Ra. This passes through her body during the night, and she returns it to the world at dawn by 'giving birth' to Ra.

▶ A religious calendar
The ceiling of the hypostyle hall in the temple of Esna, built between the first and third centuries AD, is decorated with astronomical scenes. A calendar shows the dates of religious feasts, some of which match the dates of the agricultural cycle. Others, like the Feast of Opet at Thebes, were associated with particular deities.

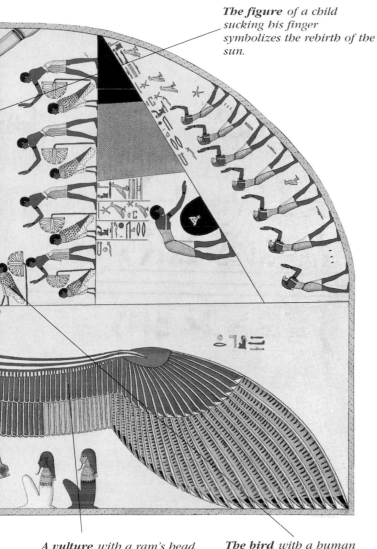

The figure of a child sucking his finger symbolizes the rebirth of the sun.

A vulture with a ram's head, possibly the goddess Nekhbet, dominates the image.

The bird with a human head represents ba, the soul of the deceased.

◄ **The morning sun**

The Egyptians gave each image of the sun a different name. In the morning, when it rose after travelling through the body of Nut, it had the appearance of a scarab beetle pushing the solar disc, and was called Khepri; in the evening, when it set, it took on the appearance of an old man, and was known as Atum.

INSIGHT

The Dendera zodiac

The picture below is a reproduction of a stela from a ceiling in the temple of Hathor, another sky goddess, at Dendera. Sculpted in relief and dating from 50 BC, the sandstone monument is now in the Louvre, Paris.

The slab shows a zodiac of a celestial sphere travelled by the stars and planets and divided into 12 equal sections. Invented by the Babylonians in the fifth century BC, and then taken up by the Greeks, the zodiac appeared in Egypt only at the end of the third century BC.

The figures around the edge of the circle represent the 36 10-day periods, or 'decades'. Above their heads are the 12 signs of the zodiac, including Pisces and Taurus, as well as the constellations known to the Egyptians.

The first depiction of the zodiacal signs, with the 10-day periods, was on the astronomical ceiling of the tomb of Senenmut, chief steward to Queen Hatsheput, at Deir el-Bahri (1463 BC). Zodiac reliefs similar to the Dendera zodiac were commonly engraved in temples and on sarcophagus lids during Greco-Roman times.

The Nile calendar

The Egyptian calendar, based originally on the annual cycle of the River Nile, had three seasons of four lunar months:

akhet: the flood season
thoth: 19 July – 17 August
paophi: 18 August – 16 September
athyr: 17 September – 16 October
sholiak: 17 October – 15 November

peret: the growing season
tybi: 16 November – 15 December
meshir: 16 December – 14 January
phamenoth: 15 January – 13 February
pharmouthi: 14 February – 15 March

shemu: the harvest season
pashons: 16 March – 14 April
payni: 15 April – 14 May
epiphi: 15 May – 13 June
mesori: 14 June – 13 July

plus five extra 'epagomenal' holy birthdays:
14 July: Osiris; 15 July: Horus; 16 July: Seth; 17 July: Isis;
18 July: Nephthys

The night sky

This drawing by Ippolito Rosellini replicates part of the ceiling of the funeral chamber of Sety I (1294–1279 BC) in the Valley of the Kings. The constellations and divisions of the sky are represented as mythological divinities. In the top part of the drawing, the constellations are aligned and by observing their positions the Ancient Egyptians determined the duration of the hours of the night. Various constellations associated with the 10-day periods, or 'decades', are depicted at the bottom.

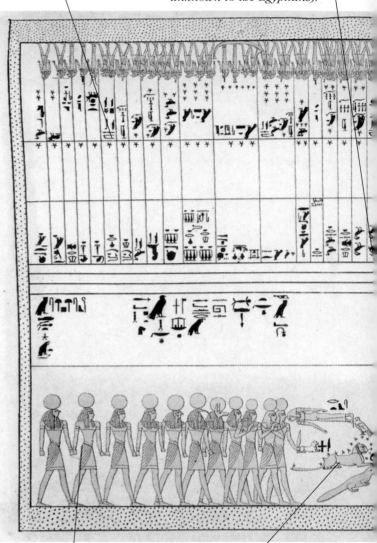

The night hours are shown at the top.

A human figure with arms spread wide possibly represents the Swan constellation (although swans were unknown to the Egyptians).

Deities flank the northern constellations in the lower half.

The Lion constellation is easily identified.

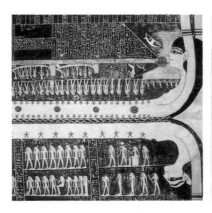

▶ **Day and night**
The ceiling of the sarcophagus room in the tomb of Rameses VI (1143–1136 BC) is decorated with pictures and inscriptions taken from the *Book of the Day* and the *Book of the Night*. These texts relate the nocturnal travels of the solar disc, representing the sun god Ra, through the body of the sky goddess Nut.

▲ **The march of time**
While births and deaths were dated by the reigns of the pharaohs, the peasants of Ancient Egypt based their yearly calendar on the flow of the Nile. Today, however, the flow of the river and its annual cycle is carefully controlled by the Aswan Dam.

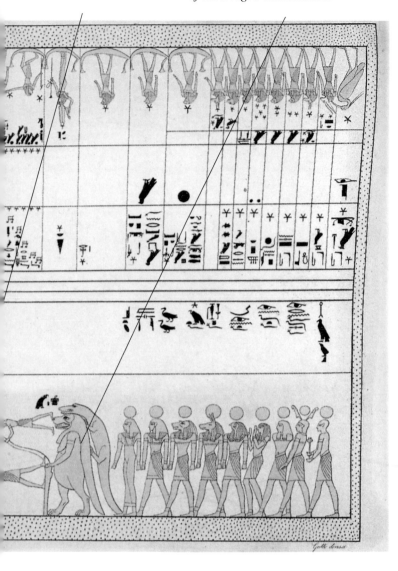

The bull represents the Great Bear constellation.

The hippopotamus carrying a crocodile is a complex representation of the Dragon constellation.

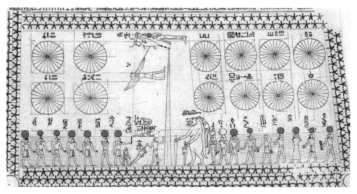

▲ The astronomical ceiling of Senenmut

This painting from the ceiling of the tomb of Senenmut, Queen Hatshepsut's favourite courtier – and possibly her lover, according to some Egyptologists – shows the first astronomical ceiling in Ancient Egypt. By studying the position of the stars, it has been possible to date the ceiling accurately to 1463 BC.

The picture indicates the position of the constellations visible over the different months of the year, the 12 circles with their spokes symbolizing the 12 months. Star charts, it was believed, enabled the deceased to tell the time of night or the date in the solar year.

▼ The sun's night voyage

The reproductions from the *Book of the Earth* which decorate the walls of the funeral chamber in the tomb of Rameses VI (1143–1136 BC) show the gods Ra and Osiris, associated with the rebirth of the dead, and 12 women, personifying the 12 hours of the night.

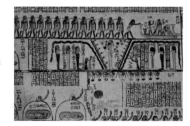

▲ The solar clock, c. 1500 BC

The time between the first and last hours of the day was measured by a gnomon. When the front of the gnomon is directed to the sun, its shadow is projected onto the back of the instrument. The accurate time is determined by both the length and direction of the shadow.

The missing link

The birthdays of the five gods (born only through the intervention of Thoth, the god of knowledge, who provided five extra days of light), took the Egyptian year back to its beginning – 19 July on our Gregorian calendar. This was the date of the rising of Sirius, the brightest star in the sky, which was personified by the star-crowned goddess Sopdet. Surviving textual accounts of this event (and its observation) form the basis of the traditional chronology of Egypt.

However, there remained a discrepancy between the civil year and its divisions – which gave the Egyptians a reasonably accurate means of measuring time – and the solar year, which was six hours longer. In effect, the difference meant that the civil year and the seasonal year coincided precisely just once every 1,460 years. This hardly bothered most Egyptians, and it was not corrected until the Ptolemaic period, when the notion of a 'leap year' (one extra day every fourth year) was introduced by Ptolemy III, dating the New Year from 29 August.

▼ The Aztec calendar

Located in the National Museum of Anthropology in Mexico City, Mexico, the famous sun stone or Aztec calendar offers a Mesoamerican explanation for the origins and early history of the world. The centre of the umbo or boss is occupied by Tonatiuh, the sun god. The four rectangles surrounding him evoke the four eras experienced by humanity during its history.

In the central circle are the gods corresponding to the 20 days of the Aztec month, while the two snakes in the outer circle symbolize the celestial dome. The Aztecs believed that the sun required blood for fuel and, according to some Spanish chroniclers, between 20,000 and 50,000 people a month were sacrificed in order to placate it.

Measuring Time

Amazingly simple devices were used in Ancient Egypt for the measurement of time. Surviving water and sun clocks show that only a very inexact determination of day and night times was possible.

The Ancient Egyptian year had 360 days and was divided into 12 months of 30 days each, as well as into 36 months each containing 10 days. At the year's end, five days remained which were considered to be 'outside' of the year, and the birthdays of Osiris, Isis, Horus, Seth and Nepthys. Each year was a quarter day shorter than the solar year, so an extra day was added every fourth year to compensate for this.

Day and night

Day and night were each divided into 12 'hours', whose length varied according to the season. From the New Kingdom (1550–1069 BC), daylight hours were measured by a sundial (setshat) of which there were two varieties: one involved measuring the length of a shadow and finding its value on a corresponding table; the other measured the progress of a shadow against an inscribed scale.

The night hours were measured from the New Kingdom onwards with a water clock (clepsydra), which was invented by the astronomer Amenemhat 'for the glory of King Amenhotep I'. This equated the passage of time with the amount of water that ran out of a hole in the base of a container.

A baboon sitting on the water clock is one of the manifestations of Thoth, god of time.

The clepsydra measured the passage of time by the depth of the water that slowly ran out of a hole in the base.

◄ The water clock
The water clock was generally used to measure the passage of the night hours. This stone container tapers towards the bottom, where there is a small opening, often decorated with a figure of Thoth. The interior of a water clock was inscribed with 12 rings, each representing the passing of an hour. The outer surface was frequently decorated with pictures of the deities of heavenly bodies.

◄ The sundial
This pylon-shaped sundial worked by reading the sun's shadow against the 12 inscribed divisions. A small rod was placed in the hole, with the position of its shadow giving an approximation of the time of day. It is impossible to say whether such devices were actually used, or whether they served only as a model or as a votive offering.

Sety I raises his hand in a gesture of worship and presents the daughter of the sun god with a water clock.

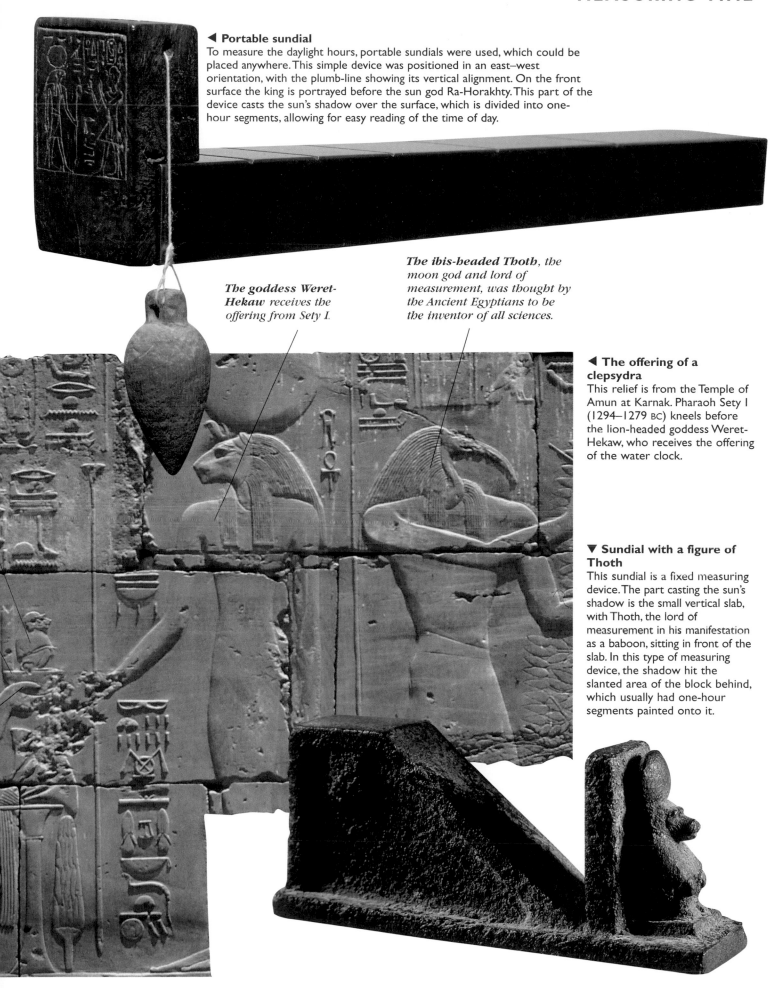

◄ Portable sundial
To measure the daylight hours, portable sundials were used, which could be placed anywhere. This simple device was positioned in an east–west orientation, with the plumb-line showing its vertical alignment. On the front surface the king is portrayed before the sun god Ra-Horakhty. This part of the device casts the sun's shadow over the surface, which is divided into one-hour segments, allowing for easy reading of the time of day.

The goddess Weret-Hekaw receives the offering from Sety I.

The ibis-headed Thoth, the moon god and lord of measurement, was thought by the Ancient Egyptians to be the inventor of all sciences.

◄ The offering of a clepsydra
This relief is from the Temple of Amun at Karnak. Pharaoh Sety I (1294–1279 BC) kneels before the lion-headed goddess Weret-Hekaw, who receives the offering of the water clock.

▼ Sundial with a figure of Thoth
This sundial is a fixed measuring device. The part casting the sun's shadow is the small vertical slab, with Thoth, the lord of measurement in his manifestation as a baboon, sitting in front of the slab. In this type of measuring device, the shadow hit the slanted area of the block behind, which usually had one-hour segments painted onto it.

Medicine

Athough the Ancient Egyptians attempted to find remedies for their ailments, they knew little about the functioning of the human body and were unable to predict or tackle the causes of an illness.

Our knowledge of Ancient Egyptian medicine comes essentially from medical papyri and a number of tomb and temple decorations. The Ebers papyrus and the Edwin Smith papyrus – both named after the collectors of the documents – are the most important and date from the beginning of the New Kingdom (1550–1069 BC). The first is like a medical encyclopedia, which lists the various ailments a doctor might encounter on his daily rounds and offers advice on treatments. The second, dealing almost exclusively with fractures and wounds, lists 48 types of injury and lesion and the appropriate treatments. The process of mummification, which was carried out by priests, seems to have contributed little to the knowledge of human anatomy or medical practice in general.

The flint knife was held in the priest's right hand.

The priest held the end of the penis in his left hand.

▲ ▼ Medicine jars and instruments
The Egyptian pharmacopoeia included natural ingredients from the animal, plant and mineral worlds, stored in ceramic jars (above). Among the instruments found in tombs were forceps and spatulas (below), some of which were inscribed with magical spells or the symbols of protective gods.

▶ Scenes of circumcision
A number of tomb and temple reliefs depict this ancient ceremony. This relief dates from the Old Kingdom (2686–2181 BC) and was found in the tomb of the vizier Ankhmahor (c. 2300 BC) at Saqqara.

Circumcision – a religious ritual

This operation, which probably dates back to prehistoric times, was part of the sacred initiation that marked the passage from adolescence to adulthood. It was performed on boys from the age of about 10 to 14. The simple operation, however, was not without risk, notably from infection. It was carried out by a priest who, at the same time, recited magical incantations. Because of its ritualistic nature, a flint, rather than a metal blade, was used.

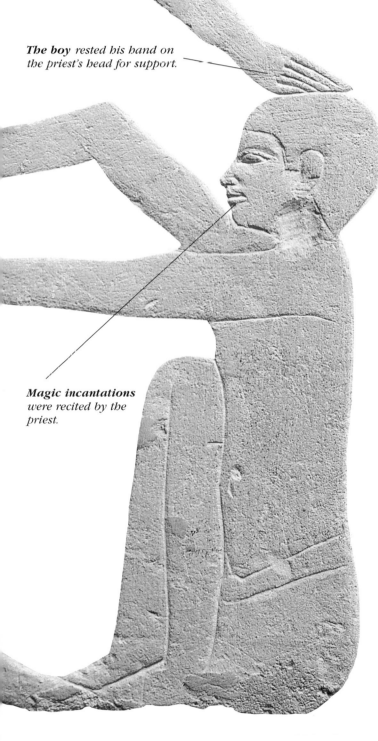

The boy rested his hand on the priest's head for support.

Magic incantations were recited by the priest.

◀ **Ptah, god of healing**
When ill, the Egyptians not only used medicines, but also made appeals to the gods. Ptah, regarded as one of the creators of the world, was the patron of craftsmen and also the protector of doctors.
Here, he is depicted wearing a skull cap and with a straight beard. In the Late period (747–332 BC) he was attributed with healing powers and, in this role, is often depicted as a naked dwarf who repels dangerous creatures, such as serpents and scorpions, and cures the victims of their bites.

INSIGHT

Eye complaints

The Ancient Egyptians frequently suffered eye complaints due to their constant exposure to intense sunlight, sand and dust. Blindness was also common, as this relief from Tell el-Amarna of blind temple musicians shows.

A great many eye remedies appear in the medical papyri. Bat's blood, for example, was used to treat eyes because it was believed that this creature's 'night vision' could be transmitted through its blood. This treatment was rarely successful. However, some problems of the retina were more effectively treated with ox liver, which contains vitamin A; today, liver extract is still used to cure eye problems associated with this vitamin deficiency.

Because of the limited knowledge of anatomy, surgery did not go beyond an elementary level, and no internal surgery was undertaken. Most of the medical instruments found in tombs or depicted on temple reliefs were used to treat injuries or fractures, which were possibly the result of accidents incurred by workers on the pharaohs' monumental building sites. Other implements were used for gynaecological problems and in childbirth, both of which were treated extensively in the medical papyri.

◀ A man in pain
This bronze statuette of a sick man racked with pain dates from the New Kingdom (1550–1069 BC). Although Egyptian physicians were generally unable to say what caused an illness, they attempted to treat its symptoms. Medical texts dating back to about 1500 BC suggested dill in a pain-killing mixture based on wine mixed with a small quantity of raisins and dates. The concoction was boiled and strained before being taken for four days. Dill also appears in an ointment to relieve headache, and in a poultice for neck pain.

Surgical instruments
The temple of Sobek and Haroeris at Kom Ombo in Upper Egypt, near modern Aswan, has provided important evidence about Ancient Egyptian surgery. This relief from the enclosure wall, which depicts commonly used surgical instruments, is from the Roman period.

Cautery for sealing wounds

Specula for viewing the inside of the body

Urethral catheters for male adults

Cautery for sealing wounds

Saw

Flat double hook

Dental pliers or bone nippers

Bone saw

Probe (instrument inserted into a cavity for exploration)

Forked probe

Catheter (used for extracting fluids)

Pipette for drawing off fluids

Phial for enemas

Clamps for holding or separating tissue

Pipette for applying ointment

Cranioclast (used for breaking up the head of a dead foetus within the uterus)

Dental forceps

Knife

Lancet for opening veins

Scoop

Jars or mortars for grinding medicines

◀ **Juniper, a natural remedy**
This ingredient is frequently quoted in Ancient Egyptian medical papyri for both internal and external use. The Ebers Papyrus recommends that its oil, mixed in equal parts with 'white oil', be taken for one day to cure tapeworm. A juniper ointment, based on goose fat, was also used as a treatment for headaches.

DOCUMENT

Medical papyri

These documents, inscribed on papyrus in hieratic script, were essentially collections of remedies written for the medical practitioner. Along with the specific treatments, they also included spells and incantations, indicating the close link between magic and medicine.

The various medications were identified by a heading, often in red, which outlined its use and described the symptoms of the complaint, its treatment and the way in which the remedy was to be administered. The example (below) is from the Chester Beatty papyrus which deals with digestive problems.

The incantations were combined with the administration of the remedy, so that if the latter proved ineffectual, the help of the gods was at hand. Deciphering many of the texts has been difficult because of the inability to identify both the ailments and the ingredients used in the cures.

Pliers for extracting teeth or bone fragments

Phial

Scales. This instrument is from the Roman period. The Egyptians prescribed medicine according to volume and not weight

Phials for enemas

Flask for cupping

Scissors

Flask for cupping

Bandages

Sponge

Double-headed probe

Scalpels

Textile Production

Tomb paintings and models, as well as surviving pieces of cloth, tell us all about Egyptian clothmaking, from the preparation of fibres through spinning yarn to weaving and dyeing textiles.

The weaver sits at the loom using a shuttle to weave the weft threads through those of the warp.

L inen, from the fibres of the flax plant, *Linum usitatissimum*, was the principal cloth used in Ancient Egypt. Flax was not a native plant – it came from the Levant – but was already being cultivated in the Nile Valley by around 5000 BC, as scraps of fabric have been recovered from tombs of that date. Other fragments of cloth found in tombs of the Predynastic period (5500–3100 BC) testify that woollen yarn – from both sheep and goats – was also used, but wool was never as popular as linen. Cotton from India and imported silk did not reach Egypt until the Ptolemaic Dynasty (305–30 BC), while mohair, from the wool of the angora goat, was not introduced until the seventh century AD.

Getting the thread

The production of linen yarn from flax was a long, complicated process, beginning with the early harvesting of the flax; the younger the plant, the finer the fibres. Plants were pulled from the soil, rather than cut with a scythe, to maximize the length of the fibres. The dry stalks were soaked for several days to loosen their hard outer layers, then dried in the sun before being beaten to shreds and pulled through two sticks to clean the fibres of any woody detritus. The fibres were then hand-spun into yarn, a job usually reserved for women.

▲ Linen from the New Kingdom
Depending on the thickness of the yarn, and the closeness of the weave, Egyptian linen could vary in quality from rather coarse, everyday stuff like this, to the sheer, diaphanous material used to make the clinging robes depicted in sculptures and reliefs.

Lengths of yarn are being measured out to make warp threads for the loom.

The spinners gather their threads around the spindle below the whorl – a disc that acts as a flywheel.

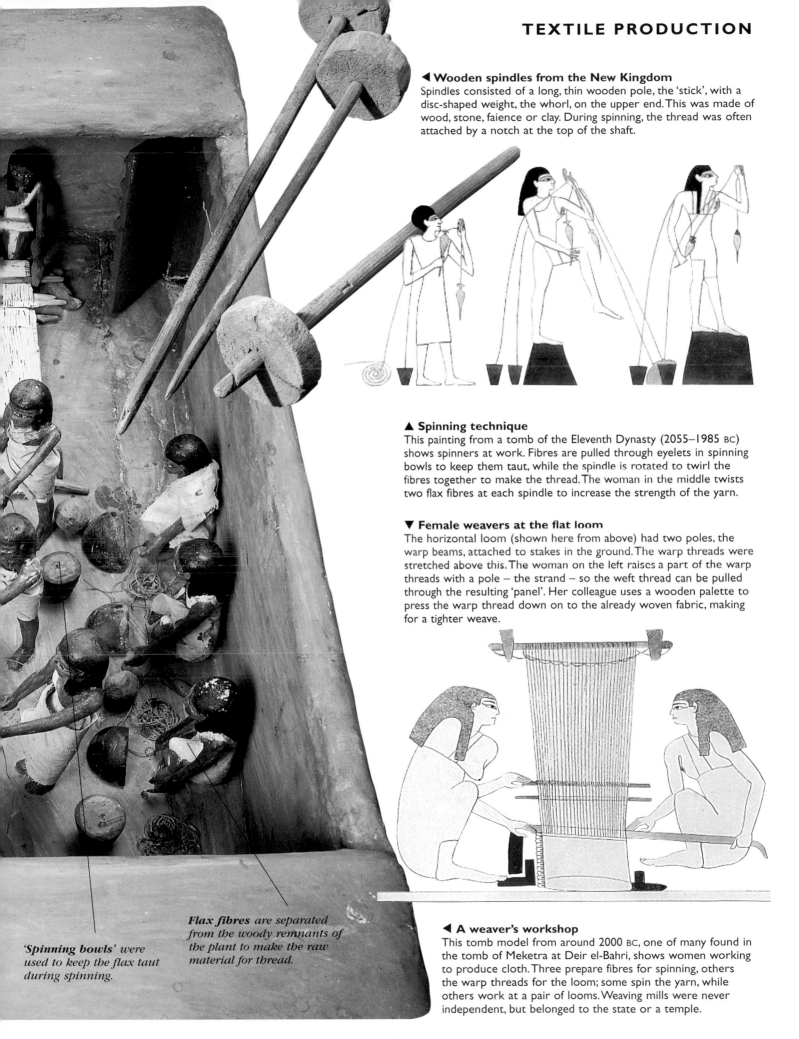

◀ Wooden spindles from the New Kingdom

Spindles consisted of a long, thin wooden pole, the 'stick', with a disc-shaped weight, the whorl, on the upper end. This was made of wood, stone, faience or clay. During spinning, the thread was often attached by a notch at the top of the shaft.

▲ Spinning technique

This painting from a tomb of the Eleventh Dynasty (2055–1985 BC) shows spinners at work. Fibres are pulled through eyelets in spinning bowls to keep them taut, while the spindle is rotated to twirl the fibres together to make the thread. The woman in the middle twists two flax fibres at each spindle to increase the strength of the yarn.

▼ Female weavers at the flat loom

The horizontal loom (shown here from above) had two poles, the warp beams, attached to stakes in the ground. The warp threads were stretched above this. The woman on the left raises a part of the warp threads with a pole – the strand – so the weft thread can be pulled through the resulting 'panel'. Her colleague uses a wooden palette to press the warp thread down on to the already woven fabric, making for a tighter weave.

Flax fibres are separated from the woody remnants of the plant to make the raw material for thread.

'Spinning bowls' were used to keep the flax taut during spinning.

◀ A weaver's workshop

This tomb model from around 2000 BC, one of many found in the tomb of Meketra at Deir el-Bahri, shows women working to produce cloth. Three prepare fibres for spinning, others the warp threads for the loom; some spin the yarn, while others work at a pair of looms. Weaving mills were never independent, but belonged to the state or a temple.

INSIGHT

A splash of colour

Coloured textiles were a rarity in Ancient Egypt before the New Kingdom (1550–1069 bc), when various dyeing techniques began to be used on a much larger scale. For pigment, the Egyptians used natural ochres to produce red, yellow and brown, and plant dyes such as woad for blue and sea-wort for red. Threads, rather than whole pieces of cloth, were dyed, and the colourful yarns were used to weave geometric patterns into fabrics (below left, on a piece of linen from Deir el-Medina), or to decorate the neckline or seam of a tunic. If the fabric was intended to robe someone of high rank from the royal household, figurative motifs might also be woven into it. In the Coptic period (between the division of the Roman Empire in AD 395 and the Islamic conquest of Egypt in AD 641), coloured cloth became abundant, as wool – much easier to dye than linen – was increasingly used for everyday purposes in Egypt. Robes of the time were decorated with wide ribbons and bands – with coloured, mainly figurative motifs woven into them (below, from the sixth or seventh century AD). As well as images from the natural world, motifs on textiles took inspiration from Christian symbolism or were based on Hellenistic geometric elements.

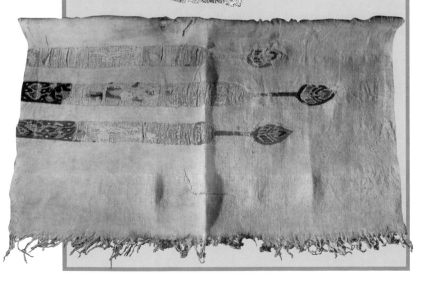

Two kinds of loom were used in Ancient Egypt. The horizontal flat loom, typically used by women, was the simpler of the two. Only the two poles of the warp beams had to be attached to the ground. The main drawback was that fabric woven on it could never be longer than the loom itself. The vertical upright loom – only used by men, according to tomb paintings – was more complicated. The two warp beams could be turned, allowing the weaver to roll up the woven fabric, and therefore make much longer bolts of cloth.

Weaving techniques

The prevalent technique used to make cloth was simple linen weaving, interlacing warp and weft threads. This one technique could produce a wide variety of cloth, depending on the thickness of the yarn and the quality of the weave. It was quite common to vary the pattern by bunching together two or three threads in the warp and weft, a style now known as panama weave. In the Eighteenth Dynasty (1550–1295 bc), a style now called gobelin weaving was introduced, where several coloured weft threads are used in producing figurative patterns.

The woven fabric was then washed and folded, and the quality of the finished cloth was categorized according to its sheerness and the looseness or density of the weave. The best quality went to make fine clothes; another grade was preferred for bandaging mummies, and so on for various other purposes.

◄ Mats and baskets

This relief shows plant stalks being prepared for weaving into a mat or basket. Egyptian basket- and rug-makers used a range of plants, mostly palm ribs and different types of reed, but also wheatstraw, halfa grass, raffia, bullrush and papyrus. Techniques of coiling, twining, weaving and plaiting were used. Reliefs and tomb paintings that show mats being made suggest that they were mainly the work of shepherds, who plaited them in the open air while watching over their flocks.

► A modern craft

Young Egyptians today learn techniques of making carpets and wall hangings very similar to those developed by their distant ancestors, knotting them or weaving them in what has become known as the gobelin technique. A rectangular, horizontal frame is used in this tapestry work. The warp threads are stretched across it, and the desired pattern is then either knotted in, using short lengths of coloured yarn, or woven into place using several small weaver's shuttles.

Baskets of material, newly wrung out, are taken away to be dried in the sun.

Washed cloth was wrung out by hand – usually by a man – to speed up the drying process.

► Ready for use

The final step in textile production, shown in this New Kingdom tomb painting, was to wash the cloth. On the right, a boy dips a piece of cloth in a washtub. In the middle, a man who has already wrung several washed lengths of material passes them to a woman crouching on the floor. She readies them for drying.

Boiling water was used to wash the cloth, which was then sun-dried, a treatment that bleached it white.

Boats in Ancient Egypt

Such was the significance of the Nile to the economic and spiritual prosperity of Ancient Egypt that boats, from simple papyrus skiffs to large wooden vessels, were built from Predynastic times.

The geographical structure of Egypt, with its narrow ribbon of fertile land stretching along the Nile, made shipping an immensely important means of travel, communication and trade from the earliest times. Egyptians first made boats in the New Stone Age, between 6000 and 5000 BC, and ceramic models of boats have been recovered from tombs of the period. These early boats were small skiffs made from bundles of dried papyrus. From 4000 BC to the start of the Early Dynastic period in 3100 BC, boats were a popular decorative motif on pottery.

Wooden boats

Finds from tombs of the Naqada II period (3500-3100 BC) show that carpenters already practised techniques that could be used to make wooden boats, but the oldest known examples are no earlier than *c*. 3000 BC – 20 wooden boats, up to 20m long, were recently discovered in the royal necropolis of the Early Dynastic period at Abydos. They were part of the funerary equipment of a king, presumably so that he could use them to sail across the sky in the company of the sun god.

The papyrus bundles are made watertight by being lashed together under pressure.

◀ **The raw material**
The stems of *Cyperus papyrus*, which grow to a height of around 3m (10 ft) in a season, were the prime boat-building material of Ancient Egypt. The stems were dried and made into bundles, which were lashed together with ropes, themselves fashioned from the plant's fibres. The outer stems were also used in the weaving of sandals, mats and baskets, while other parts of this versatile and abundant plant provided writing materials, food and medicine.

▶ **Traffic on the Nile**
The River Nile was of central importance to Egypt as a means of communication as well as being a source of fish and other food from Predynastic times. Fishermen built skiffs and barges from which to launch their nets, while other river users included the pleasure boats of the wealthy, craft transporting goods, livestock and people, funerary barges and even the divine barges that carried statues of the gods on ritual journeys.

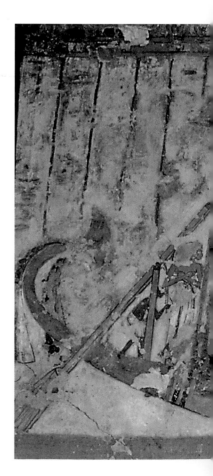

The papyrus rope used to tie the bundles is tightened using the whole body as a brace.

Teamwork allowed a serviceable boat to be put together relatively quickly.

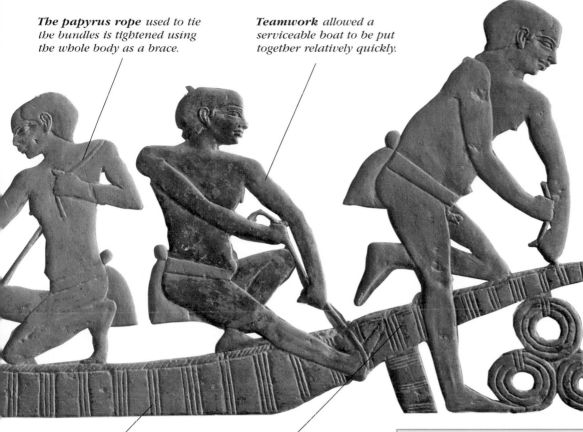

◄ **Papyrus boats**
The primary boat-building material grew in abundance all along the banks of the Nile, while the construction method was simplicity itself: even the poorest Egyptian could afford a papyrus boat. Nobles used these speedy, manoeuvrable craft for hunting birds, fish or hippos in the shallow wetlands of the Delta, while peasants saw them as a way to fish in the Nile or take produce or livestock to local markets. Most papyrus boats were little skiffs for one or two people, using poles – as in modern punts – or oars for propulsion and steering. Large papyrus barges, up to 17m (55 ft) long (any longer and the limitations of the materials would have made the boats unstable), were built using much the same techniques as the skiffs. They had wooden plank decks and two ranks of around a dozen oarsmen. Some were equipped with rectangular sails.

A wooden deck reinforced the interior of larger papyrus barges.

The raised prow and stern make the keel-less barge navigable in shallow waters.

DOCUMENT

Vessels built of plants

The shallow-water craft made by the Ancient Egyptians from bundles of papyrus form part of a tradition of building boats from fibrous plant stems that is at least as old as the earliest civilization in Mesopotamia and persists today anywhere in the world where there are inland waters to navigate and wood is scarce.

Construction techniques have hardly changed since reed boats plied the Tigris and Euphrates in the fourth millennium BC, or the early Chinese used such craft to explore their great rivers. Ancient Egyptian fishermen would be quite at home in the small reed skiffs used today (below) for inshore travelling on Lake Titicaca in the virtually treeless High Andes.

From then on, wooden boats – pleasure barges, funerary barques, cargo ships and, later, seagoing trading ships – plied the Nile alongside frail skiffs of papyrus, the boat-building material of choice for fishermen and the poor. Between 3100 and 3000 BC, Egyptian boatmen adopted the sail, which had been in use in Mesopotamia since 3500 BC. Sometimes the rectangular sails replaced oars, and sometimes complemented them. With the prevailing wind in the north, ships set sail to go upstream; oarsmen were used on trips downstream. A boat shown under sail in a relief is moving south. If the sail is furled, it is headed north.

Wooden boats were built in boatyards, essentially woodworking businesses that took on other commissions. Boats were made of native wood from sycomore fig trees and acacia, or imported timber such as conifers from Lebanon.

A developing craft

Remains of real boats – such as the royal barge made in Lebanese cedar found in a pit dug into the pyramid complex of Khufu (2589–2566 BC), or the Middle Kingdom boats unearthed in the necropolis at Dahshur – along with the wooden scale models placed in tombs, enable us to trace the history of navigation on the Nile and to measure the rather slow progress of boat-building technology. Cabins, awnings and other details can be seen on all kinds of models.

The picture is rounded out by tomb reliefs of boats being built, wall paintings of the general traffic on the river and temple-wall depictions of gods – or at least their statues – travelling in water-borne ritual procession.

▶ **A dignitary's craft**
This painting is from the Theban tomb (TT261) of Khaemwaset, a high official who lived in the Eighteenth Dynasty (1550–1295 BC). It shows his wooden boat, which is covered with decorative paintings. In the centre is the cabin in which Khaemwaset would have sheltered from the sun during his trips on the Nile. The large rudder oars at the stern are painted with protective wedjat eyes, while the curved stern ends in a papyrus umbel. Sailors, dressed simply in short loincloths, are unloading a cargo of sealed jars. These probably contain wine; other scenes in the same tomb depict wine-makers at work.

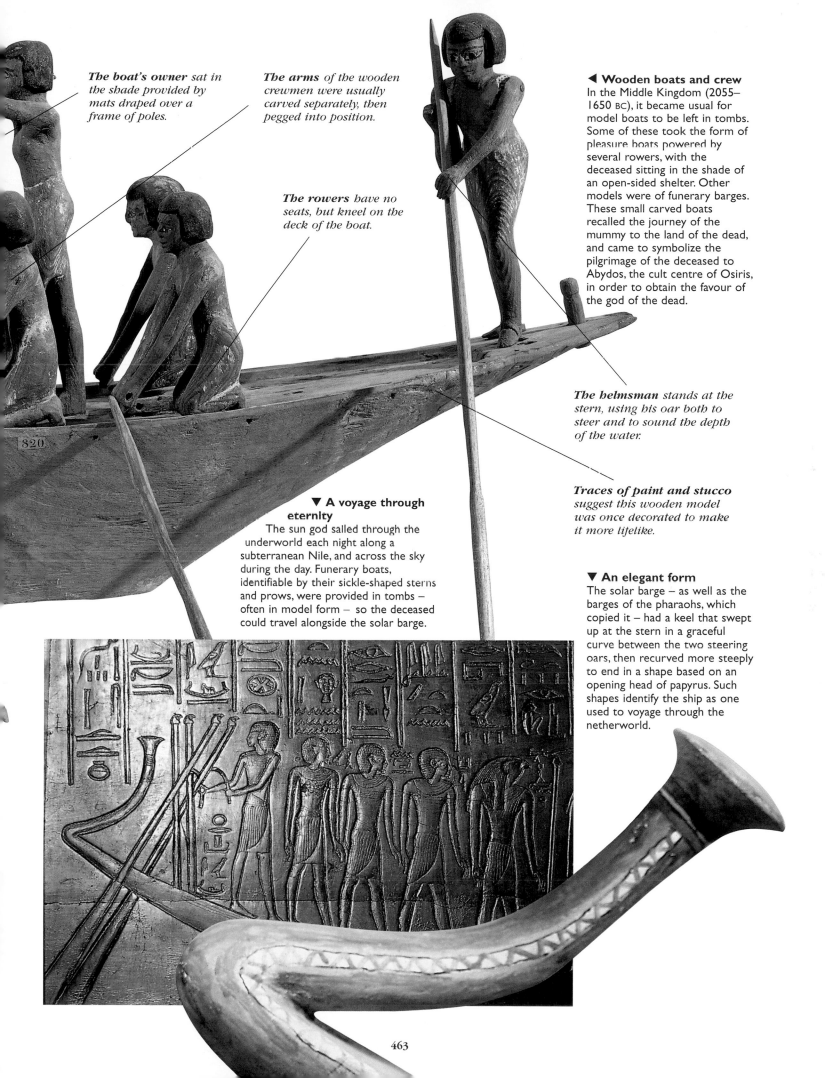

The boat's owner *sat in the shade provided by mats draped over a frame of poles.*

The arms *of the wooden crewmen were usually carved separately, then pegged into position.*

The rowers *have no seats, but kneel on the deck of the boat.*

◀ **Wooden boats and crew**
In the Middle Kingdom (2055–1650 BC), it became usual for model boats to be left in tombs. Some of these took the form of pleasure boats powered by several rowers, with the deceased sitting in the shade of an open-sided shelter. Other models were of funerary barges. These small carved boats recalled the journey of the mummy to the land of the dead, and came to symbolize the pilgrimage of the deceased to Abydos, the cult centre of Osiris, in order to obtain the favour of the god of the dead.

The helmsman *stands at the stern, using his oar both to steer and to sound the depth of the water.*

Traces of paint and stucco *suggest this wooden model was once decorated to make it more lifelike.*

▼ **A voyage through eternity**
The sun god sailed through the underworld each night along a subterranean Nile, and across the sky during the day. Funerary boats, identifiable by their sickle-shaped sterns and prows, were provided in tombs – often in model form – so the deceased could travel alongside the solar barge.

▼ **An elegant form**
The solar barge – as well as the barges of the pharaohs, which copied it – had a keel that swept up at the stern in a graceful curve between the two steering oars, then recurved more steeply to end in a shape based on an opening head of papyrus. Such shapes identify the ship as one used to voyage through the netherworld.

Weapons

The earliest arms, such as spears and battle-axes, differed little from hunting weapons or the tools used by craftsmen. Later, specific weapons were developed, their design often influenced by foreign invaders.

Soldiers of the Old and Middle Kingdoms (2686–1650 BC) were fairly inadequately equipped. The only development in weapons since Predynastic times had been the replacement of flint blades with those of copper. The heavy infantry carried wood and leather shields, copper-headed spears and swords. The light infantry were armed with bows and primitive arrows made from a bronze alloy and reed shafts. Troops had neither protective helmets nor armour. It was not until the New Kingdom (1550–1069 BC) that the design and quality of weapons were improved.

▼ The pharaoh's arsenal

In a tomb in Thebes, Kenamon, steward to king Amenhotep II (1427–1400 BC), had depictions made of the items used in battle by the pharaoh. Bows, arrows, quivers, swords, daggers, battle-axes, clubs and maces, a chain-mail tunic, shields and helmets are all shown.

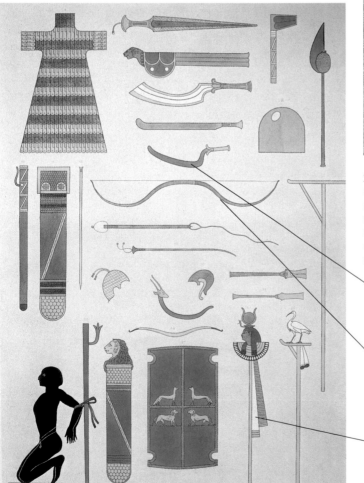

The Egyptian bow *was triangular in shape during the New Kingdom, and replaced the double bow, which was more difficult both to use and to manufacture.*

The khepesh *was a curved bronze sword used in the New Kingdom.*

The double-curved bow *was a potent weapon in the hands of the Nubians.*

Ensign holders *identified the various units of the army.*

An armourer *carves the wood for the bow with an adze.*

▼ Predynastic weapons

Copper was not used in the manufacture of weapons until Dynastic times (c. 3100 BC). The arrow points and knife and dagger blades, which were very sharp, were made of flint. The blades were secured to a handle made of wood or chased precious metal, as on this dagger.

◀ Bronze dagger
Used for hand-to-hand fighting, the earliest Egyptian daggers had flint or copper blades riveted to a decorative handle. Later, bronze daggers were cast as one piece and were consequently stronger.

▶ The quiver
Spare arrows were carried in quivers that were worn over the shoulders and held with a strap. This cylindrical model dates from the Middle Kingdom (2055–1650 BC). Quivers were later fixed to the sides of chariots to make the archer's task easier.

▶ The slicing axe
The earliest axes consisted of half-moon, copper blades set in a wooden shaft. The long blade was used in a slicing movement, rather than in the chopping motion of later battle-axes.

Arrow tips were cast in bronze for attachment to reed shafts.

▲ The armoury
During the New Kingdom, expeditions for trade and conquest to the Near East and the Sudan created a considerable demand for arms. The northern capital, Memphis, saw incredible growth in the number of armouries and arsenals under Rameses II (1279–1213 BC).

▶ The khepesh sword
In the Second Intermediate period (1650–1550 BC) and at the start of the New Kingdom, the Egyptians adopted certain weapons from their Asian neighbours. These included the curved sword known as the khepesh. The king was often seen wielding it in combat. Both the blade and handle of the khepesh were made entirely of bronze.

▲ The battle-axe
It is often hard to distinguish between the battle-axes wielded by soldiers and the tools used by carpenters. The earliest metal axes had a half-moon-shaped copper blade, but bronze blades, like the one above, appeared around 2000 BC.

Foreign influences

The New Kingdom marked an important turning point in the quality and efficiency of Egyptian weapons. During the Second Intermediate period (1650–1550 BC), Egypt was invaded by an Asian tribe, the Hyksos. They introduced the war chariot and spread the use of the horse. The Egyptian army adopted this new equipment and formed a special army corps, the 'chariot regiment', made up of chariot drivers and the fighters they carried.

By the New Kingdom, the Egyptian army had begun to adopt the superior weapons and equipment of their enemies – the Syrians and Hittites. The triangular bow, the helmet, chain-mail tunics and the khepesh sword became standard issue. Equally, the quality of the bronze improved as the Egyptians experimented with different proportions of tin and copper. Iron, however, although used by the Hittites, took a long time to appear in the Egyptian armoury. Later, foreign mercenaries also brought their their own arms and battle tactics.

INSIGHT

The war chariot

In the Second Intermediate period (1650–1550 BC), the Hyksos invaders from Palestine introduced the war chariot into Egypt, revolutionizing the art of warfare in the Near East. The chariot was mounted by two men – a driver and a soldier armed with bows, arrows and spears. It consisted of a wooden frame with wooden or leather walls. An axle was fixed at the back, supporting two wheels.

Two horses were harnessed to the shaft, at the end of which was a double yoke. The lightweight Egyptian chariot was swift and easy to handle, and in battle it could quickly cut through the enemy lines.

This relief, on the outside wall of the hypostyle hall at Karnak, depicts King Sety I (1294–1279 BC) triumphant after a campaign in Syria-Palestine. The horses pulling his chariot are magnificently armoured and adorned with plumes.

The pharaoh at war

The pharaoh was both Minister of War and Commander in Chief of the army, and often led his troops in battle. His was more than simply a practical role, however, as his presence represented the rule of Egypt and therefore order in the universe.

Since Early Dynastic times, the pharaoh has been depicted striking down the enemies of Egypt with a mace or battle-axe, as in this painted relief of Rameses II (1279–1213 BC) restoring harmony to the world created by the gods.

The Nubian prisoner is identified by his black skin.

The Asiatic soldier wears a pointed beard.

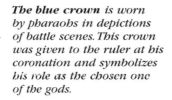

The blue crown is worn by pharaohs in depictions of battle scenes. This crown was given to the ruler at his coronation and symbolizes his role as the chosen one of the gods.

This battle-axe is typical of the axe's trapezoid shape during the New Kingdom.

◄ The shield
A wooden shield, covered with animal skin, was the chief defensive weapon of Egyptian soldiers. Chain-mail tunics, made of bronze 'scales', did not appear until the New Kingdom.

► Spears
Developed by hunters at the end of the Predynastic period (c. 5500–3100 BC), the spear underwent very few changes over the centuries. As with other weapons, however, the flint head was later replaced by copper, then by bronze.

▲ Expeditionary forces
The soldiers sent by Hatshepsut (1473–1458 BC) to the land of Punt (in southern Sudan) were armed with spears, shields and axes.

◄ Mercenaries
The Egyptian army supplemented its numbers by recruiting foreign mercenaries, who fought with their own weapons. Here, Nubians wear a protective leather net.

The Libyan is recognizable by his clothing.

Writing

According to their own writings, there was no better nor important job in Egypt than that of a scribe. Their importance is not surprising in a culture whose administrative structure seems to have been complex. Early in Egyptian history a number of government departments were established to manage the storage and supply of food, the labour force and building projects, finances, and legal matters, and there was a separate department of scribal administration. Many people wealthy enough to build themselves a substantial funerary monument held scribal titles, and the records recovered from the village occupied by the workers responsible for the tombs in the Valley of the Kings show that the scribe's role in this project was very important.

Useful evidence

Historians have reason to be grateful to the scribes. Their existence has in many cases given us an insight into the lives of people whom we can only speculate about from the archaeological record. For example, inscriptions in temples can tell us the function of various parts of these buildings. With all Egyptian written sources, however, one must exercise a degree of caution: we are using them for a purpose not envisaged by their authors. For example, monuments were not inscribed in order to record information but in order to achieve a purpose, which may have been to ensure that rituals would have a continued existence even if nobody was there to perform them, or to claim responsibility for constructing a particular part of a temple.

Written records
Illustrating the importance of writing in the study of ancient Egypt, these illustrations show (clockwise from far left) the Rosetta stone, hieroglyphs on a fragment of the sarcophagus of Djed-Thoth-ef-Ankh, and a statue of a scribe – a key member of Egyptian society.

The Rosetta Stone

During Napoleon Bonaparte's Egyptian campaign (1798–1801), one of his officers made a momentous discovery when he overturned a stone inscribed in three scripts, which provided the key to the deciphering of Ancient Egyptian hieroglyphs.

Napoleon's Egyptian expedition in 1798 was not merely a military one to cut off the Suez trade route to the Indies, the main source of British wealth. It also had a cultural and scientific purpose. Napoleon took with him mathematicians, economists, artists, architects, musicians and engineers to make a study of the country in every detail. In this, he was notably successful, although his military campaign was a disaster.

In British possession

Soon after landing in the country, the French fleet was destroyed by Nelson in the Battle of the Nile (1 August 1798). Three years later, the French army was defeated by the British near Alexandria and forced to hand over all the Ancient Egyptian antiquities its forces had gathered together. Among them was the Rosetta Stone, discovered in 1799 by François-Xavier Bouchard, who was an officer in Napoleon's engineering corps.

▼ Jean-François Champollion

In 1801, the French left Egypt with engravings of the Rosetta Stone. Using these copies, Jean-François Champollion (1790–1832) began to decipher the hieroglyphs in 1822. In 1828, as a member of a Franco-Tuscan expedition, he visited Egypt and Nubia in the company of his friend and fellow Egyptologist Ippolito Rosellini (1800–1843). In this painting of the pair in Egypt, Champollion is seated in the centre with Rosellini standing to his right.

DOCUMENT

A triscripted document

The Rosetta Stone is inscribed with a decree of 196 BC by the priests of Memphis bestowing special honours upon the pharaoh Ptolemy V Epiphanes (205–180 BC). It was for services rendered to the temples, including the reduction of taxes. The text has been reconstructed thanks to the discovery of copies of the same decree on other stelae of the same period. Written in three scripts – hieroglyphs, Demotic and Greek – the Rosetta Stone became the key to deciphering hieroglyphs.

Alphabetic signs used to write the royal name of Ptolemy in a cartouche were the first hieroglyphs identified by Champollion.

Greek text features the name of Ptolemy V, which Champollion compared with the hieroglyphs in the cartouche.

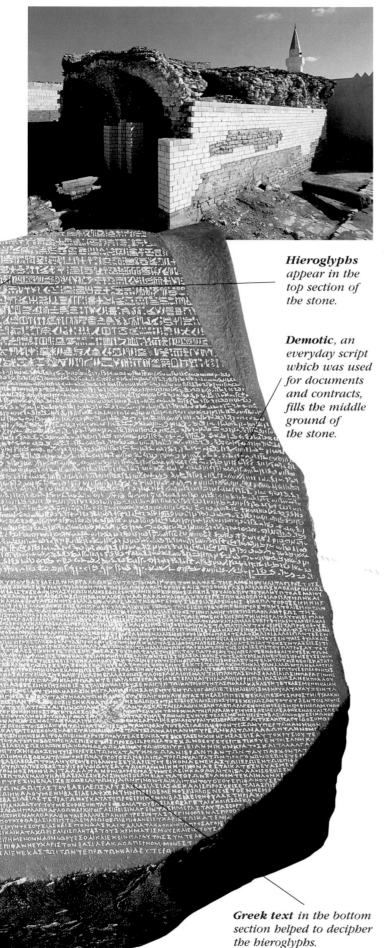

◄ The Rosetta fortress
Rashid, or Rosetta, a town on the Nile Delta close to Alexandria, is the site of a medieval fortress, which the French called Fort Julian. In 1799, French soldiers in the engineering corps received orders to strengthen the fortifications against a possible attack by Turkish and English troops. During the excavation work, Lieutenant François-Xavier Bouchard noticed the stone embedded in a wall. Aware of the importance of his discovery, Bouchard notified his superiors. The Rosetta Stone, one of the many antiquities seized by the British as spoils of war, is now in the British Museum in London.

► The key to understanding hieroglyphs
The Rosetta Stone is a slab of grey granitoid about 1.14m (3¾ft) high. Re-cut in Islamic times before being incorporated into the fortress wall, the stone was formerly in an open vault, surmounted by a winged disk depicting various gods.

Hieroglyphs appear in the top section of the stone.

Demotic, an everyday script which was used for documents and contracts, fills the middle ground of the stone.

Greek text in the bottom section helped to decipher the hieroglyphs.

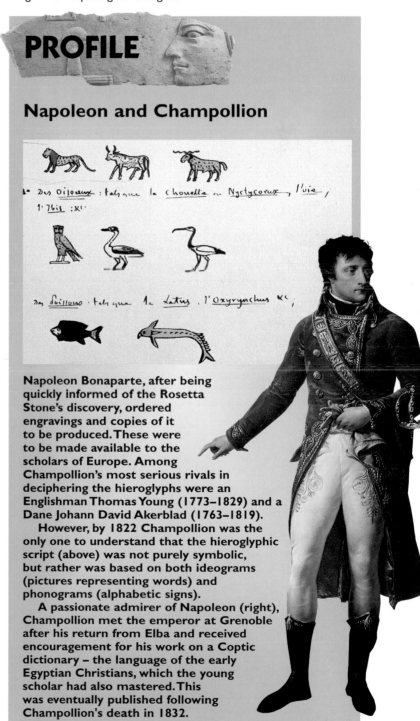

PROFILE

Napoleon and Champollion

Napoleon Bonaparte, after being quickly informed of the Rosetta Stone's discovery, ordered engravings and copies of it to be produced. These were to be made available to the scholars of Europe. Among Champollion's most serious rivals in deciphering the hieroglyphs were an Englishman Thomas Young (1773–1829) and a Dane Johann David Akerblad (1763–1819).

However, by 1822 Champollion was the only one to understand that the hieroglyphic script (above) was not purely symbolic, but rather was based on both ideograms (pictures representing words) and phonograms (alphabetic signs).

A passionate admirer of Napoleon (right), Champollion met the emperor at Grenoble after his return from Elba and received encouragement for his work on a Coptic dictionary – the language of the early Egyptian Christians, which the young scholar had also mastered. This was eventually published following Champollion's death in 1832.

Reading Hieroglyphs

Hieroglyphs on monuments and papyri combine both art and language, and are arranged in different ways. The direction in which they are read follows certain rules, although there are exceptions.

Ancient Egyptian hieroglyphs are found in texts from the beginning of pharaonic times, around 3000 BC. They were written in rows, which could be read from left to right or right to left, or were arranged in columns, which were read from top to bottom. To work out the direction in which a particular text is to be read, it is necessary to look at the animal or human figures, which always face to the right or the left. If the figure faces right, the hieroglyphs are read from right to left, and vice versa.

Exceptions to the rule

These rules were sometimes broken, however, because of the artistic nature of hieroglyphs and their religious and symbolic significance. When replicating texts that most people recognized – such as sacred texts or offerings formulae – a harmonious composition was deemed more important than the strict rules of orientation.

▲ **Writing in columns**
On the walls of temples and tombs, hieroglyphic script generally appears in columns. The example above, from the Ptolemaic period (332–30 BC), is read from right to left.

Orientation of other ancient scripts

When Egypt was conquered by the Greeks and Romans, the Egyptians adopted their languages, both of which are written from left to right (below right, in a Latin manuscript). Coptic, the language of the Christian period (c. AD 395–641), combined the Greek alphabet with six further signs taken from demotic (a cursive Egyptian script) and was also written from left to right. After the Islamic conquest in the seventh century, Arabic became the national language, and remains so today. Arabic (below centre, in an extract from the Koran) is read from right to left. A number of other modern writing systems, such as Chinese and Japanese, are orientated this way. The text below left is Chinese, arranged in columns and read from right to left.

The goose is shown facing right, meaning that this section of text is read from right to left.

The sun disc divides the inscription into two parts written in opposite directions.

The bee faces left, indicating that this part of the text is read from left to right.

◄ **Writing in lines**
Hieroglyphs were also written in horizontal lines, as on this pyramidion of Amenemhat III (1855–1808 BC) which is from his complex at Dahshur. This striking example illustrates the versatility of the hieroglyphic script, arranged here in two different directions.

▲ **Changing direction**
There are instances where hieroglyphs are orientated in the opposite direction to the one that the figure is facing. This is sometimes found where standardized inscriptions are used, such as in offerings formulae. In the example above, the hieroglyphs are read from right to left.

▲ **Horizontal rows**
On this relief, the hieroglyphs are written in horizontal rows. As all the figures face right, each of the six rows is read from right to left.

Two horizontal lines of hieroglyphs decorate the base of Amenemhat's pyramidion.

Hieroglyphs from Life

To create the signs for their writing, the Ancient Egyptians took their inspiration from the world around them. They transformed animals, plants, natural elements, household objects and buildings into hieroglyphs.

Around 2000 BC, there were some 700 hieroglyphs in 25 categories, as well as a group of unidentified signs. When forming the signs that comprised their writing system, the Ancient Egyptians rejected the use of abstraction, and took the many elements that became hieroglyphs from the world around them.

Elements from everyday life

The most complete sections are those devoted to people and to parts of the human body, but animals and birds form another important category. Other groups include tools used by peasants and craftsmen, weapons for hunting or warfare, boats, crowns, jewels and sceptres.

The objects of everyday life, such as furniture, tables or food, form other groups, as do the sky and the sun. Buildings were represented in plan and elevation and, as new forms and functions were created, a hieroglyph

▲ **The forearm**
This denotes the phonetic sign 'ain', which is conventionally pronounced 'a'.

▲ **The owl**
This depicts the phonogram 'm'.

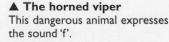

▲ **The horned viper**
This dangerous animal expresses the sound 'f'.

▲ **The sun**
The solar disc is shown as a circle with a dot in the centre. It is pronounced 'ra'.

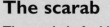

DOCUMENT

The scarab

The symbol of rebirth, the scarab, in the form of a dung beetle, is the hieroglyph used to denote the word 'kheper', meaning 'becoming or transforming oneself'. The dung beetle (*Scarabeus sacer*) rolls a ball – the shape of which is a reminder of the solar star – from which it takes its nourishment and in which it lays its eggs. When associated with the solar disc, the word kheper designates the transformations of Ra. The sun disappears at night as an old man into the underworld and is reborn on the horizon in the morning as a scarab.

◀ **The beetle pushes a ball of dung with its hind legs.**

◀ **The throne name of Thutmose III, Menkheperra, means 'Longevity is the manifestation of Ra'.**

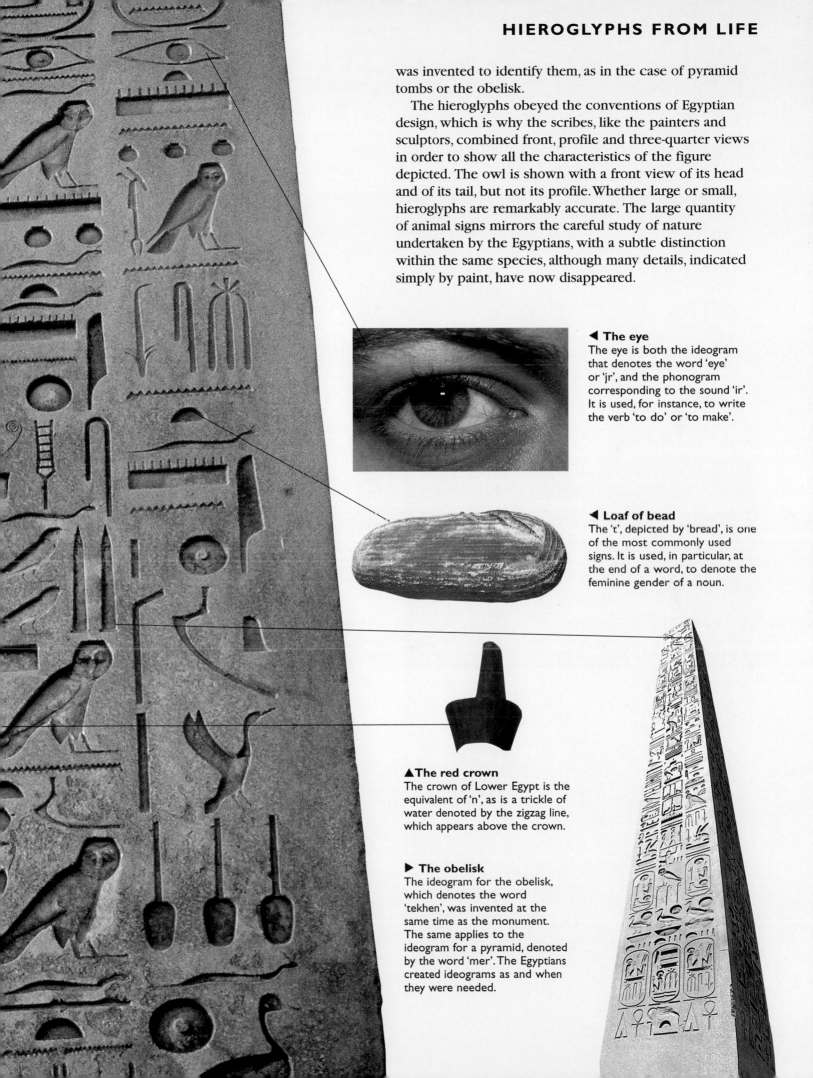

was invented to identify them, as in the case of pyramid tombs or the obelisk.

The hieroglyphs obeyed the conventions of Egyptian design, which is why the scribes, like the painters and sculptors, combined front, profile and three-quarter views in order to show all the characteristics of the figure depicted. The owl is shown with a front view of its head and of its tail, but not its profile. Whether large or small, hieroglyphs are remarkably accurate. The large quantity of animal signs mirrors the careful study of nature undertaken by the Egyptians, with a subtle distinction within the same species, although many details, indicated simply by paint, have now disappeared.

◀ The eye
The eye is both the ideogram that denotes the word 'eye' or 'jr', and the phonogram corresponding to the sound 'ir'. It is used, for instance, to write the verb 'to do' or 'to make'.

◀ Loaf of bead
The 't', depicted by 'bread', is one of the most commonly used signs. It is used, in particular, at the end of a word, to denote the feminine gender of a noun.

▲ The red crown
The crown of Lower Egypt is the equivalent of 'n', as is a trickle of water denoted by the zigzag line, which appears above the crown.

▶ The obelisk
The ideogram for the obelisk, which denotes the word 'tekhen', was invented at the same time as the monument. The same applies to the ideogram for a pyramid, denoted by the word 'mer'. The Egyptians created ideograms as and when they were needed.

Magical properties

Like all pictures, hieroglyphic designs were invested with magical powers. The Ancient Egyptians believed that words had the power to create – it was enough to pronounce the name of an object or being to give it tangible life.

Reading a carefully inscribed word on the walls of a temple, which was a sacred place, therefore became very dangerous, particularly if it was the name of a harmful god, such as Seth, the murderer of Osiris, or the serpent Apophis who, from the distant margins of the created world, threatened the sun each morning. To prevent these divine creatures from entering the human world, the signs representing them were often scored across or stabbed with many daggers.

Not all hieroglyphs have been deciphered: there are still some signs the meanings of which are not known.

▼ Sacred inscriptions
Hieroglyphs covered the walls of temples, recounting the deeds of the pharaohs and gods. Although the signs were drawn from life, their meaning was incomprehensible to many Ancient Egyptians.

Sacred writings

Hieroglyphs, as sacred signs, were used to 'decorate' certain sarcophagi. Apart from their decorative function, the hieroglyphs formed inscriptions that had the magical potency attributed to speech by the Ancient Egyptians.

'Hem', a biconsonantal phonogram, was linked to an everyday activity – the washing of clothes.

The hieroglyph of the stoneware jar with handle, when used as a phonogram, was pronounced 'khenem'.

The sign that depicted a wicker basket was associated with one of the pharaohs' titles. It was the biconsonantal phonogram 'nb'.

One of the parts of the human body, the mouth, indicated the consonantal phonogram 'r'.

◄ The sculptor's trial
Sculptors had to make several trial attempts to achieve precision in hieroglyphs, as many vary only in small details, as in the case of various species of bird.

▼ Animal reality
The many species of animal provided a great source of inspiration for the Egyptians when they invented hieroglyphs.

Among the birds represented, the quail had the phonetic value 'waw' and corresponded to the letter 'u'.

Certain sounds could be represented by various hieroglyphs. The 'm', for example, was depicted by an owl or by the rib of a gazelle.

A piece of folded cloth led to the invention of the sign indicating the letter 's', although the word from which it derives is not known.

The natural world was represented by hieroglyphs depicting a bundle of reeds, and was pronounced 'is'.

The various species of snake were minutely detailed, as in the case of the horned viper.

INSIGHT

The cross, then and now

Many hieroglyphic signs were already used in antiquity as jewels and amulets. The ankh was the symbol of life, and, as such, its use was widespread. However, it was important not only to the Ancient Egyptians, but was also adopted early on by the Coptic Christians of Egypt as their unique form of cross, called the *crux insata*. Today, many people still wear it round their necks as a protective amulet, and, in modern Egypt, many of the caretakers of monuments carry a key with the handle in the shape of the ankh (right).

Temple reliefs frequently included the ankh. This example (below) from Hatshepsut's temple at Deir el-Bahri shows the was sceptre, djed pillar and ankh sign on the basket hieroglyph.

◀ **The grouping of signs**
Some hieroglyphs could indicate a word, but generally it was the combination of various signs that formed a title or a proper name. This was the case with the sun disc, 'ra', and the goose, 'sa', which together formed the royal title 'son of Ra': sa-Ra.

◀ **The survival of inscriptions**
Hieroglyphs were used in inscriptions down to AD 535, when the emperor Justinian ordered the closing of the Temple of Isis at Philae. By then, however, the script had been in disuse for some time.

The Egyptian Alphabet

Egyptian hieroglyphic writing is a pictorial script with a huge number of characters: 24 of these stand for what we would recognize as letters; others stand for complete words or combinations of consonants.

The earliest known use of hieroglyphs, the Ancient Egyptian form of writing, dates from around 3200 BC; the last inscription was in AD 394. For much of this time, the Egyptians relied on around 1,000 signs, although this increased sixfold in the Ptolemaic (332–30 BC) and Roman (30 BC–AD 395) periods.

The first step towards transforming Egyptian from a spoken to a written language was to use stylized word pictures – known as logograms – to represent objects or ideas. The word 'mouth', for example, was represented by a picture of two parted lips, while a wavy line was used to represent the word for water.

Pictures into sound

While this was fine for most common nouns and some verbs, there were real problems in representing such abstract concepts as 'luck', 'health' or 'life', or actions such as 'think' or 'do'. The solution was to adapt certain logograms to represent sounds, rather than things, so that

| f | p | r | $ḥ$ | t |

these 'difficult' words could be spelled out phonetically. These 'sound signs', or phonograms, made up a sort of alphabet, although there are many more signs in Ancient Egyptian than in modern alphabets.

The Ancient Egyptian language was written entirely without any signs representing vowels. In this way, the language resembles Hebrew and Arabic, both of which are written as true consonant scripts. One sign suffices for all words with the same sequence of consonants, even words with quite different meanings, although we can assume they were actually pronounced differently.

| r^c | $s3$ | $sἰw$ | mn | mr |

Although we can never be sure exactly how Ancient Egyptian sounded, we can get an approximate idea by studying Coptic, the language that grew out of it. Coptic,

▶ **Expressions of immortality**
Hieroglyphic inscriptions on temple walls, graves and other monuments were both decorative and sacred, always destined 'for eternity'. Parts of the text of the *Book of the Dead*, for example, were inscribed on sarcophagi.

This illustration shows a fragment of the sarcophagus of Djed-Thoth-ef-Ankh, preserved in the Egyptian Museum in Turin, with a selection of the hieroglyphs explained. Here the text runs up and down in columns, while in other cases hieroglyphs were written on horizontal lines, usually, but not always, from right to left.

This phonetic sign represents the consonant m

This sign is a determinative, meaning to 'go forwards'

This sign represents the consonant n

This phonogram represents two consonants, written as d̠3

The hieroglyph for 'man' is used here as a determinative

A two-consonant phonogram, written as i3bt

The hieroglyph of an ostrich feather representing the sound š, used in this case to write the name of Shu, the god of air and sunlight

A phonogram of two consonants, written as ir

Another phonogram with two consonants, written as hr

A phonogram with three consonants, written as ntr

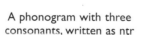

This phonogram of two consonants is written as k3

The logogram for 'papyrus roll' is used as a determinative for abstract concepts and states

This two-consonant phonogram of a hare is written wn

which is written in the Greek alphabet and some signs from demotic (the everyday script that was used from about 600 BC), and used vowels, is the closest connection we have to the long-dead language of Ancient Egypt.

New meanings

Phonograms were taken from the existing supply of logograms. The chosen ones lost their distinctive pictorial

bit   'nh   nfr   chc   hpr

meaning, but gained a new value as a sound. There were 24 signs for single consonants in the hieroglyphic alphabet. Each came from a logogram for a word pronounced in the Ancient Egyptian language with that consonant. The sign for 'mouth', for example, stood for the sound 'r', and that for 'water' for the sound 'n'. The Ancient Egyptian alphabet also contained about 100 phonograms representing two consonant sounds, such as 'pr' or 'mn', and around 50 more representing a series of three consonants, such as 'nfr' or 'bit'. In order to vocalize these multi-consonant signs, Egyptologists put an 'e' between each one; 'nfr' is pronounced 'nefer'. Some of these consonants do not exist in English and cannot be directly transcribed into the our Roman alphabet. Additional points and strokes, known as diacritical signs, are used to express many of them.

Determinatives

A third category of sign found in hieroglyphic writing is the 'determinative'. These characters – which, like phonograms, were based on logograms – were put at

child   eat/think   god   Uraeus/goddess   town

the end of words written in phonograms to differentiate words that would otherwise look exactly the same. A word for a person, for example, would be followed by the sign for a man or a woman, while a verb of movement would be accompanied by a pair of running legs. As any group of consonants can represent several different words, making sense of an inscription depends both on context and the correct interpretation of determinatives.

Determinatives also help comprehension in another way. As they invariably appeared at the end of words (as hieroglyphs generally read from right to left, this means on the left), they served to separate words from one another. Otherwise, Ancient Egyptian completely lacks word spacing and indeed any sort of punctuation.

WRITING

THE ALPHABET

SIGN	WRITTEN	SPOKEN	PICTURE MEANING
	3	a	vulture
	ỉ	i or y	reed
	ʿ	a	forearm
	w	w or u	quail chick
	b	b	foot
	p	p	stool
	f	f	horned viper
	m	m	owl
	n	n	water
	r	r	mouth
	ḥ	ḥ	courtyard
	ḥ	ḥ	rope
	ḫ	kh	placenta
	ẖ	kh	the belly and tail of an animal
	s	s	bolt (for a door)
	ś	s	folded cloth
	š	sh	pond
	ḳ	k	hill slope
	k	k	basket
	g	g	stand (for a vessel)
	t	t	loaf
	ṯ	tj	tethering rope
	d	d	hand
	ḏ	dj	cobra

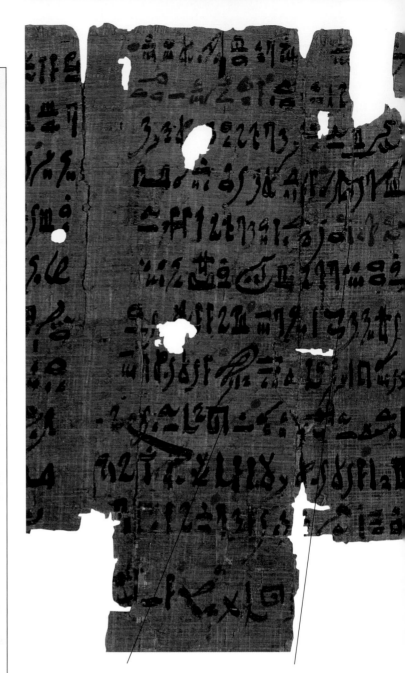

This single consonant sign has the value ḥ.

Characters in red indicate the start of a new section.

While hieroglyphs were mainly used for inscribing religious texts, especially tombs, the scribes adopted the hieratic script for more everyday purposes. This flowing script, based on the hieroglyphs, was used in business and administration from around 2700 BC.

Holy and eternal

It may seem remarkable that such a complex, unwieldy system should survive for so long. This may be because the long years of study required to master it contributed to the privileged, élite position of the scribes, or because hieroglyphs were seen as a gift from the gods; to alter or abandon them was seen as an act of sacrilege.

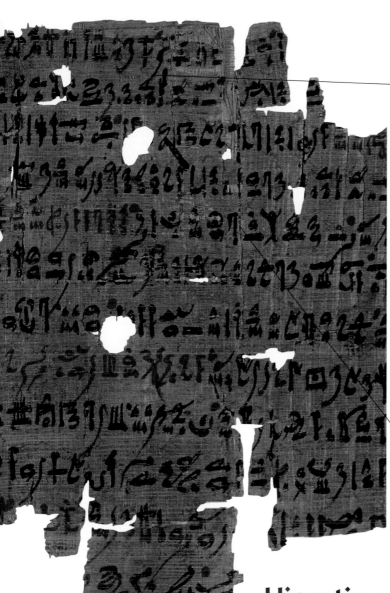

◀ **Everyday writing**
The simplified form of writing, known as hieratic script, was developed for practical, everyday use. The majority of the papyrus texts that have come down to us are in hieratic script.

Until the Middle Kingdom (2055–1650 BC), it was written in columns. After this period, the script was generally laid out in horizontal lines from right to left, as here.

This character for š is more or less identical to the hieroglyph.

Hieratic script

This pictorial script was used to record business transactions and could be written more rapidly than the cumbersome hieroglyphs.

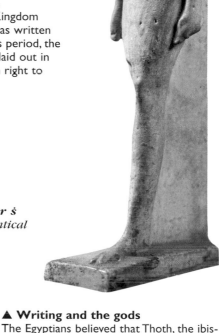

▲ **Writing and the gods**
The Egyptians believed that Thoth, the ibis-headed god of wisdom, and the goddess Seshat gave them the hieroglyphic system. Many of the phonetic characters have magical or symbolic meaning, in addition to their literal one, and were used for amulets, for example; this dual function is preserved in the word 'hieroglyph', which comes from the Greek, and means 'sacred carving'.

DOCUMENT

The cartouche

While Ancient Egyptian writing generally lacks punctuation, there is one convention that was of great use to early translators, such as François Chabas (1817–1882, right). This was the habit, from the Fourth Dynasty (2613–2494 BC) onwards, of enclosing the birth names and throne names of pharaohs in an oval shape that represented a loop of rope. When Napoleon mounted his expedition into Egypt in the early years of the nineteenth century, his soldiers dubbed the device a cartouche, or cartridge, because of its bullet shape.

With the phonograms for the royal names written in a cartouche – the one at near right is for Tutankhamun – the process of deciphering and reading hieroglyphs was greatly speeded up.

Hieratic Script

Several different scripts developed from Egyptian hieroglyphs. One of the most important, called 'hieratic' by the Greeks, was the everyday writing in Egypt for nearly 2,000 years.

Hieroglyphs, the most famous and earliest type of Egyptian writing, were well suited to monumental inscriptions, but not to everyday use. Hieratic writing, which developed from them, is a script. Its more rounded outline made for quicker, more flowing writing.

Simplified signs

The hieratic signs that appeared around the end of the Early Dynastic period (*c.* 2686 BC) were simplifications of hieroglyphs. Although the original hieroglyphs can still be identified, the hieratic shapes are less precise and complex, and can be joined together, unlike hieroglyphs, which always have a space between them. The difference between hieratic script and hieroglyphs is similar to that between handwriting and printed capital letters. Hieratic remained the Egyptians' everyday script until it was replaced by demotic in the seventh century BC.

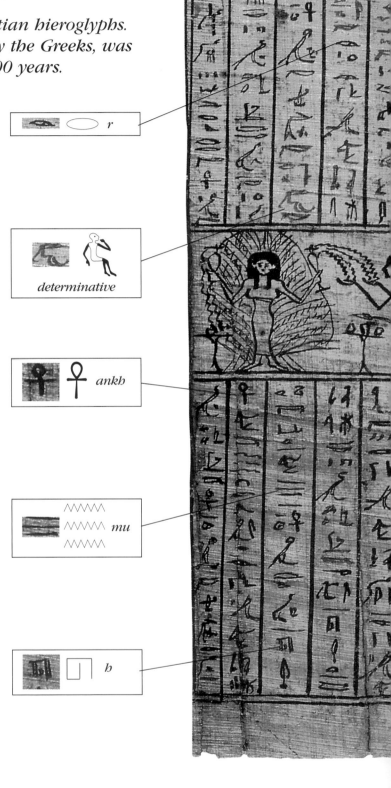

r

determinative

ankh

mu

h

◀ **Remarkable longevity**
Hieroglyphs were used throughout pharaonic history. For much of this time, the number of symbols used was relatively small, but in the Ptolemaic and Roman periods it grew from 700 or so to around 6,000. This form of writing became extinct only with the closure of the Egyptian temples by the Romans in the fourth century AD.

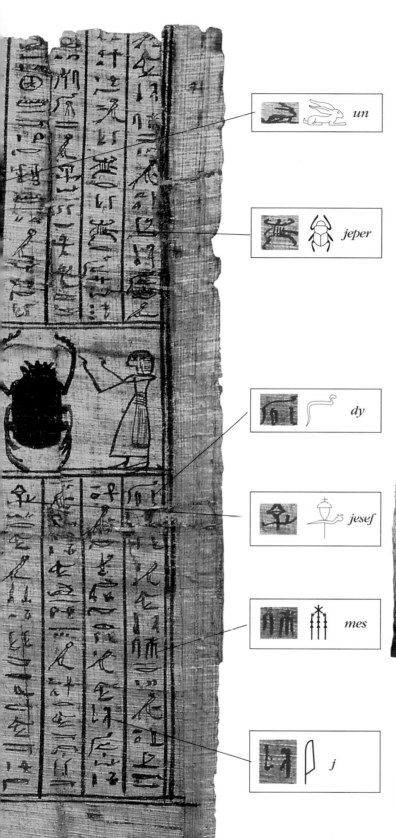

		un
		jeper
		dy
		jesef
		mes
		j

▲ Hieratic script in religious texts

Although hieratic was used at first mainly for secular literary and administrative purposes, it became the main choice for religious texts after Alexander the Great conquered Egypt in 332 BC and ushered in 300 years of Greek rule. This example is from the *Book of the Dead*.

▶ Hieratic script on papyrus

Writing hieratic script on papyrus was much easier than using hieroglyphs, as the scribes' brush strokes could flow across the surface. Scribes preferred to use it for all those administrative tasks that required speed.

◀ Taking notes

Ostraca – pieces of limestone or shards of broken clay pots – were used rather than the more expensive papyrus to make notes or in the teaching of writing. Hieratic script was usually employed when writing on ostraca.

▼ A letter to the dead

This bowl from the First Intermediate period (2181–2055 BC) bears a message in a form of hieratic script from a mother to her dead son, and was found in his tomb. It asks his help in protecting the family from its enemies. This rare object is now in the Louvre in Paris.

From the beginning, hieratic was a completely phonetic script, with each sign representing a sound rather than a word or idea. It was always written from right to left. Before the Eleventh Dynasty (2055-1985 BC), the symbols were usually arranged in columns; after that date, they were written in horizontal lines.

Scribes often developed individual styles of writing, but in the Middle Kingdom (2055-1650 BC), two noticeably different types of hieratic script evolved. In literary texts, the signs were precisely written and more attractive to look at, while 'abnormal hieratic', used in administrative and economic documents and texts, employed more flowing and schematic signs for speed of writing. During the New Kingdom (1550-1069 BC), the signs were further rounded and simplified, becoming more and more 'polished'.

The beginning of demotic

An even simpler and more cursive script, called demotic by the Greeks and 'sekh shat' (writing for documents) by the Egyptians, developed out of abnormal hieratic. In the Twenty-Sixth Dynasty (664-525 BC), it replaced hieratic, except in sacred or funerary texts, which were still written in the 'literary' style. Hieratic was used for this purpose well into the Ptolemaic period (332-30 BC), and the Greeks, unaware of its mainly secular history, gave the script the name 'hieratic' (priestly), to distinguish it from demotic writing.

Hieroglyph	Hieratic	Transcription	Hieroglyph	Hieratic	Transcription	Hieroglyph	Hieratic	Transcription
		a			p			s
		j			f			sch
		jj / y			m			q
		a			n			k
		u, w			r			g
		b			h			t
					ḥ			ṯ, t
					ḫ			d
					ẖ			ḏ

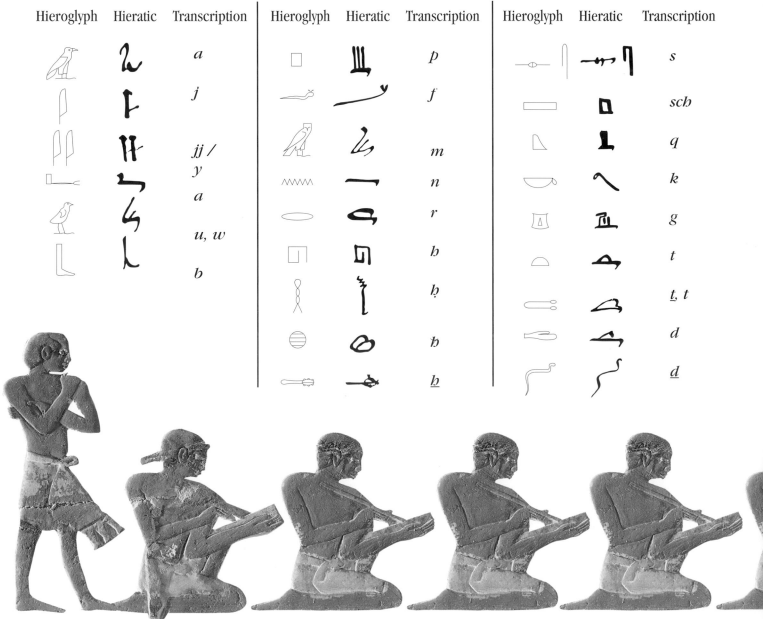

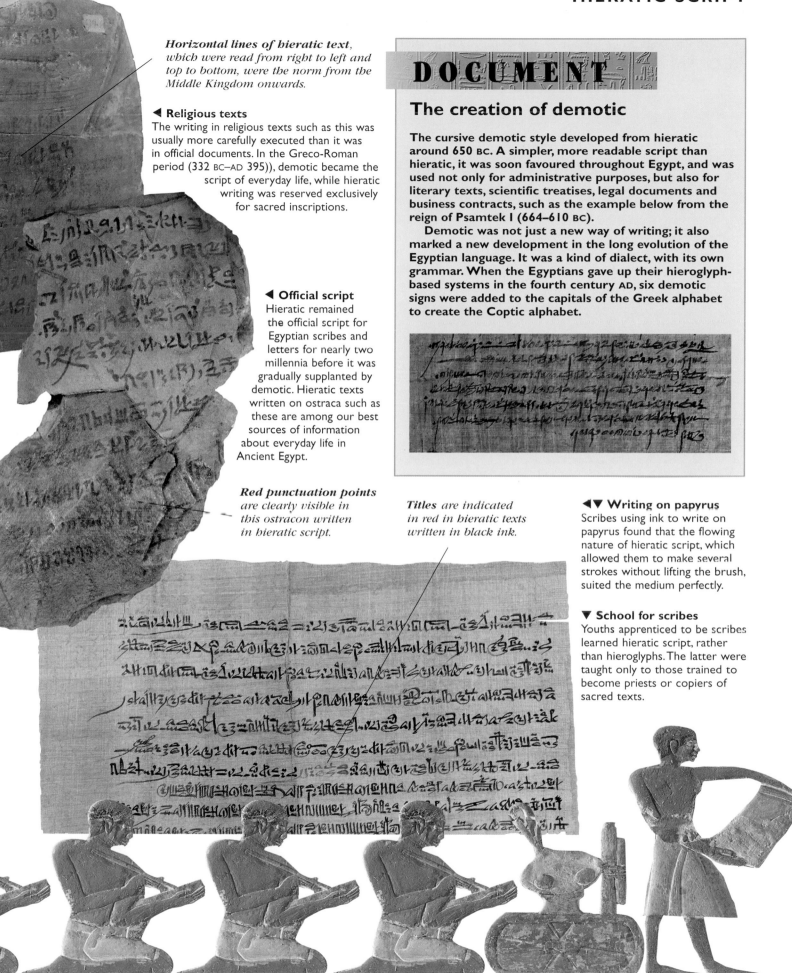

Horizontal lines of hieratic text, which were read from right to left and top to bottom, were the norm from the Middle Kingdom onwards.

◀ Religious texts

The writing in religious texts such as this was usually more carefully executed than it was in official documents. In the Greco-Roman period (332 BC–AD 395)), demotic became the script of everyday life, while hieratic writing was reserved exclusively for sacred inscriptions.

◀ Official script

Hieratic remained the official script for Egyptian scribes and letters for nearly two millennia before it was gradually supplanted by demotic. Hieratic texts written on ostraca such as these are among our best sources of information about everyday life in Ancient Egypt.

Red punctuation points are clearly visible in this ostracon written in hieratic script.

Titles are indicated in red in hieratic texts written in black ink.

DOCUMENT

The creation of demotic

The cursive demotic style developed from hieratic around 650 BC. A simpler, more readable script than hieratic, it was soon favoured throughout Egypt, and was used not only for administrative purposes, but also for literary texts, scientific treatises, legal documents and business contracts, such as the example below from the reign of Psamtek I (664–610 BC).

Demotic was not just a new way of writing; it also marked a new development in the long evolution of the Egyptian language. It was a kind of dialect, with its own grammar. When the Egyptians gave up their hieroglyph-based systems in the fourth century AD, six demotic signs were added to the capitals of the Greek alphabet to create the Coptic alphabet.

◀▼ Writing on papyrus

Scribes using ink to write on papyrus found that the flowing nature of hieratic script, which allowed them to make several strokes without lifting the brush, suited the medium perfectly.

▼ School for scribes

Youths apprenticed to be scribes learned hieratic script, rather than hieroglyphs. The latter were taught only to those trained to become priests or copiers of sacred texts.

Coptic, the Script of the Christians

Coptic was used in Egypt between the end of the Roman period (c. AD 395) and the Arab conquest (c. AD 641), and still survives in the religious services of the country's Christians.

The Egyptian language underwent a great deal of change in its 4,000-year history. For most of the pharaonic era, hieroglyphs were used, with hieratic as their cursive form. By the Twenty-Sixth Dynasty (664–525 BC), demotic replaced hieratic in commercial and bureaucratic documents, and by the Ptolemaic period (332–30 BC) it appeared on stelae such as the Rosetta Stone. Finally, during Egypt's Christian phase, Coptic script developed.

A Greek and Egyptian script

Christianity in Egypt emerged in the form of monastic communities, often in desert regions, and this characteristic gave rise to a need for written communication – for example, translating the Bible and conducting business affairs. Hieroglyphs could not be used as they were symbols of paganism, based on the same principles that had been employed to represent the old heathen gods and goddesses. The new church, therefore, adopted the Greek alphabet, with the addition of six letters derived from demotic to allow the transcription of intrinsically Egyptian sounds, and thus created the Coptic script.

▼ **The end of paganism**
The advent of Christianity meant the death of the Ancient Egyptian pantheon. In AD 535, the Byzantine emperor Justinian I sent soldiers to the temple of Isis at Philae, the last refuge of the old religion, to convert it into a Christian church.

▲ The monastery of St Anthony
Although Islam is the state religion, there are still Coptic communities in Egypt. The Monastery of St Anthony is one of the oldest in the country, and the monks here observe rituals that have remained largely unchanged for 16 centuries.

◄ A funerary stele
The distinctive Coptic cross dominates the surface of this funerary stele. Above it, a short inscription reads 'no one in the world is immortal'.

▼ Coptic dialects
Coptic was not a single, unified language, but was made up of at least six dialects. The most common form was Sahidic, which originated in Upper Egypt.

The jackal-headed god Anubis leads the deceased to Osiris, the god of the underworld.

A short inscription in Coptic lists the name of the deceased and the date of his death.

◄ The survival of ancient beliefs
At the beginning of the Coptic period (c. AD 395–AD 641), before most of the ancient temples had been closed by Theodosius the Great (AD 379–395), new Christian beliefs existed alongside the old religion of Egypt. This stele shows the gods Anubis and Osiris greeting the deceased in the underworld, yet features an inscription in the Christian language of Coptic.

THE COPTIC ALPHABET

LETTER	NAME	PHONETIC VALUE	LETTER	NAME	PHONETIC VALUE	LETTER	NAME	PHONETIC VALUE
Ⲁ	alpha	*a*	ⲗ	lambda	*l*	Ⲯ	phi	*ph*
Ⲃ	beta	*b*	ⲙ	mu	*m*	Ⲭ	chi	*ch*
Ⲅ	gamma	*g*	ⲛ	nu	*n*	Ⲯ	psi	*ps*
Ⲇ	delta		Ⳅ	xi	*ks, x*	ⲱ	omega	*o*
Ⲉ	epsilon	*e*	ⲟ	omicron	*o*	ⲱ	shaj	*sch*
Ⲍ	zeta	*z*	Ⲡ	pi	*p*	Ⳅ	faj	*f*
Ⲏ	eta	*e*	Ⲣ	rho	*r*	ⳍ	hori	*h, ch*
Ⲑ	theta	*th*	Ⲥ	samma	*s*	Ⳉ	dshandsha	*tsch*
Ⲓ	iota	*i, j*	Ⲧ	tau	*t*	Ⳓ	shima	*c, kj*
Ⲕ	kappa	*k*	Ⲩ	upsilon	*u, w, y*	ⲧ	dij	*ti*

Peacocks, Christian symbols of eternal life, appear at the top of the stele.

A depiction of a Christian chapel dominates the stele's surface.

▶ **The stele of Sabek**
This richly decorated funerary stele from Upper Egypt provides an example of the type of abstract design that was a feature of Coptic art. Beneath the image of a chapel, framed by peacocks and interlaced patterns, is an inscription which gives the name of the deceased and the date of his death, as well as a short prayer.

◀ **Information about the deceased**
The inscriptions on Coptic funerary stele are characteristically very short. On this stele from the eighth century AD, just the name of the deceased appears, above a stylized depiction of a building.

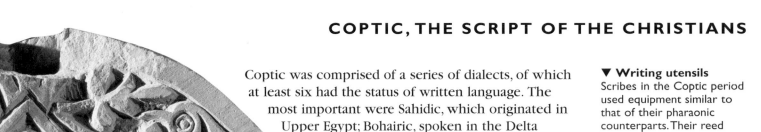

Coptic was comprised of a series of dialects, of which at least six had the status of written language. The most important were Sahidic, which originated in Upper Egypt; Bohairic, spoken in the Delta region; and Fayyumic, the version found in the Fayum and its environs. Of these, it was Sahidic that developed into the standard form of the language.

Coptic in Christian services

The Arab conquest of Egypt in the seventh century AD signalled the demise of the Coptic language. The Christian script was pushed aside in favour of Arabic, the tongue of the new Islamic rulers. By the seventeenth century, Coptic had ceased to be spoken even in the most remote villages of Upper Egypt.

However, as late as 1936, the Coptic specialist Werner Vycichl found people living near Luxor who claimed to speak the language within the family. It also still exists in certain parts of the Coptic Christian service, although much of this has been translated into Arabic. Furthermore, Jean-François Champollion's knowledge of Coptic was a key factor in enabling him to decipher the hieroglyphs of the Rosetta Stone and unlock the mysteries of the ancient language of the pharaohs.

A short prayer has been inscribed, as well as the deceased's name and the date of his death.

▼ Writing utensils
Scribes in the Coptic period used equipment similar to that of their pharaonic counterparts. Their reed pens and inkwells were kept in leather cases such as this one, which bears an image of St George.

◀ The monasteries
Christianity in Egypt began life in the form of monastic communities established in the wilderness of the country's desert landscape. Monasteries such as St Anthony's and St Paul's were founded by early Christians who had fled from religious persecution at the hands of the Roman rulers. The monks were instrumental in the development of the Coptic script – a means of written communication without the taint of paganism inherent in hieroglyphs.

Writing Materials

In Ancient Egypt, scribes recorded harvests, taxes and salaries, and transcribed sacred and secular texts. They were identified with the tools of their trade, which went with them to their tombs and were shown in reliefs and paintings.

Scribes carried the tools of their trade wherever they went – in the countryside, the granaries and even on the field of battle, where it was their duty, once the fighting was over, to count the number of enemy dead. The scribe's brushes, palette, pigments, papyri and other writing materials were stored in a box of wicker or wood – sometimes used as a writing support – or in a leather container for ease of transport.

The scribe's palette was a rectangular piece of wood (sometimes stone) some 30 x 6cm (12 x 2½in), with a central groove or slot to hold reed pens or brushes, and a couple of circular wells in one end. One was to hold red pigment, obtained from red ochre, and was used for headings and highlighting important words. The other was for a black pigment, based on charcoal or lamp black, in which the main text was written.

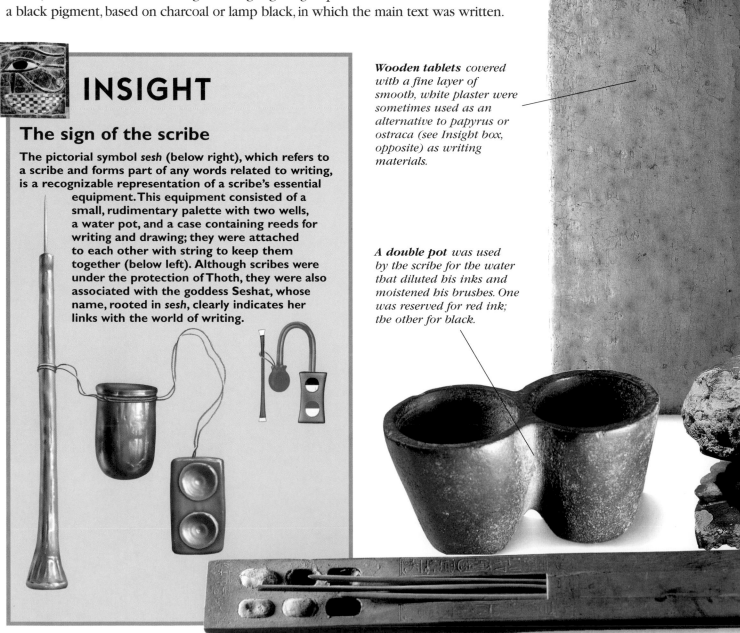

INSIGHT

The sign of the scribe

The pictorial symbol *sesh* (below right), which refers to a scribe and forms part of any words related to writing, is a recognizable representation of a scribe's essential equipment. This equipment consisted of a small, rudimentary palette with two wells, a water pot, and a case containing reeds for writing and drawing; they were attached to each other with string to keep them together (below left). Although scribes were under the protection of Thoth, they were also associated with the goddess Seshat, whose name, rooted in *sesh*, clearly indicates her links with the world of writing.

Wooden tablets covered with a fine layer of smooth, white plaster were sometimes used as an alternative to papyrus or ostraca (see Insight box, opposite) as writing materials.

A double pot was used by the scribe for the water that diluted his inks and moistened his brushes. One was reserved for red ink; the other for black.

The painters who created vignettes to decorate papyri, such as those in the *Book of the Dead*, required a wider range of colours, and had palettes with extra wells for blue, yellow, white or green pigment. Before beginning work, a scribe had to prepare his inks. Pigments were supplied in the form of bars or round 'cakes', from which a piece was broken off and reduced to powder using a stone crusher and mortar. The scribe then put a little pigment on to a wetted brush and mixed it with water on the palette to obtain the required consistency.

INSIGHT

Signed and sealed

The Egyptians who knew how to read and write – basically, the scribes or civil servants and various royal dignitaries (all of them men) – exchanged a great deal of correspondence. Clay tablets or ostraca (pieces of polished pottery or limestone) were often used for brief notes and functional letters, but more important communications were written on sheets of papyrus rolled or folded to form a letter, complete with the names of the sender and the addressee.

The letters were secured with personal seals pressed into a small piece of fresh clay. These seals were also attached to legal deeds, as a means of proving their authenticity. Hieroglyphs identifying the owner of a personal seal were cut into the seal's surface in order to leave a pattern in relief in the clay.

The seals took various forms. They were often found on the back of a scarab or set into a ring like a precious stone. Others were in a custom-made triangular form, with a hole for the finger (below). The cylinder seal, which was widespread in Mesopotamia at the time, was found less frequently in Egypt.

Royal seals were often made of precious metals, gold or silver, but the most usual and functional material was glazed earthenware, as in the seal below.

◀ **Scribe statues**
From the time of the Old Kingdom (2686–2181 BC), princes and other dignitaries commissioned statues that showed them sitting cross-legged in a posture associated with scribes, with a papyrus unrolled across their knees. Some are shown reading, as here, and some writing. The purpose of such statues was to imply that their subjects were scholars.

Natural pigments came in cakes that were first powdered, then mixed with water.

Small pigment pots stored the crushed materials ready for dilution and use.

This palette has six pigment wells and a slot to take the scribe's reed pens.

A flat mortar and a crusher were used to pulverize the pigments.

The writing material used by a scribe depended on the job he was doing. For notes that were not to be kept or for rough drafts, scribes used an ostracon, a piece of limestone or a fragment of pottery polished up for the purpose, or incised a text in wet clay. Children and apprentice scribes normally practised on wooden tablets covered with a layer of plaster.

Using papyrus

Generally, papyrus was reserved for administrative texts, religious books, letters and literary or scholarly works. It was costly to make and a far more valuable material than paper is today; unneeded texts were often erased so that the sheets could be re-used. Scribes used special tools to prepare papyrus. A wooden smoothing tool or polishing stone was rubbed over the sheets to ensure an even writing surface, while a bronze blade was used to cut pieces off the precious papyrus if it was to be used for a letter or inscription of only a few lines.

▼ **Domestic details**
The scribes of Deir-el-Medina, the village of the workers who built the tombs in the Valley of the Kings, left thousands of ostraca on which they noted trivial details of everyday life. These included reasons for the absence of workers, ration accounts and questions to the oracles. Today these texts are an invaluable insight into the lives and concerns of ordinary Egyptians.

Scribes at work

In Ancient Egypt, scribes found employment in just about every sector of the economy, including agriculture, crafts, trade, mining, building and quarrying. They were also an important part of life in the temples, where they were involved with copying and creating religious texts, and in the army, where they listed the conscripts, for instance. The model below comes from the tomb of Meketra, who lived under the pharaoh Mentuhotep III (2004–1992 BC), and shows scribes noting down the number of cattle raised by various farmers.

Papyrus rolls were used for the important business of the cattle census.

A supervisor oversees the scribes' work from a nearby seat under the colonnade.

The cross-legged position was not used by all scribes. This man has one knee raised and one leg folded beneath him.

The scribes' palettes, containing wells for red and black ink, have been carefully placed on the boxes in front of them.

▼ Storing papyri
Records written on papyri were protected from decay by keeping them in boxes or sealed vases. This jar successfully preserved documents in demotic Egyptian and Greek from the second century BC until today.

▶ Rough sketches
Writing materials were not just for documents. An artist has used this papyrus to sketch birds and animals. The grid of red ink over the drawings suggests they were intended to be copied onto another medium, such as a wall.

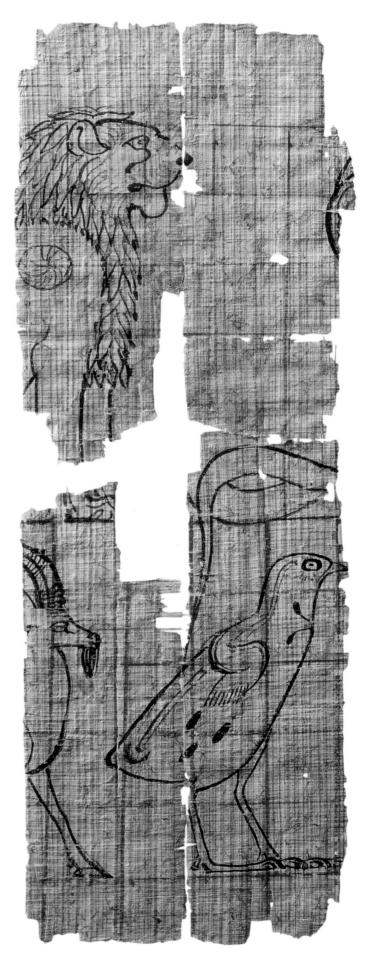

Making Papyrus

Paper is an Egyptian invention. While most modern paper is made from tree pulp, Egypt's writing materials were made from a reedy plant that grew abundantly in the swampy areas of the Nile Valley. The finished product was exported to the Middle East and Greece.

Great thickets of papyrus grew in the swamps and marshes of the Nile Valley, particularly in those of the Delta, from prehistory to throughout the time of the pharaohs. It was the heraldic plant of Lower Egypt, and is often depicted with the lotus, the heraldic plant of Upper Egypt, as a symbol of the unification of the country. The densely packed, reedy expanses provided a habitat for many species of birds and animals. Several tomb murals and reliefs show the teeming life among the papyrus as part of hunting and fishing scenes.

A versatile plant

The ancient Egyptians saw this reed – which grew so abundantly out of the life-giving mud of the Nile – as a symbol of youth and joy, but also found many practical uses for it. The lower part of the plant could be eaten as a vegetable, while the fibrous inner bark, or bast, was used to make rope, baskets and sandals, or was woven into a coarse cloth used for sails and the loincloths of the poor.

A genet – a small, cat-like carnivore – is hunting birds in the papyrus thickets.

This owl is protecting its young from an attack by potential predators.

▶ The scribes

From the time of the first pharaohs, rolls of papyrus were used by professional writers called scribes. They used reed brushes and red and black inks to write their texts in hieratic script, derived from hieroglyphics. In a land where few people were literate, scribes were the officials and administrators, members of the élite, and the profession was often passed from father to son.

Seated on the floor with his legs tucked beneath him, the scribe held the papyrus roll on his knees and rolled it to the right. His loincloth served as a pad as he wrote from right to left in single columns.

▼ The banks of the Nile
The tangled undergrowth of the muddy banks and swamps surrounding the Nile teemed with wildlife. It provided food and shelter for migratory birds, as well as native species, and the abundant birdlife in turn attracted other animals. Egyptian tomb paintings often return to the themes of hunting and fishing in the papyrus thickets. Pictures such as this appear in even the earliest tombs of the Ancient Kingdom, known as mastabas.

◄ The papyrus plant
The papyrus (*Cyperus papyrus*), which is a member of the reed-grass family, has stems that are triangular in section and grow up to 3m (10ft) tall. It was once common in the wetlands of the Nile, but the draining of the swamps and overcultivation in the past mean that, today, extensive areas of papyrus are found growing wild only in its upper reaches in Ethiopia and Sudan. Small areas are also cultivated in Egypt to make replica documents for tourists.

Brightly coloured butterflies represent the teeming insect life thriving in the papyrus.

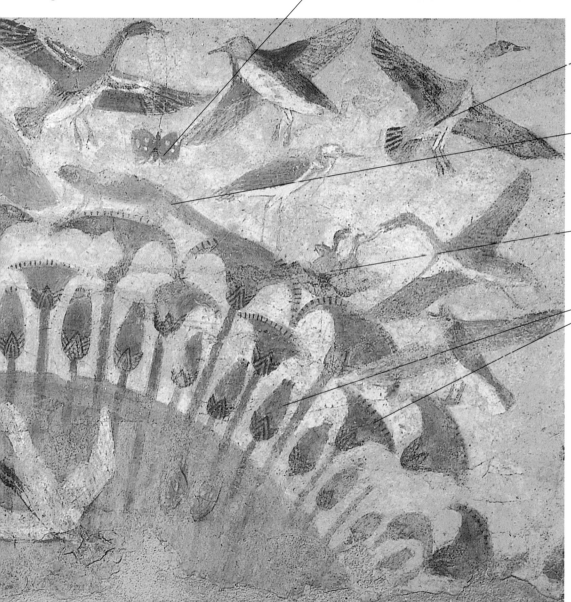

*A **wild duck** takes flight from the papyrus reeds.*

***An ichneumon**, an African relative of the mongoose, creeps through the reed bed seeking its prey – small birds and eggs, as well as snakes.*

***Several birds** make their nests in the reed beds between the papyrus heads.*

***The leafy heads** of the papyri are shown at various stages in their growth cycle.*

▼ Stylized decoration
Stylized versions of the papyrus were often used as decorative motifs. The umbrella-shaped head of the plant (insignificant flowers rise from the centre of each rosette of leaves) changes shape as it grows. Open papyri and closed buds alike are shown in reliefs, paintings, amulets and jewellery, as well as in the capitals of stone columns, clustered together in long rows in imitation of the Nile's reed beds.

DOCUMENT

Making a papyrus roll

Making a roll of papyrus was a complex business involving a good deal of skilled labour. Papyrus was used primarily for important documents because of the costs of production. Scribes also wrote on leather sheets, on wood covered with plaster and – most inexpensive of all – on chips of limestone or broken pottery.

1. First, the stem was cut into pieces of roughly the same length, and the outer layers were peeled away. The inner pith was then cut lengthways into strips.

2. Two layers of strips went into each sheet of papyrus. Several strips were laid alongside each other, then another layer was laid at right angles to this. The two layers were not interwoven.

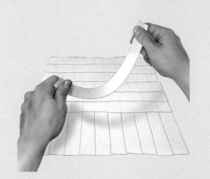

3. Both layers were moistened, then firmly beaten together, breaking down the fibres and gluing the layers together in a single sheet with a felt texture. This was left for several days, under weights, to dry out.

4. The final step was to use a flat stone to polish the sheets to a smooth writing surface, then to trim their edges. The finished sheets were glued together to make a roll ready for use.

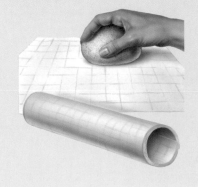

The papyrus harvest

Fully grown papyrus plants were sought out by the harvesters.

Bundles of the stalks could be tied together to make lightweight boats or rafts. These were useful for hunting in the shallow waters, but did not last long, as the stems became waterlogged.

A pliable material

This ability to take up water was a positive advantage in the most important use of the plant. The pith of the stems was fashioned into a fine, pale and pliable writing material that was used in Egypt from at least the time of the First Dynasty – the oldest surviving piece of papyrus is from a tomb of about 3000 BC – until the final takeover of paper some 4,000 years later.

The name of the plant is a testament to its importance. 'Papyrus' derives from *pa-en-per-aa*, 'belonging to the pharaoh'. The king had a monopoly over the manufacture and sale of papyrus for writing materials. Although the plant was grown from seed in Cyprus, Palestine and Sicily in ancient times, Egypt – its natural home – remained the principal source of fine writing materials for the whole of the Mediterranean region.

Freshly cut papyrus stems are bundled together to be taken back to the river bank.

▲ A valuable resource
Papyrus was the most important writing material for officials recording economic transactions, and for literary texts. Completed rolls were stored in large jars to protect them from insects and the weather. While officials generally wrote only on one side, papyrus rolls were so expensive that they were often recycled (sometimes much later) by writing on the back.

Boats made from papyrus stems lashed with papyrus rope carried the harvesters through the marshes.

Muddy, waterlogged soil provides the ideal growing medium for the reed-like papyrus plant.

Surprisingly little is known for certain about the cultivation of papyrus, but it is reasonable to assume it was harvested, as it is now, mainly in spring or summer. Murals and reliefs from Ancient Egypt show how the stalks were pulled from the water, cut and transported in bundles to the workshops (see above).

Complicated process
Fresh papyri, in good condition, were needed to create fine quality writing material. Strips of the inner part of the stems were compressed into sheets that were usually no more than 45cm (18in) long. These sheets were then fixed together to form rolls of varying lengths. The standard roll of papyrus had around 20 sheets, but they could be more extensive; the longest known roll is over 40m (130ft) long. The inside of a papyrus roll was written on first; the other side was often left blank.

INSIGHT

Papyrus today

In the first millennium AD, papyrus was slowly replaced as a writing material first by parchment, then by paper. Today, however, tourists can buy papyri made and inscribed with ancient motifs (below), using similar methods to those in Ancient Egypt.

Temple Inscriptions

The hieroglyphic texts accompanying the reliefs on temple walls are much valued by Egyptologists as they describe what is going on. Their original purpose, though – like that of the images they accompany – was essentially magical, rather than informative.

Egyptian temples were not places of congregation and prayer like churches or mosques. Access to the temples was forbidden to ordinary Egyptians; hieroglyphs were not intended to edify casual visitors.

In the Old and Middle Kingdoms, inscriptions were usually limited to a bare commentary on what was depicted in the reliefs. Only in the New Kingdom did sacred scriptures, magical formulae and other, more secular texts make their way on to the walls. From then on, every bit of space between reliefs was filled with text.

Magical powers

The reliefs would show the everyday cult business of the temple, such as the replenishment of the offerings altars, as well as more occasional rituals carried out by the king – or, more likely, a priest acting in his name. These secret ceremonies were meant to perpetuate the creation of the world and maintain the order created by the gods.

Inscribing its text on a temple wall heightened a ritual's power. The hieroglyphs had the power to perpetuate through eternity the performance of the rituals they described. If the cult were to fade away, the Universe would still function, thanks to the power of the texts.

▶ The white chapel of Senusret I
Built by the Twelfth-Dynasty pharaoh Senusret I (1965–1920 BC), this barge sanctuary in the precincts of the Amun temple at Karnak was dismantled in the middle of the New Kingdom (1550–1069 BC), and its stones used as infill on the third pylon. It was rebuilt in the twentieth century. The pharaoh stands face to face with Amun, manifest as Amun-Ra and Amun-Min, in the reliefs on its square pillars. The texts identify the king and the gods and evoke the ritual exchange between them.

❝ *Year 30, 4th month of the akhet season, day 1. The appearance of the good god in the temple of Amun … His Majesty was looking for something splendid for his father Amun-Ra, as he determined the first sed festival for his son resting on his throne and announced numerous (sed festivals) for him in Thebes.* ❞

(Jubilee inscription)

A pharaonic cartouche *encloses two names: Senusret and his throne name, Kheperkara.*

Amun-Ra *stands before the pharaoh in this relief. The inscription, part of a rite of adoration, reads 'Praise the god four times.'*

The nomes of Egypt *are personified in the reliefs on the barrier walls. The accompanying texts list the name and size of each nome.*

▼ Relief from Kom Ombo

Most of the reliefs at the double temple at Kom Ombo, north of Aswan, were created in the reign of Ptolemy XII Neos Dionysos (80–51 BC). The names of the pharaoh appear in cartouches guarded by the two titular gods of the temple – the falcon-headed Haroeris, an aspect of Horus, and the crocodile god Sobek.

◄ Obelisk of Thutmose III

The columns of text covering this Eighteenth-Dynasty monument tell its history. The stone was hewn from the quarries of Aswan in the reign of Thutmose III (1479–1425 BC), but he died before it was erected. It lay in a workshop in Karnak until Thutmose IV (1400–1390 BC), its originator's grandson, had his own cartouche added to it and erected the obelisk east of the temple. At just over 32m (105ft), it is the tallest obelisk ever erected in Egypt, and now stands in Rome.

***The Horus name** of Thutmose III is followed by a sign for 'two ladies', referring to Nekhbet and Wadjyt, the protective goddesses of Upper and Lower Egypt, respectively.*

***The names of Thutmose IV**, who had the obelisk erected at the Karnak temple, are carved in columns on the side of the monument; those of his grandfather are in the centre.*

> 66 *He had it made as a monument for his father Amun, the lord of the two countries, by erecting two large obelisks for him at the front of the temple, with a pyramidion of djam gold ... so that he be blessed with life like Ra in all eternity.* 99
>
> (*Obelisk inscription*)

▼ Images and text

In the temples of the New Kingdom, colourful reliefs of kings and gods engaged in rituals covered most vertical surfaces. The columns of the mortuary chapel of Rameses III at Medinet Habu provide some of the best preserved examples. On the right, Rameses offers, according to the inscription, jugs of milk. On the left, identified by name as well as their attributes, are the deities Amun-Min and Isis.

WRITING

By far the most common subject for a temple relief is the king and the god standing face to face, with a short expository text identifying the occasion. The pharaoh, whose names and titles are contained in a cartouche, makes an offering to the god, to sustain him and ensure his well-being. The offering may be material or spiritual, and is often defined in the title of the scene, such as 'Consecrating the white bread' or 'Worshipping the god'.

In return for the offering, the god grants the sovereign gifts to help him in his role as ruler of Egypt: life, stability, power, health and, above all, happiness. On this exchange – which often ends with an offering of Maat, or natural harmony and balance, to nourish the god – depends the maintenance of the order created by the gods.

As well as temple ritual, the reliefs and texts provide a great deal of information about other religious occasions, such as festivals, as well as royal ceremonies including the coronation and the sed festival or jubilee, at which the king reaffirmed the legitimacy of his rule.

▶ **Making an offering**
The chambers around the inner sanctuary of a temple depicted scenes of everyday ritual. Here, at Luxor, Amenhotep III (1390–1352 BC) offers beef, including the prized foreleg, to Amun, the temple deity. Reliefs always show the pharaoh carrying out rituals, although, in reality, a high priest usually did this on his behalf.

> *Beginning of the records of the victory of the king of Upper and Lower Egypt … which he gained over the land of Khatti and Naharina, over Karkemish and the land of Qadesh.*
>
> (Report of the Battle of Qadesh)

Oval shields *enclose the names of the cities conquered by the pharaoh.*

Cartouches of Thutmose III *are still partially visible on the ruined wall in front of the king, who wears the red crown of Lower Egypt.*

Conquered cities *are named on the chests of bound prisoners led to the king by the goddess of the west.*

Campaign journals and king novellas

Among the more secular subjects for temple reliefs are the military exploits of the king. Each victory represents a symbolic triumph over the chaotic forces that were a constant threat to the world. Texts accompanying these reliefs are naturally more elaborate than those in offering scenes. New Kingdom pharaohs, such as the conquering Thutmose III, Sety I and his son Rameses II – or even Rameses III – used temple walls to narrate their military campaigns in some detail.

Sometimes, the inscriptions take a more literary turn. A good example is the poetic report of the Battle of Qadesh in *c.* 1274 BC, and the great victory claimed by Rameses II. Such tales about the deeds of individual rulers are usually structured in the same way; this form of composition is today described as the king novella.

▲ Naming the gods

Although gods depicted in temple reliefs can sometimes be identified by their appearance or headdress, they are always named in the inscriptions to avoid confusion. Several gods, for example, had the head of a falcon; this one is Horus, son of Isis (Harsiese). Inscriptions were also necessary to distinguish goddesses such as Hathor and Isis, who were often shown with the same robe and hairstyle.

◀ Campaign reports

The reliefs on the seventh pylon at Karnak, built by Thutmose III (1479–1425 BC), bear the image of an oversized pharaoh smiting his enemies, a traditional scene symbolizing the conquest of chaos by order. In this case, though, the texts list the conquered peoples and evoke the very real campaigns led by the pharaoh to build his empire in Syria-Palestine and the Levant.

▶ Unchanging style

Temple inscriptions in Ancient Egypt were always in hieroglyphs, even when the country was ruled by Persian, Greek or Roman pharaohs. Later temple inscriptions had more information than earlier ones, and the number of signs used grew from around 700 to more than 6,000. The secret of reading these texts was lost soon after the temples were closed in AD 391.

Coffin Texts

The ritual texts and magic spells known as the Coffin Texts *were used from the First Intermediate period (2181-2055 BC) until the Middle Kingdom (2055-1650 BC), allowing ordinary people the same access to funerary rites - and the afterlife - as the pharaoh.*

The *Coffin Texts* are a group of more than 1,000 spells of a religious nature, which were written in hieroglyphs or a cursive script on wooden coffins in the First Intermediate period and in the Middle Kingdom. Most of these inscribed coffins were found in necropolises in Middle and Upper Egypt.

The texts, a collection of ritual texts, hymns, prayers and magic spells, which were meant to help the deceased in his journey to the afterlife, originated from the *Pyramid Texts*, a sequence of mainly obscure spells carved on the internal walls of the pyramids of the Old Kingdom. The *Pyramid Texts* were exclusively for the king and his family, but the *Coffin Texts* were used mainly by the nobility and high-ranking officials, and by ordinary people who could afford to have them copied. The *Coffin Texts* meant that anyone, regardless of rank and with the help of various spells, could now have access to the afterlife.

▼ Coffin of Khnumhotep
The interior of this wooden coffin of an early Twelfth-Dynasty governor is decorated with *Coffin Texts* inscriptions, along with paintings of food offerings. The exterior is ornamented with horizontal and vertical bands of hieroglyphs, and with two wedjat eyes (eyes of Horus). These are painted on the east-facing side at the level of the head and allow the deceased to observe the world outside.

The written formulae were designed to help the deceased in his journey to the afterlife.

The coffin, made of durable wood, represented the eternal dwelling-place of the deceased.

▼ Pyramid of Amenemhat III
It is not known what texts were used in the coffins of the pharaohs of the Middle Kingdom (2055–1650 BC). Most of the kings of this period were buried in pyramid tombs, such as the one in Hawara of Amenemhat III (1855–1808 BC), which were looted by grave robbers not long after interment. The wooden coffins, along with their inscriptions, were burnt at the same time.

◀ **Mereru's coffin**
The inside of this coffin, discovered in the necropolis of the nomarchs of Asyut (one of the nomes of Upper Egypt), shows hieroglyphic extracts from the *Coffin Texts*, along with painted depictions of several everyday objects needed for survival in the afterlife. These include shields, a quiver, and a bow and arrows. Above them on a table sits an offering of two cooked ducks, complete with platters.

INSIGHT

The democratization of the afterlife

During the Old Kingdom (2686–2181 BC), only the pharaoh was guaranteed a place in the afterlife – in death, he was identified with Osiris and transformed into a god, with his journey to the afterlife facilitated by spells, such as those in the *Pyramid Texts*.

With the collapse of the Old Kingdom due to civil war and instability, the power of the provincial governors, or nomarchs, increased. They assumed some of the rituals associated with the pharaoh, among them the benefit of having funerary texts included in their burials. In this way, they, too, could have access to the afterlife, along with the pharaoh. Consequently, from the First Intermediate period (2181–2055 BC) through to the Middle Kingdom (2055–1650 BC), nomarchs such as the Twelfth-Dynasty governor of Asyut were buried in local necropolises in coffins decorated with funerary spells. Some of these were derived from the royal *Pyramid Texts*, while others were spells from different regions.

Ordinary individuals also wanted access to the afterlife, and to overcome the numerous dangers lurking in the underworld by using the same magic texts and rites. Gradually, throughout the Middle Kingdom, the use of *Coffin Texts* became more widespread.

A new feature, not found in the *Pyramid Texts*, was the use of pictorial vignettes. By the end of the Middle Kingdom, the *Coffin Texts* had fallen into disuse – to be replaced by a new guide to the afterlife, the *Book of the Dead*.

The wedjat eyes enabled the deceased to look out at the world from which he had passed, and also to see the rising sun.

◀ **Offering formula**
The 'hetep-di-nesw' (a gift which the king gives) was a prayer asking for offerings to be brought to the deceased. It was often written on the exterior of a coffin, as here. Usually, the first line of the formula asks for the king to make gifts to the gods Osiris or Anubis; it then lists the various items of food and drink required.

The *Coffin Texts* appear not only on coffins, but also sometimes on the walls of the burial chambers and on papyrus rolls and mummy masks. They were usually written in black.

As it was impossible to write all the texts on one coffin, the owner of the tomb chose the particular extracts he wanted. Some spells were used more often than others and came to be associated with particular necropolises. High-ranking individuals of the Thebes region, for instance, used spells addressed to Osiris, while the necropolis at el-Bersha in Middle Egypt principally used texts from the *Book of Two Ways*, a sort of guide book to the underworld.

Paths through the underworld

Illustrated by a map depicting roads and canals, the text of the *Book of Two Ways* relates the journey that the deceased must take in order to arrive at the place of his rebirth. Knowledge of the spells and possession of the map meant that the deceased, like the pharaohs in times past, could negotiate the dangers of the underworld and achieve eternal life.

DOCUMENT

From the *Coffin Texts* to the *Book of the Dead*

The *Coffin Texts* were partly the inspiration for the *Book of the Dead* of the New Kingdom (1550–1069 BC), when the spells were written on papyrus rolls. Some of the formulae point to the 'negative confession of sin', which can be found in a more developed form in the *Book of the Dead*. The deceased had to deny having sinned in his life and underwent a trial before a court of gods to prove his purity and innocence. Only if his denial of sin was accepted did the deceased proceed to eternal life in the underworld.

Some coffins depict a map of the underworld with various demonic creatures. The texts accompanying this map, known as the *Book of Two Ways*, gave precise instructions about how to overcome the dangers posed by these creatures. The 'guiding' function of the *Coffin Texts* gradually became more important from the Second Intermediate period (1650–1550 BC) on and was eventually incorporated in the *Book of the Dead*, the use of which became more widespread than that of the *Coffin Texts*.

As this 21st-Dynasty papyrus (right) shows, the texts were illustrated with vignettes.

In a funeral procession, people carry offerings and tomb furnishings for the deceased to use in the afterlife.

Illustrations and texts are rendered directly on to the wooden walls of the coffin.

The colour of the inscriptions is mostly black - as in the manuscripts written on papyri - with red headings.

Horizontal friezes between the text columns depict people with a variety of funerary offerings.

The vertical columns list the objects needed by the deceased for the afterlife.

The texts are written in cursive hieroglyphs, a style similar to but slightly different from the hieratic script.

◄ Iqer's coffin
This coffin from the late Twelfth Dynasty was found in Gebelein, south of Thebes and the site of a Middle Kingdom temple of Hathor. Only its interior has been preserved. The decoration includes horizontal friezes of figurative designs showing people with offerings, together with scenes of the burial rites. The texts between the friezes are inscribed in black.

INSIGHT

The gods of the *Coffin Texts*

The gods appearing in the *Coffin Texts* mainly belong to the group associated with creation and, in particular, with the creation myth of Heliopolis centring on the sun god Ra. Geb (the earth) and Nut (the sky), Shu (air) and Tefnut (moisture) feature prominently, along with Nephthys, Isis and Osiris, and their son Horus. The most dangerous enemy was Apophis, a giant serpent, who symbolized the forces of chaos and evil. Hathor (below, as the cow goddess with human face and cow's ears) also appears in texts from Gebelein, where she was the main deity.

Osiris, as god of the dead and the afterlife, is very often represented, and, as part of the democratization of funerary religion, the deceased himself sometimes appears as Osiris.

References to other creation myths are found in some texts. One is that of Hermopolis Magna, which attributes the creation of the world to four pairs of gods in the shape of snakes or frogs, symbolizing different aspects of the chaos before creation.

Above: The image of the kneeling Isis with raised arms as a gesture of protection is a common coffin decoration.

Left: Osiris, god of the dead, is one of the most familiar coffin motifs.

Administrative Papyri

Egypt's prosperity was founded on a stratified, centralized bureaucracy with a network of scribes throughout the country. These functionaries kept accounts and made reports on countless papyri, which provide insights into the social and economic life of Ancient Egypt.

The oldest written comments in Egypt were of a bureaucratic nature: small labels with details about the funerary equipment in the kings' tombs of the 'Zero' Dynasty (c. 3150–3100 BC). While scribes would make preliminary reports or notes using ostraca, pieces of stone that were later discarded, the more important administrative files were written on papyrus. These were stored in the archives of the government institutions and the temples, which had their own bureaucracies. All administrative papyri were written in cursive hieratic or (from the seventh century BC) demotic script. Hieroglyphs were too cumbersome for the needs of everyday life.

The great central repository of all this information was the office of the vizier, which collated and classified papyri concerning the stewardship and allocation of land, the level of the annual flood, the collection of taxes, the careers of bureaucrats and reports on local administration, as well as the results of judicial disputes.

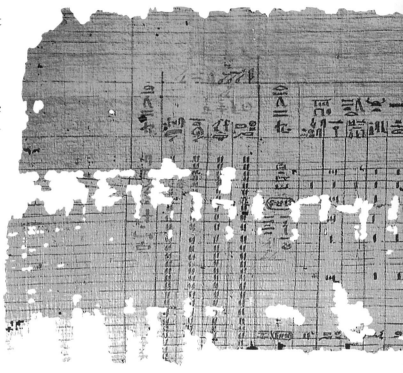

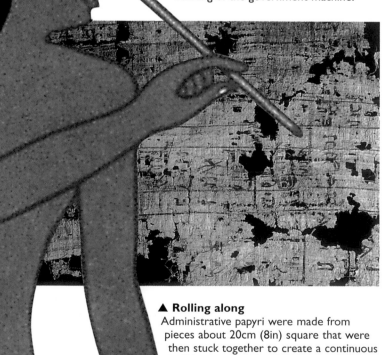

◀ **The ubiquitous scribes**
Huge numbers of scribes – rarely, if ever, separated from their palettes and brushes – were the cogs that ensured the smooth running of the government machine.

▲ **Rolling along**
Administrative papyri were made from pieces about 20cm (8in) square that were then stuck together to create a continuous roll long enough for the purpose the scribe had in mind.

506

▶ Early hieratic
Papyri recovered from the funerary complex of the Fifth-Dynasty pharaoh Neferirkara (2475–2455 BC) at Abusir are the earliest known documents written in hieratic script. At this stage the signs were still fairly close to the hieroglyphs from which they derived.

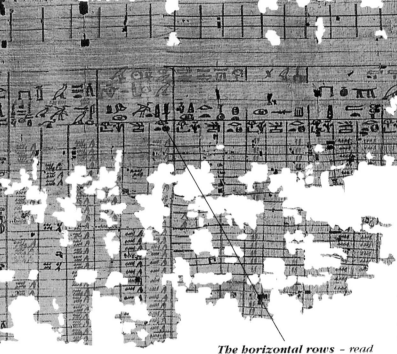

A monthly account of the offerings delivered to the funerary temple is the subject of this fragment of papyrus.

A cartouche bearing the king's name identifies the beneficiary of the offerings brought to the temple.

◀ The Abusir papyri
The numerous administrative papyri found in the funerary temple of Neferirkara at the necropolis of Abusir, north of Saqqara, are devoted to temple business. There are accounts of the food, unguents and fabrics offered by the temple, and texts that lay out the daily lives of the priests who worked there. These priests benefited from the solar temple built by Neferirkara at nearby Abu Roash. The custom of highlighting important passages by using red ink rather than black was already established at this stage.

The horizontal rows – read from right to left – name the offerings, and the vertical columns give their number.

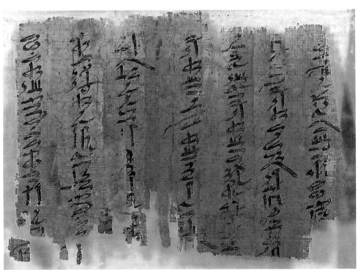

◀ The temples of Abusir
Each royal pyramid in the Abusir necropolis had its own mortuary temple with a priesthood and administrators dedicated to the service of the dead king.

▲ The evolution of hieratic
This document from a temple archive at Thebes from the New Kingdom (1550–1069 BC) highlights the changes in hieratic script since the Old Kingdom.

Page numbers in *italics* refer to
illustrations; page numbers in **bold**
refer to the main reference

Abu el-Haggag Mosque 270, *295*
Abu Roash 28, *256*
Abu Simbel temples **316–19**
  colossi 85, *133, 310, 311, 315*
  moved to higher ground 85
  sanctuary *433*
Abusir *30, 507*
Abydos
  cenotaph 56
  inscriptions 20-1
  Osiris *107*, 118
  royal cemetery *26*
  stelae *216*
  U cemetery 21
Achaemenid *94*
Actium 99
administration **388–9, 506–7**
adzes *194, 195*
Aegean Islands 45
afterlife, democratization of 102, **503**
afterlife, god of *see* Osiris
Aha, Pharaoh 22, *26*
Ahhotep I, Queen 59, *63*
Ahmose I, Pharaoh 59, *59, 63, 353*
Ahmose Nefertari *353, 363, 375*
Ahmose, Princess 68
Akerblad, Johann David *471*
akh **178–9**
Akhenaten, Pharaoh **74–7**
  art **298–301**
  family 80, *344, 352*
  foreign policy 87
  garbage remains *384*
  Luxor temple 292
  necropolis 78
  relief work *210*
  religion 65, 65, 108, *111*, 114, 142
  society *362*
  stelae *215*
akhet season 166, *446*, 448
Akhetaten 74, 75, 78
alchemy *147*
Alexander IV, Pharaoh 97
Alexander the Great **96–7**, *114, 115*, 294
Alexandria 96, 146, **328–33**
alphabets **478–81**, *488*
Amanunet 112
Amarna
  art **298–301**, *303*
  as capital 65
  end of 80
  fashion *375*
Amarna Letters 75
Amaunet *103, 149*
Amduat 309
Amenemhat (astronomer) 449
Amenemhat I, Pharaoh *48*, 52
Amenemhat II, Pharaoh 49
Amenemhat III, Pharaoh 49, *49, 473*, 502
Amenemhat IV, Pharaoh 49
Amenemope, Pharaoh *241*
Amenhotep (architect) 288
Amenhotep I, Pharaoh *68*, 68, 276, *278*
Amenhotep II, Pharaoh 90, *105, 345*, *432, 464*
Amenhotep III, Pharaoh **289**
  building 64-5
  hunting *414*
  Luxor temple 292
  mortuary temple 274, **288–91**
  offerings to the gods *500*
  religion 74
  sed festival *165*
  sphinx *254*
  statues *223*
  wives *352*
Amenhotep IV, Pharaoh *see*
  Akhenaten, Pharaoh
Ammonios *336, 337*
Ammut *198, 200*
amphorae *233, 234, 407*
Amratian period 16-17, *124*
amulets *175, 181, 183*
Amun **104, 112–15**, *293*

and Amaunet *103, 149*
  cult reduced 74
  king of the gods 44, 45, 75, 80, 170
  Opet festival 166-9
  statues *220*
Amun-Kamutef 112
Amun-Kematef 112
Amun-Min *104, 113, 168*
Amun-Ra 71, 102, 108, **113**
Amun-Ra temple
  enlarged 53, *83*
  fertility scenes *139*
  hypostyle halls *312*, 466
  magic protection for 57
  relief work *210*
  sacred lake *173*
  sanctuary *326*
  sphinxes *113*
  wealth and power 65, 90, 114, 205
Amurra 86
Amyrtaios 95
Anat 58, 86, 146
Anat-her Heka-khasw, Pharaoh 61
Anatolia 144
Anedjib, Pharaoh *26*
Anedjti 118
Anen *432*
Ani *160*
animals
  husbandry **396–9**
  mummies 182
  necropolis **154–7**
  sanctification 156
  slaughtering **400–3**
ankh *79, 114, 336, 477*
Ankhenesmeria 35
Ankhesenamun, Queen 80
Ankhesenpaaten, Queen 80
Ankhtify *38*
anthropoid coffins 227
Anubis **104**, *118*, 126, *174, 195*
Anuket 126
Apepi I, Pharaoh 61, *63*
Aphrodite *122, 147*
Apis 102
Apis bulls 95, **104**, *152–3*
Apollo *158*
Apophis 124
aprons *374*
Arabic *473*
Archimedes 333
Archimedes screw 15, *392*
architects *253, 439*
areas 438
Ariandes 95
aristocracy 348, 362, 363, *365*
Aristotle 96
Armant 45
armies 364, **422–5**
arrowheads *16, 464, 465*
art **202–5**, 390, 493 *see also* painting
  techniques; relief work; wall
  paintings
    artists' village **278–83**
    portraits of Fayum **334–9**
    rock art *16*
Artaxerxes 95
Ashait, Princess *370, 379*
Asia Minor 96
Asiatic settlers 58
Astarte 58, *122*, 144
astronomy 171, **432–5**, *448*
Aswan *13*, 56, 250
Aswan Dam *15*, 448
atef crown 58, *118*
Aten 65, *65*, **74–7**, *111, 115*, 300
Athena *122*
Atum *254*, 447
Augustus *311*
Avaris 58, 59, 62, *124*
avenues 255
Awibra *see* Hor I, Pharaoh
axes 465
Ay, Pharaoh 80, *81*, 81, *196*, 272
Ayrton, Edward 302, *308*
Aztec calendar *449*

Ba **178–9**
Baal 58, *117*, 124, 144

Babylon 75
Badari 236
Baghdad 59
Bahr Yussef canal *12, 40*
Bak *210*
Bakenrenef, Pharaoh 93
balances *443*
bandages *127, 175*, 176, 182, *183*
bankruptcy 36
barges *115, 164, 173*, 248, *461*
barley 395
bas *136*
basins *383*
baskets *459*
Bastet **104, 136–7**, *156*
bathrooms 382
battle-axes 465, 467
beards 70, *119*
Beautiful Festival of the Valley 114, 287
beds *243, 244*
beef *168*, 396, 400
beer 373, 395, **408–11**
beginning of the world 103
Behdet *108*
Belzoni, Giovanni *131, 311*, 317
benu-bird *83*, 256
Bes **104**, *141, 142, 373, 380*
Bintanat 312
Birket Habu 272
birth houses 342
birthdays of the gods 448, 449
black *138*
blindness 453
blue crown *84*
boats *33, 390*, **460–3**
body care **382–5**
Boghazköy *59, 60*
bolts *355*
Bonaparte, Napoleon 470, *471*
Book of Gates 83, 303, 308, *309*
Book of Kemyt 346
Book of the Dead 91, *104, 107, 116*, *150, 160, 198*, **504**
Book of the Earth 449
Book of the Two Ways 504
books of stone *see* stelae
Bouchard, François-Xavier 470, *471*
boundary stelae *215*, 437
bows *464*
brains 180
branding animals **397**
bread *186, 187*, 395, **408–11**, *475*
Breasted, James 72
breastfeeding 342
breweries *410*
brothers 352
Bubastis **104**, *136*, 156
Buhen fortress 46, *47*, 54, *57*
'bull' palette *19*
Burckhardt, Jean-Louis 317
Burckhardt, Johann Ludwig *311*
bureaucracy **388–9, 506–7**
burial chambers *249*
Burnaburiash II, King 75
Busiris *107*
butchery **400–3**
buying and selling 360
Byblos 34, 45, 132
Byzantine period *339*

calcite greywacke 34
calendars *441*, **446–9**, *450*
Cambyses II, Pharaoh 94-5
camel caravans *420*
camels *14*
Canaan 86
Canopic deities 126
Canopic jars *127, 160, 174*, 176, *180*, *181*, **184–5**, *234*
Canopic Way *332*
canopies 182
Canopus *184*, *332*
capstones *249*, 250
carpenters *460*
carpets *459*
Carter, Howard 81, *163*, 239, 301, 423
cartonnage *175*
cartouches 20, *26*, 52, **481**

catfish *23*
cats 136-7
cattle 396, *396*
causeways *249*
cedar 242
cenotaphs 56
ceramics *17*, **232–7**
ceremonial names *19*
Chabas, François **481**
chain of command 362-4
chairs *242, 243*, 244
Champollion, Jean-François 470, *471*, 489
chaos 366
chaos, god of *see* Seth
chariots 58, *415*, **422–5**
charms *175*
Cheops *see* Khufu, Pharaoh
chests *177, 185*
chests of drawers *245*
chickens 401
childbirth *104*, *140*, 142, 342
childhood **342–5**
children 121, *344, 347*
Christianity 122, **486–9**
circumcision 344, 452, *453*
city life **358–61**
civil servants **388–9**
class society, development of 18
clay *233*
cleanliness *173*, **382–5**
Cleopatra VII Philopator, Queen 98–9, *365*, 406
Cleopatra's Needle *333*
clepsydra *450, 451*
cloisonné technique *230*
clothes **374–7**
coffin chapels 228
Coffin Texts 39, **502–5**
coffins *183*, **224–9**
colonnaded halls *325*
colossi at Karnak *312*
colossi at Tanis *314*
Colossi of Memnon *272, 274*, **288–91**
combs *385*
commemorative stelae 217
copper 34, *386*, *464*
Coptic church *336*
Coptic language *471, 473*, *478-9*, **486–9**
corn *394*
corn mummies *117*
Corpus Hermeticum 147
cosmetic palettes 18, **19**, *208, 381*
cosmetics **378–81**
cotton *456*
craftsmen *143*, **278–83**, *348, 361*, 390
creation *103*, 103, *107*, **148–50**, *505*
Crete 55, 59
crimes 368
criosphinxes *255, 270, 275*
crocodiles *107, 157*, 414, *415*, 415
crooks *84, 201*
crux ansata 336, *477*
cubits *436*, 437

daggers *464, 465*
Dahshur 54, *178*
Dakhla Oasis *35, 51*, *149, 418*
Darius I, Pharaoh *94, 95*, *419*
Darius III, Pharaoh 96
Dashur 28, 56, *60*
date palms *12, 420*
dates *440*
d'Avennes, Emile Prisse 71
day and night 449
dead, gods of *see* Anubis; Osiris
'decades' *446*, 447
Deinokrates 332
Deir el-Bahri necropolis 44, *61, 67*, 67
Deir el-Bahri temples *163*, **264–9**
Deir el-Hagar temple *149*
Deir el-Medina *145, 175*, 274, **278–83**, *358*
Demeter *122*
demotic script *471, 473, 479*, **484–5**
Den, Pharaoh *26, 162*
Dendera temple 99, *131, 132, 132*, *133, 147, 435, 447*

Description de l'Egypte 131
deserts 418
destruction, goddess of *see* Sekhmet
determinatives **479–80**
dignitaries' tombs 284
dill *454*
Diocletian *333*
Dionysos *147*
diplomatic language 75
discipline *346*
divine kingship, god of *see* Horus
divine mother *see* Isis
divine tribunal 176
divorces 350, 373
djed pillar *116, 126*
Djedefra, Pharaoh 28, *29*, 108, *256*
Djedi *282*
Djehutyhotep *444*
Djer, Pharaoh *26*
Djet, Pharaoh *25, 26*
Djoser, Pharaoh 28, *29, 30*, 30, 162, *163, 179*, 248
domesticated animals 16, **396–9**
donkeys *398, 421*
doors *355*
double containers *235*
double crown 22, *54*
Dra Abu el-Naga *58*
dress 79
dromedaries *14*
dromos *255*, **325**
duality, concept of 124
Duamutef *174, 185*
Duat 110
dung beetles *231*
dwarfs 262
dyes **458**
dynasties 11
0 Dynasty **20–1**
1st Dynasty *22, 26,* 111, *244*
2nd Dynasty 27, 28
3rd Dynasty 28, *30, 218*
4th Dynasty 28, *30, 107, 172,* 220, *227*
5th Dynasty 28, *31, 107, 234, 249,* 368
6th Dynasty 28, *34–5, 36*
7th Dynasty 37, 38
8th Dynasty 37, 38
9th Dynasty 38
10th Dynasty 37, 38, 50
11th Dynasty 37, *39,* 40, *45,* 48, 50, 271
12th Dynasty *45, 45,* 48–9, 52, 62, *227*
13th Dynasty *58,* 60, *178*
14th Dynasty *58,* 60
15th Dynasty 61
16th Dynasty *61, 62*
17th Dynasty *58,* 61, 62, *117*
18th Dynasty
  Canopic jars *181*
  coffins 228–9
  end of 82
  golden age **64–5**
  hunting 414
  religion *106, 196*
  sphinx *255*
  tombs 284
  weaving 458
19th Dynasty 65, 84, *124, 197,* 414
20th Dynasty *92, 124*
21st Dynasty 91
22nd Dynasty *41, 93, 93*
23rd Dynasty *93, 93*
24th Dynasty *93, 93*
25th Dynasty 93, *103,* 114
27th Dynasty *94, 145*
30th Dynasty *255*

Early Dynastic period *see* Thinite Period
earthquakes 290
Eastern Thebes **274**
Ebers papyrus *452, 455*
ebony 242
eclipses *435*
Edfu temple *125, 132,* 160
education 344, **346–9**
Edwin Smith papyrus 452
egg models *148*

el-Lisht *52, 53*
el-Qasr *361*
el-Qurn *288*
Elements (Euclid) 333
elements of life 112
Elephantine 56, *105, 431*
embalming *104,* 174–6, **180–3**
Emery, W.B. 155
emmer 395
encaustic technique *334, 336*
end of the world 103
ennead *107*
equal rights *373*
Esna *105, 446*
eternal life, god of *see* Heb
Euclid 333
Euphrates 68
everyday life **340–1**
  afterlife **502–5**
eyes *29,* 380, *381,* 384, *453, 475 see also* wedjat eyes

fabrics 17
faience *233,* **237**
false doors *215, 287*
farming **392–5**
  beginning of 16
  cereal growing *285*
  children *343*
  domesticated animals **396–9**
  everyday life *348, 348*
  women's role *372, 372*
fashion **374–7**
father of pharaohs *113*
Fayum oasis *12,* 17, *40,* 53, *60, 334*
Fayum portraits **334–9**
feathers 176, *198, 200*
Fed, stele of *24*
feet *383*
feluccas *15*
female rulers of Ancient Egypt 70–1
fertile soil, god of *see* Khnum
fertility, gods of *see* Min; Osiris; Renenutet
fertility symbol 152
Festival of Opet 114
final separation 192
First Intermediate Period **36–43**
  afterlife 503
  Canopic jars *185*
  chronology 38–9
  end of 44
  monarchy collapses 364
  mummy masks 238
  religion 102
fishing *15, 285,* 412, *460*
flails *201*
flax 395, *456*
flint tools *16,* 18
flour *410*
food **186–9,** 362–3
forearm *474*
foreign gods **144–7**
foreign rule *see* Second Intermediate Period
fortresses 46–7, 54, *419*
fruit *189*
fruits of the soil **392–5**
funeral corteges **190–3**
funerary barges *248, 463*
funerary texts *224*
furniture *177, 192,* **242–7**

game meat *400*
games *342, 344, 348*
garden parties *354*
gardens *354, 357, 358*
Geb *103, 107,* 116, *120, 129, 505*
Gebel el Arak dagger *16, 21*
Gebel el-Silsila *83*
geese *401, 414*
Geese of Meidum *246*
Gemenefhorbak *198*
geometry 333, *437, 439*
Gerzean period **17–18**
Giza *12,* 28, *30,* **32–3,** *204*
'glazes' *237*
goats *398*
gobelin weaving *458, 459*
gods **102–7**
  birthdays 448, *449, 450*

flesh, hair and bones 175
lesser deities **140–3**
marriages **353**
naming *501*
of the Nile 13
gold 34, *50, 170,* 230, 238, **386–7**
goldsmiths **386–7**
Graefe, Erhard 67
grain measures *364, 441*
granaries *394*
granite 250
grapes **404–7**
grave robber papyri 66
Great Pyramid at Giza 28, **32–3**
Great Sphinx 28, *217, 249,* **256–8,** *258*
Greco, El *339*
Greco-Roman times
  fashion 375
  law 369
  mummy masks *239, 240*
  portraits of Fayum **334–9**
  religion *158*
  sphinx 259
  stelae 219
  writing 483
Greece 96, *122,* 259
Greek gods 146–7
green skin 117
gryphons *94*
guardians 128

Hadrian *291*
hair care 385
hairstyles *338*
Hapy 13, 102, **105,** *127, 160,* 174, *184*
harems 352
harmony, goddess of *see* Maat
Haroeris 157, **158**
harpists *287, 417*
Harpocrates *143, 158,* 160
Harsomtus *105*
harvests *348, 365, 372, 393,* 107
Hathor (goddess) **105, 130–3**
  beer *409*
  foreign gods and *145*
  funerary aspect *320*
  Isis and *122, 123*
  shrine **269**
  temple *283, 317*
  wine *405, 407*
Hathor, Pharaoh *21*
Hatnub 34
Hatshepsut, Queen **70–1**
  mortuary temple *44, 113,* 264, *265,* **267,** *274, 353*
  obelisks *69*
  as pharaoh *72*
  sarcophagus *123*
  sed festival 162, *163*
  stelae *219*
Hattusas (Boghazköy) *60, 87*
Hattusilis *353*
Hauhet *103*
heart scarabs 175
heart, weighing of **176, 198–201**
  judgement of the dead 102, *104,* 367
  'negative confessions' 102
  scales *366, 367*
  scarabs *231*
  scribes *107*
Heb *135*
heb-sed coat *20*
heb-sed festivals 75, *143,* **162–5**
hedjet crown *125*
Heh *103*
Heka *142*
Heka and Hemet *38*
Heket 13, *142, 342*
Heliopolis *103, 107,* 108, *256, 505*
Helios 102
Hellenic Confederation 96
Hemaka *25*
Hemiunu *389*
Henuttawy, Queen *91*
Hera *259*
Herakleopolis Magna 37, **40–1**
herdsmen *396–7*
Herihor 326

Herihor, Pharaoh 20, 90–1, *91*
Hermes *147*
hermetic tradition *147*
Hermopolis Magna *103, 147,* **148–50**
Herodotus *12, 95, 152, 373, 392,* 442
Heron 333
Heryshef *40, 41*
hes-vases *170, 187*
hetep *189*
hetep-di-nesw *196*
Hetepheres, Queen *30, 32*
Hetepsekhemwy, Pharaoh *27*
Hibis temple *94, 95*
Hierakonpolis 17, 18, *18, 19,* 20–1, *34*
hieratic script *481,* **482–5,** *507*
hieroglyphs
  alphabet **478–81**
  deciphering **470–1**
  first *19*
  from life **474–7**
  reading **472–3**
high priests *391*
high relief *210*
hippopotamus hunting 59, 63, 414, *414, 415,* 415
hippopotamuses 125
Hittites *60,* 75, 85, *86–7, 87*
holy birthdays 448, *449*
Homer 270, *328,* 332
Hor I, Pharaoh *60, 60, 178*
Horakhty *159*
Horeau, Hector *43*
Horemakhet 158
Horemheb, Pharaoh **82–3**
  Amun and *115*
  family 77, *77*
  as general 81, *81*
  Horus and 128
  legislation 366
  mourners *190*
  prisoners of war *43*
  relief work *209*
  temples *272*
  tomb furniture *242*
  tombs **302–9**
  wall paintings *205*
Horus **105, 128–9** *see also* wedjat eyes
  Coffin Texts 505
  cult of **158–61**
  family 116, *117–18*
  as infant *121*
  opening of the mouth *197*
  and Seth *125*
  symbol *111*
  temples *18*
Horus falcon *23*
'Horus kings' 20
hour priests *171*
hours *449*
houses *280,* **354–7,** *358*
Houses of Life *171*
Hunefer *195*
Huni, Pharaoh *218*
'Hunters' palette' *412*
hunting *285, 358,* **412–15**
hygiene **382–5**
hypostyle halls **325**
Hyskos *58,* **58–61,** 64, *117,* 124

ibexes 412, *413*
ibises *154*
Ibu *225*
ideograms *471*
Idout, Princess *401*
Idrimi, Pharaoh *65*
Ihnasya el-Medina *40*
Ihy (child god) *132, 133*
Ihy I, Pharaoh *60*
Imeretef *351*
Imhotep *29,* 248
imiut *118*
immigration *see* Hyskos
Immortals *95*
Imsety *160, 174, 185*
incense *378*
Ineni *276*
inner sanctuaries **325**
inscriptions 20–1, **498–501**
inspectors of priests *172*
Instruction of Amenemhat I 53

intaglio 208, **213**
Intef I, Pharaoh 37, 39, 40, *60*, *227*
Intef II, Pharaoh 37, 39
Intef III, Pharaoh 39
interior decoration 355
Intermediate Periods 11 *see also* First Intermediate Period; Second Intermediate Period; Third Intermediate Period
internal organs 160, 180, *181*, **184–5**, *198*
intestines *174*, *185*
inundation **13–14**, 102, *105*, *148*, **428–31**
inundation, god of *see* Hapy
invasions 65, 88–9
Iput, Queen 34
Ipuy *226*
Iqer *505*
irrigation *15*, *392*, *428*, *442*
Irtisen *390*
Irukaptah *400*
Isis **106**, **120–3**
    Coffin Texts 505
    family *103*, *116*, *117*, *138*
    marriage **353**
    representations *182*
Israel in Egypt (Poynter) *135*
Issus, battle of 96
Iteti *172*
Iti *382*
Itjer *218*
Itjtawy 53, 58

jackal masks *175*, *180*
Jerusalem temple 92
jewellers **386–7**
jewellery **230–1**, *335*, *373*
joiners *253*
judgement of the dead 176, **198–201**, 367
Julius Caesar 98–9, *99*
juniper *455*
Junker, Hermann 262
justice, goddess of *see* Maat
Justinian 122, *486*

Ka *21*, *60*, *134*, *168*, **178–9**
Ka-aper statue **260–1**
Ka, Pharaoh 20
Kadesh *144*, *144*, *145*, 146
Kagemni 31
Kamose, Pharaoh 58, 59, 61, *63*, 63, 217
Karnak *see also* Amun-Ra temple
    colossi *312*
    columns *212*
    festival hall 73
    Khons temple *91*, *275*, **324–7**
    monuments *43*
    obelisks *69*, *71*, 72
    ramps *445*
    Red Chapel 73, *164*
    sphinxes *255*, *292*, *293*
    White Chapel *49*, 53, *113*, *139*, *498*
Karomama *375*
Kauket *103*
Kawa *43*
Kawit, Queen *209*, *390*
Kek *103*
Kenamun *345*
Kerma 56, *237*
Kha *282*, *439*
Khaemeaset *462*
Khafra, Pharaoh *30*, *220*, *222*, *249*, **256–8**
Khaneferra *see* Neferhotep I, Pharaoh
Kharga Oasis *95*, *418*
Khasekhemra, Pharaoh *see* Neferhotep I, Pharaoh
Khasekhemwy, Pharaoh 27, 28
Khendjer, Pharaoh 60
Khentamenti *116*, *118*
khepesh *464*, *465*
Khepri *108*, *109*, **111**, *446*, *447*
Kheruef *165*
Khety I, Pharaoh *38*, 40
Khety IV, Pharaoh 39
Khmun *147*
Khnemtneferhedjet, Princess *49*

Khnum **105**
Khnum-Ra 108, *109*
Khnumhotep *502*
Khons *104*, *112*, 293
Khons temple *91*, *275*, **324–7**
Khufu, Pharaoh 28, *30*, 30, **32–3**
Khui 35
Khyan, Pharaoh 61, *62*
kilns 234
king of the gods *see* Amun
Kingdoms 11 *see also* Middle Kingdom; New Kingdom; Old Kingdom
King's protector *see* Horus
knives *464*
kohl *29*, *379*, *380*, *380*, *381*, *384*
Kom el-Shugafa catacombs *333*
Kom Mer 126
Kom Ombo temple *107*, *135*, *157*, *210*, *499*
Kyphi *378*

labour 35, *444*, *445*
Laburna II, King 87
ladders 248
Lake Moeris 40
Lake Nasser 47
lakes *359*
languages *485*, **486–9**
lapis lazuli *113*, 230
Late Period **94–5**
    law *369*
    mummy masks 240
    religion *104*, 121, *123*, 126, 136
law **366–9**
leap years 449, 450
leather *402*
Lector Priests *181*
lengths, measuring *437*, 438
Leontopolis 93
leopard skins *370*, *375*
Lepsius, Karl Richard *302*
lesser deities 140–3
Letopolis *158*
letters *491*
levelling *251*
levers *443*, *444*
library of Alexandria *331*
Libya *23*, *51*, *67*, *89*, *92*, **92–3**
life after death **174–7**
lighthouse of Alexandria *328*, *329*, *330*
limestone quarries *250*
linen garments *177*, *456*
lion sphinx *62*, *254*, *256*
lions' tails *374*
lip tints *381*
literature 53, *59*, *348*
livers *174*, *185*
logograms *478*
loincloths *163*, *374*
looms *457*, *458*
lotus flowers *13*, *144*, *150*, *151*, *199*, *379*, *385*
love, goddess of *see* Hathor (goddess)
low relief *210*
Loyalist's Instruction 53
lunar eclipses *435*
lungs 126, *127*, *174*, *184*
Luxor *167*, *168*, *255*, *271* *see also* Thebes
Luxor temple **292–7**
    location *271*, *272*
    monuments *315*
    processional colonnade *294*
    relief work *81*
    sacred barge *96*
    unity *275*

Ma *151*
Maat *82*, 102, **106**, *200*, 366
Maat, concept of *366*
Macedonia 96
magic 57, *476*, 498 *see also Coffin Texts*
Main Deposit *21*
malachite *380*
Malkata *165*, 272
mammisis *133*, *141*
manicures *383*
manpower *444*, *445*

Marathon 95
Mareotic *406*
Mariette, Auguste *104*, *153*, 155, 246, 260
Mark Anthony 99
markets *360*
marl *233*
marriage 344, **350–3**, 373
Maspero, Gaston 67
mastaba tombs *30*, *31*, 214, *218*, *246*
mathematics **436–9**
mats *459*
measurements **436–9**
meat *186*, *398*, 400
Medamud temple 56, *57*
medical papyri *454*
medicine **452–5**, *454*
Medinet el-Fayum 157
Medinet Habu nilometer *431*
Medinet Habu temple
    Amun-Min *113*
    entrance *46*
    exterior walls *88*
    inscriptions *499*
    location *272*, *274*
    monuments *43*
    relief work *89*, *212*
Meggido, Battle of 73, *425*
Meidum 28, *218*, *246*
Meketra *492*
Memnon colossi *272*, *274*, **288–91**
Memnon, song of *290*, *291*
Memphis
    armouries *465*
    as capital 24
    colossi *314*
    foreign gods 144
    founding of 22, *26*, 34
    monuments *314*
    necropolis 28, *143*
    religion *103*, 118
Menena *343*
Menes 22, 26
Menkaura, Pharaoh 28, *30*, 36, *221*
Mentuhotep I, Pharaoh 38, 39, 40
Mentuhotep II, Pharaoh 48, **50–1**
    Amun 112
    mortuary temple *44*, *264*, **266**
    statues *163*
    unification 37, 40, *41*, 44
Mentuhotep III, Pharaoh 48, 51
Mentuhotep IV, Pharaoh 48
mercenaries *35*, 37, 92, 95, *467*
Merenra, Pharaoh 28, *31*, 35
Mereret's pectoral 55
Mereru *503*
Mereruka 31
Merineferra *see* Ihy I, Pharaoh
Merire-mennefer 31
Meritaten, Queen 77
Meriuserra Jaqob-her, Pharaoh 61
Meroitic period *237*
Merykara, Pharaoh 39
Mesher 89
Meshkent *142*
Mesopotamia *21*, *461*
Meteti *344*
Meyer, Ludwig 257
Michael, St *201*
middle-classes 56, *360*, 363
Middle Kingdom **44–57**
    afterlife *503*
    chronology 48–9, 60–1
    Coffin Texts 502
    fashion *375*
    founding of 40, *41*
    mourners *193*
    mummy masks *240*
    religion *90*, *103*, 107, 108, 119, *133*, **269**
    statues 222
    stelae *216*
    writing *484*
midwives *342*
migrant confederation *see* Sea Peoples
migratory birds *178*
military campaigns *501*
militias *364*
milking *397*

Min **138–9**, *144*
minerals 34, 42
minor gods 140–3
mirrors *379*, *384*
Mitanni 68, 72, 73, 75, 353
modern festivals 167
Modigliani, Amedeo *339*
mohair 456
monasteries *489*
monogamy 350
Montet, Pierre *93*, *314*
months 446
Montu *45*, *50*, 57, **106**, *143*, *162*, *272*
Montu-Ra 108
moral education **347**
Morgan, Jaques de 55, *60*
morning sun *159*, *447*
mortar *253*
mortuary temples *249*
motherhood 130
    goddess of *see* Isis
mourners 176, *177*, 190–2
mouth, opening of *180*, *192*, **194–7**
mouths *476*, *478*
mud bricks *354*
mummification **180–3**
    gods of *104*, 174
    length of 190
    natural 181
    Osiris resemblance 102
mummy masks *174*, *175*, 182, *183*, *229*, **238–41**
music *169*, *286*, *287*, **416–17**
Mut *104*, *112*, *149*, 293, **371**
Mutemwija *176*
Mutemwiya *289*
Muwatallis, King 87
myrrh 180

Nakht's tomb **284–7**, *377*
names 178, *481*
Napoleonic expeditions *131*
Naqada *17*, *18*, *20–1*
Naqada I period 16–17, *124*, 236
Naqada II period **17–18**, *212*, 236, *460*
Narmer palette *19*, *21*, 22, *383*
Narmer, Pharaoh 21, *21*, **22–3**
natron 180, 181
Naunet *103*
Nebamun *412*
Nectanebo I, Pharaoh *255*, *292*, 293, *294*
Neferhotep I, Pharaoh 60, *193*
Neferirkara *507*
Neferkare, Pharaoh 38
Nefertari, Queen
    colossi *133*
    as principal wife *84*
    role of *371*
    temples 85, **316–19**
    tomb **320–3**
    wall paintings *85*
Nefertem 150
Nefertiabet, Princess *370*, *440*
Nefertiti, Queen 76, **78–9**, 298–301, *352*, *375*
Nehmetaway 95
Neith 22, *320*
Neithotep, Queen 26
Nekhbet *55*, 98, *200*, *229*, *301*, *319*
Nephthys *107*, **124–7**
    Coffin Texts 505
    family *103*, 116
    headdress *123*
    manifestations *182*, *190*
    turquoise flesh 230
Neset 28, *29*
neshmet *193*
New Kingdom **64–89**
    capital 271
    ceramics *232*, 234, *235*
    coffins *226*
    fashion 374, *375*
    foreign gods 144
    funerary texts 224
    law *366*, 368
    mortuary temples 264
    mummy masks 238, 240
    Nubia *43*, *43*
    perfumes *380*

religion 65, 74–7, 90, 106, 107, 108, 111, 123, 124, 126
sarcophagi 225
sphinx 223
statues 221, 222
wall paintings 287
weapons 466
writing 484
New Valley 418
night sky 448
Nikare, Pharaoh 62
Nile 12–15, 193 see also inundation
Nile, Battle of 470
nilometer 13, 14, 428–31
Nimlot 93
Nimrod 259
'nine bows' 318
nobility 348
Nofret 247
nomarchs (provincial governors) 34, 35, 36, 36, 503
nomes 55, 141
nub 386
Nubia
    annexation 310
    cataracts 13
    ceramics 237
    conquests of 54
    and Egypt 42–3
    fortresses 14, 46–7
    gold 34, 50
    independence 51
    mercenaries 35, 37
    Nubians 42, 51
    temples 310
numbers 436–8, 440–1
Nun 103, 148, 429
Nut 107
    Coffin Texts 505
    daily cycle 110
    family 103, 116, 120
    personification 102
    Ra and 446
Nynetjer, Pharaoh 27
Nyuserra, Pharaoh 30, 31

oars 462
oases 418–21
obelisks 204, 248, 249, 292, 333, 475
Octavian 97, 99
Odeion 332
Oedipus 259
offerings to the dead 186–9, 192, 196, 440
offerings to the gods 156, 173, 403, 500, 500, 503
officials 362
officials' necropolis 284
Ogdoad 104, 148–51
oils 177, 181
ointments 136, 286, 385
Old Kingdom see also Khufu, Pharaoh; Pepy I, Pharaoh
    afterlife 503
    cattle 396–7
    chronology 30–1
    domesticated animals 398
    end of 14
    fashion 375
    hunting 414
    jewellery 387
    mummy masks 238
    oases 420
    obelisks 249
    private sculpture 260–1
    religion 28–9, 102, 118, 133
    sculpture 262–3
    statues 222, 246–7
    wigs 372
Opet festival 83, 166–9, 275, 293, 294
oracle of Amun-Ra 97, 420
Osiris 102, 107, 116–19
    Coffin Texts 505
    family 103, 106
    as god of the dead 200
    headdress 22
    marriage 353
    mythology 102, 120
    and the priest 172
    profile 118

transformation into 229
Oskoron I, Pharaoh 92, 93, 151
Oskoron II, Pharaoh 93
Osorapis 146, 152
ostraca 492
ostrich feathers 196
overseers 391
owls 474
ox meat 186, 187, 188
Oxyrhynchos 119

Pa Demi 278
pain-killers 454
painting techniques 336
paintings see wall paintings
palm widths 437
paper 494
papyrus
    administrative papyri 506–7
    boats 460, 461, 497
    making 494–7
    preparation 492
    uses 13
Papyrus Abbott 66
Papyrus Amherst-Leopold III 66
Park of Pan 331
peace treaties 85, 87
peacocks 488
peasants 363, 365
pectorals 201
pedicures 383
Pedubastis, Pharaoh 93, 93
Peleset 89
Pepy I, Pharaoh 28, 31, 31
Pepy II, Pharaoh 28, 31, 36
peret season 446, 448
perfumes 377, 378–81, 384
Peribsen, Pharaoh 27
peristyles 325
Persepolis 94
Persians 94–5, 145
personality 178
pesesh-kef knives 194, 196
Petrie, Flinders 236, 334
pets 157
Pharos of Alexandria 328, 329, 330
Philae temple 120, 122, 213
Philip Arrhidaeus, Pharaoh 97
Philip II, King 96
phonograms 471, 478, 479
physical characteristics 178
physics 442–5
Pi-Ramesse 85
Piankhi 91
pigments 491
Pinedjem 67
Pinudjem I, Pharaoh 90, 91, 326
Piramesse 312
Piy, Pharaoh 93, 217
pleasure, goddess of see Hathor (goddess)
ploughing 393
Poem of Pentaur 87, 87
polygamy 351, 352
Pompey 98
Pompey's Pillar 333
population figures 365
portraits of Fayum 334–9
potter's wheel 232, 234
poultry 398, 401
Poynter, Sir Edward 135
Predynastic period
    ceramics 234, 236
    history 16–21
    religion 124, 130
pregnant women 342
Priest kings 90–1
priests 140, 156, 170–3, 359, 377, 383, 391
primeval eggs 148
princes' education 348
prisoners of war 43, 67, 88, 364
professions 348, 372
property rights 351
provincial governors see nomarchs (provincial governors)
Psamtek I, Pharaoh 485
Psamtek II, Pharaoh 95
Psamtek III, Pharaoh 94
pschent see double crown
Psusennes I, Pharaoh 91, 91, 187, 239

Psusennes II, Pharaoh 92
Ptah 107
    manifestations 104, 141, 152, 453
    Shabaqo Stone 103
    syncretism 119
    Tutankhamun necklace 135
Ptah-Sokar 123
Ptah-Sokar-Osiris 119, 143
Ptahshepses 36
Ptolemaic Period 99, 333
    foreign gods 146, 147
    mummy masks 239, 241
    religion 104, 115
Ptolemy I, Pharaoh 97
Ptolemy I Soter, Pharaoh 99, 102, 146, 146, 152, 329
Ptolemy II, Pharaoh 333
Ptolemy III, Pharaoh 449
Ptolemy IV Philopater, Pharaoh 283
Ptolemy V Epiphanes, Pharaoh 470
Ptolemy VIII Euergetes, Pharaoh 99
Ptolemy XII Neos Dionysus, Pharaoh 98
Ptolemy XII, Pharaoh 434, 499
Ptolemy XIII, Pharaoh 98
Ptolemy XIV Philopator, Pharaoh 98, 99
Ptolemy XV Caesarion, Pharaoh 98, 99
Punt 34, 71, 467
purification ceremonies 196
pylons 325
Pyramid Texts 28, 31, 120, 248, 502
pyramidions 249, 250
pyramids
    construction 248–53
    Middle Kingdom 52, 53, 54
    Old Kingdom 28, 30, 31, 32–3

Qa'a, Pharaoh 26
Qadesh 73
Qadesh, Battle of 85, 86–7, 274, 292, 310, 423, 424
Qar 31
Qasr el-Ghueida 419
Qasr el-Labeka 419
Qasr Ibrim 47
Qebehsenuef 160, 174, 185
quails 477
quarries 204
queens of Ancient Egypt 70–1
quivers 465
Qurna 67

Ra 107 see also Amun-Ra
    cyes 130, 134
    manifestations 102, 104
    secret name 106
    sun cult 108–11
Ra-Horakhty 110, 110, 112, 159, 160, 316
Raettawy 143
Raherka and Meresankh 263
Rahotep 246, 247, 383
Rameses I, Pharaoh 83
Rameses II, Pharaoh 84–5
    Abu Simbel temples 316–19
    Battle of Qadesh 86–7
    coffin 224, 225
    colossi 318
    family 155, 345
    Herakleopolis Magna 41
    Luxor temple 292, 294, 295, 297
    marriages 353
    monuments 65, 310–15
    population figures 365
    Ramesseum 84, 274, 315, 423
    sculpture 205
    stelae 214, 215
    temples 43, 318
    weapons 466
    wife see Nefertari, Queen
Rameses III, Pharaoh
    relief work 122
    Sea Peoples 65, 88–9
    temples 46, 272, 326
    wall paintings 277
Rameses IV, Pharaoh 66, 221, 225
Rameses VI, Pharaoh 81, 448, 449
Rameses IX, Pharaoh 66, 66, 327, 435

Rameses XI, Pharaoh 67, 90, 108, 277
Ramose 192
ramps 252, 444, 445
rams heads 255
Raneb, Pharaoh 27
Rassul brothers 67
Red Chapel 73, 164
red crown 22, 23, 475
Rekhmira 196, 222
relief work 204, 208–13, 500
Renenutet 140–1, 407
Reshef 144, 144, 145
resins 175
Restoration Stele 217
resurrection 102, 119
    god of see Osiris
reunification 37, 50, 50–1
Rhind Mathematical Papyrus 59, 61, 436
Rhoda 430
rishi coffins 227
ritual ablutions 383, 383
ritual run 163, 164
ritual slaughter 401
Roberts, David 47, 57, 125, 277
rock art 16
Roman period
    fortresses 419
    mummy masks 241, 381
    Nubia 42
    oases 421
    portraits of Fayum 336–7
    religion 147
    sarcophagi 227
    'song of Memnon' 290
    temples 122, 311
Rome 98, 123
Rosellini, Ippolito 293, 414, 448, 470
roses 337
Rosetta Stone 217, 470–1
royal families 362, 363
royal seals 491
rubbish 384

Sabek 488
sacred barges 115
sacred writings 476
sacrifices 196
Sahara 11
Sahura, Pharaoh 30, 31
sailing 462
Sais 93, 94
Sanakht, Pharaoh 28, 30
Sanam 43
sandal carriers 388
Saqqara 22, 28, 30, 60, 154–5, 248
sarcophagi 176, 177, 224–9
Sardinia 89
satraps 95
scaffolds 252
scales 201, 443
scarabs 111
    hieroglyphs 474
    jewellery 231
    Middle Kingdom 61, 62
    New Kingdom 69
    ram-headed scarab 108
    symbolism 109
sceptres 84
schendyt 374
Schiaparelli, Ernesto 320
science 426–7, 442–5
Scorpion I, Pharaoh 20, 21
scribes 29, 364, 388, 438–9, 485, 494
    writing materials 490–3
sculpture see statues
sea battles, earliest depiction 89
Sea Peoples 65, 88–9
seals 491
seasons 446, 448
Second Intermediate Period 58–63
    chronology 60–1
    mummy masks 240
    religion 124
    sarcophagi 227
sed festivals 162–5
Sedment el-Gebel 41
Sehel Canal 55
sekhem sceptre 199
Sekhemib, Pharaoh 27

Sekhemrakhuitawy, Pharaoh 60
Sekhmet 104, 130, **134–5**, 142
sem priests 171, 194, 196
Sema-Tawi 84
Semerkhet, Pharaoh 26
semi-precious stones 386
Semite caravan 440
Semna fortress 54
Seneb and family **262–3**
Sened, Pharaoh 27
Senenmut 267, 389, 449
Senetites 262, 263
Sennedjem 175
Sennefer 357, 405, 411
Senusret I, Pharaoh 43, 48, **52–3**, 112, 139, 498
Senusret II, Pharaoh 49
Senusret III, Pharaoh 43, 45, 46, 49, 49, **54–7**, 162
Sepa 28
Septimius Severus 290, 291
Serabit el-Khadim 132
Serapeum 104, 146, 152, 153, 154, 154–5, 331
Serapis 102, 104, 146, 146, 153
serdab 179
serekhs 20, 21, 26, 134
Serket 142, 142
servants 176, 189, 283, 364, **376**, 391
Seshat 143, 490
Seth **24**, **107**, **116**, **124–7**
    Baal and 58, 144
    depiction of 117
    family 103, 120
    and Horus 128
    Horus and 105
Sethankhte, Pharaoh 129
setjats 438
setting sun 447
Sety I, Pharaoh 86, 87, 113, 124, 124, 131, 204, 210
    hunting 414
    tomb 277, 448
Seuserenra see Khyan, Pharaoh
sexuality, god of 104
Shabaqo Stone 103
shabtis 176, 283
shadows 178
shadufs 15, 392, 442
shaving 385
sheep 398
shemu 393
shemu season 446, 448
shen sign 123, 200
Shepseskaf, Pharaoh 28, 30
Shepsi 366
Sherden 89
Sheshonq I, Pharaoh 41, 92–3
Sheshonq II, Pharaoh 92
Sheshonq III, Pharaoh 93, 93
shesp ankh 254
shields 467
Shu 103, 505
siblings 352
sickles 393
sidelocks 263, 344
Sidon 97
silent trade 71
silk 456
Sinai 34
singers of Amun 371
sisters 352
Siwa Oasis 114, 419, 420
skin colour 117, 119, 207, 246, 247, 308
sky, god of see Horus
slaughtering **400–3**
sleds 251, 442, 444, 445
Smendes, Pharaoh 90
Smenkhkara, Pharaoh 76–7
Smenkhkara, Pharaoh (Nefertiti) 79
snake bites 142
snakes 474, 477
snakes, god of 104
Sneferu, Pharaoh 28, 30, 30, 32, 218, 246, 248
soapstone 233
Sobek 60, **107**, 157, 415
Sobek-Ra 107
Sobekemsaf II, Pharaoh 67

Sobekhotep IV, Pharaoh 60, 60
Sobekhotep (scribe) 61
Sobekneferu, Queen 49, 58
Sobkensaf 368
society **362–5**
Sokar 118, 119, 143
solar barges 110, 463
solar clocks 449
solar cult 102
solar eclipses 435
soldiers 47, 364, 464–7
Sopdet 448
soul houses **356**, 403
soups 402
southern harem 168
sowing 393
spears 467
speos 83
Sphinx of Djedefra 29
sphinxes **254–9**
    avenue of 292
    New Kingdom 70, 223
    Second Intermediate Period 62
spindles 457
spinning 456–7
St Anthony 487
stability 364
statues **179**
    materials 204
    moving 288
    Old Kingdom **246–7**
    royal statuary **220–3**
    sculptors 222, 223
    statuettes 121, 176
    substitute bodies 205
stelae **214–19**
step pyramids 248
stomachs 174, 180, 185
stone-cutting tools 250
stonemasons 204
stoneware jars 476
Strabo 153, 155
streets 358
Sudan 46
sun cult 108–11
sun god see Ra
sun hieroglyph 474
sun sanctuaries 150
sundials 449, 450, 451
Suppiluliumas, King 75
surveys 250
Susa 94
swords 464, 465
sycomore trees 260, 354
syncretism 102
Syria-Palestine 55, 58, 68, 69

Taa II, Pharaoh 58, 59, 61, 63
Taharqo, Pharaoh 43, 325
Takelot I, Pharaoh 93, 375
The Tale of Sinhue 48, 52, 53
Taniotic 406
Tanis 62, 93, 314, 431
Tasa 236
taverns 410
Taweret 13, 140, 142, 342
Tawosret, Queen 129
taxation 96
Tefnut 103, 505
Tell el-Amarna 75, 78, 217, 298
Tell el-Dab see Avaris
tempera 206, 336, 338
temples 140, 205, 433
Tenti 351
Teti, Pharaoh 28, 31, 31, 34
Tetisheri 59, 61
textile production **456–9**
thanksgiving offerings 121
Thebes **270–5**
    as capital 58
    festivals 114
    growth of 44
    Middle Kingdom 81
    as power base 37
    religion 103
    sphinx 259
Theodora 339
Theodosius 331, 487
Thinis 20, 24
Thinite Period (Early Dynastic Period) 11, **24–7**, 105

Third Intermediate Period 41, 90–3, 126, 151, 240
Thoth **107**
    cult site 103, 147, 155
    manifestations 102, 450
    wife 95
threshing 394
thrones 231, 244
thumb widths 437
Thutmose I, Pharaoh 64, **68–9**, 278
Thutmose II, Pharaoh 70
Thutmose III, Pharaoh **72–3**
    family 64
    marriages 353
    mortuary temple **268**
    obelisks 499
    regency 70–1, 71, 113
    sanctuary 265
    sarcophagus 227
    stelae 139, 217
    throne name 474
    Tomb 320 67
Thutmose IV, Pharaoh 254, 256, 258
Thutmosis IV, Pharaoh 176
Ti 373
Tiberius 132
time measurement **450–1**
Tiy 289, 352, 352
Tiys, Queen 74, 74, 165
Tjenenyet 143
toiletries 384
Tomb 320 67
tomb robbers **66–7**, 90, 276
tools 16, 17, 176, 250
town life **358–61**
trade 34, 45, 59, 60, 71, 85
Trajan 132, 133
trappers 414
truth, goddess of see Maat
Tuna el-Gebel necropolis 154, 155
Tura quarries 250
turquoise 34, 132, 230
Tushratta, King 75
Tutankhamun, Pharaoh **80–1**
    Canopic chest 184
    chariots **423**
    coffins 190, **228–9**
    family 77, 77
    hunting 414
    Luxor temple 292
    mummy 177
    mummy mask 64, 239, **301–2**
    necklace 134–5
    pectorals 126, 230, 231
    reign 65
    sarcophagus 211
    stelae 217
    tomb furniture 243, 244, 245
Tuyu 241
tweezers 385
'Two Ladies' 26

Umm el-Qa'ab cemetry 21
Unas, Pharaoh 28, 31, 34
underwater archaeology 328
unguent pots 378, 380
unification **22–3**
    heraldic emblem 84
    renewed 37, 41, 50, 50–1
    in sight of 21
Upi 86
upper-classes 363, 365
Upper Egypt 20–1, 98
uraeus 72, 84
Userhet 389
Userkaf, Pharaoh 31

Valentino, Rudolph 108
Valley of the Kings 274, **276–7**
    location 64, 273
    tomb robbers 66, 67
Valley of the Queens 67, 85, 273, 274, **320–3**
valley temples 248
vegetables 189, 395
viceroys 49
Victory Stele 217
vines 404–7, 421
Virgin Mary 122

viziers **388**
    fashion 365, 377
    law 368
    Middle Kingdom 51
    role 56, 359, 368
volume 438
votive stelae 217
vowels 478
Vycichl, Werner 489

wab priests 171
Wadi es Sebua temple 43
Wadi Hammamat 16, 34
Wadjet 129, 201, 229
Wadjyt 99, 150
Wadjyt cobra 301
wages 282, 362
wailing women 190
wall paintings **206–7**
    condition 205
    deterioration 322
    first recorded 18, 19
    food 188
    Gerzean period 18
    importance 175, 277
    oldest 19
war chariots **422–5**, 466
war, god of see Montu
Waset 271
washing sets 382
washrooms 382
water carriers 282, 392
water clocks 449, 450
water raising 442
weapons 58, 59, **464–7**
weaving 456–7
wedjat eyes **129**, **161**
    coffins 225, 226, 503
    as offerings 108
    as protection 110, 183
Wegaf Khuitawyra, Pharaoh 60
weights 438
Weneg, Pharaoh 27
Wenennefer 217
Weni 35
Wepwawet 23, 191
weret hekaw 195
Western Desert 418
Western Thebes **274**
wet nurses 345
wheat 395, 439
White Chapel 49, 53, 113, 139, 498
white crown 22, 23
wicker baskets 476
wild bulls **415**
windows 355
wine **404–7**, 421
wisdom, god of see Thoth
'wisdom texts' 347
women, role of **370–3**
women's fashions 376
women's skin colour 247
wood 31, 242
wooden boats 462–3
wooden coffins 226
wooden stelae 219
wool 456
workers' village **278–83**
working classes 359, 360, 360, 361, 363, **376**, **390–1**
workshops 390
writing 20, **468–9** see also hieroglyphs; scribes
    everyday **482–5**
    materials **490–3**
    tools 177
writing, gods of see Seshat; Thoth

Xerxes, Pharaoh 95

years 446, 450
Young, Thomas 471
Yuya 238

'Zero' Dynasty **20–1**
Zeus 97, 102, 115, 146, 146, 259, 329
zodiac 434–5, 447